MUSIC IN HISTORY

*There is no truer truth obtainable
By man, than comes of music.*
Robert Browning

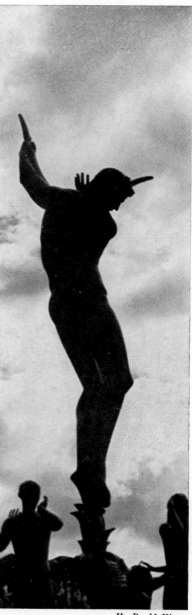

ORPHEUS, THE
GOD OF MUSIC
Statue by Carl Milles
in Stockholm

H. D. McKinney

MUSIC IN HISTORY

The Evolution of an Art

THIRD EDITION

Howard D. McKinney and W. R. Anderson

AMERICAN BOOK COMPANY *New York*

FOREWORD

None of the arts—and this is especially true of music—has developed in a void, unassociated with its time and period. Music reflects the temper of the time that gives it birth, and has a definite relationship to the political, economic, and cultural conditions that surround its composers and practitioners. To understand music, it is necessary to know something of the forces that have shaped and conditioned the various epochs of its growth. And so all the music discussed in this book is placed against the backgrounds of its time and co-ordinated with some of the other arts—painting, literature, sculpture, and architecture—in an attempt to show it as an integral element of the general spirit which informs the whole exterior and interior world of a period.

Because of its very nature music, insofar as the average individual is concerned, is a matter more of emotional significance than of intellectual understanding. Therefore, except for the specialists, real interest in music begins with the eighteenth century. While recognizing this fact, the authors have provided an adequate treatment of the music written before that time, incorporating some new perspectives on the backgrounds out of which eighteenth- and nineteenth-century music developed. Naturally, the music of these two centuries receives full treatment. This edition also gives a great deal of attention to the exciting developments of the present century, and there is an attempt to evaluate their probable place in music history.

The pedagogic aim of this edition, as of earlier editions, is to help prepare the reader to participate more fully in the total musical experience. For the limitless pleasures of good music are founded, in part at least, on understanding: it is with the halls of music as with the inn in the proverb—the fare is as good as the sojourner brings with him.

Because of circumstances, most of this revision has been the work of the first-named of the co-authors.

HOWARD D. McKINNEY

W. R. ANDERSON

ACKNOWLEDGMENTS

The authors herewith offer thanks to the following, who have kindly given permission to reproduce copyrighted material. Specific credits for illustrations are given with the pictures themselves.

American Book Company for selections from *Fluctuation of Forms of Art,* Volume I of "Social and Cultural Dynamics" by Pitirim A. Sorokin and *The National Mind* by Michael Demiashkevich.

Breitkopf & Härtel, Berlin, for the selection from *Geschichte der Motette* by Hugo Leichtentritt. By kind permission of Breitkopf & Härtel, owners of the copyright.

The Clarendon Press, Oxford, for extracts from *The Works of Lucian of Samosata,* translated by H. W. and F. S. Fowler and *The Mediaeval Stage* by E. K. Chambers. By permission of The Clarendon Press, Oxford.

The Cordon Company, Inc. for the extract from *An Intellectual and Cultural History of the Western World* by Harry Elmer Barnes.

Covici Friede, Inc. for the excerpt from *Fool of Venus; The Story of Peire Vidal,* translated by George Cronyn.

F. S. Crofts & Company for the paragraph from *Hellenic Civilization* by Maurice Croiset, translated by Paul B. Thomas.

Dodd, Mead & Company, Inc. for selections from *International Cyclopedia of Music and Musicians; Debussy, Man and Artist* by Oscar Thompson; and *Palestrina, His Life and Times* by Zoe K. Pyne. All are reprinted by permission of the publishers, Dodd, Mead & Company, Inc.

Gerald Duckworth & Co., Ltd. for the extract from *Southern Baroque Art* by Sacheverell Sitwell.

E. P. Dutton & Co., Inc., New York, for selections from *The Caedmon Poems,* translated by Charles W. Kennedy; *Monteverdi; His Life and Work* by Henry Prunières; *Gluck* by Alfred Einstein; *Letters of Mozart,* edited by Hans Mersman and translated by M. M. Bozman; and *Raggle-Taggle* by Walter Starkie.

Newman Flower for the extract from *George Frideric Handel.*

Harcourt, Brace and Company, Inc. for an excerpt from the Introduction to *The American Songbag* by Carl Sandburg.

William Heinemann, Ltd. for a selection from *Giuseppe Verdi* by Francis Toye.

Henry Holt and Company, Inc. for a selection from *The Social Forces in German Literature* by Kuno Francke.

Houghton Mifflin Company for the poem from *A Tropical Morning at Sea* by Edward Rowland Sill and an extract from Virgil's *The Aeneid,* translated by T. C. Williams.

Kegan Paul, Trench, Trubner & Co., Ltd., London, for the excerpt from *Gustav Mahler* by Bruno Walter.

Alfred A. Knopf, Inc. for the selection from *Franz Schubert and His Times* by Karl Kobald, translated by Beatrice Marshall; *Memoirs, 1808–1865, of Hector Louis Berlioz,* translated by Rachel and Eleanor Holmes and revised by Ernest Newman; and *Jean Sibelius* by Karl Ekman.

H. Laurens Publishing Company, Paris, for the selection from *Le Ballet de Cour avant Lully* by Henry Prunières.

J. B. Lippincott Company for an excerpt from *The Civilization of Babylonia and Assyria* by Morris Jastrow.

Liveright Publishing Corporation for the lines from *Collected Poems of H. D.* (Hilda Aldington), published by Liveright Publishing Corporation.

London *Observer* for selections by Basil de Sélincourt, April, 1933, and William Glock, July 26, 1936.

Longmans, Green & Co. for a passage from *The Theatre* by Sheldon Cheney.

The Macmillan Company for selections from *Art and Society* by Herbert Read; Gluck's Preface to *Alceste* in *Music & Nationalism* by Cecil Forsyth; *Beyond Good and Evil* by Friedrich Wilhelm Nietzsche, translated by Helen Zimmern; *Music Study in Germany* by Amy Fay; and the map adapted from *A Political and Cultural History of Modern Europe, Volume I,* by C. J. H. Hayes. These selections are used by permission of The Macmillan Company, publishers.

Music & Letters, London, for the selection by Eva Mary Grew, January, 1938

New York Herald Tribune for the item by Lawrence Gilman; the Schönberg item translated by J. D. Bohm; and the item signed "J. S., May 25, 1939."

The New York Sun for the article by W. J. Henderson.

The New York Times for the excerpt from Olin Downes's interview with Ernest Bloch, January 22, 1939.

Novello & Company, Ltd., London, for the extract from *The Organ Works of Bach* by Harvey Grace.

Oxford University Press, London, for selections from *The Music of Bach* by C. Sanford Terry and *The Oxford History of Music, Volume I,* edited by H. W. Wooldridge.

Oxford University Press, New York, for the quotation from Shaw's translation of *The Odyssey* and the poem by Ford Madox Ford from his *Collected Poems.*

Duncan Phillips, author, for part of his article on Giorgione from *The Enchantment of Art.*

G. P. Putnam's Sons for selections from *The Dance; A Short History of Classic Theatrical Dancing* by Lincoln Kirstein.

Random House, Inc. for a paragraph from *Beloved Friend* by C. S. Bowen and B. von Meck.

G. Schirmer, Inc. for selections from the following articles in *The Musical Quarterly:* "The Social Condition of Violinists in France before the Eighteenth Century" by Marc Pincherle, "Music and the Centenary of Romanticism" by Julien Tiersot (in which he quotes from Victor Basch), "Gluck and the Encyclopaedists" by Julien Tiersot, "Haydn and the Viennese Classical School" by Guido Adler, "Early Spanish Music for Lute and Keyboard Instruments" by Willi Apel, and "Polyphonic Music of the Gothic Period" by Rudolph Ficker.

Charles Scribner's Sons for selections from *The Dawn of Conscience* by James H. Breasted and *The Opera, Past and Present* by William F. Apthorp.

Bernard Shaw and Constable & Company, Ltd., London, for quotations from *Music in London.*

Sheed and Ward, Inc. for the selection from *In Search of Mozart* by Henri Ghéon.

Ives Washburn, Inc. for the selection from *Dufay to Sweelinck* by Edna R. Sollitt.

CONTENTS

THE TWENTIETH CENTURY

THE ARTS IN HISTORY

THE ARTS IN HISTORY

Art must be recognized as the most certain mode of expression which mankind has achieved. As such it has been propagated from the very dawn of civilization. In every age man has made things for his use and followed thousands of occupations made necessary by his struggle for existence. He has fought endlessly for power and leisure and for material happiness. He has created languages and symbols and built up an impressive fund of learning; his resource and invention have never been exhausted.

And yet all the time, in every phase of civilization, he has felt that what we call the scientific attitude is inadequate. The mind he has developed from his deliberate cunning can only cope with objective facts; beyond these objective facts is a whole aspect of the world which is only accessible to instinct and intuition. The development of these obscurer modes of apprehension has been the purpose of art; and we are nowhere near an understanding of mankind until we admit the significance and indeed the superiority of the knowledge embodied in art.

We may venture to claim superiority for such knowledge because whilst nothing has proved so impermanent and provisional as that which we are pleased to call scientific fact and the philosophy built on it, art, on the contrary, is everywhere, in its highest manifestations, universal and eternal.

Herbert Read: *Art and Society*

THE VALUE OF HISTORY

We must have a knowledge of what has been going on and how and why it came to be, if we are to be as wise and as happy as possible—in a word, if we are to possess the world in which we live. The sum of such knowledge,

3

order made out of a vast number of facts, the significant separated from the inconsequential, is what we call *history*—social, economic, political, and cultural.

That the present generation is making an earnest attempt to summarize the course of those events which have brought about its social, economic, and spiritual crises is evident from the titles of many of the new books constantly appearing in bookstores and the types of articles that are published in the better magazines. It is also beginning to realize the necessity of attempting an understanding of the supersubstantial heritage of the human race, if it is ever to escape from its present sense of spiritual insecurity and loss of confidence in the future. The best of several possible ways of attaining such an understanding is through learning something of the nature of this spiritual heritage given us by our forefathers—to possess it, in the words of Goethe, by looking upon its history not merely as definite and literal information on what has been accomplished in the past, but rather as a description of the social, political, and artistic milieu out of which grew the music, painting, architecture, and sculpture of the various periods, and which explains how they came to be what they are.

DIVERSE PHILOSOPHIES OF HISTORY

The idea of the division of man's achievements into certain definite periods has been used in historiography since early times. The philosophers of Greece—Plato, Aristotle, and the rest—thought of human developments as occurring in a series of historical cycles, which always returned to the original starting point. The Middle Ages looked to the ancients as the source of all wisdom, and so the historical outlook was a static one. It was the rationalistic seventeenth century, led by René Descartes and his followers, which developed a philosophy of history based on the idea of a cultural evolution, the various elements of which were closely integrated.

Prior to the nineteenth century, the most enthusiastic exponent of the doctrine of history as progress was the Marquis Marie Jean de Condorcet, who tried to show "through reasoning and through facts that nature has assigned no limits to the perfecting of the human faculties, that the perfectibility of man is truly indefinite, and that the progress of this perfectibility, henceforth independent of any power that might wish to arrest it, has no other limit than the duration of the globe on which nature has placed us."

The philosophers of nineteenth-century Romanticism added their individual conceptions to this idea of history as a series of periods, each representing definite progress. The need for a science based on the facts of human relationships rather than on the abstract reasonings of philosophers was first expressed by Count Claude Henri de Saint-Simon and developed as a system by his pupil and associate, Auguste Comte. In the latter's *Positive Philosophy*, published in 1851–1854, history is divided into epochs, each of which shows socialized progress. It was Herbert Spencer in England who merged the idea of such sociological progress with the new theory of cosmic evolution. From this resulted the materialism and confidence in progress so largely current up to the time of the First World War. The doubts arising from the collapse of this optimism have led to a number of other theories of sociological fluctuations.

With or without the concept of "perfectionism," most anthropologists, sociologists, and historians have used some scheme of periodizing—of dividing historical changes into certain phases in each of which there is definite social and cultural integration. Let us put it in another way: the observer, as he watches the long scroll of history unroll before his eyes, is impressed by the fact that there are certain periods when man's achievements in science, philosophy, religion, and the arts indicate that there were characteristic patterns in thinking and acting, patterns which are repeated and which show that the various phases of activity were part of one living unity and the manifestation of one spirit. This was recognized by the eighteenth-century philosopher Turgot when he said: "The same senses, the same organs, the spectacle of the same universe have everywhere given to men the same ideas, just as the same needs and the same propensities have everywhere taught them the same arts." An impressively documented sociological study by Dr. Sorokin of Harvard University has gone so far as to maintain that the theories of social and cultural development generally held are not valid, and to suggest a new classification of the fluctuation of the forms of art, systems of truth, ethics, and law, as well as those of social relationships, war, and revolution. But even such a sociological theory as this depends for its validity on the fact that the various phases of the cultures studied are logically and closely integrated. Sorokin states that not only the arts but all the main components of a culture—its science and philosophy, its ethics and law, its forms of social, political, and economic organization—are interrelated and have changed their form at the same time and in the same direction.

Most historians of art have followed some such periodizing as a matter of course and have evolved in the process a great many "catalogue histories" of painting, architecture, music, and so forth. These are of importance if one wishes to know who painted a certain picture and when he did so, how many operas Boïeldieu wrote, how many symphonies Stamitz produced, or where the great buildings of the world are located; but they give little understanding of these things as works of art. Art, even considered in the most abstract way, is the result of the desire of the artist to create something that will satisfy himself through the manipulation of certain arrangements of shape, size, mass, time, and so forth—what the aestheticians call *beauty*. And all the arts, especially music, have tended to express the sense of beauty in certain periods according to definite ideals. Which means that the conception of beauty has been a constantly changing idea during the ages, one that has altered itself to suit the ideals of the historical period during which it was produced. It means also that, in order to appreciate the manifestations of a work of art, we should know the general life and thought of the period which brought it into being, and we should know how the sonata, the sonnet, the cathedral, the painting, reflecting this life and thought, are related to the other intellectual products of the time.

THE SEVENTEENTH CENTURY, A PRACTICAL EXAMPLE

A concrete example may help to make this clear. No period in the history of Europe was more active in liberating man's powers and shaping our modern life than was the seventeenth century. It was then, we must remember, that some of the greatest discoveries in science were made: when Francis Bacon set the current of man's thoughts turning toward material things, after it had dwelt so long on spiritual ones; when Galileo, the creator of experimental science, swept the heavens with his telescope, discovering the Milky Way to be a track of countless separate stars and the moon a dead satellite owing its light merely to a reflection of the sun's rays; when Isaac Newton, through the observation of an apple's fall, worked out the laws of universal gravitation; when Harvey published his discovery of the circulation of the blood and Pascal his treatise on vacuum. This was the time when Shakespeare, Milton, Corneille, and Molière lived and wrote; when Rubens, Rembrandt, Velásquez, and Van Dyck carried out to the full the traditions which had been handed down by the masters of the Renaissance. If we realize all this and can sense something of the great intellectual curiosity of the period, something of its tremendous zest for living, then we can understand the developments that took place at this time in music. It was during this era that the Italians invented and developed their colorful and spectacular *new music,* the opera. In Venice, church music of gorgeous quality and luxuriant richness was being produced for both choirs and orchestras. In St. Peter's in Rome, Frescobaldi, the greatest organist of the time, was playing to crowds of thousands of people; so great was his popularity that his audiences followed him from city to city. In England, a musical culture so varied and rich that it has never again been equaled in that country was in full flower; everywhere instruments were freeing themselves from the shackles of being merely "consorts for the voice" and were developing a new and outstanding kind of expression for themselves; it was at this time that the violin came into its own and the keyboard instruments first attained their popularity. All this was part and parcel of the daring, experimental attitude of mind that was common to the age, an attitude which completely changed during the next hundred years but which explains the operas of Monteverdi, the church music of the Gabrielis and Schütz, the instrumental works of Corelli and Purcell.

"BIGGER AND BETTER"

It is through describing the characteristic thought and feeling of the various periods in history and the sense of form and ideals of beauty manifested in the art works of these periods that a history of art can best help one to share the delight of those who produced them. In the writing of such a history, the traditional precedent of periodizing may be followed, provided it is realized that overlapping is unavoidable and that pigeonholing everything exactly and definitely is impossible. The concept of rationalists and early sociologists that history is a series of episodes inevitable in their progress must also be avoided. It is not a matter of a sort of grand triumphal procession from something simple and elemental to the superior and complex result which we know today. Such a conception has been rudely upset by recent events in all phases of life; and recent discoveries show that it has always been absolutely untenable insofar as art is concerned.

Until 1895, the outstanding intellects of western Europe had dedicated themselves definitely to the conviction that the culture of their time represented the highest to which man had attained—that everything which had been produced before the beginning of history could only be primitive and insignificant in comparison with the developments that had taken place since, which culminated in the glories of the nineteenth century. Then, from a French scholar, there came accounts of a newly discovered series of rock paintings in Spain and France, paintings which showed that the men living in the ice age, thousands of years before our era, had possessed a significant culture and produced an art so advanced as to be not far removed from that of modern times—an art to which later sculptors and painters were to turn for inspiration.

Many historians of art have planned their works according to this concept of inherent growth, a growth in which "individual events and men sink into insignificance in comparison with the drama of which they are only acts and actors" (Daniel Gregory Mason). Without making any attempt to settle the question of creative evolution, we can undoubtedly say that such a concept is not true. If it were, it would be necessary to consider the Gregorian chant (a type of music which we have come to appreciate as one of our most precious tonal treasures), or the secular and sacred polyphonic music of the Renaissance, or even the works of the great Sebastian Bach, as merely steps in an orderly progress from the primitive music of the savages to the contemporary "perfection" of Stravinsky and Schönberg. And we should have to think of the lovely lute songs of the seventeenth century as being but the early products of an evolutionary process which was to lead to the later glories of Schubert and Wolf, whereas these early songs are fully developed entities, beautifully expressive of their time and period.

The best thought on the subject, while recognizing the reality of the spiritual development of the human race, regards history as a process of flowering rather than one of continual progress, one of practical and cultural change rather than of constant improvement. Such changes are due to a number of causes; but they do not necessarily make any one period greater or more developed than another. Faure has said that the Egyptian civilization was the equal of any which has yet appeared on the earth; and from many aspects this is true, though it reached its zenith, you will remember, in the fifteenth century B.C. There is no good reason why we should try to think of the music of Palestrina either as superior to or inferior to that of Beethoven. Our enjoyment of either is enhanced if we know why the music of each is typical of the religious, social, and general intellectual trends of the time in which it was written and how it differs from the other things of the same period. Then we realize why it affects us as it does.

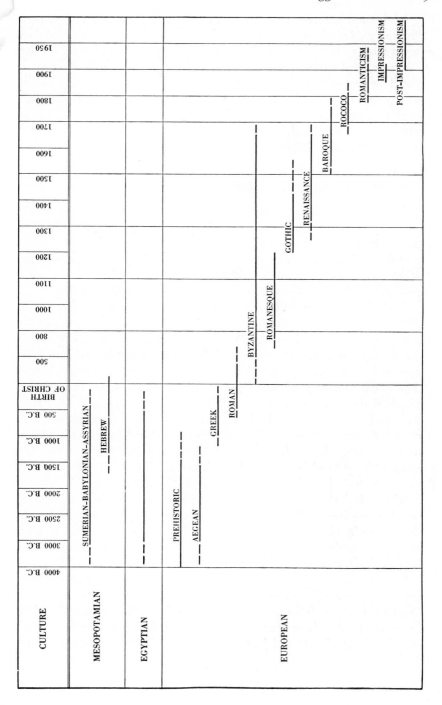

Malvina Hoffman, the American sculptress, has said in her autobiography, *Heads and Tales,* that the beauty of the Greek civilization
as revealed to her in the architecture and sculpture in Athens made her
"stagger, as if under a series of blows," a statement which all lovers of
visual beauty will understand. But she does not infer that this beauty
was greater than that which was made manifest during the Renaissance
or than that which is being produced today. It was simply different,
suggestive of the ideals of the culture which gave it birth. And so it
has been through all history.

DANGERS TO BE REALIZED

There are, of course, certain dangers in any attempt to integrate the
arts; the process is not so simple as it seems. In the course of development, each art has naturally followed certain technical procedures
peculiar to itself, which may or may not have their counterparts in the
other arts; and an attempt to interpret these according to the same
principles is bound to result in confusion and misunderstanding.

And there are other difficulties. For one thing, history refuses to be
divided arbitrarily: at the time when the Gothic period was gradually
losing its force and vigor, the Renaissance was nearly at its height and
the Baroque was in the process of being born. Likewise, certain styles
appeared earlier and developed more rapidly in some countries than in
others: the Gothic ideal arose in the north and was never fully understood in the south of Europe; the Baroque was essentially an Italian
style and never really reached England at all; and we are apt to think
of the Rococo as a purely French influence. Nevertheless, the clearer
understanding that results from an integrated treatment of the arts
against the general background of history justifies the employment of
such a historical method, no matter what the difficulties.

In making the differences between the various periods as clear as
possible, we have followed the usual procedure and chosen the epochs
shown on the chart on page 9 as most representative and of scope wide
enough to include all the materials pertinent to the treatment of our
subject. The dates given are, of course, only approximate.

Various classifications of the arts have been made during these different culture periods. Without maintaining that it can be absolutely
justified, we have followed the conventional distinction, usually taken
for granted today, between what have come to be known as the "major"
and the "minor" arts and have confined our discussions to the former

as being more highly expressive and self-sufficient than the latter. The difference between these two groups may be realized by comparing the finest products of the silversmith or the cabinetmaker with the best architectural, musical, or literary productions. When we refer in general to *art,* we mean the arts of music, the dance, architecture, sculpture, painting, and literature.

Naturally, in a book which treats of one special art—in this case, music—it will be necessary to deal with it at much greater length than with the others. But it must always be remembered that, if we are really to understand the development of any single art, we should consider its history against the background of the period which produced it and the other arts which developed at the same time. Otherwise we get nothing but a sort of "catalogue history" of interest and importance to specialists, but of no real significance in understanding the cultural achievements of the past, in appreciating the artistic expressions of the present, or in prophesying the developments of the future.

It is on such a premise that this book has been written.

THE CONJECTURAL BEGINNINGS

THE ORIGINS OF ART

*Art is a product of civilization; its natural call-
ing is to bear witness to the civilization of an
age and the culture of a people.*

Richard Strauss in his *Recollections and Reminiscences*

ART—WHAT IS IT?

Philosophies differing widely in point of time and conception of ideas have been in general agreement as to the importance in the life of man of that which we have come to call *art*. From the time of man's earliest existence on earth, even perhaps before he had developed a written language, he has been possessed of an impulse to surround himself with beauty. Sometimes he seems to have been largely concerned with merely making designs for the pure pleasure of creation; at other times he has tried to provide himself with beautiful examples of the things he had to use every day. As he has developed in experience, he has attempted, through the expression of his emotions, to establish some sort of contact between himself and the outer world—"to bring into order the whole world of the gods."

We can find these various aspects of art in the earliest phases of human development and can trace them through all conditions of society. As man emerges from the dark chaos of the prehistoric centuries and starts to form tribes, cities, nations, through all the simple as well as the complex processes which have transformed and shaped his life and made and destroyed his civilizations—the power and magnificence of the Egyptians, the glory that was Greece and the grandeur that was Rome, the turbulence and strife of the Middle Ages, the splendor of the Renaissance, the exuberance of the Baroque, the grace of the Rococo, the warmth and sentiment of the Romantic years, into the machine age of today—there has persisted this simple yet essential impulse of man to produce art. Man seems to have been endowed from the first with a certain intuition which has impelled him to create things according to the laws of proportion and rhythm and has enabled him to invest his symbols and sounds with eternal beauty and mystery.

15

Yet, because words are necessarily such poor instruments for conveying thought, the same expressions being sometimes employed for diametrically opposed ideas, and because in this case the ideas themselves are so intangible, any exact definition of art seems impossible, although many have been attempted. The Alexandrian philosopher Plotinus, writing in the third century after Christ, said that art deals with things that are beyond human definition; nevertheless, his successors through the ages have spent a great deal of time and energy trying to explain just what they considered art to be and how it affects the human consciousness. It remains today, however, like electricity, one of those great forces which have tremendous influence on our lives and yet elude all attempts at satisfactory definition.

A work such as this, based as it is upon the premise that art is one of the supreme achievements of human endeavor and a representative activity of human history, has naturally to inquire, at least briefly, into the possible origins of this activity in man. Art has remained essentially the same in spirit throughout the centuries of its existence; and so, if we learn something of the interplay of forces to which it owes its beginnings, we can understand more about its essential characteristics and be able to explain some of its later, more complex developments.

There are two main sources for the materials of such a study: first, the speculations of the anthropologists[1] and the archaeologists[2] regarding those remains of prehistoric art that have come down to us—such things as the pictures drawn and painted on the walls of caves and on rocks in the various parts of Europe and Africa which were inhabited by the Stone Age men and their descendants, as well as the many artifacts that they left behind them; and second, the observation of such primitive societies as still exist, living an elementary hunting life in the wilds of Africa and the other places of the globe not yet pre-empted by civilization.

THE ORIGINS OF ART

If we strip art of the intellectual connotations which civilized man has given it and try to see it, as far as we can, from the viewpoint of mentalities many epochs removed from ours, we realize that it is an

[1] In its fullest sense *anthropology* means the study of man in general, his relation to his physical character, environment, and culture; in practice it is usually limited to the study of man in the earliest stages of his advance to full development.

[2] *Archaeology* treats of man's past life and activities as shown by the relics and monuments he has left behind him.

activity of the senses, "elemental as the primary emotions of love, hate, and fear." We can reasonably conclude that such an activity arose in different localities as the result of a number of varied influences. Among these most usually considered are the following:

1) It was the result of an innate desire of prehistoric man for ornamenting and decorating himself, thus providing, through such means as painting or tattooing his body and decorating it with various ornaments, the sort of pleasure in adornment that is to be observed in all modern primitive peoples. This impulse was naturally transferred to the utensils and implements used by early man.

2) It was designed to serve some definitely utilitarian purpose; that is, the painting of pictures, the making of sculptured objects, the practice of dancing, even self-adornment were phenomena connected in various ways with such elemental activities as the obtaining of food, the making of war, and the propagation of the species.

3) It came from the impulse to imitate nature and the pleasure to be derived therefrom; some of the earliest theories of the origin of art maintain that man is naturally an imitative animal, delighting in providing imitations of natural sounds or likenesses of himself and his surroundings, and in thus being able to recognize the original in his copies.

4) It was the expression of some kind of sex-consciousness, a theory that has been strongly emphasized by the ideas of Sigmund Freud and his followers.

5) Art is largely important as an adjunct to religion—a theory which seems to explain many of the details of the art with which we are primarily concerned. The amazing diversity of forms taken by civilized man's supernatural religions, a diversity that has often developed into strongly opposed theologies, suggests the depth and significance of the vital factor of *imagination* in religions as well as in art.

6) It expressed some emotional necessity which has no direct connection with ordinary life, a theory which goes far to explain the importance of art as a factor in human history because of its power to stir feeling, arouse emotion, influence attitudes, and affect thought.

There are many who argue that no one of the foregoing explanations, or any of them combined, suffices to account for the emergence of the arts, and that these may be simply an essence of the expression of what man, in any stage of his development, has felt about his relationship with the world he knows and with any other which he may imagine to exist. But it is hardly necessary to dogmatize regarding such a long-continuing, universal, and diverse force as art. From its very beginnings,

man's creative tendencies in art seem to have taken two definite directions, the ideological leading to abstractions and the utilitarian leading
to achievement of material, realistic form. The proportion of each of
these has varied in the different arts in different countries at different
times: at one period there has been a dominance of one ideal; at another,
the opposite has prevailed. But if we can realize that from the very first
these aims have existed concurrently and that both have been important
factors in the production of art, we shall avoid many of the misunder-
standings which often arise in reading works on the appreciation of art.

THE BEGINNINGS OF MUSIC: RHYTHM

Among the earliest peoples, the arts which we have come to distinguish as music, poetry, and the dance were united in one common
whole, the regulating force of which was rhythm, a factor which determined alike words, music, and dance figures. This united art played as
important a role in the ideological and religious life of these early people
as it did in their everyday existence.

In his book *Arbeit und Rhythmus* Karl Bücher has established the
fact that the dance was a constant and persevering feature of the life of
primitive man. "All people dance," he says,[3] "dance till they are in a
frenzy and their physical powers exhausted, often until the dancers sink
fainting to the earth." Such a dance might have developed out of some
sort of uncoordinated, spontaneous movement of the body, perhaps
arising from a surplus of animal vigor, resulting in the kind of capering
and flinging about of the body, with accompanying shouts and cries,
that we see when a boy and his dog take their morning walk together.
Or the early dancers may have imitated the appearance and movements
of animals as they had observed them while hunting, a procedure which
can be observed in the play of young children and which illustrates Aristotle's theory as to artistic creation being an imitation of nature.

But whatever the beginnings, nothing in the way of art was achieved
until some sort of control was applied to such movements. By applying
the principle of the rhythmic beat (the repetition of a measured sequence of strokes or sounds), our progenitors systematized and coordinated the movements of their dances so as to make them pleasurable and
effective. That there is a psychological effect in the repetition of rhythms

---

[3] Another writer on early music, Wallaschek, has said that there has never been dance
without music of some sort.

for the production of emotional states was probably discovered early. The hypnotic effect of monotonous repetition and the exciting effect of acceleration of speed and vehemence can still be observed in the ritualistic dances of primitive peoples—both orgiastic dances and war dances. The realization of these effects may well have been the source of dance rhythm. At any rate, rhythm probably antedated melody, since it seemed capable of satisfying both emotional and intellectual instincts of primitive man, such as were shown in his simple ordering of the objects he strung into a necklace or the making of patterns in his drawings.

AN ADDED FACTOR: MELODY

Many theories have been advanced as to how man first began to make melody. Herbert Spencer thought that singing was the result of some intense emotion influencing the organs of speech and respiration so strongly as to produce sounds, a fact that is shown by our natural grunting while working or screaming when in pain. Darwin thought that it originated in some sort of love call from man to his mate. Grosse believed that song, as we have suggested of the dance, was some form of play. Others have thought that it may have resulted from some biological necessity or the attempts of the members of a group to coordinate their work so as to make it most effective.

There is probably some truth in all these ideas. As Sorokin has well said, it is likely that primitive people sang when they became excited or when they had an overabundance of energy or merely because they enjoyed it, because singing and dancing are pleasant and biologically useful. But, undoubtedly, one of the principal uses which primitive man found for music and dancing was in the performing of acts of magic. Religion was of great significance in the life of prehistoric society, just as it is today in primitive communities. In its practice, as we have pointed out, one of the chief activities was that of the performance of certain occult formulas and prescribed rituals in order to obtain the favor of the gods. These rites seemed to have been carried out according to certain contracts which it was believed the gods had revealed and to which man had agreed. Some of the tribes came in time to believe that the objects of their desire could be obtained through the potency of the magic rites themselves, without participation of the gods. It was in this manner that music came to be thought of as having a special meaning.

Combarieu maintains that, if we are to believe the evidence of modern primitives, there were in these prehistoric societies magic dance incantations for all purposes—for communicating with the spirits, for subduing animals, for obtaining rain or good weather, for inspiring love, for aid in childbearing, for assuring the birth of a boy, for obtaining vengeance, for bringing back the spirits of the dead, for appeasement of evil spirits, and so on. We have no idea, of course, as to the musical nature of these incantations, aside from assuming that they were much like those used among modern primitive peoples. But there is little doubt that prehistoric man attached definite significance not only to the sounds themselves but to the religious-magical values they represented.

So, too, with the dance movements associated with these rites. Savages have a large number of magic dances, many of which are accompanied by both vocal and instrumental music—dances of the chase, where the figures imitate animals such as kangaroos, bears, wolves, and otters; war dances, in which the actual movements of battle are imitated in order to inculcate courage and insure victory; dances for celebrating the conclusions of treaties between tribes, and so on. One of the most important writers on the origins of civilization, Lubbock, says that among savages and uncultured people the dance was never thought of as an amusement without significance but always as a serious occupation and a necessary factor in all the activities of communal life.

THE USE OF INSTRUMENTS

From the very beginnings of his music-making, man was furnished by nature with two very serviceable instruments, his voice and his hands. The wind instruments which he developed, flutes and reeds, are but "prolongations" of the voice, means to increase its natural force and quality. So the various percussive instruments which he made—drums, castanets, and so forth—were developments of the idea of clapping together his hands or beating in gorilla-fashion on his breast, for the purpose of indicating rhythm. The origin of the stringed instruments was possibly the hunter's bow with which he shot his arrows. Even today the savages in Africa speak of the bow as the source of all music.

Modern archaeological research has unearthed some instruments which certainly belong to the earliest years of man so far known: a double pipe, probably made of human bone, in Mesopotamia; and a form of stone xylophone recently discovered by the French in Southeast Asia. It appears that all of the musical instruments which appear first in history originated in Asia and were quickly distributed over the then known world.

MUSIC IN THE

LIFE OF THE NEAR EAST

Thy dawning is beautiful in the horizon of heaven,
O living Aton, Beginning of life!
When thou risest in the eastern horizon of heaven
Thou fillest every land with thy beauty.

From a hymn by Amenhotep (Ikhnaton)

THE CRADLE OF CIVILIZATION

There is a wide and so far unexplained gap between the arts we have described as having been produced by primitive man and those created by the earliest "civilized" peoples. What happened in between has long been the subject of continued research on the part of eager archaeologists anxious to solve the riddle of how the cave man developed into the Egyptian architect or the Sumerian poet. As Durant has remarked in his *Story of Civilization*, there are not many finer things in man's rather sorry existence than this noble curiosity, this restless passion for understanding his past.

These researchers have come to the conclusion that the beginning of civilization took place in the restricted area lying at the eastern end of the Mediterranean somewhere around 5000 B.C.[1] As to just which civilization was the earliest to develop or what people first evolved the idea of conscious art, opinion seems divided. Both the Mesopotamian valley and the Egyptian valley have their supporters among the scholars; but the majority of opinions at present seem to favor the first and to suggest that at the time our Stone Age forefathers in Europe were still without written language or organized communities, there had developed in the Mesopotamian peninsula a technique of life which was later transferred to posterity intact in all its essentials.

[1] Professor Woolley of the University of Pennsylvania, in his researches at Ur, estimated that the Sumerians appeared to have reached civilization by 4500 B.C.

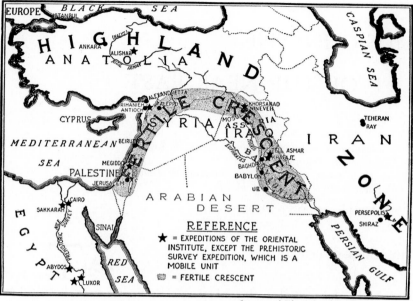

Courtesy of The Oriental Institute of Chicago

Directly east of the Mediterranean Sea lies the so-called Fertile Crescent, the region where the early civilizations worked out the techniques of life which they transmitted to the modern world through Greece and Rome.

THE SUMERIANS

One of the great romances of archaeology, a science in which there is much more of romance than the layman generally realizes, has been the recent unearthing of this civilization which represents the first evidences we have of anything like a complete culture and which was, until these investigations were undertaken during the latter part of the last century, entirely unknown. The manner in which this discovery was made seems almost fantastic.

During their study of the cuneiform writing of the Babylonians, archaeologists gradually became convinced that much of this writing, because of its non-Semitic character, must have been borrowed from an earlier race; and, without knowing that such a people had actually existed, the scholars posited them and gave them the name Sumerians.

This theory was first proved through the work of two English archaeologists who uncovered the sites of a number of cities in which a presumably pre-Babylonian race had lived: Ur, which was already rich and powerful in the year 3000 B.C., Eridu, and Urak. The civilization was given the name Sumerian, as we have noted; owing to the fortunate fact that, by the time it made its appearance on the rapidly changing stage of history, the art of writing had been fully developed, we have been able to reconstruct this earliest of civilizations in detail.

THE SIGNIFICANCE OF MUSIC AMONG THE SUMERIANS

As has been true all through its history, one of music's principal uses in this early civilization was in connection with religion. We have already spoken of the fact that primitive man was certainly cognizant of the peculiar capacity of music for stirring the emotions. A Sumerian clay tablet of the twenty-sixth century B.C. attributes the same power to it:

To fill with joye the Temple court
And chase the Citie's gloome awaie,
The harte to still, the passions calme,
Of weeping eyes the teares to staie.
Translated by Francis W. Galpin [2]

There was only the loosest sort of political unity in the Sumerian government, each group maintaining its own priest-king and acknowledging the power of an emperor only when one arose with personality enough to make them his subjects. So in the Sumerian religion there was no universal god but, rather, a number of deities belonging to the different city-states and associated with the various phases of human activity.

Most of these gods lived in temples, where they were liberally provided by their priests with money, food, and even wives. In addition to the gods, there were spirits, beneficent as well as evil, seeking to possess the Sumerian soul. Music was used in the worship of these temples, where the priests were wont to deliver the revealed word of the god to the people with the solemn accompaniment of the harp, a fact which

[2] In his book *The Music of the Sumerians and Their Immediate Successors, the Babylonians & Assyrians.* This is by far the most exhaustive study yet made of the music of these early peoples. In it Galpin appraises the effect of Sumerian music and song and states definitely that the Sumerians or their compatriots, the Akkads, had discovered a means of writing down their music centuries before the Greeks, to whom we have hitherto looked for the earliest efforts in this direction, evolved their systems of notation.

The book contains an example of a Sumerian hymn of creation transcribed into our modern notation by Galpin, who thinks that it was based on a seven-tone diatonic scale with the fourth step augmented—C,D,E,F#,G,A,B,C—and that its rhythm and stress were entirely dependent on the words, which must have been delivered, in part at least, in a sort of free recitative.

It should be added that scholars do not agree on this matter. Dr. Curt Sachs in the *Archiv für Musikwissenschaft,* April, 1925, maintains that this notation, found on a tablet at Assur, shows the Sumerian scale to have had a nonchromatic pentatonic basis.

A LARGE TEMPLE LYRE FROM UR   (about 2700 B. C.) The bull's head is of gold, with lapis-lazuli beard and shell inlays.

caused this instrument to be thought of as that of the "decision of fate." There were, likewise, music forces of liturgists and psalmists, both men and women, in the temples, trained to sing and play in praise of the god. A late account describes these forces as consisting of an orchestra, led by a harp, with a seven-stringed lyre, a two-stringed lute, pipes, and so forth, and a large group of singers.

That there was Sumerian secular music as well as sacred music is shown clearly by a catalogue which has been found of a music library of the time, listing, in addition to liturgical and psalmodic music, folk songs for craftsmen and shepherds, poems of victory and heroism, and love songs for both sexes. All these, according to Galpin's ideas, were without the modal characteristics which are to be found in later music and would sound more congenial to modern ears than would, for instance, the music of the Greeks.

Their musical scale is not the only thing in the Sumerian culture which would seem congenial to modern man, for many Sumerian ideals were absorbed by later peoples and so have become the common heritage of the ages. The exorcising power of music, later exemplified by the playing of the Hebrew shepherd David before King Saul; the attribution of some of man's powers to animals, an idea which persisted in the Orpheus legend and which is to be found as late as Gothic times, when the sculptors and wood carvers loved to depict animals playing instruments; the "blowing-up of the trumpet in the new moon," a later religious practice of the Hebrews; the story of the Flood, adopted by the writers of the Old Testament—all these were part of Sumerian consciousness and so were absorbed into history.

The significant fact for musicians, however, is that the Sumerian art when it first appears in known history occupies a position that was not very different from that of later times. In other words, when music made its advent, it was as a fully established art, one which played an important role in the life of its time and established its standing for centuries to come. It was used in connection with religious services; it was thought to possess definite powers of magic; officially it was recognized by the state and religious authorities, although there are evidences that it was likewise pursued for pleasure's sake, in a "wine, woman, and song" sense; it was both vocal and instrumental, employing the services of many instruments, among them harps, lyres (both these types favorite instruments for accompanying the voice), flutes, drums, reed pipes, double as well as single, and, in a later, more decadent phase, trumpets, timbrels, and rattles (sistra); it passed through various developments, reaching a "golden" period, after which it became more and more sensual. In all these characteristics it differed little from its use in the other civilizations which appeared in the Near East—Egyptian, Babylonian, Assyrian, and Hebrew.

THE EGYPTIANS

A modern archaeologist has said that we know more about the details of the daily life in the Egypt of the fourteenth century B.C. than we do about those of England in the fourteenth century A.D. But such knowledge, unfortunately, does not extend to the field of music. There are two reasons: first, the fact that the Egyptians interested themselves a great deal more in the arts of sculpture and architecture than they did in music; and second, the fact that the musical practices were largely in the hands of the priests, who regarded them as magical and sacred

influences in the lives of the people and hence as something to be carefully and secretly protected. No change or development was to be
thought of. They would not even take the chance of revealing their
secret by writing it down. As in other early cultures, the whole musical
system of Egypt was subjected to such "rigid religious and hierarchal
laws that it remained at its primitive form . . . and represents an im-
movable block which resists the assault of the centuries" (H. Wollett).[3]

We have already said that scholars are not agreed as to the priority
of Sumerian to Egyptian civilization and that some of them, notably
the great American Egyptologist Breasted, consider that it was the other
way about—that whatever ideas of agriculture and civilization the
Sumerians may have possessed came to them from Egypt. However it
may be, with the exception of music, the Egyptians developed what
they may have borrowed from their neighbors to the northeast into a
civilization which was not only one of the most robust and powerful
but also one of the most polished in history. In spite of the advanced
conditions in agriculture and industry which were to be found in ancient
Egypt, its remarkable developments in science and letters, its well-
organized system of government, with a longer record of duration than
any other people has since attained, its advancement of science and education, the greatest achievements of Egyptian civilization, everything
considered, were its architecture, sculpture, painting, and applied art.
It is quite possible, as Faure has said, that "Egypt, through the solidar-
ity, the unity, and the disciplined variety of its artistic products, through
the enormous duration and the sustained power of its effort, offers the
spectacle of the greatest civilization that has yet appeared on the earth."
And Herr Ranke in his introduction to the book which gives the best
of all possible records of this civilization, *The Art of Ancient Egypt,*
agrees that this art, in the course of the transformations which it underwent during the three kingdoms,[4] represents one of the greatest achievements of human creation.

THE ARTS OF EGYPT

During the whole period of Egyptian history, from its earliest fixed
date of 4241 B.C., art seems to have served the material and spiritual

---

[3] He is writing of Chinese music, but his statement applies with equal truth to Egyptian.

[4] The term *kingdom* is not used here in its usual sense; it refers, rather, to long periods
of time, each of them comprising several dynasties. The usual division is as follows:
Old Kingdom, 2980–2475 B.C.; Middle Kingdom, 2160–1788 B.C.; New Kingdom,
1580–1150 B.C.

Archives Photographiques

FRAGMENT OF A SUMERIAN BAS-RELIEF This shows what is evidently a religious procession. Several of the figures bear in their hands utensils
which were dedicated to the rites of that time. Underneath, two figures provide accompanying music: one seems to be singing, and the other playing a
large lyre similar to that discovered at Ur.

needs of the people: each tomb or statue or carving had a definite purpose to serve. The chief use of art was in religion, where it was employed to manifest the belief of man's continued life after his existence here upon earth. The tombs of the prehistoric chieftains were filled with objects which were thought to be of use in their life after death. The huge Old Kingdom Pyramids of Cheops and Khephren were attempts to memorialize the names of their creators in an impressive fashion that man could never forget, as well as to provide an eternal resting place for the bodies of these god kings. The rock tombs of the Middle Kingdom, the mural paintings and funerary statues, the figures and articles of jewelry and utensils placed in the tombs, which now give us a detailed picture of the life of the time, all fulfilled the same purpose of serving the dead. It is in the New Kingdom that the greatest glory is to be found: royal funerary temples hidden in out-of-the-way valleys; temples at Luxor and Karnak built for the luxury-loving monarchs in honor of the foremost of all gods, Amon; beautiful fresco paintings adorning the tomb walls with scenes from real life; and curiously modern sculptural portrait heads and figures.

One of the outstanding developments of this New Kingdom was the attempt of the "heretic king," Ikhnaton, to abandon the traditional religion and social organizations which he had received from his fathers in favor of a monotheism which transcended national bounds. This spiritual and social rebellion brought about an aesthetic revolution which, instead of following the impersonal conventions of the traditional sculpture and painting, inspired a series of portrait sculptures which are among the most amazing and enjoyable things in the whole range of the art. But Ikhnaton, a poet and a visionary rather than a practical ruler, was far ahead of his time, and after him Egypt returned to the old order of imperialism and artistic convention. The priests deliberately destroyed all the manifestations of Ikhnaton's reforming spirit and saw to it that the old order of privilege and prosperity was restored. Slow decay ensued, a decay which paralleled the gradual lessening of the energy of the nation, a decay which, however, was stayed long enough for the artists and sculptors and poets of the Saite period (663-525 B.C.) to gather together the traditions of their great predecessors, and so prepare them for transference to the Greek, Persian, and Roman conquerors who were to come.

Thus rooted in the religious conceptions and practical needs of the people, Egyptian architectural and sculptural art flourished. We can hardly say the same about Egyptian music.

THE PLACE OF MUSIC

There is abundant evidence in the tomb paintings, bas-reliefs, and so forth, that music played much the same rôle in the lives of the Egyptians as it had in those of the Sumerians. During the first and second kingdoms, the priests looked upon it as invaluable in approaching the gods and in invoking their aid for assuring immortality. As in Sumeria, these priests lived in the luxurious temples of the gods; they ate and drank the sacrifices and libations offered to the gods; their considerable revenue was derived from the rental of temple lands and the fees which they demanded for their services; they were exempt from most taxation and from all enforced labor. Such prestige, together with their learning, gave them a position of great influence. In time, they came into concurrence with the civil power. The king was looked upon as the chief priest of the faith, and thus both Church and State, as in so many later civilizations, secured continuance.

The chief duties of the priests were the performance of rites and the invocation of spells designed to secure the help of the gods. Among the rites with which we are familiar was one which Plato thought must have been invented by a god, for its "ingenuity was entirely divine"—the Dance of the Stars. This was a special sort of ritual, evidently designed to show the whole cosmic order rather than to supplicate any special divinity, and it was danced entirely within the temple precincts, without audience. Kirstein (in his book *The Dance, a Short History of Classic Theatrical Dancing*) describes its choreography as probably devised by astronomer priests and centering about a fixed altar which represented the sun, the dancers, clad in brilliant robes, making signs of the zodiac with their hands and turning rhythmically from east to west, following the course of the planets. After the completion of each circle, the dancers remained immobile in representation of the constancy of the earth. Thus, by combining miming and plastic movements, the priests represented the harmonies of the celestial system and the laws of the universe in a manner which must have been much like that of the modern abstract ballet. Bands of female singing dancers were kept in all the temples for the honoring of the god, and the royal and princely houses maintained similar groups, which were often used for secular purposes as well. Thus, music existed in the life of the Egyptians, as in that of the other early civilizations, as an accessory but not as an independent art.

Flutes and harps (the latter an Egyptian invention, first found in the monuments of the fourth dynasty, the time of the building of the Pyramids) were the chief instruments used. At first, hand clapping accompanied the dances. To this was later added the more subtle means of accentuating the rhythm afforded by the sistrum (a sort of rattle that was made of wood, porcelain, or enamel) and the drum, both of which instruments first appeared about 2500 B.C. If we are to judge by appearances, these religious rites demanded slow music and graceful dances.

But music during the so-called Old and New Kingdoms was no prerogative of the priests. A picture dating from 4000 B.C. shows a secular use of the flute—a child in a fox's skin trying to attract the attention of other animals by playing a flute (the Orpheus concept again!). And Ptah-hotep, prime minister of the fifth dynasty and, incidentally, author of the oldest work on philosophy known to us, gives a description of how he enjoyed his music while being barbered, manicured, and pedicured. There is an atmosphere of almost Hollywoodian luxuriance about the scene—pet animals, including monkeys, wander about as he sits in his palace; there are flowers and fruits in front of him, servants wait on him, and musicians play for him.

NEW-KINGDOM LUXURIANCE

The New Kingdom marked the zenith of Egyptian glory: Thutmosis III in a series of fifteen campaigns made his country the master of the world then known, conquering and annexing the Syrians and drawing their enormous wealth into Egypt for the creation of art and for the preparation of new conquests. It was during this period that Asian luxuries were introduced—such instruments as the cithara with its five to eighteen strings, played either with a plectrum or the fingers; the oboe; the guitar, with two or three strings and a long neck (thought to be so effeminate by the priests that they tried to prohibit its use); the harp, which in its earlier form had been only about five feet high and possessed six or eight strings, now taking a larger form, having ten, fifteen, or even twenty strings and a highly decorated frame ornamented with inlays of gold, silver, or lapis lazuli; and the drum, which was enlarged and, together with the trumpet (of small scale and sounding, according to Plutarch, like the "bray of an ass"), was used for military purposes. Music lost its former simplicity, and the dances evidently became much livelier. Significant is the fact that, beginning with the New Kingdom, the bas-reliefs show only women as flute players. Instrumental music, at least, seemed to have become the sole

THE BLIND HARPER   Accompanied by strings and flutes, the blind harper plays and sings his song of the mystery of death, while a priest offers sacrifice. The words of the song are inserted above. This is the finest record now extant of music's place in the life of ancient Egypt. (XVIII Dynasty, about 1350 B.C.; from a limestone relief).

privilege of feminine musicians, perhaps because it was considered beneath the dignity of men.

We see, in the mural tomb decorations of this period, fashionable people sitting at banquets and being amused by flute players and dancing girls. We hear the song of a blind harper, accompanied by flutes and strings, a song filled with the inscrutable mystery of death:

The generations pass away,
While other remain,
Since the time of the ancestors,
The gods who were aforetime,
Who rest in their pyramids,
Nobles and the glorious departed likewise,
Entombed in their pyramids . . .
Their place is no more. . . . .

Behold the places thereof;
Their walls are dismantled,
Their places are no more,
As if they had never been.

None cometh from thence
That he may tell us how they fare;
That he may tell us of their fortunes,
That he may content our heart,
Until we too depart
To the place whither they have gone.

Translated by Breasted in *The Dawn of Conscience*

But there is no reason to believe that the collective mind of Egypt dwelt only thus imaginatively on the long sleep of death; for Weigall has shown conclusively that the Egyptians were at heart a gay people, given to the pleasures of this life. If their speculation led them to ponder the inevitility of death, they came to the conclusion that while man is here on earth he might as well enjoy himself. And so, this Egyptologist insists, there was in Egypt sunshine, laughter, and feasting as well as mystic contemplation. Music was a means for increasing enjoyment: there are hieroglyphs signifying "songs of the harem" and "songs by domestic singers" as well as "songs by the singers of god." We know even the names of some of these pleasure-providing singers; and the boasts of Snefru and Remery-Ptah that they have "fulfilled every wish of the king by their beautiful singing" sound strangely like those of later times!

THE BABYLONIANS AND THE ASSYRIANS

There remains little to be added regarding the music of the powerful Babylonian and Assyrian civilizations which developed out of the earlier Sumerian beginnings in Mesopotamia, the fertile land between the rivers. The relationship of these three cultures is a difficult one to establish, for there was a great deal of warfare, conquest, and interpenetration.

Essentially traders, businessmen, and warriors, the Babylonians achieved more success in science than in art: their commerce made necessary the development of mathematics, and out of their religious beliefs came the foundations of the modern sciences of astronomy and medicine. It was their laws that became the pattern for all ancient society. Their legends, through adoption by the Hebrews, became known to the whole world. Yet in the visual arts and music they accomplished little that was new. Because of the necessity for using bricks as building material, there being no stone available in the flat country of Babylonia, the Babylonian architecture was heavy and uninspired. Painting never acquired any importance as an independent art; and sculpture, with the exception of some fine bas-reliefs, remained undeveloped, stereotyped, and crude; the best artistic results of the Babylonians seem to have been achieved in ceramics, glazed tile, and pottery. Their music is but an elaboration of Sumerian practices. They used, perhaps, more and bigger instruments—harps, citharas, lutes, single and double flutes, reeds, trumpets, drums, cymbals, and tambourines. As in Egypt, the singers sang and the orchestras played both in the temples and in the palaces of the rich; but again, no examples of Babylonian music have come down to us, and so we know nothing of its character.

Shortly after Nebuchadrezzar's death in 562 B.C., the Babylonian empire fell apart and thus became a ready prey for Cyrus and his conquering Persians, who captured it in 538 B.C. and made it an essential part of their ambitious imperial scheme. Then, two hundred years later, came Alexander; and through him the cultural elements of the civilization of the Land between the Rivers were dispersed to become a part of the heritage of mankind.

The great man of Assyria, the imperial power to the north, was Ashurbanipal (?-626 B.C.), whose empire at the height of its power embraced Assyria, Babylonia, Armenia, Palestine, Syria, Phoenicia, Sumeria, and Egypt. This empire was founded, as all such domains must be founded, on military power. It recognized frankly that government is the "nationalization of force," and its chief contributions—if

SCENE FROM AN ASSYRIAN WALL RELIEF   The relief is one from the time of
the empire's greatest glory under Ashurbanipal, 668—626 B.C.

they can be called contributions—to the progress of man were in the
art of war. So we can hardly expect any important developments in
Assyrian art. Except in their magnificent bas-reliefs, filled with scenes
from their wars and hunts, the Assyrians did not distinguish themselves
as artists. They copied or imported everything from Babylon.

The one outstanding illustration of the use of music in the Assyrian
civilization is the great decorative relief (now in the British Museum)
from the time of Ashurbanipal, showing the royal musicians celebrating
the triumphant return of the king from one of his wars. In this procession are players on double flutes and harps, a player on a percussive instrument, and singers, one of them, according to Combarieu, holding
his hand to his throat in such a way as to produce the nasal tone so
characteristic of Oriental music, the others marking the rhythm by
clapping their hands.

THE HEBREWS

The history of the Semitic people, the Hebrews, has become familiar
not so much because of their importance as a people as through the
influence which they exerted on the later history of the world. As someone has said, they did not make history; history made them. They were
settled on a narrow strip of land bordering the Mediterranean, between
Egypt and Assyria, and their country was the natural high road between these powers. Their significance is due to the fact that, influenced

by the great civilizations to the south and east, they produced a written literature, a history of the world which records their developing concept of God, a collection of laws, songs, and religious rites, all of which were incorporated into the Christian Bible and thus became known to the whole Western world.

The music of the Hebrews was probably similar to that of their neighbors and largely bound up with the ritual of their worship. It was King David who assigned to one of the Hebrew tribes the sole duty of providing music in the temple, although there had long been a special caste of "singers with instruments of music, psalteries, harps, and cymbals." It was the Levites who sang and played and danced before the Lord; and many of the texts which they probably used are to be found in the Psalms.[5] These are of interest to us today not only because of the superb lyricism of their poetry, but also because they represent the sort of liturgical texts that were probably used by the Egyptians and the Babylonians. Commentators believe, for instance, that the rolling lines of the Twenty-fourth Psalm were a liturgical chant performed when the ark of the covenant arrived in front of the Temple, the priest singing half of each verse, and the choir the remainder:

The earth is the Lord's and the fullness thereof,
the world and they that dwell therein.
For he hath founded it upon the seas;
and established it upon the floods.

It is the opinion of scholars that the last four verses of this magnificent psalm are the oldest:

Lift up your heads, O ye gates, and be ye
   lifted up, ye everlasting doors;
And the King of Glory shall come in.
Who is this King of Glory?
The Lord strong and mighty, the Lord mighty
   in battle.

[5] Modern research seems to show that Solomon's Temple (which he built on Mount Moriah, a broad plateau east of Jerusalem, in order to provide a fitting setting for the sacrifices of his people to Jehovah and a permanent shelter for the ark of the covenant) consisted of a group of buildings surrounded by a strong fortress wall and surmounted by a high, golden-roofed tower. This tower, about two hundred feet high, contained the holy inner chamber where rested the tablets of the Ten Commandments; before it was an inner court which contained the great altar where the priests offered the sacrifices of animals and crops, required three times a year of every Hebrew. It was probably before this inner court that the musical ceremonies of the temple took place. The Levites, who were the singers (under King David 4000 men out of a tribe of 38,000 were musicians), "being arrayed in fine linen, having cymbals and psalteries and harps, stood at the east end of the altar, and with them an hundred and twenty priests sounding with trumpets."

And again, in ecstasy:

Lift up your heads, O ye gates, even lift them
up, ye everlasting doors;
And the King of Glory shall come in.
Who is the King of Glory?
The Lord of Hosts, he is the King of Glory.
Selah.

These magniloquent lines call for mighty music. How impressive they must have sounded accompanied by the sweep of harps, the sound of trumpets, and the clash of cymbals! Then it must have been that the "trumpeters and singers were as one, to make one sound to be heard in praising and thanking the Lord; and when they lifted up their voice with the trumpets and cymbals and instruments of music . . . the house was filled with a cloud, even the house of the Lord. The glory of the Lord had filled the house of God."

The Hebrews believed that all music possessed this magic power. The prophet Samuel, when he anointed Saul to be king, said to him: "It shall come to pass . . . that thou shalt meet a company of prophets coming down from the high place with a psaltery and a tabret and a pipe and a harp before them; and they shall prophesy. And the spirit of the Lord will come upon thee, and thou shalt prophesy with them and shalt be turned into another man." And it was when the "evil spirit from God was upon Saul that David took a harp, and played with his hand; so Saul was refreshed, and was well, and the evil spirit departed from him."

The Bible gives many evidences that secular music and dances were likewise commonly employed by the Hebrews; war and work songs, laments and rejoicings are mentioned. Wandering minstrels, of whom Jubal, the "father of all such as handle the harp," was first, sang to the people. After such national triumphs as the passing of the Red Sea or the conquering of Goliath by David, there was rejoicing in song, with dancing and tambourine beating by the women.

It is interesting to speculate as to the nature of this music. The more recent research which has been done along this line has been able to establish definitely the character of the liturgy used in the ancient Hebrew synagogues or meetinghouses established by the Hebrews at the time of their Babylonian captivity (586-538 B.C.).[6] There were

---

[6] These stood in somewhat the same relation to the Temple as the modern parish churches to the Cathedral. At the time of the destruction of the Temple in 70 A.D., there were over 400 of these meetinghouses in Jerusalem alone. They were the scenes of the preaching and worship of Jesus and of St. Paul.

portions of Scripture taken from the Pentateuch and the Prophets, sung in free rhythm to traditional tunes of a highly decorated character (the process was called *cantillation*) in a manner strongly resembling the later practices of the Christians. There was also the great *Shema* or Credo; and there were special prayers and psalms for various occasions. Certain scholars, particularly A. Z. Idelsohn and Lazare Saminsky, have proved, to their own satisfaction at least, that the synagogical modes and melodies used by the modern Transcaucasian Hebrews are much the same as those in use during the great days of Hebraic worship. These Babylonian and Persian communities of Hebrews were established long before the beginning of the Christian era and have kept themselves isolated from European influences. Their religious songs and cantillations reveal an astounding similarity of melodies and scales, entirely different from those used by the Hebrews whose religious music has been subject to Arabic and European influences. And so their religious music probably established a real contact with the traditional practices of pre-Christian times.

Canon Douglas (in his fine book *Church Music in History and Practice*) has summarized the essential features of this Hebraic Bible music, features which were taken over by the early Christians into their musical practices:

(1) The basic principle of monotonic recitation, or what we call *chanting*
(2) Congregational refrains to the singing of the Psalms
(3) Elaborate musical exfoliations (melismata) on certain vowels
(4) The establishment of the principle that the rhythm of the music depends on the rhythm of the prose
(5) A musical style of noble dignity, sharply distinguished from secular melodies.

Undoubtedly the accounts of Hebraic magnificence and importance as given in the Books of Kings and Chronicles have been exaggerated by patriotic writers in an attempt to show that a small, provincial people was able to keep up with the magnificence of its rich and powerful neighbors. But even if this is true, the Hebraic ritual and music, representing, as they well may, something of the characteristics of the music of the other civilizations of the Near East, deserve our special consideration. For they are the nearest elements that we possess to a living link with that great past.

THE ART AND MUSIC OF THE FAR EAST

It should be remembered that the diverse cultures of the Far East—China, Japan, India, and the Islamic Orient—have pursued their own courses of musical development, though on quite different lines from those of the West. Only recently have sufficient investigations shown the importance of these Eastern musical systems. Nevertheless, it is important not to overlook the significance of Eastern ideals, which tended toward the development of subtle and complex arrangements of scales, ornamentation, and rhythm, rather than, as in the European system, of polyphonic and harmonic enrichment.

The art of China is still underestimated by the great majority of Europeans, for the reason that it has for so long remained entirely a sealed book to them. In all its ramifications, covering a period of at least four thousand years, it is essentially mystical and symbolic rather than realistic and objective. Chinese music is based, like most other Far Eastern systems, on a five-tone scale, each note of which is considered to have its own essential importance *per se,* without regard to its relationship to the other tones of the scale. These various pitches, as well as the texture of the materials which produce them, are all involved, in the Chinese mind, with a complex set of symbols having social, political, and cultural implications. It is therefore not to be wondered at that the European is apt to find classic Chinese music monotonous.

In the music of India, on the other hand, the individual tones have little significance in themselves but derive their meaning from their position in the scores of *ragas,* or set melodic patterns making up this music. The ragas have the power, according to Indian philosophy, of arousing emotions and feelings motivating human conduct; therefore Indian music, though impersonal, has definite emotional connotations. Like the Chinese music, this expression of Hindu culture is entirely monophonic, or one-voiced. Its rhythmic structure is fairly complex, and the vocal part is often highly ornamented. The music is closely associated with a conventionalized style of dancing, replete with postures and gestures, which are for the Indians symbolic and evocative.

The music of the Islamic tribes in North Africa, Arabia, and Persia is, like their architecture, highly decorative rather than functional. This music, while strongly rhapsodic, is concerned with arabesque-like ornamentations, consisting of groups of coloratura melodies.

After this necessarily very brief glance at the musics of the Orient, we resume our tracing of the backgrounds of European developments.

THE MUSIC

OF THE HELLENIC AGE

The nodding promontories, and blue isles,
*   And cloudlike mountains, and dividuous waves*
Of Greece, basked glorious in the open smiles
*   Of favoring heaven: from their enchanted caves*
Prophetic echoes flung dim melody.

Shelley: "Ode to Liberty"

I cannot rest from travel: I will drink
Life to the lees . . .
For always roaming with a hungry heart
Much have I seen and known: cities of men,
And manners, climates, councils, governments,
Myself not least, but honored of them all . . .
I am a part of all that I have met;
Yet all experience is an arch wherethro'
Gleams that untravel'd world, whose margin fades
Forever and forever when I move.

Tennyson: "Ulysses"

THE SOURCES OF HELLENIC
THOUGHT AND CULTURE
With the entrance of Greece into the arena of history, a new force made itself felt in the world: a force which, by casting off the dead weight of the superstitions of the past and by developing an insatiable curiosity for penetrating the unknown future, achieved in a few short centuries a cultural supremacy which, spreading over western Europe, has remained down to this day one of man's greatest heritages. While largely devoted to intellectual speculation, this spirit of free inquiry of the Greeks enabled them to make important contributions to the sciences as well as to the arts. It was Pythagoras who, about 550 B.C., after experimenting with strings, first founded the science of mathematical acoustics and

ORPHEUS PLAYING HIS LYRE TO THE THRACIANS   The original dates back to the fifth century B.C.

discovered the octave; and the other Greeks made many fundamental contributions to the sciences of astronomy, medicine, and biology—contributions which, generally speaking, were not transcended until the seventeenth century. It is interesting to speculate as to what might have happened if this intellectually curious people had been possessed of a greater inclination for real scientific experimentation.

Modern historians like to remind us that these unique contributions which Greece passed on to later civilizations were by no means original with her but were based on the rich inheritances which she, in her turn, had received from earlier peoples. It was Egypt and Mesopotamia which, as Barnes has said, cleared the road and set up the cultural and intellectual signposts for the civilizations that were to follow; and through her whole history Greece maintained constant contact with her eastern neighbors, a fact which explains many of the characteristics of her art.

There were three sources which influenced the development of Greek culture as we know it: first, that which developed on the island of Crete in the Mediterranean between 2700 and 1400 B.C.; second, that of the mainland of Greece, centering at Mycenae and Tiryns, the bearers of this culture being the wandering tribes of fair-haired Aryans who came into Greece around 2500 B.C.; and third, the Phoenicians, those Semitic sea-traders and wanderers who roamed the whole Mediterranean from their bases at Tyre and Sidon. All three of these sources stand in the background as a sort of preludial introduction to the great symphony whose opening movement begins with the development of classic Greece.

THE MINOANS

Excavations made by the British archaeologist Sir Arthur Evans at the beginning of the present century show conclusively that a brilliant civilization had begun in the island of Crete as far back as the Bronze Age (around 2700 B.C.) and that its early developments coincided with those of the Old Kingdom in Egypt. Evidently a high degree of culture grew up early, and these pre-Grecian people achieved some astonishingly beautiful results in painting, sculpture, and such minor arts as bronze working and pottery making. The centers of this Cretan or Minoan culture were the great court cities of Knossos and Phaestos, as well as such industrial towns as Gournia and small market places scattered over the whole island. Its chief feature was the huge palace of King Minos, built at Knossos about 1700 B.C., a structure which, like the later palace of Louis XIV at Versailles, evidently housed not only the monarch but his whole court as well.

Examination of these Cretan remains has given us important information regarding this almost forgotten civilization. We know that it must have been rather a Sybaritic one supported by a flourishing Mediterranean commercial trade, confined to the court and aristocratic circles, and delighting in all sorts of luxurious surroundings. It produced great festivals and shows and indulged in a kind of bull-fighting much like that which developed later in Spain. That there were dances and gymnastic displays is certain, Crete being looked upon by the writers of antiquity as the cradle of their dances. One of the earliest ritualistic dances was found in the so-called "Hymn of the Kouretes" (young men just come to maturity), discovered at Palaikastro in Crete. The archaeologists have found terra-cotta figures, dancing in circles, which date from the sixteenth century before Christ; and frescoes of dancing ladies have been found decorating the walls of the palace of Minos. Indeed, the excavations made by Evans and others show that this whole vast structure must have been filled with a life that was generously enlivened by the arts; and there is no reason to think that music played a less important part in the civilized life of Minos at Knossos than it did in that of contemporary Babylon.

THE MYCENAEANS

The most recent archaeological discoveries support the idea that there arose, contemporaneously with the Minoan civilization in Crete, a purely Greek culture on the mainland, the result of the coalescence of the Aryans who came into the country from southwestern Asia Minor around 2500 B.C. with its previous inhabitants. This mainland civilization advanced rapidly and without apparent interruption, especially after it had come into contact with the Minoan culture of Crete. It centered at Mycenae and Tiryns on the Peloponnesian peninsula; and the latest excavations show that not only did these mainland Greeks absorb much from Crete, but that around 1450 they actually established their supremacy of the island, taking over the centers outside Knossos and eventually causing the destruction of the palace itself about 1400. All the archaeological evidence points to the fact that, during its later period, Knossos was Greek and that the later stages of pre-classic Greek civilization developed under the domination and supremacy of Mycenae, the mainland city which later was to become famous as the capital of the Homeric king Agamemnon, from which he set out for the Trojan wars. The quality of the Mycenaean civilization, which later spread about the Aegean and Mediterranean and reached the coasts of Asia Minor, Cyprus, Syria, Palestine, and Egypt, as well as those of southern Italy, is only beginning to be realized. The Mycenaeans evidently enjoyed great commercial prosperity and long-continued peace; their weapons, elaborately worked gold and silver cups, carved ivories, graven jewels, and polychrome pottery now coming to light show that this pre-Homeric Mycenaean civilization was important artistically as well as materialistically. And the recent deciphering of what had hitherto been their unintelligible writing from the fourteenth century shows conclusively that the Mycenaeans had developed a new and distinct language from that which had been previously used in Crete and that this language, "fashioned to agree with the economic system of the mainland," is really the earliest form of what later was to become classic Greek.

It is reasonable to suppose that music must have played a role in the life of this Mycenaean civilization, as it had in that of the Minoans. Aside from the fact that a few instruments have appeared in the excavations, it is known that music played a real part in the life of the antecedent Aryans as they wandered about Europe and Asia Minor. They have been well called a vocal people, for by way of enlivening their

The Louvre

LADY OF AUXERRE
One of the oldest
Greek statues known

wanderings they would foregather for communal feasts, on which occasions, in addition to a great deal of eating and drinking, there would be
entertainment by the national poets, the bards. Their minds crowded
with the memories of the great events of tribal history, these poets recited and sang their poems for their fellows, accompanying themselves
by playing the lyre. Thus originated that great series of epics and sagas
which has contributed so much to the world's enjoyment: *The Iliad*
and *The Odyssey* (attributed to the late Mycenaean poet Homer), as
well as the subsequent European *Nibelungenlied* and the *Kalevala*.

Historians have been wont to maintain that this Mycenaean civilization which had been established on the mainland of Greece was destroyed by the Dorians, another branch of the Aryan stem, descending

upon Greece from the north some time before 1000 B.C. and capturing
its centers of civilization. Evidence does show that Mycenae and Tiryns
and other similar sites were burnt at the end of the Bronze Age, but
Professor A. J. B. Wace, the leader of the British excavations at
Mycenae, thinks that there is no sign of any real interruption of cultural development. On the other hand, there is clear evidence, he
thinks, that in many parts of Greece, from the later days of the Bronze
Age right through the periods of transition down into the days of
classic greatness, there was a steady development of culture, with nowhere any such break as is envisaged by a concept of a "Dorian invasion." If the Dorians did return, or if there was an influx of fresh
barbarians into Greece, no racial or cultural break occurred in its development, but only political disturbances resulting in the overthrow of
those in power. And Wace maintains that what the historians and
archaeologists have called the pre-Grecian "Dark Ages," when the
inhabitants of the mainland are supposed to have forgotten how to read
and to have degenerated in culture, are dark only because so far we have
little evidence—archaeological, cultural, or linguistic—of the real state
of the civilization of this time. In reality, it was then that there were
slowly laid the foundations of the religious, social, and artistic developments which made possible the "Greek miracle" of the fifth century B.C.

THE PHOENICIANS

Ethnologists seem to be completely baffled as to the origin of the
Phoenicians, the people who in pre-Hellenic times lived on the narrow
strip of land along the east coast of the Mediterranean, whose ships
sailed every known sea, and whose bartering merchants were to be found
in every port. They were probably a western branch of the Semitic tribes
of Arabia who had conquered Sumeria and helped set up the Babylonian
empire. Forced by the geographical position of their country to make
their living from the sea, they became the means of spreading the culture of Asia Minor among the countries of Europe.

As early as 2800 B.C. we find their ships in the Mediterranean, and
they soon became the busiest merchants in the world. They manufactured various sorts of artistic objects—glass, metalware, jewelry, and so
forth; and they became well known for extracting from the sea animals
along their coasts the famous purple dye which was much in demand.
In addition, they transported the products of India and the Near East to
all the cities along the Mediterranean, carrying in return metals, ivory,

and wood, as well as slaves for the service of those who could afford them. Their two great cities, Tyre and Sidon, rose to a place among the richest and most powerful in the world; according to the account of the prophet Ezekiel, they were "perfect in beauty and in them was sealed the sum of all wisdom." Their culture and art, drawn from Egypt, Crete, and the Near East, were carried abroad, along with their goods and merchandise; and we owe a great debt to this commercial people for introducing the Egyptian alphabet to the nations of antiquity.

Music seems to have occupied much the same place in their civilization as it did among their neighbors: we hear of its use at princely feasts, played on the same instruments as in Egypt and Assyria. The Phoenicians used the aulos, a kind of double-reed pipe made of wood with mouthpiece of ivory or metal, which was later very popular in Greece. It is thought that those elements of theory and practice which entered the Greek music system from the East, elements which survived in the names of two of the Greek scales, the Phrygian and the Lydian,[1] were transmitted through the Phoenicians.

THE ARTS IN GREECE

Not only Hellenic art but also European literature begins on a note of epic grandeur, the Homeric poems. It is quite appropriate that the origin of such grandeur should be shrouded in mystery: whether or not there was a blind poet by the name Homer, who, according to popular legend, composed the two great epics *The Odyssey* and *The Iliad*, no one knows. Probably these epics were the result of the long accumulation of many generations of Aryan ballads, which may have been set down by one man sometime during the eighth or seventh century B.C. These great works deal with the adventures of the early Greeks in their warfare with the Minoans and tell of the last years of the siege of Troy, and of the adventures of Odysseus upon his return from these wars.

Written in flexible hexameters (lines of six feet), these two epics have given rise to a great deal of discussion as to just how they were presented in Homeric times. We know that they were accompanied by the lyre, an instrument originally made by stretching strips of an animal's skin over a tortoise shell and adding branches from the side, joined by a

[1] Phrygia and Lydia were two of the nations which became powerful in Asia Minor, in the district to the east of Assyria, sometime after the ninth century B.C. They linked the civilization of the ancient Hittites, who came from India, with that of Greece. Whatever the Phrygian or Lydian musicians had inherited or found out as to the structure of instruments or schemes of tonality had its echo or application in Greece.

Furtwangler-Reichold: Griechische Vasenmalerei

GREEK SCHOOL   (From a vase now in Berlin) This vase, dating from the youth of
Sophocles, shows boys being taught to read, write, recite poetry, sing to the aulos, and
play the lyre.

crosspiece. Probably the words were delivered in a free sort of recitative,
accompanied by the lyre. When in later centuries the renditions of the
Homeric epics had become events of national importance, the *rhapsodes,*
those who made the renditions, wore distinguishing costumes—long
flowing cloaks of crimson when they recited *The Iliad,* blue when they
declaimed *The Odyssey.* The accompaniment consisted of a prelude

played on the lyre, a modest unisonal background for the voice,[2] and interludes between verses, with a postlude at the end of the performance.

The word *music* is of Greek origin (*mousikē*) and meant originally *of the Muses;* it was applied to a combination of poetry, music, and dancing, of which poetry was considered the ruler, music an accompaniment, and dancing an integral part and not a mere spectacle.[3] Although such an association limited its own development as an art, it made music of tremendous significance in the life of the people. We have seen how the epics of Homer were always declaimed to musical accompaniment; other uses of music in this heroic age of Greek history, an age which extended down to 600 B.C., were in connection with religious and civic festivals, a fact that is commemorated by the survival of the names of the various musical forms used.

The mixed races which had settled on the islands and the lands bordering the Aegean Sea had, by the seventh century, founded a number of cities, the most important of which were Athens, Sparta, Corinth, Thebes, Samos, and Miletus. The last named, situated in Asia Minor, was the most important of them all. These cities grew rapidly in size and significance, but they never formed any strong political coalescence. Among the chief influences which gave them a certain amount of common interest and which held them together in a political sense was their religion. Basically borrowed from the cults of preceding civilizations, the Greek religion early developed its own rich mythology and striking theogony. In many of their dealings with the spirits who became their gods, the Greeks made music a necessary feature, regarding it as a sort of charm between man and the Invisible, and as possessing special effectiveness for their communications with the naturalistic inhabitants with which they had peopled Olympus, the home of their deities.

A number of accompanied chants, which went by the general name *nomos,* were used in honor of the various members of this pantheon. Special forms of these were used on occasion: the *dithyramb,* at festivals of Dionysos, the wine god, wild and boisterous; the *paean,* a chant to Apollo, the god of music; *prosodies,* marchlike chants used to accom-

---

[2] The term *harmony* employed by many of the Greek writers on music always meant accompaniment at the unison. Chords, harmony, and counterpoint in our modern sense did not exist in ancient times. Plato speaks of the introductions to these accompanied poems (*nomos*) as having been composed with "remarkable art."

[3] Among the Greeks the term *musician* had a special significance, one somewhat similar to that of the eighteenth-century *honnête homme*: a well-rounded individual rather than a specialist. The study of music with the Greeks meant a training in singing and playing, dancing and verse. It was considered to be the backbone of education and to be closely associated with ethical and moral principles.

pany religious processions; *threnodies,* perhaps the most primitive of all the chant forms, employed in lamenting the death of an individual *(The Iliad* closes with three magnificent examples sung on the death of Hector); songs of joy and thanksgiving, used after recovery from illness or for invoking the protection of the gods in matters of health or in the midst of battle or as part of a religious ceremony at a banquet.[4]

THE FIRST OF THREE GREAT PERIODS: THE ARCHAIC

In the Homeric days, the worship of these pantheistic people centered about smoking open-air altars and included the enjoyment of song and dance, with sound of pipe and lyre. As they progressed toward a more unified culture, the Greeks designated certain spots, such as Delphi, as sacred places; and people came from far and near to sacrifice to the gods, to consult the oracle who was supposed to reside there, and to enjoy themselves generally while attending to their religious duties. Gradually permanent buildings arose in these sacred places—shrines, "treasuries," and monumental temples designed to give an appearance of dignity and impressiveness. The spontaneous games and play, the dancing and the singing of earlier days were developed into huge festivals in honor of Dionysos, Apollo, Aphrodite, or some other deity, festivals which came to be considered among the most important functions in the country. At first these festivals were concerned with elaborate pantomimic dancing celebrating events in the life of the gods or of the human heroes who were raised almost to the rank of deities. There are long lists of these dramatic dances performed for celebrating such events as the birth of

[4] Nothing gives the real character of these early religious rites better than does Homer's description of such a banquet:
"Then they orderly employ'd
 The sacred offering. washed their hands, took salt cakes; and the priest
 With hands held up to heaven, thus pray'd:
 O thou that all things seest . . .
 Hear thy priest, and as thy hand, in free grace to my prayers,
 Shot fervent plague-shafts through the Greeks, now hearten their affairs
 With health renewed and quite remove th' infection from their blood.
 He pray'd; and to his prayers again the God propitious stood.
 All, after prayer, cast on salt cakes, drew back, kill'd, flay'd the beeves,
 Cut out and dubb'd with fat their thighs, fair dress'd with doubled leaves,
 And on them all the sweetbreads prick'd. The priest, with small, sere wood,
 Did sacrifice, pour'd on red wine; by whom the young men stood,
 And turn'd, in five ranks, spits . . . which, roasted well, they drew.
 The labor done, they served the feast in, that fed all to satisfaction.
 Desire of meat and wine thus quench'd, the youths crown'd cups of wine
 Drunk off, and fill'd again to all. That day was held divine,
 And spent in paeans to the Sun."

THE PARTHENON AT ATHENS

Zeus, the marriage of Zeus and Hera, or the battle of Apollo and the python.[5] They were always performed to music. The aulos, the flute, and the cithara were the instruments employed, and there seems to have been a background of singing. Gestures were used as means of heightening the effect of the words that were being sung. It was out of beginnings such as these that the popular Attic drama, both tragic and comic, developed.

The character of this early music was, of course, entirely religious. There was not a hint of the subjects with which the later Greek *mousikē* was so concerned—romantic love, or man's gigantic and helpless struggle against the Invisible. The choristers, always men, sang their parts in unison (the Greeks had no idea of part music as we know it), with the instruments playing the melody either in unison with the voices or an

[5] One of the old authorities, Meursius, names over two hundred dances known to him. He refers in many cases to steps rather than to whole dances; but in any event the number is large. There were athletic, military, religious, and social dances.

THE DORIC TEMPLE AT PAESTUM   (middle of the fifth century B.C.)

octave above them, sometimes using a simple variation. The combination of instruments beloved of the ancient civilizations, such as string,
wind, and percussion, were not used by the Greeks. They especially
stressed simplicity. Considering the large audiences which heard their
musical performances, the means they employed seem meager enough
—from sixteen to twenty-four choristers and dancers and one or two
auloi.

The other arts were as much concerned during this archaic period
with religious and mythological subjects as was music. In both painting
and sculpture the technique employed was simple in the extreme and
made no attempt to create a visual illusion of the objects rendered. The

subjects used were the gods and incidents in Olympian life, straight-forwardly and almost geometrically conceived. Architecture was largely concerned with the erection of temples serving the gods and the dead, simply and yet beautifully proportioned, of modest style, and using with great effectiveness the Doric column, an architectural feature which, because of its structural and organic unity, has never been sur-passed for beauty. So, down to the sixth century B.C., we may say that the great concern of all the arts was that of the conveying of religious and ideational concepts.

THE SECOND PERIOD: THE LYRIC AGE

Then there came a change. With the gradual expansion of the city-states, the leadership of which was strongly maintained by the Ionians on the western coast of Asia Minor and on the adjacent islands, trade became more general, wealth increased, and intellectual interests became general. Man was no longer concerned only with his gods but began to take more interest in himself. Consequently, art became more personal, expressive, emotional, and visual. This was the great age of lyric poetry (the very derivation of the term *lyric* shows that this poetry was written to be sung). The poets Archilochus, Simonides of Ceos, Sappho the Lady of Lesbos, Anacreon, Pindar, and the great Athenian lawgiver Solon sang with such ecstasy and beauty as to insure for their songs a permanent place in the affections of lovers of poetry; all of the poetry was sung, much of it by solo voices accompanied by the lyre. Such things as the odes which Pindar wrote commemorating the victories of athletes in the games which by this time had become so essential a part of the religious festivals were chanted by a dancing chorus, the move-ments of which were carefully prescribed.

CULMINATION IN THE GOLDEN AGE

The Golden Age of Greek life and art came during the sixth and fifth centuries B.C., when Athens, after turning back the invaders from Persia who were intent on conquering Greece, assumed the leadership of all the Greek cities and established herself as the head of the Delian League and the center of Greek life and culture, attracting money and scholars and artists from the entire known world. During this fabulous period there occurred such a development in the drama, sculpture, and archi-tecture as the world has never experienced since. Originating in the

THE THEATER AND TEMPLE OF APOLLO AT DELPHI   These are beautifully situated on the slopes of Mt. Parnassus.

mimetic dances and chanted choruses of the religious festivals, especially
those connected with Dionysos, Greek drama, from its earliest stages
musically accompanied, may be said to have started with the works of
Aeschylus (525–456 B.C.), who was the first playwright to introduce
individual characters into his plays and thus make them capable of

expressing personal ideas. Before his time, one character delivered formal speeches against a background of the chorus, which commented upon the action for the benefit of the spectators. Aeschylus kept the chorus but reduced its importance, for he could carry on the action by means of his few characters.

From the time of these early Aeschylean plays, the Greek dramas were always chosen in open competition and produced at the time of the great religious festivals, which included, in addition, processions, games, religious rites, and contests in singing and playing. Participation in these festivals was looked upon as a religious rather than a social exercise, and during the spring days on which they were held the Greeks put aside their other affairs for the time being. They loved competitions of all sorts, dramatic and musical as well as athletic, and no greater honor could come to one of them than the prize, a vase or a wreath, given to the winner of one of these play competitions.

Greek plays[6] were given in outdoor amphitheaters that were built in natural beauty spots about a circular stage, structures wonderfully suited to their purpose. Originally merely a circle of benches about a level earthen stage tamped smooth for dancing, by the fifth century these structures had developed into gently sloping tiers of seats arranged about the *orchestra* and set into the slope of a hill in such a way as to provide a beautiful and extensive view beyond the limits of the stage. On the far side of the semicircular orchestra there was built the *skene*, a simple, two-storied building which served as a background for the actors and the chorus. The scenery was rudimentary, and there were few properties. The actors were originally amateurs, the poet always acting in his plays and writing the music for them as well as the lines. By the time of Aeschylus, acting had developed as a separate art, and the poet called in other specialists to help in producing his play. The actors wore masks and used a chanted recitative, making necessary a slow-timed and artificial style.

The chorus, with its members chosen from among the free citizens, played an important role throughout the development of Greek drama. Until the time of Euripides its interludes of music, poetry, and dance were an essential part of the dramatic design, and a definite plan was always followed as to its use. After a spoken *prologue* came the *parados,* or chorus entrance, an impressive procession led by *coryphees* or leaders and accompanied by aulos players. Two by two its members came into

[6] Exclusive of fragments, forty-seven of these Greek plays have survived—seven of Aeschylus, seven of Sophocles, nineteen of Euripides, eleven of Aristophanes, and three of Menander.

the orchestra, their pace slow and majestic, their faces proudly serious, their flowing robes forming a sort of visual bas-relief against which the action would be played out. The rhythm of this entrance was that of a march, and the words sung were always anapaestic. Defiling around the circular orchestra, the members finally came to rest in front of the skene, to remain there until the end of the drama, commenting from time to time on its development in solemn chant, lively song, or graceful dance. Through it, often, the dramatist expressed his ideas on religion.

The action of the play was developed by means of a series of *episodes* between the characters, interspersed with these *stasima* or musical chants. As there was no division into intervals, the play going on from its beginning to its inevitable and frequently awful conclusion, some such relief from the stormier heights of the action was absolutely necessary. In the earlier works, these dance-song episodes constituted the main design of the drama; and even in the time of Euripides they were beautifully decorative additions to its structure. Such a chorus as this from *Iphigenia in Aulis* may not be necessary to the development of the plot; but what a lovely accessory it must have made when chanted and danced!

May no child of mine
Nor any child of my child
Ever fashion such a tale
As the Phrygians shall murmur,
As they stoop at their distaffs,
Whispering with Lydians,
Splendid with weight of gold—
Helen has brought this,
They will tarnish our bright hair.
They will take us captives
For Helen . . . if men speak truth.

But still we lament our state,
The descent of our wide courts.
Even if there be no truth
In the legends cut on ivory,
Nor in the poets
Nor the songs.

Translated by Hilda Aldington

The choreography of the chorus interpreted the sense of the words it sang. The dancing was not dancing as we know it; for it possessed none of the characteristics of the modern ballet or social dance—no *pirouettes* or *pointes* or *demi-pointes*. There was no coupling of figures among the

State Museum, Berlin

A GREEK DANCER
FROM A FIFTH-CEN-
TURY RELIEF

dancers, for there were no women interpreters; the movements were measured and graceful, well-proportioned and carefully balanced, and made use of the hands in a plastic manner that was suggestive of sculpture. It must have been a superb art, this dancing of the Greek chorus; and we find ourselves brooding with Euripides, who asks,

Will they ever come to me again, ever again
The long, long dances,
On through the dark till the dim stars wane?
Shall I feel the dew on my throat, and the
*   stream*
Of wind in my hair? Shall our white feet
*   gleam*
*   In the dim expanses?*

The Bacchae, translated by Gilbert Murray

Sophocles (496?–406 B.C.) introduced more characters into his dramas —he wrote over a hundred and won productions for eighteen of them—

and so was able to achieve more of a dramatic plot in the modern sense, through the development of climax and suspense and the expression of conflict between his protagonists. Although the characters gave vent to emotions that were personal and individual, they did so in a manner that had universal significance. The story of Oedipus the King, doomed by the gods to marry his own mother, as it proceeds from disaster to disaster, is characteristic of Sophocles's treatment and is as simple, inevitable, and dignified as the sculptured figures of his contemporary, Phidias. With Euripides (480–406 B.C.), the individual, personal element became even more pronounced: the dramatic conflict was drawn between men and not gods; feminine characters were humanized; and the element of love was for the first time adequately treated. Euripides was in fact a romantic artist, emphasizing the personal and expressive, in rebellion against the classic restraints of his predecessors. He was the last of the great tragedists. After him came Aristophanes and the writers of comedy, who, in dealing with the ordinary social problems of living, held them up to the ridicule of the multitudes.

The character of the music changed with that of the drama. No longer concerned with purely sacerdotal aims, it became more human and elaborate, and there crept into it an evident desire to please as well as to edify. The classic balance, so carefully maintained between the chorus and the actors in the works of Aeschylus and Sophocles, was gradually destroyed by the introduction of more individual performers and the use of music expressive of the passions and the emotions. In Euripides, whenever an emotion was expressed by one of his heroines, the regular dramatic rhythm gave place to one more adaptable for lyric singing. Such a love song as the following, for instance, must have called for a musical utterance far different from that used in the classic dramas:

One with eyes the fairest
  Cometh from his dwelling,
Someone loves thee, rarest,
  Bright beyond my telling.
In thy grace thou shinest
Like some nymph divinest,
In her caverns dewy:—
All delights pursue thee,
Soon pied flower, sweet-breathing,
Shall thy head be wreathing.

Translated by Shelley

THE VICTORY OF SAMOTHRACE (about 300 B.C.)

MUSIC IN PRIVATE LIFE

It should not be thought that because the Greek citizen was so interested in the music and dancing used in religious and public festivals he neglected them in private life. On the contrary, we find that from the earliest days the Greeks loved to participate in and watch these dances. We remember the famous description of the "chain dance" in *The Iliad,* one of the first accounts of dancing that we have:

And with great skill he made a dancing floor, like that which Daedalus had done in broad Knossos for blonde Ariadne. These youths and maidens worth many oxen were dancing, holding each other's hands by the wrist. Of these some wore delicate linen dresses and others golden swords hanging from silver belts. At one time they moved rapidly in a circle with cunning feet, right easily, just as when a potter, seated, tries the wheel fitted to the hand, to see whether it runs; at another time they moved rapidly in file.

And a great crowd stood round the charming dance, enjoying the spectacle; and amongst them a divine bard sang to the cithara; and two tumblers, when he began his song, whirled about in the middle.

And again, this time in *The Odyssey,* Homer tells of the love of his people for dancing:

They leveled the dancing ground, making its ring neat and wide. The herald arrived with the minstrel's singing lyre. Demodocus advanced into the cleared space. About him grouped boys in their first blush of life and skillful at dancing, who footed it rhythmically on the prepared floor. . . . Then Alcinoüs ordered Halias and Laodomas to dance, by themselves, for never did anyone dare join himself with them. They took in their hands the fine ball, purple-eyed, which knowing Polybus had made them, and played. The first, bending his body back, would hurl the ball towards the shadowy crowds: while the other in his turn would spring high into the air and catch it gracefully before his feet touched ground. Then, after they had made full trial of tossing the ball high, they began passing it back and forth between them, all the while they danced upon the fruitful earth. The other young men stood by the dancing and beat time. Loudly their din went up.

Translated by T. E. Shaw

In later times there came a sharper distinction between the professional dancers, who appeared at such functions as dinner parties and banquets, purveying entertainment and amusement to the guests, and the amateurs, who danced for pleasure, in either social or religious groups. Speaking generally, the Greeks were by nature participants, in contrast to the later Romans, who were always spectators and therefore naturally looked on the professional musicians and dancers as little better than courtesans.

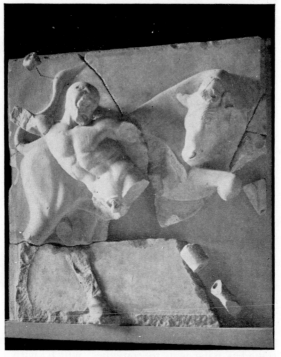

The Louvre

A GROUP FROM THE
TEMPLE OF ZEUS, OLYM-
PIA

THE THIRD PERIOD: DECLINE

After the Golden Age all the arts—music, the drama, sculpture, and architecture—underwent changes that paralleled those which took place in the religious beliefs and the civil practices of the various city-states. After the earlier devotion of the arts to purely religious purposes, there came during the great Athenian period a happy balance between religion and pure art, an equilibrium which was lost during the so-called Hellenistic times, after Athens had lost her supremacy and the center of Hellenic culture had moved to Alexandria and the cities of Asia Minor. The political and economic stability which had been the background of the period of Athenian greatness passed, and there came transformations in all phases of Greek life. Athens, and, with her, all Greece, came on troublous times. The philosophers—Plato, Socrates, Aristotle, and the rest—tried to explain the reasons for these adverse circumstances. Instead of the Olympian objectivity of the sculpture of Phidias and his contemporaries, we find an increasing desire for the achievement of grace and beauty, a desire which finally brought about a sentimentality that was about as antipodal to the severe virility and

THE OLYMPIEION   (second century A.D.)

graceful serenity of the fifth century as can be imagined. The older
tragedies gave way to comedies, which, with their spirited and witty
satirization of contemporary foibles and their absorption in the controversial issues of the day, made existence seem more bearable, if less
sublime. Architecture became more and more colossal and grandiose, the
Corinthian order being preferred above others because it seemed so exuberant and afforded chance for theatrical effectiveness.

Music became more secular, sensual, and individual: the main aim of
the musician of the fourth century seemed to be, as Aristoxenus said,
"to get the applause of the multitude." No longer concerned with religious ceremony or dramatic expression, the musician was principally
interested in developing, with an ever-increasing complexity of technique, the theme of the common man and his everyday affairs. Profes-
sionalism among both the composers and the performers increased. The
dramas had to be commercially sponsored, and traveling companies were
formed for playing them throughout Greece. The auloi were capable of
"rivaling the trumpet's tone"; large citharas with as many as fifteen
strings were used; all sorts of liberties were taken with the scales and
rhythms; instrumental music became disassociated from choral music,

and large concerts, with hundreds and even thousands of players, were given. Program music came into vogue, and at all the festival games competitions between virtuoso artists were instituted, musicians coming to compete from all parts of the world then known. It has been estimated that at some of the games organized by Alexander the Great as many as three thousand artists came together. Music, in a word, became a popular, sensual means for pleasure, indulged in for its own sake and cultivated more as a social fad than as an inherent necessity of life. Aestheticians and philosophers such as Aristotle, Aristoxenus, and Plato wrote of music, some of them dealing with speculations as to its nature, others with its psychological powers.

It is impossible to speak of Greek music as if it were an art possessing uniform characteristics. Within the space of some seven hundred years, it passed through a cycle which, beginning with the stark simplicity of the Homeric epics, developed into the dithyrambic lyrics and religious chants of the classic age. Later came the marvelously coordinated unity of the fifth-century music-drama-dance form, the humanization of the Hellenistic period, which led eventually to the completely commercial and social debasements of the Alexandrian times. Modern European music has passed through much the same sort of changes, but it has taken nearly two thousand years for the process. When we speak of Greek music, we think of that of the Golden Age, without realizing, perhaps, that the later periods of its history brought changes as demoralizing and debasing as any that have occurred in later times.

Perhaps this is as well. For, as Alfred Einstein has pointed out, the knowledge which we have of the place which music occupied in Greek life, together with our wonder at the highly developed style which it eventually reached, has suggested to us that it must have possessed a unique and exalted character. It was this valuation which so strongly influenced later centuries, from the Middle Ages down to the time of Wagner, by "blazing up at important crises and stirring men's minds"; and its effect has been all the more potent in that no concrete examples of the music have survived. For all practical purposes, the music of the Greeks remains the "dim melody" of which Shelley sings.[7]

[7] A few melodic fragments have survived, fifteen in all. But these are of little value for conveying any real idea of what Greek music of the Golden Age sounded like, for they are mostly from later periods, some of them dating from the Christian epoch. And there is no agreement as to how they should or could be interpreted by modern musicians. We are still very much in the dark as to how Greek music actually sounded. Such experiments as have been made in recreating it according to classic Greek theories suggest that it is the voice of West Asia and the Orient that we would recognize in this music rather than that of Western Europe.

The Louvre

A SATYR SUSPENDED ON A
PINE-TREE TRUNK (second
century)

A SUMMARY

There is no calculating the debt which Western civilization owes to
Hellenic culture. Taking the material advances which had been made
before their time as a basis, these people of Ionia, Aeolis, Doris, and
Athens[8] developed a set of intellectual and emotional concepts which,
in their freedom from superstition and intolerance, their bold hypotheses
regarding the universe, their balanced rationalism, and their challenge
to the future, have never been surpassed. It was their ability to combine a definite feeling of humanity with a high degree of imagination
that enabled the Greeks to produce such expressive and lasting art. The

[8] It was the poets, philosophers, and intellectual inhabitants of these and a few other
Greek states who made the great contributions to the progress of civilization attributed
in general to the Greeks. The majority of their city-states, as Barnes reminds us, were no
more cultivated than the regions of the Hottentots.

Attic citizen, altogether a very human individual,[9] while he may have possessed few of the qualities of the superman that have been attributed to him, nevertheless exemplified in his everyday life such real devotion to the principles of truth and beauty and such freedom of mind as to make his conduct a desirable prototype for all time.

The education of Greek citizens was such as to make them aware that what we call "culture" was an essential part of living and not something that was to be extraneously sought after, once the material demands of life had been taken care of. It has been said that every free man in Athens could play the aulos; and he was also trained to take his part as a member of the chorus in the drama. The plastic and architectural beauties of the Athenian Acropolis were matters of ordinary experience to these men. No wonder that creative art flourished as it did, and reached heights of excellence that have seldom been equaled or surpassed!

OUR TECHNICAL HERITAGE FROM THE GREEKS

Inasmuch as it was the Greek conception of intervals, scales, and modes that affected all later music, the reader of music history should know something regarding it. Pythagoras, a Greek mathematician, has the distinction of being the first man in history to explain the laws of proportion in music—how changing the length of a vibrating body affects the pitch of the musical tone it gives. Experimenting with sounding strings, he found that dividing them in half raised their pitch an octave; and this he established as the most important relationship in music. Dividing his string at a point two thirds of its length, he found, would raise the pitch by a perfect fifth; and this he considered the second important relationship of intervals. Dividing the string at three quarters of its length, he raised the pitch a perfect fourth; and this he established as another fundamental relationship.

These intervals of an octave, a fifth, and a fourth remain today, twenty-four hundred years after the experiments of Pythagoras, the fundamental intervals of music. The other ratios established may be stated as follows:

Octave—1:2; fifth—2:3; fourth—3:4; major third—4:5; minor third—5:6

[9] It was Plato who told of some Athenian gentlemen who debated during the course of a banquet as to whether they should spend the night in revelry or in philosophic discussion. They decided on the latter, but the end of the discussions found at least two of the guests under the table!

A GREEK GATEWAY

The unit of the system devised by Pythagoras was the tetrachord, a group of four sounds, its name being derived from the early four-stringed form of the cithara or the lyre. There were three kinds of these tetrachords: the *diatonic,* composed of tones and half tones as in our modern system; the *chromatic,* made up of an interval greater than a tone (minor third) and two half tones; and the *enharmonic,* derived from the East, in which a major third and two quarter tones were used. The diatonic genus was that most often used, especially in vocal music; but after the Golden Age, when music became progressively more and more complex, the chromatic and even the enharmonic genera crept into vocal use, after they had long been very popular with the instrumentalists.

Tone Tone Semitone	Minor Semi- Semitone tone	Major Quar- Quar-
Diatonic	third tone	third ter tone ter tone
	Chromatic	Enharmonic

The basis of Greek scale theory was the difference in the position of the semitone within the two tetrachords that were used to make up the note series of an octave. Thought of in a descending series, as was customary with the Greeks, there were three possible arrangements, each of them named after a different Greek tribe:

Dorian: tone, tone, semitone
Phrygian: tone, semitone, tone
Lydian: semitone, tone, tone

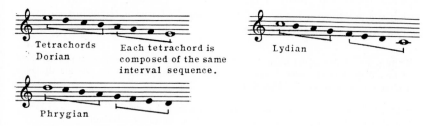

Tetrachords
Dorian   Each tetrachord is composed of the same interval sequence.

Lydian

Phrygian

These constituted the most important scale patterns used by the Greeks; others, among them the Mixolydian, Hypodorian, Hypophrygian, and Hypolydian, were derived from these principal scales. The very fact that tone and word were inseparable in Greek music and that the time of the music depended upon the prosody of the words makes any idea

of polyphony improbable, although harmony was seemingly known. Greek music seems to have been largely monodic, or one-voiced, because this type of music was simple, and simplicity was an essential aspect of Greek aesthetic thinking. Harmony was probably felt to be impure.

There is not enough evidence to show which of these scales the Greeks considered the ideal for melodic expression. We moderns must always remember that they did not use these scales, as we do ours, as foundations for harmony, but only as a sort of framework into which the melodies were fitted. The difference in general pitch and in the intervals used, as well as the fact that the melodies clustered about different centers in the different modes, gave the Greeks their doctrine of *ethos*, which regarded each mode as capable of a distinct general impression. The Dorian, for example, was considered suitable for virile, energetic music; the Lydian was thought to be effeminate and likely to induce poor morals. The modes which came from the East were used for amusement purposes, for banquet and dance music.

Much of the treatment of the subject of music on the part of the Greek philosophers consisted in elaborations of the idea that these various scales were capable of calling forth definite emotions within the listener. The aesthetic doctrine of the ethos, established by the Pythagoreans, was later given great attention by Plato and Aristotle,[10] who considered music as a valuable and important factor in educating the people; and later the Peripatetics developed it still further. In the second century of the Christian era, Ptolemaeus compiled a summary of the whole philosophic and aesthetic theories of the Greeks which served as the basis of later treatises by the Romans. So the Greek theoretical conceptions regarding music have affected our present system in ways of which we are hardly conscious. Even the doctrine of the ethos survives in the investigations which have been made into the possibilities of

---

[10] "By some of them [the modes], as for example the Mixolydian, we are disposed to grief and depression; by others, as for example the low-pitched ones, we are disposed to tenderness of sentiment." (Aristotle)

" 'Which of the Harmoniai [modes] then are soft and convivial?'
'The Ionian,' he replied, 'and Lydian, and such as are called relaxing.'
'Can you make any use of these, my friend, for military men?'
'By no means,' replied he.
'Then, it seems, you have only yet remaining the Doric and the Phrygian. I do not know,' said I, 'the modes; but leave me that mode which may, in a becoming manner, imitate the voice and accents of a truly brave man, going on in a military action, and every rough adventure.' " (Plato: *The Republic*)

music as a therapeutic agent, possibilities about which modern scientists by no means agree.[11]

Some scholars maintain that the most important discovery in Greek music was the invention of musical notation—a way of designating by written symbols the notes which were being played or sung. Some of the Eastern peoples may have antedated the Greeks in this, but the Greek system is the first clearly defined musical notation in history. Each sound could be registered in two ways, one for instruments and one for voices. The characters used were mostly derived from the Greek alphabet, there being 16 instrumental signs, capable of showing quarter tones, and 24 vocal ones. Some of these had slight rhythmic significance, although in the vocal music the rhythm depended entirely on that of the words. In general, we may conclude that rhythms meant much more to the Greeks, so far as the general effect was concerned, than did melody. Aristides Quintilian, a writer of the third or fourth century A.D., basing his observations on the work of the Greek philosopher and musical theorist Aristoxenus, said that rhythm is masculine, melody feminine, and implied that the latter must always be subordinate to the former.

In this, as in other matters concerning Greek music, we can only theorize; all possibility of recovering the expressive value it once possessed has been forever lost.

[11] The Greeks had no doubts, however. It is reported that Thaletas of Crete destroyed the power of an epidemic through the sweetness of his lyre playing. Contemporary with the very important discoveries which the Greeks made in science and medicine, as well as in music, we find such curious theories as those of Aesculapius, who treated disorders of the ear with music; Theophrastus, who testified to the value of soft aulos music (it had to be in the Phrygian mode) for the relief of pain; and Caelius Aurelianus, who claimed that the agonies of sciatica could be mitigated through music.

ROMAN MUSIC

Let others melt and mold the
breathing bronze
To forms more fair, aye, out of
marble bring
Features that live; let others plead
causes well;
Or trace with pointed wand the
cycled heaven,
And hail the constellations as they
rise;
But thou, O Roman, learn with
sovereign sway
To rule the nations.

Virgil: *The Aeneid,* translated by
Theodore C. Williams

THE ROMAN SPIRIT

The incidents which constitute the Roman episode in history are well known to everyone and hardly need retelling here. They represent, broadly speaking, the attempt of a nation made up largely of landowners and farmers to capture and control the entire European world. It started with a small city-state on the banks of the Tiber around 400 B.C., the first territorial additions to this tiny beginning being made because of the necessity of keeping off the enemy from its borders. Once started by the suppression of its neighbors, the Etruscans, a race which had come from the East or North and settled in central Italy, this accretive process never ceased until, at the time of its greatest extent, the Roman Empire embraced such widely separated territories as Britain to the north, Spain to the west, Egypt to the south, and Mesopotamia to the east. In addition to the Etruscans, the Greeks and the Carthaginians and the Gauls were overcome and amalgamated into this enormous world state. Such a process of conquest and subjection was made possible, of course, by using a tremendous force of arms; and in order to form the innumerable legions necessary for their conquests, the patricians, or the older landowning class, granted more and

A ROMAN GATEWAY It would be difficult to find a better illustration of the essential difference between the spirit of Greek and Roman art than two gateways formerly in a Berlin museum. The first (see page 64), built in the second century B.C. in a Greek colony in Asia Minor, reflects the calm spirit and austere restraint of the best Greek art. The second, from the Roman colony of Milet, built about 150 A.D., is obviously copied from the Greek style; but in comparison it is grandiose and overlavish.

more power and political privileges to the plebeians, or the free citizens of the middle class. The continuing wars and increasing possessions multiplied the wealth of all, including that of a third class which quickly arose, the business and official class, made up of merchants, politicians, bankers, and moneylenders.

A background such as this, of military conquest, narrow-minded and hidebound aristocracy, petty officialdom, political intrigue, and social corruption on a large scale, does not offer a promising field for cultural development. The Roman intellect was at bottom, Barnes says, a farmer's intellect. And he attributes to its lack of imagination and flexibility not only the fact that Rome never produced any distinctive creative art —excepting a grandiose type of structural engineering—but also the fact that she was never able to cultivate sufficient commercial enthusiasm and financial wisdom to carry the tremendous load of world empire which she assumed. And so her doom was inevitable.

Nevertheless, the riches and the power acquired by the Romans, together with the fact that the presence of one sovereign political power enabled widely spread peoples to exchange and merge their cultural contributions, produced what one historian has called the most successful and extensive assimilation of culture achieved up to that time. Rome's great contributions to civilization were, of course, in the fields of law and politics. But the art fields were all enriched by Roman contributions of such a character as to affect strongly the generations that followed.

The austere beauty and the fine restraint characteristic of the best Greek art made little appeal to Roman taste, it is true; and when the Romans copied Hellenic models, they usually chose those of a decadent period, for they loved grandiose magnificence more than artistic restraint. Building was largely devoted to providing large public meetinghouses and law courts (basilicas), baths, theaters, sports arenas, monumental bridges, commemorative arches, and superb aqueducts. A desire for Gargantuan grandeur seemed to be an overwhelming passion: the great Circus Maximus, a sort of "multiple political club, lounge, social rendezvous," had accommodations for hundreds of thousands of spectators.

Sculpture was devoted largely to a literal copying of personal attributes—the making of a huge number of portrait busts of senators, generals, and merchants—or to some sort of elaborate architectural ornamentation. The best examples combined some of the Greek ideals with an inherent desire for naturalism, but as a whole they were not very

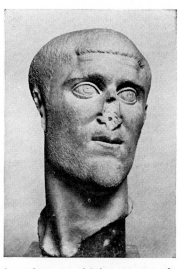

State Museum, Berlin

THE EMPEROR MAXIMINUS   A fine example
of the Roman portrait bust

impressive. It was this architecture and sculpture which so strongly
affected nineteenth-century European and American art. No visitor to
Paris, London, or New York can help realizing how architects and
sculptors have based some of their most monumental creations on these
Roman models. In painting, the Roman artist tried to attain the same
naturalistic effects, simulating the appearance of depth by the devices
of perspective, and achieving some important atmospheric results.

The Greek dramas were not imitated. Instead, we hear of farces given
by the *mimi,* and of pantomimic dance dramas divorced entirely from
words, and of the gorgeous spectacles of circus and arena which, controlled and exploited by the politicians, constituted one of the most
powerful influences in Roman life. Artists were looked on as minor personages, many of them being slaves who had been captured from subject countries celebrated for excellence in learning or creative ability.

BORROWED IDEALS

So, not much is to be expected in the way of musical development on
the part of the Romans. They borrowed their ideas and ideals from the
Greeks, but instead of developing them, they degraded them. Their
poetry was not recited to musical accompaniment as it had been, at least
in classic times, in Greece. In their productions of drama there was no
orchestra or choir, the monodies of the actors being accompanied only
by the aulos; these actors did not always sing their own parts but kept

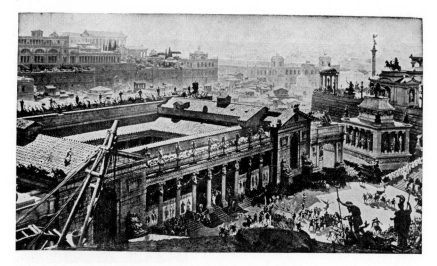

RECONSTRUCTION OF THE CIRCUS MAXIMUS, ROME

the declamation and dialogue as speaking roles and hired a singer for the choral parts. One of the chief uses of instruments was in warfare, the cornu and the tuba being especially developed for this purpose. In the dance pantomimes into which the old tragedies had deteriorated, and which became more and more popular as they became more and more licentious and obscene, instruments were used for accompaniment. The band consisted of players on the tibia (a sort of double flute), the Pan-pipe (syrinx), the lyre, and cymbals; and each player had two metal plates fastened under his foot, so that he could mark out the time and thus keep the band together.

Enough has been written about the splendors and terrors of the Roman public games with which the consuls, and afterwards the emperors, won the favor of the people—at their own expense. These imperial side shows might include anything that was exciting enough or barbarous enough to form an absorbing spectacle: chariot races and gladiatorial combats, fights between slave-manned galleys in the flooded arena, hundreds of trumpeters playing in a chorus, wild African lions let loose to be shot by specially imported archers, and so forth. Sad to relate, music played an ignominious role of accompaniment to all this Roman splendor, dismayingly like that which it occupies in similar Holly-woodian revels. All the noisy instruments they could find were used by the Romans in providing music for these spectacles, including tubas,

horns, and organs, the latter being known in Alexandria as early as
100 B.C.

In the Augustan times and afterwards, art began to be cultivated by
"the" people—both nobles and *bourgeoisie*. Artists and singers and
players were sought after by Roman society and often received the
favors of princes. A knowledge of music was looked upon as essential to
social climbers, and by the time of the first century A.D. all the former
prejudices against professional artists had disappeared. Music was even
cultivated by the emperors. We remember Nero's aspirations along
this line; he devoted much time and patience to the cultivation of his
"feeble, veiled voice," as one of his contemporaries described it, by
going through long periods of fasting or of eating only pears and by
exhibiting other foibles peculiar to singers.

Loving to appear in public as a singer, Nero inflicted himself upon
audiences all over Italy; and in order to be sure of his reception, "he
chose young men of the equestrian order, and about five thousand
robust young fellows from the common people, on purpose to learn
various kinds of applause, called *bombi, imbrices,* and *testae,*[1] which
they were to practice in his favor, whenever he performed. They were
divided into several parties and were remarkable for their fine heads of
hair, were extremely well dressed, with rings upon their left hands. The
leaders of these bands had salaries of forty thousand sesterces allowed
them" (Kirstein: *The Dance*).

Nothing better illustrates the depths of degradation to which Roman
art finally descended; for here, as Kirstein has remarked, we have the
spectacle of a spontaneous actor directing artistic applause, rather than
spontaneous applause given to an artistic actor! Legend has given a final,
aesthetically consistent denouement to this demoniacal career in the
story of Nero's setting Rome aflame for the sheer enjoyment of tragic
beauty, and fiddling while he watched it. Such a legend may have little
historic basis but it shows into what disrepute music had fallen during
the first century A.D.

---

[1] The term *bombi* was derived from the humming of bees and meant a confused din
made by the hands or mouth; *imbrices* meant the sound of rain or hail on the roofs;
testae, the smashing of terra-cotta jars. Here are old ideas which have been neglected by
the modern purveyors of applause, the *claques!*

MUSIC

IN THE EARLY CHURCH

Music is a two-edged sword; capable of quelling the passions, so of giving mortal wound to virtue and religion; and therefore should always be in sober hands. . . . Quick and powerful, and penetrating the minutest parts of the body and inmost recesses of the spirit, when employed under the banner of religion; but likewise searching and irritating every evil thought, and intention of the heart, when debauched in the service of immorality and profaneness. What ought to kindle a devout affection may blow up every evil desire into a flame, may be the fuel and incentive for vice.

From an eighteenth-century sermon

THE EARLY CHURCH

The history of the world has seen nothing more dramatic than the sudden reversal of the fortunes of that devoted group of religionists who took the name Christians during the first centuries of the present era. Jesus of Nazareth, who was considered a god by many of his followers, but who was looked upon by the Roman officials of the time as simply another of the fanatical Judeans who had given them so much trouble, was crucified in Jerusalem in the year 30 A.D. About thirty years later another Hebrew who had taken part in the spread of the religion of Jesus, Saul of Tarsus, was put to death in Rome. In another ten years Jerusalem itself was razed to the ground and its inhabitants scattered over the face of the earth. Hundreds of its people were paraded through the streets of Rome as prisoners in celebration of what the Romans must have considered the end of the Judean fanatic and his religion.

But they were wrong: Christianity increased rapidly in popularity and in numbers during the first three centuries of its existence. The rea-

74

sons why it was able to achieve such significant triumph over its powerful rival religions are many and complex. It happened to fit the needs of
its time better than did any of the others; it possessed an assured and
positive dogma; and it owed a great deal to the splendid organizing and
disciplining power of the missionary Paul, as he was called after his conversion from Judaism. It was he who took the rather metaphysical
teachings of Jesus, addressed as they had been to a small circle, and
adapted them as the basis for a well-organized religion of universal
appeal.

It would be apart from our purpose to attempt any complete account
of the details of Christianity's triumph over Roman paganism. It is sufficient to note the fact that from a simple communal society formed from
the followers who were left after the Crucifixion of Christ—a society
that had no need of extensive organization, for it expected Jesus to return
soon to earth—Christianity developed rapidly, especially among the
urban middle class, during these first years, and in the process aroused
the strong suspicions of the Romans. Any comparative study of religions
will show that many of the fundamental doctrines which Christianity
adopted during these years of its early existence are common to most
of them and were inherited directly from the beliefs of the Hebrews,
who, in turn, borrowed them from earlier prototypal religions. The Hebrews also contributed to Christianity the fundamental idea of a Jehovah
God and the hope of a Messiah to save humanity from its sins—an
idea which Breasted has traced to Egyptian philosophy. The scholastic
Greeks of the early Christian centuries introduced the element of abstract reasoning into the very personal, intimate teachings of Jesus. In
their hands, as has been said, Christian theology took on the color of
Greek metaphysics, centering about Jesus and his place in the world
rather than about Plato and his conception of truth. The religious practices of the Greeks contributed also to the shaping of parts of the Christian ritual, notably the rites of the Eucharist and baptism. The Persians
are thought to have been the first to believe in man's immortality, a
belief that was absorbed into Christianity through its becoming a
constituent part of the Hebrew faith. Rome itself made a mighty contribution to the new religion, that of its policy of organization and
administration: as the Christian Church spread over the eastern and
central parts of Europe, it effectually adopted for its own purposes the
system of administration that had been found to work well within the
empire. Drawn from all parts of the world, borrowing its ideas from all
known cults, Christianity was able to impose such a strong element of

emotional symbolism and didactic persuasiveness into its teachings as to make them quickly popular.

During its earliest days the Church had little interest in art of any kind; for not only were many of the converts of the new faith drawn from the middle class, who were unused to artistic expression, but also in the minds of these early members of the Church, art stood for everything to which the new faith was opposed. It was the symbol of a godless, corrupt, pagan, and doomed world—a world to which the early return of Christ would bring a merciful close. Music especially was associated with the Antichrist, and painting was used merely to represent visually some of the events connected with Old Testament history.

THE "HYMN OF JESUS"

There are only the vaguest indications of the actual use of music in the Church during these first centuries. Not content with merely taking over some of the usages of the synagogues which had sprung up in all the important towns in Asia Minor, Syria, and even in Rome itself after the destruction of the temple in Jerusalem by the Roman Titus, the new religion early began to develop its own chants. Besides the Hebraic psalms, these early Christians sang hymns similar in character to those connected with the Greek mysteries and used for the same purpose, that of invoking the god and coming into exalted, mystic contact with him. There is a definite record of such a hymn in the Apocryphal "Acts of John" known, according to the Catholic Dictionary, to St. Augustine; it is supposed to date from about 160 A.D., and from its content we are justified in imagining that the music used must have been of a Hellenic nature and that not only music but dancing formed a part of the liturgical practices of the new sect:

> *Before Jesus was taken by the Jews and unbelievers who hold to Satan's law, he gathered us together and said: Before I am delivered over to them, let us sing a hymn to the Father. We will then go to them, together. Then he asked us to form a circle: we took each by the hand, he being in the middle and said: Amen, Follow me; and he commenced the hymn.*
>
> Jesus: *Glory be to the Father (and we who were circling him responded):* Amen. [*Thus let it be.*]
> Jesus: *Glory be to thee—the word. Glory be to thee—the grace.*
> Disciples: *Amen.*
> Jesus: *Glory to thee—the Holy Ghost—praise be to thy glory.*
> Disciples: *Amen.*
> Jesus: *We praise thee, Father—we render thanks to thee, light where no shadows dwell.*

Disciples: *Amen.*
Jesus: *Of that unto which we render thee thanks I speak—to be saved is my desire and I desire to save.*
Disciples: *Amen.*
Jesus: *To be delivered is my desire, and I desire to deliver.*
Disciples: *Amen.*
Jesus: *To be blessed is my desire, and I wish to bless.*
Disciples: *Amen.*
Jesus: *To be born is my desire, and I wish to engender.*
Disciples: *Amen.*
Jesus: *To be nourished is my desire, and I wish to nourish.*
Disciples: *Amen.*
Jesus: *To hear is my desire, and I wish to be heard.*
Disciples: *Amen.*
Jesus: *To understand is my desire, with all my intelligence.*
Disciples: *Amen.*
Jesus: *To be cleansed is my desire, and I wish to cleanse.*
Disciples: *Amen.*
Jesus: *Forgiveness is our* choragus [*dance leader*]—*to sing is my desire, let us dance together.*
Disciples: *Amen.*
Jesus: *I wish to be grieved for, weep you all.*
Disciples: *Amen.*
Jesus: *I am thy light, ye who see me. I am the gate, ye who enter.*

The twelve disciples now dance.

Jesus: *Those who do not dance will not comprehend what shall befall.*
Disciples: *Amen.*
Jesus: *Then all of you join my dance. You who dance, see what I have accomplished.*

We know that the spontaneous, ecstatic sort of songs that are characteristic of rather primitive religious rites (and which survive in the Negro camp-meeting extemporizations and Salvation Army gatherings of today) had a part in the early worship of the Church; they were accepted as a valuable adjunct to the services by Paul himself, who, however, insisted that they be intelligible to the rest of the congregation. None of the melodies of this period have survived; but they were probably of small compass and employed a simple form of melismatic decoration.

The third century was a period marked by a slow strengthening and a gradual development of the Church's resources. As the social and economic conditions of the Roman Empire became progressively worse, in spite of the reorganizing reforms and efficient administration of a few emperors, the collapse of that once powerful institution was seen to be inevitable; but there was little change in its official attitude toward the

PAINTINGS FROM AN EARLY CHRISTIAN CATACOMB IN ROME The subjects
are figures from Christian mythology painted in Roman terms.

Christians. The members of the new sect were regarded at all times
during these early centuries of the Church's existence with suspicion
and dislike in the empire and were subjected to intermittent persecutions
in the hope of breaking their morale. But in vain: the Christians continued to flourish especially in Alexandria and the eastern part of the
empire; important communities were founded, and many of the rich
and learned professed the new faith.[1] By the year 300 the problem of
the Christian Church was not so much that of defying the imperial
power of Rome as it was of securing a unity of organization for itself.
This was the great period of heretical discussion. There arose so many
diverse opinions as to what should constitute the essential doctrines of
the Church that its very life was threatened. For it was obvious enough
that, if the new organization was not to split up at the very beginning
of its existence into a number of irreconcilable sects, each differing from
the others in some essential way, some method of repressing these individualistic spirits must be found. And so it was necessary to deal

[1] "Let cruelty, envious or malignant," cries Cyprian, "hold you here in bonds and
chains as long as it will; from this earth and from these sufferings you shall speedily come
to the Kingdom of Heaven." (C. H. Dawson: *The Making of Europe*)

summarily and harshly with such heresies as Arianism, a dispute revolving around a difference of interpretation brought about by the change of a single letter in one Greek word; Gnosticism, an attempt to make the Christian faith conform to Greek metaphysics; Montanism, which preached the immediate second coming of Christ; and many others of a similar nature. One of the historians of this period has made the statement that these quarrels within the Church "made five or six times as many martyrs in fifty years as the pagan emperors had in two hundred and fifty years!"

DEMONIAC SONGS

Some of these heretical sects used propaganda songs, which they introduced on occasion into the worship of the Church, perhaps something in the manner in which the Salvation Army makes such effective use of modern melodies and rhythms. One of the problems of the early Church Fathers was how best to deal with such matters; indeed, they were sorely troubled as to what the general attitude of the Church should be toward this disturbing matter of music, so popular with the people and so pagan in its associations. They realized well enough its power to arouse feelings and stir passions;[2] they heard on every side its secular use, in work songs, sailor chanteys, lullabies, and so forth, and were worried about the effect which this sort of music might have on the hearts and minds of the faithful. They knew that the pagan shows and pantomimes were still popular with church members, both young and old, and they ranted about the "demoniac and satanic songs" to be heard on such occasions. St. John Chrysostom observes bitterly that if a youth of the time was asked to sing a psalm, he wouldn't know one; but if he was asked to hum one of the popular revue songs from the current pantomime, he would be sure to have it by heart! The councils of the Church tried to counteract these evil influences by decreeing that no person connected in any way with a circus or pantomime could be baptized and that any church member attending the theater on holy days would be excommunicated—rules which, if they had been strictly enforced, would have thrown half of Christendom, including a good part of the clergy, out of the Church's communion:

From east to west, in Constantinople, in Antioch, in Alexandria, in Rome, the mimic drama flourished, uniting together old pagans and new Christians in the one common enjoyment of pure secularism.

Allardyce Nicoll; *Masks, Mimes and Miracles*

[2] "Nothing so lifts the soul, gives it wings, frees it from earthly things, as a holy song, in which rhythm and melody form a true symphony." (St. John Chrysostom)

THE PROBLEM OF INSTRUMENTS

Another problem which taxed the ingenuity of the Fathers was that concerned with the use of instruments in the services; if some of their rulings seem strange to us today, we must always remember the infelicitous association which music had for them. In the beginning, all the Christian musical practices were vocal, if for no other reason than the very practical one that it was necessary to use great caution while conducting the services; and so no loud instruments could be tolerated. Later on, the lyre and the cithara were allowed, at least in private meetings; but even Clement of Alexandria, one of the most broad-minded of the early churchmen and one well versed in all the amenities of instrumental music, went on record to the effect that the Christians did not need to use instruments in their services, their word "being peace and not the psaltery, trumpet, aulos, and cymbals of those who prepared for war." The early bishops did not hesitate to compare the aulos to the evil serpent which tempted Mother Eve, and we read of their inveighing against such pagan uses of music as those in a church in Asia Minor, where they beat the hands, sounded little bells, and employed choreographic movements of the body in accompanying the holy chants.

The Old Testament contains, of course, numerous references to the use of instruments in the worship of God's house; and the tortuous and symbolical means of explaining these away on the part of the good Fathers of the early Church make amusing reading. The injunction of Holy Writ to "praise God with the timbrel and the dance and all instruments of music" meant, according to their ingenious explanations, that the "members of the body are like strings in accord in praising the Lord, and its thoughts like cymbal's chime." St. Basil saw in the ten strings of the psaltery a likeness to the Ten Commandments, and therefore that instrument was permitted, especially since it was severe-looking and in no sense resembled the instruments used in theatrical performances. Moreover, its upper strings were the ones which resounded the best, and not the lower, as in the lyre and the cithara; therefore it represented a higher, purer form of music, and its use might be condoned.

Since music was the only one of the arts even mildly approved by the early Church, it seems probable that its emotion-releasing effect was much more powerful than if it had been one amongst various arts serving as the handmaid of religion. We can thus better understand the anxiety of the early Church Fathers to rationalize (as we would now say) the effects of music and to explain them away in symbolic terms.

AN EARLY CHRISTIAN CHURCH: ST. CLEMENTE, ROME In the center of the
nave is the space reserved for the singers.

THE CHURCH'S POSITION

Out of all these backgrounds there crystallized very gradually the
general psychological attitude which the Church assumed towards music
—an attitude which was to influence the history of the art for the next
thousand years and shape its general development for an even longer
period. With the Greeks, music was thought of as a moral and political
force, capable of exerting a tremendous influence on the lives of the
people; but it was also used as a means for giving pleasure. The Church
Fathers, who were strongly influenced by Greek thought in so many
things, adopted only part of this attitude. To them, as to the Hebrews,
all art was justifiable only in the sense that it could be made to serve
God; they never thought of it under any circumstances as existing for
its own sake. Therefore it must be brought under the control of the
Church. Even pleasure in its use for the glory of God was to be frowned
upon: an early manuscript now in the Library at Vienna tells of an
Egyptian abbot named Paulo, who, at the beginning of the fourth

century, retired to the desert with some of his followers and of how one of them, on being sent to Alexandria on business, returned with accounts of the scandalous goings-on in the churches there—the praises of God were actually being sung. Thereupon the old monk held forth on the iniquity of seeking divers melodies and diverse rhythms for the worship of God. "When we stand in the presence of God we should assume an attitude of contrition and not employ the voice of praise. Can there be any spirit of penitence in a monk who, in church or cell, makes his voice resound like that of a bull?" So even the honest pleasures of the anchorite enjoying the fine resonance of his cell as he sang the praises of his Creator were to be denied him.

All these early chants of the Church, most of them confined to the settings of the Psalms, were probably simple in character, their melodies confined to the limits of the tetrachord and with no definite feeling of tonality. Athanasius (296?-373), who formulated the doctrine of the Trinity that was finally adopted by the Church, ordered that the Psalms were to be sung with so little variety that they sounded, according to St. Augustine, more like speaking than singing. There was an evident effort on the part of the early authorities to keep the use of music simple and avoid all extravagances.[3] Not only was music to be confined to the worship of God, but its use in this connection must be so carefully controlled that no suggestion of its paganistic implications might appear.

It was not until after the triumphant emergence of Christianity from the catacombs and its adoption as the Roman state religion that a more liberal attitude prevailed and ritualistic music assumed something of the importance it deserves in the worship of the Church. But that is another story and belongs to another chapter.

---

[3] The fourth-century abbot Silvain, in rebuking a monk who had confessed to having fallen asleep during vigils, said that undoubtedly his sin was the result of too much fancy psalm chanting. Song, he maintained, had sent many a man (and some priests as well) to hell, so impure were the passions it aroused.

THE HISTORICAL PAST

MONODIC MUSIC OF
A THOUSAND YEARS

Music in the Church

*Take nonspecialists in music and non-Catholic
clergymen; take contemporaries, whether farmers, laborers, college students, college professors,
journalists, scientists, etc. Play the records of the
Gregorian chant on a phonograph without telling what it is, and then ask the listeners whether
they like it or not. I venture to say that at least
95, if not 100, per cent would answer negatively.
And in a sense they could not be blamed. Because, from the standpoint of a sensually audible
criterion, the chant is no music at all; it is something queer, unenjoyable, primitive, dry; in
brief, it has none of the earmarks of what we
are accustomed to style music—neither measure,
nor harmony, nor polyphony.*

Pitirim A. Sorokin: *Fluctuation of Forms of Art*

ART IN THE EARLY CHURCH

I t was the fourth cen-
tury which brought about the dramatic change in the fortunes of the
Christian religion that was to make it one of the greatest forces in
European civilization. In the beginning years of this century, members
of the strange new sect were being thrown to the lions in the arenas
because of their refusal to bow down to the gods of the Romans; before
the century was out, the same gods were thrown down and dragged in
the dust during the festivities attendant upon the crowning of a Christian emperor. The citizens of Rome of the year three hundred were
accustomed enough to the sight of the persecution of the Christians.
Not many years later, the descendants of these citizens were crowding

the Christian altars, praying to their new God for the forgiveness of their pagan fathers. The change came suddenly, almost in the manner of a theatrical climax—one decade, furtive secrecy and clandestine worship; the next triumph, victory, and honor.

By the year 300 A.D. the Christians had become so numerous that the Roman emperors realized further persecution would be useless. In 311 the emperor Galerius revoked the edict of persecution and introduced an era of tolerance. In 313 Constantine signed the famous Edict of Milan, an act which legalized Christian worship throughout the Roman Empire. He moved his capital from Rome to Byzantium, which was later called Constantinople, and from there he directed the practical realization of his dream of a Holy Roman Empire and pushed it onto the world stage. In 337, just before his death, this first Christian emperor received the rites of baptism at the hands of a bishop of the Church. Twenty-five years later, his nephew Julian died, after making a vain attempt to re-establish the pagan religion in Rome, murmuring, so the story goes, *Vicisti, Galilaee* (Thou hast conquered, O Galilean).

For nearly two hundred years, during which time the Church was able to consolidate her gains and lay the firm foundations for her future developments, she rejoiced in her triumph; then in 476 came the banishment of the last of the Western emperors (whose name was, ironically enough, Romulus Augustus the Little) and the final collapse of the Roman civilization under the impact of the invading barbarian hosts. For a number of centuries the future of Church as well as State seemed dark enough; "Western European culture retrogressed to the level of the Cretan and Mycenaean civilizations" (Barnes) which had preceded both Greece and Rome. But the years between the conversion of Constantine and the coming of the Lombards form one of the great epochs in the Church's history and one of tremendous importance to art. It was during this first brilliant flush of its power and wealth that the foundations of Christian liturgy, legendry, and art were laid, the site of these early developments being Byzantium.

At the time the emperors of the West were still officially engaged in persecuting the followers of Christ, the Church in the East had already come to a state of maturity as a result of cultural traditions that reach back to the beginnings of history. We are sometimes likely to forget that the very beginnings of Christianity are Asian—Christ and the Judeans lived in Palestine, not in Europe. So, too, the backgrounds of Christian culture are Eastern and not Western. It was in Egypt, with its capital at Alexandria, the center of the learning of the time, in Syria,

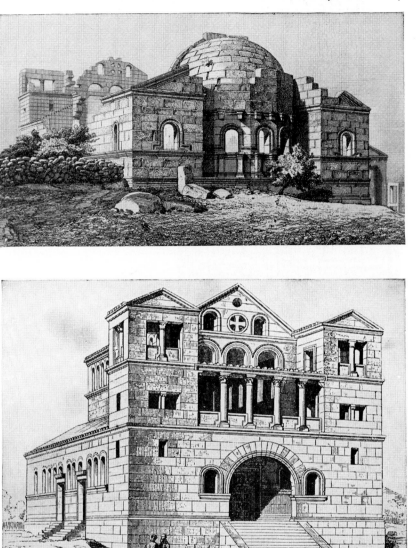

AN EARLY CHRISTIAN-BYZANTINE CHURCH   At the top is shown the rear view of the ruins of the basilica at Turmanin in North Syria, built during the sixth century; at the bottom, a front view of its reconstruction.

KING DAVID AND POPE GREG-
ORY   A Byzantine ivory miniature

with its mixed Hebraic, Greek, and Mesopotamian inhabitants, and in Persia that its first important development took place. Long before the Western Church dared to worship openly above ground rather than in the dark catacombs and secret places where it had furtively gathered, the Church in the East had started on a brilliant period of growth, a development which made necessary new buildings and suitable textiles, murals, and sculptures for their decoration, as well as elaborate liturgies and appropriate music which could be used in the services.

Out of the attempt to meet these artistic needs of the Church, there came a glorious amalgam: the influence of the art of the Orient (an influence which, of course, was strongly felt in this part of the world) —with its love for color, its stylized patterns, its rigid conventions, its sensuous feeling for mystical expression—was blended with the demands and ideals of the new religious sect and the remains of the Greco-Roman tradition. The result was the style which has come to be known as Byzantine, a style with so many cross-purposes and varying racial characteristics as to make any attempt at exact classification impossible. Cheney has characterized it well by saying that it was Christian in purpose and Oriental in expression. The churches which these Asian Christians built had Eastern domes and Eastern barrel vaults; they were

decorated with painted murals and tapestries whose flattened composition, peculiar iconography, rich color, and closely intertwined motives
all suggest an Eastern origin; their walls were covered with mosaics—
designs worked out by setting small squares of colored glass or stone
into a cement foundation. Everything about this art—its depths of infinite color, its sumptuous richness suggestive of the gold and jewels
and spices of the Orient—aroused the spirit of mystic exaltation and
emotional fervor which the Church wished to cultivate. So, in spite of
later attempts on the part of Europeans to purge the Church of this
gorgeous Eastern art, it exerted a strong influence on religious developments from the second century clear down to the twentieth century.

Not the least important of these influences has been that on music.
Most modern investigators are agreed that it was here in these Eastern
communities that the type of Church music which has come to be
known as the Gregorian chant had its origin; and that it was later introduced into the Roman Church, there to become one of the great
foundation stones on which the structure of European music was
erected. Anyone familiar with this chant as it is still used in the Roman
Catholic Church[1] today is often startlingly reminded of these Eastern
influences by the frequent use which is made of the rich, florid vocal
figures of the type known as *melisma*—a term which has come to be
used for any decorative passage in which the original melody is spun
out into embellishments. The people of the East have always had a
strong predilection for this sort of vocalization, as we have heard in the
music of India and the Orient. It was the practice in all the Eastern
religions for the cantor (the trained leader of the choirs) to embellish
the melodies he sang. The musicians of the early Church adopted the
same idea, and melismatic singing, in which oftentimes a veritable
torrent of florid vocalization occurs, has been a constituent part of
Christian music from earliest times.

SOURCES OF EARLY CHRISTIAN MUSIC

We have but to listen to some of the traditional chants of the Hebrew
liturgy to realize how close is the bond between early Christian and
Hebraic music. In our discussion in an earlier chapter, we have stated
the features which were taken over into the music of the Christian
Church from the practices of the Synagogue. Prominent among these

[1] It has also made notable progress in the present-day Anglican communion in Great
Britain and the Episcopal Church in the United States.

THE FRONTISPIECE
OF THE *ANTIPHO-
NARY OF ST. GREG-
ORY* It illustrates Pope
Gregory dictating to an
amanuensis.

was the singing of the Psalms and Canticles, a feature of the oldest
portion of the Church's liturgy, used in the so-called "Offices of the
Hours" performed at fixed times during the day and night. The Church
kept the responsorial character of the Hebraic psalmodic singing, a
phrase sung by the solo cantor or precentor being answered by the choir
or congregation; and this practice has been maintained to the present
day.[2]

A comparison of the music system of the early Christian Church with
that of the Greeks will also reveal many likenesses. It can easily be
shown that some of the Christian chants resemble the Greek melodies
that have been preserved, and there is little doubt that the general
musical traditions of those lands at the eastern end of the Mediterranean, traditions which the new sect derived from the Greek practices,
had a great deal to do with the forming of the earliest music used in
its worship.

[2] It may be that we have here the beginnings of "prima donnaism," for it is clear
historically that the cantor in both synagogue and church employed a certain element of
melismatic coloratura.

In fact, it has come to be generally agreed that the music which came into use in the Church is an elevation of materials received from three sources the Hebraic synagogical liturgy, the usages of Greco-Roman antiquity, and the spontaneous developments that occurred among the early Eastern and Western congregations. In the true sense, the early Christian music was the result of the cross-breeding of paganism, Hellenism, and Christianity.

THE MYSTICAL POWER OF GREGORIAN CHANT

But, we must always remember, there was something more: the raising of music from a secondary to a sovereign role in the life of the early Christian peoples came about because of a recognized spiritual necessity. If we listen carefully to such a chant as that which has become traditional for use on Holy Thursday,[3] a setting of the words "Christ became obedient for us unto death, even to the death of the cross; for which cause God hath exalted him and hath given him a name which is above every name," we shall note that the general effect is that of a quiet, simple statement in which the melodic and textual divisions accord exactly. From time to time there are melismatic embellishments of the melody which give it added intensity, as if the simple melodic line could not sufficiently express the emotional fervor of the words. It is evident enough that the Church was able to create out of the material it borrowed from earlier sources an art which is distinctly its own, a perfect medium for the conveyance of its ideals and doctrines. The first part of this chant suggests, as clearly as does anything in pictorial art, the humiliation and sufferings of the cross; the second, the triumphal exaltation of which this suffering was the necessary preliminary. Thus the unknown composers of this melody would sum up the doctrine of the Church as to the efficacy of the redemption of mankind through Christ's death upon the cross.

In listening to this music we find ourselves far removed from the secular surroundings and hurrying bustle of the world. It is a fitting counterpart to the beauty of the architecture, the majestic, varicolored pageant of the ritual, the visual impressions of the incense mounting to heaven like the prayers of the righteous, with which the Church surrounded her worshipers from early times, seeking thereby to supplement and stimulate their natural emotions and lift them out of themselves into a region completely detached from everyday existence.

[3] *Christus Factus Est.*

THE DEVELOPMENT OF PLAINSONG[4]

It must not be thought that all the chants of the early Church were as fully developed or as expressive as this. The history of early Christian music is inextricably bound up with that of the development of the liturgy—that is, the public rites and services used in the Church's worship. The earliest of these liturgies, together with the music used in it, came out of the East; and for the first few centuries of the Church's existence, innumerable local and territorial liturgies were used, all of them different—Syrian, Egyptian, Persian, Byzantine, Gallic, Hispano-Gallic. Even the Roman liturgy, which later supplanted the others and remains today (with a few exceptions[5]) the standard in the Roman Catholic Church throughout the world, was at first Greek in form and language. By the seventh century this had become homogenized, had adopted Latin as its official language, and had gathered to itself a vast body of effective music of scope wide enough to cover the needs of all those who participated in the services. By this time, bishop, cleric, choir, and congregation each had an important and individual part in the common worship, with a definite type of music adapted to the particular requirements.

There was, first of all, the essentially dramatic dialogue, set to simple chants, which took place between the Celebrant of the Mass (the official name of the Eucharistic Sacrifice and of its liturgy of prayers and ceremonies) and the entire congregation. Then there were the more elaborated chants sung by the choir, set to psalm texts, with refrains varied for the seasons and feasts of the liturgical year—such things as the Gradual and Alleluia responds, the Introit and the Offertory. Finally, there were those parts of the Mass (three in number at this time, the *Kyrie eleison,* the *Gloria in Excelsis Deo,* and the *Sanctus*[6]) designed for singing by the congregation alone and therefore set to very simple chants, which strongly contrasted in character with those sung by the trained choir.

[4] This term is usually applied to the whole traditional ritual melody of the Western Church; it is derived from *cantus planus,* implying a plain melody without counterpoint, and is used interchangeably with the term "Gregorian," which comes from the name of one of the greatest exponents of the chant, Gregory the Great, elected Pope in 590.

[5] Notably the Ambrosian liturgy, still in use at Milan, and the Mozarabic rites in Spain; each of these has its own peculiar type of music, differing from Gregorian plainsong.

[6] The first of these was taken bodily from the Greek liturgy; the second and third were adaptations from Greek and Hebrew sources. The final details of the Mass as we know it today were not complete until the eleventh century, by which time two other portions were added, the *Credo* and the *Agnus Dei.* These portions are referred to as the Ordinary of the Mass, and to them are added the choral parts with variable texts, called the Proper —introits, graduals, alleluias, and so forth.

THE *ANTIPHONARY*
OF ST. GREGORY
open at one of the anti-
phons

These developments were not accidental; they came about over a long period of time and through the agencies of a number of individuals. Leaders in the movement were (1) St. Ambrose, Bishop of Milan, the man generally credited with introducing the musical usages of the Eastern Church into the West (he it was who brought order out of the great confusion arising from the use of so many liturgies and who codified, from the usages of the time, four scales to be used in singing); and (2) Pope Gregory, who at the end of the sixth century again had the entire matter reviewed, added four more scales, and collected and recast, in his *Antiphonale Missarum,* the whole repertoire of chants then available.

An important factor in this standardization of the plainchant during these centuries was the great Roman *Schola Cantorum,* a school of singing founded, according to tradition, during the fourth century, immediately after the Edict of Milan, which officially freed the Christians from Roman persecutions. For nearly eight hundred years this institution maintained its identity and helped spread the traditional manner of singing the music of the Church throughout all her domains, even as far afield as England. As Douglas puts it, in all that welter of migration, war, political turmoil, and social transformation which we call the Dark Ages, the "Song Schools of many a monastery and cathedral, faithful children of a great mother, preserved the ideals and advanced the practice of purely religious music. We are in their debt today for a very large part of what is best in our choral worship."

TECHNICAL CHARACTERISTICS OF PLAINSONG

The chants contained in the Gregorian *Antiphonale Missarum* still stand as a model and standard for the worship of the Church. But their melodies are bound to sound somewhat foreign to modern ears, and their general lack of rhythm, in the sense in which we understand it today, accentuates this strangeness. As we listen to these melodies, we are conscious of the fact that they seem to have been designed to emphasize the modulations of the natural speaking voice, like the changes in pitch of the voice of any speaker who has to make his words carry through large spaces—for instance, a train announcer in a huge modern terminal. No more practical means could have been found for the conveying of thought throughout the reaches of the large churches of the time. The chants use musical scales that are entirely diatonic (that is, made up of only tones and half tones), thereby giving the senses a feeling of peaceful assurance that is far removed from the restlessness and strivings of secular music, with its colorful variety of chromatic intervals. There are no wide skips or nervous leaps in melody; everything proceeds by steps which suggest the quiet inflections of the voice in normal speaking. None of the effects of modern rhythm, with its regularly recurring stresses of accent, are present here; our impression is rather that of a wavelike flow of melody, uniting the various textual elements into a series of intelligible phrases. There are delicate dramatic effects, but nothing that is strained or overpowering. The whole feeling of this music is one of secure peacefulness, yet of strange mystery. All its elements—melodies, rhythm, and dynamics—flow from a single idea, simply because they sprang from the mood which best expresses this idea. They do for the text what faith does for the reason—carry it beyond its own limitations. According to the ideals of the Church this chant music has been made the true language of the worshiping soul.

Whereas modern music makes most frequent use of but two scales—the major and the minor, each of which has its own characteristics—the Church chant used eight scales, each with its individual flavor. The different feasts of the Church year vary naturally in mood—some joyful in character (Christmas and Easter), some hopeful (Advent), some sorrowful (Lent), some triumphant (Ascension). So the music that was composed for these various occasions was joyful, hopeful, sorrowful, triumphant in turn and those who composed the chant melodies employed different scales to express the mood. They considered the first and second scales ("modes," they called them) as producing music of a "discreet, restrained, grave, contemplative character." The third and fourth they regarded as the modes of ecstasy, giving as much an impression of humanity as this impersonal music ever gave. The fifth and sixth modes, strongly resembling our modern major scale, they thought of as imparting a bright and spirited character to the music, filling it with hopeful buoyancy. The seventh, according to an authority, was the mode of solemn affirmation. The eighth mode was the "musical expression of that serenity of mind which is the characteristic feature of the wise." It is certain that our modern ears will never hear all that these old writers felt in their ancient scales; but it is interesting to know how they believed in these various possibilities and chose their modes carefully to suit the type of expression they wished to convey.

It is obvious enough that theoretical conceptions such as these were transplanted from the ideals of the Greeks. The two men who seem to have been largely responsible for transmitting these classical conceptions of musical theory into the Middle Ages were the Late Roman philosophers, Boethius and Cassiodorus,[7] both of the sixth century. Somewhere in this process the names of the Greek modes, *Dorian, Phrygian, Lydian,* and *Mixolydian,* were misapplied to the medieval scales, so that what in Greek music had been called *Dorian* was called *Phrygian* in medieval music, and what had been known as *Lydian* was called *Ionian.* This false nomenclature was generally adopted and remained as the basis of musical theory for many centuries, the error being retained in order to avoid still further confusion. Boethius and Cassiodorus were thoroughly convinced of the validity of the Greek ideal of ethos in music, and their writings contain complete enumerations of the moral powers of music, its exhilarating and calming effects—ideals which were adapted to their needs by the Fathers of the Church.

The medieval theorists developed also a system of notation, at first merely using *neumes,* small signs placed above the words, giving a

[7] Boethius, a minister at the court of Theodoric the Great, wrote five books on music, *De musica,* which remained the standard textbooks on music during the Middle Ages in Europe. Cassiodorus, who also had a public career at Theodoric's court in Ravenna, retired into a monastery where he had collected all that he could find of the fast-disappearing ancient culture, in order that he might preserve as much of it as possible for posterity.

Names	Neumes	Notations	
Single Notes		Gregorian	Modern
Virga jacens	—		
Punctum	▪		
Virga recta	/ /		
Groups of two notes Pes or Podatus	♩!		
Clivis	⌐		
Groups of three notes Scandicus	!		
Climacus	/∵		
Torculus	∫		
Porrectus	∿		
Group of more than three notes Scandicus flexus	∵⌐		
Porrectus flexus	∿⌐		

A TABLE SHOWING HOW THE NEUMES WERE NAMED, AND THEIR EQUIVALENTS IN NOTATIONS visual representation of the rise and fall of the melodies. Out of this came our modern notation, the greatest step forward being taken in the time of Guido d'Arezzo, a noted Benedictine theoretician of the eleventh century, when there was adopted the simple device of placing the neumes on lines representing fixed pitches.

As used by the medieval theorists, the Church scales made use of the same notes that we employ in our major scale—C, D, E, F, G, A, B, C—each mode commencing on successive notes of the scale and extending over the compass of one octave. Thus:

Four Principal Modes

First (Dorian): D, E, F, G, A, B, C, D
Third (Phrygian): E, F, G, A, B, C, D, E
Fifth (Lydian): F, G, A, B, C, D, E, F
Seventh (Mixolydian): G, A, B, C, D, E, F, G

Four Secondary Modes

Second (Hypodorian): A, B, C, D, E, F, G, A
Fourth (Hypophrygian): B, C, D, E, F, G, A, B
Sixth (Hypolydian): C, D, E, F, G, A, B, C
Eighth (Hypomixolydian): D, E, F, G, A, B, C, D

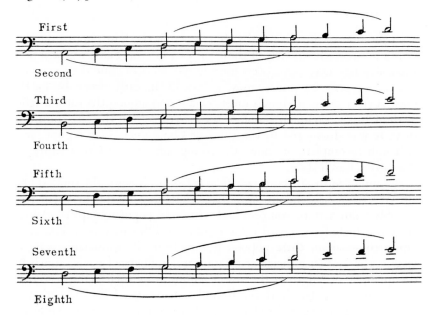

Later, Glareanus, a sixteenth-century theorist, added four more modes
—the Aeolian, starting on A (with its derived Hypoaeolian), and the
Ionian, starting on C (with its derived Hypoionian).

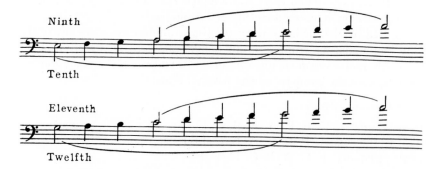

NOTE. It may be added that, since the secondary modes (*plagal,* Gregory called them)
were borrowed from the principal modes, there was bound to be some overlapping. For
example, although the Dorian and the Hypomixolydian modes use the same notes (see
page 97), the latter is in reality the Mixolydian mode extended in a different compass.
Therefore the melodies written in it have a different nature from those in the Dorian
mode.

EARLY HYMNS

In addition to the chants, the churchmen of the East wrote a number
of hymns after the models of those sung in Greece. Some of these non-
Biblical songs may have been used in the services; but they were designed primarily for private uses, at least in the early times. By far the
most ancient piece of church music extant and among the earliest relics
of the Christian religion is one of these hymns from the late third century. It was discovered in the ruins of Oxyrhynchus, in Egypt, and,
although incomplete, it shows the strong influence of Greek music on
the early Church style.

A simpler form of hymn, which was later to become the standard for
all Western Christendom, was that originating in the East (derived
possibly from Semitic sources) and written in popular couplets. Apparently one melody was used for a number of different verses. The interesting thing about these popular hymns from the musician's point of
view is the fact that their versification was influenced not so much by
the quantity or length of the vowel sounds as by their being patterned
according to regular rhythmic formulas made up of an alternation of
accented and unaccented syllables. Such a hymn as this of St. Ambrose,

Bishop of Milan, calls for a simple musical structure that is very much like that of the later folk songs and is entirely different from that of the freer chant melodies:

Ae - ter - ne re - rum con - di - tor, Noc -
tem di - em - que qui re - gis Et
tem - po - rum Das tem - po - ra, Ut al - le -
ves fas - ti - di - um.

From Hymnary of Pairis
(Bibl. Colmar 442)

These hymns became extremely popular with the people when introduced into the services, for they represented something in which the whole congregation could heartily join. Many of them were written in the East. Their authors included men who are well known in ecclesiastical history, and their vogue extended into the sixth century.

A modern writer, Dom Cabrol, has imaginatively described the use of these hymns in the services of the Church of St. Sophia in Constantinople—that magnificent structure, an everlasting monument to the glory of Byzantine art, which was built by the emperor Justinian in the sixth century in an attempt to create a single building that should stand as the largest and finest in Christendom:

These poems, conceived in the quiet of the cloister, were sung amidst surroundings and by congregations of great splendor: into the Church of St. Sophia came the people of Constantinople, together with the emperor and his brilliant cortege of officers, priests, dignitaries, and ladies of his palace. Here in the midst of a most astonishing profusion of precious marbles, mosaics, gold and silver decorations, the liturgical office commences. The priests defile in long processions, their ranks reaching even to the throne of the patriarch, that second ruler of the land.

The moment arrives for the singing of the poet friar's hymn: the master of the choristers gathers his forces and prepares to direct their singing; the reader mounts the tribune, holding in his hand a roll of parchment on which the poem is written in clear, brilliant colors. The people come to attention, for they love this part of the service. The liturgical spectacle has renewed their ancient faith and made them ready for the inspiration that comes from music. Their eagerness is real; the song commences, line succeeds line, verse follows verse, the words outlined and made more significant by the appealing melody. The opening lines suggest with vividness the liturgical significance of the day; the succeeding stanzas are more general in their meaning. The singers reply to the reader, the scene being enlivened by the appearance in the dialogue of varied characters: the angels, the prophets, the saints of both the Old and the New Testament, Adam, Noah, the good Joseph, even the devils themselves, speak one to another. It is in reality a mystery, the form which the later Latin Church was to develop centuries after.

Translated from Dom Cabrol: *Le Cardinal Pitra,* Paris, 1893

It was Ambrose,[8] Bishop of Milan and defender of the faith against the Arian heretics, who introduced these hymns into the Western usage. He wrote a number of them which breathe a spirit of clarity and optimistic confidence. Many of the great Occidental Church Fathers followed his example and made contributions to the liturgy of the Church in the way of Latin hymns full of austere beauty, yet pulsating with warm religious fervor. Gregory the Great (540?–604), Venantius Fortunatus (in the second part of the sixth century), Magnentius Arabanus Maurus (776–856), and St. Thomas Aquinas (1225?–1274?), "perhaps the most perfect master of lyric thought which the Occident ever possessed" (Max Fischer: *Mediaeval Hymns*), all wrote ardent, fervid poems which were popular in their day, but only a few of which, unfortunately, have found their way into Christian usage.

GROWING MAGNIFICENCE IN ART AND RITUAL

Music was not the only art to be strongly influenced by the opulent splendor of the East. During the great golden age of Byzantium, the Roman Church split officially with the Eastern Church, but there came out of the great producing centers, Constantinople, Salonika, Nicaea, Ephesus, and the rest, such a flood of ivories, illuminations, textiles, goldsmith's work, and colored enamels as to transform completely the

---

[8] The most comprehensive source of information regarding the early music of the church is St. Augustine of Hippo, who, around 388, wrote a long treatise, *De musica,* which shows how great was the difference between the ancient and the modern conceptions of music. The early musicians concentrated their attention largely on the rhythm and meter of the Latin verses they set. Augustine states in detail the differences between twenty-eight varieties of metrical feet; nevertheless, he admits that the melody has certain purely musical laws of its own which it should obey. It is upon his authority (in his *Confessions*) that St. Ambrose is credited with organizing the music of the Western European Church.

Fotografo Scansani Walter

ST. AMBROSE The original mosaic is in the Biblioteca Ambrosiana in Milan, Italy.

whole European conception of art. Prominent among these Byzantine influences was that which affected the building of churches: through all Christendom there arose magnificent buildings which combined the plan of the basilicalike structures of the West with the love for glowing colors and rhythmic patternings of the East. The result was what one historian of art has described as "the most glorious manifestation of colorfulness in the whole of world architecture." We get some idea of the glories of this period from such churches as those which have survived in Ravenna, on the east coast of Italy, or in Palermo, Sicily—cities which borrowed their artists from Byzantium—with their enormous spaces, their glowing mosaics spread over all the available walls, and their characteristic stiff formalism. (See the picture on page 107.)

LATER PHASES OF GREGORIAN HISTORY

With the completion of these buildings, there arose the necessity of providing a more colorful and elaborate liturgy for the services held in them. We have already described in some detail the full collection of music suitable for this purpose available at the beginning of the seventh century. The crude and widely varied chants and songs of the earlier

THE INTERIOR OF SANTA SOPHIA, CONSTANTINOPLE

days gave way at the time of Gregory to a homogeneous and coherent body of music, which fitted the Latin text like a glove and was of extraordinary beauty. We know the names of some of the composers of the chants of this great period, which lasted until the tenth century. It was during this time that many of the chants in use today were written, characteristic ones that have come down to us being those comprising the two mass settings, *Orbis factor* and *Lux et origo,* to be found in *The Kyriale,* the authorized Vatican collection of chants.

The eleventh century saw a veritable throng of new composers; but none of them achieved the simplicity, the grandeur, and the originality of the earlier epoch. Technique was developed at the expense of clarity and direct appeal, the composers delighting in "difficult intonations and eccentric melodies which mounted high and descended low." During the twelfth century, St. Bernard of Clairvaux, the Church's great mystic, issued an *Antiphonaire* and a *Gradual,* collections and anthologies of chants which contained some new materials and certain modifications of the older usages. The names of most of these composers have been lost; we do know, however, the writer of the melody for such a hymn as the Easter *Victimae Paschali*—Wipo, chaplain of Conrad III.

It was during this period that there developed under the aegis of the Western Church two forms which were frequently interpolated into the Mass: the *sequence,* a text fitted to elaborate melismatic melodies suitable for a solo voice, the words emphasizing some particular phase of the liturgy or celebrating some special occasion; and the *trope,* additional words supplied to the liturgical text, making a devotional comment on it, set in such a way as to provide a syllable for each note of the chant used. These forms are no longer largely used, since they are felt to be out of character with the traditional style of the Mass.[9] But they are of great historical interest, for out of them grew the liturgical drama, the beginnings of the modern theater. Certain of the Easter and Christmas sequences and tropes were treated in the form of dramatic dialogues, with questions put by one priest and answered by others or by the choir. These in turn became the medieval Miracle and Mystery plays with which the Church sought to dramatize her essential doctrines.

[9] It was the Council of Trent (1545-1563) that ruled against the abuse of these liturgical additions: the use of tropes was forbidden, but four sequences were allowed to remain—the *Dies Irae,* the *Veni Sancte Spiritus,* the *Victimae Paschali,* and the *Lauda Sion.* Later another, the *Stabat Mater dolorosa,* was added.

Not being allowed in the Gregorian service books, the tropes were collected in great books called *Tropers.* These show the advances made for centuries.

The decadence of the chant began in the fourteenth century and was due largely to the influence of the new measured, contrapuntal style, which had by this time become popular. By the seventeenth century this decadence was complete, each diocese adopting its own practices of chanting, thus insuring complete confusion throughout the Church. The Council of Trent tried vainly to remedy matters, but things went from bad to worse. The seventeenth and eighteenth centuries, fruitful enough insofar as the production of measured music is concerned, saw the nadir of plainchant. Its rhythm became heavy and measured; influenced, of course, by the other music, it introduced sharps and flats so as to make the traditional melodies conform to the major and minor modes and free them entirely from the bonds of the ecclesiastical tones. It was not until the comparatively recent careful study by such experts as Dom Jumilhac, Dom Mocquereau, and Dom Pothier that anything like the honorable traditions of the earlier centuries has been restored. Even after all the study which these modern Benedictine monks have made of the ancient sources, there remains a great deal of difference of opinion as to how Gregorian chants are best interpreted.

GREGORIANS, A UNIVERSAL LANGUAGE OF THE SOUL

For those who have the spiritual interests of the Church at heart, this music stands as a means for an exalted type of religious expression, an expression which, by providing liturgical beauty, helps the congregations to love truth and practice goodness. For the historian, the vital simplicity and melodic severity of this music is of interest because it instituted strong foundations upon which many of the later developments were erected. Yet we need not go to the Gregorian chants for either religious or historical reasons alone; for they possess beauty as pure music, even though it is a beauty, as Prunières has rather plaintively remarked, that demands a certain initiation on the part of the hearer. The very process of listening without sharing the ecstasy of these chants or taking an intimate part in their essence is derogatory to appreciating their full beauty. The art of the Christian Church in music, as is true of so many other kinds of art, demands a certain quality of exhilaration that must be recaptured if we are to understand it fully and really like it. And this is particularly difficult in the case of an art so far removed from reality and modern thought as this music of the first ten centuries of the Christian era.

The Gregorian plainsong fulfills two great roles and represents two well-defined moments in music. In its own right and in its many varied

Archives Photographiques

HIGH MASS IN THE CHAPEL OF SAINTE CHAPELLE, PARIS Fifteenth-century
miniature from the *Heures* of the Duc de Berry

forms, it stands as music of special beauty and great sincerity of expression, the sung prayer of the Church in her intercourse with God. One of the greatest modern exponents of the chant, Dom Mocquereau, whose research as to the way in which it should be interpreted has gone far toward restoring its pristine beauty, has said of this music: "It appeals to what is highest in the soul; its beauty and nobility come from the fact that it borrows nothing, or as little as possible, from the world of the senses." The Gregorian chant represents also the basis for all the great changes that were wrought in the music of the period from the eleventh to the sixteenth century. To know it in each of these capacities is greatly to enrich our musical experience and heighten our sense of musical perspective.

Music Outside the Church

It is self-evident that the germ of all music lies in folk music. Music existed for thousands of years before the coming of the professional and academically trained composer and has continued to develop since, quite apart from his activities. Every form of vocal and instrumental music we possess has developed out of folk song or dance.

Percy Scholes

THE UNIVERSALITY OF FOLK MUSIC

French writers on music assume that the history of secular music begins with the troubadours and trouvères. If we are to believe such modern German historians as Moser and Mayer, the Nordic races were largely responsible for the familiar principles underlying all popular music. According to a present-day Italian, influenced no doubt by the ideology of the time, his people have always been first in every phase of musical development; therefore, without question, they must have produced the first composers of what we have come to call *folk music*. And the English, with their customary reticence, simply point to the account of a medieval traveler, one Giraldus Cambrensis, who, while journeying through Britain in the twelfth century, heard the people singing their own part

THE BYZANTINE CHURCH OF S. VITALE IN RAVENNA (526 A.D.) This shows
the altar, choir, and presbytery. Notice the mosaic of Justinian's Procession.

songs: so there must have been popular music in Britain long before
that!

As a matter of fact, no such chauvinistic claims need be made for the
origin of folk music; for human beings have always been fundamentally
the same everywhere and have had a common spontaneous desire to express themselves in song and dance. They have composed tunes as they
worked and have danced while they played, the men roistering together
in taverns and inns and the women crooning their little ones to sleep
with lullabies in much the same fashion the world over. The characteristics which separate the music of the various countries became gradually
fixed, not because of any great differences in the nature of the peoples
but because of the social circumstances in which they lived. The songs
of the people of France are different from those of Germany and England not because the *genus homo* is fundamentally different in France
from what it is in Germany or Great Britain, but because the people
we call French, through their inherited prejudices, traditions, beliefs,
and the history that is back of them, are so different from those we call
Germans or Englishmen.

No one knows, of course, when secular music actually began. There are direct references in some of the Greek plays which show that certain songs were then known and sung by everybody; but there must have been popular songs long before this. We can reasonably assume that they existed in the earliest days of music and were sung by the people of civilizations which appeared at the very dawn of history. It is not unreasonable to suppose that the laborers in the Egyptian and Babylonian civilizations had their work and play songs; and we know for certain that there was folk music among the Hebrews and Greeks—work songs, rhythmic chanteys for the oarsmen, and so forth. But it is not until early medieval times that we have evidences of the important role which music played in the lives of the common people.

THE CHURCH'S OPPOSITION

The activities of the Christian Church of the fourth, fifth, and sixth centuries were largely concerned with the conversion of the various peoples with whom it came into contact—first the Romans themselves, then the huge hordes of Celts, Teutons, and other pagan tribes of northern Europe. Hundreds of thousands of those who accepted Christianity as a religion understood it hardly at all but accepted it merely as a means for convenient or temporal advantage in their relationships with Rome. These people, although adhering outwardly to the doctrines of the Church, still kept many of their old beliefs—beliefs in supernatural spirits, household deities, the powers of magic, and so forth. It is in the vigorous discourses which the Church dignitaries found it necessary to make on the subject of these pagan survivals among the Gallo-Roman Christians that we frequently come upon mention of the music and dancing which went on outside the Church; aside from these pronouncements, secular music was not recognized by the ecclesiastical authorities.

Evidently horrid and pagan practices were mingled with the observation of certain Christian feast days, especially those which the Church found it wise to synchronize with former religious festivals, such as Mid-summer's Day, May Day, and St. John's Day. From the time of the fourth century down to the fifteenth, we hear a great deal about the diabolical practices of dancing and singing at such times. What is more, these *cantica diabolica, amatoria, et turpia* were sung and danced in the churchyards—the only common gathering places the people had—and sometimes even in the churches themselves. In these dances the people joined hands and moved around in a ring, with one of the women acting as leader. "As a cow which precedes the rest carries a bell on its neck," writes a medieval observer, "so the woman who sings and leads the dance has the Devil's bell bound to her neck. For the dance is round, the Devil is its center, and all turn to the left, because all are going to eternal death. When the Devil hears the sound, he is reassured, and says, 'I have not lost my cow yet.' " (The Church considered the Devil as the inventor and ruler of dancing, and for this reason struggled so valiantly to keep out of her music all suggestiveness of popular rhythms.)

The Church Fathers tried their best to stop such profane songs and carols, as the ring dances were called, by making announcement that disaster was sure to follow in the wake of those who participated in them. Their warnings were sprinkled with accounts of people being struck dead, consumed by fire, stricken with disease, and so on, but their efforts were all in vain. The evil practices still went on. There are stories of priests who, exasperated by the heathen conduct of their parishioners, were brought to the extremity of cursing them, so that they were to dance for a whole year. This the dancers had to do, sinking exhausted on the ground and dying after their release from the curse. Giraldus Cambrensis tells of an English priest who became so obsessed with the rhythmic refrain of one of the dance songs, which he had heard the people singing all night long, that at morning mass he involuntarily substituted for the words *Pax vobiscum* the opening line of the song, *Swete Lemman dhin are*—"Sweet love, thy lover needs thine aid." The consternation of his superiors and the delight of his congregation can be imagined.

All the later medieval folk songs and dances were the survivals of these pagan ritualistic performances. The earliest music we have of this kind, dating from the thirteenth century, shows a strongly rhythmic character. No wonder that it was beloved of the people and obnoxious to the Fathers of the Church!

SACRED FOLK MUSIC

But not all this folk music was of such a diabolic tinge. The Venerable Bede (673–735) tells in his famous *Ecclesiastical History of the English People* of a lay brother in one of the English monasteries, Caedmon by name, who received in the year 680 the "free gift of song, for which reason he never would compose any trivial or vain poem. [The same Caedmon is looked upon by scholars as the father of English poetry.] For having lived in the secular habit until he was well advanced in years, he had never learned anything of versifying; and for this reason sometimes at a banquet, when it was agreed to make merry by singing in turn, if he saw the harp come towards him, he would rise up from the table and go out and return home. Once having done so and gone out of the house where the banquet was, to the stable where he had to take care of the cattle for the night, he there composed himself to rest at the proper time. Thereupon one stood by him in his sleep and saluting him and calling him by name, said, 'Caedmon, sing me something.' But he answered, 'I cannot sing, and for this cause I left the banquet and retired hither, because I could not sing.' Then he who talked to him replied, 'Nevertheless thou must needs sing to me.' 'What must I sing?' he asked. 'Sing the beginning of creation,' said the other. Having received this answer, he straightway began to sing verses to the praise of God the Creator."

This song, out of the dream of Caedmon, may be said to be the first known English poem; as translated by Kennedy, it runs:

Praise we the Lord
Of the heavenly kingdom,
God's power and wisdom
The works of his hand;
As the Father of Glory,
Eternal Lord,
Wrought the beginning
Of all his wonders!
Holy Creator!

Warden of men!
First, for a roof,
O'er the children of earth,
He stablished the heavens,
And founded the world,
And spread the dry land
For the living to dwell in.
Lord Everlasting!
Almighty God!

These songs of a religious nature were popular in all the countries in medieval times and were widely sung by the people. The gentle St. Francis of Assisi was an important leader in developing the taste of the ordinary people for such songs. He founded singing societies, the *laudisti,* each of them under the direction of a *capitain;* and the mighty sweep of the lines in his own song calling upon all things to praise the Lord—Sun, Moon, Earth, and even Death—shows how effective these *laudi* (songs of praise) could be. They were generally very simple in structure, with a refrain at the beginning and at the end, and were sung in unison.

It was natural enough for the people themselves to imitate, in some of the songs they made up, the style and language of the Church. We find that many of the earliest folk songs we know, for example *Christ ist erstanden* and *Gelobet seist du, Jesu Christ,* end with the Greek expression *Kyrie eleison*—"Lord have mercy on us." From earliest times this phrase was one that the Church encouraged its congregations to sing; and so the people took it for their own, often setting new words to the Kyrie melodies they knew and always ending them with this plea for mercy. Later they translated Latin hymns in the vernacular (*O filii et filiae* is an example), sometimes mixing Latin and vernacular phrases in a most incongruous and quite amusing fashion.

But beyond this they did not go for some time. In the twelfth century, even if the common people had been able to imagine a different world of their own, one entirely outside the influence of the clergy and the nobility, who would have thought of recording these imaginings? The thoughts and feelings of gentlemen were, of course, another matter, one worthy of record. And so we have handed down to us the songs of the troubadours and trouvères, the minnesingers and minstrels, songs that still have a fascination after the lapse of many centuries. These will be discussed in another chapter.

monk or another. With enough voices and instruments, their effect in the resonant Romanesque interiors must have been indeed impressive:

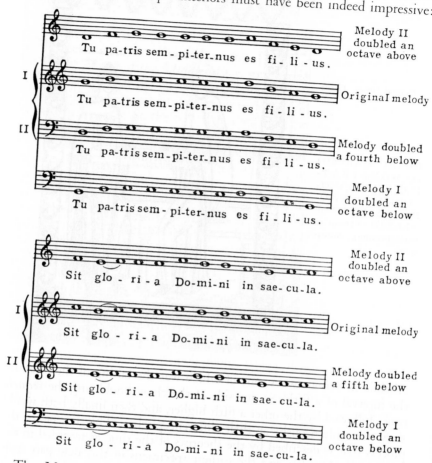

The *Musica Enchiriadis* also gives suggestions for the use of other kinds of polyphony, in which the added parts do not duplicate the given melody in strict parallelism. These were the first steps taken toward making the various parts independent. The late Canon Douglas compared the importance of these steps in the annals of music history with the momentous occasion when the American Wilbur Wright made his first flight in a self-propelled airplane. Both these experiments permanently transformed the usages of man and opened up vistas that had before been undreamed of.

As we have mentioned earlier, Giraldus Cambrensis (Gerald of Wales), writing toward the end of the twelfth century, described a custom of popular singing in parts of Wales and North England that does not differ greatly from the uses of the theoretical treatises of the time. This custom, introduced perhaps from Scandinavia, seems to have been long established and consisted of not more than "two varieties of pitch in the voices, one murmuring the lower, the other the upper part, in a manner both soothing and delightful," according to Cambrensis. The Welsh, however, did not utter the tunes uniformly, as was the practice elsewhere, but "manifoldly, and in many manners and notes; so that in a multitude of singers, such as it was the custom of this people to gather together, so many songs are to be heard as there are singers to be seen, and a great diversity of parts, which finally come together in one consonance." This latter would seem to indicate, even if we make the necessary allowance for reportorial exaggeration, a much freer practice than the methods of uniform progression described in the theoretical writings of the churchmen.

These worthies seem to have been strangely silent in respect to the developments of symphonious singing, which took place toward the end of the Romanesque period. Guido[2] wrote, as has often been recorded, a detailed description of the methods of organum employed in his time (the beginning of the eleventh century), which suggests that the two voices had acquired some individual freedom, not always keeping at exactly the same intervalic distance from each other, with now and then a suggestion of contrary movement. But from the time of his death (1050) until the beginning of the twelfth century, no description of contemporary methods has been found; however, several specimens of the work of that period have been discovered by the musicologists. These indicate that great progress toward a real art of composition was made during this time and that the foundations for future developments were firmly laid. Broadly speaking, the three chief types of developing polyphony came to be known as *Organum, Conductus,* and *Motet.* These styles were carried over into all music employing several voices instead of one.

Organum developed from the very simple parallelisms we have illus-

[2] Guido, a Benedictine monk of the monastery of Pomposa near Ravenna, Italy, is credited with a number of important "discoveries" in music, among them being the system of teaching sight singing by means of *hexachords,* groups of notes with the tones and semitones arranged exactly alike. He is supposed to have given us the sure foundation upon which our modern system of notation is built—the exact fixing of the pitch of the neumes or notes by means of lines a third apart. See examples on page 96.

trated, through a stage of freer time values in which one part often used several notes against each note of the plainsong. Imitation and ornamentation played a great part in such developments. Conductus moved more in solid chordal blocks. Pérotin was a notable exponent of this style, in which the words might be either sacred or secular. Here, as in all fashions and shapings of the period, there was constant experiment. The essence of the Motet style was the use of two or more different sets of words at once. The tenor, holding to a familiar or, at any rate, known melody, would repeat it rhythmically. We deal with these in the next chapter.

The Early Gothic Music

*How high the sea of human happiness rose
during the Middle Ages we know now only
from the barriers built to restrain it.*

Gilbert K. Chesterton

TWELFTH AND THIRTEENTH CENTURIES

The Gothic era, in many respects one of the greatest ages in the history of the world, grew naturally out of the Romanesque. Once referred to by the enlightened intellects of the Renaissance as *barbare,* the twelfth and thirteenth centuries stand for us today as a period of intellectual and spiritual awakening comparable to the time of Pericles in Greece. Within a few generations they brought forth the Crusades, the Gothic cathedral, and Thomas Aquinas. The great names of the Gothic period are legion: Abélard, John of Salisbury, Bernard of Clairvaux, Roger Bacon, Duns Scotus, St. Francis of Assisi, St. Dominic, Dante. These were the centuries which produced the *Chanson de Roland,* the Arthurian romances, and the *Divine Comedy.* Never before or since have architects and builders been fired with such zeal or produced such results: it has been carefully estimated that between the years 1170 and 1270 eighty great cathedrals and nearly five hundred churches of cathedral dignity were built in France alone, among them some of the greatest structures ever reared by man. Here is the paradox of a religion that

A. ...otographiques

CARCASSONNE   The medieval town in southern France dates back to the twelfth century.

was concerned with otherworldliness being able to manifest itself in so much beauty that was of this world: architecture, sculpture, music, joined in a magnificent symphony of which the leading theme was *Deus vult*.

Those most familiar with this period, however, assure us that Gothic art was not only mystic and otherworldly; it was also concerned with expressing satisfaction and joy in the abundant life here below. Out of a very limited population, youths by the tens of thousands flocked to the great teachers of that era; and out of the ensuing intellectual ferment there came the universities, centers of learning in the various countries: Paris in France, Bologna in Italy, Salamanca in Spain, Oxford and Cambridge in England. No one who has read the history of the Crusades, those exciting adventures in religion, art, love, and conquest, can maintain that they were concerned only with holy aims! Even the cathedrals were not entirely dissociated from worldly relations: they may have been built to the glory of God, but they were also monuments of local pride and gathering places for the processions, pilgrimages, and even secular festivities of the people of the time.

It was a complex and paradoxical period; its leitmotiv was unquestionably religious in character, in spite of the fact that the nobility were developing a conception of life and art independent of, and even contradictory to, that of the Church. This new freedom of thought, characterized by the struggle between State and Church which runs through the whole period, is but another manifestation of the Gothic spirit and had a powerful and, indeed, irresistible influence on the striking development of the individual which took place in the fourteenth and fifteenth centuries. There had arisen by this time a great body of secular songs and ballads, the influence of which on later music is only beginning to be realized and the importance of which is hardly suggested by the few examples that have come down to us. The songs of the troubadours and trouvères have long been appreciated for the quality of their poetry; their music is likewise worthy of our attention, combining as it does both the religious and the popular characteristics of the time and so reflecting the life and the spirit of medieval Europe.

No one who has ever heard or sung the old English round, *Sumer is icumen in,* supposed to have been written by a monk of the early thirteenth century, can doubt that it represents a new spirit in music, one which was trying wings for much finer flights than had so far been attempted. This marvel of the Middle Ages remains, alas, alone as something extraordinary, beyond the range of time. It is a song about the freshening season of the year that sounds quite modern in scale. Although three parts had long been the limit, this is written in six parts, four of which are in canon, each taking up the tune a little after the others; it stands as an intricate and formal piece of construction that finds no parallel until more than two centuries later, the two lowest parts repeat over and over a "ground bass," a short passage that does not vary and that goes with the canoning of the four upper parts to make a gay, open-air piece that is as delightful in spirit as it is clever in craftsmanship.

Although this piece seems to stand alone, the manuscript which contains it (now in the British Museum) has also a list of other music that links it definitely with the work of composers writing at that time in Paris. We can say truly enough that the freshened spirit and clever workmanship of this rondel is representative of the new Gothic feeling that entered the world with the twelfth century. The Crusades of the preceding years had brought stimulating contact with the East; and, with the gradual revival of general prosperity, commerce developed, merchants became more important, and towns arose whose inhabitants, although they were always united by their religion, nevertheless developed a new sense of independence that had no direct relation with the Church.

ABBEY CHURCH OF ST. DENIS One of the earliest Gothic churches, this still stands outside Paris.

The visible world became a more pleasant place to live in, for life was felt to be more enjoyable for its own sake. Religion warmed to the influence of St. Francis of Assisi and his followers, who were more popular for their humanism and love for man and nature than they were for their asceticism. A characteristic result of this new spirit in religion and life was the *laudi spirituali*, popular devotional songs with poems in the vernacular. Originally composed for singing confraternities that had sprung up in Florence and other Italian cities, these were also used by bands of itinerant pilgrims who, as flagellants and penitents, wandered over the countryside. The melodies of these congregational-type hymns scarcely changed their character until the seventeenth century; adapting the form of dialogues, the *laudi* became the basis for the later oratorio, as we shall see. Similar songs (*Geisslerlieder*) were also sung in Germany, especially during the terrifying mid-fourteenth-century days of the Black Death.

Learning was increasingly cherished, and it, too, realized the grandeur and significance of nature and of man in all his activities. The Romanesque world had been largely in the hands of the monks; that of Gothic times centered in the communes, the large towns which sprang up everywhere in France and England, their inhabitants friendly to both bishop and king and yet not dependent on either.

THE CATHEDRAL, THE GREATEST EXPRESSION OF THE GOTHIC ERA

We have already remarked on the strong sentiment for religion which pervaded all classes of society at this time: its greatest expression was the Gothic cathedral of the twelfth and thirteenth centuries. One of the first complete expressions of this type of architecture may be seen at the very gates of Paris, in the royal abbey church of St. Denis, where many of the kings of France sleep their long, last sleep. Instead of the massive walls and heavy pillars which the Romanesque builders found necessary for their huge structures, the Gothic architects, by developing the Romanesque system of construction, were able to turn their fanes into armatures of stone, with slender piers soaring aloft and merging into pointed arches that seem to reach up into boundless space. In place of the small windows in the thick-walled Romanesque structures, these builders of the north filled every interstice of their buildings with glowing glass, whose gorgeous colors were expressive of their warm faith. There remained nothing of the heavy gloom of the monastic churches, everything about these communally built structures being light and animated.

From the Ile de France, Gothic architecture spread over most of Europe. Such buildings as Notre Dame in Paris, the cathedrals of Chartres and Amiens, and York Minster in England express this new, freer spirit of the times in their design and in the decorative glass, carving, and tapestry. The people could not read, but they had spread before them a marvelous fabric, which expressed their love for God and their joy in humanity; the Gospel story was narrated for them in thousands of sculptured images. No other such symbolization of faith has ever been

THE GOTHIC INTERIOR Chartres has "armatures of stone, with slender piers soaring aloft and merging into pointed arches that seem to reach up into boundless space."

ANALYSIS OF GOTHIC
CONSTRUCTION Rheims
Cathedral (from Gailha-
baud)

achieved as in these Gothic buildings; a contemporary writer expressed
it thus:

*My beloved son, thou hast approached God's house in all faith, and adorned
it with such abundant comeliness; and having illuminated the vaults of the
wall with divers works and colors, thou hast in a manner shown forth to the
beholders a vision of God's paradise, bright as springtide, with flowers of every
hue, and fresh with green grass and leaves, refreshing the souls of the saints*

with crowns proportioned to their divers merits, whereby thou makest them to preach his wonders in his works. For man's eyes knoweth not whereon first to gaze: if he looks up at the vaults, they are as mantles embroidered with spring flowers; if he regard the walls, there is a manner of paradise; if he considers the light streaming through the windows, he marvelleth at the priceless beauty of the glass and the variety of this most precious work. Work, therefore, now good man—kindle thyself to a still ampler art, and set thyself with all the might of thy soul to complete that which is yet lacking in the gear of the Lord's house, without which the divine mysteries and the ministries of God's service may not stand.

Quoted in *Burlington Magazine,* September, 1912

THE GOTHIC SPIRIT IN ART

It is this spirit of achievement in creation, of trying to acquire a unity of expression through using an infinite variety of means, that is most characteristic of these Gothic times: it pervaded every form of artistic activity. To the thirteenth-century artist, the thousands of details in a Gothic cathedral were simply means for expressing the essential unity of his faith. So with the illuminators who spent their lives in decorating the manuscripts of the period; they loved to work into their designs all sorts of seemingly eccentric and unrelated details, representations of beasts and birds and flowers that had no connection with the text they were illustrating. Yet to these artists nothing was unimportant; they saw significance and beauty in all things and were able to "sense the infinite in the particular." The sculptor loved to crowd every possible space with his figures, feeling them all to be component parts in a unified design. The glassmaker wrought out of gorgeous bits of color intricate patterns that were expressive of the universality of his beliefs.

EARLY GOTHIC MUSIC

The makers of music followed exactly the same ideals. If we examine some of the music of the thirteenth century—a large amount of which has been preserved in a manuscript, the *Antiphonarium Mediceum,* now in the Laurentian Library, Florence—we shall find the same attempt at elaborate construction and infinite detail that appears in the visual arts of the time. The unknown composers of this music were really craftsmen working at their melodic ornamentation in precisely the same way as the illuminator did on his manuscript or the goldsmith on his monstrance. For the first time we find in this music a strong contrast in rhythm between the parts: above a rigid, unmeasured *tenor* (the original melody) there has been constructed a decorative melismatic series of notes—we can hardly call it a melody—which completely throws the original into the background.

We have always to remember that this music, like the music which preceded it, derived a great deal of its effect from the surroundings in which it was performed and that it was deliberately shaped accordingly. This *organum purum,* one of the most important forms of music at the time, with its completely free upper voice, whose part the singer could and did decorate by improvisation, was largely cultivated at the Abbey of St. Martial in Limoges, at Chartres, as well as in Paris, which later became the principal center for polyphonic music during the Gothic era, as it had long been of architecture.

Here we first learn of definite composers: the two earliest mentioned are Léonin and Pérotin, both of whom lived and worked in Paris about 1200, a little before its intellectual center, the famous Sorbonne, was founded. Léonin was the choirmaster at Notre Dame and wrote a whole cycle of *organa pura* for the various occasions of the church year, calling it *Magnus liber organi de Gradali et Antiphonario.* This was somewhat remodeled by his follower, Pérotin, who likewise wrote some three-part and four-part organa. The most famous of these are the four-part *Viderunt* and *Sederunt* organa: of colossal dimensions, they are full of tremendous rhythmic energy. Their powerful massed tones and chords, sung by both men's and boys' voices and played on various sorts of instruments, must have had a tremendous effect in the wide, resonant spaces of the Gothic cathedrals. As Dr. Ficker has described it, "Above a syllabic chant of mystic profundity there flows a far-flung stream of interwoven tones, now like shadowy, fugitive apparitions, now swelling to an orgiastic rout." Again the Gothic love of elaborated construction and infinite detail is felt expressing the might of a religious idea; and we can well credit an ancient report concerning the effect of this music on the common people, who "listened in awe-stricken and trembling admiration to the strident creaking of the organ bellows and the shrill clangor of the cymbals, the harmony of the flutes."

There arose the necessity for finding some means of more exactly writing down what the composer wanted to be sung and played; for down to this time the manuscripts were able to serve only as a sort of sketch and were not by any manner of means a precise indication for the performers as to numbers and kinds of singers and instrumentalists, tempi, dynamics, tonalities, accidentals, and so on. The performers really improvised on the bare outline left by the composer, and the effect they achieved depended largely on their own artistic abilities.

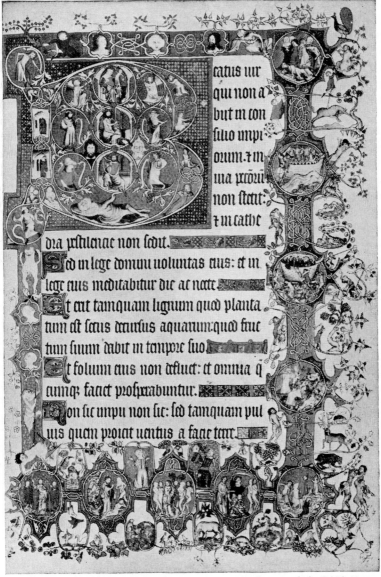

GOTHIC ART The Beatus Page from the Psalter of the St. Omer Family is a fine example of Gothic illuminated manuscript showing a multitude of seemingly unrelated details.

The science of musical notation advanced rapidly during this time; the neumes representing groups of notes, which had first come into practical use during the seventh century, now became more precise as to pitch and were no longer mere reminders of the general course of a melody. (See first example, page 135.) This exactitude as to pitch was increased by the use of a line (*staff* or *stave*) to define the exact pitch of the note; other lines were added, and in time there was established the standardized stave of four lines with the neumes scattered among them. (See second example.) During the ninth and tenth centuries, interest began to develop in a notation that could also record time values with some exactitude; and by the time of Léonin, the use of "measured music," in which sound lengths were accurately measured, was general, although there was great variety in the signs that were used to indicate it. (See example three). These systems were worked out in detail by the theorists and taken up gladly by the composers, who then could demand from the performers a more exact rendering of what they had conceived than had been possible under the purely improvisatory method.

One of the outstanding features of all this music was the use of a liturgical melody for a *cantus firmus*—that is, the melody around which the composer wove his other parts. There was a good psychological reason for this, for these liturgical melodies possessed for the devout congregations an ideal significance, one far removed from things of the world; hence any music built on them was lifted beyond the realm of mundane expression into an atmosphere of spiritual significance. But in the early part of the thirteenth century composers began to use original melodies for their *cantus firmus,* so that the whole piece was pure composition. This resulted in what was called the *conductus.* Pérotin has left us many of these compositions, in which the cantus is freely invented and no longer consists of long-held notes but possesses plenty of rhythmic variety, with the added voices keeping the same fundamental rhythm that underlies the cantus.

THE MOTET

Pérotin was evidently a man of many parts, for not only did he write voluminously and effectively in the Gothic forms already mentioned, but he is credited with being the initiator of the chief form by which Gothic music of this period became famous, the *motet,* a term not to be confused with its use by later composers. The difficulty of providing structural unity between the various parts of the organa led to the adop-

Neumes without staff (tenth century)

Gothic choral notation on a three-line to four-line staff (eleventh century)

Gothic choral notation on five-line staff (fourteenth century)

DIFFERENT TYPES OF NOTATION

tion of this motet form as described by a writer of the thirteenth century
(Johannes de Grocheo, quoted in Leichtentritt's *Geschichte der Motette*):

*The motet is made up of several interwoven voices which have either their
own texts or kind of syllable division, and which sound together in consonances.
There may be three or four of these interweaving voices, each of them having
its syllables, with the exception of the tenor, which in some motets has a text,
in many others does not.*

*The various parts have different names: tenor, motetus, triplum, quadruplum.
. . . The part upon which the others are built, as a house is built upon
its foundation, is the* tenor; *it determines the character and the size of the
motet, just as foundation does the building.*

The voice immediately above the tenor is called the motetus; *it usually
begins on the fifth above the tenor and keeps about that relationship to it,
although it may go to the octave.*

*The voice which begins at the octave above the tenor and keeps about that
same relationship to it is named the* triplum: *whenever necessary, however, the
triplum may go either above or below this range.*

The quadruplum *is a voice sometimes added to make the harmony perfect,
although there are some motets having only three voices in which the harmony
may be said to be perfect.*

Thus we have a real architectural structure made up of a number of
seemingly incongruous members, unified according to Gothic ideals,
in somewhat the following manner:

(To us it may seem anything but unified to have the tenor an instrumental part based on a Gregorian motif, *Veritatem* . . . , the motetus singing a melody to the words *Verbum caro factum est;* and the triplum one to *Salve virgo nobilis.* But to the Gothic artist it was evidently the height of reasonableness.)

The true characteristic of these Gothic motets was this placing-together of the most incongruous elements, each voice often having a different text, sometimes in a different language. Just as the illuminator called into being a peculiar set of fantastic creatures, half real and half unreal, which had no direct connection with the text of the manuscript he was illustrating, and the architect his fantastic race of gargoyle demons, so the musician did not hesitate to intermingle the most startlingly varied elements in his motets. Dr. Ficker describes one which has a tenor part based on a fragment of a Gregorian chant, set to the word *regnat* (he reigns), thus providing a sort of constant underlying reminder of God's sovereignty. The *motetus* sings a text suggestive of a moral lecture addressed to a roistering drunkard, exhorting him to change his ways, the implication being that otherwise he cannot expect to escape the chastening hand of Him who reigneth over all; and the *triplum* has a melody similar to the *motetus* without any text at all; it may have used the same words.

Even this fragmentary connection is often lacking. Secular words and melodies were added to the most solemn tones of a Gregorian-chant *tenor;* there was thought to be nothing incongruous in the combination of a Latin hymn in praise of the Virgin with a drinking song in a second part and an erotic love song in a third, and in the placing of all this above a *tenor* based on a slow-moving Gregorian melody. There is a famous thirteenth-century motet with its *tenor* a Kyrie from a Gregorian Mass, its *motetus* having reference to the birds that sing in the spring, tra-la, and its *triplum* descriptive of the perils of bigamy! Later motets written in the so-called Burgundian style often had the melody in the upper voice, this being the only one with words, the other parts being accompanimental, often played on instruments—in reality, a monody accompanied by two subordinate voice parts.

To try to comprehend all this we must again recall the peculiar mental attitude of the age and all the incongruities of the other arts. Typical also were the scenes of ribaldry and frivolity that were often enacted in the churches on great feast days, which it is difficult to reconcile with the spirit that created the beautiful interiors. The congregation did not hesitate to burlesque the sacred mysteries to such an extent that, during the twelfth century when celebrating the "Feast of the Ass,"

AN ENGLISH GYMEL (thirteenth century) A specifically English type of two-part writing.

they would in procession bring an animal into the church. Then, with much drinking and reveling, they would proceed to represent the flight into Egypt. After a rollicking hymn, set to one of the Church's melodies, in praise of the ass, a Mass would be celebrated, with imitations of the animal's braying interpolated at suitable places. In the same spirit of naïve realism, the sculptors and wood carvers working in the cathedrals did not hesitate to use all sorts of peculiar and amusing animal and human monstrosities in their designs. So we should not wonder too much at the Church's attempt to draw within her circle all phases of human activity, trying thus to make them subserve her own purposes and unifying them insofar as the attitude of the time was concerned. Whilst Paris remained the chief center of experiment and development in these new technical styles, they were employed also in the provinces of France, as well as in Spain and in Britain, where, indeed, they may well have originated.

The only secular music of this time that we know was the special kind of songs written and composed by the *goliards,* rascally students and uprooted clerics who wandered about through England, France, and Germany during the last half of the tenth, the eleventh, twelfth, and early thirteenth centuries. These *carmina,* although they covered a wide variety of subjects, were chiefly concerned with wine, women, and song; they were written in a mixture of popular and classic Latin with music whose character we can only surmise, since it has been preserved largely in staffless neumes.

USE OF INSTRUMENTS

Those who live in one age can never fully understand the music of another: for example, we who are accustomed to instrumental music that has reached an advanced stage of development find it almost impossible to realize how primitive its earliest stages must have been. These beginnings are to be found in the period under discussion; it must be remembered that, although the scores did not always lay forth the parts for instruments as well as voices, instrumental accompaniments were freely used during this period. (The subject is treated in more detail in another place.) But there is plenty of evidence in the sculptures and pictures of the period that instruments often played along with the voices in these polyphonic compositions, and we have examples of some of them that have both prelude and postlude for instruments alone. Organs were certainly used in the churches, together with such bowed instruments as fiedels and viols, and, in addition, lutes, harps, reed instruments, and trumpets. All these added their not overdelicate tones to the harmony, sometimes to the critical disapproval of the more sensitive-eared listeners. If a voice part had not its singer or a sufficient number of singers, instruments were used to fill in; there seemed to be no hesitancy in spoiling the effect of the vocal lines. But we can hardly say that the instrumental parts as yet assumed any real independence.

It is extremely difficult for us, with our present-day conceptions of tone color and harmonic relationships, to realize what this music must have sounded like to the Gothic ear. It is impossible to be certain of the exact types of sounds produced by the instruments of the Middle Ages, or to recreate the effects achieved by their sounding together in the resonant interiors in which this music was performed. It is much better to imagine, as Ficker has suggested, how the "metallic boy voices were mingled with all the gentle tintinnabulation of the glockenspiel, cymbals, triangle, etc. then in use, together with the dulcet tones of the viols, while the long-sustained notes of the lower parts were sung by smooth tenor voices supported by manifold wind instruments." Then we can perhaps get an idea of the dazzling effect of these Gothic motets and organa. "Fancy yourself," he bids us, "attending one of the great assemblies of the estates honored by the regent's presence and accompanied by the most lavish display, for which the courts of France and Burgundy were then conspicuous. All the bewildering splendor radiated by the cerebral action finds an echo in the scintillant rhythms and interlinked tones of this music."[3]

The Music of Chivalry

I can play the lute, the violin, the pipe, the bagpipe, the syrinx, the harp, the gigue, the gittern, the symphony, the psaltery, the organistrum, the regals, the psaltery, the rote. I can sing a song well and make tales to please young ladies and can play the gallant for them if necessary. I can throw knives into the air and catch them without cutting my fingers. I can do dodges with string, most extraordinary and amusing. I can balance chairs and make tables dance. I can throw a somersault and walk on my head.

Les deux Menèstriers, Bodleian Library, Oxford

THE TROUBADOURS AND THEIR FELLOWS

The songs of the troubadours were the direct result of a wave of emotionalism which swept over Europe during the twelfth century, an emotionalism that was engendered by the new contacts which the Europeans made with the East and its highly developed civilization. The Moorish conquest of Spain and the seven crusading journeys[4] that were made in order to

---

[3] For those who would pursue further the spirit of this fascinating time, we recommend two books: *Mont-Saint-Michel and Chartres* by Henry Adams and *Cathedral; A Gothic Pilgrimage* by Helen H. Parkhurst.

[4] Even a casual reading of history shows how confused were these centuries of the Crusades. "The most distant islands and savage countries," writes a historian of the time, "were inspired with the same ardent passion. The Welshman left his hunting, the Scotchman his fellowship with vermin, the Dane his drinking party, the Norwegian his raw

A GRIM REMINDER OF THE POPULARITY OF THE CRUSADES   Crac-des-Chevaliers, a vast fortress that was built in the twelfth century on a thousand-foot eminence near Homs in Syria, was for over a hundred years one of the outposts of the Knights of St. John of Jerusalem, who built it with the help of artisan pilgrims from France.

rescue the Holy Land from the profane hands of the infidel occasioned a new interest on the part of the aristocratic European world in the more delicate and refined things of life: poetry and music began to be cultivated for themselves, and a new code of chivalry, with ideals of fealty to God, King, and Lady, was adopted:

A Dieu mon âme,	*My soul to God,*
Mon cœur aux dames,	*My heart to the ladies,*
Ma vie au roi,	*My life to the king,*
L'honneur pour moi.	*Honor for myself.*

The center of this romantic influence was France; but it had no peculiarly nationalistic background and spread rapidly through all Europe, producing some great literature and poetry in France, England, and Germany. Its chief spokesmen were the troubadours (as they were called in the language of the south), the trouvères (the term used in the north—both *troubadour* and *trouvère* have the same significance, that

fish" in order to help rescue the Holy Places of the East. Perhaps the most monstrous folly of all the seven crusades was that of the Children, in 1212, when scores of thousands of youths were persuaded to embark on this "holy mission," only to find themselves in the end sold into slavery, their goal still unrealized.

TWO JONGLEURS, FROM A TWELFTH-CENTURY MANUSCRIPT At the left is a shawm player and at the right a juggler. According to tradition each jongleur had to be able to play at least nine instruments.

of inventing or making poetry), and the minnesingers (as they were called in Germany). These were men born sometimes in high estate, sometimes in low, who gave their lives to the production of poetry and music in celebration of the beauty and loveliness of women, for the purpose of reciting deeds of chivalry and relating epic tales, both of men and of gods. The medieval biographer of William, Count of Poitiers, the earliest troubadour mentioned in history, said of him that he was "one of the most courteous men in the world and one of the greatest deceivers of ladies—a valiant knight in warfare and bounteous in love and gallantry. And he knew well to sing and make poetry, and long time went through the world beguiling ladies"—a description which could be made to serve for most of his successors! The names of some four hundred troubadours and two hundred trouvères have come down to us, as well as a great deal of their poetry, consisting of ordered sequences of couplets and refrains, together with a number of the melodies they used.

The fact that these musician-poets treated subjects which were quite outside the Church and upon which the clergy frowned, and which therefore found no place in the process of education that was entirely monopolized by the Church, was a tremendously important influence in the secularization of music. The nobles, increasingly reacting against the dominance of the Church, began to look elsewhere for artistic materials and found them in the common songs and dances of the people.

While the troubadours were essentially poets, they usually composed the melodies of their songs; but it was obviously important to the dignity of a nobleman that he should have an attendant trained to perform his master's works. These accompanists and musical scribes (the more skillful of whom acted as "ghosts" for their masters) were called *ménestrels* or *jongleurs;* being of the common people, they would naturally be influenced by popular melodies. Someone has called them the beloved vagabonds of the thirteenth century, for they passed constantly from one world to another, from noble castle to rustic inn.[5]

[5] The minstrels "wandered at will from castle to castle, and in time from borough to borough, sure of their ready welcome alike in the village tavern, the guildhall and the baron's keep. They sang and jested in the market places, stopping cunningly at a critical moment in the performance to gather their harvest of small coins from the bystanders. In the great castles, while lords and ladies supped or sat around the fire, it was theirs to while away many a long bookless evening with courtly *gests* or witty sally. At wedding or betrothal, baptism or knight dubbing, treaty or tournament, their presence was indispensable. The greater festivities saw them literally in the hundreds, and rich was their reward in jewels, in costly garments, and in broad acres.

"They were licensed vagabonds, with free right of entry into the presence chambers of the land. You might know them from afar by their coats of many colors, gaudier than

Such songs as these, taken from the manuscript of an unknown jongleur of the thirteenth century and now in the National Library, Paris, show this folk influence clearly enough. They were probably dance songs of the time, popular with commoner and noble alike.

I

Je me che-val-choi-e Par-mi un pra-el,

De joste une ar-broi-e Lez un or-mis-sel.

Là tro-vai grant joi-e: Pas-tore en l'ar-broi-e,

En sa main fres-tel chante un son no-vel.

II

L'au - trier m'iè - re le˙ - vaz,
Ne sui gaire es - loi - gnaz,

Sor mon che-val mon-taz Sui por de-duire a-laz
Can me sui ar-res-taz, Et des-sen-di en praz

[1.
Lez u - ne prai - e - ri - e:
[2.
Sor une en - te flo- _ri - e.

any knight might respectably wear, by the instruments on their backs and those of their servants, and by the shaven faces, close-clipped hair, and flat shoes of their profession. This hen-speckle appearance, together with the privilege of easy access, made the minstrel's dress a favorite disguise in ages when disguise was imperative."

E. K. Chambers: *The Mediaeval Stage*

Sometimes the minstrels used in the midst of the song a phrase intended to be sung as a sort of response by a group of singers or dancers.
Notice, for instance, this ballade:

A l'en-tra - da   del   tens clar,   *E - y - a,*

Per joi - a   re - co - men-çar,   *E - y - a,*

E   per je - los   ir - ri - tar,   *E - y - a,*

Vol la re - gi - na mos-trat Qu'el 'es si a - mo -

ro - sa   *A   la   vi',   A   la   vi -*

a, Je - los,   *Lais - saz nos,   Lais - saz nos,*

Bal - lar   en - tre nos,   En - tre nos.

TYPES OF TROUBADOUR ART

The gallant music of the troubadours, written for use in court and
castle, was something quite different. Springing out of the current chiv-
alric romanticism, the same spirit that produced the Arthurian romances, these troubadour songs fall naturally into two groups: *chansons
à personnages,* general in manner and written according to strict conventions; and *poésie courtoise,* addressed by the troubadour directly to
his lady. Included in the *chansons à personnages* were various conventional types: *chansons de toile,* work songs; *chansons de malmariée,* a

most fruitful subject; *pastourelles; chansons de danse,* like those already mentioned; *reverdies,* or spring songs; and *chansons d'aube,* morning songs. The more personal utterances of the poet were marked by passionate, often extravagant, devotion to the service of love; the troubadour, anxious to establish himself in favor with the lady of his choice, spent a great deal of his time imploring her favor in carefully designed stanzaic schemes:

Lady, if Mercy help me not, I ween
That I to be thy slave am all too mean,
  For thy great worth small hope to me has given
Aught to accomplish meet for dame so rare—
Yet this I would, and nowise will despair;
  For I have heard, the brave, when backward driven,
Strive ever till the conquering blow they deal,
So strive I for thy love by service leal.

Though to such excellence I come not near,
Nor eke of one so noble am the peer,
  I sing my best, bear meekly Love's hard burden,
Serve thee and love thee more than all beside,
Shun ill, seek after good whate'er betide;
  Wherefore, methinks, fair dame should liefer guerdon
With her dear self a valiant knight and true,
Than the first lord that haughtily may woo . . .

Raymond of Miraval

And more to the same purport. If the fair lady decided to "guerdon with her dear self" the valiant knight, a ceremony was arranged, modeled on that of a vassal pledging himself to his lord. "The lover, kneeling down with clasped hands before his lady, vowed fidelity to her; she then lifted him up, gave him a ring, and kissed him, as a token that she 'retained' him." Such a union, strange as it may seem in the light of today's monogamous ideals in marriage—for the troubadour's lady was almost sure to be the wife of someone else—was considered so solemn a matter as to call for blessing by a priest.

Indeed, the whole period is difficult of modern comprehension; if we are to realize the beauty of some of these troubadour songs, we must detach ourselves from present-day connotations and immerse ourselves in the atmosphere evoked by the accounts of the lives of these gallants. (It was the custom of medieval times to head the collection of a troubadour's poems with the story of his life; and so we have plenty of contemporary evidence available.) Take, for example, such a biography as that of Raimbaut de Vagueiras (*d.* 1207), one of the most distinguished of the Provencal poets, whose lively *Estampie* is quoted later on:

Raimbaut de Vagueiras was the son of a poor knight of Provence, of the Castle of Vagueiras, one named Peirors, who passed for mad. And Raimbaut became a jongleur, and abode full long with the Prince of Orange, William of Baux. Well did he know how to sing and to make coblas and sirventes; and the Prince of Orange did him great good, and great honor, and advanced him, and made him to be known and prized of all good folk. And afterwards, Raimbaut departed from him, and gat him to Montferrat—to the court of my Lord the Marquis Boniface, and therein dwelt full long, growing in wisdom, in knowledge, and in prowess. And he became enamored of the sister of the Marquis, the which hight my Lady Beatrice, wife of Lord Henry of Carret, and he made many fair songs, calling her therein, "Fair Knight," and men weened she loved him well. Now well have ye heard who was Raimbaut de Vagueiras, and how he came to honor, and by whom; but now I will tell you how that when the Marquis had dubbed him knight, Raimbaut became enamored of my Lady Beatrice, sister of the Marquis and my Lady Azalais of Salutz.

Greatly did he love her and desire her, having care that none should know of it, and much did he spread abroad her fame, and many a friend did he win for her. And she was wont to bear herself full graciously towards him, yet the while he was dying for desire and fearfulness, for he durst neither beseech her for her love nor show that he strove therefor, until as one sore pressed, he told her that he loved a lady of great excellence, yet durst not make known the goodwill and love he bore her, nor seek for hers in exchange, in such fear was he of her great excellence; and he besought her for God's sake to tell him whether she held it meet that he should speak his mind, or he should die loving the lady privly. Then that noble lady—my Lady Beatrice—when she heard this, and knew the goodwill he bore her, having also ere now full well perceived that he was, from great yearning for her, nigh unto death, was moved by love and pity, and spake, and said:

"Raimbaut, full meet it is that the true love of a gentle lady should fear to show his love, but or ever he die, I read him to tell it to her, and pray her to take him for servant and lover; and I will warrant, that if she be wise and courteous she will in nowise hold it for an ill and shameful thing of him; rather will she prize him the more, and hold him the better man for it. Likewise I read you to speak your mind and will to her you love, and to bid her take you for her knight, since you are such as no lady in the world should scorn for knight and servant; for my Lady Azalais, Countess of Saluza, suffered Peire Vidal, and the Countess of Burlatz, Arnaut de Marvoil, and my Lady Maria, Gaucelm Faidit, and the Lady of Marseilles, Folquet; wherefore I give you counsel and license that you, by my word and surety, may beseech her for her love."

Then Raimbaut, hearing the counsel and assurance she gave, and the license, that she promised him, told her she was verily the lady that he so much loved, even she of whom he had sought counsel; whereat my Lady Beatrice told him that he was come in a happy hour, and that if he strove after worth, and after the doing and speaking of good things, she would indeed choose him for knight and servant. So Raimbaut strove to the uttermost to increase her fame, and it was then that he made the canzona which says: "Now demand of me her bearing and demeanor."

And after this it befell that the Marquis, with his host, passed over into

*Romania, and with great help from the Church conquered the kingdom of
Salonica, and then it was that Raimbaut, for his valorous deeds, was made
knight, and there the Marquis gave him rich lands and revenues, and there also
did he die.*

Unlike Raimbaut, most of these poet-musicians were of knightly origin; but whether of humble or noble birth, they all conformed strictly
to the aristocratic style of their period. In addition to those already mentioned the most famous of them were Bertran de Born, who lived
around 1180; Peire Vidal (1175–1215), perhaps the most celebrated of
the whole lot, known everywhere as the "terror of husbands"; Bernard
de Ventadour (1201–1253); and Gaucelm Faidit (*d.* 1220). The trouvères were able to include kings in their number, notably Richard Cœur
de Lion[6] (1157–1199) and Thibaut, King of Navarre (1201–1253);
but the most famous of all the northern singers was the hunchbacked
minstrel Adam de la Halle (1238?–1288), whose little pastoral play *Le
Jeu de Robin et Marion* is one of the landmarks of French dramatic history. The centers of this musical culture of the Middle Ages were the
courts of Provence, Toulouse, and Poitou, and of the dukes of Flanders
and Brabant, as well as of the kings of England, France, and Spain.

How much of the art of the troubadours was of their own invention
and how much came from their paid assistants, the jongleurs, we cannot
tell.[7] Probably the latter, who wrote down the music, made a far greater

[6] Richard's interest in minstrelsy is one of the pleasantly accepted legends of history.
Just how many songs he did write is open to question; but there seems no reason to doubt
the authenticity of the one which still survives in the Laurentian Library, in a manuscript volume of Provençal poetry. This was probably composed in 1193, when the king
was a captive in an Austrian castle on the Danube and seems to have been written with
some definite tune in mind:

"Never can captive make a song so fair | "My men and barons all, full well they
As he can make that has no cause for | know,
care, | Poitevins, English, Normans, Gascons,
Yet may he strive by song his grief to | too,
cheer. | That I have not one friend, however
I lack not friends, but sadly lack their | poor,
gold! | Whom I would leave in chains to save
Shamed are they, if unransomed I lie | my gold,
here, | I tell them this, but blame them not
　　A second Yule in hold. | therefor;
 | Though I lie yet in hold. . .

"Sister and Countess God give you good cheer!
And keep my Lady, whom I love dear;
For whom I lie in hold."

[7] A contemporary account describes a troubadour's voice as being "so supple that the
nightingale was amazed to hear it." But there is plenty of evidence that such vocal gifts
were by no means usual, the troubadours leaving to their jongleurs the singing of the
songs they had composed. Wolfram von Eschenbach confessed that he could neither read

RICHARD THE LIONHEARTED AND HEINRICH VI While Richard was the prisoner of the Emperor (1193–1194), he wrote his *Reis Rizard*.

contribution to the history of music than did their masters; but it was the masters who were the glamorous figures, the men who received all the honor and glory, and so it is their names that have become attached to the whole movement. The jongleurs accompanied these songs by some instrument, usually the vielle (a bowed instrument, the direct ancestor of the violin) or the harp. In writing down the songs after they had perfected them, the scribes used a notation of the plainsong type; nor write—a statement perhaps somewhat exaggerated for effect—but we do know that the troubadour Ulrich von Liechtenstein dictated his songs to a scribe. There are conflicting reports concerning the ability of the jongleurs. An early ecclesiastic said that many of his own brethren that were charged with uttering the noble words of God took less care and were far less keen about their work than were these players of the cithara and the flute. Petrarch, writing to Boccaccio in 1366, says: "They [that is, the jongleurs] are men of spirit, far from mediocre, gifted with good memory—very lavorious sort of persons with plenty of cheek," a description which might well be used of some of their modern descendants! Guiraut de Cabreiar was probably more concerned with rhetorical effect than with stating the truth, when he said to his jongleur: "You play the viol vilely; you sing even worse; you can't make a beautiful final cadence to save your life; even less can you contrive embellishments." But these complaints are rather common, especially against bad singers, so the technical efficiency of the musicians was probably none too good.

REINMAR, THE FID-
DLER He plays for
dancing (from the Ma-
nesse Manuscript, Heidel-
berg University Library).

but this was defective, for while the rise and fall of the notes was shown, their length was a matter of rough rule, regulated by the syllables to which they were set. And so there has resulted a great deal of confusion in the modern transcription of these early songs and dances, most authorities letting the melody change occasionally to two and four pulses to the measure, instead of keeping it always in three, as suggested by the regular alternation of long and short syllables in the texts used.

Set to words according to modern principles of accent, and using melodies that are strongly suggestive of our present-day major and minor scales, the troubadour songs make a more definite appeal to most of us than do the mystic chants of the Church. Again there are many theories to explain the provenance and the popular appeal of troubadour and trouvère song. This type of song may have come from Spain, where Moorish influence can so often be traced; religious *conducti* or folk dances and songs may have played their part, these themselves originating in the songs of the Church. Here, as in other places and times, Church and folk influenced each other, and it is strongly debatable (as in the famous hen-or-egg-first problem) which had the prior effect. But it would be reasonable to suppose that the Church's dominant power gave it preferential influence, even on the music of the troubadours.

Gustave Reese has classified the main formal types of these songs and has suggested that they derive from the litany, the rondel, the sequence, and the hymn. Briefly, it can be said that these varied delicate works of art, in which music and poem are indivisible, resulted from variants in the arrangement of sections of poetry and melody in stanzas and refrain. A number of different forms resulted; the most important were

1) The epic type, known as the *chanson de geste*
2) The strophic type, the *laisse*
3) The *rotrouenge,* with a solo part, the finish of which provided a refrain for the audience
4) The *chanson avec des refrains,* a variety of choruses, each of them taken from a familiar song
5) The *rondeau, virelai,* and *ballade,* all of which became prominent later on
6) The *estampie,* which developed into an instrumental dance.

Contrast, for example, this estampie of Raimbaut de Vagueiras, based on a courtly dance rhythm, with the music of the Church which we have already heard:

Kalenda maya
Ni fuelhs de faya
Ni chanz d'auzelh ni flors de glaya
Non es quem playa,
Pros domna guaya,
Tro qu'un ysnelh messatgier aya
Del vostre bel cors, quem retraya,

Plazer novelh qu'Amors m'atraya,
E jaya
Emtraya
Vas vos, domna veraya;
E chaya
De playa
L'gelos, ans quem n'estraya.

It is the age-old, yet ever-new complaint:

The joys of May, the new leaves on the trees, the songs of the birds, the blossoming of the flowers—all these can mean nothing to me, my noble and lovely one, until I see your messenger come with some token of your love for me, till I see my jealous foe struck by the lightning of your wrath.

A suggestion of modern tonality and rhythm is present in the two well-known little lyrics from Adam de la Halle's *Robin et Marion: J'ai encore un tel pâte* and *Robin m'aime.* These were undoubtedly popular melodies of the day, preserved for posterity by the charm of the art of this trouvère. That these fragrant reminders of this gallant period can still please is evidenced by the fact that they often are placed on modern programs. Perrin d'Angicourt's charming *Quand voi an la fin d'estey* and Blondel de Nesle's *A l'entrant d'esté* (both available in the *Anthologie Sonore*) are perhaps more of their period; they show clearly enough the influence of Eastern ideals and have a decidedly courtly atmosphere.

The texts of many of these lovely songs of the Provençal poets and musicians have luckily been preserved. Some of them have great simplicity, such as this, fresh as the breath of spring itself:

Quand le rossignol chante—qui nous charme par son chant—
Pour ma belle, douce amie—Je vois mon cœur rossignolant—
Jointes mains je la supplie—Car jamais je n'aimai tant;—
Je sais bien, que, si elle m'oublie—C'en est fini de mon bonheur.

Translated into modern French by J. Beck

Others are stormy and turbulent like Peire Vidal's

Atressi co.l perilans
Que sus nn' laiga balansa . . .

As a mariner, sea-tossed,	*Beneath her beauty's mask*
Capsized in desperate plight,	*If I could know her mind*
Gives himself up for lost,	*I'd have no need to ask,*
Yielding to craven fright,	*Is she no more than kind,*
Then sees a sudden light	*And am I somewhat blind,*
And feels a rescuing hand	*To steer my passion's bark*
Drawing him safe to land;	*Through the uncharted dark,*
So I, distraught, downcast	*Trusting to her regard*
By heavy doubt, and long	*Without assurance? Dear*
Love-hungry, find at last	*Lady, be not so hard,*
A splendid theme for song.	*But make the sailing clear!*

Translated by George Cronyn

Unfortunately, many of the tunes to which these songs were sung have been lost. In the case of the trouvères we are most fortunate, for oftentimes several of their melodies are found set to the same words.

THE GERMAN COUNTERPART

We have spoken of the minnesinger as the German counterpart of the troubadour and trouvère. In reality, the minnesinger, literally a love singer, was a somewhat later development in point of time, and his art lasted almost a whole century longer than that of his French brothers in song. The whole of this German art was tinctured with a religious ele-

THE MINNESINGER HEINRICH FRAUENLOB　(*d.* 1318) (From the Manesse Manuscript, Heidelberg University Library).

ment, for the delicacy of the love sentiment allowed it to be, in part,
sublimated into a worship of the Virgin Mary; and this element is accentuated in the songs of the minnesingers by their melodic derivation

A SINGING TRIAL OF THE MASTERSING-ERS In this seventeenth-century miniature the markers are sitting at the left on the podium; in the pulpit at the right, the candidate is singing; the mastersing-ers are in the foreground.

from Church sources. Thus, we have another link between secular and sacred song, the modes of the Church exercising their restraining influence on the music, which in the troubadour minstrelsy had shown a well-developed tendency to step into the path of what we know as the major keys.

The most famous minnesinger was without doubt Walter von der Vogelweide (*c.* 1170–1230). Many of his poems are known today, none of them more personal or characteristic than the one beginning:

Unter den Linden,
An der Heide,
Wo ich mit meiner Trauten sass,
Da mögt ihr finden,
Wie wir beide
Die Blumen brachen und das Gras.
Vor dem Wald mit süssem Schall
Tandaradei!
Sang im Tal die Nachtigall.

Translated by Ford Madox Ford

Under the lindens on the heather,
There was our double resting place,
Side by side and close together
Garnered blossoms, crushed, and grass
Nigh a shaw in such a vale:
Tandaradei!
Sweetly sang the nightingale.

One of the few authentic melodies of Walter's is that of a *Crusader's Song,* written during his journey to the Holy Land in 1228, only two

HANS SACHS (1494—1576)
He was the most famous of the
mastersingers — *"Schumacher
und Poet dazu."*

years before his death. The music is suggestive of Gregorian influence, and the words express the lyric joy of the poet on at last reaching the goal of his desire—the Holy Land.[8]

The *Meistersinger* (mastersingers) carried on the art of the minnesingers, though with less brilliance, from about the middle of the fifteenth century to the early part of the seventeenth. They were local musicians of the bourgeois class, organized into guilds according to strict rules and regulations, and they allowed the artificiality and stiffness of these academic bonds to hamper their music. There were definite gradations of rank in this order—apprentice, pupil, singer, poet, and master —each of them subject to careful examination as to the ability of the candidate. Although Hans Sachs of Nuremberg, the best known of the mastersingers, wrote some beautiful melodies that are strangely suggestive of the later chorales, most of the work of these bourgeois musicians was uncouth and prosaic, the satisfaction of rules being more important to them than the expression of poetic or musical thought. Wagner's glorious opera, *Die Meistersinger,* draws a genial portrait of their weaknesses.

[8] Wagner brings the medieval spirit of chivalry and the culture of this period strikingly before us in his operas *Tannhäuser* (in which is staged a contest of song and poetry for the hand of a lady) and *Lohengrin.*

DANCE SONGS OF THE TIME

The period of the troubadours produced also a definite art of instrumental music in the aristocratic and courtly dances that were so popular. As Dr. Sachs has asked, what more significant expression of this peculiar world of love and intrigue could be found than these *fêtes galantes,* when during the dances the barriers between knights and the ladies they loved were temporarily dropped? Modern research has made available some of this music and has shown how strong was its pull toward a regular rhythmic pulse.

Among the most interesting of these medieval dances described by Johannes de Grocheo, in his contemporary treatise on popular music,[9] is the *ductia*—a light, rapid tune that falls and rises gracefully and thus is well suited for both singing and dancing. A good example has been preserved in a manuscript now in the Bodleian Library at Oxford. It is of the thirteenth century and consists of a number of short *vers* (verses) with the melody ending in a half close; the same tune is then repeated, ending in a full close on the tonic. During each repetition the dancers evidently returned in their steps to where they had begun each *vers.*

Another dance described by this author, who seems to have been a professor in the Sorbonne, is the *stantipes,*[10] which he says was so difficult of execution that it "served to restrain the youths from wicked thoughts." An amusing example of *stantipes,* with a primitive contrapuntal second part, is preserved in the British Museum. The *saltarello* and *Lamento di Tristano* came from Italy. The latter had a changing rhythm and was the sort of compound dance that is still found in country districts. The *vers* was in triple time, according to Sachs, and probably marked a step in which the whole company participated. The *rotta,* which followed, was in lively double time, and suggests an interlude for individual steps and interpolated pantomime.

There are a few other medieval dance tunes known today, but these we have mentioned are representative. It does not require a great deal of imagination when listening to their music to re-create the colorful background of courtly chivalry and graceful intrigue; and in their peculiar instrumentation we hear again the voice of a fascinating age long forgotten.

[9] Johannes de Grocheo was a music scholar and writer of the thirteenth century who lived in Paris. His *Theoria* is a rich source of the forms of medieval music.

[10] The Latin term for a medieval dance piece played before courtly listeners; it was called *estampida* in the Provençal dialect, and Boccaccio calls it *stampita.* It was played *stehenden Fusses* (in place) in contrast to the *ductia,* where the players led in a round dance.

A Transitional Period

The period which carried Europe from scholasticism to humanism, once regarded as arid and sterile, is now looked upon as one of the great turning points in intellectual history. It marked the actual transition from medievalism to the modern age. . . . The older conception of a sudden classical "renaissance" in the fifteenth century, and of an almost precipitate development of natural science between 1550 and 1700 has been supplanted by a more truly historical perspective which stresses the continuity of cultural development between the late twelfth and the fifteenth centuries.

Barnes: *An Intellectual and Cultural History of the Western World*

THE FOURTEENTH AND
FIFTEENTH CENTURIES

One of the consistent phenomena of history is the appearance between eras of exceptional physical, mental, and spiritual activity (such as the one we have just been considering) of what may be called *fluctuational periods*—zones of a comparatively undetermined quality, sharing the characteristics of both the preceding and the following epoch without having any decided ones of their own. Feeling the stirrings of the new times ahead, and yet unable to throw off the trappings of the old ones behind, these fluctuational periods are likely to be marked by attention to *law* rather than to *spirit*. In an attempt to hide the lack of real motivating forces, they are concerned with the development of technical perfection, of learning for its own sake, of oversophistication. Some historians consider the fourteenth and fifteenth centuries, lying between the apex of the Middle Ages and the High Renaissance, as such a period.

The medieval concept of the world was that of its being a God-inspired mystery which was capable of being expressed in terms of great beauty; that of the Renaissance was that it was rather a man-made rationality, worthy of cultivation for its own sake. In between there came these two centuries. Because both the old and the new were present in them, the old slowly perishing, the new slowly struggling for life, they were troubled enough. Symbolic is the fact that they produced

DANSE MACABRE IN THE CHURCH OF LA CHAISE DIEU,

both Dante's *Divine Comedy,* designed, as someone has said, largely for preparing the reader for the life to come, and Boccaccio's *Decameron,* which had as its purpose the preparation for life on this earth.

Gone was the sustaining faith of the eleventh and twelfth centuries; in its place arose a type of intellectuality which has made the term *scholasticism* one of contempt. The soaring Gothic beauty of the medieval churches degenerated into an overdeveloped, flamboyant style, which suggested a technical art of decoration rather than a spiritual means of expression. There developed a fashion for strict, artificial lyric forms in poetry, which, although possessing a certain charm, were not very significant in content. The Church seemed to have lost its hold on heaven as well as its grip on earth. The clergy were often corrupt beyond belief, some of them actively practicing piracy when not engaged in reading their services; ecclesiastical preferment was openly obtained by a process of barter and trade; the papacy had lost its moral and political power, not to speak of its spiritual significance, and at one time three popes were engaged in the edifying spectacle of trying to excommunicate one another.

Moreover, in these centuries occurred the Black Death and the Hundred Years' War between France and England. It is difficult to say which was cause and which effect; but to these two major catastrophes in man's history can be laid a great deal of the gloom, the sin, and the suffering of this period. Between them these two cataclysms cost Europe uncounted thousands of its inhabitants, drained it of a great deal of its wealth, and deprived it of manners and morals, faith and reason. No wonder that a favorite theme of the time was the brevity of life and the consequent need for immediate pleasure. The *danse macabre* became a sort of universal symbol: in verse and wall paintings and actual dance ceremonial, every type of society was portrayed—pope, emperor, cardinal, prince, archbishop, baron, lady, squire, abbot, prior, lawyer, scholar, deacon, merchant, monk, thief, physician, minstrel, and common workingman—marching forward in a sort of inevitable parade, each in his place according to his rank, with Death dancing grotesquely

Haute-Loire, France (by an unknown artist of the fifteenth century)

among all, questioning them and demonstrating the certainty of his final triumph.

But we must not overemphasize the dark side of the picture; if the old was dying, the new was being born. For out of the confusion and disillusionment of these years there came new ideals. New political units —the states—emerged, shaped by the common national sentiment of the various peoples and governed by central rulers. The medieval unifying forces which had held sway for so long—the Holy Roman Empire, the Catholic Church, the feudal system—gradually lost power and influence in the face of these new concepts. There was another factor in the decline of medieval ideals during this time: the development of commerce and the consequent growth of a prosperous bourgeois class with its particular ideology. The commercial relationships of these trading merchants led "straight to the discovery of America and the origins of the modern age."

Nowhere is the dual nature of the period better shown than in the art it produced. On the one hand, there was the interest in virtuosity and a tendency to be content with a sort of sensuous enjoyment mixed with a touch of humorous and ironical philosophy, a let-us-drink-and-be-merry-for-tomorrow-we-die attitude. We have mentioned some of the characteristic results of this—the flamboyance of the northern architecture, the technical perfection and artificiality of fourteenth-century poetry. A symptomatic portrait is that given by the gilded youths of Boccaccio's *Decameron,* who while away their time in the pleasant countryside near plague-stricken Florence telling stories and singing ballads.

On the other hand, these centuries mark the rise of a new interest— or, better, a renewed interest—in man as an individual and a curiosity regarding the world in which he lives. The religious concepts of the Middle Ages are no longer completely satisfying; artists begin to portray man as a natural, human being and not merely as an abstract religious symbol. This is the period of the great sculptors Ghiberti, Verrocchio, and Donatello, the latter one of the great realists of Italian art; of the painters Giotto, Masaccio, Uccello, and Fra Filippo Lippi, a

A THIRTEENTH-CENTURY ROSE WINDOW

distinguished line which brought the art out of its medieval limitations and, by concentrating on such matters as draughtsmanship, color, and perspective, laid the foundations for its modern development. In Italy Brunelleschi and his follower, Michelozzo, designed buildings which show a definite attempt to return to older, more humanistic ideals. In literature, Chaucer and Boccaccio introduced a new secular spirit derived from a wide knowledge of the world and its inhabitants. The poets Petrarch and Villon infused new feeling into old forms and represent the humanistic tendencies of the time, as does Dante its more medievalistic aspects. In music we find a strong consciousness of the traditions of the past, as well as a great enthusiasm for the new expressive powers which suddenly opened up. Philippe de Vitry's treatise, *Ars nova,* was much more than a mere proclamation of a new art; it provided a fresh outlook by emphasizing new rhythmic schemes and secured thereby a significant advance in emotional expressiveness and humanistic interest.[11] His ideals were carried on by the Florentine organist, Francesco Landino, and the intricate developments of the Netherlandish polyphonic composers.

There were a number of reasons for the exhaustion of the burning, driving intensity of the Gothic spirit of creative enthusiasm which came toward the end of the thirteenth century. First of all was the feeling of doubt and often complete agnosticism engendered in the minds of many churchmen by the teachings of the Greek scholastic philosophy which preceded the Renaissance. Then the frightful ignorance and open corruptness of the clergy made the Christian religion an object of scorn and derision over the whole of Europe. The long years of struggle between France and England caused most of the wealth which these countries had formerly lavished on the building and decoration of churches to be levied for the purposes of war. And, as a tragic climax, came the paralyzing horrors of the Black Death, the terrible pestilence which originated in China, spread over India, Asia Minor, and Egypt, and reached Europe in 1347.

These physical events in the history of Europe had a marked effect on man's spiritual development, for with the weakening of the authority and power of the Church, upon which man had learned to lean for so long, there came a corresponding unfolding of man's personality. No longer entirely dependent on either Church or State, man began to realize how he could make his own spiritual approach to God and find his own place in the world about him. It was a time of stirring interest and teeming ideas, this close of the medieval period; there came, after

---

[11] It is in De Vitry and other theorists of the *ars nova* that we first find the rule which so strongly affected all music written after their time—that of forbidding consecutive fifths or octaves in two parallel contrapuntal parts. This was in direct contrast to the general practice of the time. These theorists also emphasized the necessity of using the so-called *musica ficta*—the introduction of extra-modal sharps or flats—"for reasons of beauty" or "by reason of necessity." Thus *musica ficta* became *musica vera et necessaria*.

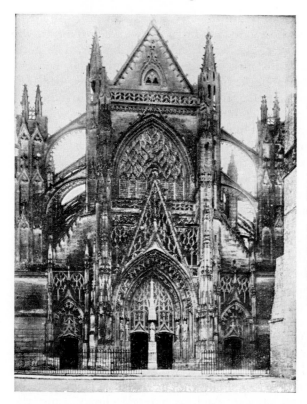

Archives Photographiques

FLAMBOYANT
GOTHIC ARCHITEC-
TURE — La Trinité,
Vendome, France. What
an overinsistence on
technique did to the
Gothic style: this
twisted, crackling façade
is far removed from the
quiet, exalted beauty of
Chartres.

a long time of subordination to the wishes and desires of the Church, a release of new power, a zest for the realities of life, and a love for the things of the world. This spirit was everywhere manifest, but especially in Italy; and it had its reflection in art, as might be expected. No longer satisfied with the composite expression of the Cathedral, the individual began to seek out ways to express his definite and personal viewpoint. The emphasis was thus shifted from a collective, symbolic, and, therefore, impersonal spirit of artistic expression to a more subjective, realistic, and personal one. From this time the individual begins to stand out more and more in art, and the period of the so-called "easel picture," made by a single artist for a single person, begins.

THE RISE OF ARTISTIC PERSONALITIES

It was not until the fourteenth and fifteenth centuries, then, that definite personalities began to emerge in Christian art—among others, the painters Giotto, the Van Eyck brothers, with their curiously wrought Gothic multiplicity of detail, the gentle Memling, the sculptors Donatello and Ghiberti, and the musicians Guillaume de Machaut in the north and Francesco Landino in the south. But before tracing the achievements of these earliest individual composers, it will be interesting to note briefly an attempt made by the Church to reassert something of its old authority and to reinstate something of its old austere beauty into its ritual. From Avignon, the French city to which the papacy had been temporarily withdrawn, Pope John XXII issued in 1324 his famous decree on the misuse of music in the churches. In this he attempted to take the art back to where it had been four hundred years before; for the only intervals he would allow in the Church were the octave, the fifth, and the fourth. The language of this document, which in purpose was much like that of the later *Motu proprio* issued by Pius X, is clear:

> *Certain disciples of the new school, much occupying themselves with the measured dividing of the* tempora, *display their prolation in notes which are new to us, preferring to devise methods of their own rather than to continue singing in the old way; the music therefore of the divine offices is now performed with semibreves and minims, and with these notes of small value every composition is pestered. Moreover, they truncate the melodies with hockets,[12] they deprave them with discants, sometimes even they stuff them with upper parts made out of secular songs. So that often they must be losing sight of the fundamental sources of our melodies in the Antiphonal and Gradual, and may thus forget what that is upon which their superstructure is raised. They may become entirely ignorant concerning the ecclesiastical tones, which they already no longer distinguish, and the limits of which they even confound, since, in the multitude of their notes, the moderate risings and temperate descents of the plainsong, by which the scales themselves are to be known one from another, must be entirely obscured. Their voices are incessantly running to and fro, intoxicating the ear, not soothing it, while the men themselves endeavor to convey by their gestures the sentiment of the music which they utter. As a consequence of all this, devotion, the true end of worship, is little thought of, and wantonness, which ought to be eschewed, increases.*
>
> *This state of things, hitherto the common one, we and our brethren have regarded as standing in need of correction; and we now hasten therefore to banish those methods, nay, rather to cast them entirely away, and to put them to flight more effectual than heretofore, far from the house of God.*

[12] It may be added in passing that the *hocket* was a musical embellishment popular at the time, consisting of a quick alternating of the same melody between two parts. It was thus satirically described by a contemporary writer: "Sometimes thou mayest see a man with an open mouth, not to sing, but as it were breathe out his last gasp, by shutting in his breath, and by a certain ridiculous interception of his voice to threaten silence, and now again to imitate the agonies of a dying man, or the ecstasies of such as suffer." Dr. Curt Sachs makes the happy suggestion that the *hocket* may have been due "to the same impulse to dissolve coherent masses and surfaces that urged the architects of later Gothic times to distintegrate their walls and spires into lace-like openwork."

Wherefore, having taken counsel with our brethren, we straitly command that no one henceforward shall think himself at liberty to attempt those methods, or methods like them, in the aforesaid Offices, and especially in the canonical Hours, or in the solemn celebration of the Mass.

And if any be disobedient, let him, on the authority of this canon, be punished by a suspension from office of eight days; either by the Ordinary of the diocese in which the forbidden things are done or by his deputies in places not exempt from episcopal authority, or, in places which are exempt, by such of their offices as are usually considered responsible for the correction of irregularities and excesses, and such like matters.

Yet, for all this, it is not our intention to forbid, occasionally—and especially upon feast days or in the solemn celebrations of the Mass and in the aforesaid divine offices—the use of some consonances, for example the eighth, fifth, and fourth, which heighten the beauty of the melody; such intervals therefore may be sung above the plain cantus ecclesiasticus, *yet so that the integrity of the* cantus *itself may remain intact, and that nothing in the authoritative music be changed. Used in such sort the consonances would much more than by any other method both soothe the hearer and arouse his devotion, and also would not destroy religious feeling in the minds of the singers.*

The Oxford History of Music, Volume II, 1901 Edition

THE CASUISTRY OF THE FALSE BASS

It may well have been that the attempt of the Church to simplify its music at this time was the origin of what was known as *faulx bourdon* (false bass).[13] In an attempt to circumvent this decree of Pope John's, the Church musicians developed a method of organizing which consisted in inserting a third voice between a simple two-part organum at the fifth. This was written at an equal distance from the outer voices and thus resulted in the interval of a third with each:

But—and here is where the ingenuity of frustrated man shows itself —in singing such an arrangement, the lowest part was given to a high voice, which would transpose it up an octave, and it would sound thus:

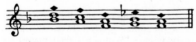

This resulted in an agreeable series of consecutive thirds and sixths, which were not in accord with John's decree, as well as a fourth, which

[13] Often spelled *faux bourdon* or *faburden*. Other authorities give different versions of its origin.

CHOIR GALLERY IN THE CATHEDRAL, FLORENCE, 1433-1438 (by Donatello)

was; but officialdom evidently closed its ears and was satisfied with what its eyes suggested was obedience to the letter of the law, since the highest part was always written as a false bass below the others. This use of parallel thirds and sixths was really a form of improvisation and is thought by some authorities to have originated in England, where it received the name *gymel* as early as the eleventh century. At any rate, it marks a definite growth of the harmonic sense in music, and it spread over the whole of Europe by the end of the fourteenth century.

The development of *faulx bourdon* was not the only sign that music was beginning to strain at the leashes which had so long been imposed upon it by the Church. As we have noted earlier, sometime between 1316 and 1325 Philippe de Vitry, bishop, poet, and composer, issued a work to which he gave the proud title *Ars nova* (*The New Art*); and this gave the name to the whole century, which was a period of steady development and humanizing of the art. And there took place a remarkable change in rhythmic procedure, for the theoreticians awakened to the possibilities of duple time, which the composers then began to use as well as triple time, which had up to this time reigned supreme. The contrast between long and short notes became more clearly established. One of the unifying principles characteristic of the motets in-

THE INSPIRATION OF GUILLAUME DE MACHAUT Attributed to an unknown painter of the court of Charles v, this scene from a contemporary miniature represents Love bringing Sweet-thoughts, Pleasure, and Hope to Machaut.

cluded in De Vitry's *Ars nova* is their isorhythmic structure—that is, their different voices were composed as variants upon one rhythmic pattern that remained uniform throughout, even though the notes sung might be longer or shorter in one part than in another. There was a further development of music forms and a tendency to use more and more instrumental music; the whole movement was, in fact, a continuation of liberating influences initiated by the troubadours and trouvères.

MACHAUT, A TYPICAL GOTHIC COMPOSER

The life of Machaut, who lived from 1305(?) to 1377, was an extremely brilliant one. Born in Champagne, he became a courtier in the service of the warrior king, John of Luxembourg and Bohemia, and later entered the service of the French court. An important figure in the development of the technique of writing French verse, Machaut, in addition to his musical activities, became a canon of the Church and, when he died, was considered the most influential spiritual leader of his time. In music he expressed himself most freely in the composite *ballade-rondeau-virelais* form, the most important secular form of the period and extensively used for well over a century. It consisted of a vocal song or duet set to several verses of rather elaborate and stilted poetry and supported by one or two purely ornamental added parts. Machaut's best essays in this form show clearly enough, even to our modern ears, that he attempted to practice what he preached—that "he who writes and composes without feeling spoils both his words and his music." His greatest achievement was the writing of a musical setting of the Mass, probably the first one ever to include the entire Ordinary.[14] For years this was an almost legendary work, unknown even to musicologists; now it has been gathered together from various fragments and different sources and appears in various recorded versions. In form it is a gigantic motet in the medieval sense, its four voices weaving a constructional unity out of a confusing number of tangled architectural elements in true Gothic fashion. Because of its length and the fact that the various parts are connected by means of a melodic nucleus, it represents better than any other single work the Gothic conception of collective expression and so should be heard by everyone who would know what this music was like. But in it are present, too, an impassioned melodic movement and a rhythmic liberty characteristic of the *ars nova.*

A CONTEMPORARY COLLECTION

Preserved in the same manuscript as the so-called *Roman de Fauvel,* one of the outstanding works of early French literature, is a collection of *rondeaux* and other vocal works, all but one of them in one part, by Jehannot de l'Escurel. Their style is suggestive of the *ars nova.* This particular *roman,* one of a number of similar medieval poems dealing with tales of war and adventure, dates from the beginning of the fourteenth century and is particularly important because it contains a rather unusual combination of the literature, painting, and music of the time.

THE ARS NOVA IN THE SOUTH

We have already suggested the special importance of Italy and Italian painters in the new humanizing movement of the fourteenth and

[14] The Mass deserves special attention as an "art form," for it was the first of the larger forms to develop and has been of great importance in the history of music. Down to the time of Machaut the Ordinary of the Mass—that portion which is invariable whatever the seasons of the Church's year—had been sung to plainsong melodies but not combined in any fixed work. (The fact that modern editions group these Gregorian chants in fixed Masses should not confuse the issue; they do so purely for convenience. Such groupings are arbitrary and vary in different editions.)

Machaut's was the first entirely composed Mass; its settings of the *Kyrie, Gloria, Credo, Sanctus,* and *Agnus Dei* constitute a new fivefold art form comparable in importance, as Douglas says, to the great parallel form which evolved from instrumental dance music —the symphony. A large number of composers followed Machaut's example, among them some of the greatest in music. Bach's noble *B Minor Mass,* one of the world's masterpieces of choral art, is a direct descendant of this Gothic work of the fourteenth century.

ADORATION OF THE MAGI   by Stephan Lochner

fifteenth centuries. We must always remember that this was the time
when Dante, Petrarch, and Boccaccio did so much there to free man
from the stultifying and often hypocritical interpretations of the medieval theologians and to awaken in him a new delight in the things of
this earth. It was natural that the *ars nova* should thrive in this southern clime; a new style of writing developed in which fifths, unisons,
and octaves were evidently forbidden and which was strongly influenced by the popular music of the day. A large number of forms were
used, the composers contriving settings to fit such contemporary poetic
forms as the *madrigal* (derived from troubadour poetry and representing the art song of the period) and the *ballata* (a composition for
combined singing, playing, and dancing). The Italian love of elaborate
fioriture (embellishments) in melody is everywhere evident in these
works, and frequent use was often made of instrumental preludes,
interludes, and postludes. One of the most popular forms was the

caccia, apparently derived from the older French *chace.* This was a canon for two voices (in Italy it had a third, free, part), its text descriptive of some animated scene such as a hunt or the cries to be heard in a street.

The records of the time show an amazing fecundity on the part of at least thirty composers in northern Italy, there being extant hundreds of specimens of the work of this period. Among the names that have survived are those of Vincenzo da Rimini, Giovanni de Cascia, Jacopo da Bologna; but at the head of all is Francesco Landino, the organist of San Lorenzo in Florence (*c.* 1325–1397), "blind of body but enlightened in spirit, one who understood both the theory and practice of his art, the best singer of his time, a player of every instrument and especially the organ, by means of which he was wont to delight his many listeners," to use the words of a contemporary writer. Over a hundred and fifty of his works have come down to us, written in all the forms used at the time and showing the characteristics which made them so popular during the composer's life. A contemporary writer, Giovanni da Prato, has, like Boccaccio, left behind him a clear picture of Florentine life in his romanza, *Il paradiso degli Alberti;* included in this are stories of Francesco and a description of an occasion when the blind musician played his love verses so sweetly that the listeners' hearts "almost burst from their bosoms." But Francesco's chief glory—like that of many another composer who followed him—came from his skill as a virtuoso organist and his powers of improvisation. A number of the works of this composer, as well as others of the Italian *ars nova,* have been preserved in the so-called *Squarcialupi Manuscript* now in the Laurentian Library at Florence.

The fifteenth century saw a further intensification of this late Gothic spirit of humanism. The love for grace and susceptibility to form, which is natural to the Italians, produced new loveliness in the art and music of the south, and these ideals were retransferred to the artists of the north. If we look at the fifteenth-century pictures of such Italian painters as Fra Angelico and Fra Filippo Lippi, we shall see in them the same love for harmonious color, attention to exquisite detail, refined grace, sweep of rhythmic line, and spirit of lyric happiness that are found in the works of the Flemish Van der Goes and Memling and the German Stephan Lochner. This is natural enough, for during the century in which they worked, communication between the flourishing trade centers of Italy and Flanders was frequent, and the artists of one country mingled freely with those of another. This explains the cosmopolitan influences so strongly present in the music of Guillaume Dufay, a composer born in the Low Countries, who traveled and studied as a youth in Italy and who spent most of his life as composer to the rich and art-loving dukes of Burgundy.

BURGUNDIAN MASTERS

The duchy of Burgundy, a territorial organization which comprised parts of modern France, the Netherlands, and Belgium, was a country dominated by French influence and civilization. Its court at Dijon was French in nature; its intellectual language and predilections were French; its duke was the first peer of the realm and exerted a great deal of influence on the internal policies of France. The great artistic centers of the country, however, were its rich and populous cities in the Low Countries—Brabant, Flanders, and Hainault; and it was here that the celebrated Burgundian School (often called the School of the Netherlands) originated. For many years the music in these wealthy cities of Philip the Good and Charles the Bold, the two outstanding members of the Burgundian ducal family, was considered by contemporary critics to be the best in the world, quite the equal of the famous painting and sculpture fostered by these art-loving dukes. The centers for the music were the churches and chapels maintained by the princes. The chapel service of Philip the Good, modeled on that of the Papal Chapel, was for nearly a century the most important influence in the cultivation of the music of the time.

The great theoretical writer of the end of the fifteenth century, the Netherlander Tinctoris, recorded the fact that the origin of the School of the Netherlands, that school which has meant so much to the development of music, was in England and associated it with the name of John Dunstable (*c.* 1370–1453). The still-existing *Old Hall Manuscript,* dating from the reign of Henry v in England (1413–1422) and containing 138 compositions by English composers, would seem to be further proof of this fact. With Dunstable there begins a new feeling of euphony, largely achieved by the use of thirds and sixths; he stands at the beginning of a technical line of development which culminated in Palestrina. That Dunstable enjoyed an enormous reputation amongst his contemporaries all over Europe is evidenced by the fact that most of his works have survived in continental, rather than English, libraries.

It was his pupils Binchois and Dufay who carried his ideas to the kingdom of Burgundy and developed them there. The rich ducal

Courtesy of St. Edmund's College, Old Hall, near Ware, Herts

A PORTRAIT OF THE *OLD HALL MANUSCRIPT,* c. 1480.

patrons of this country made it possible for Dufay to settle in the city
of Cambrai from 1450 to the end of his life and to devote his time to
both composition and travel. His life there seems to have been that of
a great personage, honored and respected by all of intellectual and
artistic Europe. He was connected with the Cambrai Cathedral and
wrote a great deal of church music for its choirs; but he did not confine
himself to this style, and his use of the secular forms of the period,
particularly the *chanson française,* the most favored form of aristocratic
music, shows some of his most characteristic attributes. These *chansons*

DUFAY AND BINCHOIS (from the miniature "Le Champion des Dames")

were the northern counterparts of the Italian secular forms and, like them, were governed in structure by literary formulas. Dufay cultivated all types of these, writing *ballades, rondeaux,* and *virelais* with equal ease and success. He must have been particularly happy in his work at Cambrai and made it one of the great musical centers of the time.

The achievements of Dufay were all characteristic of music's general trends; in one of them he took the art a long way forward on the road leading to the modern devices of the sonata and the symphony. He was the first to use the unifying scheme of basing the different sections of his Mass settings on one melody, a *cantus firmus* that was sometimes secular, sometimes sacred in origin; by building all his sections around this one theme, he gave his work as a whole a musical unity that was comparable to the liturgical unity provided by the words.

It has become customary with music historians to group Dufay with Dunstable and Binchois to form a so-called first phase of a Netherlands School. Gilles Binchois (*c.* 1400–1460) was a soldier turned musician, a pupil of Dunstable, and the *maestro di cappella* of the Burgundian court of Philip the Good. He composed some fifty Masses and a number of sensitive *chansons* which had a strong influence on South German song writing as late as the sixteenth century.

The oftener one hears the music of these Burgundian masters, strange as it seems at first to modern ears, the more one realizes that it was but part and parcel of the vivid life of its time. In writing of Dufay's music, a modern Dutch critic has said that it is necessary, if we are to

OCKEGHEM CON-
DUCTING A CHOIR

appreciate it to the full, to picture ourselves in the setting of the court
of Philip the Good in Dijon, with its Gothic rooms covered with
multicolored tapestries and filled with elaborate and infinitely varied
costumes, the hats and headdresses original almost to the point of extravagance. Only then can we realize that Dufay's music, with its
delicate melodic parts and slightly dissonant counterpoint, was just the
type to please an aristocracy which prided itself on being fully abreast
of the times, eager to take up the newest and finest creations.

One of Dufay's enthusiastic contemporaries speaks of him as having
written the "first music worthy of being heard." Most modern listeners
would probably reserve this honor, insofar as it implies emotional
expressiveness in music, for Josquin des Prés, who lived from 1450 to
1521. Midway between these masters stands Johannes Ockeghem,

Dufay's principal pupil, who until recently has been regarded chiefly as a composer largely given over to the working-out of ingenious technical problems—to the "cultivation of crabbed canons," as one writer has put it. Recent research and the publication of a great deal of his music, however, tend to absolve Ockeghem from such a stigma. He and his contemporaries did write some music that reminds us of tonal puzzles to be solved by the application of intricate rules; but they also wrote much that is beautiful and worthy to be classed with the best music of their time.

Ockeghem and his pupils represent a later phase of the Netherlands School, one that is characterized chiefly by a greater use of complex, canonic writing and the desire to develop a polyphonic movement from a single melody according to definitely prescribed rules. These composers made wide use of the practice of employing a *cantus firmus* for all the movements of their Masses.

Jacob Obrecht (1430–1505) represents still another phase of the Netherlands School, one in which the art of contrapuntal construction grew less complex under the influence of the Italian composers of the south. His counterpoint has been described as "clean and clear" and does not contain the rhythmic subtleties of some of the other later Netherlanders.

JOSQUIN DES PRÉS, CREATOR OF A UNIVERSAL EXPRESSION

But all these men are entirely overshadowed by Josquin des Prés, a pupil of Ockeghem, who, like Dufay, was a man of international importance, having been born in the north but active for much of his life in Italy and France. He employed all the constructive skill and craftsmanship developed by his predecessors, and he was able to impart much more expressiveness to his music.

Like Beethoven, Josquin lived and wrote in two epochs: in him was united the Gothic ideal of art, the ability of creating a universal expression out of a multiplicity of individual elements, with that of the Renaissance, the idea of creating art for its own sake. He may be said to have been the first composer to express in music the ideals of the Renaissance. His imagination was able to seize on the spirit of a text, whether solemn or majestic, passionate or serious, secular or sacred, and to express it with something like definite exactness. Luther's remark on Josquin, who was his favorite composer, sums it up well: "He is the master of his notes: they have to do as he bids them; other composers have to do as the notes will."

Altogether, Des Prés wrote more than thirty Masses, besides many motets and secular *chansons;* even in his own day his work was regarded as unique, and every other composer of the period was affected by it. In many respects his music is suggestive of the peculiar beauty that is to be found in the paintings of his contemporary countryman, Hans Memling. Both these artists had a simple charm of style and a decided novelty of expression that made them stand out far above the general artistic level of their time. Both happened to serve the Church, for the influence of that powerful factor in the development of art was still very potent; yet both men were interested in making their art beautiful as art, developing its technical resources not merely for the joy of craftsmanship, but so that with it they could increase its human expressiveness. Thus were they true forerunners of the Renaissance.

There were other men in other countries who showed that they also were able to combine constructive skill and carftsmanship with profound emotion. Among these were the pensive Pierre de la Rue (*d.* 1518); the Frenchmen Mouton and Compère; the Germans Finck, Paumann, Isaac, Senfl, and Agricola; and the English composers Robert Fayrfax and John Taverner. Indeed, there were so many brilliant contemporaries of Josquin that Einstein has suggested that the highwater mark of genuine church music should be placed here at the very threshold of the Renaissance rather than later, as is customary, at the time of Palestrina.

Of all these national composers affected by the internationalism of the Netherlands School, Heinrich Isaac (*d.* 1517) was perhaps the most significant. Like some of the others, Isaac was actually Flemish in origin and received much of his musical experience in Italy. But as he was essentially German in spirit, we will have more to say about him and his contemporaries in a later chapter. Fayrfax and Taverner pursued somewhat insular ways, as might be expected; but even they, "accounted the prime musicians of their nation," show traits of the internationalism of the Netherlands School.

A great deal of the influence which these late Gothic composers exerted on one another came about through the invention of music printing at about this time: the work and style of one man was thus made immediately available to the others. Ottaviano dei Petrucci perfected a process of printing music from movable type in Venice in 1498, about fifty years after Gutenberg's first work; and three years later this

ADORATION OF THE MAGI   by Hans Memling, contemporary of Des Prés

printer issued a comprehensive collection of motets by Josquin and his contemporaries. Although Venice long remained the center for the printing of music, the invention rapidly spread over all Europe and had an incalculable effect on the development of the art, even though the printed examples were so expensive as to make them within the reach of only the richest patrons, such as princes, both worldly and spiritual.

THE GOTHIC PERIOD IN GENERAL

Thus the Gothic period, which began within the cloistered walls of the Church, ended in a burst of rich and joyfully exuberant humanistic invention that was a fitting precursor of the Renaissance. Through it all is manifest the same spirit, a conscious joy in the seeking of elaboration and complexity, a richness and vitality, a love for brilliance that was manifested in the use of colors in the illuminating of manuscripts, in the glitter of gold and jewelry, in the richness of architectural ornament, in the sweep of melismatic melodies. For most of these medieval artists, art was that which could be applied to those practices which contributed toward and produced the necessities of life, to use the expression of St. Thomas Aquinas; and for most of the period, the greatest necessity in life was man's religion. The usefulness of architecture was therefore that of providing a beautiful setting for the worship of God; the object of the figurative arts was to illustrate suitable religious teachings and history; and music, as it gradually took on sensuous charm and rich complexity, as well as a touch of humanistic feeling, did so the better to exemplify the truth and beauty of religious experience.

A contemporary glimpse of the artistic outlook of this whole period may be had through the eyes of the already-mentioned theorist Tinctoris, Latinized name of the musician Johannes de Verwere, a Fleming who lived from 1446 to 1511 and was active at the court of Ferdinand I in Naples. He says:

Before I began to write, I strove to equip myself with the necessary knowledge of the various things pertaining to music, partly through listening to others and partly through my own incessant work. However, I do not write to bring honor to myself, but for the benefit of others who wish to study music, and further in order not to bury the talent which God has bestowed upon me. And therefore I have now undertaken to write briefly about counterpoint—which is made up of well-sounding consonances—in God's honor and for the use of those who are striving for skill in this excellent art. Before I proceed now with the work, I will not hide the fact that I have studied what the ancient philosophers, such as Plato and Pythagoras, as well as their successors, Cicero, Macrobius, Boethius, and Isidore, believe concerning the harmony of the spheres. Since, however, I have found that they differ very much from each other in their teachings, I have turned from them to Aristotle and the more modern philosophers, and no one shall make me believe that musical consonances arise through movements of the heavenly bodies, for they can only be produced by means of terrestrial instruments. The ancient musicians, Plato, Pythagoras, Nicomachus, Aristoxenus, Archytas, Ptolemaeus, and many others, indeed including Boethius himself, dealt exclusively with the consonances, and yet we do not know at all how they arranged and classified them. And if I must now refer to that which I have seen and learned I must confess that some old compositions of unknown composers have come into my hands, pieces that sound quite simple and tasteless, so that they rather disturb than please the ear. However, what surprises me especially is that only in the last forty years are there compositions which, in the judgment of the specialist, are worth listening to. Today, however, we have blossoming forth, quite apart from the large number of famous singers— whether it be on account of heavenly influences or particularly zealous studies —an almost unlimited number of composers, for example Johannes Ockeghem, Johannes Regis, Antonius Busnois, Firminus Caron, Guilelmus Faugues, and all can boast of having had as teachers the musicians who died recently, Johannes Dunstable, Egidius Binchois, and Guilelmus Dufay. Nearly all the works of these masters excel in pleasant sound; I never hear or look at their

*compositions without rejoicing in them or being instructed by them, and
therefore I, too, in my own compositions, adhere entirely to the approved style.*

Translated by Coussemaker

The composers of this period have often been charged with being too
closely bound by the many constructive devices they employed. The
charge can easily be overurged; most of their music must be heard with
an ear to the parallels which can be drawn between the architecture and
the music of this period. Medieval resources in imitative writings were
carried far—to canons, direct or reserved, inverted or time-changed, and
to the utmost possibilities in the exploitation of repeated rhythmic
patterns. All these have their exact parallels in the great Gothic buildings. The fact that the most subtle devices were sometimes referred to
by their composers in an oblique way reminds us of the practices of the
architect-masons who built the cathedrals and who did not hesitate to
insert a gargoyle, a carved caricature, or a tiny rebus in stone to provide
enlightening contrast and change.

The Instruments of the Middle Ages and Their Music

*Madame Music, she of the little bells
And her clerks full of songs
Carried rebecs and viols
Psalteries and little flutes.*

Henri d'Andeli: *La Bataille des VII Ars* (13th Century)

OBSCURE ORIGINS

To the modern mind,
the term *music* means sounds produced on instruments. How often we
hear the distinction made in describing the forces employed in some
concert, between *musicians* and *singers!* Our present-day musical practices are so predominantly instrumental that popular opinion is inclined
to designate musicians as those who are able to play some instrument
or other, while vocalists are assigned to a sort of intermediate twilight
zone of benevolent toleration, as being occasional necessary accessories
to a well-established fact. Yet we have seen that the early developments

Photo Houvet

MUSIC (from Chartres Cathedral) In these figures we see represented the two popular medieval traditions regarding the origin of music. There are countless examples in medieval art of representations of King David as the incarnation of music, striking bells which are suspended above him: thus, the medieval artist follows the tradition of his time that Tubal, the descendant of Cain, invented music by striking resonant bodies with hammers of different weights. At Chartres, beneath each of the figures representing the arts, is seen the seated figure of a man engaged in writing or meditation; the sculptor has followed the other popular tradition of the time as to the origin of music. The figure is probably Pythagoras, to whom the "Greeks attributed this invention," in the words of a writer of the period.

in Western European music were almost entirely vocal in character; the modern predominance of instrumental style is a comparatively recent thing, dating from about the beginning of the eighteenth century.

Up to the sixteenth century, instruments were used only as accompaniments for vocal music or interchangeably with it. Such an idea as letting instruments express their individuality or voice their independence was never even thought of. We shall see how the lute music of Spain and France was the first purely instrumental music ever written, in the sense that it showed the real possibilities of instruments as means for expressing musical ideas. A little later the organists succeeded in working out a style well suited to their instruments, and they in turn were followed by the writers for the clavichord and the harpsichord.

MINIATURE FROM THE UTRECHT PSALTER (860 A.D.) This miniature illustrates the One Hundred Fiftieth Psalm.

During the seventeenth century, a genuine type of orchestral music developed out of the court and popular dances of the time, and then followed the deluge of music for instruments, both solo and ensemble, that has continued down to the present.

But what happened before this era of instrumental precedence set in? It is obvious enough that instruments have existed from the earliest periods of history, and there is plenty of evidence that man has always enjoyed himself playing them. Why was instrumental music, then, so slow in developing in comparison with that used by singers?

We have already speculated a bit as to the ways in which the various types of instruments may have been introduced to man; beyond this it is hardly necessary to go, aside from mentioning the fact that the historical records of all the early civilizations are full of references to the ways by which man learned to use these instruments of music. The Greek account of the invention of their national instrument, the lyre, is characteristic: Mercury found one day a tortoise of which he took the shell, made holes in the opposite sides of it, and passed cords through them. His instrument was thus complete, with one cord for each Muse.

We have also referred to the fact that when music first appeared in known history, among the Sumerians, it was produced by a wide variety of instruments: the harp, the lyre, the flute, the reed pipe, the drum, and even the trumpet. As we have seen, instrumental music played an important part in the great civilizations that grew up along the banks of the Nile and on the Assyrian plains of western Asia. We know a great deal about the instruments used by both the Greeks and the Romans; but there is little definite information as to just how and when the ancestors of the various instruments we use today were introduced. It is quite certain that at the beginning of the Christian era musical instruments of every kind were excluded from the services of the Church; yet one of the miniatures in the manuscript of an illustrated ninth-century Psalter, now in the library of the University of Utrecht, provides a lively picture of singers and players against a decorative background suggestive of a church mural, these figures being evidently engaged in providing music for Christian worship. Sometime between the third and the ninth century stringed, wind, and percussion instruments came into general use in the Church. The organ, which the early Christians had associated with their Roman persecutors, must early have been introduced into the Christian service, for it was in special favor with the Church during the ninth century, if we are to judge by the important place given to it in this famous medieval miniature. It forms the central feature of the illustration from the Utrecht Psalter, with its two players greatly concerned over the wind supply that is being furnished by four hard-working blowers.

INSTRUMENTS IN MEDIEVAL PAINTING

Our most reliable source of information regarding the use of instruments during the Middle Ages is that left behind by many of the painters of this period. They show stringed instruments, such as lutes, guitars, mandolins, psalteries, harps, and fiedels, in amazing and confusing profusion; wind instruments, such as flutes, schalmeis, trumpets, and horns; percussive triangles, xylophones, and drums; and, in addition, organs and organistrums, commonly known as hurdy-gurdies. These were gut-string instruments with both drone and melody strings, the latter being sounded by a revolving wheel. All these instruments were played, if we can trust the contemporary painter's powers of observation, in any sort of combination, being sometimes used with, and sometimes without, singers.

When we find in a twelfth-century manuscript in the British Museum a depiction of Christ surrounded by twenty-four elders playing various instruments—organs, psalteries, oliphants (carved horns), fiedels, harps, and so on—it may mean nothing more than that these particular instruments happened to please the artist's fancy; but we are certain of the fact that they must have been used at the time.

Hans Memling, the contemporary of Josquin des Prés just at the beginning of the great choral era, has left us two pictures that he painted for the decoration of an organ case in a Spanish church. These

DECORATION FOR AN ORGAN CASE BY MEMLING (1430—1495)

    1   2   3   4   5

contain depictions of the instruments that we may safely conclude to
have been in common use at that time (1480).

(1) *Psaltery* (Zither). Introduced into European music somewhere
around the eleventh or twelfth century and much used as an accompanying instrument. When a keyboard was added, the psaltery became
the harpsichord of Renaissance music.

(2) *Tromba marina* (Nun's fiddle). A peculiar, one-stringed instrument, whose thick, heavy string was played in its "harmonics" only, by
touching its nodes rather than by stopping it in the ordinary way.
Rather mercifully, now obsolete, for its tone was loud and brassy. Used
until the time of Mozart.

(3) *Lute.* Probably of Oriental origin, introduced into Europe around
300 A.D. With pear-shaped body and from 6 to 13 strings, this became
one of the favorite Renaissance instruments and was made in many
sizes, the four-stringed *chitarra* being the smallest and the *chitarrone*
(often with 24 strings), the largest.

(4) *Trumpet.* A relic of the Roman military instruments, its clear
piercing tone being of great effectiveness for outdoor use. Gradually it
increased in length and folded on itself.

(5) *Bombart.* The ancestor of our modern reed instruments, descended

The fifteenth-century painter depicted contemporary instruments.

   6   7   8   9   10

in turn from the Asian *schalmei*. This double-reed instrument was used by both Greeks and Romans and came into new significance at the beginning of the second century A.D., when it developed into a complete family, called *shawms* or *pommers*. This was the nucleus of the ensemble groups before the strings assumed their modern pre-eminence.

(6) *Busine*. The ancestor of our trombone and an instrument of great length. A "slide" was added about the end of the fourteenth century, and the altered instrument was called a *sackbut*.

(7) *Trumpet*.

(8) *Portative organ*. We first hear of the organ in the third century before Christ. It is the only instrument that shows a continuous development from very early times. These small organs, with one or two sets of reed pipes and capable of being carried about, were very popular for home use.

(9) *Harp*. One of the most widely diffused types of instruments, in use (as we have seen) from the earliest days of man's history.

(10) *Fiedel*. A representative of the generic bowed string family from which have descended our modern violin, viola, cello, and bass. Called by various names, this type of instrument was in wide use during medieval and Renaissance times.

SECULAR USES

There is likewise much iconographical evidence that the instrumental style was popular in the secular music of the Middle Ages, both for furnishing the accompaniments for such songs as the troubadours used and for the dances of the people. The great *Heidelberg Songscript,* for instance, by far the most valuable of the minnesinger manuscripts, shows that various forms of the fiedel family, psalteries, harps, shawms, drums, and even glockenspiels were in common use in Germany during the fourteenth century. And the charming miniatures of the thirteenth-century Codex of the time of Alfonso x in Spain, in the library of the Escorial, show that the same instruments were used there.

The music for the medieval dances was probably played on combinations of instruments that would sound to modern ears, to paraphrase Rabelais, "above the pitch, out of tune, and off the hinges"—not least because of the age's taste for drone basses produced by bagpipes, fiedels, portative organs, and organistrums. Strings and wind and brass instruments were all mixed together in a sort of neutral style of rendition. Later, in the sixteenth century, after Italian violinists had established the primacy of their instruments, a mixed orchestra of bowed instruments became the popular medium for the interpretation of dance music.

THE ORGAN

A word is necessary regarding the most popular instrument of the medieval period—the organ, the instrument that shares with the sixteenth-century lute and the viol the distinction of beginning what may be called the reign of free, independent instrumental music. The Romans used the organ in their theatrical spectacles, building it of considerable power and blowing it with compressed air. The Christians, once their antipathy was overcome, made the organ serve as an accompanimental instrument in their services from the fourth century on. In the great Gothic age of cathedral building, the organ played its part in the magnificent ritual of the Church, being at that time an instrument of several keyboards and pedals, with twenty or more sets of pipes. Amiens Cathedral, for example, had in 1429 an organ of three keyboards, with forty stops and a pedal keyboard. Since on these organs one key usually controlled a number of pipes sounding in parallel fourths and fifths and octaves (sometimes as many as ten or, later, twenty), a whole series of tones was produced each time a single key was played; thus on C being

A RENAISSANCE COURT DANCE: "THE DANCE WITH FLAMBEAUX" (From a wood engraving by Dürer)

sounded on one of these ten-pipes-to-a-key instruments, there would be heard the ascending sequence C-G-C-G-C-G-C-G-C-G!

There were also small organs called *portatives* and *positives,* capable of being carried about, some of them being played and blown by the same person. The organ was ready for its literature before composers had fully developed any idea of what we today think of as instrumental style. One would have thought that the variety of color to be obtained from even a few sets of pipes might have suggested more diversity in writing for the keyboard than it actually did. Except for differences in mechanical perfection, the organ has remained practically unchanged from medieval to modern times.

Around the middle of the fifteenth century, while the organ in southern Europe remained much as we have described it above, the instrument in the north was developed much beyond the fourth-fifth-octave level. These northern, Gothic organs had several keyboards and a small number of stops which could be used to bring out solo melodies.

The Germans, the French, and the English have been, until recent times, the most passionate lovers of the organ, and these nations have done a great deal toward achieving its perfection. Their organ lofts brought forth many of their finest musicians, both practical and theoretical, and from the sixteenth century on there gathered round the parish church and cathedral a busy, fruitful activity. This tradition of the organist as the center of music-making dates back to the time of Henry de Saxonia, organist of the Chapter of Notre Dame, in the early fifteenth century. It has been for long one of the strongest and most beneficial influences in the musical life of the various nations—an influence now broken, alas, as individual music-making is everywhere being weakened by the supplying of music from central founts, much in the manner of such everyday commodities as water and electricity. Neither organ nor organist is of great importance in the musical life of the present.

THE NATURE OF THE MUSIC

Wooldridge has remarked that the history of instrumental music during the Middle Ages is one of the most tantalizing problems before the student of musicology. There is, as we have just seen, sufficient evidence in the other arts that music at this time was a very lively business; the hosts of lutes, organs, flutes, and brass instruments displayed in the pictures and referred to in the literature—Chaucer alone has a long list of such references—must have had something played on them. But what? How fascinating it would be to know, for instance, what sort of music was used by that lively group depicted in the Utrecht Psalter and whether the evident anxiety of the pair of organists and the tremendous labor of the quartet of blowers was due to the faulty mechanisms of their instruments or to the heavy demands of the music used!

Undoubtedly most of the music employed by the players of this time was never written down but was transmitted from master to pupil, becoming somewhat modified and changed in the process. For there was not the same incentive or necessity for writing down the music played by a single instrument that there was for vocal music needed for a number of performers; and the processes of printing did not come into general use until somewhat later.

It was this unknown and unwritten music that formed the basis of the first complete compositions that enable us to see something tangible

A GOTHIC MANUSCRIPT SHOWING INSTRUMENTS OF THE PERIOD   Done by a French illuminator of the early fifteenth century, this shows a Tree of Jesse bearing various instruments in use at the time. In order from left to right these are:

Schalmei (ancestor of the oboe)
Trumpet
Busine (ancestor of the trumpet)
Harp
Rebec (ancestor of the violin)

Mandolin
Flute
Fiedel (viol)
Pair of drums
Lute
Psaltery

amidst the mists of the medieval instrumental music—the well-developed, completely independent instrumental works found in the fifteenth-century German organ books and the Italian and Spanish lute collections of the early sixteenth century. So the few fragments of the earlier time that have survived and have found their way into the various libraries of Europe are worth special attention.

The chief sources of information so far discovered are a fourteenth-century *chansonnier* now in the National Library in Paris, which contains a number of the *estampies*—dance tunes; the so-called *Roberts-bridge Fragment* in the British Museum, containing six pieces for the organ, three of them purely instrumental, three transcriptions of motets, with the upper voices "colored" or varied in a simple way; and a few miscellaneous transcriptions of vocal works and dances. It may be said, in general, that these lamentably few survivors of what must have been a considerable literature show:

First, that the organ was used more during the Middle Ages than has been generally thought—it was Guillaume de Machaut who first called it the King of Instruments—and that much of the music played on it must have been vocal music taken bodily from the various settings of the Church's service. An early fifteenth-century *Liber organisatoris* defining the duties of the organist of Notre Dame, Paris, states specifically that part of such duty shall consist in playing on certain occasions the Kyrie, the Gloria, the Sequences, the Sanctus, and the Agnus Dei.

Second, that when the organists did play in what might be called instrumental style, there was very little difference between that music and what was written for the voices—perhaps the upper melodic voice might occasionally be given a little different treatment suggestive of what came to be known later as *variation*.

Third, that in the case of music played on the other instruments, either singly or in combination, no general distinction can be made. All the instruments used could seemingly be combined without regard to qualities of timbre or of sonority; and they were given the same sort of music the vocalists used. Any voice part was played by any instrument that had the requisite compass. But we remain unsure as to even such fundamental facts as the tempo in which this music was played, or to what extent the written notes were decorated at the performer's pleasure. As Ficker has said,[15] the ear perceives little of these technical refinements, for the composer was able to bring on new harmonic and melodic shades and intensifications which gave the impression of the music's being consistent throughout.

[15] In *The Musical Quarterly*, Vol. XV, p. 483.

THE RENAISSANCE

Causes and Effects

*By the grace of God light and dignity
have been in my time restored to letters,
and now I see therein such improvement
that at present I would hardly be admitted to the first class of primary pupils,
I who in my prime was not unjustly regarded as the wisest man of the age. . . .
The whole world is full of savants,
learned teachers, ample libraries, so that
it seems to me that not even in the time
of Plato, Cicero, or Papinian was there
such faculty for study as one sees now.
Now all studies are restored, the languages installed: Greek, without which it
is shameful for man to call himself a
scholar, Hebrew, Chaldean, Latin. These
exist in elegant and exact printed books
invented in my time by divine inspiration, just as, on the other hand, artillery
was by diabolical suggestion.*

François Rabelais, 1532

VARIED INTERPRETATIONS

If any proof is needed that
history, like life itself, cannot be made to fit exactly into the separate
periods into which we so carefully divide it in order to bring its events
into something resembling order, it will be found in this epoch, the
Renaissance. For this important period, stretching over an indefinite
era—some historians include both the late fourteenth as well as the
whole of the seventeenth century within its borders—presents a new
aspect each time a different interpretation of it shifts our angle of
approach. To Rabelais it was obviously important as a period devoted
to the resurrection of classic learning, the development of scientific

invention being a secondary and retroactive influence. To others the Renaissance has meant the period of man's renewal of interest in himself and the world he lives in, enabling him to look on life as a thing of joy in itself and not merely as a preparation for an existence to come. Many look on the epoch as one in which there took place a tremendous process of social, economic, national, and spiritual upheaval which found its most powerful outlet in the field of religious controversies. The pragmatist sees the Renaissance as the time when man began to become interested in the mechanical conception of life and in making his knowledge of natural forces conform to physical laws. Man established the fact that the earth is round and moves about the sun and so had the courage to sail in search of adventurous proof into regions before unknown. The historian of art thinks of this time as one in which man awoke to the fact that beauty is worth cultivating for its own sake and not merely as a means for serving other objects.

We have already tried to show all this, as well as the fact that the forces which reached their culminating peak at the beginning of the sixteenth century—the height of the Renaissance movement—had been gradually at work centuries before. So that while we speak of Renaissance ideals as having developed during the sixteenth century, in reality they were formed away back in the Middle Ages; and likewise they stretched far ahead into the future, giving promise of what was to come in the modern world in the way of literature, science, and political freedom. In the words of its most eloquent interpreter, the Renaissance was a process of transition, fusion, preparation, and fresh endeavor, which affected all phases of man's activities and which laid the foundation of much of our spiritual and mental existence today.

Among the many material explanations which are generally given for the Renaissance are such things as the fall of Constantinople to the Ottomans in 1453 and the consequent flight of her scholars to the West, bringing with them the knowledge and art of Greece and the ancient East; the voyages of discovery of Columbus, Da Gama, and Magellan; the inventions of the printing press and gunpowder. There is little question that all these were factors contributory to this great intellectual upheaval which came to a head in the sixteenth century; but, again, it is extremely difficult to distinguish between causes and effects. Did the invention by Gutenberg, for instance, or whoever it was that first used movable type for printing, come about through the increased curiosity of the Renaissance man and his desire to acquire more learning, or was it one of the reasons for his achieving individualism and liberation from the ideals of a past age? There is a simpler explanation than those usually advanced for this *volte-face* in man's thinking which, perhaps without adequate reason, and certainly without exact definiteness, we have learned to call the Renaissance.

As Sir Charles Oman has said in his interpretation of this much-discussed period *(The Sixteenth Century)*, once wonder, mystery, and spiritual values are removed from the life of man, it is inevitable that he becomes a materialist. If he can no longer look on the teachings of established authority as implicitly valid and begins to realize that his own ideas and thoughts are of value and worthy of his attention, he becomes an individualist. And this is exactly what transpired in the fifteenth century. The preceding periods had created new mental outlooks for man; instead of having an essentially spiritual concept of life, a concept which demanded imaginative rather than intellectual thinking, there arose new incentives for living, such as the acquiring of worldly wisdom, material gains, and temporal power. The Renaissance tended to heap scorn on the rags of the medieval "romancer"; new dreamers arose, but their world was one of business and politics rather than of the spirit. Italy, through her fortunate geographical situation, became the center for all this tremendous activity and for the financier who made it possible. Various city-states, such as Florence and Venice, emerged and became rich and powerful; their *condottieri* of government and politics were the strong men of the time. It was a period of great vitality, strong forcefulness, hard business, and extreme cruelty; and in it arose many strange contradictions.

Freed from the leading strings of the Church, man began to look about him, peering into every corner of the universe and demanding an answer to all its riddles. In the process he spared neither prince nor pontiff and did not hesitate to question the authority of both State and Church. Learning, which in the Middle Ages had been considered as important only for churchmen, began to be cultivated for its own sake. The old classic writers had, of course, not been unknown to the school and church men of medieval Europe; but these dignitaries had read such authors as Aristotle, Pliny, Virgil, and the rest for what they could teach in the way of manners and morals. It was the discovery of the Renaissance, as Chambers has so well pointed out in *The History of Taste,* that these classics were beautiful as literature and not merely useful as moral teachings. To the medieval scholar, Cicero was a writer of essays having a moral leaning, and Virgil was famous because he was thought to have foretold the coming of Christ; to the men of the

GOTHIC FOURTEENTH-CEN-
TURY PIETÀ (From the Elisa-
bethenkirche in Marburg)

Renaissance, Cicero was again one of the great orators of all time, and
Virgil was "crowned anew with the laurels of the poet." Thus was the
pagan humanism of the classic civilizations revived and cultivated for
its significance as a factor in human life and happiness. Beauty was
worth cultivating for its own sake and not merely for what it could
teach. And all the fine arts—architecture, painting, sculpture, literature,
and music—were assiduously cultivated and fostered by the rich and
enthusiastic patrons of the period.

A PLASTIC ILLUSTRATION

No better example of this difference in spirit could possibly be found
than that shown by the three pieces of sculpture illustrated here—the
first from the fourteenth century, Gothic in every line and feature; the
second from the transitional fifteenth century; the third from the sixteenth century, typically Renaissance in line and proportion. All have
the same subject, even the same pose: Mary, the mother of Christ,
holds in her lap the dead body of her Son after its removal from the
cross.

The unknown artist of the Gothic period has made his figures dis-
tressingly gaunt and angular—the body of Christ is elongated out of

FIFTEENTH-CENTURY PIETÀ   by Benedetto da Majano

all proportion to the conception as a whole. But he has emphasized the religious significance of his work: the dead Christ is the Saviour of the world, who has suffered an agonizing death for its sins; and Mary is a mother sorrowing for her beloved Son and also for man in general.

In Benedetto da Majano's treatment there is not so great a concern with religious ideas: the figures have more human grace and interest; they are not so symbolically powerful but for that reason are perhaps more "artistic." There can be felt here an interest in the individual, a concentration on the expression of the sculptor's conception that was not found in the earlier work. This is not to say, of course, that these had reached the state in which we find them in Michelangelo's rendering of the same subject a century later.

What an entirely different conception is Michelangelo's! The whole effect is one of graceful balance and lovely proportion, the representational significance being quite secondary. The dead body resting in the flowing luxuriance of the robe is that of a young Greek Adonis, beautiful in its lines and perfect in its modeling; the proportion of the figure of Mary is carefully arranged and nobly executed, but there is no intensity of suffering or shadow of agony in her beautiful classic countenance.

RENAISSANCE SIXTEENTH-CEN-
TURY PIETÀ   by Michelangelo—in
Rome

Even her outstretched hand suggests the need of the sculptor for compositional balance—the idea of art for art's sake—rather than any sense
of emotional expressiveness. Here, modeled so that anyone who runs
may read, is the real difference between the Middle Ages and the
Renaissance: these sculptured figures are more eloquent than any words.

WHAT THE RENAISSANCE DID FOR MUSIC

Certain very definite achievements in music may be credited to the
sixteenth century, each of them representative in a different way of
these multifarious ideals of the Renaissance:

First. The continued development of the woven, contrapuntal style,
which had had its beginnings in the Gothic centuries, to a point where
it was capable of completely expressing both the humanized religious
emotion of such composers as Palestrina and Victoria and the secularized sophistication of such pagan humanists as Monteverdi and Gesualdo.

Second. The cultivation of music for varied instruments and the development of styles well suited to their individual requirements. This
change came about through the gradual secularization of art that occurred during the Renaissance, the mechanical conceptions which began
to prevail at this time, and the passion for law and order then general.

For the musical instrument is nothing but a mechanical tool, and its use necessarily imposes definite limitations and patterns according to which music can be put together.

Third. The complete breaking-away from the traditions of the past in the development of harmony as we know it today, notably exemplified in the opera, a form which resulted from the desire of its originators to imitate the classic Greek drama and which led to the modern harmonic sense. By this we mean the conception of music as being the result of vertically grouped tones instead of the product of horizontally inter-woven melodies. This harmonic way of thinking is based on natural physical laws, for the notes which go to make up a simple chord are the mechanically selected natural overtones of the note on which the chord is built. This was but another manifestation of the awakening Renaissance interest in the physical laws of nature.

One of the most striking differences between the music of the Renaissance and that of the earlier periods was the realization, from 1500 on, that the various voices were integral parts of a whole, whereas the earlier polyphonists thought of the parts in their compositions separately, writing them one after the other, with no attempt to fuse them into a component whole.

The Renaissance in Italy

The Italy of the Renaissance, with its magnifi-
cent palaces, its classically ornamented build-
ings, its terraces and gorgeously decorated
galleries, this enchanted the nobles of France,
the lords of England, and the rich men of
Spain and Germany.

Albert Malet: *Nouvelle Histoire de France*

AN ARTIST OF THE RENAISSANCE

The traveler to modern Italy is likely to look on Florence as the one city which most fully represents the life and spirit of the Renaissance. He is usually taken to the great building in the center of the lovely city, the Medici Palace, built by the most famous of all Florentine families, and is shown there, spread out on its walls, the colorful depictions of Renaissance life as

C. C Stover

RENAISSANCE ITALY

painted by Gozzoli. There are three pictures supposed to represent the journey of the three kings to Bethlehem; in reality these are gorgeous depictions of life in Florence at the time of the Renaissance. They contain all the local celebrities of the period, decked out in their gay clothes, placed against a background studied from the natural surroundings of Florence, the figures being chosen from the Medicean circles. If Florence, as has so often been remarked, is the heart of the Renaissance, these Gozzoli pictures represent the heart of Florence and should be seen by all those who would understand this period in Italian history.

We have already described the changes in spirit brought about by the fourteenth and fifteenth centuries. Italy at that time was made up of a number of small, entirely independent states, each of them maintaining a separate existence. In the north were the domains of Savoy, Milan, and Modena, all of them under the sovereignty of dukes. The rich and powerful republics of Genoa, Venice, and Florence were under the power of merchant princes of the Medici type—bankers and businessmen who had been powerful enough to seize the government of their cities and dictate their policies. In central Italy were the Papal States, with their center at Rome; and in the south, the kingdoms of Naples and Sicily struggled to hold their own against the more power-

JOURNEY OF THE THREE KINGS (First Episode) by Benozzo Gozzoli   The picture is founded on the historical meeting in Florence in 1439 of an episcopal council for the uniting of the Eastern and Western churches. The figure of the third Magus is that of Lorenzo de' Medici.

ful republics to the north. It was the demand for splendor on the part of these various rulers, together with the attempt of each prince and tyrant to outdo the others in the magnificence of his local surroundings, that so markedly advanced the arts of architecture, painting, and sculpture at this time. The result was the production in enormous profusion of some of the most glowing pictures, monumental architecture, outstanding pieces of sculpture, and exciting literary works the world has ever seen in any one country or during a comparable period.

THE RESULTS IN MUSIC

In the art of music the effects were not so happy. After the striking works produced in Italy under the inspiration of the Ars nova—the *ballate, madrigals,* and *caccias* of which we have spoken—there came during the first part of the fifteenth century a decided slump in musical production and invention. Taught and stimulated by the Florentine

pains to show what may be expected of the gentleman musician: he must possess a good voice, sing well at sight, and be able to accompany himself on various solo instruments.

In this book of Castiglione's a reference of special interest to the historian is that in which he speaks of a solo performance which consisted of reciting poetry to the accompaniment of an instrument, so as to heighten the beauty and increase the significance of the words. It has long been thought that this sort of *recitativo*, which later influenced the writers of opera, had been devised by Vincenzo Galilei, the father of the famous astronomer, in an attempt to imitate what he considered to have been the musical practices of the Greeks. But here is a reference showing that this usage was common before Galilei's employment of it.

THE RENAISSANCE MADRIGAL AN ITALIAN DEVELOPMENT

The most important manifestations of the Renaissance spirit in music, developed in these circles described in detail by Castiglione, were the sixteenth-century *madrigal* and *motet,* works which show a much more complete sense of unity and balance than can be found in the earlier contrapuntal forms depending upon a calculated, artificial device to hold them together. These newer forms were unified by the composer's imagination rather than by the perfection of his technical powers. They followed the poetic demands of the text, with plenty of contrast and expressiveness in the working-out of their motives. In his monumental work on the Italian madrigal,[1] Einstein points out the difference between the music of the fifteenth and that of the sixteenth century by saying that the former had been full of ingenuity and intellectual contrivance (as we have seen in Machaut and Obrecht), while the latter was the result of a directly sensuous, poetic expression of an idea. And he goes on to add that these two contrasting attitudes were finally united later on in the music of Sebastian Bach.

We have already seen something of the effect of the *ars nova* in Italy during the fifteenth century. It was in protest against this involved contrapuntal style from the north that the native musicians of Venice, Florence, and Rome developed types of their own: the *frottola* (little fruit) and the *villanella*. The latter has been described by Thomas Morley, the English composer, as "clownish," a somewhat boorish satire on the aristocratic order of a love song. Then there was the *villota,* one of the dance-song types from Italy, with a clear-cut melody and accompanying parts below it.

[1] *The Italian Madrigal* by Alfred Einstein, Princeton: Princeton University Press, 1949.

Courtesy of The National
Gallery, London

FROTTOLE SINGERS
by Roberti

It is the obviousness of these *frottole* and *villanelle* and their repetition of the same music for many verses that irked the taste of the cultured literary and musical circles of the time. In an attempt to develop these simple forms, the prominent composers of Italy, many of them church musicians from Flanders and the Netherlands, may be said to have founded the madrigal style. The new works which they developed may be looked upon as the logical elaborations of the *madrigali* of the fourteenth century (of which Landino's madrigal has been cited as an example), carried out in the manner of a period two centuries later. Naturally these later works were richer in technical achievements because of the additional experiments which had taken place in the meantime. Using the free-flowing, melodious *frottole* as bases, composers like Willaert and Arcadelt brought to bear on them the full force of their invention and technical facility. The result was what we have come to know as the *madrigal,* a form that was originally cultivated by musicians alone and intended for an intimate circle of connoisseurs and amateurs such as gathered at the courts of the princes and in the academies of the time. In this sense the madrigal was essentially chamber music, performed by but one musician to a part. There were literally no listeners to this type of performance, for everybody participated. But there was also a more social aspect of the madrigal, cultivated by the above-mentioned *académie,* institutions which pursued art for art's sake, giving concerts at which madrigals were sung for the joy of perform-ance in company. This entertainment aspect of the madrigal was distinct from what might be called its purest manifestation as chamber music.

It seems that at the beginning of their Italian history, madrigals were sung *a cappella*—that is, without instrumental accompaniment. But gradually instruments were admitted to their performance, either to supply a concentrated support to a solo, or to double all or some of the vocal parts. Out of this practice came the instrumentally accompanied solo madrigal as a rival to its purely vocal form—another example of the inevitable trend towards monody.

The new style spread like wildfire in the aristocratic circles. The earliest madrigals were published in 1533, and from that time onward for a number of years there poured out of Italy a steady stream of these works. That the same spirit animated the composers in the other coun-tries may be seen from the table on page 261, which lists the names and dates of the principal madrigal composers in the various countries.

No better description of the characteristics of this form could be found than that given by the composer of some of the best English madrigals, Thomas Morley, in his book *A Plaine and Easie Introduc-tion to Practicall Musicke,* written in 1597:

> The best kind of light musicke is termed Madrigal . . . a kind of musicke made upon songs and sonnets such as Petrarcha and manie poets of our time have excelled in. . . . As for the musicke it is next unto the Motet the most artificial and to men of understanding the most delightful. If therefore you will compose in this kind you must possess yourself with an amorous humor . . . so that you must in your musicke be wavering like the wind, sometime wanton, sometime drooping, sometime grave and staide, otherwhile effeminat, you may maintaine points and revert them, use triplaes and shew the verie uttermost of your varietie, and the more varietie you shew, the better shal you please.

The sensuous delight experienced by those who wrote and sang these madrigals came through the clever manipulation of means rather than from any deep expression of feeling. From its very beginning, the form of the music was free enough as regards structure: the composer would take verses of any meter that appealed to him, usually a stanza of some five or six lines chosen from a lyric, pastoral, or amorous poem, although he sometimes set words of a grave character. Here are two examples:

Cor mio, montre vi mire	*O bellezza mortale!*
Visibilmente mi transform' in voi;	*O bellezza vitale!*
E transformato poi	*Poi che si teste un core*
In solo sospir' l'anima spiro.	*Per ter inasce e per te nato* **morte.**

. . .

In pride of May	*Then, Lady dear,*
The fields are gay	*Do now appear*
The birds do sweetly sing;	*In beauty like the spring;*
So Nature would	*I will dare say*
That all things should	*The birds that day*
With joy begin the spring.	*More cheerfully will sing.*

The composers dealt with such words line by line, even breaking them into phrases, thus dividing their work into definite sections. The parts were usually written for four or five voices, in both harmonic and contrapuntal style, the latter often of very involved and curious workmanship. The chief distinguishing mark of the madrigal was its marvelous rhythmic freedom, no matter how complicated the weaving of the various parts. Each voice followed the meter of the verse with absolute accuracy, sometimes in slow, sometimes in quick tempo, according to the dictates of the words. The prevailing atmosphere of the poem was caught in a sort of stylized musical paraphrase, and there were often curious attempts at what may be called word painting: "long festoons of thirds were woven about such expressions as 'chains of love'; sighs were translated by pauses and breaks in the melody; the idea of duration, of immobility, was expressed by the holding of a single voice, the others carrying their parts relentlessly. The voices rose on such words as 'heaven,' 'heights'; they fell on the words 'earth,' 'abyss,' 'hell.' The notes scattered in silvery groups round the words 'laughter,' 'joyous,' 'gay,' etc.; tears are expressed by audacious discords and unexpected modulations" (Prunières: *Monteverdi*). There was a good deal of imitation among the various parts, but it was hardly ever strict in the sense of the mechanical canons and devices of the earlier church music. Everything was free, yet strongly conventional; expressive, yet severely intellectual; imaginative, yet purely artificial. The madrigals were indeed a happy compromise between pure, spontaneous

CON GRATIA ET PRIVILEGIO
Della Illuftriſsima Signoria di Venetia, & di tutti li Prencipi
Chriſtiani, come ne i loro priuilegi appare.

In Venetia appreſſo di Antonio Gardano. · 1 5 5 9·

Foto Fiorentini—Venezia

ADRIAN WILLAERT (from the woodcut portrait in his *Musica nova,* 1559)

utterance and calculated ingenuity. Considering their restricted field, no more perfect art form has been devised.

Having invented the madrigal, the Italians achieved great distinction in writing it. All the outstanding composers, including even Palestrina, wrote in this style. As we might expect, there is a vocal flow, a directness of expression, and a dramatic intensity in these Italian madrigals that was never quite equaled by the composers of the other nations.

Historians trace the development of the Italian madrigal in three periods. The first includes two prominent Flemings, Philippe Verdelot (1500–1565) and Jacob Arcadelt (*c.* 1505–*c.* 1557), besides Constanzo Festa (*d.* 1545), who is generally considered the first Italian composer of madrigals. The work of these men is largely homophonic and quiet in expression. A good example of its spirit, in fact the only one to survive insofar as popular knowledge of their work goes, is Arcadelt's piece upon the subject of the dying swan, *Il biano e dolce cigno* (1539), with its somewhat acrid comment upon humanity: "More geese than swans now live, more fools than wise"; this sentiment was reflected in

Orlando Gibbons's setting of the same words near the very end of the madrigalian period, almost a century later.

The classic period of the madrigal is considered to include the work of the outstanding composers Adrian Willaert (*c.* 1480–1562) and Cypriano de Rore (1516–1565), both Flemish-Venetians; Philippe de Monte (1521–1603); Andrea Gabrieli (*c.* 1510–1586); Orlando di Lasso (*c.* 1530–1594); and Palestrina (1525–1594). Einstein considers De Rore to be the central figure of the madrigal, an uncompromisingly serious composer to be compared to his contemporary, Michelangelo, in the significance, character, and influence of his work. In these composers we find an intensification of unity between text and music, a richer and more consistently polyphonic texture, usually in five parts (the earlier school had commonly written in three or four parts), and a more vivid use of imitative devices.

The last phase in the historical development of the madrigal includes the names of a number of composers whose works stand in strong contrast to the self-contained forms used earlier. Among them are Luca Marenzio (*c.* 1553–1599), Gesualdo (1560–1613), and Monteverdi (1567–1643). The style of these men is still more elaborate; it is experimental, often mannered, and, in the case of Gesualdo, chromatically exaggerated.

Einstein describes Marenzio as a virtuoso, the purest of artists, and a writer of music for connoisseurs. Both sensual and austere, he chose texts both pastoral and pathetic from Plutarch and other contemporary poets. In his works the madrigal becomes "more of a symphonic structure in the service of the text." He wrote nine books of madrigals and in his late work displayed an extreme plasticity of tempo that often pushes expression to the limits of good taste. He also wrote some pieces in which the top voice freely declaims, while the others support it in fairly solid harmony.

The chromaticism and violent declamation of the erratic Gesualdo, Prince of Venosa, extreme for that age, suggests his classification as a real Mannerist, complete with the usual autobiographical confessions. Claudio Monteverdi, one of the great geniuses of all music, who also used chromaticism audaciously, added an unexampled realization of moods and a versatility of expression which make his madrigals the high-water mark of the whole movement. Especially noteworthy as representing in almost perfect form the ideals of the Renaissance is his madrigal sestina *Le lagrime d'amante al sepolcro dell' amata* (Tears of a Lover at the Tomb of His Loved One), a cycle of six madrigals set to

STATUE OF BARTOLOMMEO
COLLEONI   General of the Ve-
netian Republic (modeled by
Verrocchio)

a carefully constructed lot of texts based on arbitrarily designed rhyme
schemes—the whole thing designed for the same sophisticated audience
as were Ariosto's *Orlando Furioso* and the paintings of Botticelli. In the
later development of his career as a composer of opera, Monteverdi
often returned to the madrigalian style; a notable example of this is his
dramatic scene in madrigal form arranged from his opera *Ariadne*.

It is Monteverdi who stands as the greatest man of this epoch, an
important link between the old and new styles of the sixteenth and
seventeenth centuries; for not only did he carry the polyphonic vocal
style to great heights, but he also proved himself to be the father of
modern dramatic and orchestral music. He is the first composer to
whom those whose experience with music has been limited to the works
of the eighteenth and nineteenth centuries can listen with real pleasure
and understanding. His music, in whatever style it was written, was
essentially dramatic, romantic, and adventurous. Realizing that no one
could go further than he had in the madrigalian style, he made, as
Prunières has said, a complete *volte-face* and laid hands on the aristocratic spectacle that had been invented and laboriously carried out by
his Florentine contemporaries, turning this humanistic plaything into
the modern music drama. Of this, more in another chapter.

A particularly interesting figure of the period is Orazio Vecchi (1550-1605), who was, as Einstein describes him, a poet-musician, "a merry and pious priest, . . . a man of broad culture, . . . an altogether original figure, but not a revolutionary." He wrote serious madrigals and gay *canzonette,* in some of which he was parodistic, quoting even the revered Palestrina; in another vein, he did not hesitate to suggest the speech of a drunken man. He created figures from the *commedia dell' arte,* notably in his *Amfiparnasso,* a full-fledged madrigal comedy in sketchily dramatic form, introducing all the familiar characters: shepherds and shepherdesses, Pantaleone, the Doctor, a Spanish Captain, and the comic servants. In this *commedia harmonica,* Vecchi tried to suggest dramatic developments while attempting no visible action on the stage and keeping entirely within the older contrapuntal forms. This rather simple composition is such as a party of noble amateurs would enjoy producing for their own amusement.

SACRED MUSIC OF THE SIXTEENTH CENTURY

But the interest of the period is by no means confined to secular music. Perhaps in no other field did the flame of genius burn so brightly in this era of creative activity as it did in the field of sacred music. The three great names Palestrina, Di Lasso, and Victoria represent figures of pronounced individuality, their works being definitely the expression of their own personalities, as well as the culmination of all the brilliant experiments of the Netherlands composers; they may be said to be the final symbols of the Renaissance spirit in music. Palestrina will always stand as the composer of an ideal type of church music, humanely harmonious and yet purged of all unnecessary objectiveness. Having completely mastered the technique of his predecessors in this field, he had a perfect means for the expression of those mystic, exalted ideals that are so unlike anything else in all music. While the other composers of the time were equally proficient in sacred and secular styles and wrote for both instruments and voices, Palestrina confined himself almost entirely to choral music. His manner of writing *a cappella* (that is, for voices, unaccompanied) is so pure, and so completely adapted to the beauties of the human voice as a musical instrument, that it is impossible to think of his music as being rendered by any other medium. There is a peculiarly unearthly quality about it. Palestrina was not characteristic of the time in this aspect of his genius; and in listening to the melting transcience of his harmonies, we seem lifted completely beyond the confines of time and space. But we must always remember that this music as printed today is something quite different from that which was sung in Palestrina's time; for, strange as it may seem to us, the singers of the period were accustomed to add all sorts of variations and embellishments to the composed score, according to their taste and desire. And so what seems to us as being detached and unworldly must have sounded quite different in the actual renditions of the period.

The Renaissance in France and the Netherlands

Outside of Italy the art of the Renaissance appears to have been, at least in its origins, an art of importation—an importation which had many different aspects.

Colombier: *L'Art Renaissance en France*

THE RISE OF FRANCE AS A WORLD POWER After long years of impoverishment brought on by wars with England and anarchy within her own borders, France began in the fifteenth century to try to establish herself as the dominant power of Europe. Louis XI, a royal despot if there ever was one, ruled from 1461 to 1483. In what had formerly been a decrepit monarchy, he dealt a final blow to the system of medieval feudalism and, by stringent administrative reforms and an active policy of territorial acquisition, was able to put his country in condition for foreign conquests. His son, Charles VIII, by marrying Anne of Brittany and thus adding this duchy to the French Empire, continued his policy. He was the first to invade Italy, making a temporary conquest of Naples at just about the time Columbus set forth on his memorable voyage of discovery.

Charles died without leaving any male heirs and was succeeded by a distant relative of another branch of the House of Valois—Louis XII, known as *le père du peuple*. In alliance with the Spaniards, who in the sixteenth century were the great people of Europe, Louis conquered Milan and Naples, and then, in league with other powers, tried to

THE RENAISSANCE
TOMB OF FRANCIS I
IN THE CHURCH OF
ST. DENIS, PARIS
Compare this tomb with
the Gothic tomb of
Philippe Pot, page 210.

deprive the Venetians of their holdings on the mainland of Italy. The final result of all these wars and intrigues was the expulsion of the French from the Italian peninsula in 1512. This, however, did not end Italy's troubles.

Louis was succeeded by his brilliant cousin, Francis I. Reigning from 1515 to 1547, this gentleman king held the throne during the great years of the Renaissance and proved himself an ideal man for the time. He patronized all the arts, and it is pleasant to record that literature, music, sculpture, and architecture flourished mightily during his reign. The long series of Italian campaigns of his predecessors, together with his own attempts to recover and hold parts of Italy, brought France into direct and vital contact with the ideals of the Renaissance. It was Francis who made attempts to transport bodily some of the most famous of the Italian artists, bringing home with him Leonardo da Vinci, who died soon afterwards; Andrea del Sarto, who did not stay long; and others.

TOMB OF THE "GRAND SÉNÉCHAL" PHILIPPE POT　The new spirit in the Gothic is shown in this fifteenth-century work.

THE INFLUENCE OF ITALY

Long before this, however, as early as the reign of Louis VIII, Italian sculptors had come to France and had made a deep impression there. The Gothic figures of the French *imagiers* gradually forsook their peculiarities of style and Christian feeling and took on more of that ideal cast of beauty which was fostered by the Florentine study of the antique. Nowhere can it be seen so clearly as in the Church of St. Denis, Paris, already mentioned as one of the earliest Gothic structures in France and a sort of French Westminster Abbey, containing, as it does, the tombs of French kings and notables until almost the time of the Bourbons. In walking through the array of tombs in the old abbey church, we pass gradually from the Gothic world to that of the Renaissance; and this change in form corresponds to the change in thought between these two periods. The sculptors of the Middle Ages have fixed the royal figures in humble, recumbent positions, showing them pitiable in death, and surrounding them with figures of sinister *pleurants,* mourners over the royal decease. In the tombs of the sixteenth-century kings, Louis XII and Francis I, the figures are not in the least suggestive of death, but of glory and power; these beautiful sculptured figures, modeled after classic sources and placed against a background recording the exploits of the king, are not Christian but pagan. Theirs is no temporary tomb, where man awaits his final resurrection in faith and hope; rather is it a triumphant monument assuring him of worldly immortality after his brief and brilliant career on earth.

So, too, with architecture and painting. The traveling artists who were so numerous in the early days of the Renaissance, the Italians invited to France by private individuals, the French artists who returned home from Italy with their luggage full of copies of Italian art—all these gradually effected such a penetration of Italian methods into northern art as to revolutionize European tastes completely. This, of course, could not have been done had not the Renaissance mind outgrown the conceptions of the Gothic era. Architects had invented the Gothic cathedral to suit the religious requirements of that time; the feudal castles and fortresses were built to fit the necessities of a warlike period; and the artists of the thirteenth century had a definite system of iconography by which they expressed concurrent religious beliefs. But when Christian faith had diminished so that huge communal churches were no longer necessary, when monarchical France made feudal fortresses no longer compulsory, men turned their architectonic energies into building great houses in the Italian Renaissance style, their chief aim being the creation of beauty. And the sixteenth-century painter responded to the collective taste of his time by using humanistic and classic subjects rather than religious ones, and by painting in a way which showed that beauty was worthy of cultivation in itself rather than merely as a universal language for the propagation of the faith.

Thus two styles, one the result of long tradition, the other introduced through the charm of a foreign novelty that happened to fit well the natural aptitude of the country, both benefiting by a return of national energy, flourished in France from the time of Charles VIII to that of Henry II—roughly from the latter fifteenth to the middle sixteenth century. But the new style, founded on a wider and more humane base, permeated by a spirit of law and order, gradually triumphed: rejecting all ideas of compromise, it completely eliminated the other style—sometimes with unfortunate results—severing forever the ties which had so long bound a united Christian people and its universal religious art.

MUSIC FOLLOWS THE OTHER ARTS

During this period of transition, music followed the same tendencies. We have considered the outstanding characteristics of Gothic music—

the elaborate craftsmanship, the perfection of a style consisting of an ingenious and skillful weaving-together of various voices, resulting in a sort of universal expression of personal concepts, and the definitely religious quality which closely associated it with the services of the Church.

Gradually there came out of Italy other ideals which led eventually to the complete secularization of the art: the substitution of instruments for voices in one or more of the woven parts; the compression into an accompaniment, capable of being played on a single lute, of the polyphonic parts of the older style (Italian lutenists had published such arrangements as early as 1508); the consequent shifting of the relationship between the parts, with the constant development of the idea of a chief melody and accompanying voices; and the gradual tendency to use more and more a chordal rather than a purely contrapuntal type of writing. This penetration of Renaissance ideals can be seen very clearly in the music of France, but it affected that of other countries as well.

During the later Middle Ages in France, there developed a peculiarly nationalistic type of expression, the *chanson,* which may be said in general to correspond to the Italian madrigal. The earliest examples we have of the chanson, by Busnois and De la Rue, are as simple in structure as the Italian *frottola,* and even clearer and more concise in expression. Gradually, as the Italian influence made itself more and more felt, these compositions became more elaborate, with involved counterpoint, and often bristled with the artificial devices of the artistry of the time. The chanson of the middle of the sixteenth century was a highly sophisticated composition, set to various kinds of texts, mostly amatory. Referred to by a contemporary writer as *lascives, sales, et impudiques,* and by a modern writer as "airy, sprightly, and full of pretty babblings," these compositions are truly French in nature, having fresh, lively melodies, pleasing wit, spirited words (very often indelicate), and piquant rhythms.

As might be expected, the chansons were mostly composed according to the old tradition of writing in several simultaneous melodic lines, each of them requiring an individual interpreter. They often showed a peculiar tendency toward tonal painting—a tendency that was later to reappear in a more elaborate form in French music. Clément Jannequin (*c.* 1485—*c.* 1560), best-known composer of the chanson, wrote several celebrated program pieces, notably the *Bataille de Marignan* (descriptive of the defeat of the Swiss by Francis I in 1515, and ending realistically with a Swiss cry of defeat, in dialect: "Everything is lost, by God!"); the *Cris de Paris,* depicting the street noises of the time; *La*

A FRENCH RENAISSANCE CHÂTEAU OF THE SIXTEENTH CENTURY

Chasse, in which we are present at a court hunt; and, best of all, *Le Chant des oiseaux,* a piquant description of a bird concert, with naïve references to the amorous customs of the period. Other well-known writers of the chanson were Claudin de Sermisy, Claude le Jeune, Guillaume Costeley, and Charles Tessier. Characteristic works by each of these will be found in the list of recordings on page 721.

Unquestionably there were various ways of performing these works. The usual one was to assign each part to an individual voice, the whole composition thus being sung; but often some of the parts were given to instruments, the resulting effect being partly vocal and partly instrumental. We have plenty of evidence that these chansons were also played by instruments alone, with a result that must have been pleasing, for their general style is quite neutral and not dictated by any considerations of voice or instruments, either bowed or wind. Musical archaeologists have discovered in old libraries pages of chanson music with the first words of a poem at their head but with no words under the staves, thus showing that they were copies made for purely instrumental use, with no thought of vocal execution.

Courtesy of Musée Carnavalet

"GUINGUETTE" AT THE TIME OF FRANCIS I   The setting is in the environs of the
Quai St. Bernard, Paris.

The earlier chansons were largely polyphonic in nature, each voice
being of equal importance and having individual interest. Later on,
we find many, affected by the Renaissance ideal, in which this purely
polyphonic interest has been displaced by a melody in one of the parts,
with the others serving a subordinate role. Evidently this was the sort
of thing that was favored at the height of the French Renaissance under
Francis I. Claudin's *En entrant en ung Jardin* was certainly sung this
way, as were most of the works in Pierre Attaignant's *Trent-cinq livres
contenant chansons,* published in Paris from 1538 to 1549. There is a
charming picture in the Musée Carnavalet showing a *compagnie* of
the period gathered in the country just outside Paris. We can imagine
the three musicians of this picture playing and singing Claudin's
happy song, the vocalist supplying the melody and indicating the
rhythm with his hand for his accompanists, who play the other parts
on flute and lute.

Such a development of new senses of vocal and instrumental relationships, as well as those between preponderant and subordinate voices,
led directly to our modern ideals of harmonic music. Another factor
that greatly heightened this development was the reduction of the

accompaniment of the chansons to a form suitable for playing on the lute, a great number of such arrangements being made and printed in France. The first collection was issued by the celebrated printer Attaignant, who seems to have had exclusive possession of the field, in 1529; he called it *Très brève et familière introduction,* and it contained a large number of arrangements of chansons in the manner of the Italian lutenists. Twenty-five years later there appeared another under the title of *Hortes Musarum,* and again, in 1571, Adrian le Roy and Robert Ballard, *imprimeurs du Roy,* issued a third. Thus in a period in which the printing of music was by no means common, there were issued in France within less than fifty years three great collections of these lute songs. With real melodies of a rich character and definitely subordinated accompanimental parts, they did much to tune man's ear to the harmonic sense of tone to which it later became so accustomed. The French musician of the later sixteenth century was thus as strong an influence in disseminating the ideals of the Italian Renaissance as were his brother artists—the sculptors, the painters, and the architects.

RELIGIOUS MUSIC OF THE RENAISSANCE

Sixteenth-century France, as anyone who knows the history of this brilliant country will remember, was far from being united in matters of religion. The latter half of these hundred years was given over to a cruel series of wars between Protestants and Catholics, in which the leaders of both parties, as well as two of the French kings, fell by the hands of assassins. It was a generation of intolerance of opinion and barbarity of action, each side striving to force its beliefs on the country as a whole; and yet this religious strife had a stimulating effect on music.

During the first part of the century, the music of the established church was able to resist most of the infiltrations that had so affected the character of the chanson and the madrigal. Jean Mouton (*d.* 1522), a pupil of Josquin des Prés's, was the outstanding composer of Catholic church music at this time. He was a singer in the royal chapel choirs of both Louis XII and Francis I and was a composer who developed a virtuoso contrapuntal technique while maintaining a natural gift for simple and grand effects.

The next important name in the Netherlands School of church music of this time is that of Philippe de Monte, who was described in 1555 as "without any contradiction the best composer in the whole land," although we today no longer rank him with his contemporaries, Di Lasso and Palestrina. Like his compatriots, De Monte shows strong Italian influence in the 38 Masses and 318 motets that have survived. In all of these, the ideals of the earlier Flemish contrapuntal masters are combined with the puissant use of color, dramatic effectiveness, and melodic charm that are so characteristic of the Italian style. De Monte's European reputation was such that he was appointed Imperial *Kapell-meister* to the Emperor Maximilian in 1568.

During the second half of the century, Orlando di Lasso (or Orlandus Lassus) came into his own as a composer. Born in Mons about 1530, he traveled over all civilized Europe during the course of his life and so learned to adapt himself quickly and easily to different national styles. In spite of his fluency and facility in writing, he was a composer of definite individuality, one whose brilliant achievements in both sacred and secular music are too little known. In no other composer is the influence of the Renaissance so clearly evident. He took the old Josquinian counterpoint as the basis for his writing, and on this he imposed the decorativeness of the Italian madrigal style together with its dramatic chromaticism, mixing with them a dash of Venetian passion and color. The result is irresistible. He was able to achieve a happy apposition of polyphonic and homophonic effects and expressed his strong religious beliefs with a joyous exaltation and an *élan* that is robust and human in comparison with the mysticism of his contemporary, Palestrina.[2] The effect of Di Lasso's music is powerful and inevitable, brilliant to the last degree; its imagination is above all the other writing of the time. If, as is so often done, we are to liken Palestrina to the tranquil Raphael, Di Lasso must be compared to Michelangelo in his heroic strength and variety of expression.

[2] Lehman Engel has made the following pertinent comparison between these two great men: "Palestrina's work was closely associated in every sense with the past, while Lassus's was greatly affected by his own present. Through it he reached out toward the future. His works are far more varied and cover a wider range than do Palestrina's, and his aesthetic and emotional approach is personal and warm in contradistinction to Palestrina's, which is remote and impersonal. Lassus often wrote 'light' music intended purely as entertainment and often wrote to texts which were bawdy and even pornographic. He set out to succeed in a world in which there was only superlative success or obscure servitude. His success was a complete one in competition with some genius and much near-genius. Viewed today Lassus's work bears the stamp of inspired greatness, and his quality of workmanship is unexcelled by any later master. He combined the skill of the Netherland craftsman with the more profound and deeper personal sentiment of the rising German art. One wonders whether the overwhelming success of his life in art was not due to rather than in spite of the unceasing hectic demands made on his talents."

THE BAVARIAN COURT CAPELLA UNDER THE DIRECTION OF DI LASSO
(from Hans Mielich Kodex in the Staatsbibliothek, Munich) Di Lasso sits at the clavier;
around him are the players on viol and gamba, lute, zinke, bassoon, and trombone;
the singers make up the background.

There are over five hundred motets for 2, 3, 4, 5, 6, 7, 8, 10, and even 12 voices in his great collection *Magnum opus musicam*. Perhaps the best example of his poetic, lively style of motet writing is his *Alme Deus,* written originally to secular words. He wrote also a number of Masses and settings of psalms. Especially effective are his settings of the seven so-called "Penitential Psalms," filled as they are with the deep anguish of his soul.

FRENCH REFORMATION MUSIC

A peculiar outgrowth of the Renaissance influence in France was the production of Protestant religious music which followed the break with the established church. We shall see in our discussion of the Renaissance in Germany what a tremendous influence the Reformation had on the development of music there: Luther gave a great deal of time and attention to its cultivation for his new ritual. But the Protestant leaders in the other countries were not so artistically minded. Zwingli excluded music entirely from the services of his church, and Calvin limited it to the unisonal singing of psalms, thus, as he believed, emulating the ancient Hebrews in excluding all secular and human elements from the worship of the church. In France, where the Calvinistic movement gained considerable headway, two poets of the time—which, in general, was an exceedingly prolific one for French poetry—furnished metrical translations for these psalm settings favored by the Genevan reformer: Clément Marot, previously given to writings of a decidedly frivolous nature, and Théodore Beza. The musical settings were largely the work of Claude Goudimel, who during his early life had set many a Catholic Mass to music (but who gave up his life in defense of his new faith in the massacres following St. Bartholomew), as well as of Claude le Jeune, who likewise wrote a great deal of secular music.

For the actual church service these men wrote an adaptation of what was known as the *chanson mesurée,* secular songs composed according to the strict requirements of verse, their syllables being sung simultaneously by all voices. There resulted a simple sort of four-part chordal harmony, built around a melody placed in the tenor. Except for this latter fact, these Huguenot psalm settings sound very familiar to modern ears, their syllabic treatment of the words and general style being that known to generations of singers of Anglican hymns or Presbyterian psalms. These simple settings were the only ones allowed by

Calvin in his church, and Goudimel and Le Jeune composed a great number of them, some of which are still to be found in our hymn books.

But even Calvinism could not entirely discourage the love for artistry which had been fostered by the current ideals of the *cinquecento*. The French Protestant composers realized that it was not enough to write music for the faithful in order to direct their minds and thought toward higher things. It was necessary also to furnish music which could be sung with some of the aesthetic pleasure and sense of satisfaction that was to be derived from the other arts of the time. And so they produced another type of music, using a much more elaborate style and requiring greater skill in its execution—music not to be sung in church, as Goudimel said, but for the praise of God in the home. These richly polyphonic settings seem to take on an added impulse of freedom and suggestion of artistry from their increased movements. One or another of the parts takes little flights around the voice which holds the melody. Nothing is overdone; and all is charming, simple, and seemly, as befitted the spirit of Calvinistic reform.

INSTRUMENTAL MUSIC AND DANCES

The lute music of the sixteenth century may be regarded as the first really independent instrumental music. We have observed that the instrument was very popular during this period, and it was natural that an independent type of music was developed for it alone. This was done, as we shall see, in Spain; but its use spread rapidly to every other country. All Europe during the sixteenth century seemed seized with a desire to play the lute. France, with its cultivation of all the luxuries of the world, was no exception, and its lute music possesses a delicate refinement that sets it off from the rest. Attaignant published (1529) the first book of lute music, *Dix-huit basses danses,* and this was quickly followed by others, notably by John Baptiste Besard's *Thesaurus harmonicus,* containing original and arranged works by all the great lutenists of the time. The lute style reached its culmination in France in the seventeenth century, when Gaultier published a series of pieces which exhausted the instrument's possibilities, combining all the rhythmic and melodic effects of which it was capable.

In 1589 a priest in Langres, writing under the pseudonym of Thoinot Arbeau, published a celebrated treatise on dancing, the *Orchésographie,* which gave not only the description of the various steps then in vogue but likewise a notation of the different tunes to which they were danced. Many of these tunes were played on the lute, others on various sorts of brass, wood-wind, and string instruments. About the middle of the century, a troupe of Italian violinists came to Paris and established themselves in the favor of the French court; this troupe came to be known later as the *vingt-quatre violons du Roy,* the most famous dance band in history. From that time, all the court dance music was played by orchestras of bowed instruments, another instance of the Italian shaping of French taste.

The most popular of these sixteenth-century dances[3] seems to have been the *basse danse,*[4] its graceful steps being danced by two people. Always associated with this was the *tordion,* an "after-dance" contrasting in rhythm and style and marked by leaping jumps. Another popular dance was the *pavan,* with its pendant *galliard.* The "steps of the *pavan* and the *basse danse* are slow and heavy, those of the *galliard* and *tordion* light and graceful," says the *Orchésographie.* The *branles* were lively round dances executed by a whole ring of dancers, circling first one way around and then the other, and gradually increasing in speed. These were often gathered into suites of *branles,* made up of sets of varying liveliness. There was also the lively *canaries,* with its tapped effects; and processional *marches* also came into the dance category.

France's great role in the development of music and art during the sixteenth and seventeenth centuries was that of cultivating what she had received in such great abundance from her meridional neighbor, impressing this music and art with the peculiar grace and charm, the clarity and balance that we have come to recognize as peculiarly her own.

---

[3] At the present time it would seem that the oldest printed book on the dance is the copy of an anonymous treatise, *L'Art et instruction de bien danser basse danse* (now in possession of the Royal College of Physicians, London), originally published by Michel Toulouze at the sign of *La Corne du cerf,* Paris, probably as early as 1496. This is now issued in a modern reprint, as is another pamphlet of about the same time, *The manner of dancing of bace dances after the use of France and other places, translated out of the French in English* by Robert Coplande, the original of which is in the Bodleian Library. Both of these are of fascinating interest to students of early music and dances.
[4] The *basse danse* is supposed to owe its name to the gliding motion of the feet that was used, in contrast to the dances in which the feet were lifted from the ground. The name may suggest nothing more than its lowly origin.

The Renaissance in Spain

*Spanish art is wanting in continuity of de-
velopment; its changes are invariably stimulated from without. It would carry us too far
to attempt to explain this lack of initiative
and creative power by racial qualities, by
political history, or by the contempt for the
worker with his hands. Similar phenomena
are seen among the nations that lie at a distance from the main focus of European civilization; they show the same zeal to keep up
with the procession by a prompt adoption of
new methods and inventions, and to keep
step, at least ostensibly, with their more
favorably situated sisters.*

Carl Justi

THE ROOTS OF SPANISH ART

A study of Spain
will ensure the art lover at least one thing—a new leaf in the album
of his experiences," begins a well-known historical sketch of Spanish
architecture, sculpture, and painting. The art lover will be able to
recognize all the familiarities of the Romanesque, Gothic, and Renaissance styles, but with a strange difference; for added to the characteristics of these schools as he knows them in Italy, France, and
Germany are certain traits derived from the creations of the country's
ancient conquerors, the Moors and the Arabs, which give them that
spirit which we can call "Spanish." The Arab taste exerted a strong
influence on architecture, modifying the Gothic and Renaissance styles
throughout the country. The native feeling for plastic art was strongly
touched with it, and it was combined with Italian, French, and even
German ideals in various parts of the peninsula. Spanish painting,
grounded securely on an Italian-Flemish foundation, owes its peculiar
genius for fiery energy and truthful realism to this distinctive blend of
racial qualities.

As in the other European countries, Spanish art has been inextricably
bound up with the political history of the empire. The story is quickly

told, being largely one of a few powerful, and not particularly brilliant, monarchs. The sixteenth century was the great epoch of Spanish history, an epoch that opened in 1469 with the marriage of Ferdinand and Isabella and the consequent union of the kingdoms of Castile and Aragon. Thus was laid the foundation for what might have been the world's most powerful kingdom; but the expulsion of the Jews and the Moors—the two most useful and enterprising races of the country—made such an eventuality impossible, in spite of Spain's discovery of America and the consequent opening-up of undreamed resources and wealth.

The outlook of the Isabelline artists was purely Gothic, as the churches, sculpture, and painting of the time show clearly enough. Mixed with this Gothic taste was a love for fantastic splendor and elaborate design, which we have spoken of as derived from the Arabs. In 1516 the Hapsburg, Charles v, became emperor and reigned over Spain for a period of forty years, conquering in that time Mexico, Peru, Chile, and Tunis and extending the Spanish borders until they included a good part of the Old World as well as most of the New World. It was during this apogee of Spanish power that the ideals and principles of Italian Renaissance art began to be felt in the land; beginning with the brilliant *plateresque* sculpture and architecture, which was Gothic in form and Renaissance in detail, this Italian influence made itself felt in all parts of the country, achieving notable results in painting, literature, and music.

The cause for the rapid decline from these dizzy heights of political and material power has been suggested—the unreasoning bigotry and stupidity of an iron-handed tyrant, who tried to stay the progress of thought and the natural evolution of the ideas originating with the Renaissance. The religious controversies were bad enough; but in their wake came the destruction of the great Armada that was to have stood as the symbol of Spanish mastery of the seas, the loss of Portugal, and the insurrections at home in Catalonia. Before a century was out, the once proud empire was permanently crippled and forever doomed.

Because of this brief, dazzling flash of power and riches, her romantic history, and her remarkable ethnological constituency—made up as it was of Iberians, Celts, Basques, Goths, Arabs, Moors, and Jews—Spain was able to achieve an influential position in the history of art. Not only did she produce some of its greatest men, such as Velásquez, Cervantes, and Victoria, but, as modern research is beginning to show, her contact with Asia during the Middle Ages was far more direct than that of any other nation and profoundly influenced all European art.

THE MAIN DOORWAY OF THE COLEGIO DE SAN GREGORIO   A fine example of
Spanish plateresque architecture, the college was built in Valladolid during the sixteenth
century.

SPAIN'S PLACE IN MUSIC

The first that we hear of music in Spain is in connection with dancing, which has always been one of the country's chief amusements. Martial, an early writer, described the castanetted rhythms of the dances of Cádiz as being "wild and lascivious." Dances and danceable music may be said to have constituted the dominant influence in Spanish music up to the fifteenth century; as a matter of fact, dances such as Martial described may still be seen in the mountainous regions of Andalusia in the south, their rhythms persuasively conveyed by the Moorish gypsies.

But the Moors left behind them more important evidences of a musical culture than merely rhythms. We have shown in the section on the music of the troubadours how the latest Spanish research on the subject indicates that Spain received with open arms and developed to a point of great beauty the Arabic music brought in at the time of the invasion of the Moors.[5] In the universities founded by the far-seeing Moorish princes of Granada, musical theory was made the subject of profound study, the result being that the peculiar melodic physiognomy of this Arabic music left a profound influence on the folk music of Spain. It is difficult for modern musicians to realize what an enormous amount of this didactic literature was produced by these Spanish pedagogues, a literature which was based not on the ideas that other medieval writers had developed from their study of Greek theory, but which was entirely different, being influenced by medieval Arabic forms and enriched through practice.

This gave Spanish music from an early period a rhythmic and melodic character which it otherwise would not have possessed. Some of this literature was devoted to the plainchant, some to instrumental music, its express purpose being that of the practical training of pupils in all branches of the art. It was one of these Spanish theorists who, around 1480, conceived the idea of tempering the twelve semitones of the scale, one of the foundation stones upon which the system of modern music has been erected.[6] Another, in 1565, wrote a method for teach-

[5] The greatest collection of these Arabic tunes extant is that made by Alfonso the Wise at the end of the thirteenth century, *Las Cantigas*. Formerly supposed to have been influenced by the troubadours, Ribera interprets them as corresponding to the lyric and rhythmic system of the Spanish Moors and says that they were probably set down by a Moorish musician employed by Alfonso.

[6] In this connection it is necessary to remember that during the course of music's development there have been a number of varying schemes for arranging sounds into the

ing the playing of keyboard instruments, giving fingering and other similar details. In 1553, Diego Ortiz, *Kapellmeister* to the Duke of Alba, published a course in the forming of variations over a given bass, this being the popular way of improvising music for the court dances of the time.

That the sixteenth-century Spanish educators in music were familiar enough with the work of their European predecessors and confreres is evident from such a treatise as that of Fernando Esteban, which includes quotations from such representative non-Spanish composers as Philippe de Vitry, Guillaume de Machaut, Dunstable, Dufay, and Ockeghem. The Spaniards studied this counterpoint assiduously and were thoroughly conversant with all the details of its craftsmanship, a fact that can be proved by a look at their works. But their background made them more interested in preserving the poetic value of their texts than were the writers of France and Italy, who did not seem particularly concerned when the meaning of the words they set became entirely lost through the intricate and involved weaving of the parts. In the Spanish *romances* and *villancicos,* the two forms most popular in the sixteenth century, the composers achieved a happy blend of the craftsmanship of the scholastics and the individual flavor and characteristic features of the popular Arabian and Moorish music. Dr. Sachs has expressed it thus: when the composers of one of these sixteenth-century works contemplated the words of a romance recounting the exploits of that glorious past that is undying in the memory of every Spaniard, or of a lyric *villancico* containing a poetic idea many times repeated, he seemed to forget all about the bounds imposed by strict polyphony. Fired by the spirit of the words, he created a vigorous and almost

most workable order. These have been based on differing acoustical plans adopted as the result of experiments by theorists, which reach as far back as the sixth century B.C., when the Greek Pythagoras first investigated the basic mathematical ratios between the different series of ordered sounds which came to be grouped into the *modea*. It became necessary to modify slightly the intervals making up the various scale patterns, because an interval whose mathematical ratio made it sound perfectly "in tune" in one scale could not be incorporated into another without sounding "out of tune." Hence arose what are known as systems of "temperament,"—that is, means of distributing these inaccuracies, inevitable in any system that is to allow free passage from key to key, so as least to offend the ear. Developing from the Pythagorean system, the chief types of temperament which have been adopted have been (1) "equal temperament," in which only the interval of the octave is exact, all the others being slightly inaccurate, but none so much so as to distress the average ear; (2) "mean tone temperament" (in use from about 1600 to 1800), in which a few intervals are absolutely accurate, the rest not, making it practicable to use some, but not all, keys without distress; (3) "just intonation," in which all the intervals are dead in tune, making passage from one key to another impossible.

entirely independent melody that combined both aristocratic and popular elements.

Thus we have the peculiarly Spanish phenomenon of composers who, having made their bow to European tradition and having written their works in the international three- and four-part forms, lost no time in issuing versions for solo voice, with an accompaniment by a sort of guitar lute known as the *vihuela,* an instrument that was used by high society as well as by the musicians of the lower classes.

Representative composers of secular works during the golden age of Spanish music were Fuenllana, Gonzales, Vasquez (whose charming *villancico, Vos me matasteis,* can well stand as a representative example of the whole period), Pisador (who published a *Libro de musica de vihuela* in 1552), and, above all the others, Antonio de Cabezon, an outstanding composer of clavier music, and Luis Milan, the greatest of all Spanish writers of instrumental music. Milan was the first to write specifically for the *vihuela;* his pieces in the *Libro de musica,* published in 1536, are perfect examples of the virtuosity which marked this sixteenth-century instrumental style. Milan was also a poet, courtier to the Valencian sovereigns, and an outstanding performer on the lute, which, because of its suitability for outdoor use, had secured such a firm hold on Spanish affection.

THE POPULAR LUTE

The most popular of Renaissance instruments, the lute, as employed in Spain, was built like a flat, pear-shaped guitar and had six pairs of strings, tuned a fourth apart. Its tone was not very powerful but was capable of a great delicacy and sweetness of utterance. Its possibilities were limited by the mechanical difficulties of fingering, which made possible only combinations of simple polyphony and detached chords. But its sharp-cut, accented tone emphasized the rhythmic features so characteristic of dance music; thus, while tradition made it an aristocratic instrument, its practical possibilities made it a popular one.

The place which the instrument held in the life of its time[7] may be

---

[7] This instrumental family included members of various sizes, from the large *theorbo* to the small *mandore.* The Spanish lute *(vihuela)* had a body somewhat resembling a modern guitar. It is interesting that Leonardo da Vinci, going to the court of Milan in 1482, was known as a musician as well as a painter and that he took with him at that time a silver lute of his own making, shaped like the head of a horse. Marsilio Ficino, the famous humanist scholar, died, according to tradition, with his lute in his hands.

gathered from a seventeenth-century description, *A Recreative Praeledium to the Lute Part of Musick's Monument, or a Remembrancer of the Best Practical Musick both divine and civil that has even been known to have been in the world*, by Thomas Mace:

Beloved Reader, you must know,
*   That Lutes could Speak ere you could so;*
There has been Times when They have been
Dicoursers unto King and Queen;
To Nobles and the Highest Peers;
And Free Access had to Their Ears
Familiarly; scarce pass'd a Day
They would not Hear what Lute would say:
But sure at Night, though in their Bed,
They'd Listen well what then She said.
*   She has Discourses so sublime,*
No language yet in Any Time
Had Words sufficient to define
Her Choice Expressions so Divine
*   Her Matters of such High Concern*
No Common Folks can It discern
'Twas ne'er intended for the Rude
And Boisterous—Churlish—Multitude;
But for Those Choice-Refined-Spirits
Which Heav'nly Rapture oft Inherits.
(See pictures, pages 201, 246.)

Milan's great lute fantasias, which he called *pavanes,* are perhaps the greatest music ever written for the instrument. Taking their general form from the Italian dance, they strongly suggest the romantic fire and earnest sincerity that are typical of the best Spanish art.

CABEZON

The beginning of the sixteenth century shows efforts on the part of the composers in all countries to experiment with instrumental contrapuntal music; but none of them can compare in actual artistic results with the Spaniards. Outstanding among the writers of clavier music was the blind musician Cabezon, whose works were collected and edited by his son, under the title *Obras de musica.* This collection, published in 1578, some years after the death of the composer whose name it bears, is one of the most significant works of Spain's golden age in music. It contains a number of pieces for *tecla* (keyboard instruments), as well as others for the harp and *vihuela,* some of them playable interchangeably on all these instruments. There are also contrapuntal pieces invented or written over liturgical melodies, variations, and *tientos* (toccatas).

"No one who seriously studies the works of Cabezon is likely to feel that any praise of him is exaggerated. To associate him with Bach signifies more than the expression of an unconsidered admiration. It points to an inner relationship that links the Spanish master more closely to the great German than perhaps to any other musician. In any event, I know of no one among the clavier and organ composers of all time who, by reason of musical spontaneity, profundity, and exalted seriousness of purpose, austerity and sublimity of thought, and —last but not least—complete contrapuntal mastery, more properly belongs in his company" (Willi Apel: *Musical Quarterly*).

MORALES AND VICTORIA

The other great names in Spanish Renaissance music are Cristobal Morales, born in Seville about 1512, and Tomás Luis de Victoria, born about 1540. Both these men wrote church music and lived their productive years during the time of the Spanish ascendancy. Their art shows little of either Gothic or Moorish influence, being strongly Renaissance in its character; yet it cannot be said that there is nothing Spanish about it. Both men were influenced by their surroundings, just as was El Greco, the Greek artist who lived in Spain and whose paintings may be said to express the essence of Spanish character. All these men studied and absorbed the European technical methods of their predecessors. The point is that they were able to feel like Spaniards. No one who has heard even such a short work as Victoria's sublime motet *O vos omnes* could ever mistake his style for that of one of his Italian contemporaries, any more than he could think of El Greco's super-religious combinations of asceticism and ecstasy as being anything but intensely Spanish.

Victoria felt that music should be devoted entirely to the aim and end for which it was originally intended—"the praise and glory of God"; and he carried out this ideal to such an extent that he refused altogether to write secular music. In this respect it is important to remember that the Renaissance did not have the same freeing influence in Spain as it had in the other countries of Europe. Racially conscious and integrated to an almost unbelievable degree after his long fights against the Moor and the consequent saving of Europe for the Chris-

THE DEAD CHRIST by El Greco

tian religion, the sixteenth-century Spaniard felt himself a man chosen of God for the special purpose of upholding his true religion.

Consequently, there could be none of the questioning of faith that occurred in the other countries, a fact which explains much of the ardor and fire of Victoria's music and of El Greco's painting. The Spanish at the time of the Renaissance still maintained the medieval conception that this world is a mere interlude between birth and a glorious, all-important afterlife. Their whole point of view regarding art and life was that of loyal allegiance to the Church, their strong, burning faith feeding their natural ardor and increasing their native intensity.

Critics speak of El Greco as a painter whose temperament was un-usually sympathetic to the religious ecstasy of sixteenth-century Spain. There is a peculiar quality about his composition, an excitement and intensity about his method of depicting light, an ability to make us feel that his figures defy all natural and materialistic laws, that give his pictures their atmosphere of mysticism. "Where painting touches upon the ecstatic and the supernal," says Cheney, "El Greco is master above all others."

The same may be said regarding Victoria. In Rome, where he seems to have spent much time, he came into contact with the other great musical giants of the period; but he remained true to his national feeling and continued to incorporate into his music the fiery mysticism that was so characteristic of the Spanish soul. In all his piquant settings we hear a strong personal conviction, as well as his national temperament. It is as if he had been able to catch the elevated thought and devout mysticism of his contemporary, Palestrina, and infuse into them his own passionate nature. He wrote extensively in all religious forms, and his works should be much better known today than they are; only occasionally do we have opportunity of hearing them, even in the service music of the Church. A more intimate study would convince us that we have in these sixteenth-century composers, Palestrina and Victoria, two companion figures such as are so familiar to us in the eighteenth-century Bach and Handel.

The Renaissance in England

They have no fancy, and never are surprised into a covert or witty word . . . but they delight in strong earthy expression, not mistakable. . . . This homeliness, veracity, and plain style . . . imparts into songs and ballads the smell of the earth, the breath of cattle and, like a Dutch painter, seeks a household charm, though by pails and pans.

Emerson on the English

ELIZABETHAN ENGLAND

It was the sixteenth century that saw the development of England from a medieval city-state into the beginnings of a great world power. The twenty-four-year reign of Henry VII, marked as it was by careful thrift and hard toil, did much to repair the ravages of the preceding century and lay the foundation for the glories to come. Under a series of rulers remarkable

KING HENRY VIII—
artist unknown (Head
from Holbein's portrait)

for their individuality rather than for their ability—Henry VIII, a strange combination of artistic ability, intellectual shrewdness, and bestial vitality; Mary Tudor, an embittered woman whose devotion to her Catholic faith brought the country to the brink of revolution; Elizabeth, a clear-headed, unscrupulous ruler who was able to maintain herself for so long a period by "meeting the extremes around her with her own extremes of cunning and prevarication"—these hundred years are exceedingly important in English history. During them England's trade and seamanship, her learning, literature, art, and music developed enormously; moreover, taking whatever she needed from the various elements of the European Renaissance, England was able at this time to produce literature, music, even a church that were peculiarly her own and that reflected her characteristics. Everything at the time tended to increase this feeling of independence and insularity in the growing empire. The development of the language, the establishment of a fleet that was able to command the mastery of the seas, the successful break with Rome and the consequent establishment of the Church of England—all contributed toward the fostering of that confident self-esteem which has remained until this day one of the country's most striking characteristics.

Shakespeare, born in 1564, only six years after the accession of Elizabeth, and therefore a typical Elizabethan, puts it thus:

This royal throne of kings, this sceptr'd isle,
This earth of majesty, this seat of Mars,
This other Eden, demiparadise;
This fortress built by Nature for herself
Against infection and the hand of war;
This happy breed of men, this little world;
This precious stone set in the silver sea,
Which serves it in the office of a wall,
Or as a moat defensive to a house,
Against the envy of less happier lands;
This blessed plot, this earth, this realm, this
    England.

That this was the spirit of the era and not a mere megalomaniac embroidering of language by a poet may be gathered from a contemporary passage from the *Memoires des sages et royales Œconomies d'Estat de Henry le Grand,* written by Sully, the powerful minister of that famous French king, in the early years of the seventeenth century:

It is certain that the English detest us with a hatred so strong and widespread that one is tempted to regard it as one of the inborn characteristics of that people. More truthfully, it is the outcome of their pride and presumption, there being no people in Europe more haughty, more disdainful, more intoxicated with the notion of their own excellence. If they are to be believed, reason and wit exist only amongst themselves; they worship all their own opinions and scorn those of other nations; nor does it ever occur to them to listen to others or to question their own. Actually this characteristic harms them more than it does us. It places them at the mercy of all their fancies. Ringed by the sea, they may be said to have acquired all its instability.

THE REAL CULTURE OF THE ENGLISH

A retrospective and perhaps more unbiased glance at the England of that period suggests that her people may have had good reason for this "pride and presumption." London, the center of the country then as now, was already a city of some three hundred thousand souls, with well-laid-out streets, an important money exchange, many permanent theaters, and a well-functioning educational system. The city was thronging with business and vibrant with pleasure; the country was becoming dotted with large and comfortable manor houses, built in a peculiar blend of Gothic and Renaissance forms; the average educational level was high: both men and women read Latin poets, studied mathematics and science, composed and sang music.

An accurate picture of the times is given by Morley in his *Plaine and Easie Introduction to Practicall Musicke* (1597):

> *Supper being ended and Musicke bookes, according to the custome, being brought to the table, the mistresse of the house presented me with a part, earnestly requesting me to sing; but when, after many excuses, I protested unfainedly that I could not, every one began to wonder, some whispering to others, demanding how I was brought up.*

London was a center of culture, which, while it followed the general ideals of its Renaissance archetypes, became essentially national. The court and its circle read the poems of Philip Sidney, Thomas Wyatt, Edmund Spenser, and Christopher Marlowe—all of them obviously patterned after Italian Renaissance models, yet as English in their fresh spontaneity and peculiar imagery as the Sussex downs or the chalk cliffs of Dover. The plays of Shakespeare and Marlowe, although they used themes common to the time and sounded its general sensibilities, can hardly be thought of as being anything but English. And while the influence of foreign models is strongly shown in the music of the sixteenth century, in no other art did the native craftsmen achieve more notable success in establishing a characteristic style of national expression.

ENGLISH MADRIGALS

The madrigals of the Elizabethan Age, the fairest musical treasure England possesses, are copied clearly enough after Italian models, as regards both their contrapuntal intricacy and their harmonic simplicity. Tradition has it that Nicholas Yonge, a singer in the choir of St. Paul's Cathedral, London, first introduced the Italian madrigal into England. He published a collection of these foreign imports translated into English in 1588 and another in 1597. It was Thomas Morley who imitated in England the *balletti per cantare, sonare e ballare* (ballets for singing, playing, and dancing) of the Italian Gastoldi.

The English madrigal composers—Morley, Dowland, Byrd, and the

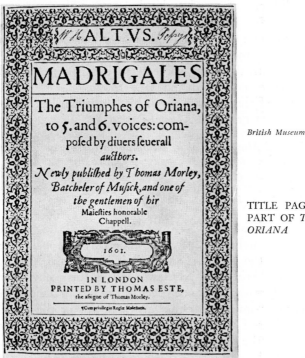

TITLE PAGE OF THE ALTUS
PART OF *THE TRIUMPHES OF
ORIANA*

rest—were able to infuse into their compositions a certain robustness
and straight-forwardness, as well as a sweetness, freshness, and humor,
that mark them as characteristically English. Called by various names
—ballet (having a strong rhythm, infectious melody, and a fa-la refrain), canzonet, song, and ayre—these English madrigals were sung
and played during the late sixteenth and early seventeenth centuries.
They were generally published as separate part books and sung by
small groups of amateurs seated about a table. The singers employed a
wide latitude of interpretation and presentation, often supplying missing vocal parts by means of instruments and embroidering the written
melodies with various kinds of improvised ornamentations. Set by
brilliant and versatile composers to a splendid lot of lyric poetry that
had been written during this golden age of English literature, it is no
wonder that the madrigal in England achieved such an astounding
perfection and popular success.

The madrigal was but one of the many forms in which William
Byrd (1542–1623), organist of Lincoln Cathedral and Elizabeth's

Chapel Royal, was completely at home. Thomas Morley (1557–*c.* 1603), who may well have been a friend of Shakespeare since he wrote certain songs for the Bard's plays, devoted a great deal of attention to graceful ballets. Perhaps the greatest master of the whole English madrigal school was John Wilbye (1574–1638), resident from his twenty-first year at one of the great Elizabethan country houses, Hengrave Hall in Suffolk; his sixty-five works in this form may be said to represent the madrigal, both in the British and foreign types, at its very best. Thomas Weelkes (*c.* 1575–1623), organist of Chichester Cathedral, ranks next to Wilbye as a madrigalist according to present-day estimates. Orlando Gibbons (1583–1625), organist of Westminster Abbey, together with his contemporaries John Ward and Thomas Tomkins, foreshadows the end of the madrigal style in his superb *The Silver Swan,* considered by many to be the loveliest thing of its kind ever written.

The most important collection of English madrigals was *The Triumphs of Oriana,* a collection made in honor of Queen Elizabeth by twenty-three different composers under the editorship of Thomas Morley. In obvious imitation of an earlier Italian set of similar character which had appeared in Venice, each of the compositions in this collection ends with the rather fulsome phrase, *Long live fair Oriana,* in homage to the queen. The best-known of these Oriana madrigals is probably Weelkes's *As Vesta Was from Latmos Hill Descending.*

ECCLESIASTICAL MUSIC

The English church music of this time was affected by the constantly changing religious complexions of the different monarchs. When Henry VIII made up his mind to have a national church of his own entirely outside the pale of the papacy, it became necessary to adopt the creed and the ritual of the Established Church to fit the needs of the national one. Christopher Tye and Thomas Tallis happened to be the leading composers at the time and so were entrusted with the task of modifying the chants and composing the "anthems" for the new rite. With Henry's son and successor, Edward VI, there came a definite Protestant reaction. Mary Tudor, daughter of Henry, who succeeded to the throne on the early death of Edward, was a Catholic and took constant opportunity to force her ideals on the country. With Elizabeth, her successor, came the final adoption of the Thirty-nine Articles of faith, which, by retaining certain Catholic rites and leaning strongly toward a moderate Protestantism, effected a typically English compromise.

These rapid and constant changes in official belief did not particularly affect the exterior lives of the composers of church music, however. Tallis was a gentleman of the Chapel Royal during the reigns of Henry VIII, Edward VI, Mary Tudor, and Elizabeth and seemed able to write Catholic motets and Protestant anthems with equal ease. Byrd, an ardent member of the Catholic Church, "withoute which I beleeve there is noe salvacon for me," as he wrote in his will, composed a great deal of music for the Anglican services; and so the authorities were content to ignore his personal beliefs. But there is no question that Byrd's best music was written for the church in which he believed so thoroughly; for he felt that there is a "certain hidden power in the thoughts underlying the words themselves, so that as one meditates upon the sacred words and constantly and seriously considers them, the right notes, in some inexplicable fashion, suggest themselves quite spontaneously." His finest work was his great five-part Mass, which, as one English critic claims, is "without a parallel in the whole field of English church music and is only equaled by the highest flights of the greatest masters in other lands."

Before considering the instrumental music of this century in England, it will be well to add a note regarding two aspects of this sixteenth-century choral style that is not well understood by the choirs who today are attempting to sing it. The first is that the modal influence is still strong in this sacred and secular music, but not paramount, so that a curious mixture of key feelings is characteristic. (This is apart from personal traits of the composers, such as Byrd's use of major and minor thirds in conjunction.) The other element has already been mentioned—the rhythmic freedom necessary for an adequate reproduction of the music. As the independent melodic lines were woven together, so were the meters. The performers sang from music which had each part printed on a separate line, without bars, or a bar line was put in merely to clarify some point of accent. One singer did not see the other parts; only his own was before him. This demanded much higher reading skill than in a modern part song of equal difficulty, where, if we are getting into a tangle, we can always see what the other parts are doing and have a chance to pick up our place a few bars ahead.

In general, the fitting of words and notes was far purer in madrigalian times, though there were then some differences of word stress

A RENAISSANCE FIVE-PART MADRIGAL   The copper engraving by "L'ouie" indicates that there were parts for voices, lute, and viola da gamba.

in the language. Hence comes the chief technical difficulty in getting singers to perform madrigals really well. They have been so long tied by the leg to bar lines that, like prisoners freed, it is some time before they can enjoy their freedom.

ENGLISH RENAISSANCE MUSIC FOR INSTRUMENTS

Instrumental music was closely associated with choral music during the Renaissance, as we have seen; it was often used for accompanying the voices, the instrumentation following very closely the various vocal parts. If any of the voices happened to be missing, they were actually supplied by various instruments; thus, vocal and instrumental parts were inextricably mingled, and it may be taken for granted that the same work was hardly ever performed twice in the same way.

But gradually the instruments began to live a life of their own; transcriptions of madrigals and dances were made for them; and compositions were written in which they were used to form a prelude, an inter-

VISSCHER'S VIEW

lude, or a finale to vocal works, as well as to supply the accompaniment. The lute did not seem to achieve so great a popularity in England as it did on the Continent; the viol was the instrument largely affected by "gentlemen in privat meetings." Having six strings and played on the knee rather than under the chin, viols were made in all sizes and were kept in sets or "chests" in properly appointed domestic establishments of the time. Tastes varied as to the sizes of viols that made up these chests; but there were usually six of them: two basses, two tenors, and two trebles, "all truly and proportionately suited."

It may be said, in general, that the music used for these families of instruments, called "consort music" (a mixed collection of instruments being known as a "broken consort"), was essentially transplanted vocal music. The favorite form of viol consort music was the fantasy or "fancy," a sort of instrumental madrigal in which one instrument after another takes up the principal melody, all of them being engaged in making a real contrapuntal contribution to the whole. There was no attempt to provide strong contrasts between sections, as was done in the instrumental suites based on popular dance tunes; the "fancy" composers were content to work toward a cumulative climax, as did the fugue writers a century later. Thomas Morley, in his *Plaine and Easie Introduction to Practicall Musicke*, describes the earliest type of "fancy": "When a musician taketh a point at his pleasure, and wresteth and turneth it as he list, making either much or little of it according as shall seeme best in his own conceit. In this way more art

Courtesy of Folger Library, Washington

OF LONDON, 1616

be showne than in any other musicke, except changing the ayre and leaving the key, which in fantasy may never be suffered."

One of the special types of fantasy was the *In Nomine,* which was based on a definite cantus firmus:

It would appear that the title was in the nature of a dedication, rather than having any definite association with the Benedictus of a Mass, in which the Latin words of the title occur. This theme, at any rate, was very popular among English composers, just as was, for example, *L'Homme arme* with the Flemish. Literally hundreds of these fantasies were written by the English composers of this century, the most notable being those by William Byrd and Thomas Weelkes. Music for the broken consort, combinations of viols, lutes, flutes, and so on, did not become popular in England until the early part of the next century, when such collections as Morley's *First Book of Consort Lessons* (1611) began to appear.

England's great contribution to the development of instrumental music was made in the type of music written for keyboard instruments. Organs and harpsichords were the favorite instruments at the court of Henry VIII, who himself was able to play well on the lute and harpsichord and sing from book at sight, as well as draw the best bow in England and joust marvelously, according to contemporary description.

WOMAN PLAYING THE CLAVICHORD by Jan Van Hemessen It has been suggested that this is a portrait of Eleanor of Portugal, sister of Emperor Charles v. It is obvious from this and other pictures of the time that the playing technique of the Renaissance was quite different from that of today!

We get an intimate picture of the position of music in sixteenth-century England from some of the dispatches sent home by Sebastiano Giustiniani, an ambassador of the seigniory of Venice to Henry's court, and quoted in Rawdon Brown's translation *Four Years at the Court of Henry VIII*. Describing some of the May Day festivities at Greenwich Palace, the writer tells how the king went to dinner, and "by his Majesty's order, the ambassadors, and we likewise, dined in his palace, with the chief nobility of this land. After dinner the ambassadors were taken into certain chambers containing a number of organs and harpsichords and flutes and other instruments, and where the prelates and chief nobles were assembled to see the joust which was then in preparation; and in the meantime the ambassadors told some of these grandees that I was proficient on some of these instruments; so they asked me to play, and knowing that I could not refuse, I did so for a long while, both on the harpsichords and organs, and really bore myself bravely, and was listened to with great attention. . . . The prelates who were present told me that the king would certainly choose to hear me, as his Majesty practices on these instruments day and night, and that he will very much like my playing."

Later on, a friar, Dionisius Memo, who was organist of St. Mark's, Venice, came over to London; Giustiniani sent word of his visit to Venice and described his arrival "with a most excellent instrument of his, which he has brought hither with much pains and costs. I presented him in the first place to the Cardinal, telling him that when your Highness heard of his wanting to quit Venice for the purpose of coming to his Majesty, you gave him gracious leave, which you would not have done had he intended going anywhere else. His Lordship chose to hear him in the presence of many lords and *virtuosi,* who were as pleased as possible with him; after which his right reverend Lordship told him to go to the King, who would see him very willingly, employing many words of flattering commendation. He afterwards went to his Majesty, who, knowing he was there, sent for him immediately after dinner, and made him play before a great number of lords and all his *virtuosi.* He played not merely to the satisfaction, but to the incredible admiration and pleasure of everybody, and especially of his Majesty, who is extremely skilled in music, and of the two Queens [Catherine of Aragon and Margaret of Scotland]. My secretary was also present, who highly extolled the performance, and told the King many things in his praise as it went on, mentioning how much favor he enjoyed with your Highness and all Venice, which had been content to deprive itself for the satisfaction of his Majesty, with many other very suitable words, so that said Majesty has included him among his instrumental musicians, nay, has appointed him their chief, and says that he will write to Rome to have him unfrocked out of his monastic weeds, so that he may merely retain holy orders, and that he will make him his chaplain."

Fortunately for us, a collection of organ music of this time has survived, one belonging to a master of the choir at St. Paul's, London, during the reign of Mary Tudor, daughter of Henry VIII; and so we have a good idea of what the music sounded like which these composers wrote for organ and harpsichord. There are over a hundred compositions in the collection, many of them obvious transcriptions of vocal motets and madrigals; others are manipulations of chant melodies, some of them in purely vocal style, as well as a number of *In Nomines.*

KEYBOARD INSTRUMENTS AND THEIR MUSIC

There were two general kinds of keyboard stringed instruments in use at this time: the struck type (clavichord) and the plucked type (harpsichord, spinet, and virginal). It is impossible to determine which of these was developed first; both were in use until after the time of Bach. The principle of the clavichord is seen from the painting by Van Hemessen.

The strings, strung from right to left, were struck by brass tangents placed at the end of each key. One string could serve several tangents, since they acted as does the finger on a violin string, stopping off a portion of it, the resulting pitch depending on where the string was hit. The tone of this instrument was tiny, but it was capable of a pleasing *vibrato (bebung)* obtained by moving the finger on the key. Gradations of relative loudness and softness could also be obtained by regulating the force of the stroke of the fingers on the keys.

In the harpsichord type of instrument, the key mechanism actually plucked the string by means of a quill or a leather plectrum set in a "jack." A much louder tone was produced; but it was one that could not be varied except by bringing into action an entirely different set of plectra, actuated by another keyboard. There might also be "stops" which actuated strings sounding octaves above and below the normal pitch.

Of the harpsichord there was an upright form, but the one best known in pictures and paintings is that in which the strings stretched from front to back, after the manner of the modern grand piano. The English *harpsichord* is *clavicembalo* or *cembalo* in Italian and *clavecin* in French. The square instrument, in which the strings were stretched from right to left, was called the *virginal(s)*[8] or *spinet,* the latter term also furnishing the root of various southern European forms of the instrument's name. The virginal(s) was perhaps more popular than the harpsichord in England.

In their wide use, the two forms of the plucked-string keyboard instrument of the Renaissance could be likened to the piano of today, which, it must be remembered, was not invented until 1709. It was the Italian instrument maker Cristofori who first successfully developed the complicated hammer action of the modern piano.

William Byrd, by far the greatest musician of the time in England, richly endowed in his ability to write both sacred and secular and both vocal and instrumental music, was the first composer in any country to develop the real potentialities of these stringed keyboard instru-

[8] The origin of this word is disputed: some authorities dubiously associate it with Elizabeth, the Virgin Queen, who was a great player on the instrument; it may have meant simply an instrument for young ladies, an idea given color by the fact that the first music printed for the instrument in England was called *Parthenia* (Songs for Maidens) and had on its title page a picture of a young lady playing.

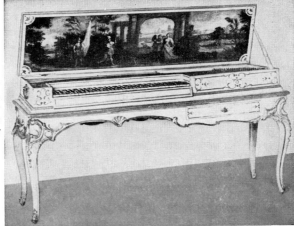

A GERMAN HARP-
SICHORD OF THE
EIGHTEENTH CEN-
TURY, built by the
instrument maker
Christian G. Hubert

ments. Based in general on continental models, Byrd's compositions use all the forms then current, but in such a manner as to make them characteristically English. Typical of one sort is his little suite which he called *The Earl of Salisbury,* made up of two of the court dances, a pavan and a galliard, published in the first book of keyboard music ever to be printed in England—*Parthenia or The Maydenhead of the first musicke that ever was printed for the Virginalls, composed by three famous Masters, William Byrd, Dr. John Bull, and Orlando Gibbons, Gentilmen of his Majesties most Illustrious Chappell.*

Byrd and Bull, the latter nicknamed the "wildly whirling," wrote many sets of variations, one of the earliest purely instrumental forms which did not imitate in any sense the polyphonic vocal style of writing. There is a plausible story that this form originated with the Spanish composers and was brought to England during the time of Mary Tudor, whose husband was Philip of Spain, thus naturally bringing the two countries into very close touch with each other. These variations began with a simple tune, which was played through a number of times; only, instead of making the repetition exact, the composer or player added a few ornaments made up of passage work and instrumental figures, or he even made some changes in the tune for the pure pleasure of "falsifying the expectation of his own ear." Byrd and Bull were not content with merely mechanical variations but infused a poetic idea or program into a few of their pieces. Byrd's *The Bells* and his variation on *The Carman's Whistle* are good examples of this, each of them using a poetic conceit as the basis for our interest in the music, and each working up the interest in the variations until a climax is reached. Farnaby's *The New Sa-Hoo,* on the other hand, is an example of the variation form used without a poetic program; it is simply the manipulation or "paraphrase" of a well-known Dutch tune of the time.

Of a slightly different nature was another order of variated piece which built on a ground bass *(basso ostinato),* a form much cultivated later, notably as the "passacaglia" famous from Bach's and Brahms's treatments. The name explains the idea: a brief theme is often repeated, usually in the bass, while upper parts weave music about it. The style derived from a vocal form of three centuries earlier.

Such short numbers as Farnaby's *A Toye, His Dreame,* and *His Rest* and Peerson's *The Fall of the Leafe* show these early English virginalists searching for expressive possibilities in the new technique they were developing for their instrument. These were early predecessors of the "piano poems," which became so popular later on and were written by hundreds of composers from Schumann to Debussy. All these works mentioned are, as we might expect, short and simple in form, for the matter of lengthy development of ideas had not yet been thought of.

Still other forms used by these early instrumental writers were the descriptive piece, such as Byrd's *The Battle,* copied from Jannequin's famous *Battle of Marignan* and attempting to produce on the instrument the same rather futile imitations of trumpets, drums, war noises, and so forth; and the *Divisions on a Ground,* consisting of a florid embellishment of a short bass tune. Norcome's *Divisions for Lute and Viol* is a good example. Byrd's *The Bells,* already mentioned, is interesting in that it is a combination of three of these early styles, for it is written over a short ground bass of two notes and is a series of nine variations, each of them vividly descriptive of the pealing of various types of bells, large and small.

It was customary to make collections of these pieces, and most of our direct knowledge of the English instrumental music of these Renaissance centuries comes from such anthologies. Some of these were in manuscript, such as *The Fitzwilliam Virginal Book* (containing, besides English compositions, arrangements of music by prominent continental composers), *Benjamin Cosyn's Virginal Book, My Lady Nevells Booke* (all of whose forty works are by Byrd); others were printed, such as the *Parthenia.* The publisher of the latter dedicated the work to Elizabeth, daughter of James I, then king, the same Elizabeth who later became the wife of the "Most High and Mighty and

Magnificent Prince Frederick, Elector Palatine of the Reine," and progenitor of the present reigning house of England. This publisher begs
Elizabeth to remember that if she (who was a pupil of Byrd's) will
only vouchsafe her "white hands," the music "will arrive with more
pleasure at ye princely ears of your Grete Fredericke."

LUTE SONGS

There remains to be said a word regarding the lute songs that were
so popular in England in the palmy days of her music-making, adaptations of the Spanish type of *romances* and *villancicos,* collections of
which were published in Spain as early as 1536. Similar books appeared
in England, the form reaching its height in the lute songs of John
Dowland, a cosmopolitan Englishman, who traveled all over Europe
making his music known. These solo songs were really madrigals of a
simple type, the melody of which was capable of being sung by a solo
voice, while a lute, usually played by the singer, supplied the other
parts. In Dowland's collections, published in the early part of the
seventeenth century, optional choral parts were provided, so that if
desired the accompanying instrument or instruments could be dis-
pensed with, and purely vocal renditions given. The lute was often
reinforced by some instrument with more sustaining power, such as
the viola da gamba. The lute songs were extremely popular in their
day. A contemporary readily admits "prick song [contrapuntal music]
to be a faire musicke, so it be done upon the booke surely and after a
good sorte. But to sing to the lute is much better, because all sweetness
consisteth in one alone [that is, lies in one solo part]; and singing to
the lute with the dittie (methinke) is more pleasant than the rest, for
it addeth to the words such a grace and strength that it is a great
wonder" (Castiglione's *Il cortegiano*). Such "singing with the dittie,"
moreover, greatly strengthened the growing favor of the harmonic over
the polyphonic style and marked the beginning of the solo art song, a
development which in time led to the masterpieces of Schubert, Schumann, and Brahms.

MUSIC AN ESSENTIAL OF LIFE

It is difficult for us today to realize how general was the practice of
music in Renaissance times. In Elizabethan days England was much
more of a common community than she has ever been since: all classes

© *Foto-commissie
Rijksmuseum, Amsterdam*

THE   SERENADE   by
Judith Leyster shows a
typical Renaissance lute.

were brought together in comparatively close contact, family and servants, patrician and plebeian, peer and commoner, city man and country
dweller. The unifying social cement which held together all cultural
life was music, the one thing which all people could enjoy together. As
yet the common majority could read little and write less. The art of
literature did not come into being in England until the end of the
century, when the ability to read and write became more general because of the establishment of the grammar schools. But all the people
knew and practiced music; the leisure time of all classes was taken up
with music and dancing in those pre-radio, pre-television days. The
court had its own instrumental and vocal performers, as we have seen,
king and courtier uniting to make music; the great town and country
houses had their madrigals, both vocal and instrumental; the working

man had his own "neat and spruce ayres, common tunes being known by the boys and working people singing in the streets, among them many excellent and well-contrived," writes Mace. "Every troublesome and laborious occupation useth musicke for solace and recreation; hence it is that manual labourers and mechanical artificers of all sorts keepe such a chaunting and singing in their shoppes—the tailor on his bulk, the shoemaker at his last, the mason at his wall, the ship boy at his oar, and the tinker at his pan."

And these classes mingled rather freely in their music-making; there are many examples in the literature of the period of families playing and singing together with the servants. The traditions of the bards and minstrels were still strong enough to make a talent for music an open sesame to higher degrees of social rank. Fifteenth-century English poets were all of them musicians capable of singing their verses to the lute. Even in the next century, when each of these twin arts began to pursue more of an individual existence, because of the gradual creation of a new order of readers and the growing intricacies of musical style, poems were always written by those whose lives had a musical background. "Hee who cometh with words set in delightfull proportion either accompanied with or prepared for the well inchaunting spell of Musicke" was a poet. The cultured composers of early music for instruments were in the habit of taking popular tunes of the day as themes for their pieces, as Byrd did in his *Carman's Whistle*. Everywhere music was being produced in fact as well as in fancy; England was, indeed, "a nest of singing birds."

It is hardly necessary to dwell on the unfortunate picture that follows: the outbreak of civil war; the strong social influences of Puritanism, with its general scorn for beauty and its austere days of Scripture reading and psalm singing; the importation, after the monarchy had been restored, of foreign music and musicians to please and entertain the people. Gradually music was divorced from the ordinary activities of Englishmen, and these became more and more concerned with the production of material wealth; the cultivation of music drifted into the hands of specialists and professionals, many of them from other countries. As the Industrial Revolution spread its pall of dirty smoke, ugly cities, and social distintegration over the country, the men of one class no longer cared about those of another, either as to how they lived or how they amused themselves. At the height of Victorian prosperity and imperialistic megalomania, music in England was at its lowest ebb. The nest of nightingales had become a blackened ruin, silent amongst the "dark satanic mills."

The Renaissance in Germany

*But for him [Luther] there would have been
no seventeenth century of German competition, and so no Johann Sebastian Bach; from
which it follows that there would have been
no Beethoven, Wagner, or Brahms. For if it
is too much to say, simply and directly, that
all Teutonic art music proceeds from the
Lutheran chorales, it is not too much to say
that all Teutonic art music proceeds from the
sources which the Lutheran chorales first explored and so first made vitally and progressively "popular."*

Eva Mary Grew: *Music & Letters*, January, 1938

GERMANY'S EARLY BACKGROUND   We have become so
accustomed to thinking of Germany as one of the outstanding musical
nations that it is difficult to realize that in the two centuries we have
been considering—the fifteenth and the sixteenth—the art of music in
this country was extremely backward in its flowering in comparison
with its position in Flanders, Italy, Spain, and England. A brief glance
at the country's political development will help to explain it. We have
seen that art seems to flourish best under a rich, powerful, and more or
less centralized form of government, but Renaissance Germany offered
almost exactly the opposite conditions. If we look at a map of the
Europe of 1000 A.D., two centuries after the time of Charlemagne, we
find that what had been the eastern part of his great empire had become broken up into a large number of sections, each of them ruled by
a duke, who was a king in all but name. By the thirteenth century,
St. Louis in France had been able to weld together a real monarchy out
of what had been the western part of Charlemagne's domains; but no
such unification came in Germany until the nineteenth century. In a
political sense, there was no Germany at all during the fifteenth and
sixteenth centuries, only a great number of duchies, held loosely together by a kaiser who played the rather grandiose role of Holy Roman
Emperor, but who in reality, as Voltaire said, was neither holy,
Roman, nor emperor. Each of these independent states and principal-

ities differed greatly from the others, and there was little idea of co-operation or reciprocity among them.

THE LIEDER

That there was unmistakable racial bonds, however, is proved by the large number of *lieder*—contrapuntal compositions corresponding in general character to the *chansons*—that were produced at this time in all parts of Germany, especially in the south.[9] These works, with their wide range of expression from a simple, sincere naïveté to a noble grandeur, are unmistakably German and could have been written by no other people. They filled a deep-rooted need in the people for some sort of simple, straightforward means of expressing their natural romantic feelings, and so became extremely popular. The first collection of these lieder, a manuscript known as the *Lochheimer Liederbuch*, consisting of a number of three-part arrangements, was made in the middle of the fifteenth century. Later many printed collections appeared.

Those who seek the real basis for the later pre-eminence of German music and musicians will find it here in these fifteenth-century and sixteenth-century contrapuntal songs, for they combine a deep sentiment, which arises out of the spirit of the folk, with a method of expression that is robust and strong yet surprisingly effective. The lied was based on a *cantus firmus,* usually taken from one of the old traditional folk melodies. The practice of the composers was to place this in one of the parts and weave about it other voices which, while closely matching its general style and melodic line, at the same time amplified and developed it. Instead of the rather pretentious architecture of the Italian madrigal, we find in these German polyphonic settings a new intensification and enhancement of the spirit of the simple folk song.

As was true of their more elaborate Italian and French parallels, the lieder were mainly love songs; but in such collections as that of the art-loving Nuremberg physician, Georg Forster, who from 1539 to 1556 published no fewer than five anthologies containing nearly four hundred lieder, we find occupational songs, reflective expressions of an ennobling nature, what might be called political songs, and plenty of drinking and convivial songs. Composers sprang up all over Germany; early names, among a large number of unimportant craftsmen, are Von

[9] Strictly translated, the word *lied* means simply "song." Its use, however, is generally restricted to the German-Austrian products of the Romantic era, from about 1780 on. These Renaissance compositions in Germany were an entirely different type of music and must not be confused with the later lieder.

THE EMPEROR MAXIMILIAN by
Burgkmair, 1508

Fulda, Stoltzer, and Finck. Gradually there was formed a sort of school
of these lieder composers, centering in the imperial court of Maximilian
at Innsbruck[10] and the ducal courts at Stuttgart and Munich. The
important men of these groups were Heinrich Isaac (born in Holland,
c. 1450–1517), Ludwig Senfl (*c.* 1492–1555), and Arnold Bruck (*d.*
1545).

The best way to realize the peculiar qualities of these works and how
much they contain of promise for that which was to follow is to study
in some detail a few characteristic examples. Good to begin with are
Isaac's two songs of farewell, probably written on his taking leave of the
Innsbruck court: *Zwischen Berg* ("'Twixt mountain steep and valley
deep the road runs free and wide"), vigorous, proud, and full of hope
for the future; and *Innsbruck, ich muss dich lassen* ("Innsbruck, I
now must leave thee"), filled with a nostalgic longing for the past.
Hofhaimer's sorrowful *Meins traurens ist ursach* ("The reason for my

[10] We possess striking records of the enlightened glories of Maximilian's court in some
treatises written by his own hand, *Sir Teuerdank* and *Der Weisskunig,* as well as in
Dürer's famous series of woodcuts showing various phases of the court life, including its
musical forces.

sorrow") shows the ability of these composers to use a simple, imitative polyphony to enhance the original heartfelt beauty of the German popular song. In such a setting as *Ach Elselein, liebes Elselein,* Senfl combines two well-known folk melodies in a masterly fashion.

GERMANY VERSUS ITALY

But these rather slender expressions of native composers could not hold their own against the strong tide from the south: the latter half of the sixteenth century saw a complete dominance of Italian culture in German life. The knowledge of Italian art developed by the general practice then in vogue—of all German artists spending their apprentice years in Italy—as well as the employment of a great many foreigners, especially musicians, by the German courts, broke through the old barriers and stimulated the imitation of foreign models. The results, however, were never satisfactory. For the German masters, no matter how much they might study Italian styles, never were able to assimilate Italian ways of thinking. They might pay homage to the Renaissance ideals, but they were never able to disguise completely their essentially northern mentality. And they were never fully appreciated by their own people. "How I shall shiver for the sun," wrote Dürer from Venice; "here I am loved, at home I am a parasite."

Albrecht Dürer (1471–1528), the greatest of the German painters, is a case in point: he was pre-eminent not because of his technical methods of composition and coloring, learned from the Italians, but because his genius was great enough for him to express honestly and directly those conceptions which reveal the soul and atmosphere of Germany. His followers, overwhelmed by the popular influence of the Italian art of the time, were never able to advance beyond the point of copying Italian mannerisms. Falling between two stools, their work is of little importance.

What is probably the most important single example of German art of this period stands in St. Sebald's Church in Nuremberg, a city which still gives in its rows of picturesque, high-gabled houses a unique picture of a typical German Renaissance town. In the early years of the sixteenth century the most celebrated German artist in bronze, Peter Vischer, finished here his beautiful shrine in honor of the saint whose name the church bears. Within the architectural framework of the saint's coffin are a number of statuettes which show how strongly the native Germanism of the creator was influenced by Italian ideals. But

THE TOMB OF ST. SE-
BALD, NUREMBERG

even in a master work of this kind there seems to be no real amalgama-
tion of styles: classical deities find themselves in such strange company
as the twelve apostles and the four cardinal Christian virtues.

Music offers an exactly parallel case. Because of the existence of a
number of important foreign figures who sojourned in Germany,
among them Orlando di Lasso, who spent the latter part of his life as
court musician in Munich, and Scandello, who was master of the elec-
toral chapel in Dresden, the Italian influences reigned supreme during
the latter part of the sixteenth century in Germany. It was the fashion
for the art patrons of the time to affect Italian styles; and German composers did their best to furnish what was wanted, attempting to mix
certain Italian ingredients with the native products that had formerly
been so much in favor.

But they were hardly more successful than the artists had been. The works of the sixteenth-century German composers who affected the Italian style, often using Italian words, were not always effectual. Hans Leo Hassler (1564–1612) and Jacob Handl (1550–1591) came nearest to success in their assimilation of Italian models. Hassler was able to combine much of the characteristic German introspection and naïveté with Italian grace and swift charm. Such a simple thing as his little strophically composed *Mein G'müth ist mir verwirret, das macht ein Mägdlein zart* ("A tender maid's the cause of my confusion") is perhaps most typical of this composer, who was a worthy predecessor of Schütz and Bach. We cannot help feeling that he was most successful when he was most German, as in his *Mein Lieb will mit mir kriegen* ("My love would do me battle"). Handl, who became known by the Latin form of his name, Jacobus Gallus, was one of the choristers in the Imperial Hofkapelle and shows the influence of the Venetian choral school in his writing for double choir, his love for all sorts of echo effects, and his bold use of chromatics for expressive purposes. But in general it seems, as a German historian has remarked, that during the last years of the sixteenth century the native blossoms which earlier had flowered so luxuriantly in the native soil and had given real promise of a completely native flora, dried up and withered. The Italian importations and blossoms had an easy conquest.

PAUMANN AND HIS FOLLOWERS

Some fifty years before Vischer and his sons began to erect their monument in St. Sebald's, a blind virtuoso by the name of Conrad Paumann (*d.* 1473) played the organ there. The following lines are taken from a contemporary poem and show Paumann to have been the most remarkable man in the city:

Dass ter ein Meister ob allen Meistern ist . . .
Wollt einen Meister der Kunst man krönen
Er trug dann wohl eine goldne Kron'.

For he is a master above all others . . .
If a master of Art were to be crowned,
It would be he that deserves a golden crown.

This remarkable man was the shining light in the German music of the time; he left behind him a large work with the formidable title *Fundamentum organisandi,* the oldest instruction book on instrumental composition in existence, containing transcriptions of church melodies,

TITLE PAGE OF *SPIE-GEL DER ORGELMA-CHER UND ORGAN-ISTEN* (1511) This woodcut shows how music was played in the German churches of the time.

lieder, and dance tunes for the organ or clavier. (An earlier fragment for organ—the so-called *Robertsbridge Fragment* of the fourteenth century in the British Museum—has already been mentioned. Its main feature is the coloration of the upper voice in a manner suggestive of the later German composers, only much simpler.) The pieces in this anthology of Paumann's show very definitely the peculiar fascination which these German artists found in the decorative and ornamental aspects of Renaissance art. Just as the German architects decorated their façades with such eye-filling features as elaborate doorways, ornamented gables, carved figures, and gay friezes, without ever really assimilating the fundamental principles of Renaissance architectural design, so Paumann and the organists who followed him *kolorierten* (colored) their melodies, overlaying them with superficial ornament without affecting their organic growth. In Germany the organ was developed as a means for aiding such coloration. Schlick's *Spiegel der Orgelmacher und Organisten* (A Mirror of Organbuilders and Organists), published in 1511, tells of the free combining of solo stops to give new tone colors and combinations.

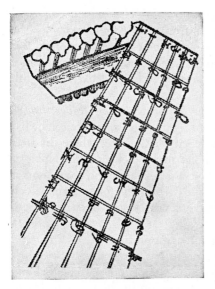

LUTE FINGER BOARD RELATED TO
TABLATURE NOTATION (from *Musica
getutscht*)

ITALIAN TABLATURE (from *Libro
primo d'intavolatura di Chitarrone*)

Tablature can perhaps best be described by saying that it was a system of notation
which told the player not which musical tone he was to think of, but actually just where
he was to put his fingers on his instrument. The staff notation we use was originally
developed for singers and defines relationships of pitch; that is, it shows the singer or
player the pitch distances between the various notes represented on the staff. Tablature,
on the other hand, was a purely mechanical system, showing the player, by various devices, where he was to put his fingers in order to reproduce the music that had been
thought of by the composer. Many sorts of tablature have been invented: these were in
use at different times and in various countries. Some of them are still employed, such as
the guitar tablature of Spain, the mandolin tablature of Naples, and the ukulele tablature
of America.

A page of tablature music, as can be seen from the accompanying illustrations, looks
like a collection of musical staves, with numbers on the lines instead of notes; in lute
music, the lines of the staff represented the strings of the instrument, the figures showing
which fingers should be placed on the frets to produce the notes. The rhythm was
usually indicated by note values placed above the lines.

A number of other instruction books followed, giving both theoretical and practical materials for the use of the musical amateur, who was
beginning to assume an important place in German musical life. These
books (the most famous of them were Virdung's *Musica getutscht,*
1511, and Schlick's *Tabulaturen . . . uff die Orgeln und Lauten*)
make little distinction between music for different instruments, one of
them maintaining that "what you have learnt to play on the lute, you

can easily learn also on harp, psaltery, or viol." The influence of vocal music also is strong in these early instrumental books, many of the pieces being merely ornamented transcriptions of popular motets. But gradually during this period there were worked out the principles of a real instrumental style, principles most effectively used by the English composers.

This early instrumental music, beginning with the *Robertsbridge Fragment,* was written in a system of tablature notation somewhat similar to that which had been developed for the lute, where the frets on the neck of the instrument were designated by letters of the alphabet and several supplementary signs. The organ tablature (used also for other keyed instruments) was likewise written on one stave, which gave the top voice in notes. The other, lower, voices were designated by letters.

Many of these German composers, in addition to writing secular and instrumental works, did a number of things for the service of the Catholic Church, which organization, in spite of internal political and sectarian strife, maintained a dominant position in the religious life of the country as a whole. Isaac, who had drunk so deeply at the well of Flemish music, was a prolific composer of Masses, and one of the most treasured examples of early music is his *Choralis constantinus,* a complete setting of the offices for the ecclesiastical year. Hofmeyer, Paminger (whom Luther called a *musico inter primos*), Hassler, Aichinger, and Jacobus Gallus (Handl) were important men of the period in this field. The last is considered by historians one of the most important figures of the whole period, often being called, not without reason, the German Palestrina.

THE REFORMATION IN GERMANY

The most important manifestation of the Renaissance spirit in Germany was, of course, the Reformation. The natural temperament and intellectual endowment of the German people made such a response to the individualistic and humanistic ideals of the period inevitable. This break from the established church had its real inception in the struggle of the spirit of man for self-expression. The historians have become fond of saying that such a change in ideals was inevitable and that the currents from which flowed the Reformation were so much older than Luther that, if he had not appeared to head such a revolt, some other reformer would have arisen. In other words, the nailing of the Ninety-five Theses attacking the alleged wickedness of the Catholic Church

NORTH GERMAN
CHURCH MUSIC
(1556)   Woodcut from
the title page of Her-
mann Finck's *Practica
musica*

to a door at the University of Wittenberg in 1517 by one of its professors, Dr. Martin Luther, was only the physical act which precipitated a spiritual revolution long in preparation and which the spirit of
the century as manifested in this particular people had made unavoidable. The results of this revolution, we are constantly being reminded,
were by no means uniformly beneficial; some of them were disastrous
insofar as the development of cultural interest was concerned.

ITS EFFECTS UPON MUSIC

All this may be true; but as musicians and art lovers, we should be
thankful that it was Luther who captained such a revolt and not someone like Calvin or Knox, who brought about a religious revolution in
the northern countries which was largely concerned with economic,
political, and social ideas and had no thought for art at all. Out of the
happy combination of Luther the musician and Luther the reformer
came one of the most notable contributions made by the Germans to
music, the Protestant chorale. It was a cardinal point in Luther's reform
that each individual was capable of a direct relationship with his God,
a doctrine which repudiated the representative ideals of the medieval
Church, which had allowed access to Christ only through the special
mediation of his deputies, the clergy. And so in the worship of this
Protestant body, each man had his own part to play, a part which could
not be taken by another individual, be he priest or chorister.

In his evangelical ritual, therefore, Luther provided for liturgical

AN EARLY CHORALE BOOK   open at Luther's tune *Ein Feste Burg*

forms that gave the congregation opportunities for direct participation in the service. Instead of merely participating in the Mass by listening to it or by having small portions of it to sing, the members of the Protestant congregations were given hymns to sing before and after the sermon, at the beginning and at the end of service. Thus the chorales, those magnificent, majestic expressions of the religious principles of the new church, came into being. In their creation, Luther played a direct part; Eva Mary Grew's tribute, quoted at the head of this section, shows exactly the tremendous significance of this contribution to later developments in music.

LUTHER AS MUSICIAN

Luther was a good musician, although seemingly without interest in any of the other arts. He regarded poetry as purely utilitarian and was entirely oblivious of the arts of form; traveling through Italy at the height of the Renaissance, he had not a single word to say about the beauty being created on all sides of him. He played both flute and lute, understood the principles of polyphony (Josquin des Prés was his special idol), and was on good terms with a number of the leading German composers of his day. So he chose wisely the hymns which his congregations were to sing: some of them originated from Gregorian chants, others from earlier sacred folk songs; some came from contemporary secular melodies ("the devil has no right to all the good tunes," said Luther); a number were especially composed, some of them attributed to Luther himself. It was because of his musical talents and unflagging interest that these chorales became the foundation stone of music in Germany, their style affecting all her later composers from Bach to Brahms and Wagner.

Luther was artist enough to realize that the untrained singers of the congregation could not utilize anything but the simplest music; and so, in addition to providing hymns which had a strong melodic part for the people to sing, he had polyphonic arrangements made of these chorales in the current style of the German lieder. For he felt that when "natural music is heightened and polished by art, there man first beholds and can with great wonder examine to a certain extent (for it cannot be wholly seized or understood) the great and perfect wisdom of God in his marvelous work of music, in which this is most singular and indeed astonishing that one man sings a simple tune or tenor (as musicians call it) together with which three, four, or five voices also sing, which as it were play and skip delightfully round this simple tune or tenor and wonderfully grace or adorn the said tune with manifold devices and sounds, performing as it were a heavenly dance so that those who at all understand it are moved by it, must be greatly amazed and believe that there is nothing more extraordinary in this world than such a song adorned with many voices."

In 1524 Johann Walther, Luther's friend and musical adviser, published, at Wittenberg, his *Church Chorale Book* containing a number of these arrangements with the melody in the tenor part and the other voices woven about it in the fashion so quaintly described above. A later collection, the *Neue deutsche Geistliche Gesange* of Georg Rhaw, published in 1544, contained numbers by all the composers of the early Reformation period, among them Arnold Bruck, whose impressive setting of Luther's words *Aus tiefer Noth* ("In deepest need") may be taken to be representative of the deep feeling and sincere artistry of these German Protestant contrapuntal settings.

Two of the most important figures in the development of the chorale were the Berlin cantor Johann Crüger (1598–1622), whose *Praxis pietatis melica* contained hymn tunes afterward used by Bach, and the already-mentioned Michael Praetorius (1571–1621), *Kapellmeister* to the Duke of Brunswick. Sometimes Praetorius made chorale arrange-

THE SIXTEENTH-CENTURY NUREMBERG   by Dürer (1471—1528)

ments in the simplest two- and three-part style, sometimes in what can only be called a chorale motet or concerto style for voices and instrument, after the fashion imported into Germany from Italy by Hans Leo Hassler.

THE ARTISTRY OF THE CHORALE

Later on, the tune made its way into the upper or soprano voice, and the settings became more suitable for congregational use, finally resulting in the kind of arrangements which Johann Sebastian Bach made a century later and which are among the finest things in all music. In these comparatively simple little pieces in harmonic style, with their masterly part writing, there is a wealth of poetic utterance and a strength of emotional expression that has never been surpassed. "Nothing in music is more wonderful, perhaps more surprising, than the power and grip which these chorales have over all classes of musical listeners and over the singers themselves. . . . These simple four-part compositions . . . have, in fact and in the supremest degree, a religious and mystic effect upon the hearer that cannot be analyzed or explained" (Hannam). They are Germany's outstanding contribution to Renaissance art.

A Table Showing the Most Important Madrigal Composers of the Sixteenth Century				
FLEMISH	ITALIAN	FRENCH	ENGLISH	GERMAN
Willaert[11] *c.* 1480–1562		Jannequin *c.* 1485–*c.* 1560		
Gombert 1495–1570	Festa *c.* 1495–1545	De Sermisy *c.* 1490–1562		
Verdelot[11] 1500–1565				
Arcadelt[11] *c.* 1505–*c.* 1557	A. Gabrieli *c.* 1510–1586			
De Rore[11] 1516–1565				Scandello[13] 1517–1580
De Monte[11] 1521–1603	Palestrina 1525–1594			
Di Lasso[12] *c.* 1530–1594		Le Jeune *c.* 1528–1602		
	Vecchi 1550–1605	Costeley 1531–1606		
	Marenzio *c.* 1553–1599		Byrd 1542–1623	Regnart 1540–1600
	Gastoldi *c.* 1556–1622		Morley 1557–*c.* 1603	Lechner 1550–1606
	Gesualdo of Venosa 1560–1613		Pilkington *c.* 1562–1638	Eccard 1553–1611
	Anerio 1560–1614		Dowland 1563–1626	Hassler 1564–1612
	Monteverdi 1567–1643		Bateson 1570–1630	
			Tomkins 1573–1656	
			Wilbye 1574–1638	
			Weelkes *c.* 1575–1623	
	Frescobaldi 1583–1643		Gibbons 1583–1625	

[11] These men were Netherlanders who worked in Italy.
[12] Di Lasso wrote in the Italian, French, and German styles.
[13] An Italian who introduced the madrigal style to Germany.

VIEW OF TOLEDO by El Greco

of the greatest of all Manneristic painters; sometimes it was disciplined and mannered to the point of self-effacement, as in the pictures of Pontormo and Bronzino. And often it was exaggerated and aggressive, as in the flamboyant works of Benvenuto Cellini, the Florentine goldsmith, sculptor, and musician.

Even the giant Michelangelo was so obsessed in his tremendous frescoes (such as *The Last Judgment* on the rear wall of the Sistine Chapel) with the idea of portraying stark terror that he became almost incoherent, while the uncomfortable restlessness of some of his late architecture and sculpture shows a complete neglect of the classic Renaissance ideals of unity and coherence. The strained, stilted prose style of this century can be tolerated best if we think of these contemporary movements as characteristic of Manneristic art. Even Shakespeare, universal artist as he usually seems, had certain strong Manneristic characteristics; the artificiality, affectation, and desire for strange, original effects that mark so many of his later works and which have puzzled so many of his admirers can readily be explained by the fact that he did not hesitate to cater to the definitely Manneristic tastes of his time. And John Donne, the so-called metaphysical poet, shows, at least in his earlier poems, such a strong desire to break through the classic bonds which had restrained the Renaissance poets that he can be understood only if we consider him as a real Mannerist, obsessed with the imminence of death and decay, even while striving for all sorts of unusual and startling effects.

MANNERISTIC TENDENCIES IN MUSIC

The art of music during this time shows the same Manneristic tendencies toward the destruction of balance and proportion and the same desire for overstrained, rather artificial effects that we find in the other arts. Even the composers and interpreters of the High Renaissance delighted in inserting all sorts of complicated rhythmic patterns and distorted melodic contours into their music, as we have already observed. It is very evident, if we are to judge by some of the descriptions contained in such treatises as Morley's *Plaine and Easie Introduction to Practicall Musicke* (1597), that the simple, balanced, and stately effects of the polyphony of the High Renaissance were never heard in the form that their printed scores suggest. The singers of that time were experts, as Sachs says, in dissolving the plain notation on their music sheets into all sorts of mannered graces and coloraturas.

There were many features of the music of this period that closely parallel the Mannerist developments in the other arts, developments which strove to break down the spirit of the preceding Renaissance by destroying its ideals of proportion, balance, and unity, and which often resulted in a deepened and more personalized expressiveness. Chief among these was the effort to transcend the expressive limitations of the Renaissance polyphony that resulted in such works as Vecchi's *Amfiparnasso* (1594–97); the experiments of the Florentine *Camerata*, which developed into the invention of the opera around 1600; and the revolutionary evolution of the expressive qualities of the various instruments.

The madrigals of Monteverdi may also be used as an illustration of the gradual emergence of the new spirit of revolt and insistence upon the imagination as the source of the creator's inspiration, which marked the whole Mannerist development in art. Prunières, in his book on Monteverdi, describes this well by likening the music of Ingegneri, Monteverdi's master, to a carefully tended and correctly designed Renaissance formal garden. Under Monteverdi's guardianship, however, weeds invaded the flower beds and wild flowers raised their perfumed blossoms insolently above the complicated designs of the boxwood. Monteverdi's earlier madrigals, while possessing real personal color, are entirely suggestive of the Renaissance; his later works, strongly influenced by the contemporary attempts to develop the expressive powers of music, could be called Mannerist in their use of new resources and the insistence upon the importance of the imagination.

Writing in 1600, a noted critic of the time accused Monteverdi and his followers of being preoccupied with "delighting the senses rather than satisfying the reason." And he went on to deprecate those artists who desire to "call everything into question instead of following the paths of the masters." To which Monteverdi replied, in characteristic Mannerist fashion, that other systems of harmony exist than those used by those old masters who had been exclusively concerned with the structure and the adjustment of the different parts in accordance with the possibilities of music. He further added that it was the intent of the moderns "to seek above all else to translate into living expression the emotions suggested by poetry."

GESUALDO THE MANNERIST

But the most striking example of a musical Mannerist, as regards both his life and his art, was Don Carlo Gesualdo, a member of one of the oldest Spanish families in the Kingdom of Naples, who held the title of Prince of Venosa. Born at Naples in 1560, he devoted himself passionately to music from his early manhood and grew up in the midst of a brilliant Renaissance court circle given over to the pleasures of the time—art, music, and dalliance. He wrote and had published six books of madrigals (a seventh was published posthumously) containing 150 pieces, as well as three books of church music. Many of these madrigals were advanced beyond the wildest dreams of his contemporaries; for the purpose of vivid expression, Gesualdo employed chromatic progressions that foreshadow the dissonances and affective devices peculiar to the music of much later times. His exaggerated subjective expressionism, his weighing-down of the text with all sorts of harmonic allurements, his strange, weird "false relations" (which sound even to our ears much like the music of Wagner, Schönberg, and Stravinsky) delighted his contemporaries because they were so much part and parcel of the aesthetic tendencies of the time. Numerous editions of these madrigals were issued in various parts of Europe, and, in the words of an eighteenth-century historian, eulogies were bestowed upon their author by persons ranking high in literature as well as music, many of them speaking of the Prince of Venosa as the greatest composer of their time.

It must be added that Gesualdo somewhat heightened the appeal of his bold, artistic style by the Manneristic details of his private life. In 1590 he had his beautiful young wife murdered, not without provocation, as one recent commentator has wryly observed, her lover shot, and a child killed whom he suspected of not being his own. After these deeds Gesualdo took refuge in his castle, later fleeing to the court of the Estes at Ferrara. It was while he was there that he came into close association with Lizzasco Luzzaschi, head of the Estes court music, an association which Einstein holds responsible for the development of the more eccentric side of Gesualdo's genius.

But, whatever the reason, the madrigals making up his fourth, fifth, and sixth books have a harmonic audacity and a distorted expressiveness that resemble the bold disregard for natural form, the strong, dramatic visual distortions to be found in the paintings of Gesualdo's great contemporary, El Greco. Both these Manneristic artists have been strongly criticized for exactly the same reasons: their distortions, their "forced, affected, and disgusting" changes of mood, their overdoing of contrasts, and their exaggerated treatment for the sake of expressiveness. It is only when we consider them against the Mannerist background of their period that we begin to realize their true worth. Listen to one of Gesualdo's madrigals, such as *Io pur respiro in così gran dolore* or his *Resta di darmi noia,* and compare it with such a picture of El Greco's as his painting of Toledo, the Spanish city of his adoption, where all the external forms and figures seem to be dissolved on a swirl of airy, yellowish light and an abstract sense of unreal space, and you will have a wonderful idea of the similarity between these two Mannerists. Like the best of their contemporaries, they would be what Einstein calls "insufferable Mannerists" if, in their predilection for the extreme, they had used their style for the sake of style alone. But when we think of their exaggerations and distortions as means for conveying their strongly significant feelings, we have to realize that they are both genuinely great artists.

It is obvious that the interest in the music of Gesualdo since the 1950's has arisen largely through realization of his significance as a Mannerist composer. For years this Prince of Madrigalists was a shadowy figure in the history books; as a result of the enthusiasm of a group of southern Californians in discovering, studying, and performing some of the approximately two hundred Gesualdo compositions that have survived, there has come a new understanding of this complex and emotionally charged music, as well as the discovery that it is a perfect example of the self-conscious, exaggerated, affected Mannerist art of its period. Included in this group were Aldous Huxley, Igor Stravinsky, and Robert Craft, all of whom made important contributions to the growing Gesualdian enthusiasm. Craft, who calls Gesualdo the musical Mannerist par excellence, has shown, through a number of outstanding recordings, how this music should sound, with its extremely difficult problems of intonation, its constant striving for dramatic effect, and its desire, above all else, to be expressive.

Gesualdo died in Naples in 1613. He marks the end of the long development which began with Willaert, a development which Einstein describes as ending in a blind alley: "beyond the peaks yawns the abyss; as their escape was cut off, the desperate ones lost themselves in lofty aspirations." Later, new life came with the paintings of the Carracci and Caravaggio, and the operatic music of Monteverdi, a life that was evidenced by a more popular and easily comprehended spirit, which was in strong contrast to the calculated, intellectual character of the Mannerists. With this new spirit we arrive at the Baroque.

THE OVERTURE
TO THE
BAROQUE

General Background of the Baroque Period

The sixteenth century followed Michelangelo's manner and turned it into Mannerism. The seventeenth appreciated the terribilità *of his spiritual conflict and made Baroque out of it.*

Nikolaus Pevsner: *An Outline of European Architecture*

THE SEVENTEENTH
CENTURY

We have seen how the sixteenth century, which had opened with the feeling of joyous exaltation and great hope that we find expressed in much of the art of the High Renaissance, closed in a period of doubt and disillusionment, with many of the countries of Europe torn and divided, fighting at one another's throats for their very existence—a period of reaction which produced another characteristic reaction: when old beliefs have been discarded, old faiths destroyed and the new ones installed in their place have proved to be inadequate and insufficient, as was the case in the century which followed the Renaissance, there seems to be but one thing left for man to cultivate—action. And so the seventeenth century turned out to be a time of tremendously buoyant physical, intellectual, and artistic activity. Perhaps no other period in the whole development of European civilization has been so strongly dominated by a spirit of optimistic action as was that which stretched, roughly speaking, between the beginning of the seventeenth and the middle of the eighteenth century—the era which we have come to think of as the Baroque.

One of the most brilliant periods in all history, standing squarely at the crossroads between medieval and modern times, this was an age of real achievement, strong hope, and vigorous actuality. During its course, man, struggling out of the mystic darkness of the Middle Ages, made new sallies into the unknown and began to devise new ways of overcoming it. Stimulated by the liberating influences of the Renaissance, he began to realize the power of his intellect and to use it in every possible field of endeavor. Whitehead has well called this the century of genius, an era so rich intellectually that it has provided us with most of the mental capital upon which we have been living ever since.

Certainly no other single period in man's existence has been more active in liberating his powers or in giving him the foundations upon which to build his life. It was then that some of the greatest discoveries in science were made, by such investigators and philosophers as Francis Bacon, Galileo, Isaac Newton, Harvey, and Pascal; when such artists as Milton, Corneille and Molière, Ben Jonson, Dryden, and Pope lived and wrote; when Rubens, Rembrandt, Velásquez, and Van Dyck carried to full fruition the traditions and manners of the Renaissance painters; when the Gabrielis, Schütz, Bach, and Handel added so much glory to the art of music. Out of this Baroque spirit of active curiosity and buoyancy there came the invention of such instruments as the telescope, the microscope, the periscope, the barometer, the thermometer, and the pendulum clock; such modern concepts as the laws of motion and those of speed and light; and acceptance of such intellectual processes as the differential calculus and logarithms in mathematical calculations. And out of this spirit of confidence and optimism there developed a concept of the world that not only demanded the perfecting of the individual, of society, and of mankind, but, through emphasizing the power of the reason and the intellect, actually attempted the herculean task of realizing such perfection!

When the Baroque era began, Europe was strongly divided nationally and had become more and more secularized after the long period of domination by the Church centering in Rome. Spain, which in the early part of the seventeenth century had been the leading power of Europe, lost her important position. The domination of Italy, the natural home of the Renaissance world of secular, religious, and artistic activities, was replaced by that of France and England. In England the rights of men to rule as special representatives of God were questioned, fought over, and finally disposed of. And, although these rights were seemingly more firmly established than ever in France during the reign of Louis XIV, they were finally abolished during the Revolution of 1793. In a time marked by good zest in living as well as in thinking, the *bourgeoisie* of Holland and the Lowlands grew rich and prosperous. A spirit of adventurous discovery brought fabulous returns in colonizing to all the great European powers.

The Church, sobered by her losses in the Reformation, determined to reassert her power and authority and, in an attempt to manifest her worldly opulence as well as to depict her hoped-for heavenly glory, enlisted the service of the arts, especially the arts of painting and architecture. Under the patronage of such a powerful influence as the Jesuits (The Society of Jesus), these arts became buoyant and extrovert, colorful and startling often to the point of being what seems to us today theatrical and overdecorative. Instead of following the ideals of the Renaissance, which stipulated that reason should be the determining influence in the production of art, the creators of the Baroque period, stimulated by the demands of the Church for architecture and painting of swelling movement, lively color, and above all else, of startling effects of light and shade, tried to mystify or even confuse reason—to drown it out and get rid of its restraining processes, as Friedell has said, through a process of "artistic neurosis."

And so there was produced the dramatic design for the Church of the Gesù in Rome, a building which was planned as the epitomic symbol of the growing power and glory of the Church. This particular structure became the prototype for hundreds of Baroque churches scattered over the European landscape during the succeeding century. On its walls, tumbling over each other in their anxiety to impress and overwhelm the beholder, are multitudes of cherubs, saints, and angels grouped about the symbol of the Holy Name of Jesus, which bursts in a glow of radiant light from the center of the picture. So crowded and so violent is the movement of the figures that they are thrust outside the frame and down into the interior of the church; this violence is, of course, intentional and is meant to mystify the beholder as he wonders what is real and what is illusion in the spectacle before him. Not far away in another Roman church is Bernini's sculptural realization of the mood of mystic exaltation and fervid rapture felt by the sixteenth-century Spanish Saint Theresa, an angel transfixing her body with an arrow of ecstasy as she dreams of heavenly felicity and bliss.

Anderson

THE MAGNIFICENT INTERIOR OF THE CHURCH OF THE GESÙ, ROME

Yet an age which produced such powerful exponents of reason as Francis Bacon, who first enunciated the principles of the scientific method of inquiry; Descartes and Pascal, who began the study of mathematics in order to reckon quantities and have an instrument for the handling of facts; and Newton, who inaugurated a scientific revolution by his creation of the differential calculus and by his experiments in physics and astronomy, could hardly altogether dispense with the idea of rationalism in its art. In an age in which the scientific mind established itself in every phase of human activity—politics, religion, philology, the natural sciences—it was inevitable that reason and control should act as a restraining influence in whatever artistic creation took place.

So we have the two great extremes of sensualism and rationalism present in the art of the Baroque. On the one hand, there was the interest in this buoyant, optimistic, passionate expression; for man, who had been merely "beautiful" to the artists of the Renaissance, now became warmly human and strongly endowed with feeling and passion. Art was made to express this by the most obvious means, and the whole world, even the Church, was made into a sort of theater in order to present in the most forceful and impressive way, often with what seems unnecessary exaggeration and exorbitant expressiveness, the sensualistic aspect of humanity. On the other hand, there was the realization that above all else in the activities of man there must be reason; as Descartes put it, "we should busy ourselves with no object about which we cannot attain a certitude equal to that of the demonstration of arithmetic and geometry." It was the control and restraint inspired by such ideals of rationalism that kept the art of the time within bounds, no matter how strong its pull in the contrary, sensualistic direction.

These seemingly heterogeneous aspects of the century—an active, buoyant, delving curiosity; an optimistic outlook expressed by the doctrine that this was the "best of all possible worlds," one in which perfection was really possible and in which God acted for the supreme good, provided it was not contrary to the demands of reason; a determination to know scientifically as well as to experience the world in terms of theatrical illusion—all of these were welded together into a cultural tendency that affected all phases of man's activity. It manifested itself in a new emphasis upon man, his "torments, his convulsions, his manias, and his abysses," and the expression of his feelings in new ways, especially in the art of music. Yet this concept of sensualistic reality was always regulated by a delight in formal restraint. For, in many of its various aspects—its attempt to substitute illusion for reality, its attention to the details of dress and deportment, its love for logical thinking, the careful correctness of its manners—the Baroque was an age of formality. It is the tension between these elements, between buoyant, exhilarating expression which was often passionate to the point of strain and expressive to the point of exaggeration, and the restraint which was imposed upon any expression by the rationalistic ideals of the time, that constitutes the very essence of the spirit of the Baroque. It expresses, as no other single style can, the never-ending struggle between the active creative force and recalcitrant matter.

The use of the term Baroque[1] came into the general field of art criticism from the special field of architecture, where it was first used by critics of the seventeenth century to suggest a type of building that, since it did not correspond to the classic Renaissance rules regarding balance and proportion, seemed to them absurd or grotesque. From this rather derogative original association, it has gradually spread over into the other fields of art criticism and now has come to be used to describe the type of virile, powerful art peculiar to the seventeenth

[1] The term probably comes from the Spanish or Portuguese word descriptive of the large, irregular pearls which inspired the goldsmiths of the time to fashion all sorts of irregular and grotesquely extravagant jewelry.

the arts of this one period. The new energy which this spirit injected into the intellectual and artistic life of its century resulted in a vivid, emotionally expressive kind of art which is as strongly evidenced in the painting as it was in the architecture, in the literature as it was in the music of the time. This epoch produced a *corpus* of art, a tolerance of opinion, and a graciousness of living that has never been surpassed.

The Birth and
Development of the Opera and Oratorio

So let me die,
Why must I, who have trusted in thee,
Feel the blows of such a cruel fate
And suffer so bitter a fortune?
Ah, let me perish, let me die!

THE BIRTH OF A NEW ART

We have only to read such words as those quoted above, voicing the lament of the unhappy Ariadne and sung by one of the characters in Monteverdi's opera of that name, written in 1608, to realize that a new spirit has come into music, one quite different from the ideals of such works as we have so far been considering. Monteverdi was able to clothe these words, filled as they are with self-pity and expressive of the utmost despair, ardent passion, and longing for death, with music which so heightens their emotional effect and emphasizes their natural intensity as to make us realize that at this point we have come to the beginnings of the modern period of music. For here is a musical setting which makes an immediate appeal to our hearts, just as it did to the hearts of the people in 1608, when, as a contemporary account puts it, "there was no one in the audience who was not greatly moved; none of the ladies present, at the singing of the beautiful 'Lament,' could withhold their tears of sympathy, so filled with vehement passion was the music, and so movingly was it sung."

In listening to this Lament of Monteverdi's, the most casual hearer will realize that its composer was not concerned with any process of weaving sounds together so as to secure the generalized, abstract type of musical beauty which we found in the madrigals. Here the musician has come to a more direct grip with life and has been able to translate his experience into music which is moving in the same sense that Beethoven's or Wagner's music is. We find that there are also clear-cut technical changes: all the involved contrapuntal feeling is gone; the accompaniment has taken on a chordal, harmonic form; there is a clearly defined difference between the vocal and the instrumental parts. In 1605, we must remember, composers like Wilbye, and even Monteverdi himself, were writing madrigals—plenty of them—of the usual sort; and here, but a few years later, there suddenly emerges an entirely new form, one filled with a quite different feeling.

The actual change from one style to the other was sudden enough; but it was made inevitable by the artistic ideals which the Renaissance had set in motion, and there were in the music of the sixteenth century many presentiments that it was coming. The discovery of the best physical means for conveying this new aspect of personal emotion and dramatic intensity in music was, like so many of the world's important discoveries, something in the way of an accident; but years before the first opera was invented in 1600, composers were striving to inject a more dramatic and expressive spirit into their music. Among them, as we have seen, were Luca Marenzio and Gesualdo of Venosa, who introduced dissonances into their madrigals in order to make them more effective, and Orazio Vecchi, who attempted what has since come to be known as a "madrigal opera"—a drama of three acts in which the entire text was set in five-part madrigal form.

In his book on *The History of Taste,* Frank Chambers has pointed out that the natural and inevitable result of the whole Renaissance movement was the emergence of the ideal of Classicism. This spirit in art was brought about through the revival of interest in the older classic civilizations and the pursuant formation of a set of principles derived from the study of these civilizations for the guidance of contemporary artists in their creative activity. Outstanding among such classic ideas was that which declared that art should attempt above all things to imitate nature. As Giovanni Lomazzo, whose *Trattato dell' Arte pittura, scultura ed architettura,* published in 1584, was a formulation of the ideals of Italian classicism, said: "All the arts have the same end, intending nothing else than to resemble things as near life as may be.

An emotion represented in a picture should be able to arouse the same emotion in the beholder; a laughing picture will arouse laughter, grieving cause grief, wondering arouse wonder, etc." In brief, art should essay to imitate natural things, idealizing them, and supplying, if need be, any defects that might exist. It is easy to see why, then, with this spirit of naturalism so strongly current, the writers of the late Renaissance became impatient with the restrictions laid on them by the purely contrapuntal type of music and sought an expression that would be more direct and personal.

ITS SOURCES

The discovery of how best to do this came through a characteristically Renaissance effort to imitate the musical ideals of the ancient Greeks and to add some contribution to Italian drama which would make it comparable to what Spanish and English writers had done in that field. Along about the eighties of the sixteenth century, a group of amateur antiquarians began to investigate the manner in which the Greeks might have used music in their dramas, thinking thus to be able to increase the expressiveness of contemporary musical declamation. These men, bound together in an artistic circle, the *Camerata*— composers, singers, and instrumentalists—were thoroughly familiar with the music of their times; and they realized that it was not suitable for the purpose they had in mind. A few specimens of early Greek music were available to them, in fact, almost as many as we have today. Although none of this group could read this music, it inspired Galilei, father of the famous astronomer, to attempt an adaptation of a part of Dante's *Divine Comedy* in what he conceived might have been the Greek manner of composing dramatic music.

This pleased the fellow members of the *Camerata* so well that two of them combined to produce a whole drama with music. Rinuccini, a poet, wrote a dramatic poem, *Dafne,* which was set to music by Jacopo Peri, director of music to the Florentine court. This was produced in one of the great houses of the nobility in Florence in 1597 and was, in turn, so well received that its author and composer united in another similar enterprise, the writing of a *dramma per musica* on the classic Eurydice theme. It was first played on the occasion of the wedding of Maria de' Medici and Henry IV of France in 1600 and constitutes the first opera the music of which has come down to us, that of *Dafne* being lost.

Thus was born not only a new type of music[2] but an entirely new era. These dramatic musicians working in Florence at the beginning of the seventeenth century thought that they were reviving the glories of the Greek classic drama. What they actually did was invent a musical form which made possible the direct expression of personal feeling on the stage, its music being a close reflection of the ideas and emotions of the text. So was opened the door leading to modern musical expression. When *Eurydice* was published, Peri wrote a Preface giving the reasons for what he had tried to do. It explains, better than can any description, this new kind of writing. It is quoted in part here:

Before offering you this music of mine, I think proper to make known to you what led me to invent this new kind of vocal writing; since reason must be the beginning and source of all human doings, and he who cannot give his reason at once lays himself open to the suspicion of having worked at haphazard. Although our music was brought upon the stage by Sig. Emilio del Cavalieri, with marvelous originality, before anyone else I know of, it nevertheless pleased Signori Iacopo Corsi and Ottavio Rinuccini (in the year 1594) to have me set to music the play of Dafne, written by Sig. Ottavio Rinuccini, treating it in another manner, to show by a simple experiment of what the song of our age is capable. Wherefore, seeing that I had to do with Dramatic Poetry, and must accordingly seek, in my music, to imitate one who speaks (and doubtless no one ever yet spoke in singing), it seemed to me that the ancient Greeks and Romans (who, in the opinion of many, sang the whole of their tragedies on the stage) must have made use of a sort of music which, while surpassing the sounds of ordinary speech, fell so far short of the melody of singing as to assume the shape of something intermediate between the two. And this is why we find in their poems so large an use made of the Iambic Metre, which does not rise to the sublimity of the Hexameter, albeit it is said to overstep the bounds of ordinary speech. Therefore, abandoning every style of vocal writing known hitherto, I gave myself up wholly to contriving the sort of imitation (of speech) demanded by this poem. And, considering that the sort of vocal delivery applied by the ancients to singing, and called by them vox diastematica (as if held in check and kept in suspense), could be somewhat accelerated, so as to hold a mean course between the slow and deliberate pace of singing and the nimble, rapid pace of speaking, and thus be made to serve my purpose (as they, too, adapted it to the reading of poems and heroic verse) by approaching the speaking voice, called by them vox continuata, as has also been done by our modern composers (if perhaps for another purpose); considering this, I also recognized that, in our speech, some sounds are intoned

[2] This new kind of music received several names. Sometimes it was called *Le Nuove Musiche* (The New Music), from the title of a book of songs written in this style by Caccini; sometimes it was given the title *Dramma per Musica* (Drama through Music); and Peri and Rinuccini called their work a *favola in musica*—a musical fable. The best generic term to use in describing it is *monody*, meaning that it is based on the principle of one voice accompanied, instead of many voices intertwined.

in such a way that harmony can be based upon them and that, in the course of conversation, we pass through many others which are not so intoned, until we return to one which is capable of forming a new consonance. And, having regard for the accents and modes of expression we use—in grief, rejoicing, etc.—I have made the bass move at a rate appropriate to them, now faster, now slower, according to the emotions to be expressed, and have sustained it through both dissonances and consonances [tra le false, e tra le buone pro- porzioni], until the speaker's voice, after passing through various degrees of pitch, comes to those sounds which, being intoned in ordinary speech, facilitate the formation of a new consonance. And I have done this . . . to the end that the employment of dissonances shall diminish, or conceal that advantage of which ancient music may perhaps have had less need. And finally (though I dare not assert that this was the sort of singing done in Greek or Roman plays), I have deemed it the only sort that can be admissible in our music, by adapting itself to our speech.

Receive it, therefore, kindly, courteous readers, and, though I may not, this time, have reached the point I thought myself able to reach (regard for novelty having been a curb on my course), accept it graciously in every way. And perhaps it will come to pass on another occasion that I shall show you something more perfect than this. Meanwhile, I shall think to have done enough if I have opened the path for the talent of others, for them to walk in my footsteps to that glory to which it has not been given to me to attain. And I hope that my use of dissonances, played and sung discreetly, yet with- out timidity (having pleased so many and worthy men), will not trouble you; especially in the sad and grave airs of Orfeo, Arcetro, and Dafne . . .

And may you live happy.

From Peri's Preface to his opera *Eurydice* (Apthorp: *The Opera Past and Present*)

In reality, the idea of thus associating music with drama was neither new nor confined to the practices of the Greeks. All nations and peo- ples have loved the drama and from its earliest days gave music a share in its representations. Holy Mother Church recognized the lessons that dramatic representation of her mysteries could teach, and we have ac- counts going back as far as the tenth century describing short liturgical dramas that were introduced into the services. During the Middle Ages the Church produced mystery and miracle plays about the lives of her great figures, as well as moralities, teaching through the personi- fication of Good, Evil, Covetousness, Charity, and the other qualities of man's mind. At appropriate places in these medieval dramas there were inserted suitable musical interludes to heighten the dramatic effects, such as, for example, the songs of the angels and shepherds and the touching lullaby by the mothers of the slaughtered innocents in the famous English Coventry Christmas play of the sixteenth century.

In Italy the *sacre rappresentazioni* (sacred dramas), special kinds of mystery or miracle plays, were important as direct predecessors of the

From Livre d'heures d'Estienne Chevalier, Chantilly

SCENE FROM A MEDIEVAL MYSTERY PLAY: "The Martyrdom of Apollonia" Notice the general details: the scene, of course, is that which would constitute the "hit" of the whole play, of the torture. In the background of the open stage upon which this is being enacted are a number of raised booths in which the other episodes would be played; to the right is Hell's Mouth, with its attendant demons, who constantly roamed about, enlivening the whole; to the left is a curtained Heaven, with its angels, waiting to receive the soul of the martyred victim. Just to the right is a group of musicians with trumpets and woodwind instruments. There is good reason to suppose that these, as well as singers, were employed in other episodes. In the center, with stick and book, stands the *regisseur,* directing the action.

opera; for at the height of their development—about the middle of
the sixteenth century—they seem to have been largely sung, with few
spoken lines, and had definite interludes which were given over to
dancing. The special channel through which these religious dramas
permeated the common, secular life of the people was the *commedia
dell'arte,* with its characters of Harlequin, Pantaloon, Pulcinella, and
the other figures which have survived only in rather faded pantomime
and fancy-dress relics. Here the ancient Greek and Roman plays, much
attenuated and liberally filled out with contemporary impromptus and
gags, were made the bases of the art. These Italian comedians traveled
abroad to France and England, and Shakespeare used more than one
of their ideas and brought to fresh life a number of their characters.
Music was an integral part of their plays.

Still another important forerunner of the opera was that traditional
Renaissance social entertainment, the masque—a combination of poetry, vocal and instrumental music, dancing, pageantry, acting, elaborate costuming and scenic decoration, the whole treating, in the most
elaborate and lavish manner possible, classic and allegorical subjects.
The form seems to have developed first in Italy, possibly having its
origin in the huge processions put on by the Renaissance princes, consisting of long lines of men on horseback, carrying torches, wearing
masks and fantastic costumes, and accompanied by musicians. It passed
rapidly to France (the popular *ballet de cour,* of which no less than
eighty were given during the twenty-year reign of King Henry IV, was
really a masque) and reached its highest perfection and elaborateness
in Elizabethan England.[3] The instrumental musicians used in these
tremendous spectacles were scattered about the scenes in association
with various groups of dramatic characters, a fact which may have led
to the traditional grouping together of certain instrumental timbres and

[3] Francis Bacon has left an interesting description of the contemporary masque in his
essay, *Of Masques and Triumphs:* "These things are but toys, to come amongst such
serious observations. But yet, since princes will have such things, it is better they should
be graced with elegancy than daubed with cost. Dancing to song is a thing of great state
and pleasure. I understand it, that the song be in quire, placed aloft, and accompanied
with some broken music [an accompaniment furnished by a band in which the instruments were not all of one kind]; and the ditty fitted to the device.

"Acting in song, especially in dialogues, hath an extreme good grace: I say acting,
not dancing; and the voices of the dialogue would be strong and manly (a base and a
tenor; no treble), and the ditty high and tragical; not nice or dainty. Several quires,
placed one over against another and taking the voice by catches, anthem-wise, give great
pleasure. . . . Let the songs be loud and cheerful, and not chirpings or pulings. Let the
music likewise be sharp and loud and well placed."

thus laid the foundations for later developments in the orchestra. There were both choruses and solo parts in monodic style for the voice.

There were other Italian Renaissance ingredients which had a determining influence on the final flavor of the whole: (1) the carnival songs, ribald and licentious stanzas directed at the ladies present at these festival masques, which were later toned down and treated in a dramatic fashion; (2) the choruses and dances from the pastoral dramas, which, modeled on the classic Latin eclogues, became the delight of the fashionable sixteenth-century world; and (3) the madrigal comedies, attempts to dramatize and unify in one continuous and developed piece the short, lyric madrigal type of writing of which Vecchi's *L'Amfiparnasso* is the classic example.

There is a great deal of confusion among the writers of musical history as to just how and when all these various elements were fused into the form we know as *opera*. Some of them give great prominence to Poliziano's *Favola di Orfeo,* produced at the court of Mantua sometime between 1472 and 1483, as being an important forerunner of the form. An Italian musicologist, Tirabassi, claims that the little 34-page *Orfeo dolente* by Domenico Belli, choirmaster of the Church of San Lorenzo in Florence, is the first opera. Sometimes Peri's *Dafne* is given this honor, sometimes *Eurydice* by Peri and in part by Caccini. Such matters may well be left to the scholars; it is important for the general reader, however, to realize what a desire for novelty there was in the air at the time. As a Florentine musician put it, "The one thing everyone agreed on was that, since the music of the day was quite inadequate to the expression of the words and its development actually repugnant to the thought, means must be found in the attempt to bring music back to that of classical times, to bring out the chief melody so that the poetry should be clearly intelligible" (Soni, writing in 1640).

Once the form was started, there were problems of all sorts to be solved: how best to carry on a dialogue to music; whether to let the music be continuous or to intersperse it with speaking; what part the chorus, hitherto paramount, was to play; what sort of instruments should be used for accompaniment—this when no orchestral mould existed beyond that of the "chest of viols" and "broken consorts" of miscellaneous instruments. All these questions had to be decided; and it was, indeed, a matter of *solvitur ambulando!*

Opera, for the majority of people, has always been an exotic form.

THREE SCENES FROM THE BALLET *THE FAIRIES OF THE FOREST OF ST. GERMAIN,* danced at the palace of the Louvre, 1625: (1) musicians of the ballet; (2) Spanish guitar players; (3) musicians of the country

This is easily enough understood, for it is unnatural, and in its most elaborate shapes makes very heavy demands on the listener's power of attention. It is not too much to say that without a great deal of solid study, much of Wagner's work, the greatest that has ever been written in this form, must remain uncomprehended. For the mass of citizens, music is still a recreation; they always resent the idea of having to work at it, and so they will always prefer the operas which make the smallest demands. How delightful it must have been in the earliest days of opera, when everything was fresh and adventurously exciting; when the Italians, always quick in the dramatic uptake, had around them all the stimuli for such new invention: the patronage and money of the nobility, leisure and zest for experiment, and the background of Renaissance example in the other arts!

AS DRYDEN SAW OPERA

Not so many years after Peri and Rinuccini presented their first opera in Florence, the English writer John Dryden, whose experience with the stage in London gave him a particular insight into dramatic problems, wrote this description of opera:

An opera is a poetical tale, or fiction, represented by vocal and instrumental music, adorned with scenes, machines, and dancing. The supposed persons of this musical drama are generally supernatural, as gods, and goddesses, and heroes, which at least are descended from them, and are in due time to be adopted into their number. The subject, therefore, being extended beyond the limits of human nature, admits of that sort of marvelous and surprising conduct which is rejected in other plays. Human impossibilities are to be received as they are in faith, because, where gods are introduced, a supreme power is to be understood, and second causes are out of doors . . . If the persons represented were to speak upon the stage, it would follow, of necessity, that the expressions should be lofty, figurative, and majestical, but the nature of an opera denies the frequent use of these poetical ornaments; for vocal music, though it often admits a loftiness of sound, yet always exacts an harmonious sweetness; or, to distinguish yet more justly, the recitative part of the opera requires a more masculine beauty of expression and sound; the other, which for want of a proper English word I must call the songish part, must abound in the softness and variety of numbers; its principal intention being to please the hearing rather than to gratify the understanding. It appears, indeed, preposterous at first sight, that rhyme, on any consideration, should take place of reason; but, in order to resolve the problem, this fundamental proposition must be settled, that the first inventors of any art or science, provided they have brought it to perfection, are, in reason, to give laws to it; and, according to their model, all after-undertakers are to build.

THE CHARACTERISTICS OF THE FIRST OPERA

If we examine Peri's *Eurydice* in any detail, we shall find readily enough that most of the "after-undertakers" in opera used it for a model and built pretty well after its plan; all the advantages as well as the shortcomings of the later music dramas are here present in embryo. In general, the work presents a number of broad dramatic situations, with a text that gives opportunity for both histrionic incident and reflective comment. There are a number of different stage pictures to please the eye and enough stage action to hold the interest of the spectator. The ending, in defiance of the classic myth on which the text is based, is a happy one, thus establishing a license that succeeding generations of operatic writers have followed.

The music is used for heightening the dramatic expression. All music, if properly devised, can be made to intensify the expression of emotion, just as poetry does, in comparison with ordinary prose. And it has been the particular function of dramatic music ever since the *stilo recitativo* or *rappresentativo* was evolved—dry and barren as it may seem today—to make it possible for the singer to re-create the emotions of his part in a more intensified form. This recitative was indeed the real accomplishment of the new style. Its characteristics have been described by the classic scholar Giovanni Doni (1594–1647), who wrote enthusiastically: "The real delight in hearing a singer derives from a clear understanding of the text." Listen to the monologue from this opera, which begins *Funeste piaggie:* "Ye dismal hillsides, how sad ye are without Eurydice." The accompanying chords are primitive, to be sure; the elaborate mechanism of the preceding era has been swept away; but there is a simple poignancy of expression that was generally lacking in the more elegantly mannered music of the madrigals.

Peri's accompanying orchestra was a strange one according to modern standards—a harpsichord, a chitarrone (bass lute), a large lute, a viola da gamba, and, for special effects in certain parts of the score, three flutes. The harpsichord played the chordal accompaniments for the recitative, against a running background of gamba tone. Thus was established another custom which held for years after as to the proper rendition of accompaniment for recitative. In the score, only the vocal part and the bass were written out, the players filling in the chords from a sort of abbreviated musical shorthand supplied by the composer (called *figured bass*), a method which was generally used until the time of Mozart and Beethoven. In addition to supplying the accom-

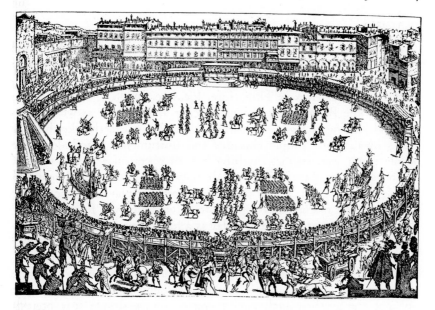

THE WARS OF LOVE   The scene represents a Renaissance spectacle produced in the Piazza di S. Croce in Florence, with text by Salvadori and music by Peri and other composers.

paniments, this orchestra (playing behind the scenes) provided a general atmospheric background for the action of the piece; for instance, Peri introduces into one of his songs short instrumental interludes for the three flutes, in an attempt to suggest the pastoral quality of the text, the flute having been the favored instrument of the Greek shepherds. Here is the direct ancestor of all the means for providing emotional color, so richly developed by later operatic composers. Furthermore, there were a number of massed choruses and dances, all of them being integral parts of a dramatic action. The music for these was written in a curious mixture of a primitive attempt at harmonic effects and a use of the older madrigalian counterpoint. The principles of monodic choral construction, so effective in the later operas, had not been sufficiently worked out to be applied here with effectiveness.

The men of the *Camerata* were not mere theorists, however; they were all practical men, each one following the dictates of his own temperament: Caccini was interested in the development of singing, Cavalieri in the provision of suitable music for the stage, Peri and Rinuccini in the perfection of dramatic expression. It was out of their combined efforts that opera was born; and it is not correct to say, as is often stated, that it was merely "theories that brought about opera."

ORATORIO

To the same year, 1600, belongs the first performance of what came to be known as *oratorio,* Cavalieri's *La Rappresentazione dell' Anima e del Corpo* (*The Representation of the Soul and Body*), which introduces such characters as Time, Life, Pleasure, Intellect, as well as the Soul and the Body, and employs dancing and scenery, as well as acting and singing. Its general features were almost exactly like those of Peri's opera, with simple choruses and instrumental interludes. The whole thing was, in fact, nothing but an opera on a sacred subject, performed in a church. Thus both these styles, opera and oratorio, grew from one stem, as did the ancient mystery plays and the secular dramas.[4] Later oratorio developed into a form different from the early dramatic *rappresentazione* and today is a form entirely devoid of theatrical elements. It seems decidedly to be declining in favor, after a long prosperous period, while opera, generally speaking, is holding its own. The two arose out of different manifestations and purposes, from the same instinct for drama and for the deployment of the solo voice: opera at first for the courtly circles, oratorio for the simple. It is interesting to see how their positions have been reversed.

POPULAR INFLUENCE ON OPERATIC STYLE

The emergence of opera as a popular form of entertainment (the first opera theater being opened in Venice in 1637) brought pressure on composers to please their paying patrons. Now very rarely in history have the masses, however good their upbringing, been fond of long and complex pieces of music. Generations went to the building-up of a public for Wagner; and even today it is the commonest thing to hear people declare that they cannot stand his long works. An educated public for any kind of opera has to be developed slowly; and the instinct of every member of it, in the beginning, is to enjoy short patches of anything, but not to wish for either very long or very involved scenes. Great elaboration came only with the multiplication of orchestral resources and the use of the leitmotiv. But although the practice of the period up to Monteverdi had been to keep most of the pieces of music short, the possibilities of operatic freedom tempted composers to try longer flights. Here the popular taste was influential, and that taste has always shaped a great deal of the world's opera, so that the

---

[4] The word *oratorio* comes from *oratory,* the establishment in which St. Philip Neri, the founder of the Order of the Oratorians—an order of priests without vows—held his religious dramatic representations.

memory of nine-tenths of operagoers is concerned with particular airs which can be readily carried in the memory and hummed. The supreme example of almost a whole nation's likings is that of Gilbert and Sullivan, the only operatic material for which the British people are ever likely to care much. Those clever works abound in short, crisp, aphoristic passages, in gaiety (and occasionally simple pathos), qualities which delight without putting much strain on mind or spirit or ear. Giving all due praise to these works, which have been the lifelong joy of millions, nevertheless, to most of their devotees, operas such as Mozart and Wagner wrote are almost as foreign as those of Monteverdi.

MONTEVERDI

We can say that this composer was the first to write a great opera, although *Il Santo Alessio* of Steffani Landi (*c.* 1590–*c.* 1655) is of real importance in the later development of opera, particularly *opera buffa*. Bridging two epochs, Monteverdi is the outstanding representative of this greatest change in style that music has ever seen. Born in Cremona in 1567, he became the chief musician at the court of Gonzaga in Mantua, whence he went to St. Mark's, Venice, where he became *maestro di cappella*. Having achieved a superb technique in the writing of the contrapuntal style, he was the ideal man to breathe the breath of life into the rather stilted and ineffectual new form of the opera. We may call him the most advanced polyphonist of the sixteenth century, for many of his works foreshadow the changes that were to come later. And he was also the first man of the seventeenth century to endow the rather arid inventions of the modernists with something of the rich heritage of the past. "In either century, the new or the old, he was undisputed master."

If we look at some of the music from this composer's opera *Orfeo*, first produced in Mantua in 1607 and readily available in modern reprints, we shall see what a genius could do in the way of dramatic, descriptive music and orchestral effects. We can see here how completely changed was Peri's dry *stilo rappresentativo*. With Monteverdi it becomes a powerful, dramatic medium, suggestive of the intonation of impassioned speech. How boldly and well this composer expressed the spirit of naturalism that was abroad in his time is readily seen in such excerpts as the Lament from *Ariadne* (already quoted), the expressive song of Orpheus when he learns of the death of Eurydice, from *Orfeo*, and the song of the Nurse, from his last opera, *Poppea*. In all these we find striking use of dissonances, a use which must have seemed extremely harsh to Monteverdi's contemporaries, if we can judge by the following diatribe of one of them:

These new composers believe that they have done everything when they satisfy the ear. Day and night they spend their time at their instruments, that they may try out the effects of pieces interlarded with dissonances—the fools. They never realize that these instruments betray them. They seem to be satisfied if they can produce the greatest possible tonal disturbance by bringing together altogether unrelated elements and mountainous collections of cacophonies.

Monteverdi did not hesitate to use these dissonances, moreover, as "unprepared discords," thus firmly establishing our modern ideas of key relationships and sounding the death knell of the older modal systems of tonalities. We find him struggling, also, with problems of form and achieving some remarkable results in the way of working out something to take the place of the elaborate imitative devices of the earlier polyphony. Certain repetitions of phrases (as, for example, in Ariadne's Lament), suggestive of the later leitmotiv, a real distinction between narrative recitative and lyric aria, and such a strictness of invention as is evidenced in his monody *Ohime, ch'io cado,* where he makes use of a set of melodic variants over a fixed bass, are portents of the great things which followed in the next two centuries. Monteverdi provided his operas with a characteristic prelude, in which the instruments sound effectively, and his connecting instrumental *ritornellos* and *sinfonias* are a definite part of his dramatic development. To put it briefly, we have here the beginning of the evolution of modern music.

But we should not think of this composer as a mere theoretician, of interest only as an innovator. We have already quoted a contemporary account of the first performance of *Ariadne* in Mantua, an account which leaves no doubt as to Monteverdi's ability to move the people of his time. Monteverdi was one of the first geniuses in music. Finding a newly created form ready for his use, he was able to stamp his own individuality on it and make it a vital and moving thing. Nef has said that in no other period of music's history has there been such a strong urge toward directness and naturalness as in the first half of the seventeenth century. And, he adds, no modern *verismo* has been produced of the rank of Claudio Monteverdi, who may well be placed beside his contemporary, Shakespeare; just as the latter lets each of his characters use his own individual speech, so the Italian dramatist uses "demonic and raging passion as easily as grace and tender fervor."

Baroque
Instrumental Music

What passion cannot music raise and quell?
  When Jubal struck the corded shell,
His listening brethren stood around,
  And, wond'ring, on their faces fell
  To worship that celestial sound.
Less than a god they thought there could not dwell
  Within the hollow of that shell
  That spoke so sweetly and so well.

Dryden

THE RISE OF IDIOMATIC
INSTRUMENTAL MUSIC
The new ideals of Baroque expression in art strongly affected the indigenous style of music which was being evolved for instruments at this time. The development of new and more expressive instruments, as well as the evolution of new styles of music for them to play, were characteristic results of the new Baroque demand for more impressive and emotional expression. During the Renaissance, instruments had only been expected to provide sharply differentiated tone colors for the various parts that were woven together in contrapuntal fashion; with the rise of the new monodic *stilo rappresentativo* and the demands for rendering all shades of emotional intensities, the older, more impersonal types of instruments such as shawms, rankets, cromornes (early European instruments with double reeds) disappeared and their places were taken by the much more flexible flutes, oboes, bassoons, and cornetti (short wooden horns with finger holes). Attention was also paid to increasing the range and tessitura of all instruments in order to insure expressiveness; and the interest gradually shifted, especially in Italy, from wind to string instruments.

It was out of Italy that there came the one instrument which has had so much to do with the development of modern expressive performing technic—the violin, as well as the types of music that were written to display its special qualities. Centuries of experiments in the construction of stringed instruments of different shapes and sizes, made out of many different kinds of materials and tuned according to different theoretical systems, had preceded the appearance of the violin. These experiments had produced such primitive ancestors as the bowed lyre, the medieval rebec, and the vielle (fiddle); by 1500 these bowed instruments began to settle into two groups: the *viole da braccio,* or arm viols, and the *viole da gamba,* or leg viols.

The violin developed out of the latter group; in order to create another, higher instrument for the Renaissance instrumental ensembles, a little viol or "violino" was designed, and this, in the hands of the northern Italian lutists, became the modern violin. The instrument makers gave the new violin higher and wider shoulders and an arched back, and they diminished the number of strings. Of all the revolutionary changes that have taken place in the history of music, none has been more striking than that in which the royal viol, with its various members speaking a soft, discreet, and aristocratic language in all registers, was supplanted[5] by the bourgeois, penetrating, and agile violin. The consensus of opinion seems to be that the violin first appeared in Brescia, in northern Italy; at least its type became fixed there during the latter sixteenth century and spread rapidly over all Europe. It was not until the members of the Amati family, in the early days of the Baroque period, began to make their beautiful instruments, which are still much sought after today, that the violin fulfilled its possibilities. By the time of Antonius Stradivarius (1644–1737), the art of violin

[5] The word is used advisedly, for in reality the violins were not the successors of the viols, both families existing contemporaneously for many years, the viols being finally superseded when public rather than private performances of music became the rule, around the end of the seventeenth century. It is not generally recognized that there were so many fundamental differences between these two families, some authorities even doubting that they had a common ancestor. The most striking of these differences are:

Viol Family	Violin Family
Tone rather veiled, dull, slow-speaking	Tone brilliant, flexible, agile
Flat back	Convex back
Sloping shoulders	Rounded shoulders
Normally six strings with fretted finger board capable of adjustment	Four strings without fretted finger board
Light strings without tremendous tension	Strings very strong and taut
Held downwards, smaller instruments between the knees, larger ones between the legs	Held in various positions, the violins under chin
Bow stick curved outward from hairs, allowing freedom in playing chord	Bow stick curved inward, making for more delicate, brilliant effects

making reached its climax and the instrument as we know it today began to be made in France and Germany as well as in Italy.

We have become so used to considering the singing violin as the instrument par excellence that it is with something of a shock that we learn with what disdain these early instruments were considered. Here is a description written in Lyons, France, one of the centers of early violin manufacture in the middle of the sixteenth century:

> *The violin is very much the opposite of the viol; its body is smaller, flatter, and it is much rougher in tone. . . . We call viols the instrument which gentlemen, merchants, and other people of quality use for their pastimes. . . . The other sort is called the violin, and it is the instrument commonly used in playing for the dance; and this for good reason, for it is easier to tune, because the fifth is pleasanter to the ear than the fourth. It is also easier to carry, which is a very necessary matter, even in conducting a wedding or a mummery. There are found few people who make use of it except those who make their living by it as a trade.*

Epitome musical des tons, sons et accords, Lyon, 1556.
Quoted by Pincherle in *Musical Quarterly*

One of the principal reasons for this disdain was undoubtedly the tremendously increased sonority of which these new instruments were capable, a sonority which assaulted the ears so long accustomed to the gentle tones of the viols. Another was that the later designs and varnishes by which the Italian makers tempered the shrillness of this *barbare* and changed its tone into the warmth we know had not yet been invented. And the fact that these early violins were played by domestics "acting by the command and for the pleasure of their masters" in dancing did not improve their social status. Baltasarini de Belgiojoso and his troupe of violinists came from Italy to Paris about 1560; and, although they captured the fancy of the court to such an extent that the leader changed his name to Beaujoyeulx and that of his band to the *Vingt-quatre violons du roy*, it was nearly a century later (1636) before such a eulogy as this could be written:

> *Those who have heard the king's twenty-four violins admit that they have never heard anything more ravishing and more effective. Hence it seems that this instrument is, of all, the most popular for the dance, as we may observe in the ballets and on all hands elsewhere. Now the beauties and the graces that are practiced upon it are so great in number that one may prefer it to all instruments, for the strokes of the bow are so ravishing that there is no greater disappointment than not to hear it to the end. Particularly when they are intermingled with trills and with easy touches of the left hand, which compel the hearer to confess that the violin is the king of instruments.*

THE BEGINNINGS OF THE CONCERTO STYLE
AN EXPRESSION OF ITS TIME

If we examine the music of the Baroque era from the viewpoint of historical expression, we will find in it exactly the same artistic propensities as can be observed in the visual art of the time: the desire to put personal, subjective feelings and interpretations into the foreground; the desire to secure larger works of more impressive proportions; and the constant effort to break through the existing boundaries, which up to that time had circumscribed the powers of artistic expression. Gradually there evolved a highly organized, richly ornamented, warmly expressive idiomatic style, one which consciously developed the possibilities inherent in both instrumental and vocal media, and which had as its aim the manifestation of individual fantasy and inventiveness.

This was a concept which contrasted strongly with the ideals of Renaissance music; these latter were based on the premise of an equal, rather impersonal type of writing for both instruments and voices and so did not stress the kind of music that was particularly expressive or that was idiomatic for any particular instrument. As a means for developing their new ideas, the Baroque composers worked out an entirely new mode of instrumental expression, the *stilo concertante* (from the Latin *to strive, to contend*), based on the principle of contrast. Out of this was to come the more modern idea of the *concerto* as a form in which a solo instrument is pitted against the resources of the whole orchestra. In their desire to achieve expressiveness, the composers of the Baroque era also discovered the peculiar appeal of *a cappella* writing, that is, music written for a vocal choir without instrumental accompaniment. And as a complement to this purely vocal type of composition, they evolved a new instrumental style which concentrated on the expressive qualities of the instruments. Still another warmly expressive medium extensively explored during this time was the solo voice—what it could do both in the way of conveying the intensity of personal feeling and as a means for the display of remarkable decorative agility of the techniques of the Italian *bel canto* style.

These new possibilities, particularly those arising from the exchange of idioms between different instruments or based on combinations of differently constituted choirs of vocalists and instrumentalists, were first developed in Venice. This city, isolated among her salt marshes in splendid grandeur at the head of the Adriatic, her people thriving on their profitable trade with the East, her artists full of a colorful zest for life, was an ideal center for such coloristic, expressive experiments.

The painting, architecture, and music that had been produced here during the Renaissance were strongly influenced by the love for color which so strongly predominated in Eastern art, a joy of life and love for display engendered by the luxurious gaiety and extravagance of her existence, combined with the intellectual and spiritual ideals characteristic of the Florentine and Sienese artists. Important painters who reflected this Venetian way of life were Giovanni Bellini, Giorgione, and Titian. The rich color, marvelous texture, strong contrasts, warm emotion, and gorgeous splendor of the works of these men may be said to be characteristically Venetian.

The new revolutionary ideals characteristic of the music of the Baroque period may be said to have been initiated by the Flemish composer Willaert, who came to Venice in 1527, and climaxed in the monumental works of Andrea and Giovanni Gabrieli, uncle and nephew, both of them organists in the Church of St. Mark's, perhaps the most typically Venetian of all the churches of that city and a colorful symbol of the close bond between its religious and civil life. The music of Giovanni Gabrieli, who died in 1612, mirrors the luxuriance of the Venice of the doges as completely as do the paintings of Giorgione or Titian. It is rich and brilliant, yet deep and profound; although much of it was written for use in the services of the Church, it is nevertheless full of glowing hues and ardent warmth.

In St. Mark's there happened to be two organ lofts, one in each of the side transepts. This circumstance was of great importance for the music of the Gabrielis, for it allowed the use of groups of musicians facing each other across the large, resonant church interior; and it led to the writing of music, both instrumental and vocal, which was based on combinations of differently constituted choirs of instrumentalists and vocalists and which offered plenty of opportunity for the display of ornamentation and virtuosity. It was here, where the sound of the instruments and voices was so effectively realized, that the *stilo concertante* was developed from the earlier many-voiced compositions of the Venetian Renaissance composers. At first there was little stylistic differentiation between vocal and instrumental writing, as can readily be realized by listening to the earlier works of the Gabrielis. But, around about 1600, these happily constituted acoustical features of St. Mark's combined with the peculiar genius of Giovanni Gabrieli to produce what we realize today as the characteristic features of Baroque music: strong, flowing melodic outline, warmly expressive dissonantal features, constantly alternating disposition of contrasting parts, and a largeness of scale and massiveness of proportion. The specific tonal contrasts of color so characteristic of this composer, are first to be observed in his *Sonata pian e forte* (1597) from his *Sacrae symphoniae* and are suggestive of the possibilities of orchestral timbre for creating emotional effects, as well as the effects of light and shade to be gained through the alternation of loud and soft passages in the performance of music. This work for the first time in the history of music indicated in its score the control of tonal intensities. It is written for two instrumental choirs, one of brass and the other of brass and strings.

In other of Gabrieli's *Sacrae symphoniae* we find writing for various combinations of voices and instruments; there does not seem to be any consistent scoring, the vocal choirs sometimes being composed of soloists, sometimes of full chorus; and the instrumental ensembles comprising various combinations of violins, cornetti (wooden horns), trombones, bassoons, and bass viols. In these compositions, as well as in Gabrieli's motets, we get for the first time the full tonal sweep and vibrant sonorities that are so characteristic of Baroque music, as well as the strong tendency towards the harmonic style that was so typical of the other great Baroque musical innovation—the opera.

BAROQUE INSTRUMENTAL FORMS

We can divide the kind of music which came to be written for the new Baroque instruments (including, in addition to the new string and wind instruments, the keyboard-manipulated clavichord and harpsichord) into three general classes:

1) Forms that were derived from vocal models
2) Dance music transplanted from its ballroom origins, which began to be considered as suitable for purely instrumental purposes
3) Idiomatic, rhapsodic forms of a general improvisatory character

In all of these, certain new principles characteristic of the Baroque were apt to determine the structure: a number of different, successive sections; the use of the variation as a means of formal extension; and the use of a patterned bass[6] above which the other parts evolved. The general desire of the Baroque taste for more monumental, ornamental, and expressive utterance helped mould these into impressive, patterned

---

[6] This bass was usually accompanied by a set of symbolic figures designating the chief intervals and chords to be formed above the bass notes. This was called *thorough* bass (old spelling for through), and its use during the Baroque was widespread.

designs which became universally used wherever instrumental music was written.

It is possible to trace the processes by which the early instrumental composers gradually transformed the purely vocal style into a type of writing that was really suited to the instruments in such keyboard arrangements as those made by Andrea Gabrieli from French chansons.[7] The main outlines of the original mould are followed, but often the notes of one or another of the voice parts is divided into shorter values, or they are re-arranged into figured patterns that decorate or elaborate the original. By the beginning of the Baroque era, the change-over from vocal to instrumental style had been fully accomplished, and we find instrumental compositions such as the *ricercar* and *canzona* existing in their own right and no longer dependent upon vocal antecedents for form and structure.

The *ricercar* (its English equivalent was the *fantasy* or *fancy*) first appeared around the beginning of the sixteenth century as a literal transcription of vocal music for keyboard or lute. It gradually took on the features which distinguish it from the other forms, centering around the management of one theme—a development which eventually led directly to the *fugue*. Andrea Gabrieli's *Ricercare Ariosi* suggest the beginning of this practice; it culminated in the great variation *ricercare* of Girolamo Frescobaldi (1583–1643),[8] who, while continuing the tradition of the earlier writer of this form, gave it special distinction because of his imaginative technic and distinctive harmony. The supreme master of the fantasy was Orlando Gibbons, who liked to contrast his various sections in rhythm and tempo; John Coperario (*c.* 1575–1627), an English composer who Latinized his name from Cooper and was court musician to James I, wrote nearly a hundred of these string fantasies. *Ricercare* appeared in collections for harpsichord and organ as well as for chamber-music ensembles, and even for voices.

The *canzona* was usually lighter and less severe in style than the contemporary *ricercar,* with a livelier rhythm which encouraged all sorts of tone repetitions. It was much less contrapuntal and often contained sections of chordal nature in different meters. Frescobaldi, who published four editions of these *canzoni* from 1625 to 1634, indicated definite changes of tempo for his different sections: *allegro* for the contrapuntal, imitative ones and *adagio* for the harmonic sections in

---

[7] A whole volume of these *Canzoni alla francese* was published in Venice in 1605.

[8] The fame of Frescobaldi as an organist was so great that when he played for the first time in St. Peter's, Rome, thirty thousand people came to hear him!

slower time. Thus he led the form directly toward the later *sonata,* a term which became synonymous with the *canzona* form by introducing into it variations on one theme for the purpose of unifying the whole. Still another important pre-fugal form of this sort, usually less restrained than the *ricercar* or *canzona,* was the *capriccio.*

We have seen from such descriptions as those contained in Thoinot Arbeau's manual *Orchésographie* (1589) that the Renaissance dance music gradually changed in the direction of sturdiness as well as loveliness. When transplanted to keyboard instruments, to combinations of strings,[9] wind ensembles, or lutes, these dance tunes were issued in collections in which all the tunes of the same type were put together; as yet there was no idea of the cyclic suite of dance tunes which finally emerged during the Middle Baroque. These collections for lute and guitar became especially popular and contributed greatly to the dissemination of the new harmonic tendencies of the period. The English madrigalists, such as Byrd and Farnaby, were particularly adept at elaborating dance tunes and ballades, providing them with such an abundance of rapid scale passages, syncopated figures, and mechanically developed ornamental patterns as to cause one modern observer to remark that their tunes were completely "atomized."

In the rhapsodic forms of instrumental music, the *toccata, intonazione,* and *prelude* were the types that became popular. Both the toccata and the prelude grew into important forms in later music-making, especially those that were written for the organ. Even the earliest toccatas[10] by Andrea Gabrieli, consisting of big, full chords and interlacing scale passages, were characteristically Baroque in nature, with decidedly expressive significance. As later developed by Frescobaldi, they became a succession of quickly changing sections charged with overflowing imagination and constantly striving for release from the binding constraint of form. His *toccata avanti l'elevazione* was designed for solemn liturgical use, to be played during the elevation of the host in the Mass. Toccatas often served other liturgical functions: the *intonazioni* were used to set the pitch for choral sections that followed, while others became rhapsodic preludes to larger pieces or existed as compositions of considerable length in dignified style.

The St. Peter's organist also cultivated the German form of improvising on a Gregorian *cantus firmus.* Such improvisatory pieces were used

---

[9] The violin was particularly appropriate for dance music because of its keen tone.

[10] "Touch" pieces as contrasted with "sounding" pieces for the strings or "singing" pieces for the voices. The Italian terms are significant: toccata, sonata, cantata.

as versets, the short organ pieces that were played as substitutes for the singing of a Gregorian verse or canticle, or as short liturgical pieces as a means for relieving the monotony of a whole service in Gregorian plainchant. Frescobaldi developed these *cantus-firmus* treatments so effectively (his collection called *Fiori Musicali* was published in 1635) that they served as stimulating models for the developing style of the young Sebastian Bach some seventy years later. Using a highly colored chromaticism and demanding a brilliant performance and an effective *tempo rubato,* the Frescobaldi compositions are magnificent examples of the extent to which the early Baroque style became emancipated from the past.

Still another type of early Baroque music needs mention here, the trio-sonata, which developed into the most important type of chamber music used during this period. These are first to be found in Salomone Rossi's *Sinfonia e Galiarde,* among the earliest examples of Barcque published books devoted exclusively to instrumental music (1607). They were written for two melody instruments of similar range and a third, supporting thorough-bass part; the first of those issued leaves a choice between violins and cornetti for the upper parts, while the figured bass was to be "realized" (or played) on a harpsichord with the addition of some bowed-bass instrument, a practice which later became general. Afterwards, specific directions were given for the use of violins, and these trio-sonatas were established in two types that became general in all countries: *church sonatas* and *chamber sonatas.*

In the north, the Hollander Jan Sweelinck (1562–1621) merged the new Italian instrumental forms with the brilliant technical resources of the English virginalists to make the giant organ *fugue* which we know so well through the works of Sebastian Bach. In addition, his variations of psalm tunes and chorales begin the long and brilliant history of this particular form, a history which again culminated in the work of Bach. Although somewhat more severe than his southern contemporaries, Sweelinck was none the less a real Baroque composer, his work constantly soaring toward an ultimate, climactic finish in a thoroughly Baroque fashion.

Sweelinck's German contemporary, Hans Leo Hassler (1564–1612), the first of the German composers to undertake an Italian journey, was a pupil of Andrea Gabrieli; as we have said, he mixed Italian style and German sentiment, as did so many other Renaissance and Baroque German artists who studied in Italy. He gave, in his *Psalmen* and *Christliche Gesang,* examples of various ways of elaborating the chorale or Lutheran hymn. But he was completely outdistanced by the great Brunswick *Kapellmeister* Michael Praetorius (1571–1621), who wrote a number of Gabrieli-like compositions of enormous scope, combining chorus, solo singers, and instruments in characteristic Baroque fashion. Praetorius's comprehensive work, *Syntagma musicum,* issued from 1612 to 1620, is our principal source of information regarding the music and instruments of this time. And his *Musae Sioniae* gives us a complete collection, containing more than twelve hundred examples, of the ways in which chorales could be treated both vocally and instrumentally. It was the pioneering work of these early German composers that paved the way for the more important developments of Schütz in the Middle Baroque and Bach in the High Baroque period.

THE MIDDLE BAROQUE

Period: 1630-1680

*In Venice I learned that the long unchanged theory
of writing melodies had set aside the ancient ideas
to tickle the ears of today with fresh devices.*

Schütz (1629)

IN ITALY

The most impor-
tant aspect of the development of the new operatic style, once it had been
invented in Italy, was the emergence of the so-called *bel canto* style, a
sort of reaction against the overexuberances of the earlier operas and oratorios, in which the demands of the poets outweighed the significance of
the musicians. Once the opera had become established as a popular form,
it was natural that a balance between its two constituent parts—drama
and music—should be established. It may be added here that the swing
between an overemphasis on one of these elements at the expense of the
other and then a restoration of a more proper balance between the two
has continued all through the turbulent history of opera. The inherent
rights of music as a constituent part of the opera form were restored
during the so-called Middle Baroque period in Italy by such men as
Luigi Rossi (1598-1653), Giacomo Carissimi (1605-1674), Pietro
Francesco Cavalli (1602-1676), and Marc Antonio Cesti (1623-1669).
Working in the various vocal forms then current—the cantata and the
oratorio, as well as the opera—these big men of the time developed a
new musical style, one in which more polished and brilliant if less
expressive melodies, simpler harmonies, and a distinct differentiation
between recitative and aria took the place of the earlier Baroque attempt
to achieve expressive utterance at all costs. In addition to the recitative
as developed by the operatic pioneers (*secco,* or dry recitative, it was
called), an effective type of accompanied (*stromentato*) recitative

301

called the *arioso,* or dramatic recitative, was evolved at this time. This gave the composer three types of vocal writing suited to different dramatic purposes: the *secco* recitative for narrative, the *arioso* for dramatic, and the *aria* for lyric or ornamental purposes.

Luigi Rossi (to be differentiated from an earlier instrumental composer) was a Roman composer who specialized in a type of music that has almost completely disappeared today—what might be called vocal chamber music. This consisted of short compositions for one or several voices, written in a composite form in which recitative, arioso, and aria were attenuated; they were intended for the salons and music rooms of the wealthy patrons of art and were by no means thought to be inferior to the opera and oratorio. Rossi wrote a great number of chamber cantatas (250 of them are still extant), many of them for one voice which both "narrated" and "acted." Carissimi, who is largely known for his oratorios, especially cultivated these cantatas and may be said to have established a type which was richly developed by later composers and which culminated in the great cantatas of J. S. Bach. Other Middle Baroque composers of cantatas were Cesti (a pupil of Carissimi), Stradella, and Legrenzi, as well as that strange, stormy Baroque figure, the composer-painter Salvatore Rosa.

The oratorio, deriving originally from the same stem as the opera and making use of the same structural elements—recitative, arioso, aria, ensemble, chorus, and orchestra—had as its distinctive feature a narrator, or *testo,* who supplied the general dramatic spirit in lieu of the operatic stage and its scenic appurtenances. The oratorio was eagerly taken up by the Jesuits in their campaign to re-establish the glory and power of the Church and to stem the powerful tides of secularization then sweeping through Europe. It was established as a thoroughly artistic form by Carissimi, who wrote a number of these works in Latin,[1] including his masterpiece, *Jephtha.* These works are characteristically Baroque in their big (sometimes double or even triple) choruses and their sweeping, declamatory, and powerfully rhythmic recitatives. Carissimi was called by his contemporaries a master of rhetorical eloquence, a description which applies equally well to his successors using this form, Charpentier in France and (later) G. F. Handel in England. Legrenzi (1626-1690) and Stradella (c.1645-1682), both of whom re-introduced massive contrapuntal choruses into their oratorios,

---

[1] Two types of oratorio were current: the *volgare,* written in Italian and often on secular, popular subjects; and the *Latin,* with themes largely taken from the Old Testament.

represent the peak of the period insofar as oratorio composition is concerned.

It was during the years around 1630 that some of the most impressive architectural expressions of the Baroque spirit were being consummated. The great church of St. Peter's in Rome, for example, one of the most stupendous of all man's creations, capable of seating nearly seventy thousand people, was finally dedicated in 1626, after having been in construction for a hundred seventy-six years. Nothing could better express the striving for grandiose and overwhelming artistic effects which was so typical of the time; and it was natural that all the arts, including music, were called upon to enrich and decorate its immense spaces. It was not at all uncommon to hear in the Roman churches of this period great polyphonic compositions for six and even more choruses, vocal and instrumental, reflecting the pomp and ceremony of the ritual as they rolled around the reverberant interiors of these huge churches.

The cathedral at Salzburg in Austria, designed by Italian architects, started in 1614 and finished in 1655, was the first great example of Baroque in that country. Following its construction, the archbishops transformed medieval Salzburg into the lovely Baroque city we know today. For the dedication of the new church, the Roman composer Orazio Benévoli (1602–1672) composed a polychordal Mass for fifty-three parts, written for two eight-voice choruses, each with its continuous accompaniment, two organs, and six instrumental ensembles— one for wood winds, three for brass, and two for stringed instruments. Even with all its doubling of parts, this tremendous work suits perfectly the massive spatial dispositions of the building for which it was written; and when heard there, with the choruses and instrumental ensembles distributed in the lofts and balconies of the enormous church, the effect is colossal, imposing—Baroque.

But it was in the field of opera that the most significant contributions of the period were made, especially in those operas composed in Venice, where as early as 1637 special houses were set aside for their performance. The first great name is Cavalli, one of the earliest composers to possess the special melodic gifts that are especially necessary in opera writing. He composed forty-two operas, including *Didone,* in which the *bel canto* aria appears fully established for the first time and whose success eclipsed that of the greatest works in the field down to that time, the operas of Monteverdi. Other Cavalli operas include *Egisto,* produced in Vienna in 1642, and *Ercole amante,* composed for the

INTERIOR OF THE CORTINA THEATER, VIENNA (1667)   The production is that
of Cesti's *Il Pomo d'oro* (from an engraving by Franz Geffels).

marriage of Louis xiv in Paris in 1662. Cavalli's fame continued unabated until it was supplanted by that of his great rival, Cesti, whose
"grand festival show piece," *Il Pomo d'oro,* remains the most typical
piece of its period, although, according to the experts, it is not as
dramatically effective as some of his other works.

A well-known engraving of the time shows the interior of one of the
theaters in Vienna during a performance of this opera.[2] Everything
bespeaks the spirit of the Baroque—the splendor of the interior of the
theater, decorated in characteristic fashion, the magnificence of the
audience, the elaborateness of the stage appointments. And, if we
examine the music of this work (or any other opera by the composers
of this period), we find a greatly increased emphasis upon choral writ-

[2] This opera was written in 1667 in honor of the wedding of Leopold i, Emperor of
Austria, mighty warrior and the founder of a magnificent operatic enterprise, which was
able to produce no fewer than an average of eight operas a year through a period of
half a century—over four hundred new works all together.

ing, everything designed from the standpoint of the singer rather than from that of the composer. The vocal lines are no longer direct and simple but have developed devices which show off the voice well; the arias are written in a carefully conscious, popular style; the harmonies are clear and distinct; the rhythms are brisk and strong; and there is a predilection for massed choral effects. *Il Pomo d'oro* and the other Baroque operas are in essence "singers' operas," with emphasis put upon melody and brilliance; plot and expressive truth are not considered as important as formerly. The operatic achievements of Cavalli and Cesti were expanded and enlarged by a later generation of Venetians, of which Legrenzi, Stradella, and Pallavicini (*d.* 1688?) seem the most important; the works of all these men already show the transition to a later and more advanced Baroque style.

Insofar as Italian instrumental music during this period is concerned, the chief activity was in chamber music, which flourished particularly in the three northern centers of Modena, Venice, and Bologna, centers in which art had always been cultivated during the Renaissance. It was during the Middle Baroque that the nature of the *sonata da camera* (a suite made up of a freely ordered series of dances) became clearly distinct from the *sonata da chiesa* (comprised of alternating slow and fast dance movements without dance rhythms), a distinction which became even more marked in later times. The best-known figures of this whole instrumental development were the Venetian Legrenzi and the Bolognese Vitali (1665-1735), who delighted in the use of the rich kind of instrumental counterpoint that became so important a characteristic of the later concerto style.

IN GERMANY

Just as surely as in the other arts, the Baroque spirit in music spread quickly from its Italian birthplace to other European countries, at least to those centers where music was loved, such as Munich and Vienna. It was the Italians who originated the style, and the composers of the other countries copied it, in opera and oratorio and chamber music. Naturally the spirit of these other countries worked upon and changed the forms somewhat, especially in the case of oratorio and cantata, because of the obvious differences in religion between the north and the south. When transplanted to Germany, these forms flourished under the patronage of the Church, particularly since the impoverished condition of the country, due to long-continued wars, made adequate support of the opera difficult. While German choral music lost something of its Italian freedom of vocal utterance, it gained much in the development of its formal side, a development which led, through Schütz, to Bach and his great Mass, Passions, and cantatas.

The connection between Italian and German musical styles was made largely at the hands of the three composers Heinrich Schütz (1585-1672), Johann Hermann Schein (1586-1630), and Samuel Scheidt (1587-1654). These masters, aided by a number of lesser lights, changed the Italian concerto of the Gabrieli type into the German chorale cantata based upon or woven around a chorale, as we know it today by the many examples left us by J. S. Bach.

Of the three S's, by far the greatest was Schütz, so far the greatest that he is called the Father of German music. He was born just a century before Bach into a world made difficult by strife and conflict; he spent much time abroad, coming into contact in Venice with the operatic developments mentioned above. He studied with Giacomo Gabrieli, whose influence on his style is strongly marked. When he went back to Germany and was made director of the music at the court of the Elector of Saxony, he sent some of the other royal musicians to Italy to benefit as he had. Schütz even put Rinuccini's libretto of *Dafne* into German for a performance at the court,[3] a performance that was probably the first operatic presentation in Germany. But opera in the Italian style did not prove to be a very congenial form to the Germans, and although there were several attempts at writing native works, notably *Seelewig,* an allegorical dramatization from the *Frauenzimmer Gesprechspiele,* set in Italian fashion by Georg Philipp Harsdörffer, with music by Sigmund Gottlieb Staden, the form did not flourish.

Schütz's great contribution to German music was in the field of the dramatic *concertato,* a type which he took over from his contemporaries and carried to great heights of accomplishment. These vocal compositions[4] were written for religious use and contain a great profusion of inspired music written for almost unlimited vocal and instrumental combinations. He was able to achieve a real difference between the type of music best suited to the solo voice and that written for choral ensembles. Like Monteverdi and his master, Gabrieli, Schütz transposed the madrigal style to sacred music, and in so doing accomplished an almost perfect union of Italian style and German words.

[3] The translation was by Martin Opitz, the great German Baroque poet of the time.
[4] It is interesting to note that Schütz never wrote any independent instrumental music.

In his larger works, such as his *Psalmen Davids,* his *Symphoniae sacrae,* and especially his oratorio-type compositions—*Auferstehungs Historie* (1623), *Sieben Worte am Kreuz,* the *Historie von der Geburth Gottes* (1644)—and the three Passions according to St. Luke, St. John, and St. Matthew (1666), he points the way directly to the great German Baroque style of Bach and Handel. The crisp chording, the taking-up of the music in one part after another, the massive effects, and the big, swelling, woven endings suggest a lively, fresh approach to the text, a sense of pomp, drama, and dignity in which we sense not only a mingling of Italian and German types of mind but also a personal grasp of the material that is the sign of real genius. In some of his latest works, such as the Passions, Schütz shows an inclination toward a severity which fortunately had little effect upon his contemporaries or pupils. He even went, in these last works, so far as to use a strict *a cappella* style for his recitatives as well as for his choruses.

In music of the secular type, the Germans seemed little inclined to follow the Italian trend towards monody. As we have seen, Hassler brought with him from Italy a knowledge of Italian part songs suitable for "singing, playing, and dancing," and tried to incorporate these into his *Lustgarten* (1601), a collection of German songs "in the manner of foreign madrigals and canzonets." Schein and Schütz followed him in this with their attempts to adapt the poetic form of the madrigal. But the chief form of German secular music during the earlier Baroque years was the *continuo lied,* an adaptation of the song literature evolved by the lutenists of the other countries. The composers of these continuo songs, such men as Albert, Selle, Rist (a poet as well as musician), and especially Adam Krieger, combined Italian love for melody with the German predilection for rhythm derived from their dance music; thus there evolved an important type of song, a type which strongly foreshadowed the later German songs of the Romantic period. The achievements of this period in opera and oratorio were largely in the hands of the Italian musicians employed in the various courts, especially those at Munich and Vienna. The only important German theater where opera was cultivated was that at Hamburg from about 1678 to 1738; the most important figure in this rather desultory development was Reinhard Keiser (1674-1739), as highly prolific a composer as he was a ramshackle adventurer.

The great significance of Scheidt as a figure in German music was in the field of instrumental writing. With him, German organ music may be said to have come into its own; his *Tabulatura Nova,* of 1624,

A SETTING FROM STEFFANI'S *SERVO TULLIO*   The opera, produced in Munich in
1685-1686, showed this forest scene according to Baroque ideals.

a vast collection of organ music written in various forms, was the first
work to show completely the different methods of paraphrasing the
German chorale melodies for the organ and thus had a strong influence,
through the later Pachelbel and Böhm, upon Bach. Scheidt's instrumental style was moulded by the peculiar tonal characteristics of the
Baroque organ, characteristics that had been carefully described by
Praetorius in his *Syntagma musicum,* with its sharply differentiated
tone colors and rather bright, penetrating, brilliant tone. This type of
organ ensemble tone has recently become quite popular with some
modern organ builders in their attempt to provide suitable instruments
for the music of the Baroque period. Johann Pachelbel (1653–1706),
a South German organist prominent in Nuremberg, was a follower of
Frescobaldi and thus transmitted the Italian traditions directly to the
German style.

Both Schein and Scheidt played a considerable role in the evolution
of the German instrumental suite. In 1617, there appeared the *Banchetto*

musicale (Musical Banquet) by Schein, a printed collection of pavans, galliards, courantes, allemandes, and triplas, or *Nachtänze;* these were gathered into sets of five each, all the dances in each set being in one key and having the same melodic theme. This gave the idea of the suite a tremendous impetus and was followed in 1621 by similar sets by Scheidt. The sequence of dances which later became so usual in the suite—allemande, courante, saraband, and gigue—is often attributed to Johann Froberger (1616-1667), a harpsichordist and organist at the Austrian court, who in his wide travels about Europe had come into contact with the keyboard music of Italian, French, and English masters. In Paris he had come under the influence of the French lutenists and their use of ornaments; incorporated into his writing, these mannerisms remained an important ornamental feature of Baroque music in Germany, even in its final, great period. In 1658 Johann Jakob Loewe supplied introductions to his suites which he called *sinfonie,* a practice which paved the way for the overture of the later Baroque suites. Froberger also wrote outstanding toccatas, *canzone,* and *ricercare* for both harpsichord and organ, formalizing and clarifying the earlier loquacity of Baroque expression.

The Germans of the Middle Baroque also showed their natural taste for polyphony in the ensemble suites which they wrote for various instrumental combinations. The works of Johann Rosenmüller (*c.* 1620-1684) in this style, with their regularly established introductory *sinfonie,* show real genius and are very interesting to modern ears. Heinrich Biber (1644–1704) wrote trio ensembles and solo sonatas for the violin, some of which are strangely suggestive of the later solo violin works of Bach and characteristically Baroque in their search for unusual and rather strained effects, often calling for different tunings of all the strings of the violin in order to gain new colors and timbres.

THE MIDDLE BAROQUE IN FRANCE

It was natural that the Baroque influence, so exactly suited to Italy and the buoyant, exuberant Italian temperament, would be somewhat modified in France by the inclination towards classic restraint, which is so strongly characteristic of the French temperament and its insistence upon the necessity for the predominance of reason and will over sentiment in artistic expression. So it was that because of their respect for tradition and their dislike of what they considered ostentatious display in bad taste, the French musicians were among the last to accept the

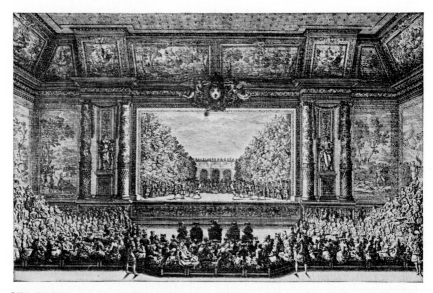

LES FESTES DE L'AMOUR ET DE BACCHUS by Jean Lepautre   The seventeenth-century spectacle — "a comedy with music" — was given in the theater at Versailles in 1664.

ornamental innovations of the Baroque style and the first to demand its restraint and mitigation.

That the French of the Baroque period regarded music as a "sonorous decoration rather than as the vehicle for the affections" is clearly evident in the *Harmonie universelle* (1627) of Father Marin Mersenne, a friend of the French philosopher Descartes; he thus describes the differences between Italian and French music, while reproaching his countrymen for their neglect of emotional expression: "The Italians express passion, intellectual ideas, and spirited emotions just as naturally as they can and with a strange violence, while we French are anxious that our music be dominated by sweetness. Music should force its way into the listener's soul to possess and lead it whither the composer wishes." Instead of developing a *stilo rappresentativo* to "create emotion in order to penetrate to the depths of human feeling," the French effected their musical reform by imitating the ancient meters in their *vers mesuré* and tried to fuse these quantitative meters of French poetry with the new Italian declamatory style in music. The result was a classic hobbling of Baroque intentions, with a real loss of expressive capacity.

The French musical Baroque style began with Louis XIII, who succeeded to the throne in 1610; it reached its climax with the Sun King, Louis XIV (1643-1715); and it gradually merged with the more emotionally disposed Rococo style after his death. French Baroque was strongly based on the dramatic developments that centered around the stage ballet, always a predominant feature in French artistic life. Modeled after the Italian entertainments of the Renaissance, these musico-dramatic *ballets de cour* consisted of a varying number of *entrées* (ballet subdivisions corresponding to scenes in opera) that were acted, and connecting *récits* that were spoken or sung. Each *entrée* was accompanied by music, sometimes by choral ensembles, sometimes by solo songs with lute accompaniment, and sometimes by ensemble music for lute and string groups. The musicians were usually professionals hidden from the audience unless they were part of the stage *décor;* oftentimes the dancers were courtiers or perhaps even royalty associated with the courts. Under the influence of Baroque taste, the *ballets de cour* became more and more decorative and grandiose, their designers indulging in all sorts of fantastic and exotic schemes to provide impressive costumes and unusual stage *décor*.[5] The composers of these ballets held influential positions at court. Among the most important of them were Pierre Guédron, successor to Claude le Jeune; Jean de Cambefort; Guillaume Dumanoir, *Roi des violons;* and Jean Baptiste Lully, born in 1652 in Florence as Giovanni Battista Lulli.

At the age of fourteen, this future Frenchman was taken to Paris and placed as kitchen scullion in one of the establishments of a court favorite. His natural gifts for music and dancing, combined with a native wit, a quick intelligence, and an ability to cope with the sort of scurrilities beloved by the French, finally gave him the position of real musical dictator in Paris, with complete control of the *grande bande* and the sole right to produce opera with all the proceeds accruing to himself and his heirs. Thus, Lully became as absolute a ruler in the

[5] Henri Prunières in his *Le Ballet de cour avant Lully* gives an interesting account of one of these early French ballets:

"The curtain, opening, discovered a *décor* representing a forest. A curious person emerged. It was 'Messire Gobbemagne, grand gonfalonier of the Isle of Monkeys,' followed by three violins 'dressed as Turks, who danced and played.' Gobbemagne drew from the wood two torchbearing pages disguised as green snails, who did monkey tricks in cadence. Then one after the other all the violins and all the torchbearers entered the hall. The violins mounted onto their stand, and the green snails, having danced bizarrely, retired. After this burlesque prologue, the action began: the enchantress Alcine came out of the forest, sounding a lute. . . . Alcine came before the king's throne and sang verses in which she was followed by her chorus of nymphs, who took up the last verse of each rhyme." (See picture, page 284.)

field of music as his patron king was in state affairs; he learned how to please the French with the many comedies-ballets he wrote for court performance. Written in conjunction with Molière, these comedies-ballets were attempts to enhance the importance of the play by detaching it completely from the ballet and thus restore the original dramatic significance of the latter. They included such famous pieces as the *Mariage Forcé* and the *Bourgeois Gentilhomme*. Lully's outstanding musicianship and energy enabled him to anticipate the needs of the public, and he was shrewd enough to use the French fondness for dancing and pageantry as the foundation upon which to build opera.

The important characteristics of the Lully operas (he wrote some sixteen in all) were their dramatic recitatives, their large and well-developed choral and orchestral forms, and their instrumental overtures, all these features taken over from his ballets.[6] Most of his music sounds dry and conventional to us today, but we must remember that for over a century it constituted for the world a model for all the instrumental music of Europe. In his dramatic arias and recitatives, there is a careful maintenance of the principles of proper declamation rather than any attempt to provide pleasing vocal melodies in the Italian fashion of the time. The arias are not greatly different from the recitatives, both being marked by classic restraint and respect for declamatory values.[7] One of his happiest inspirations—truly Baroque in every sense of the word—was the form he developed for his overtures: pompous, regal first section; a lively fugued second; and a slow, sustained finale to relieve the rhythmic tension and soothe the ear. In listening to these overtures, it does not require too much imagination to hear in their strains a suggestion of the regal Baroque elegance of the Sun King's court. The form of the Lullian overture was generally adopted by the composers of other nations and was used by them for many years.

Other outstanding features of the Lully operas, to which he gave the title *tragèdie lyrique,* that stamped themselves indelibly on the national French school were the prologues of gods and goddesses singing the praises of the king in massive chordal choruses, with all the pomp and circumstance of court etiquette; and the elevation of the orchestra to a place of greater importance than it had occupied in the Italian works,

---

[6] The single scenes of the comedies-ballets were connected by recitatives, as in the contemporary Italian operas.

[7] Lully studied the performances of the *Comédie française* to observe the accents and inflections of the great actresses appearing there in the French classics of Racine and other dramatists.

placing emphasis upon the beauties of vocal utterance. The first opera finished by Lully was *Cadmus et Hermione* (1673); other well-known ones are *Acis et Galatée* (1677), *Persée* (1682), and *Armide* (1686).

Lully was the greatest of the Baroque musical figures in France. Together with Molière, he dominated the whole dramatic situation there for years, his influence felt in every circle. The story goes that when a powerful cabinet minister of the time demanded from Lully, "How do you have the nerve to apply for a post on my committee? Did you ever do anything aside from making people happy?", the composer replied complacently, "If you could have managed to do that, you would be as satisfied about it as I am!"

In Paris the opera and ballet held such a dominating position that the other forms of vocal music—the cantata, oratorio, and church motets—did not develop too vigorously. We today are beginning to realize, however, through a number of excellent recordings recently made available, that there was another remarkable figure in Marc Antoine Charpentier (1634-1704), a native Frenchman who upheld in his own country the peculiarly Baroque style of Italy against the claims of the rather dry, classic French style of Lully, the native Italian! Inspired by Carissimi's models, Charpentier wrote an important opera, *Médée,* in 1693 and a number of "sacred tragedies" for performance by the Parisian Jesuits, as well as some French and Latin oratorios and solemn motets for solo, chorus, and orchestra similar in form to the English "anthem." Lully did some of these, too, and we find in this splendidly expressive liturgical music, with its gigantic vocal forces and orchestras complete with trumpets and kettle drums, the Baroque splendor of the court transplanted to the Church. Charpentier's other compositions include a number of Masses, a *Te Deum, Magnificats, Leçons de ténèbre* for Holy Week services, and some psalm settings.

The French lute and keyboard music of this period is especially important, since it developed instrumental idioms and fashions which were copied by the rest of Europe, as French styles in general were. One historian of the period goes so far as to say that it was the art of French lutenists of this period which made possible the marvelous clavecin music that was later produced during the Rococo era. The above-quoted authority on French music—today we would call him a musicologist—Father Mersenne,[8] considered the lute as the noblest of

---

[8] In addition to being a priest, Mersenne was a philosopher, mathematician, musician, and writer. His *Harmonie universelle* was only one of a number of books he wrote on these subjects.

all instruments, literally the instrument of kings and noblemen, since they played it so well themselves. The great number of lute music collections that had been published in France down to this time (the best known was Besard's *Thesaurus,* 1603) attest to the popularity of the instrument and the high technical standards demanded of its players.

The lute compositions culminated in the works of the Gaultiers,[9] a family of seventeenth-century lute virtuosi. The principal features of their music, especially their types of sustaining ornament and their use of the so-called "broken-style,"[10] survived in the music written for the later use of harpsichord and clavichord players. Most of the music in these Gaultier collections consisted of dances in highly stylized form, arranged in groups or suites, which were really collections of dances rather than carefully planned sequences. The basic allemande, courante, and saraband (sometimes gigue) were interspersed with other popular dance types, pavans, chaconnes, canaries;[11] *doubles* or variations on one of these dances, particularly the courante and saraband, were often included, and the whole collection was held together through the strict observance of a unity of key for all the dances. Often separate dance pieces were given suggestive and poetic names, following the custom borrowed from the English virginalists; these were not necessarily meant to convey any program meaning but rather to suggest some literary allusion. Especially popular were the *tombeaux,* or laments, written in honor of some illustrious dead person and based, in spite of their grave nature, on stylized dance patterns.

All of these features were taken over by the Middle Baroque clavecinists, the most representative of whom were Jacques de Chambonnières (1602-1672), official court player; Louis Couperin (c. 1626-1661); Jean Henri D'Anglebert (1635-1691); and LeBègue (1630-1702). Gradually, the texture of this music changed; it became richer, and its tonal range wider. The dance suite became longer, and a unity of key relationship was no longer held to be absolutely necessary. When transferred to the slower-speaking organ, this keyboard style had to be modified somewhat, especially since it seemed difficult to get away from the contrapuntal style traditional with that instrument; a great deal of attention was paid to the coloristic possibilities of the

[9] The principal members were Jacques, who played at the English court, and his cousin Denis (c. 1603–1672), called *l'illustré.*

[10] The *stile brisé* made extensive use of chords played in arpeggio fashion in order to simu'ate a continuous strand of sound.

[11] Designed as an imitation of the *sauvages des iles Canaries,* and so understandingly popular.

HENRY PURCELL

organ, this becoming a traditional feature of all the music written for the instrument. Titelouze (1563-1633) was the most important organ composer of the Early Baroque; Gigault, LeBègue, Roberday, Nivers, and Louis Couperin represent the Middle Baroque generation. Even dance patterns, ornaments and all, were introduced into the liturgical services, this practice being excused if the dances were played slowly, "in keeping with the sanctity of the church!" Altogether this was a most exciting and fruitful period for French keyboard music.

ENGLISH DEVELOPMENTS

"Dyed, but a greater musical genius England never had. Purcell began to show his great skill before the reforme of musick and while he was in pursuit of it." Thus a famous English writer of the time describes the one great English figure of the Middle Baroque. But Purcell was hardly typical; because of their northern temperament and their particular political problems, the English had espoused the Baroque style even less than had the French. This is as true of the other arts as it was of the music of this period, which for long was considered merely a lamentable degeneration of the great achievements wrought during the Elizabethan, Renaissance era. And so the

music, architecture, and literature of the Restoration period, beginning
with the return of Charles II in 1660, has not always been fairly judged
by the critics of the English-speaking world.

The most obvious connection with Italy insofar as music was concerned was that of dramatic music, especially the sort which was used
in the exclusive circles of the court for entertainment purposes. These
grandiose entertainments, called masques, as we have already said,
were made up of a combination of poetry, music, dancing, acting,
costume, pageantry, and scenic *décor* and corresponded to the big
Baroque *intermezzi* of Italy and the *ballets de cour* in France. All the
resources of the court were applied in the most lavish manner, and
these productions, which were built around mythological and allegorical subjects, united in typical Baroque fashion the talents of the
best artists, architects, and musicians of the period. Some of the greatest
authors of the masques in Elizabethan times had been Ben Jonson,
Fletcher, Chapman, Beaumont, Dekker, and Ford. Inigo Jones, the
leading architect of the Early Baroque, who had visited Italy before
1603, brought to the English stage the full developments of the
Italian stage craftsmen; working with Jonson, Inigo Jones evolved
the famous *Masque of Blackness* in 1605, the first English court
masque to match all the Baroque grandeurs of the contemporary intermezzi, and the first of a long series of such productions that lasted
until 1631. The masque became more important as a literary form
than as a musical one, and it influenced both the drama (as the plays
of Beaumont and Fletcher show well enough) and the English opera,
which may be said to have grown directly out of it.

At first, the composers of masque music were strongly influenced
by the contrapuntal style of Renaissance music; but the composers
of the Middle Baroque readily adapted the *stilo rappresentativo* to the
English language and developed a monodic style of writing. The chief
figures of these music masters of the masque were Nicholas Lanier
(*d.* 1666); the two Lawes brothers, Henry (1596-1662) and William
(1602-1645); Charles Coleman (*d.* 1664); Captain Cooke (*c.* 1615-
1672); Christopher Gibbons (1615-1676); and Matthew Locke
(*c.* 1630-1677). None of these musicians were able to reach the effective intensity of the Italians, however, even in the "songs" which they
introduced later into their scenes; and it was not until the later
Humfrey, Blow, and Purcell that we get any real expressive utterance
in English Baroque music.

Cromwell's rise to power in 1653 retarded but did not interrupt completely the development of dramatic music, even though it made necessary such subterfuge as the description of what may be called the first English opera, Davenant's *The Siege of Rhodes,* with music by Matthew Locke, Coleman, Cooke, and Henry Lawes,[12] as a "representation"! With the Restoration, Charles II brought in foreign musicians to suit his rather frivolous taste. And such native composers as Locke and John Blow (1648-1708) became firmly fixed in the Baroque, non-native traditions: the music of Blow's short opera, *Venus and Adonis* (1682), with its expressive recitatives and powerful choruses, points directly towards the work of his pupil, the "Restoration Genius," Henry Purcell (*c.* 1659-1695).

It is hardly to be wondered at that one side of Purcell's work shows the strong influence of the court, which musicians at the time were bound to flatter. It is by his other, deeper side that he ought to be judged, especially by what he was able to do in his single opera, *Dido and Aeneas,* composed for performance at a girls' school.

This little opera, like so many early works in this form, goes back to classic mythology for its subject: the story is the well-known one from the fourth book of Virgil's *Aeneid,* to which are added certain features popular in the Restoration theater. There is a rousing chorus of witches, and the original performance was prefaced by an epilogue that was very characteristic of the time. It contained such lines as these:

Here, blest with innocence and peace of mind,
Not only bred to virtue, but inclin'd;
We flowrish, and defie all human kind.

And the bad men-around-town are repulsed with vehemence:

Let the vain Fop range yon vile lewd Town,
Learn Play-house Wit, and vow 'tis all his own;
Let him Cock, Huff, Strut, Ogle, Lye and Swear,
How he's admired by such and such a Player;
All's one to us, his Charms have here no power,
Our Hearts have just the temper as before;
Besides to show we live with strictest Rules,
Our Nunnery-Door is charm'd to shut out Fools.

[12] It was Henry Lawes who set the music to Milton's *Comus,* eliciting the following tribute from the greatest of all English Baroque poets:

> Harry, whose tuneful and well-measured song
> First taught our English music how to span
> Words with just note and accent.

With an atmosphere such as this, together with limited forces (the soloists were probably brought in by the composer), it is hardly to be expected that Purcell could do his best work. *Dido and Aeneas* contains one great song which is universally known—Dido's Lament, sung before she takes her life: a masterpiece indeed, written, like so many of Purcell's themes, on a ground bass (that is, a short theme which is repeated all the time as the bass of the harmonies). The poignancy, the swift intense power of the music is beyond all praise. But apart from one other striking song, this opera is almost scrappy; everything is too short. We are just getting into a mood when it is broken off. There are excellent dances, Purcell's music being one of the deftest ever to set foot a-moving; there are some of the too-brief strokes of witchcraft music that are more fully filled out in other works. And there is, if we can get into it, a direct, English, open-air sentiment which is likable enough. This spirit is to be found most purely in some of his other songs: "Britons, Strike Home," "I Attempt from Love's Sickness to Fly," "Nymphs and Shepherds," and a score of others, every one strongly tinctured with both a personal and a national style. Purcell learned much from both the French and the Italians and always gladly acknowledged this, with a modesty that is not the least of his admirable traits. But it is for his quality of Englishness—Shakespearean in both its freshness and subtlety, not the grosser Englishness of "John Bull"—that he stands out in memory, with something of pathos, against the poor background of his time and because of the shortness of his life.

Aside from his fine sense of drama, one of this composer's most striking features was his understanding of the voice: he is like Handel in that, though probably in nothing else. Purcell was brought up among singers in the Chapel Royal and later became organist of Westminster Abbey.

Though his life was so sadly short, Purcell wrote harpsichord and string music in great abundance but with only occasional distinction; settings of Pope and Dryden odes written for courtly occasions after the fashion of Lully; church music, especially "verse-anthems" full of polyphonic richness as well as rather unexpected harmonies (it is always difficult to remember that Purcell was a half century before Bach); solo songs with fine declamatory and chromatically expressive elements; and miscellaneous hack music for masques, scenes and songs to be inserted in the plays of Shakespeare, Dryden, and Congreve.

The outstanding genius of the Middle Baroque insofar as English music is concerned, Purcell has always seemed unfortunate in his day and generation; and England was still more unfortunate in that he lived for so short a time. Today, we are coming to realize that not only was he a predecessor of the great masters of the High Baroque style, but that he had distinctive characteristics of his own, "clogged" though they be "with somewhat of the English vein," which endear his music to our ears.

In addition to Purcell, there were several other writers of church music in England of some significance during this period, most of them active after the Restoration,[13] writing anthems and settings for the liturgy of the Anglican Church. The most important of these were Pelham Humfrey (1647-1674), John Blow, Michael Wise (*d.* 1687), Jeremiah Clark (1659-1707), and the late-Baroque William Croft (1678-1727) and Maurice Greene (1694-1755).

In the field of consort or concerted music in England, that for viols and violins was most popular, the violins gradually supplanting the viols, although these latter were popular well into the eighteenth century. *Fancies* (fantasias) were the most popular form; they were written by most of the composers of the time, including the Lawes brothers, John Jenkins (1592-1678), Locke, and Purcell, whose fantasias for strings, written in 1680, may be considered as the last of this form to be composed.

That the aristocratic English of this period were as partial to dancing as their European contemporaries is evidenced by the appearance of a huge collection of *Court Ayres,* published by the Father of British Music Publishing, John Playford, in 1655 and again in 1662. These collections contained a group of more than five hundred dances, of various sorts, written by almost every well-known composer of the day. In 1650 Playford had also published a large collection of popular dance music and songs suited to the use of the middle class, called *The English Dancing Master.* In these, the violin appears in its full glory. Most of the composers contributed to this publication also, as they did to such collections as John Hilton's *Catch That Catch Can* (1652), a compilation of the peculiarly English form of the *catch* (round or canon), a rather lowly form of the convivial type of madrigal, with words usually "of the most robust indecency."

[13] The metrical psalm settings were the only church music to which the Puritans did not object.

THE HIGH BAROQUE

Period: 1680-1750

The present is loaded with the past and pregnant with the future.

Leibniz

He who would obtain something in the way of an understanding of the spirit which underlay the last years of the seventeenth and the first half of the eighteenth century, the period which historians call the High (or Late) Baroque, can do no better than read Sacheverell Sitwell's *Southern Baroque Art,* a study of the painting, architecture, and music of Italy and Spain, the real homes of this cumulative style during this time. For in this book, in grandiose, orotund prose that is as Baroque as anything in the English language may be, is set down a series of intimately detailed descriptions characteristic of this period of tremendous vitality, ardent exuberance, daring conception, and elaborate ornament.

The fact that the term "Baroque" has been given a deprecatory meaning, especially by some of the English-writing critics who never have understood it, very similar to that which was in the minds of the Renaissance worthies when they used the word "Gothic" as meaning crude and barbarian, has already been noted. This type of criticism has heaped a number of abusive appellations on the not altogether undeserving head of Baroque art, among them such expressions as cheap, tawdry, sensational, vulgar, falsely emotional, overdramatic. But such derogatory epithets, sometimes merited when applied to single examples of art and certain circumstances of creation, are certainly unfair when applied to the general characteristics of the period, for they tend to exaggerate its defects and fail to suggest the essential nature and the underlying artistic intentions which make it one of the most effective and prolific in the history of the world's art.

DAVID DANCING BEFORE THE ARK   by Sebastiano Conca

A few of Mr. Sitwell's pictures will give a better understanding of some of the definable qualities of this misunderstood time. In the church of Santa Chiara, the Pantheon of Naples, founded by Robert

possible the luxuriant type of integrated counterpoint which was quickly seized upon by all the composers of the period, beginning with Corelli and ending with Bach, for the purpose of building up large forms and impressive tonal masses. Energetic and persistent rhythmic patterns and wide-ranging melodic contours prevailed to such an extent that we come to recognize the music of this time by these features alone.

The great instrumental style to emerge during the High Baroque was the concerto style, which had gradually been taking shape since the time of the ensemble canzonas by Gabrieli. Alessandro Stradella's (1645-1682) two *sinfonia a più instrumenti* seem to have been the earliest examples of the concerto; but Arcangelo Corelli (1653-1713), generally credited with the first full realization of the possibilities of tonality in the field of instrumental music, may be said to be the composer (together with his fellow Bolognese, Giuseppe Torelli (?1650-1708) to have taken the most decisive steps in its development. We also think of Corelli as the founder of modern violin music and playing, although there had been many other composers writing real violin music before his time, including such men as Legrenzi, Vitali, and Neri. But he was the outstanding figure and so, as always happens, receives the credit of being the first all-round master of the violin, in both composition and performance.

Corelli divided the orchestra into two groups, the *concerto tutti,* or *ripeni* (reinforcing section), and a small group of solo instruments, the *concertino,* or *principale,* made up as a rule of two violins and a cello. Both these groups were supplied with an accompanying harpsichord, so that they could be physically separated and thus really made to "sound" against each other. He did not invent any new formal scheme or construction for this newly created concerto but simply transferred to it the two traditional types of chamber-music construction then prevalent in Italy—the chamber music, or *sonata da camera,* and the church sonata, or *sonata da chiesa,* the latter dropping the dance titles of its individual movements and becoming a series of free movements of alternating fast and slow character. Corelli's sonatas for violin and harpsichord, Op. 2 and 4, are outstanding examples of these *sonata da camera,* each of them consisting of four movements with a prelude at one end and a *giga,* or jig, at the other.

Corelli's twelve *Concerti grossi,* Op. 6, published in 1712, and Torelli's *Concerti grossi,* published in 1709, represent the first high point in the development of the concerto grosso, a development that was carried straight through to Bach. The same traditions were carried on by

Francesco Geminiani (1667-1762) in his Op. 2 of 1732 and his Op. 3 of 1738, using the four-movement scheme of the *sonata da chiesa* as the standard form. These works, with their alternation of polyphonic and homophonic aspects and their beautifully melodious slow movements, are striking examples of the great advances which violin music achieved within a short period. The solo concerto, in which only one soloist plays against the orchestra, is younger than the concerto grosso. Tommaso Albinoni (1674-1745), together with Torelli, composed the first of them for violin and orchestra around 1700; keyboard concertos for one instrument and orchestra, the most popular form of concertos today, came still later, both Bach and Handel writing them.

Antonio Vivaldi (1676-1741), a composer whose works seem to be coming into great favor today, judging by the items in the record catalogues, was the next in line in the development of the concerto. His works, which often treat the concertino as a group of independent soloists, stand between those of the innovators and those of the consummators of this form. A Venetian priest, Vivaldi was possessed of a keen and flashing imagination and often indulged in naïve programs for his works, programs which were really nothing but pretexts for the display of his fluent virtuosity. He standardized the concerto form into three movements, sometimes extended by an introduction. Until recently, he was largely known to listeners through the transcriptions of his string works made by Bach for keyboard instruments. But as more and more of his prolifically produced works become known (only a small part of them have been published), we are coming to recognize him as a most important Baroque figure in his own right. The number of followers of these three big names in Italian string music—Corelli, Torelli, and Vivaldi—is legion; it includes such well-known composers as Alessandro Scarlatti, Gaspanni, Manfredini, Geminiani (*d.* 1762), and Locatelli (*d.* 1764). They lead directly down to and beyond the time of the greatest of all Baroque instrumental composers, Sebastian Bach and Handel.

OPERATIC STANDARDS

The change of style in the opera of this period coincides with the rise of the Neapolitan opera school, which, up to the time of Alessandro Scarlatti (1659-1725), had been supplied largely from Venice. With this composer, there comes an entirely new type of opera: his work so gathers up all the styles and manners of his predecessors and crystallizes them into what has been spoken of for years as the *standard opera* that it is worthy of special attention. Characteristics of these Scarlatti operas as they were given in one of the five opera houses which flourished in eighteenth-century Naples were:

First, that the overture was written with regard for a definite form: it consisted of three contrasting sections, first an allegro, followed by an adagio, and finally a concluding allegro, this time of fugal character. This general scheme of three sections arranged in the order of *quick, slow, quick* survived long after the rest of Scarlatti's work was forgotten and later became the basis for many a composition by Haydn and Mozart.

Second, that beauty of vocal melody was the great desideratum; the dramatic plot was only an excuse—and usually a very poor one—for the music. A great deal of the dramatic action—the "dull parts which have to get on with the story of the play," as one writer expresses it— were sung in *recitativo secco,* a "dry recitative" accompanied by only an occasional chord on the harpsichord. Scarlatti used also a kind of recitative that was accompanied by stringed instruments, which fact infused a new color and emotional atmosphere into the opera. But what the audience awaited were the *arias,* set pieces for all the principal characters, introduced every so often and in a fixed order and used to express any emotion desired—joy as well as sorrow, rage as well as despair. They were designed not so much for the expression of emotional truthfulness as for providing a well-rounded form of aesthetic proportion. Scarlatti set the style of writing them in the *da capo* form —that is, with three parts, one of which was repeated after the second had been introduced, *a-b-a.* Nothing more typical of Baroque formalism could be found. Thus, such an opera as *Griselda* is really nothing but a series of arias for the principals in sweet cantilena or gallant coloratura, linked together by recitatives, with no ensembles or choruses of any kind.

Third, that the *castrati* type of singing predominated. Of the six principal characters which the opera demanded, the three men—and always the hero—were artificial sopranos. This fact colored the whole nature of the work, giving it a character which fitted its unreal story and its grandiose scenic conception; for nothing natural or human would have seemed congruous. The only thing which was of interest to the audience was the singing, especially that of these instrumentalized voices.

Fourth, that the singers were expected to be something in the way of creators as well; for they never sang their arias as written and were expected to introduce embellishments of various sorts into the repetition sections of their arias. The audience judged the different artists not alone by their virtuosity, but by their ability to heighten the vocal effects which had been written down by the composer. And the auditors were so trained in the niceties of vocal virtuosity that they could—and did—evaluate every point made by composer and singer. As a contemporary observer of the practice wrote:

> *Among the Things worthy of consideration, the first to be taken Notice of, is the Manner in which all Airs divided into three parts are to be sung. In the first Part they require nothing but the simplest Ornaments, of a good Taste and few, that the Composition may remain simple, plain, and pure; in the second, they expect that to this Purity some artful Graces be added, by which the judicious may hear, that the Ability of the Singer is greater; and, in repeating the Air, he that does not vary it for the better, is no great Master . . .*
>
> *Without varying the Airs the knowledge of the Singers could never be discovered; but from the Nature and Quality of the Variations, it will easily be discerned in two of the greatest Singers which is the best.*

J. E. Galliard: *Observations on the Florid Song*, 1724

Fifth, that the voices were extraordinarily beautiful. These were the real days of great solo singing, the era of *bel canto;* and the operatic scores of the time show that all the artists, and especially the *castrati*, must have possessed a virtuosity of execution which is almost unbelievable.

Sixth, that the plots were utterly barren, dramatically speaking. The subjects of the Baroque operas were always mythological in character, and although the poets attempted to make their gods and heroes live again, they usually succeeded in making them men of their own time only, dressed up to suit the occasion and singing music quite unfitted to the character of the drama, its real purpose being the display of the singer's trills and flourishes.

Scarlatti divided his time between Rome, the capital, and Naples, which was the richest and most influential city in Italy at this time. His fluent, graceful style, together with the innovations he introduced (the "Italian overture" and the *da capo* aria) and the countless composers who imitated his writing, made him the greatest influence of the early eighteenth century. With him and his followers of the Neapolitan school, who knew so well how to treat the human voice and exploit its every possibility, vocal solo song assumed a place of importance in music that it never again equaled. Other important names in this Neapolitan group were Leonardo Vinci, a descendant of the famous artist's family, Nicola Jommelli and Tommaso Traetta, who reintroduced the chorus as an important dramatic element, and Pietro Metastasio, the famous poet who wrote so many of the best librettos of this period.

THE UNIVERSAL NEAPOLITAN STYLE

It was this Neapolitan style that spread all over Europe and made the acquirement of Italian culture a fashionable fad of the life of the time and an important influence in the development of its taste. Germany came completely under its spell: Dresden, for example, the capital of the Kingdom of Saxony, was to all intents and purposes merely an outpost of Italy during the eighteenth century. The brilliant opera in this lovely city was entirely in the hands of singers from the southern peninsula. Agents of the Saxon king went to Italy and secured there a number of paintings, notably Raphael's *Sistine Madonna,* for the royal art galleries. So many Italian stonemasons and builders were working on the churches and palaces in Dresden that a special village was created for housing them. Winckelmann, the father of modern art history, went to Italy from Dresden, and the German poet, Herder, in describing this beautiful city on the Elbe, called it a *deutsches Florenz.* So with Salzburg and Vienna in Austria. In North Germany, the few experiments made in native opera at Hamburg became entirely submerged in the stream of Baroque influence that flowed so steadily from Italy. Provincial capitals like Madrid, Lisbon, Copenhagen, and St. Petersburg set up Italian operas and staffed them with Italian artists. In Paris, where Italian architects were busy creating many of the structures which have since made the city famous, the native musical forces had finally to capitulate to the charms of the music from the south. London became a devotee of the Italian style early in the eighteenth century, try as the native artists and writers might to make it seem ridiculous and "foreign"—the greatest condemnatory epithet an Englishman can use! This from Addison's *Spectator* (March 21, 1711) is typical:

> *It is my design in this paper to deliver down to posterity a faithful account of the Italian opera . . . for there is no question but that our great-grandchildren will be very curious to know the reason why their forefathers used to sit together like an audience of foreigners in their own country, and to hear whole plays acted in a language which they did not understand.*

Arsinoë was the first opera that gave us a taste of Italian music. The great success this opera met with alarmed the fiddlers of the town, who laid down an established rule that "nothing is capable of being set to music that is not nonsense."

This maxim was no sooner received but we immediately fell to translating the Italian operas; and, as there was no danger of hurting the sense of these extraordinary pieces, our authors would often make up words of their own.

The next step to our refinement was the introducing of Italian actors into our opera, who sung their parts in their own language, at the same time that our countrymen performed theirs in our native tongue . . . the lover frequently made his court, and gained the heart of his princess, in a language which she did not understand.

At length the audience grew tired of understanding half the opera; and therefore to ease themselves entirely of the failure of thinking, have ordered it that the whole opera is performed in an unknown tongue.

And an early eighteenth-century poem by Ambrose Philips, dedicated to a popular Italian singer in London in 1725, leaves us in no doubt as to his views:

Little syren of the stage,
Charmer of an idle age;
Empty warbler, breathing lyre,
Wanton gale of fond desire;
Bane of ev'ry manly heart;
Oh, too pleasing is thy strain,

Hence, to southern climes again;
Tuneful mischief, vocal spell,
To this island bid farewell;
Leave us, as we ought to be,
Leave the Britons rough and free.

What could be more characteristic of the time and place of its origin?

Alessandro Scarlatti was also supreme in the field of the chamber cantata, the élite vocal music of the Late Baroque in that it was written for a select audience of connoisseurs and did not have to depend upon popular success, as did the opera. A papal interdiction of the time to the effect that opera was a form of music not particularly conducive to public morality increased the popularity of these small-scaled chamber pieces. The wealthy patrons of the Late Baroque encouraged the writing of these cantatas, which, as Burney said, contain a "little drama entire, having a beginning, a middle, and an end, in which the charms of poetry are united with those of music, and the mind is amused while the ear is gratified." The cantatas were often extemporized by the poet, usually on some classic theme, immediately set to music by the composer, and quickly performed in the salon of the patron. Scarlatti wrote some six hundred of them, and many critics feel that in them he really shows his greatest genius. Nearly all the other opera composers of the period also wrote these cantatas, includ-

ROCOCO PERFECTION — one of the rooms in the Amalienburg, Munich

ing, above all others, Handel. As for Italian oratorio, it came completely at this period under the domination of the Late Baroque opera style and is hardly to be distinguished from it. When performed, oratorio served largely as a sort of Lenten substitute for the more worldly and glamorous opera. But it is of historical interest, in that it often displayed rich Baroque orchestral backgrounds which made much use of contrapuntal writing and which survived as the "strict style" of the next era. The most important oratorio composers of this time included such famous names as Marcello, Lotti, Vinci, and Pergolesi, in addition to A. Scarlatti.

THE RISE OF THE ROCOCO

In France a special problem of style arises during the Late Baroque period: the gradual emergence of that peculiar style (again derived from architectural practices) of light, sophisticated ornamentation which came to be known as the *Rococo,* receiving its name from the curved *rocaille* (shell) ornamentations that were its special feature. Where the Italian Baroque spirit had been powerful and forceful, the

French changed it into a delicate, almost feminine artistic style; where the Baroque had been passionate in utterance, the Rococo became playful and sentimental, suggestive of exquisite grace. As we have said, the buoyance and vigor of the Baroque were always somewhat foreign to the French nature; nevertheless, this style maintained a hold on the taste of the French court as long as *le Grande Monarque,* Louis xiv, lived. At his death, in 1715, its heavy majestic attitudes gave way in two directions: the Rococo, which, while keeping the courtly aristocratic nature of the Baroque, softened it into a charming elegance and lighthearted sophistication that exactly fitted a refined court society which was largely devoting its time to pleasure; the other direction, for which there seems to be no adequate, short descriptive title, led towards the expression of a simple, human, yet formally ordered type of art that was well suited to communicating the ideas and sentiments of the people. European historians have called this the *style bourgeois* (literally, the style characteristic of the middle class), the Germans adding the further descriptive title *empfindsam*—that is, capable of expressing feeling. It led directly to what we rather rashly and deceptively call the classic style of the following period—the music of Haydn, Mozart, and the early Beethoven. The Rococo, on the other hand, became known as the *style galant* (well-bred, a style that strives to please and is correct in its setting and bearing).

These tendencies are conspicuously present in all the art expressions of this time. Watteau's pictures, with their gay figures wistfully set against the formal background of a park, are as characteristic of the Rococo tendency as are the lightly designed palace interiors, with their graceful galleries and soft silver and ivory decorations. The later paintings of Boucher and Fragonard, and those of Chardin and Greuze, in France, of Hogarth in England, and of Morgenstern in Germany, on the other hand, show a tendency to depict naturally sentimental themes of interest to the middle class. All these artists painted pictures which may well be called bourgeois in style. This division is also clearly evident in music.

COUPERIN LE GRAND

The composer who stands at the parting of the ways was François Couperin (1668–1733), called *le Grand* to show that he was the most famous member of a large and influential family of French organists and clavecinists, which played an important part in the musical life of that country for more than two centuries. His art is completely French in manner and has been called the purest and most characteristic expression of the Gallic temperament in art. His style may be said to be an inextricable blend of the Late Baroque and Rococo traits, combining in some things the big sweep and power of the Baroque and its love of expansive outlines with the "gilt of intricate ornamentation" so characteristic of Rococo art. He wrote instrumental music, church and organ music, and a few secular vocal pieces. His vast output includes four books of harpsichord pieces, containing some 230 numbers; 42 *pièces pour orgue consistantes en deux Messes* (for many years thought to be the work of an uncle); a considerable amount of religious music, including motets, elevations, and *Leçon de ténèbres* for use during Holy Week; and some very interesting chamber music for small combinations of various instruments, including four *Concerts royaux* written as a sort of homage to his sovereign, Louis XIV. In addition to all this music, there appeared his famous didactic works: *L'Art de toucher le clavecin*, a method of teaching harpsichord, and *Régle pour l'accompagnement*, rules for accompanying.

As *Ordinaire de la Musique de la chambre du Roi* and *Organiste du Roi*, Couperin stood high in court favor and took part in the royal music activities for many years. In addition to his purely court activities, he wrote a number of ensemble sonatas, such things as *Les Nations, Les Goûts reunis*, a sort of United Nations insofar as taste was concerned, and an *Apothéose de Lully* in honor of his great predecessor. Both these show that Couperin was striving for a sort of fusion of international tastes which would, as he believed, "achieve the perfection of music." He was a prominent figure of his day and had great influence upon eighteenth-century music; but it has only been recently that he has come to the attention of the great body of listeners and his position as a leading Baroque-Rococo composer been fully established.

FRENCH ROCOCO COMPOSERS

Many of the harpsichord pieces contained in the twenty-seven "orders" constituting Couperin's complete works for this instrument are excellent examples of the characteristically Baroque "doctrine of the affections." This popular theory classified and to some extent indicated certain musical effects that were to be used to express such particular emotions as tenderness, gaiety, languor, passion, and purity. Couperin was in the habit of giving picturesque names to many of his pieces

The Scarlattis — father and son

Couperin-le-Grand

Telemann

COMPOSERS OF THE GALANT PERIOD

indicative of the emotions they were supposed to portray: *Les Lan-gueres tendres, Soeur Monique, Les Barricades mystérieuses;* and his wonderful *Les Folies françaises* consists of a whole series of short pieces, each one of which portrays an emotional mood characteristic of the contemporary French court—jealousy, coquetry, languor, virginity (a touch of sarcasm, perhaps), despair—the whole thing being an exact musical counterpart of the Rococo paintings of Watteau (1684–1721). A study of the works of these two artists, Watteau and Couperin, would give a good picture of the court life of this Rococo period.

Following him there came a number of other important French clavecin composers: Louis Marchand (1669–1732), who is supposed to have engaged in a musical competition with Bach; Louis Cléram-bault (1676–1749); L. Claude Daquin (1694–1772); and finally J. P. K. Rameau (1683–1764), the last principally known for his work in another field, that of the opera. It may be said that these men sum up the entire history of French *galant* technique. In his *Pièces de clavecin,* Rameau, the most influential of the French composers of the next generation, codified the Rococo ornaments in definite form; and his great theoretical treatise, *Traité de l'harmonie,* published in 1722, the same year that J. S. Bach launched *Das Wohltemperirte Clavier,* summarized with all the logical astuteness of the eighteenth-century Enlightenment the principles underlying the structure of modern harmony. According to Rameau, music is a "purely physio-mathematical science depending on reason, nature, and geometry."

A famous dramatic critic has said that it is characteristic for the creative Frenchman to arrive finally on the stage, no matter what his early work may have been like, for the theater has always been the center of the intellectual life of France. Rameau did not take up dramatic writing until well into middle life, but he succeeded remarkably in it, becoming the logical Rococo successor to Lully's Baroque grandeur. Following the work of André Campra (1660–1744) and André Cardinal Destouches (1662–1749), Rameau devoted especial attention to the ballet. Typically flashing in a brilliant Rococo way, although hardly ever descending to the "pastoral playfulness" that is character-istic of so much Rococo art, these ballets consisted of strings of dignified dances: minuets, gavottes, rondeaus, and so on—all revealing a capa-city for line drawing that makes them extremely effective. As is to be expected of a deep thinker on the subject of harmony, Rameau's music is notably fresh without being freakish, full of spirit, rich in variety, brilliant in color, just in diction. It is typically French, a veritable incarnation of the spirit of its race.

In his *tragédies lyriques,* as Rameau called his operas, he stands, as Bukofzer has said, like an erratic block isolated in Rococo surroundings: his attempts to achieve real dramatic truth (thus foreshadowing Christoph Willibald von Gluck) left him rather stranded in a world not ready for such expressions of the heart. And so his operas, except for occasional spectacular revivals such as that of *Les Indes Galantes,* have dropped completely out of the repertoire. Yet a contemporary was able to say of him:

> *He delivered us from the plainchant that we had been psalmodizing for over a hundred years* [*a slap at the French declamatory opera*] . . . *He presented us with a certain number of operas in which we find harmony, bits of song, disconnected ideas, clashes, soaring flights, triumphs, onslaughts, glorifications, murmurs, breathless victories, airs de danse that will live eternally.*

Much more in keeping with the spirit of the Rococo era was the development of the *vaudeville,* a comedy with spoken dialogue and music derived from outside sources, some of it quite respectable, a great deal of it not. This corresponded in a rather rough way to the rise of the *opera buffa* in Italy, the ballad opera in England, and the *Singspiel* in Germany.

Before leaving the French scene, we should add a few words about the Rococo style of the composers of chamber music in the generation following Couperin, especially about Jean Marie Leclair (1697–1764), who in his solo and trio sonatas actually achieved the fusion of Italian and French style which Couperin had attempted. He was a famous violinist and developed an advanced technique for that instrument just coming into general use; at his death, it was said that it was to him that the violin owed its acceptance in France by "decent people." His music still appeals to us today because it contains the best elements of both French and Italian Rococo style.

OPERA BUFFA

The principal Italian operatic development of this time was the *opera buffa,* created in the midst of the glory of the Baroque opera as a sort of relief and an attempt to endow the form with everyday characters, rather than with classical heroes, and to provide music that was straightforward and sincere and that was to be sung by qualified actors rather than mere singers. This developed out of the custom the opera librettists had of introducing several comic characters, toward the end of their work, in order to mitigate somewhat the artificiality and un-

AN EIGHTEENTH-CENTURY DRAMATIC PRESENTATION Leonardo Vinci's *La Contesa de Numi* (painting by Panini)

reality of their plots. This new operatic style first emerged in works by the Neapolitan composer Orefice and in the masterpiece of Leonardo Vinci (1690–1730), *Zite in galera,* which is often called the first fully developed *opera buffa.* But Pergolesi's (1710–1736) *La serva padrona* was the first to become really popular. Produced in Naples in 1733, it is a charming little work for only two singing characters and originally intended as an intermezzo between the acts of a longer drama. There is a natural humanity and sparkling wit about this work in the bourgeois style which appealed strongly to the French, for whom it was first produced in 1752, almost twenty years after its first performance in Naples. The stilted conventionalities of the Baroque style of "grand opera" had wearied the French public, which took to this new style eagerly. In fact, Pergolesi's music captured all Europe and strongly influenced contemporary instrumental developments.

IN GERMANY

We have seen how the operatic situation in Germany at this time was almost hopeless, insofar as native composition went. At Hamburg, in the early days of the century, there flourished for a few years an attempt at cultivating national opera. A number of composers tried their hand: Franck, Theile, Mattheson, Telemann, Keiser, and even Handel; but there was no patronage of an aristocratic and wealthy court to sustain the venture and direct the taste. Most of the little German courts which imitated Versailles so eagerly did not have the resources to sustain native art, and eventually the whole effort fell through for lack of suitable material. Handel's great success in this field had to come later, in London.

Much more characteristic of the late Baroque musical scene in Germany was the figure of Agostino Steffani (1654–1728), an Italian-born composer who received his musical education in Germany and served the few German courts where the Italian style was carefully cultivated. A vital and energetic individual, "honorable priest," court and chamber musician, organist, opera composer, diplomat, trusted ambassador of princes and popes, Steffani seems to have been skilled in all forms of human behavior, honoring everything he touched. His operas show the natural tendency of the Germans to express themselves contrapuntally, but they also contain features of both Italian and French derivation; such a coordination of national styles strongly influenced Steffani's successor, Handel.

Polished, sophisticated, and urbane, Steffani was connected in various roles with the princely courts of Munich and Hannover; other centers of Italian style in Germany were Dresden and, especially, Vienna, which because of its geographical situation was an especially favored city in this respect, supporting such masters as Caldara, the Bononcini brothers, Fux, and later both Handel and Hasse. Steffani's manner was described by a contemporary observer as "grave, but tempered with a sweetness and affability that rendered his conversation very engaging." No better description could possibly be given of his music, with its aristocratic, naturally graceful movement, and Baroque impressiveness.

Another characteristic development of the High Baroque-Rococo period in Germany was the rise of the *Singspiel,* comic opera with spoken dialogue. Its great center was Leipzig, where Johann Adam Hiller (1728–1804) set several translations of the English ballad operas and later wrote some *Singspiele* of his own. From Leipzig the movement spread all over Germany, concentrating in Berlin and Vienna, and attracted many composers, including even Haydn and Mozart. It became the natural ancestor of the nineteenth-century German Romantic opera.

THE GERMAN KUHNAU

A big man in the Germany of this century was Johann Kuhnau (1660–1722), the immediate predecessor of Bach as the cantor of St. Thomas's Church, Leipzig. At the time, Germany was a beleaguered land, overrun by the armies of Sweden, France, and Spain in that last great conflict caused by the differences between Catholics and Protestants. Artistically, it was completely in the hands of the Italians, for the artists from the south flooded Bavaria, Saxony, Thuringia, Austria, and even the provinces of the north: Cavalli reigned supreme in Munich, Hasse in Dresden, Vivaldi in Darmstadt, Cesti and Caldara in Vienna. German to the very core, Kuhnau struggled manfully to uphold the solemnity and the dignity of his native art against what he considered the madness of a country given over to the frivolities of the Italians, even the Church adapting its dramatic, operatic style in the settings of some of its liturgical solemnities.

Kuhnau was, in the words of one of his contemporaries, "very learned in theology, jurisprudence, rhetoric, poetry, mathematics, foreign languages, and music." He knew Greek and Hebrew, could translate works from French and Italian into German, and wrote a considerable number of original works in a vigorous and forceful style, including an amusing novel pillorying the Italians and the "Italianuses" who had deserted him for the captivating lightness of the south. His contemporaries considered Kuhnau one of the great composers of the century; he was one of the earliest to set the style for the modern sonata, and his descriptive program pieces for clavichord—*Biblische Historien,* he called them—are among the few examples outside the works of the great men—Bach, Handel, and Couperin—still remembered today.

One of these Biblical sonatas tells of Saul's madness and David's refreshing harp playing, which cured him. There are many powerful chords, uncommon for that day, and the sudden changes of mood suggest, without extravagance, Saul's stricken mind. The best known of these sonatas is *David and Goliath's Combat;* when attempting the representation of Goliath's boasting and stamping and of David's courageous defiance, Kuhnau works on a plane which may be called the median, in which a blend of imitation and suggestion is used. When he wants to show us the flight of the Philistines, he can do nothing but scurry scalically about; and the course of the stone from David's sling has to be set down by much the same means. Here Kuhnau is attempting what is either really impracticable or superficial and obvious.

There are, however, two sections of the work in which he goes much deeper and attains something of true expressive and suggestive power. One is that which depicts the Israelites' dejection and their trust in God (each section of the work is quaintly labeled in words by the careful composer). Here the chromatic dropping background of repeated-note accompaniment is genuinely poetic; above it rises a chorale tune, the plea to God. The other moment in which Kuhnau best rises above the merely imitative level is the death of Goliath; here a weighty descending figure suggests the gradual crumpling-up of the body, and another may well stand for the departing breath as the giant's life ebbs away. The end of the sonata, with its various rejoicings, takes us back to familiar dance forms of the time, and quite away from pictorialism.

In all such early program music, some of the best interest lies in picking out the various planes of effect and hearing how, on the limited instruments of the time, certain things could, and others could not, be done. We must also try to decide which, of all the things attempted, are worth while and which are not. Such a responsibility is always upon us, whether we hear the bleating sheep in Richard Strauss's *Don Quixote,* for instance, or listen to some of the extremer "absolute" music of today. What is significant, and what is not?

That he was not entirely happy in his ideas is obvious when we read the lengthy Preface which Kuhnau wrote for these Biblical sonatas, trying to explain some of their inconsistencies and discrepancies. But the instrument for which he wrote them, the clavichord, was not capable of the effects he was seeking. Small in tone, with a very simple mechanism consisting of a brass or iron plate fitted vertically to the end of each key and just striking the string when the key was depressed, it could not give a tone suited to the grandiose ideas found in these dramatic programmistic tone poems of Kuhnau. The clavichord was much better suited to sensitive and delicate music, such as came later in the time of "sighs, tears, and tender smiles"—the Rococo. But it did have an expressive quality that the harpsichord completely lacked. There were many arguments at the time as to the relative merits of these two instruments. Both Bach and Kuhnau preferred the clavichord, the latter in a letter to the famous music critic of the time, Mattheson, saying that the clavichord was the "most expressive of all keyboard instruments."

GUILD MUSIC

A peculiarly German development of the late seventeenth and early eighteenth centuries was concerted music for the special use of various guilds and corporations of musicians. These organizations had formed an important part of the musical life of France ever since the time of the minstrels and the troubadours; they had branches in all the provinces and a central organization in Paris, where their "King of the Minstrels" or "King of the Violins" ruled over the musicians of the country, much in the fashion of a modern labor leader. These corporations had a strangle hold on the performance of music throughout the whole country; and there were many quarrels with the clavecinists, lutenists, and composers who did not willingly submit to their pretensions. The whole situation, until the suppression of the guilds in 1774, strangely resembles the labor troubles of our time.

In Germany, the influence of these organizations was more beneficent: musicians in the cities and towns throughout the country united in corporations for their own benefit and protection. The "town musicians," as they were named because they were supported by the various municipalities, were called upon to furnish music for all official occasions, playing in church and in secular processions. In addition, they could be hired for private use at weddings, funerals, and so forth. Even the small towns maintained groups of trombone and trumpet players—*Stadtpfeifer*—whose duties included the playing of a chorale three times a day from the steeple of the village church and the playing of a secular program daily from the tower of the *Rathaus*. This quaint custom, which survived in Germany well into the nineteenth century and may still be found there in a few isolated examples, has had much to do with the establishment of the country's musical taste and style. For out of the chorale, there came certain elements in the music of Bach, Brahms, and Wagner and many an unknown composer.

Characteristic of the music played by these seventeenth-century German *Stadtpfeifer* is the collection *Fünff-stimmigte blasende Musik* of Johann Pezel, published in 1685, the year of Bach's birth. Much of this is solid and deeply felt music that forecasts the greater glories to come.

THE PRODIGIOUS TELEMANN

A Lulli fame has won: Corelli may be praised,
But Telemann alone above all else is raised.

. . . But who is this old man, who with his nimble pen, full of a pious enthusiasm, enchants the Eternal Temple? Listen! How the waves of the sea are roaring! How the mountains cry aloud with joy and sing hymns unto the Lord! How harmonious an "Amen" fills the devout heart with a sacred awe! How the temples tremble with the pious shout of Alleluia! Telemann, it is thou, thou, the father of sacred music . . .
Quoted by Rolland: *A Musical Tour through the Land of the Past*

These two lines of doggerel from an eighteenth-century "Who's Who in Music," Mattheson's *Ehrenpforte,* and the quotation from a contemporary poem reflect the universal opinion of the time as regards Georg Philipp Telemann (1681–1767). His contemporaries did not hesitate to place this "father of sacred music" on a plane which was considerably higher than that occupied by Johann Sebastian Bach, and yet today he is in every sense of the word a forgotten man!

Even Telemann's unexampled prolificacy, in which he was so characteristic of his time, has been forgotten. Rolland, in his interesting study of this old master, has estimated that in the twenty years which represent him at the height of his career, he produced 12 complete cycles of sacred music for all the Sundays and feast days of the year, 19 Passions

(the librettos of which were often from his pen), 20 operas, 40 serenades, 600 miscellaneous instrumental pieces for various instruments, 700
airs, etc., etc. What a man! In addition, he found time to fulfill the
duties of *Kapellmeister* and cantor in Hamburg: to provide the service
music for the five principal churches there; to direct the opera, a task
which, Rolland reminds us, was no sinecure, for there were even more
cabals and cliques than usual to render the life of an opera impresario a
difficult matter;[1] to found a series of popular concerts, which have continued in Hamburg to this day; to journey to Paris, the city of his
dreams, where he conducted some of his compositions; to publish the
first musical journal ever to be printed in Germany; to act as cor-
respondent to the Eisenach court, writing letters descriptive of the
happenings in North Germany, and to write three autobiographies containing all the details of his busy life.

Whatever our opinion may be regarding the quality of Telemann's
music, there can be nothing but wonderment as to its quantity. Like
Rolland, we cannot help being impressed with the "prodigious vitality
of a man, who, from his tenth to his eighty-sixth year, wrote music
with indefatigable joy and enthusiasm and without prejudice to a hundred other occupations!" The little of his music that is still played
shows a lively, loquacious, if not very profound, personality; it possesses
a Rococo graciousness rather than a Baroque impressiveness. In contradistinction to most of the chamber music of its time, Telemann's
Tafelmusik, a collection of concertos and chamber works, dispenses
with the *basso continuo,* a method of tying together the musical fabric
by means of some such instrument as the harpsichord or the organ
playing chords which filled in the harmonies suggested by the violoncello part. "I so contrived that the bass was a natural melody," writes
Telemann, "forming, with the other parts, an appropriate harmony,
which developed with each note in such a way that it seemed as
though it could not be otherwise. Many sought to persuade me that

---

[1] An eighteenth-century French writer, M. de la Borde, has an amusing comment on
this in his *Essai sur la musique,* published in Paris in 1780. As paraphrased by Burney in
his History, the account says that the government of an opera is painful and embarrass-
ing employment. It is necessary that the director of so complicated a machine should
know how to manage all the springs, remove every obstacle to their motion, gratify the
taste and sometimes the caprice of the fickle public, unite in one interest a crowd of different rival talents, excite emulation without jealousy, distribute rewards with justice and
delicacy, censure and punish with address, limit the unbounded demands of some by
flattery, check the independence of others by apparent concessions, and try to establish in
the interior government of this republic as much harmony as reigns in the orchestra. It
is manifest, adds Burney, that nothing but the most subtle and artful character can hope
to accomplish such Herculean labors.

I had displayed the best of my powers in these compositions." Here are the foundations of modern style.

Above everything, Telemann was a progressive; he was always attracted by the new in art and did not conceal his disdain for what he called "fossils." "One should never say to art: 'Thou shalt go no farther.' One is always going farther, and one should always go farther," he writes. He was a great student of the music of other countries —France (especially) and Poland and Italy—and through this study he introduced new ideas and fresh life into the rather stodgy German style, which, as Rolland says, was beginning to smell somewhat musty. "It would have been in danger of asphyxiation but for the great draughts of fresh air which men like Telemann let into it through the open doors of France, Poland, and Italy. . . . If we wish to understand the extraordinary blaze of music that illumined Germany from the time of Haydn, Mozart, and Beethoven, we must have some acquaintance with those who prepared this magnificent beacon; we must watch the lighting of the fire."

And nowhere can we see better that the works of the great classics are merely the logical conclusion of the whole Baroque-Rococo century than in these forgotten things of Telemann's.

IN ENGLAND

Contemporary with the vogue for Italian opera, which has waxed and waned in England to this day, was *The Beggar's Opera,* with libretto by John Gay and music arranged from various popular sources by Dr. Pepusch. Its production, in 1728, stimulated a number of similar ballad operas, in which the literary blades of the day took a hand, concocting fancies and satires and fitting them to old ballads and popular songs. As Henry Carey, one of the chief composers at the turn of the century, rather bitterly remarked:

*These handy Hirelings can, in half a **Day**,*
*Steal a new Ballad Farce from some old **Play**:*
To mangled Scraps of many an Ancient Tune
Tagg Feetless Jingle, Jarring and Jejune.
The jaded Play'rs with equal haste rehearse,
'Till Sing Song limps to Horrid, Hobbling Verse!

But nothing came of all this activity. Gay's little masterpiece alone survives to remind us of this popular vogue of the eighteenth-century operatic stage in England. The ballad opera, transplanted to Germany,

MASQUERADES AND OPERAS, BURLINGTON GATE   (an engraving by Hogarth)

and expanded and developed there, became the *Singspiel* of hallowed memory in the evolution of the German national style of opera.

Otherwise the Italians predominated until the advent of Handel, who, as we shall see, largely continued their traditions. One of the best of Hogarth's early engravings, done in 1724, bearing the title "Masquerades and Operas," admirably satirizes the Baroque-Rococo period in England with the following inscription:

O how refin'd how elegant we're grown!
What noble Entertainments Charm the Town!
Whether to hear the Dragon's roar we go,
Or gaze supriz'd on Fawks's matchless show,
Or to the Opera's or to the Masques,
To cut up Ortelans, and empty Flasques
And rifle Pies from Shakespears clinging Page,
Good Gods! how great's the gusto of the Age.

DOMENICO SCARLATTI

Though largely engaged in the production of opera, Italy also found time and opportunity for writing instrumental music. Such men as

Alessandro Scarlatti and Domenico Zipoli (*b.* 1675) wrote harpsichord music that could have been played equally well on the organ, for it shows little understanding of the essential differences in the character and sonorities of these two instruments. But with Domenico Scarlatti (son of Alessandro), born the same year as Bach, 1685, we reach forward into the sphere of virtuoso music for the harpsichord. His sonatas (*esercizi*—exercises—was his modest name for them) cover a great deal of technical ground, and some of his innovations, such as trills, arpeggios, wide skips, repeated toccata-like notes, and crossing of the hands, must have seemed amazing in their day.

A study of his sonatas (he wrote nearly six hundred of them) shows that they seem to be more concerned with technical pleasures than with poetic expression. The name "exercise" indicates the scope of these single-movement pieces but says nothing of their exciting brilliance. When we call them sonatas, we do so in the old sense of their being instrumental, as distinguished from vocal, pieces and must not confuse them with either the Corelli sonata (or suite, as it really was) or the sonata in the modern significance of the term. These Scarlatti works mark the turn of Italian music from the Baroque to the beginning of the "classic" style; most of them are built upon a single idea, although there are some signs in some of them of the emergence of a clear-cut second theme as the germ of the two-subject exposition section that came later with Haydn. But Scarlatti makes no attempt at any development of such themes beyond a little playing with rhythmic figures.

But if the Scarlatti works lack something of poetic significance, they have everything else—*élan,* brilliance, gaiety, lyricism, key daring, technical virtuosity, and rich harmonies, the last trait derived direct from the idioms then current in the Neapolitan opera school. Hearing a performance of them by a brilliant harpsichordist is a thrilling experience today and makes us realize, as perhaps nothing else can, what a shining and brilliant period theirs was. In freshness of invention and brilliance of execution, these sonatas of D. Scarlatti are the counterparts of Watteau's lighthearted grace, serene elegance, and flashing corruscation.

A re-study of the life and music of this great composer made by the American harpsichordist Ralph Kirkpatrick gives a fresh view of the extraordinary versatility of the man and the subtle sophistication of his music. Scarlatti was evidently a widely traveled man and served in various capacities as a musician in the courts of Rome, Naples, Lisbon, and Madrid. During his later years he seems to have striven to cast off his Italian roots completely, turning himself into a Spanish composer who, according to Kirkpatrick, "captured the click of castanets, the strumming of guitars, the thud of muffled drums, the harsh bitter wail of gypsy lament, the overwhelming gaiety of the village band, and above all the wiry tension of the Spanish dance."

THE FORGOTTEN GALUPPI

Since Domenico's music, the product of a really original mind, is only beginning to be known today, it is little wonder that the music of Baldassare Galuppi (1706-1785), one of the more conventional Italian composers of the period, has completely disappeared. And yet as recently as 1855 Robert Browning was able to write of this composer:

Oh Galuppi, Baldassaro, this is very sad to find!
I can hardly misconceive you; it would prove me deaf and blind;
But although I take your meaning, 'tis with such a heavy mind!

Here you come with your old music, and here's all the good it brings.
What, they lived once thus at Venice where the merchants were the kings,
Where St. Mark's is, where the Doges used to wed the sea with rings?

Ay, because the sea's the street there; and 'tis arched by . . . what you call
. . . Shylock's bridge with houses on it, where they kept the carnival:
I was never out of England—it's as if I saw it all.

Very likely it was this "Brave Galuppi" who first introduced the several-movement sonata to the world. Not being content with merely imitating his greater compatriot and contemporary who had brought the one-movement form to such a high state of perfection, Galuppi used several movements in his sonatas, the better to provide a more diversified range of emotion. He thus stands at the halfway point between the Scarlatti one-movement works and the fully developed sonatas of Haydn and Mozart. Some of his single movements are worthy of comparison with the greatest music then being produced.

A rather doubtful honor goes to another Italian writer of harpsichord music, the man who is supposed to have invented the kind of inane bass writing used in so much later piano music, even in some of the best. In order to outline the harmony without providing merely chunky chordal accompaniments, Domenico Alberti inserted this kind of bass figure in his sonatas:

And ever since, this has gone by the name of the Alberti bass.

ITALIAN INSTRUMENTAL IMPROVEMENTS

One of the strongest influences in the development of a new instrumental expressive style was the Italian improvement of instruments which took place during this period. The most epochal of these was the invention of the *gravicembalo col pian e forte,* a keyboard instrument by which qualities of dynamics from soft to loud were made possible by the mere pressure of the player's hands and fingers. This *pianoforte, fortepiano,* or finally just piano, as it came to be called, was developed out of the harpsichord by a Florentine instrument maker, Bartolomeo Cristofori in 1709; he substituted a complicated hammer-lever action for striking the strings for the older system of "jacks" containing plectra which plucked the strings and which had no control over dynamics. Other inventors in other countries improved and developed Cristofori's idea, and the piano became a sort of universal instrument during the ensuing periods.

This was also the peak period of the great Italian violin-making families, the Stradivari, the Bergonzi, and the Guarneri, whose instruments are even more prized today than they were at the time of their manufacture. With some small changes to facilitate modern technical demands, they have remained models for all succeeding generations of lutists and have had an incalculable effect on the development of the *empfindsam* style.

AND THERE WERE
GIANTS IN THOSE DAYS

The Blend That Is Bach

There were giants in the earth in those days; and also after that, when the sons of God came in unto the daughters of men, and they bare children to them, the same became mighty men which were of old, men of renown.

Genesis vi: 4

INFLUENCES ON BACH'S MUSIC

During all the time of the High Baroque and Rococo, German taste was being influenced by strong cultural forces from abroad, especially the mighty Baroque stream from Italy and the silvery Rococo trickle from France. By her special genius, Germany was able to blend these with her own ingenious qualities and provide an artistic amalgam that was not Italian, French, or even German in character, but rather universal. The best architecture in the German-speaking countries at this time was influenced by both Italian and French tastes; but there are a distinction and a universality about such interiors as Neumann furnished for various German palaces, or the decorations in the Schloss Mirabel at Salzburg, or even the Amalienburg Pavilion in the Schlossgarten in Munich which make them distinctive—the best architectural examples of their kind, regardless of country.

So it was with music. Both the French and the Italians had exerted a decisive influence on the formation of the Late German Baroque style. Based firmly on the Italian concerto and suite, as well as the organ forms derived from the north and the operatic-oratorio forms from the south, and incorporating into these the orchestral innovations of Lully, the keyboard techniques of Couperin, and the vocal as well as the instrumental *bel canto* style of the Italians, the Germans evolved a sort of universal style that overlaps all borders and defies all classifications; it is Baroque in many of its manifestations, Rococo in others, and plain bourgeois in still others. This style, combined with the happy incidence of such towering geniuses as J. S. Bach and Handel and the right chronological backgrounds, produced some of the greatest music in all history.

The list of composers who directly influenced Bach, for example, is a long one and reaches away back into the Early Baroque. Insofar as organ music goes, we can trace it easily through the three leading pre-Bach organ composers Buxtehude in Lübeck, Pachelbel in Nuremberg, and Georg Böhm in Lüneburg, to Froberger and his teacher, Frescobaldi.[1] Buxtehude, who was a Dane by birth and whose *Abendmusik* concerts made Lübeck a place of pilgrimage for all church musicians of the time, is especially important, for the young Bach worked directly with him, as we shall see, and many of the Baroque elements in Bach's music derive straight from the harmonic boldness, the wide sweeping melodies, and the profoundly stirring contrapuntal structures of Buxtehude. Johann Pachelbel transmitted the brilliant virtuoso style of the south into central Germany and also developed (in conjunction with Böhm) the contrapuntal art of paraphrasing chorale melodies. As a young man, Bach came directly into contact with the French style through his visits to the little court at Celle, a sort of minor German Versailles imitating all French taste, where French music was cultivated and French instrumental technique with its finished elegance and embellishments was favored. Out of this blend came the music of Bach; and yet, without the unfailing power which came from the strong personal religious faith that was his inheritance from German Protestantism, this music would have lost its profound subjective quality and its universal sense of truthful utterance.

In Bach we come to the culmination of one of the great epochs of the art; he represents the acme of the polyphonic grandeur and intricacy which we have been tracing from its earliest, almost instinctive, beginnings. We have seen what a world of differing spiritual and

[1] These principal figures were surrounded by a host of lesser men active in Germany and Austria. Among the most important were Georg Muffat (1645–1704), a pupil of Lully and Corelli, organist at Passau; his son Gottlieb (1690–1770); Ferdinand Fischer (1665–1746), one of whose works served as a model for Bach's *Well-tempered Clavier;* Erlebach (1657–1714), who wrote a fine collection of arias—really continuo songs; and Fux (1660–1741), the author of a standard work on counterpoint, the *Gradus ad Parnassum,* which later became famous.

human aspirations there was in this long period of development; while it was unified, externally, by the general use of woven melodies and rhythms, the era was in reality widely diversified. Nothing more unlike than the madrigals of Monteverdi and the motets and Masses of Palestrina can be imagined, even though both composers made use of the same technical means of expression. So, too, the contrapuntal music of Bach, with its marked emotion, its very personal, Protestant feeling, is far removed from the period of the Universal Church and the mysticism of passive and helpless man in the midst of untranslatable earthly trials. The lovely setting of Josquin des Prés's *Incarnatus,* which we considered in an earlier chapter, and Bach's beautiful treatment of the same words in his *B Minor Mass,* both of them outstanding masterpieces of polyphonic expression, are worlds apart in meaning.

But strongly as we may feel that this direct, personal, spiritual Bach is the real Bach, we must remember that it is not, by any means, all of him. Among the many explanations that might well be given of why he must always stand as the greatest of musicians, that of his many-sidedness is perhaps the most significant. Bigness is not synonymous with greatness, as we of this century are learning only too well; but Bach was big, broad, voluminous, and great, in the deepest and highest sense. He wrote an almost unbelievable amount of music during his long, active life; and like all the great composers, there were times in his career when the mere ease of production and the perfection of the processes of composition tended to overwriting. It seems to have been as true of him as it has been of other great workers in the arts—Shakespeare, Beethoven, Rembrandt, Rubens—that the very process of bringing into the world any masterpieces necessitates the expenditure of a tremendous amount of creative energy, some of which is inevitably diverted into channels that are not important. The very quality of the works of these men depends to a certain degree on the quantity they produced; but in the main, Bach's music-making was exceedingly profitable as well as prolific.

AN ORGANIST'S PROSAIC LIFE

The details of Bach's life are generally known. They are of particular interest insofar as they directly affected his creative output. Born in 1685, of a long line of provincial church and town musicians, in the very heart of German Protestantism, in Eisenach, Thuringia, he spent his early years in preparation for the profession which it was inevitable

THE *STAMMHAUS* OF THE BACH FAMILY IN WECHMAR   A tablet on its walls has the following inscription:
"In this house lived Veit Bach around the year 1600, and after him his son Hans Bach, both of them bakers. Hans also learned music in Gotha and became a credit to that profession. Seven generations of this Bach family have given the world a hundred practicing musicians and music scholars, and in the person of Johann Sebastian Bach, one of its greatest composers, the outstanding contrapuntist and organ player of his time.
"All honor to their memory."

for him to follow. As he lost both parents at an early age, he came under the tutelage of an older organist brother, and through him and the masters at the schools he attended, coupled with the insatiable curiosity of genius, Bach received an excellent foundational training in organ, clavier, and violin playing and came into direct contact with the choral practices of the Lutheran Church of the time. His first real position was as organist in Arnstadt, a little town not far from his birthplace, from which post he absented himself shortly after being appointed, in order to go north and learn more of his profession from Buxtehude, the great organist of his time, in Lübeck. This leave of absence became so extended that the young Bach found himself in difficulty with the church authorities upon his return, the first skirmish of a perpetual war on the prerogatives of his position in which he was engaged the rest of his life. He was a strongly opinionated, hot-headed individual, thoroughly convinced of his rights and strongly determined to uphold them, even in the face of the most duly constituted authority.

From Arnstadt, Bach went to another provincial Thuringian town,

Mühlhausen, where he stayed for a short time, and then was called to Weimar, the little town that has become known as the German Athens, as organist of the duke's court chapel. This position can hardly be said to have been commensurate with Bach's genius, but it gave him plenty of opportunity for quiet study and composition and an organ on which to play. It was during this period at Weimar, from 1708 to 1717, that he wrote most of the great organ works for which he has become famous. His own organ was small and undistinguished, but he was in demand as a virtuoso player and recitalist, and so had opportunity for playing larger instruments. Some of his masterpieces were written for such occasions, although most of them first saw the light of day in the incongruous chapel of Duke Wilhelm's castle at Weimar. Fortunately, Bach did not write for the moment. Many of his works he never heard given with anything that would seem adequate to us in the way of resources. But he seemed always to be able to hear with an inner ear and to idealize his conceptions in such a way as to make them the greatest of their kind in the literature.

AT ANHALT-CÖTHEN

The middle period of Bach's life was spent in the service of another prince, Leopold of Anhalt-Cöthen. Here he was *Kapellmeister* to the court's little orchestra. And, since there was no religious duty connected with his post and no organ to play, he interested himself in the writing of a great deal of instrumental, secular music. A good violinist, he turned his attention to that instrument and wrote for it as well as for the orchestra and the clavier. Most of his works in these fields came from this period.

In 1723, at the age of 38, Bach was elected cantor of St. Thomas's and its associated churches in Leipzig, one of the most important musical positions in Germany at the time. He spent the rest of his life there, training the singers of the choir, teaching in the school connected with the church, writing music for the weekly services, raising his large family, and generally quarreling with the authorities—not exactly what we would call an artistic milieu. Yet out of it came, for the reasons we have already noted, his greatest works, for this was his time of abundant fruitfulness in both quality and quantity. Nearly three hundred cantatas, a number of large choral works of the utmost importance, including the *St. Matthew Passion* and the *B Minor Mass,* as well as various instrumental compositions, flowed in a steady stream from his facile pen. He traveled more than he ever had in his life, going as far afield as Berlin. There he visited Frederick the Great, played for him, and sent him his *Musikalisches Opfer* as a memento of his visit. His last years, happy enough as to personal affairs, were embittered by quarrels with those in authority over him. He died July 28, 1750, at the age of sixty-five.

BACH, THE GREATER AND THE LESSER

Many present-day critics are wont to divide the hundreds of compositions left us by this composer into two general classes—what might be called the Greater and the Lesser Bach. Enough has already been said here to suggest that the former group would certainly include the majority of the religious choral works, and the latter many of the instrumental secular ones. This is probably as clear a line of demarcation as is necessary. There is no doubt that the expressive side of Bach's genius is most concentratedly shown in his sacred music—the cantatas, Masses, and Passions—and in that branch of his instrumental music most closely associated with these, his organ chorale preludes and fugues. No better example could be found of these expressive works than the *B Minor Mass*, and a study of Bach might well begin and end with this tremendous composition, one of the sublime summits in the terrain of the art.

B MINOR MASS

It grew in musical stature and favor with its creator during Bach's forty-sixth to fifty-second years of life, from 1731 to 1737. The term *Mass* is, of course, closely associated with the ritual of the Catholic Church; but the Lutheran service had its Mass as well, keeping two sections of the original six at the time its ritual was "reformed." These two, the *Kyrie eleison* and the *Gloria,* formed the rich beginning of the main Lutheran *Gottesdienst*. But, attracted by the expressive potentialities of the full Catholic text, Bach enlarged the shorter species of the Lutheran ritual to the grandeur we know today, adding the four sections, *Credo, Sanctus, Benedictus,* and *Agnus Dei,* thus bringing the whole into formal parallelism with the Roman rite. But the spirit of the work is thoroughly Lutheran, and its form makes it impossible to use it in the Catholic service.

FIRST PAGE OF THE "CRUCIFIXUS"

The additions which Bach made were taken largely from cantatas he had already composed.[2] The choral writing is commonly in five parts: for two sopranos, alto, tenor, and bass, although in the *Sanctus* and in the *Hosanna* six and eight parts respectively are employed. The orchestra contains three of the specially high Bach trumpets that are no longer present in our orchestras, besides two each of flutes, oboes, and bassoons, with strings, kettledrums, and an important part for the organ, this latter indicated in the score by a figured bass. Another instrument of which Bach was fond, the *oboe d'amore*, darkly sweet, is used at times; and the hunting horn, in the tenth number, accompanying the bass soloist and joyously acclaiming the sovereignty of the Most High, is an indication of the human sensibility that is always pulsing through this work, making us remember again the use of realism of which Bach was so fond, and suggestive of the Lutheran pietism with its overemphasis on religious sentimentalism.

The music is in twenty-four movements, comprising fifteen choruses, six solo airs (one each for soprano and tenor, two each for alto and bass), and three duets (two for soprano and alto, one for soprano and tenor). It is to be noted that Bach did not use here the operatic form of aria—that is, the regular three-part *da capo* form, since he must have realized that any mechanical repetition of a thought in a work of this kind could only weaken its significance. It is interesting to realize that, of all Bach's works, this is one which he never heard in its en-

[2] The historical origins of the various sections of the *B Minor Mass* are interesting: The *Kyrie* and the *Gloria in excelsis* (the portions which the Lutheran and Catholic liturgies had in common) were written in 1733 and sent to Friedrich August, Duke of Saxony, together with a letter of appeal for patronage, begging "that they be received not on their merits as compositions but with your Majesty's notorious generosity." He offered these two sections of the Mass as "trifling proofs of the science I have been able to acquire in music." There is no record that Augustus ever paid them any attention whatever.

The two four-part choruses, *Gratias agimus* and *Dona pacem* are to be found, with differences, in the Rathswahl cantata of 1731.

The *Qui tollis* chorus was founded on the opening chorus of a much earlier cantata, *Schauet doch*.

The *Crucifixus* was taken direct from the cantata *Weinen, Klagen* (1724).

The *Hosanna* was adapted from a welcome song to the King of Saxony (1734).

The *Agnus Dei* used materials found in an Ascensiontide cantata, *Lobet Gott in seinen Reichen*.

The structure of this great work was erected during the mature years of Bach's life; in round figures it contains some 2300 bars, about a third of which, 638, to be exact, is borrowed material. The work was not written for any special occasion, which does not mean that it is in any sense a "patchy" work. Where Bach incorporated what he had previously said elsewhere, it could have been only for the reason that he felt it adequate to the purpose of this particular composition as a whole, and that nothing new need be composed.

tirety, although he performed its first two sections with his choirs in Leipzig.

This Mass as a whole is Bach at his greatest and fullest. We hear all sides of his manifold genius, and each listener will have his favorite movement; to realize fully the master's greatness, it should be heard again and again, until it is really known by heart. This may sound like something of a heavy task, but for the right listeners it can but be a revelation of the imaginative manipulation of ideas inspired by a faith that was as natural and unquestioned as the facts of the composer's everyday existence. The student will realize in this work better than in almost any other in the history of music the truth that technique is, after all, the vital food of any composer's spirit.

This great composition was, in the fullest sense of the word, the great culmination of Bach's Baroque career. It achieved for his art what Beethoven intended the *Ninth Symphony* should do for his, and what Wagner planned, and did not quite carry out, in *The Ring of the Nibelung*.

ST. MATTHEW PASSION

Next to the Mass in the depth of its feeling and the surety of its expression comes the *St. Matthew Passion*, a work which is so "intensely felt, so deeply impassioned, so poignantly dramatic, that it seems embroidered with tears and colored with flames and blood." Of the three settings of the Passion story which Bach is known to have made, this one according to the gospel of St. Matthew is by far the richest. It is a magnificently realized and very dramatic exposition of the story of Christ's suffering and death. In it, the balance of emotion is beautifully attained. We find, as was also true of the Mass, that a tense situation is relieved, or a dark one lightened, by the placing of particular items in conjunction. If one of these is omitted, as is so often done in modern performances, it can readily be seen that the balance of sensitivity may be entirely spoiled. Conductors who have carefully studied Bach's directions tell us that his knowledge of effects—as regards, for instance, the placing of choirs, orchestra, and soloists—was remarkable, and that the moving power of his works as wholes is enhanced or weakened by close attention to his specific instructions. It seems to be the general opinion at the present that a small choir and orchestra, say, groups of forty singers and thirty players, gives a much more intimate and touching effect in the *St. Matthew Passion* than is possible with a very large body of musicians, such as usually takes part in the Mass. The place of the multitude here is in the chorales, which were meant for all to join in as a corporate act of worship.

The general form of the Passion had been in use for over a century in the German church. Schütz was the first to apply the Italian operatic style of Monteverdi and his followers to the development of a semi-dramatic piece for use in church on Good Friday, using as text the moving words of the Passion story as contained in the various gospels. He did this so effectively and sincerely that Bach, a century later, followed closely in his footsteps; the later works use the same general apparatus—recitatives to carry on the dramatic development of the story, arias of both a dramatic and a reflective nature, choruses and chorales for the congregation—as did the earlier.

In listening to a modern production of this emotionally stirring work, one of the most affecting, indeed, in all music, the hearer will probably find it difficult to recover the point of view of the worshiper of 1729, listening to this composition under Bach's direction in St. Thomas's Church in Leipzig. Here again we find that peculiar type of religious imagery which was in vogue at the time, but which has long since passed out of style. The imagination of Bach's day did not hesitate to indulge in ecstasies that seem to us as oversentimental and having no place in religious worship. Yet, we must again insist, so great was Bach's power and so sincere his expression that these textual embarrassments furnish the basis for some of his finest music, which lies essentially in a world quite apart from theological beliefs and which speaks to us today, more than two hundred years after it was written, with unaltered eloquence and changeless power.

USE OF LEITMOTIV

It was Bach's habit to use in all these choral works—the cantatas and the Mass, as well as the Passions—certain realistic motives to symbolize various ideas and images and emotions. Schweitzer and Pirro, who have gone into this matter more thoroughly than have any other writers, have pointed out wave motives, step motives, and motives suggestive of grief, despair, terror, felicity, and all the rest of the human emotions. The accompaniment to the ineffably beautiful *Crucifixus* in the Mass is built up over a stark, chromatic grief motive, which the composer uses again and again in similar places. In the aria in the *St. Matthew Passion* reflecting on the bitter picture of Jesus carrying the cross, Bach uses a stumbling, sinking motive to suggest the scene. In that part of the narrative where the Evangelist tells of Peter's suddenly remembering the words of Jesus: "Before the cock crow thou shalt deny me thrice," Bach uses a motive which actually imitates the cock's crowing. But it is exceedingly doubtful whether the sensitive listener of today, unless he is forewarned, would be conscious of all this elaborate naïve literalism. What matters to him is that this music is full of a great emotion, which transcends time and place and communicates itself to him as forcefully as it did to the listener who sat under Bach himself. It is the marvelous tone poet and master of emotional expression that impresses us; we have forgotten the eighteenth-century cantor of a Leipzig church, writing music which was wont to indulge in the simple literalism and sentimental pieties of his Baroque period.

THE CANTATAS

Any adequate study of the cantatas would take a lifetime. Carl Philipp Emanuel, Bach's second son, said that his father had written nearly three hundred such works; of these, about two hundred have survived. Most of them were written for use in the Sunday services of the churches where Bach was in charge of the music. Each cantata, written on a theme appropriate to the day in the church calendar, occupied an important place in the *Hauptgottesdienst,* or morning service. Others were written for special occasions, and a few appeared with secular words. In form, they range all the way from a series of arias for solo voice, such as *Meine Seele rühmt und preist* (No. 189) to the impressive and severe eight-movement *Christ lag in Todesbanden* (No. 4), in which every movement—introductory symphony, choruses, duets, and solos—is a variation or fantasia on the chorale tune of that name. Sanford Terry, one of the best writers on Bach, had this to say of the cantatas:

> *Their music reveals the deeps of his character, the high purpose to which he dedicated his genius . . . it is a faithful mirror in which the mind of its composer is revealed. The cantatas disclose the fact that his astonishing fecundity was controlled by searching and frequent pondering of the texts he set. They reveal the keenness and clarity with which he visualized Bible scenes and characters. How consistent and devotional, for instance, is his portrayal of the Saviour's gracious dignity! After hearing the several Michaelmas cantatas, who can doubt that Bach pictured Satan, not as Isaiah's Lucifer, the Day Star, the Son of the Morning, but as the malignant and cumberous Serpent of Genesis, the Great Dragon of Revelation? For always Bach depicts his rolling gait in*

writhing themes, which outline his motion as clearly as an etcher's pen. With what tender touches he points the scene of the Nativity! And with what poignant emotion he follows the Saviour's footsteps to Calvary!

With truth, therefore, Schweitzer observes that the cantatas are the most reliable indicators of Bach's genius and character. For their range is so wide, they reflect him from so many angles, and express him in so many moods, that they reveal his personality no less than his art . . . Bach was one of the tenderest and most emotional of men, with the eye of a painter and the soul of a poet. But the fact is fully revealed only to those who are at the pains to translate him.

Because these works are so far removed from contemporary thought, and because, in addition, they are difficult for modern choralists to manage, we have few opportunities of hearing them today. They are still sung as part of the Bach tradition in certain of the Leipzig churches and appear occasionally on programs of choral societies, completely out of character in this latter environment. Fortunately there are many excellent recordings of them.

VOICES TREATED AS INSTRUMENTS

A word may well be added here concerning Bach's treatment of the voice. Perhaps it was due to the fact that he never came into direct touch with the birthplace of the opera—Italy—or it may have been the result of his absolutely independent, forthright nature; but we never find him making any concessions to the limitations of the human voice, or writing a singer's part with the idea of giving him a grateful opportunity for technical display *à la mode italienne*. He writes a solo part for a soprano or a bass in exactly the same fashion as he would one for a violin or a cello, often using the same figures and paying scant attention to the necessity for breathing spaces, awkwardness of intervals for singing, and so on. In consequence, especially for a generation whose greatest interpretive achievements in music lie in fields other than choralism, many of Bach's arias and duets, as well as the individual parts in the choruses, seem almost impossible of adequate presentation. What Bach was interested in, of course, was the direct and pointed expression of his ideas. Whether the part which he wrote was particularly grateful for the instrument to which it was to be given or offered opportunity for virtuosity concerned him not at all. He sometimes wrote phrases which are physically difficult to sing. In consequence, we have a great deal of bad Bach playing and singing, especially the latter; and it would have been better for his reputation had Bach taken a hint or two from his contemporary, Handel, whose choral writing, although it has less expressive greatness and moving subtlety than Bach's, always lies well for the voice, and consequently makes an excellent effect.

ORGAN WORKS

The instrumental works which come closest to the great choral works in intensity of expression and poignancy of emotional speech are the organ compositions. These are touched with much the same imaginative spirit, the same Baroque intensity, and the same magnificence of style that we find in the *B Minor Mass* or in the *St. Matthew Passion.* In many of the *Chorale Preludes*—organ meditations on hymn tunes— we find just as truly as in any of the choral works Bach's spirit of yearning, of musing on man's frailty and on God's sustaining might. In their imposing magnificence, their wealth of meticulously executed detail, their magnificent rhythms and flashes of brilliant color, some of the great organ works, such as the *Fantasia and Fugue in G Minor,* are as imposing, and as truly magnificent, as anything in music.

Ernest Newman has said that for him the *Chorale Preludes* are the heart of Bach; and it is certain that they hold within them a complete world of his expressiveness. For they offered to him the sort of external stimulus which his imagination seemed to need for its richest and most fruitful release. Give him a pictorial image, or suggest a mood or present a dramatic idea, and his mind starts working immediately and gives us something that is deeply felt and beautifully expressed. The words and tunes associated with the church which he had served since his early boyhood, tunes that he had known ever since he could remember anything at all, seemed especially stimulating to him. He would take one of them, muse upon some phase of its words, and suggest its spirit in the instrumental composition which we call by the name *chorale prelude.* Most of these are program music, pure and simple, small symphonic poems for the organ.

There are many instances in these chorale preludes, as also in the choral works, of Bach's daring use of musical means that were far ahead of the practices of his time. For not only was he a writer whose expressiveness, grandeur of utterance, and perfection of form have never been equaled, but he was likewise one of the most daring and adventurous radicals of all musical history. The boldness of many of his progressions and chordal formations strikes home with telling power even today, when our ears have become accustomed to the harmonies of Wagner and Debussy, not to speak of the dissonances of Schönberg and his followers. There was nothing tentative or hesitant in his style; he was as sure of how to express himself as of what it was he wanted to express, and beside him some of the later composers—even the best ones—seem timid and halting. There is good reason for the veneration in which he has been held by great musicians: Beethoven, Brahms, Mendelssohn, Wagner, Franck—all studied his works carefully and thought of him as the father of all music.

THE BAROQUE BACH

In addition to the one hundred forty-three chorale preludes he left us, Bach wrote a considerable number of other works for his favorite instrument, among them a number of preludes and fugues. In these, he went through a typically Baroque period, of which the showy *Toccata and Fugue in D Minor* is very characteristic. Some of the other great organ works, such as the *Fantasia and Fugue in G Minor,* are a bit freer as to style and more meaty in content. The latter, written when Bach was making a trip to Hamburg in 1720, seems to have been composed to show the organists in that city how well he could handle this style, which had always been popular in North Germany. In their part weaving, in their magnificent opulence of tone, in their bold harmonies and clever manipulation of key changes, and in their freshness of invention and freedom from pedantry, the best of these organ works stand alone. They show their composer at the top of his form, the tonal genius, rejoicing in his strength and power, and wearing his learning lightly— buoyant, confident, well-knit music. All together, there are forty of these organ fugues, most of them with some sort of introductory movement, a prelude, a toccata, or a fantasia. In addition, there is a magnificent passacaglia (written on a constantly repeated theme) and fugue; some trio-sonatas, much more difficult to play than they seem and written for the instruction of his sons in organ playing; and some miscellaneous pieces, including four transcriptions of "Vivaldi" orchestral concertos.

ORGAN OR ORCHESTRA?

In recent years, there has been considerable discussion as to how these organ works of Bach may best be interpreted; and the enthusiasts who demand that they should be restricted to the instrument for which they were written have sponsored a revival of the type of organ used during

JOHANN SEBASTIAN BACH at the age of thirty-eight. (from a painting by Elias J. Haussman)

the Baroque era—an organ with sharply differentiated tone colors and light ensemble qualities which give a bright, silvery sheen to this music. It would seem, on the other hand, that much of the peculiarly Baroque sense of grandeur inherent in a great deal of this music achieves its true significance only when played on the orchestra. With this in mind, a number of transcriptions of Bach's organ music have been made for the modern orchestra; some of these, when carefully done, and when they adhere to the mood and style of the original, are marvelously effective. But, and it is a big *but*, it has become the habit of certain transcribers to attempt to heighten their effects, to increase their sonorities, and to intensify their coloring to a point where the result is overpowerfully garish—modern in a way that calls attention to the virtuosity of the transcription and the playing of it, instead of centering the attention on the content of the music. This is not good Bach, exciting and novel as the music may seem at first hearing. Schweitzer has probably thought more about the music of Bach than any other man alive today, and he says that, in listening to it, it is necessary for us to attain a composure and an inwardness which will bring to life something of the deep spiritual qualities which lie hidden there. Superficially brilliant, gorgeously colored, modernized orchestrations, played at a pace that makes adequate comprehension of the various lines of sound of which this music is composed absolutely impossible, will not help us attain this state of grace.

On the other hand, there should be no place in modern life for the dull, mechanical interpretations of Bach that are so often perpetrated by organists, with no attempt to achieve the necessary independence of part playing and no plasticity of phrasing to bring out the life inherent in this music.[3] An additional reason why these organ renditions of Bach's so often seem difficult to listen to is that the players usually choose some of his least interesting works. We have already intimated that this composer, great as he is, had his pedestrian moments—times when in the course of his busy life and the need for the performance of an incredible amount of routine labors, his powers of imagination and inspiration flagged and those of his invention flourished. It is these moments which organists so often blazon forth on their programs, forgetting that there is second-rate and third-rate, as well as first-rate, Bach. A great deal of this inferior music, turned out with the easy facility of the journalist, rather than with the inspired imagination of the poet, with its complacently jogging rhythms and easy contrapuntal embroideries of obvious harmonic progressions, is, unfortunately, what many people know and hear as characteristic Bach. The sensitive listener turns impatiently away from this journalistic small talk of a great mind, this workmanlike but uninspired prose, this by-product of an intellect, and demands the essential and incomparable truths which he knows this composer capable of expressing. He will not willingly endure these dull performances of what Newman has called the "jigging, jogging Bach" but will endeavor to find music of this composer that appeals to his imagination, kindling into life the experiences and visions which brought it into being in the mind of Bach. For he well knows that, in the use of a language of sound which possesses the "mysterious faculty of rendering thoughts with a clearness and definiteness surpassing its own natural power of expression, Bach is the greatest among the great."

[3] Surely there must be some happy medium between the two extremes so often heard in the interpretations of Bach—between those which, as one writer has expressed it, dress out the old cantor in a costume suitable for the Beaux Arts Ball, with all the opulence of color and slickness of playing of which the modern orchestra is capable, and the overascetic and dry monotony heard in other renditions. These two extremes may be heard in the records of Stokowski and Schweitzer. Neither is wholly satisfactory to an understanding listener; but, as a steady diet, the latter will prove more nourishing.

The Secular Works of Bach

*It must be by this time almost four years since
your high-wellbornness favored me with a
gracious reply to a letter addressed to you;
and if I remember that you kindly conde-
scended to ask for some news of my fate, this
shall now most obediently be done.*

*My vicissitudes from youth onward are well
known to you, up to the change which drew
me to Cöthen as Director of Music. There I
had a gracious prince who loved music as well
as he knew it, at whose court I thought to
close my earthly career. But it was so ordained
that the said* Serenissimus *espoused a Bern-
burgish princess, whereupon it began to appear as though the musical inclinations of the
said prince were to grow somewhat lukewarm,
the rather because the new princess seemed to
be something of an* amusa.

*Thus God willed that my vocation should
be that of musical director and cantor at the
St. Thomas School here, although I could not
at first accommodate myself to the thought of
being turned from a* Kapellmeister *into a
cantor.*

From a letter of Bach's, October 28, 1730

EXPRESSIONAL RELATIONSHIP
AND ORGANIZED SOUND
One careful student
of Bach's music has made the statement that at least two thirds of the
enormous quantity of music contained in the Complete Edition of the
Bach-Gesellschaft (which represents his whole life's work) is music of
an obviously expressional character, its meaning directly related to some
imaginative concept through a verbal text or a poetic program of some
sort. The other third may be said to be music of the absolute type,
making its appeal largely through its qualities as organized sound rather
than depending on expressional relationships. This is an exact reversal
of the opinions that have been generally held—for Bach is almost
always considered pre-eminently a composer of patterned, formal

music—but it is an opinion on which such Bach experts as Schweitzer and Terry agree. As we have seen, most of this program music of Bach's—using the expression in its widest sense—was written for the church; the remaining third of his output is mostly secular in character and consists of instrumental works of various sorts: for clavier, violin, flute, cello, and orchestra. Cast in the general mold of its period, much of this music moves along with all the external qualities of some of his greater works, but with little of their internal content. With the treasures of *The Well-tempered Clavier* before us, as well as some isolated movements from the orchestral and chamber works—things which represent the very best of our composer—we can hardly say that these secular compositions as a whole are inferior to the sacred ones; but they certainly contain the least treasurable side of his genius, a great deal more of the sub-Bach than of the super-Bach.

A mere outline of these works is sufficient to indicate their general nature. There are a number of orchestral works, including the *Brandenburg Concertos;* four suites and fifteen concertos for various instruments with the accompaniment of a string orchestra and a clavier; an imposing list of things for unaccompanied instruments—six sonatas for violin alone and six for cello alone, works which require superb handling on the part of modern players, who have to cope with a different type of bow than was in use in Bach's day, if they would make them interesting. There are also compositions for instruments with clavier accompaniment, including sonatas for violin and clavier and flute and clavier; and a whole horde of works for clavier alone, including the two books of *The Well-tempered Clavier* (forty-eight preludes and fugues in the various major and minor keys), and a number of fantasias, fugues, and suites.

BACH'S USE OF CONCERTO FORM

Of the so-called orchestral works, the six Brandenburg concertos, written for the duke of that name, are most familiar; they are, however, not orchestral works in the modern sense but were written for a *Hofkapelle* of the type found in most of the princely establishments in the Germany of that time, a group of string players of average ability, with a few wood-wind and brass instruments added. When played by a large modern band, as is so often done, these concertos lose their true character; for the individuality and play of the various parts are completely lost in the huge swirl of orchestral tone.

These concertos derive their very form from the nature of the body for which they were written: a few gifted soloists interplaying with the remainder of the orchestra, which probably never comprised more than twenty or twenty-five men. So they sound best when played by a small body of musicians, and are really chamber-music works rather than orchestral ones. Bach's use of this form was the same as that of his contemporaries, who tried to see what could be freshly done in the way of manipulating the old principle of contrast. In these eighteenth-century concertos, besides a variety of subjects, there was brought in a variety of people to handle them. Each of the Brandenburg concertos is scored for different instrumental combinations, the soloists being pitted against the orchestra. Contrast, argument, even conflict, these exciting new possibilities opened up. This principle had been seen at its simplest as soon as music changed from unaccompanied into accompanied singing. There was at once some other element, the instrument, that had to be reckoned with, in addition to the voice; but the latter became master, an influence which has lingered on in some of the later show concertos, where the violinist or the pianist is so obviously the master of the whole situation.

The root of the formal conception of these compositions was the idea of the interplay of individual soloists and the orchestral body as a whole, an essentially dramatic idea, exemplified in every good stage play. Uniting or dividing, the various actors show tensions and reliefs; and they are always unequally matched in dramatic power. We know the influence of a single personality. In our day, stunts and commercial publicity have twisted proportions and vulgarized values; but behind all our interest in people lies the interest in the working-out of their individual personalities—the demonstration of what they are, told in what they do and what happens to them. All life is a campaign, with its ups and downs: so, too, is a concerto. The interplay of personalities is suggested musically by the manner in which the various themes are intertwined in these early concertos. The later types, with which most music lovers of today are more familiar, extensively deploy the solo part against the much more subtle power wielded by the nineteenth-century orchestra. The later works show the full possibility of these various types of interplay in the way they use themes, in alternation of soloist and band, and in the playing-off of the various bodies in the orchestra itself. But Bach's use of the *concerto grosso*, as these early works were called, is quite typical, although we find more varied combinations in his orchestra than in other compositions of the time.

OUVERTURES

There is some confusion regarding the four works which Bach called *Ouvertures*. We generally give them the name of suite, for they comprise a set of movements of varying character, based on dance rhythms of contrasting styles. They were written for different instrumental combinations: one for wood winds and strings, one for flute and strings, and two for oboes, bassoons, trumpets, drums, and strings —the latter rather a strange orchestral *mélange,* according to modern tastes. The *B Minor Suite,* for flute and strings, is the favorite, and quite rightly so, for it has delectable parts for the soloist; it contains six movements in addition to the overture, which is itself of considerable length, written in the form which Lully invented for his series of operas which culminated about the time Bach was born. We find that Handel, too, adopted this form of the overture, consisting of a slow prelude followed by a quick movement in fugal style, and oftentimes, as if in apology for being a bit too serious, rounded off by a dance.

A SOLITARY PICTORIAL PIECE

An amusing, if not particularly important, early clavier work of Bach's is his *Capriccio on the Departure of a Beloved Brother,* written in 1704, when the nineteen-year-old boy was organist at Arnstadt and his elder brother, Johann Jakob, an oboeist, decided to forsake the quiet ways of Thuringia in order to become a military bandsman in the service of Charles XII of Sweden. This involved not only a journey, and in those days journeys were exciting enterprises, but possible dangers as a soldier; for the young king, then only twenty-two, had been a man of war ever since he was crowned at the age of fifteen and, by 1700, had defeated the Danes and was at once hurling his troops at Russia and later at Poland. So even a musician in such service was likely to smell powder; there was sufficient reason for his relatives' anxiety, and Bach put into a piece of program music an expression of their fears and their good wishes for the adventurer. Only a year or two before, Kuhnau had brought out his famous *Bible Sonatas,* landmarks in the history of pictorial suggestion in music. Bach thought that he would try his hand at the style; and the six sections of this little work show how well the young composer was able to mingle poetic suggestion and technical skill. Although he never essayed purely instrumental program music again, he seldom lost this idea of poetic suggestiveness.

In studying Bach's larger keyboard works, we must keep in mind the fact that he was much more concerned with the musical design of them than he was with the instruments on which they were to be played. In listening to some of Bach's keyboard music (apart from that for the organ), we have to remember that he thought little of whether it was to be played on the delicate, sweet clavichord, whose strings were struck by a metal "finger," or on the more powerful, potentially majestic harpsichord, with its plucked strings, two manuals (sets of keys), and various stops for giving different timbres and octave effects. It might be a valuable exercise, if one were fortunate enough to be able to hear both a clavichord and a harpsichord, to go through the set of *The Well-tempered Clavier* preludes and fugues and decide for which each is best suited.

THE SOLUTION OF A PROBLEM

Bach had always interested himself in musical science. Composers in his day were severely hampered by the system of tuning then in general use, which, in order to avoid technicalities, placed certain keys in accurate tuning at the expense of others, which became badly out of tune and so were unhappy keys for a composer to use. It was not merely a matter of writing only in one key—the annoyance developed when the composers wished to modulate to others. Bach, ever a man of bold action and determination, advocated the system of "equal temperament," then becoming known, whereby all the twelve semitones of the octave were so adjusted that none was offensively out of tune. This made all keys available; the composer's keyboard, or clavier, was now "well-tempered" or tuned; hence the name of the set of pieces which Bach wrote to celebrate, as it were, an epoch-making decision.[4] *Das Wohltemperirte Clavier* to Bach may have seemed simply a commonsense piece of business; for us, it is the work that opened up all the wealth of later music, with its absolute freedom of key change, of which, as time went on, later composers learned how to take the most delightful advantage.

So Bach brought out, in 1722 (he was then thirty-seven), his first

[4] The invention of equal temperament, and its attempt to provide a way out of the difficulties inherent in any "true" system of tuning, may be traced back to the beginning of the sixteenth century. Its introduction into general musical practice was slow, but it was greatly aided by its partial adoption by a number of composers before Bach, the best known being Pachelbel. J. K. F. Fischer's *Ariadne Musica* (1710), a collection calling for the use of nineteen of the twenty-four keys theoretically available in the tempered system, undoubtedly served as a sort of model for Bach's later, more complete work.

set of twenty-four pieces in all the major and minor keys; another set appeared later, in 1744. The two together make up what pianists know briefly as *The Forty-eight,* a work that has been well called the pianist's Old Testament, the New being the Beethoven piano sonatas. Bach wrote a prelude and a fugue for every key. Some of this first set were pieces which Bach had already composed for other purposes; some were newly written. They were done for his pleasure—sometimes to satisfy his wish to work out a piece of technique, sometimes to express a mood in a brief time.[5] The preludes, as befits their modest name, though they often contain a remarkable amount of material and science, usually work out an idea, embodied in a phrase or some musical bit of shaping that can scarcely be called a tune or a theme. There are all sorts of thoughts and moods in them; some of them are connected with their fugues only in the slightest way, as by contrast of mood.

FUGUES IN GENERAL

In studying the fugues of this remarkable collection, the listener should have a fair idea of the principles of this form, particularly of its being a structure built from a (usually) small theme, which structure grows and climaxes. Bach used a variety of fugal types. We are not to seek from him any "rules," but to gather principles, both of working out technical problems and of embodying poetic expression in fugal style. (Perhaps it may be added here, by way of definition, that the fugue *subject* is heard in turn in the several "voices" or parts—which in *The Forty-eight* means 2, 3, 4, or 5; its *countersubject* is its continuation, heard while the *subject* is being given by another voice, in the dominant, as the *answer*. Episodes carry on the action while the subject is resting from its entries, and a *stretto* occurs when an answer enters before the subject has fully ended.)

A novice, believing that the fixed rules of fugue construction should certainly be followed in such a work as *The Well-tempered Clavier,* might well ask, on finding that some of them do not follow textbook principles, "Is not Bach wrong here?" This master of fugal construction did set forth the principles of their form in a complete and scholastic way in his *Die Kunst der Fuge;* but in *The Forty-eight* we can

[5] In this connection, it is well to notice the inscription attached to the autographed copy of *Das Wohltemperirte Clavier* now in possession of the Berlin Library: "The well-tempered Clavier; or, Preludes and Fugues on every Tone and Semitone, with the major third Ut, Re, Mi, and minor third, Re, Mi, Fa. For the Use and Profit of Young Musicians anxious to learn, and as a Pastime for others already expert in the Art. Composed and set forth by Johann Sebastian Bach, at present Capellmeister and Director of Chamber-music at the princely Court of Anhalt-Cöthen."

expect as many kinds of fugal shaping as, Kipling said, there are ways of constructing tribal songs. Difference in treatment shows Bach's zest for attacking problems; and though the results are by no manner of means equal, we can find something fresh in each prelude and fugue.

FRENCH SUITES

About 1720-1722 Bach wrote some keyboard pieces, for use on either harpsichord or clavichord, for his wife, Anna Magdalena, to play, and so cultivate her skill. As might be expected, these are quite light and graceful in style and not especially severe as to content. We know them as the *French Suites,* so called because of their delicate Latin spirit, which Bach at one period took considerable pains to cultivate and which was a lightening influence on the development of his style. The title may have been given to this music by Bach's household and his friends, but it was an unofficial one. Each suite contains half a dozen or more pieces in the fashion of court dances—the foundation dances used for this type of composition in Bach's time being the flowing *allemande,* the running *courante,* the dignified, sometimes quite somber *saraband,* and the final lilting *gigue.* The fifth of these *French Suites,* for example, contains an *allemande,* a *courante,* a *saraband,* a *gavotte,* a *bourrée,* a *loure* (a dance once accompanied by bagpipes), and a *gigue.*

Any detailed enumeration of more of these instrumental works would be impossible in a book such as this.[6] The first biographer of Bach, Johann Nikolaus Forkel, writing fifty years after the composer's death, said that one needs to be steeped in this music to appreciate the genius of its author. For, he adds, the greater the work, the closer the study demanded for its apprehension; "the butterfly method, a sip here and there, is of little use." Unfortunately, the limitations of ordinary existence make anything but such a butterfly method almost impossible for all of us unless we happen to be musical scholars. But, if our "sip here and there" has included the works mentioned in this chapter, we can be sure that we have had at least an adequate introduction to this "greatest orator-poet that ever addressed the world in the language of music."

[6] Mention should especially be made of the great clavier works of the Leipzig period, the so-called *Goldberg Variations,* a long and difficult set written for a count who required some sort of musical performance to relieve his sleepless hours; the six partitas (a sort of general name for *suite*); the *Italian Concerto* and the *Partita in B Minor;* the *Musikalisches Opfer* (part of which is for flute, violin, and clavier), written in an attempt to recall to the memory of Frederick the Great Bach's skill in improvisation; *The Art of Fugue,* a series of fugues and canons on a single theme, written in 1749 and published after his death by his son Carl Philipp Emanuel.

Handel the Magnificent

I am emboldened, Sir, by the generous Concern You please to take in relation to my affairs, to give you an account of the Success I have met here. The Nobility did me the Honour to make amongst themselves a Subscription for 6 Nights, which did fill a Room of 600 Persons, so that I needed not sell one single Ticket at the Door and without Vanity the Performance was received with a general Approbation. Sigra. Avolio, which I brought with me from London pleases extraordinary. I have formed an other Tenor Voice which gives great satisfaction . . . and the Chorus Singers (by my Direction) do exceeding well, as for the Instruments they are really excellent. Mr. Dubourgh being at the Head of them, and the Musick sounds delightfully in this charming Room, which puts me in such spirits (and my Health being so good) that I exert my self on my Organ with more than usual success.

I opened with the Allegro, Penseroso, & Moderato, and I assure you that the Words of the Moderato are vastly admired. The Audience being composed (besides the Flower of Ladyes of Distinction and other People of the greatest quality) of so many Bishops, Deans, Heads of the Colledge, the most eminent People in the Law as the Chancellor, Auditor General, &ct. all which are very much taken with the Poetry. I cannot sufficiently express the kind treatment I receive here, but the Politeness of this generous Nation can not be unknown to You, so I left you judge of the satisfaction I enjoy, passing my time with Honour, profit and Pleasure.

From a letter of Handel's to Charles Jennens, writer of the libretto of the *Messiah*, dated Dublin, December 29, 1741

AN EIGHTEENTH-CENTURY PREMIÈRE

February 19, 1736, was a great night for the city of London; for it marked the first performance there of a new oratorio by Mr. Handel, the German musician who had come to England in 1710 and had had the town pretty much by the ears ever since. The theater in the Haymarket, where the performance was to be given, was crowded to the doors. It seemed as if the entire *haut monde* was present, the ladies in their

men of such equal power and opposite temperament as Bach and Handel. The life of the first was provincial and circumscribed, bourgeois in its every aspect, merely the external setting for a spiritual existence of intense reality. In this respect, Bach was a man of the Baroque —the world for him but a dream, his experience of it making him constantly yearn for an existence that was beyond the confines of consciousness. His way of escape was through a religion in which he firmly believed, instead of through the usual means of the time, a magic piling-up of unrealities and a gorgeous succession of *divertissements.* Externally, at least, Handel was more a typical Baroque figure than Bach. Vital and forceful, his life was crowded with incident and intrigue, dramatic success following crushing failure. His very appearance was characteristic—a gigantic and corpulent figure, with enormous hands and feet and a fat, bovine face enswathed in a huge wig. (The Baroque gentleman probably cultivated corpulence as a means for heightening his outward appearance of dignity and imposing grandeur.) Handel's clothing suggested his important position in life: his velvet greatcoat embroidered with brave color, his fine shirt with beruffled collar and cuffs, his walking stick with gold knob—all proclaimed him a man about town, very much concerned with practical affairs.

Before coming to London, Handel had had a thoroughly adequate preparatory career as an operatic writer. He was connected for three years with the opera in Hamburg, a more or less rough and ready establishment producing German as well as Italian pieces. From there he went to Italy, where he visited Florence, Venice, Rome, and Naples. He produced a number of operas in the prevailing mode, some of them creating a furore even among the Italians, and came into contact with the most important musical figures of the time: Corelli, Lotti, and the Scarlattis. Returning to Germany, he was made *Kapellmeister* to the court of the Elector of Hanover. One of his first official acts after taking up his duties was to request a leave of absence so that he could go to England. Here it was that he was to spend the rest of his life, for he lived in London for over forty years.

HIS OPERAS

It was inevitable that his early experience and natural bent should lead him to the writing of operas in the Italian style, especially when the demand on the part of English society was strong for this type of music. Up to the time of Handel's arrival in London, after the brief epoch of Purcell's genius (a genius which was scarcely appreciated), music had been almost entirely in the hands of itinerant Italians. Opera, although the years have proved that it is not a plant of native growth or one of which English appetites are genuinely fond, became established in London in the middle of the seventeenth century and has flourished there intermittently ever since. One of its great periods of glory was the Handel epoch. An account from one of the first issues of that ingenious eighteenth-century predecessor of our modern gossip magazine, Addison's *Spectator*, describes something of the characteristic extravagance with which these operas were produced. The work in question may well have been *Rinaldo,* Handel's first venture in this field, brought out in 1711:

An Opera may be allowed to be extravagantly lavish in its Decorations, as its only Design is to gratifie the Senses, and keep up an indolent Attention in the Audience. Common Sense however requires, that there should be nothing in the Scenes and Machines which may appear Childish and Absurd. [English practicality flying in the face of Baroque imaginative splendor!] *How would the Wits of King Charles's Time have laughed, to have seen Nicolini exposed to a Tempest in Robes of Ermin, and sailing in an open Boat upon a Sea of Paste-Board? What a Field of Raillery would they have been let into, had they been entertain'd with painted Dragons spitting wild-fire, enchanted Chariots drawn by Flanders Mares, and real Cascades in artificial Land-skips? A little Skill in Criticism would inform us, that Shadows and Realities ought not to be mix'd together in the same Piece; and that Scenes, which are designed as the Representations of Nature, should be filled with Resemblances, and not with the Things themselves. If one would represent a wide Champian Country filled with Herds and Flocks, it would be ridiculous to draw the Country only upon the Scenes, and to crowd several Parts of the Stage with Sheep and Oxen. This is joining together Inconsistencies, and making the Decoration partly Real and partly Imaginary. I would recommend what I have here said, to the Directors, as well as to the Admirers, of our Modern Opera.*

As I was walking in the Streets about a Fortnight ago, I saw an ordinary Fellow carrying a Cage full of little Birds upon his Shoulder; and, as I was wondering with my self what Use he would put them to, he was met very luckily by an Acquaintance, who had the same Curiosity. Upon his asking him what he had upon his Shoulder, he told him that he had been buying Sparrows for the Opera. Sparrows for the Opera, says his Friend, licking his lips, what, are they to be roasted? No, no, says the other, they are to enter towards the end of the first act, and to fly about the Stage.

This strange Dialogue awakened my Curiosity so far, that I immediately bought the Opera, by which means I perceived that the Sparrows were to act the part of Singing Birds in a delightful Grove though upon a nearer Enquiry I found the sparrows put the same Trick upon the audience, that Sir Martin Mar-all practised upon his Mistress; for, though they flew in Sight, the Musick proceeded from a consort of Flagellets and Bird-calls which had been

*planted behind the Scenes. At the same time I made this Discovery, I found
by the Discourse of the Actors, that there were great Designs on foot for the
Improvement of the Opera; that it had been proposed to break down a part
of the Wall, and to surprize the Audience with a Party of an hundred Horse,
and that there was actually a Project of bringing the New-River into the
House, to be employed in Jetteaus and Water-works. This Project, as I have
since heard, is postponed 'till the Summer-season; when it is thought the
Coolness that proceeds from Fountains and Cascades will be more acceptable
and refreshing to People of Quality. In the mean time, to find out a more
agreeable Entertainment for the Winter-Season, the Opera of Rinaldo is filled
with Thunder and Lightning Illuminations and Fireworks; which the Audience
may look upon without catching Cold, and indeed without much Danger of
being burnt; for there are several Engines filled with Water, and ready to play
at a Minute's warning, in case any such accident should happen. However, as
I have a very great Friendship for the Owner of this Theatre, I hope that he
has been wise enough to insure his House before he would let this Opera be
acted in it.*

Handel's success as an opera writer and producer earned for him and
his partners what we would consider to be large sums of money, even
in these days of musical entrepreneurs. But they also aroused envy, suspicion, and hatred on the part of his rivals. He had to fight for everything he gained and make his way through cliques of court hangers-on;
but, in spite of failing health and great loneliness of spirit, he never lost
courage. He ranks as one of the heroes of artistic strife and the fight
against misfortune, along with Sir Walter Scott, Poe, and many another.

Handel wrote forty-seven of these operas, in addition to innumerable
pasticci, dramatic odes, and the like; they all seem to us of today, as
Bernard Shaw has expressed it, nothing but stage concerts designed for
showing off the technical skill of singers. They have set, formal stories
mostly drawn from classic sources, little variety of scene, and hardly any
action. What dramatic qualities they possess reside entirely in the
music, all of it formalized according to the taste of the period. There is
a large number of arias, each of them with its corresponding lot of
recitative to carry on the dramatic development. These standardized
conventions, coupled with the fact that many of the soprano airs were
written for performance by *castrati,* and the tiresome repetitiousness of
their style, keep the Handelian operas off the modern stage.[7] A few

[7] Post-World War I Germany saw a renewal of interest in the Handelian operas, and
a number of them were restaged there, with various types of modern *décor.* But such
interest seems to have been but transitory, for little has been heard of them in more
recent years. It is difficult to believe that these works can ever again become part of
the operatic repertoire because of the fact that they are based on a dramatic aesthetic
which is entirely foreign to modern ideals.

airs from them have survived the ravages of time. It would seem, for instance, as if nothing could ever kill the hardy universality of such a thing as *Ombra mai fu*. Written for an opera called *Serse* in 1738, to very undistinguished words, it has been given every sort of setting imaginable and arranged for every sort of instrumental combination possible, from massed military bands to harp ensembles. "Hear me, ye winds and waves," from *Scipione* (1726), is only slightly less well known. But for modern ears the most attractive music in the operas is contained in the dances with which they were diversified. No better exhibition of Handel's peculiar qualities can be found than the suite of dances from *Alcina*, produced in 1731, and modern arrangers and composers have not hesitated to help themselves liberally to the riches to be found throughout Handel's scores and have drawn many other orchestral suites and ballets from this source.

From 1719 to 1729 Handel composed and directed operas for the newly formed Royal Academy of Music, with varying degrees of success. Rivals sprang up on all sides, the most potent of them being Bononcini, imported in 1720 as a co-director of the academy. That the public was more or less neutral in this famous artistic combat may be gathered from some of the doggerel current at the time:

Some say, compared to Bononcini
  That Mynheer Handel's but a Ninny;
Others aver, that he to Handel
  Is scarcely fit to hold a candle:
Strange all this difference should be
  Twixt Tweedle-dum and Tweedle-dee.

Yet the rivalries continued to grow. London became surfeited with the riches supplied in the way of Italian opera; and in 1729, when a new fad arose in the way of *The Beggar's Opera*, a folk piece in English, satirizing the weaknesses of the Italian style, it proved the culminating English straw which broke the Italian camel's back. The academy failed, and with it went Handel's hopes and a great deal of his money. Magnificent opportunist that he was, he immediately turned his attention to other fields of composition.

THE ORATORIOS

From this time on, Handel devoted himself largely to the writing of oratorios, although he did not give up operas entirely until 1745. In the oratorios,[8] he was able, in the words of a letter of the time, successfully to "set up against the operas. He hired all the goddesses from farces and the singers of Roast Beef from between the acts at both theaters, with a man with one note in his voice, and a girl without ever an one; and so they sing and make brave hallelujahs. And the good company encores the recitative, if it happens to have any cadence like what they call a tune" (Horace Walpole: *Letters;* written to Sir Horace Mann, February 24, 1743).

As a matter of fact, the Handelian oratorios are merely continuations of Handelian opera without staging and costuming and action; written in English, they give more attention to the chorus but treat the recitative and the aria in dramatic style, in exactly the same way as a Handel opera. They provided the composer with a popular form in which to work, and he produced them in his theaters, with the best singers and instrumentalists that he could obtain. Their librettos were taken either from classic sources—Acis and Galatea, Hercules, Judas Maccabaeus, Semele, Theodora, and so on—or from Holy Writ—Esther, Israel in Egypt, Joseph, Joshua, Samson, and the Messiah. He wrote twenty-six of them in all, most of them frankly for money; for he sensed that this type of production, with its peculiar blend of piety and passion, possessed a hold on the English public, which has never cared much for complexity in art, for what it calls "cleverness." Handel's great success entirely overwhelmed English composition and colored the people's preferences for well over a century after his death. *Messiah* has been the most potent force in all English music and is still to be reckoned with today.

Two characteristic oratorios are *Semele,* the libretto of which was

[8] Before Handel started writing his oratorios, the form did not seem to have been used at all in England. The first work to gain fame was *Esther,* written in 1720 for performance in the private chapel of the Duke of Chandos, a work which is supposed to have netted Handel some thousand pounds. It was given with scenery and costumes. Twelve years later, it was revised by Gates, Master of the Chapel Royal, and presented in the Crown and Anchor tavern for the members of a musical academy. Learning of the success of this production, the Princess Royal wished to see it performed, with scenery and action, at the opera; but the Bishop of London, who had authority over the choristers of the Chapel Royal, refused to allow them to appear in a sacred work in such secular surroundings. This so incensed Handel that he prepared an official performance, which he advertised as being by His Majesty's Command, with the information that "there will be no action on the stage, but the house will be fitted up in a decent manner for the audience, the Musick to be disposed after the manner of the Coronation Service" (a series of four anthems for the accession of George II). The performance was repeated a number of times, so successful was this new style and so perfectly did it fit English tastes. Thus, the English concert oratorio came into being, an event which was to exert tremendous influence on British taste and life.

written by Congreve, originally for operatic treatment, and adapted by Handel in 1743, and *Messiah*, written to a text compiled by a poor worm of a clergyman-secretary to Charles Jennens, one of the rich and influential art patrons of the period.[9] *Semele* is hardly known, even in England, although it contains three of Handel's most glorious arias, "Where'er you walk," "O Sleep, why dost thou leave me?" and "Now love, that everlasting boy." Its libretto is typical: the story of Jupiter's carrying off Semele when she is about to be married to Athamas and the device by which Juno, the affronted goddess of marriage, contrives to bring about the destruction of Semele by her lover's lightnings. Not exactly a story of absorbing interest in the twentieth century, whatever it may have been in the eighteenth. *Messiah*, on the other hand, is one of the most popular works in all music. When it was first produced at a charity concert in Dublin in 1742, the local reviewer remarked that "words are wanting to express the exquisite Delight it afforded to the admiring crowded Audience." Insofar as English-speaking audiences are concerned, it has been providing this exquisite delight ever since.

Messiah was actually composed in three weeks, although some of it may have been in Handel's mind before. Four of the choruses he adapted, after his not uncommon fashion, from other music of his. (It may be mentioned that he extended this plan of borrowing to the works of other composers as well, a habit which seems to have been more or less common to that time. Haste had much to do with Handel's appropriations, and Professor Dent has suggested that a certain slight mental instability from which Handel at times suffered had also something to do with them.) Speed in composition was facilitated by the lightness of the orchestration, which, as we have noted, had not then attained the heights of a complex art, though the orchestra was almost complete, as we know it today, with the exception of clarinets and the extension of the brass that we owe to the nineteenth-century experimenters, such as Sax. Slight accompaniments sufficed for many solos and for all the recitatives. The important duty of filling these up was

[9] Newman Flower, in his great book on Handel, from which several of our old prints have been taken, quotes Dr. Samuel Johnson, on being asked concerning Jennens, "Who is this conceited gentleman who lays down the law so dogmatically?" as replying:

"A vain fool crazed by his wealth, who, were he in Heaven, would criticize the Lord Almighty; who lives surrounded by all the luxuries of an Eastern potentate—verily an English 'Solyman the Magnificent'; who never walks abroad without a train of footmen at his heels, and, like Wolsey, with a scented sponge 'neath his nose, lest the breath of the vulgar herd should contaminate his sacred person."

given to the *continuo* player, who was usually also the conductor, since the separate function of this important modern-day specialist with the baton had not yet evolved. The *continuo* part was written as a figured bass and so could be quickly sketched in when composing. To a large extent, its filling-up was an art of improvisation on the part of the harpsichordist. A number of years later, Mozart took it upon himself to write out additional accompaniments to this oratorio from these figured bass parts, accompaniments which are, unfortunately, out of taste with the rest and are today seldom used.

The work contains a tremendous amount of material—three broad sections, the first concerning the prophecy of the Messiah's coming, followed by the lovable Christmas music; after it a section devoted to the sufferings and the death of the Saviour, full of deeply felt sorrow; and lastly the Resurrection section, with meditations on Christ's place in the world. There are over fifty numbers all together, although the work as a whole is seldom given. It would repay close study in detail, if one would penetrate the very essence of Handel's manner of expression.

OTHER WORKS

Of all Handel's instrumental works the best known is the so-called *Water Music,* as characteristic a thing as he ever wrote. This was a set of some twenty dances and "airs," not this time arranged from vocal works. Around them arose the pleasant story that when Handel was out of favor with George I, because he had outstayed his leave from Germany when his royal master was the Elector of Hanover, his friends arranged that this music, specially composed, should be played on a barge behind the state vessel, while his Majesty was making a triumphal procession down the River Thames in 1715. Sticklers for the truth deny this, saying that the music was written in 1717, when Handel was in full favor again. No matter; a legend is a legend, and its truth or untruth need not concern us, so long as nothing important hangs on it! The music as a whole is very rarely played, the selection generally used consisting of six numbers only. Handel scored the music for piccolo, flutes, oboes, bassoons, horns, trumpets, and strings, doubtless with an ear to the carrying effect upon the water. In modern arrangements, much fuller orchestration is employed: it is always one of the difficulties of historical estimate that we can so seldom hear old music as the composer really wrote it. Even if we had his proportion of instruments as they are used

A HANDEL ORATORIO   (from a contemporary engraving by Hogarth)

today, we should have to allow for the difference in sound. For instance, the older oboes and bassoons were coarser than ours, and, in a day when the proportions of the orchestra had not reached its finality, more of these instruments were used than today.

A final word can well be spoken for Handel's sonatas and concertos; he wrote nineteen so-called sonatas for solo instrument and several sets for two instruments with figured bass. In many of them, definite instruments are specified, but in performance one instrument was often substituted for another. These belong to an early period of the composer's life, when, as he said, he composed with great enthusiasm, "like a very devil." Although little played, they are full of splendid broad and easy-flowing melodies, with accompaniments that are simple and strong. The effect is somewhat more openhearted than in Bach's rather more austere sonatas. The cool beauty of the slow movements is always refreshing, and the athletic motion of the allegros makes it seem the simplest thing in the world to toss off such movements. Short though they are, there is much craft in them.

His best-known concertos are those of Opus 6, *concerti grossi* in the real sense of the word, employing the usual dialogue form between a group of solo strings and the full orchestral body. There are twelve of these, minor works perhaps, but full of Handel's usual melodic charm. Here, as in so many of his other works, there is a certain ruddy strength combined with a suave grace and lovely plenitude.

THE LAST YEARS

We have seen how, for over forty years, Handel and London had been enemies, his life there one long series of dramatic struggles, malicious foes, and crafty friends. It is pleasant to be able to record that in the end he triumphed and became the acknowledged master of English music.[10] But at what a cost! Worn out with the exhaustive labor and feverish haste of composition, he was just ready to celebrate his triumph when a new enemy appeared, blindness. This alone, of all his troubles, seemed to bring him despair; for it meant giving up work. His last oratorio, *Jephtha*, produced in 1752, was completed with difficulty, and by 1753 he had completely lost his sight. These last years saw many triumphant revivals of works at which London had scoffed when they were first produced, revivals which brought him in a great deal of money. But best of all, they enabled him to vindicate himself. He died in April, 1759, and was buried, after a fulsome funeral at which not a note of his own music was played, in Westminster Abbey. One of the contemporary obituary notices concluded in this fashion: "He was perhaps as great a genius in music as Mr. Pope in poetry; the musical composition of the one being as expressive of the passions, as the happy versification of the other excelled in harmony" (*Scots Magazine*, April, 1759).

[10] It is often felt that Handel's tunes have a certain Englishness about them (like Purcell's, for example) and that his imagination received refreshing impetus from British melodic forthrightness.

Such a bracketing of these two eighteenth-century masters may seem somewhat of a conceit, so different were they in many respects. But could anything be found that more fittingly describes the spirit of Handel, the great master of the Baroque, than the last stanza of Pope's "The Dying Christian to His Soul"?

The world recedes; it disappears!
Heav'n opens in my eyes! my ears
   With sounds seraphic ring;
Lend, lend your wings! I mount! I fly!
O Grave! where is thy victory?
   O Death! where is thy sting?

THE MUSICAL

DEVELOPMENTS OF THE

EIGHTEENTH CENTURY

General Background

Liberty of thought is the life of the soul.

Voltaire

THE ENLIGHTENMENT

The period between the middle of the eighteenth century and the beginning of the nineteenth was a most decisive one in European history, possessed of so many varied and significant attributes as to make it the very foundation of modern living and thinking. The warp on which there was woven the cultural fabric of these years was composed of the continuing gleaming, silver threads of the Rococo; its woof was made up of three parallel and sometimes contradictory tendencies: the atmosphere of the Enlightenment, the trend toward Classicism, and the idea of Revolution. Upon the unrelenting loom of the troubled times these interweaving threads were shuttled back and forth to form the fabric of this transitional era between the Baroque-Rococo and the Romantic periods.

By Enlightenment, whose strongest phase extended from 1750 to 1770, we mean the general emancipation of man from the shackles of authority, prejudice, and tradition brought about by freer thinking on problems which had formerly been solved by means other than purely rational ones. It included such representative figures as Locke in England and Voltaire in France. Its greatest achievement was the series of seventeen volumes produced by the French Encyclopedists, enlisting the services of the best writers of the century in increasing the interest in natural science and industry, at the same time inculcating many revolutionary ideals and inducing a general attitude of skepticism and discontent. Its most significant exponent was the German philosopher-professor Immanuel Kant (1724–1804), who felt perfectly able to answer the eternal questions as to how reality came into being with the categorical statement, "By pure reason."

The tendency toward Classicism which extended from the middle of the eighteenth century was not by any means a homogenous style, but one made up of a number of tendencies: a revival of interest in the antiquarian approach to Greek and Roman art; a reversion to a more serious and objective expression after the reign of the vital, exuberant Baroque spirit and its playful, charming concomitant, the Rococo; a striving for "noble simplicity and calm greatness" after the sophistication and insincerity of an age which began to be regarded as unnatural and somewhat degenerate. Its greatest expression was in the art theories of the German archaeologist, historian, art connoisseur Johann Joachim Winckelmann (1717–1768); and its climax was reached in one of the mightiest figures in all cultural and intellectual history, Goethe (1749–1832).

The term "Revolution" as applied to this period includes all movements which were directed at this time against the ideas and traditions which had hitherto been considered dominant and sacrosanct. It includes the spirit of revolt in social, religious, intellectual, and artistic, as well as political, fields. In the world of politics, it led to such events as the American and French revolutions; when applied to social standards it meant the overthrow of the aristocratic governing classes and the rise and protection in power of the middle-class *bourgeoisie*. It brought about the dethronement of Reason through the elevation of "feeling" and a desire to return to nature as the source of all good and the final determinant of conduct. In art, it led to an emphasis upon simplicity and passion and so gave rise to the important Romantic Movement of the nineteenth century. Revolution's greatest artistic expression was in Rousseau's *Contrat social*, which has been well called "the codebook of the French Revolution." And its crowning achievement was the appearance of Napoleon, who during practically all of this period turned the European world topsy-turvy through his ability to translate these revolutionary ideas into concrete military and political action.

THE CHEVALIER GLUCK   by
Duplessis

GLUCK AN IMPORTANT FIGURE

All these tendencies are manifested in the various changes which took place at this time in the different phases of musical development. The desire for a return to a simple, natural, passionate expression is to be most clearly observed in the operatic reforms which were instituted by the internationally active composer Christoph Willibald von Gluck (1714–1787). Born in a little village in the forests of the Upper Palatine, of humble parentage, Gluck passed the early years of his life in acquiring the cosmopolitan background that proved so useful for his later career. From Prague, where he had the beginnings of a musical education, he went to Vienna, and thence to Italy, where he lived for ten years and wrote a number of operas in the Italian style. Afterwards, he traveled to London, then to Hamburg, Denmark, Vienna, and Prague again. Everywhere he produced new works in the best Italian manner, making no particular stir beyond that of a routined, gifted musician. After another visit to Italy, he returned to Vienna, intending to settle there, where he had married a rich Dutch lady who was able to bring him a considerable fortune. But in two years he was off again to Italy, where one of his operas created such an impression that he was knighted by the Pope, receiving, so it was said, the Order of the Golden Spur and the title *cavaliere*. Returning again to Vienna, where he had been engaged as musical director to the court, he busied himself with writing French comic operas and furnishing the music for various court functions. Such was his background, one ideally suited to the demands which were later to be made on him.

THE GREAT MAN OF VIENNA: METASTASIO

The great man in opera at that time in Vienna was Metastasio, the imperial court poet and principal writer of librettos for Italian operas, the man, according to Burney, "whose writings have probably contributed more to the perfection of vocal melody and music in general than the united efforts of all the great European composers." Brought up in the atmosphere of the Baroque opera and with the opportunity of coming into direct contact with many of its principal musical and dramatic figures, Metastasio had an ideal training for his lifework. It was said that he composed his poems sitting at the harpsichord, often outlining the melodies to which they were later set. No wonder that he became the great favorite of all the Italians of the eighteenth century; settling in Vienna, he became the spoiled darling of the whole literary and musical world.

A lover of *bel canto* and all the Italian traditions, Metastasio was too great an artist not to realize the shortcomings of the Neapolitan style; and in a letter (written, as Rolland shows, some twenty years before Gluck announced the principles which underlay his reforms of the opera, in his famous dedicatory preface to *Alceste*) Metastasio placed himself on record as favoring many of the ideas later proclaimed by Gluck: the supremacy of poetry over music, the necessary importance of the drama, the power of the right sort of music to interpret the spirit of the words. Which goes to prove that as early as 1749, and in the case of so confirmed an Italian as Metastasio, reform was in the air.

It was inevitable that Gluck and Metastasio should have come into frequent contact. Fulfilling his numerous commissions for Italian operas from various sources, Gluck had set many of Metastasio's librettos. But the calm, polite, inflexibly Baroque temperament of the poet fitted ill with the strong, audacious, revolutionary spirit of the composer, who, aware of the tendencies of the time, was becoming impatient to write in a new, more naturalistic style. And when Count Durazzo, the intendant of the Vienna opera, encouraged Gluck to break from the Metastasian ideals, and the advent of a new librettist, Calzabigi, made such a break possible, the composer wrote a series of three operas—

Orfeo, Alceste, and *Paride ed Elena*—in a style which attempted to conform music with nature and reason.

Although the Viennese audiences were astounded by the novelty of these new works by Calzabigi and Gluck, they preferred the older style of writing and went on demanding operas conceived according to the earlier formulas. Gluck himself wrote several of them after finishing *Orfeo,* one of them to a libretto especially composed for him by Metastasio! His reform seemingly had little effect. Nothing daunted, Gluck turned his eyes toward Paris, attracted, no doubt, by the demands for operatic reform which had been so strongly expressed there.

THE FRENCH SITUATION

French music by this time had gone stale. For eighty years, ever since its institution under Lully, the French opera had undergone little change, its principal interest being, as we have seen, in the musical declamation of dramatic texts. The works of Lully and Rameau have been well called "tragedies in song." It seemed as if no other composer felt it permissible to write in a different style, and such a routined and constant iteration of the same ideas so irked the young intellectuals that it provoked one of them, Grimm (who afterward contributed many stirring articles to the *Encyclopédie*), to issue a pamphlet in 1752 which had as its aim the impression upon the public mind of the fact that French music was not invulnerable. In the bitter discussion which followed, Rousseau,[1] taking up the cudgels for Grimm, did not hesitate to make the defiant statement that Italian music was better than French.

As if the gods would take a hand in this *petite guerre d'intelligence,* it so happened that it was just at this time that the Italians came to

---

[1] The career of this stormy Genevan philosopher was of great importance to music, directly because of the articles he wrote about music and the works he composed, and indirectly—and of even greater importance—because of his philosophic annunciation of the principles of a new humanism, principles which helped do away with the old regime in politics and found a new one—the Romantic Movement—in art.

His polemics include such things as the *Lettre sur la musique française,* written in 1743, and the *Dissertation sur la musique moderne,* written in 1753, and contain such remarks as "there is neither time nor melody in French music because the language is not capable of either: French song is a continuous bark, its harmony crude and suggestive of the work of a student; French airs are not airs at all, nor French recitatives worth anything. And so I conclude that the French have no music at all." They include also the articles mentioned in the text, written for the great *Encyclopédie,* the errors of which were later pointed out by Rameau, and a dictionary of music (1767), which still remains an outstanding source book for those who would study eighteenth-century music and its forms,

Paris with their performance of Pergolesi's *La serva padrona,* which so took the fancy of the citizens. The whole town was astir: everyone took sides, the Encyclopedists being, of course, in the van as champions of the new, Italian dispensation, trying out their wings in this miniature musical tumult for the longer flights of universal revolution which came later. In the course of this tempest in a teapot—the lining-up of the French style of opera, with its predilection for the drama, against the Italian, with its overdevelopment of the music—many foolish things were said and written. For the Italian opera, with its long sequences of recitative and its overinsistence on vocal virtuosity, was quite as much in need of reform as was the French.

But, out of all the discussion, came a realization that some sort of reformation in opera was desirable, if not inevitable, some means by which the best qualities of both styles could be kept and blended. All the great literary minds of France began to visualize the need for a different musical order, just as they did for the necessity of a new social and economic one.

Voltaire summarized this better than any of the other writers, in the conclusion of his *Mélanges littéraires,* a collection of essays published in 1761.

> *It is to be hoped that some genius may arise, strong enough to convert the nation from this abuse and to impart to a stage production that has become a necessity the dignity and ethic spirit that it now lacks. . . . The tide of bad taste is rising and insensibly submerging the memory of what was once the glory of the nation. Yet again I repeat: The opera must be set on a different footing, that it may no longer deserve the scorn with which it is regarded by all the nations of Europe.*

Quoted in "Gluck and the Encyclopaedists" by Julien Tiersot

After a carefully launched preparatory program, Gluck visited Paris in 1773 and attempted to have his works accepted by the *Opéra.* The authorities, not anxious to encourage him and yet not willing to refuse him entirely, said they could not produce anything unless he undertook to write five new works for them. Gluck immediately accepted the proposal, writing as the first *Iphigénie en Aulide,* which was produced in April, 1774, and created a tremendous furore. With characteristic vivacity, Paris immediately began to take sides and form parties for and against the new music. When, in August of the same year, Gluck produced a French version of *Orfeo—Orphée et Eurydice*—the excitement knew no bounds. Returning to Vienna, the composer was made Imperial Court Musician by the empress, Maria Theresa.

GLUCK VERSUS PICCINNI

Two years later, Maria Theresa's daughter, the young French queen, Marie Antoinette, added further fuel to the Parisian flames by having a prominent Italian opera composer, Nicola Piccinni, invited to Paris and made director of a music school there. The real purpose of his coming was, however, to provoke a squabble with Gluck, so that everyone could take sides for or against the new style. And, although Gluck himself was too wise to become inveigled into any sort of direct competition with Piccinni, take sides everyone did, furiously and bitterly. Burney thus describes the edifying spectacle:

> *The almost universal cry at Paris was that he [Gluck] had recovered the dramatic Music of the ancient Greeks; that there was no other worth hearing; that he was the only musician in Europe who knew how to express the passions; these and other encomiums preparatory to his apotheosis were uttered and published in the journals and newspapers of Paris, accompanied with constant and contemptuous censures of Italian Music, when Piccinni arrived (1776). This admirable composer, the delight and pride of Naples, as Gluck of Vienna, had no sooner erected his standard in France, than all the friends of Italian Music, of Rousseau's doctrines, and of the plan, if not the language of Metastasio's dramas, inlisted in his services. A furious war broke out, all Paris was on the qui vive. No door was opened to a visitor, without this question being asked previous to his admission:* Monsieur! êtes vous PICCINNISTE ou GLUCKISTE?[2]
>
> *These disputes, and those of musical critics and rival artists throughout the kingdom, seem to me to have soured and diminished the pleasure arising from Music in proportion as the art has advanced to perfection.*

Burney: *General History*

This seems to have been what Gluck thought, for, after the successful production of two more operas, *Armide* and *Iphigénie en Tauride,* and the failure of another, *Echo et Narcisse,* he decided to leave Paris forever.[3] He wrote in 1780, after his return to Vienna:

> *I shall hardly allow myself to be persuaded again to become the object of criticism or the praise of the French nation, for they are as changeable as red cockerels.*

[2] At this time Benjamin Franklin was American ambassador at the court of Louis XVI and championed the cause of Gluck. When Marie Antoinette heard of this she exclaimed, "What can a man whose *métier* is to place rods on buildings know of music?"

[3] Piccinni lived on in Paris after Gluck had departed, and he later became a Professor of the Conservatoire, suffering severely in the French Revolution, as if Fate would compensate for his apparent success over a much greater rival. He wrote over 125 operas.

PICCINNI (from a contemporary portrait)

He spent his last seven years in Vienna, in almost complete retirement, a strange end to such a revolutionary life.

GLUCK'S REFORMS

In his Preface to the second of his revolutionary works, *Alceste,* Gluck tells us exactly what he tried to accomplish in his reform of the opera. He aimed at avoiding the abuses that the vanity of singers and the mistaken acquiescence of composers had allowed to creep into Italian opera: meaningless repetitions, improvisations by the soloists, orchestral interludes which broke up the continuity of the orchestration—all these were to be avoided. The great aim was that music, reinforcing the poetry, should not interrupt the action or draw attention to itself with foolish ornamentation. The music was to be like the light and shade, the coloring in a drawing, "which animates the figures without altering their outlines." The overture, he saw, ought to foreshadow the nature of the opera and prepare the listeners' minds. Orchestration throughout must be so chosen and deployed as to serve the emotion of the words and augment it. Recitative and air must not be so disparate. "A grand simplicity" was his aim—no parade of difficulties, no forced novelty, but the free breaking of any of the old rules, if the new conception of art demanded it. It is all perfectly wise, wholesome, and, to us, obvious.

If we listen to *Orpheus,* we find not a chilly Greek myth but a simple human story. There is no subplot, no complication. Orpheus, in his grief for his dead wife, Eurydice, descends to Hades to try to release her by his music. The beauty of his playing and of his singing masters the Furies—how dramatic is their first refusal!—and he is allowed to seek Eurydice in Elysium, where the chorus of Blessed Spirits is heavenly indeed. The condition is made that he must not look upon Eurydice until they are again in the world of man. His exceeding love causes him to break the rule, and Eurydice's breath departs. Here enters the one trace of older plot practice. Amor, the god of Love, takes pity on them, and, because of Orpheus's great affection, restores Eurydice to life.

In the simplicity of plot, in the use of the chorus of dark and happy spirits, in the ballet, and in its moving airs, the work is perennially affecting. The part of Orpheus, written for a male alto—here the old usage held—is now usually sung by a female, with some loss of realism. Such a work is bound, of course, to present to modern ears a good many traces of its ancestry; Gluck could not be expected to cast off all his older style: he was not aiming at novelty for its own sake. But in the closing-up of the plot, in the unity of the writing, as well as in the bold individual touches (such as the snarling of Cerberus and the tensity of the writing for the Infernal chorus), together with the ageless beauty of the ballet music in the Elysian fields and the touching "I have lost my Eurydice," known to every music lover, there is a whole new world of operatic joys. The pathos of Orpheus's appeal to the shades, with its sad melisma on "woe," strikes directly at the heart. This is no languid amusement in coloratura vocalism through an unreal plot, garnished with courtly caperings by the ballet. This is the path to a new fusion of arts, a new way of spiritual pleasure in the opera house. Gluck pursued the same path with eager enthusiasm in further Greek stories made human, *Alceste, Iphigénie en Tauride,* and the rest. He added this human touch to his instrumentation as well, making the instruments reinforce the emotional effect of the words.

It was no small virtue that the subjects of his operas were so noble. Not always, before or since, has opera lived so virtuously; but the world could hardly be expected to sustain or continue such a strain of nobility and humanity. With the exception of Mozart's and Bee-thoven's work, the opera fell back into the trough of tradition—history shows many a similar case—until the strong tide and wild winds of Romance swept it into other seas and fresh adventures.

Gluck's attempted reforms failed, in the practical sense, in that they had no immediate effect on opera; but they are important as marking the beginning of that spirit of naturalistic revolt, that stir in European intellectual life which led to the great Romantic literature and music of the first half of the next century. In his striving for naturalism and dramatic consistency, Gluck was able to create a world of illusion which forever closed the door to the past and its type of *castrato* court operas and was strongly suggestive of the great things that were to come. Like his contemporaries in other fields—the philosophers, the Encyclo-pedists, and the reformers of the eighteenth century—Gluck helped to lay the foundations for the great revolt which the inherent character-istics of the Baroque-Rococo times made inevitable.

OTHER FRENCH DEVELOPMENTS

Lully's most important successors in the writing of opera had been André Campra (1660–1740), Michel Pinolet de Monteclair (1666–1737), and André Cardinal Destouches (1673–1749); these men more or less filled in the gap between Lully and Rameau and, in addition, were active as teachers and writers of vocal cantatas, etc. Following them in the field of *opéra comique* and *opéra ballet* were a number of composers who remain today hardly more than names of interest to the historian, although in their own time they contributed a great deal to the idealization of these simpler and more natural forms of operatic expression: Jean Mondonville (1711–1772), who was chosen as the representative of the French national school to oppose the Italians during the *guerre d'intelligence* which had been waged in Paris around the middle of the century and which attracted Gluck to that city; François André Philidor (1726–1795), the best known of a famous French musical family whose members stretched through three genera-tions from 1600 to 1800; Pierre Alexandre Monsigny (1729–1817), and the Belgian André Ernest Modeste Grétry (1741–1813), whose *Richard Coeur de Lion* (1748) is still included in French operatic repertoire.

Devin du village (The Village Seer), written and produced by Jean Jacques Rousseau in 1752, was "simple" almost to the point of being artless, the four little airs of its shepherdess heroine practically summarizing the whole work. Rousseau's other attempt to solve the "learned" dramatic problem of the time, the so-called *melodrama,* was more successful. This was an eighteenth-century form in which one or two actors recited various roles in a drama in ordinary speech against the background of an accompanying orchestra, which was supposed to "contribute those traits that only music can give, the hidden depth of the soul beyond Man's actions or words." His melodrama *Pygmalion* became a sort of established model for this type of composition, a model which inspired important later composers, including Beethoven and Stravinsky, to use this form.

IN OTHER COUNTRIES

In Germany the *Singspiel,* as we have seen, had been strongly influenced by the comic operas of the English; the first important composer to employ this assimilated style successfully was Johann Adam Hiller (1728–1804), whose music in such works as *Die Jagd* (The Hunt) and *Der Dorfbarbier* (The Village Barber) so impressed Burney, when he visited Germany on his famous European trip, as to cause him to say: "Hiller's music was so natural and pleasing that the favorite airs, like those of Dr. Arne, were sung by all degrees of people; the more easy ones had the honor of being sung in the streets." Another popular writer of *Singspiele* was the Austrian Carl Ditters von Dittersdorf, whose *Doktor und Apotheker* (1786) and *Die lustigen Weiber von Windsor* (after Shakespeare's *Merry Wives of Windsor*) are still played in central Germany.

In Italy, the great exponent of this natural style in opera was Domenico Cimarosa (1749–1801), whose sparkling *Il matrimonio segreto* (The Secret Wedding) has a variety and fluidity of writing that is strongly suggestive of the Rococo, and yet in its abundance and freshness of ideas it stands as the most illustrious example of this important Neapolitan art form.

THE BEGINNINGS OF MODERN ORCHESTRAL MUSIC

The processes of ratiocination peculiar to the eighteenth-century enlightenment were not concerned with the opera alone. Two other classifications of modern music, that written for the orchestra and that written for smaller, chamber-music combinations, such as the string quartet, had their beginnings in the intellectual atmosphere of this period—the conviction that reason and order should be the arbiter of art as well as the standard of thinking.

During the course of our chronicle, we have had much to say concerning the use of instruments during the various epochs of history and have tried to show how it came about that certain of them were chosen to form the basis of the modern orchestra. Let us recapitulate briefly:

From the dawn of musical history, it has been evident that man used musical instruments of all sorts, singly and in combination; but the art of grouping instruments in some sort of logical ensembles of a definite type, such as the symphony or the chamber orchestra, and the writing of music for them, is comparatively modern, dating from the eighteenth century. Earlier than this, orchestras (using this term in its generally accepted sense of an ensemble of instruments) seemingly comprised any gathering-together of instruments which happened to be convenient. The Egyptian wall paintings, the accounts of the Greek historians, the medieval manuscripts, all assure us that these heterogeneous combinations would sound illogical and strange to our ears.

The problem of how the present ideals of orchestration slowly came to realization is one which has not been solved by modern research. Down to the end of the Middle Ages, there seems to be little information available. We get hints here and there of many different types of instruments being played, but just how or when they were used together we do not know. Gottfried von Strassburg, a minnesinger thoroughly conversant with the musical traditions of his time, credits his hero Tristan with being able to play six different instruments: the fiedel, the hurdy-gurdy, the harp, the rotta, the lyre, and the zither; but he does not tell us whether such instruments as these were ever played in combination by the minstrels. We have mentioned the rich depiction of instruments by the artists of the late medieval period; but we cannot be certain that the instruments shown were played in a concerted fashion, even when they are so depicted by the artists.

In the fourteenth and fifteenth centuries, there are historical references to orchestras, conducting, and so forth; but there was certainly no recognized standard of ensemble grouping in the various countries, and the type of music used in one place might prove quite impractical in another. When we first hear anything about what might be called an orchestra in the modern sense, we find that it was a group of mixed instruments used for accompanying vocal music and playing the same parts the singers sang. During the early Renaissance, these *consorts,* as they were called, were freely used with voices, and no distinction was made between vocal and instrumental parts, nor were any indications given as to which were meant to be played and which were to be sung. Writing of this period in 1776, Hawkins said that concerts of instruments alone were a later invention, "at least there is no clear evidence of the form in which they existed." Only gradually did composers learn that it was possible to achieve with instruments certain effects which had been quite impossible with voices; this realization was the beginning of the modern orchestral style.

We have suggested several possible influences which aided this process of learning how best to group and use instruments: the use of isolated and scattered instrumental groups in the great masques and pageants, such use showing which instruments would make the best effect when played together;[4] the popular renditions of music by folk bands of nimble-witted musicians, who would quickly grasp the principles of practicality in combining instruments[5] and the use of instrumental groups in church for accompanying services.[6]

It was not until toward the end of the sixteenth century, however, that instrumental music finally succeeded in loosening the bonds which had tied it so closely to vocal music. It was the Gabrielis of Venice who showed the possibilities of ensemble instrumental music when played alone. They discovered what the historians call *dynamic antithesis,* the effectiveness of contrast between music produced by a large and a small group of instruments, or the same group playing alternately soft and loud. Then came the idea of grouping according to their tone color, or timbre, together with the use of a changing group

[4] In his *Histoire littéraire, musicale, choréographique, pittoresque, morale, critique, facétieuse, politique et galante* of the Académie Imperiale de Musique, Castil-Blaze describes how, in a masque performed in honor of the Duke of Milan in 1489, "they changed their instruments according to the character of the music played. Each singer, each dancer, had his special orchestra which was arranged according to the sentiments intended to be expressed by his song or dance. It was an excellent plan which . . . produced a succession of trumpets, of violins with their acute tones, the arpeggios of lutes, and the soft airs of flutes and reed pipes. The orchestration of Monteverdi proves that at the time composers varied their instrumentation thus."

[5] At a later date, when traveling through Italy, the English historian Burney heard outside his inn at Brescia a "band of two violins, a mandolin, a French horn, a trumpet and a violoncello—and though in the dark they played long concertos, with solo parts for the mandolin, I was surprised at the memory of these performers; in short, it was excellent street music." And in Venice he was pleased with "an excellent band of music, consisting of violins, flutes, horns, bases, and a kettledrum."

[6] The German historian Michael Praetorius (1571–1621) tells about accompanying a church motet with the following orchestra: two theorbos, three lutes, two zithers, four harpsichords and spinets, seven viola da gambas, two *Querflöte,* and a bass viol; which, together with the vocal forces involved (two boy sopranos and an alto), gave a "marvelous, glorious resonance"!

A FLUTE CONCERT AT SAN SOUCI, FREDERICK II's PALACE   (from a painting by Adolph Menzel) The emperor played the flute with his chamber-music group every evening that he was in residence.

of instruments within the orchestral body in order to obtain varied effects. These were naturally conditioned by the inventive genius of the instrument makers, as well as by the cogitative ability of the composers. Here are some of the outstanding items in this process of development:

One of the earliest instrumental ensembles of which we have definite record is that used by Monteverdi in his opera *Orfeo* (1607). It consisted of the following instruments: fifteen viols of three different sizes, two violins, two large flutes, two ordinary flutes, two oboes, two cornets (the old wooden instruments), four trumpets, five trombones, a harp, two harpsichords, two small organs, and a regal (a portable reed organ). This combination of forty instruments probably made use of all the instrumentalists available to this court composer of Mantua; but in spite of its miscellaneousness, there is evident here the principle of the string choir as the foundation of the whole orchestral scheme.

If we examine the scores of such representative early seventeenth-century composers as Schütz and Lully, we find the gradual emergence of the wood-wind instruments as soloists; and by the end of the century the standard four-part string division had become universal: first violin, second violin, tenor viol (viola), violoncello doubling with the string bass, the latter sounding an octave lower.

Bach's scores show, significantly enough, that the brass had not yet become a separate choir in itself, that a keyboard instrument was still used to mix and bind the orchestral timbres, and that no standard procedure was followed in the grouping of the instruments. Strings, oboes, flutes, and clavier; strings, trumpets, and clavier; strings, oboes, flutes, and clavier; strings, oboes, flutes, trumpets, drums, and clavier—all such combinations alternate in a Bach score without apparent reason for any particular choice. Moreover, the functions and capacities of the instruments are little differentiated—strings, wood winds, and brass all playing the same kind of passages in ensemble or in succession.

Gluck was an important figure in the development of the orchestra as an instrument. For it was his constant experimentation with means for achieving dramatic expressiveness that led him to enrich the emotional color of his opera orchestra. He did not hesitate to use such instruments as the piccolo, the trombone, the harp, the bass drum, the English horn, and the clarinet; he investigated the tone-color possibilities of the viola and the violoncello; and he discarded the blend-destroying keyboard instrument, although it was often used in orchestras long after his time. His band functioned by choirs—that is, by unified groups set off from one another and used independently for color. It was this flexible and unified instrument, speaking comparatively, that was further enriched and developed by the Mannheim composers, as described later.

MUSIC FOR THE ORCHESTRA

During this time, there likewise developed the idea of using a definite kind of thematic material specially suited to the means and style of the ensemble. The idea grew not only out of the dynamic and color-change possibilities of the orchestra, but out of the new harmonic system introduced into music at the beginning of the seventeenth century. In other words, the orchestra developed a musical vocabulary and an expressive language of its own, capable of carrying out all the possibilities which had been gradually accumulating. The chief feature of the new language was the use of instrumental themes as material out of which the musical structure was fashioned. No longer did vocal and dance idioms serve as the sole source of material for instrumental writers. These were transformed into definite melodic themes, which were contrasted with one another and which served as the germs out of which the whole structure logically grew.

Finally, and this was definitely the work of the composers of the eighteenth century, there came the crystallization of formulas according to which musical thought was molded, the evolution of logical schemes of construction by means of which the ideas of the composer could be best expressed. If anyone would know what the eighteenth century did for instrumental music, let him compare a Bach Brandenburg concerto (which would be a fair exemplification of the instrumental ideals held up to this time) with a Haydn symphony. Bach and Handel at one end of the eighteenth century may be said to have been the culmination of the traditional style of writing and musical culture which grew out of the vocal, contrapuntal music of the past. Haydn and Mozart, at the other end, wrote in an entirely new style and employed entirely different means. What came between?

This was no sudden transformation, wrought, as the operatic inventions of the early seventeenth century had been, by a small group of experimenters. The whole of civilized Europe may be said to have taken part in it: the Italians, with their cyclic, three-movement overtures of light, fluent, harmonic style; the French, with their form of overture and suite and their galant manner of writing; and the Germans, with their peculiar capacity for expressing both the grave and the gay and their blend of philosophical reason and emotional expressiveness. All these factors interacted on one another directly and indirectly. The century was one of intense intellectual curiosity insofar as the musicians and artists were concerned, and the men in one country, in spite of the poor physical means of communication, were thoroughly conversant with the work of their contemporaries in the others.

THE MANNHEIMERS

There were certain centers, however, which seemed to be especially potent forces in this work of international artistic development. Insofar as music was concerned, the chief of these was the orchestra maintained by an art-loving prince in the little ducal court of Mannheim, a town halfway between the centers of German and French culture. We have a good contemporary account of this musical establishment of Prince Karl Theodore at Mannheim, for in 1772 the roving Englishman in search of materials for his history of music, Dr. Charles Burney, visited it, was very much impressed by its "expensive magnificence," and wrote a famous description of this experimental laboratory out of which came so many principles of modern orchestral writing and playing.

THEIR SHAPING OF ORCHESTRAL STYLE

In the effort to "surpass the bounds of common opera overtures," Johann Stamitz (1717–1757), the founder and principal composer of the Mannheim group, and the other men who worked with him in these musical experiments—Richter, Holzbauer, Toeschi, and Wendling—discovered and practiced most of the innovations which are to be found in the Haydn quartets and symphonies and which have often been attributed to him. Briefly, these are:

First, the use of the so-called sonata form (first-movement form), a kind of constructional formula which has as its basis the use of two principal themes of differing and contrasting nature, the thematic elaboration of these in another section, and their repetition in a third.[7]

Second, the addition of the minuet as a fourth movement to the three until then customary in the sonata, thus bringing in a new and enlivening element.[8]

Third, the gradual dispensing with the usual *basso continuo* (already noted in one of Telemann's works), and the increasing of the importance of the melody.

Fourth, the introduction of distinctive motives or themes, rising out of the possibilities of the instrumental style.

Fifth, the use of a simple harmonic rather than an elaborate contrapuntal style.

Stamitz's *Sonata à trois parties concertantes,* Op. 1, has been called the starting point of this new movement and should be consulted by all those who would trace the beginnings of modern orchestral writing. Although it exemplifies well enough the fact that *aller Anfang ist schwer* (every beginning is difficult), it still stands in many respects as one of the most interesting documents in music history.

---

[7] The emergence of a tentative second theme can, of course, be detected in earlier works, such as J. S. Bach's *Italian Concerto.*

[8] The minuet had long been danced at the French court, since about 1650.

THE CONTRIBUTION OF ANOTHER BACH

Just how far these Mannheim compositions may have affected or have been affected by the work of Carl Philipp Emanuel Bach (1714–1788),[9] Sebastian's second son, it is impossible to say; but, at any rate, we find in the piano works of this composer (a contemporary of the Mannheim group) the same principles of thematic and melodic development that are present in the orchestral compositions of Stamitz. In speaking of this particular Bach, Burney was moved to remark: "How he formed his style would be difficult to trace; he certainly neither inherited nor adopted it from his father, who was his only master . . . . He spoke irreverently of canons, which, he said, were dry and despicable pieces of pedantry that anyone might compose who would sacrifice his time to them." We can see now that it was the general influence of the time, together with an understanding of the work which had been done by his predecessors, that led Emanuel Bach to adopt the innovations which were being applied contemporaneously in other parts of Europe.

His general style was characteristic of much of the music written during this period. In some of his works, we find him eagerly embracing the new, fashionable language of feeling (*Empfindsamkeit*), although certain elements of the lingering Baroque style are also notable, such, for instance, as the development of a whole movement from a single theme. In other pieces, particularly those written for his royal patron, His Prussian Majesty, King Frederick II, we find him employing the *style galant*. In still others, such as some of the sonatas in his six collections *für Kenner und Liebhaber* (for connoisseurs and amateurs),[10] we find three-movement works in which the general form of the modern sonata, as we know it, is definitely fixed: an opening movement in sonata form, with two main themes, a development section

[9] In his day it was this Bach who was the important musical figure, not Johann Sebastian, as today; Mozart is said to have looked to Carl Philipp Emanuel as his musical "father." He wrote a great deal of church and chamber music, as well as works for the clavier.

[10] Loesser feels that this well-defined group of *Kenner und Liebhaber,* although not numerous, played a most significant role in the establishment of an atmosphere in the Germany of that day favorable to the development of music; it was their attitude toward music, one which treated it with a profound respect, that was almost akin to religious reverence, which came to be generally associated with the German people and which prepared the soil out of which sprang all the great composers from Bach to Brahms. These great men are, after all, but the tallest timbers of the "thick forest and rank undergrowth that grew with them out of the same nutrient soil."

and a recapitulation; a slow movement of song type, very suggestive of the spirit of the *galant* composers; and a third, jolly finale with the general character of a rondo—that is, having one theme constantly recurring.

Although Haydn seems never to have mentioned any study which he made of the works of the Mannheim groups—he must have known them, however, for they were played everywhere and looked on as models for this kind of music—he acknowledged that one of the chief influences in his musical education had been the study of Emanuel's music; and Bach, in turn, said that Haydn was the only man who really understood him. So it is possible to say that the new forms and principles which we find in Haydn's sonatas, quartets, and symphonies came directly from the piano works of Carl Philipp Emanuel Bach and indirectly from the compositions of the Mannheim composers and the men in other countries who were experimenting along the same lines.

A GENERAL FLOWERING

The important thing to keep in mind regarding this tracing of the musical developments of the eighteenth century is that in various parts of Europe the ground was being prepared for the great florescence which was to come at the end of the century. There were a number of men, important in their time, who made contributions in one way or another, to this florescence, but who have been largely forgotten except for the historians. In England, the rather innocuous "symphonies," stage entertainments, and bass songs of William Boyce (1710–1779) can be mentioned as characteristic of the rather conservative tastes of that country. In Italy, one of the earliest symphonic writers was Gluck's teacher, G. B. Sammartini (1704–1774), whose works unquestionably had a great deal to do with the final style of this type of composition. Luigi Boccherini (1743–1805) wrote chamber music—string trios, quartets, and quintets—which strongly influenced the spirit and style of his time. French music owes a great deal to Joseph Gossec (1743–1829), its first composer of symphonies and the man who applied there the orchestral ideals which had been developing in Austria and Germany. Georg Matthias Mann (1717–1750), one of the best-known Austrian organists and composers of that time; Johann Christoph Friedrich and Johann Christian Bach, two other sons of Sebastian; and others contributed to this new type of expression that was at the same time brilliant and refined, charming and intelligent, with as special a care for the manner in which it was organized as for the clarity with which it was expressed.

The style which we have come to know as eighteenth-century classical finally emerged out of a fusion of the two main forms of Rococo music—the *style galant,* with its "charming, graceful, enamoured, and gay tunes" and the *Empfindsamkeit* style, which had as its object the expression of "passions in the way they rise out of the soul." This classical style, a fine compromise between the feelings of the heart and the expressions of the intellect, began to crystallize around 1760, but it was not until the quartets and symphonies of Haydn and Mozart that it reached its culmination. The reason why their music has survived, while most of the music of their immediate precursors and contemporaries has not, is largely that they had the ability to feel more deeply and to express themselves with better logic than their fellows.

Franz Josef Haydn

When I think of the Divine Being, my heart is so full of joy that the notes fly off as from a spindle; and as I have a cheerful heart he will pardon me if I serve him cheerfully.

Haydn

This memorial to Haydn's name
Consecrates this forever a sacred spot;
His muse reminds us plaintively
That the art of this great Master,
Who joins skill of craft and depth of feeling,
Was once upon a time called "modern."

From a monument erected in Rohrau, Haydn's birthplace

THE CLASSICAL EXPERIMENTER

It was St. Paul who said, "It is the letter that killeth but the spirit that giveth life." Haydn has been credited with being the father of the modern sonata, the string quartet, and the symphony by practically every writer on the history of music. Yet, if there had been nothing more to his music than this, he would be as dead today as are the composers we have just been discussing—Johann Stamitz and Emanuel Bach. Possessing an insatiable curiosity, Haydn, through the entire course of his long life, was a constant experimenter and pioneer in his art, as quick to seize on everything that agreed with his ideals as he was to reject anything that seemed unsuited to his purpose or contrary to his spirit. But in addition to this, his music has a certain personality, a heart-warming attractiveness which shows its composer to have known life intimately and to have lived it with gusto. A formalist in art—"classicist" is the word generally used to depict his temperament—he nevertheless sensed that the important thing in music is its spiritual quality, its soul, its poignant emotion. And so his music lives today, while the music of his predecessors is brought to life only occasionally for the delectation of those interested in the historical development of the art.

There is no reason why we should attempt to minimize the formal achievements of Haydn. It was he who went forward after his contemporaries, who had helped evolve the style, had finished their work of preparation. Gathering together the various experimental threads, he was the first one to weave out of them a fabric of beautiful form, and he was able, also, to define those instruments of expression which we have used ever since. His interest embraced every field of activity—instrumental music, church music, song, opera, and finally oratorio. He brought to all his work an inquiring and practical mind, a fertile and boundless curiosity, a real imagination, a physical vigor and well-being, and a religious contentment, which make him stand out as one of the great figures in music.

HIS ACHIEVEMENTS SUMMARIZED

It may be well to state briefly just what these formal achievements of this eighteenth-century pioneer were: a crystallization of the constructive principles of the form of the symphony and the sonata, principles which have guided and influenced the work of every composer who has used these forms since; the organization of the modern instrument which we have come to know as the orchestra, basing its foundation on a quartet of strings and increasing its dynamic and color effects by the addition of wind and percussion instruments; the establishment of a definite line of demarcation between chamber and orchestral types of music (these had been much the same in style before, but Haydn established the string quartet as a distinctive instrument and showed the type of music best suited to it); the production of a style

of harmonic, instrumental writing which was as complete and satisfying and lent itself as well to all the demands made on it as did that of
the older polyphonic vocal-chorus music of the sixteenth-century writers. We are accustomed to take these all for granted and to forget that
they have not always existed.

It was his complete success in all this ground-breaking labor that
encouraged his friend and pupil, Mozart, to dub him affectionately
"Papa Haydn." This title, given with real understanding and deep
appreciation of Haydn's qualities, has taken on a rather condescending
tinge of meaning through the years, suggestive of a peruked, classic
formalist, whose music, charming enough, perhaps, has little significance
beyond its grace of line and its appropriateness of design. It was in this
sense that the nineteenth-century Romanticist, Rubinstein, liked to
refer to Haydn; but it has turned out as a shrewd observer of the time
said it would: Rubinstein has become great-great-grandfather Rubinstein, while Haydn is still Papa Haydn!

For Haydn was a seeker of spiritual as well as formal qualities, always striving to clarify his position and attain the height of those
creative powers he knew he possessed. "Ambitious, uncompromising,
energetic, patient, Haydn fought his way forward to an ideal goal not
clearly seen at first, to approach it more closely, as the faithful strive
to approach the object of their devotions. His unusual natural endowments favored the development of his native qualities and of his character as man and artist" (Adler: "Haydn and the Viennese Classical
School"). Such qualifications do not produce stereotyped, conventional art, but vital, forceful, and personal art, no matter how polished
and courteous it may be after the manner of its time.

THE WAY OF HIS LIFE

An understanding of Haydn's life helps to explain the place he
came to occupy in music. He himself felt that a divine Providence,
after equipping him with the proper mental and musical attributes,
furnished him likewise with ideal opportunities for perfecting his
genius. There was, first, his early training as a choir boy and café
musician in Vienna, where he dug out for himself the principles he
needed, largely through a study of Emanuel Bach's sonatas and Fux's
theoretical treatise, *Gradus ad Parnassum;* then there was his position
as director of the musical establishment at Weinzirl, a small castle in
Lower Austria, followed by his later post as conductor and composer

for Prince Esterházy at the latter's sumptuous palaces in Vienna, Eisenstadt, and Esterház. This post not only gave Haydn an ideal orchestra with which to experiment, but also placed him under the necessity of having to furnish compositions for this band to play.

And Haydn was shrewd enough to value these opportunities and to make the most of them, seeing no insult in having to wear a uniform or to eat with the servants at Esterház; and, when opportunity came later, through the death of his prince, to free himself from all this eighteenth-century system of patronage and to step out in the freedom of his own personality as composer and conductor in London, he was ready and fully qualified. He was as successful then as he had been formerly, receiving his honors with due humility, and not losing, in his contact with the world's great, his common touch. Among his finest compositions are the symphonies he wrote for performance in London; he conducted them himself, sitting at the harpsichord, as was the contemporary custom. Yet, with it all, he remained a simple, sincere person. When, after writing his oratorios *The Creation* and *The Seasons,* in which critics feel that he achieved the full maturity of his power, he died, full of years and honors, his only lament was that he was just beginning to learn how to compose.

HAYDN'S DISTINCTIVE QUALITIES

There are qualities in Haydn's music which make him a distinctive figure for the listener of today, a figure that stands apart from the other great men of the period, even from his two great pupils. Taking into account the circumstances under which they were written, we find that over one hundred fifty symphonies of this composer—particularly the later ones written for the London impresario, Salomon—together with his eighty-three quartets, represent a freshness of vigor and a robustness of energy that is anything but typical of the scented salon atmosphere of his period. He was able to weave into his musical fabric warp and woof of both court and countryside, but there is more of the country than of the court. He loved good, straightforward, folkish tunes and square-cut dance rhythms, a fact which gives a fresh, open-air quality to his music and makes it seem closely akin to nature. And his style of writing was well suited to such treatment. It is in strong distinction to the music of Mozart, who, although he lived the greater part of his life amidst some of the most beautiful scenery in the world, seems never to have been conscious of it or to have been affected by

A-Castle B- Guard House C-Winter Garden D- Picture Gallery
E- Master's Dwelling F- Game Houses G- Stables H- Dwellings of
Court Musicians, Opera Singers & Actors I- Guest House K-Opera House
L-Cafe M-Cascades N-N-Sun & Diana Temples O-Hermitage P-Chinese
Home Q-Q-Ring Games R-R-Fortune & Venus Temples S-Rose Garden
T-Marionette Theatre & Orangery V-Dwellings for Court Attendants
W-W-Game Houses X-Various Dwellings Y-Barracks Z-Green Houses

THE PLAN OF THE GROUNDS AT SCHLOSS ESTERHÁZ The layout shows the provision made for accommodating the Prince's musicians. Haydn lived here for many years.

FRANZ JOSEF HAYDN

it in the slightest. As a composer, Haydn betrays his country origin, for he gives us a sense of contact with the soil, an elemental and un-affected simplicity that is appealing and immediate, one to which we react unconsciously.

Then, too, there is in these symphonies a distinct reflection of Haydn's personal philosophy: he did not hesitate to ascribe his scores to God's glory or to say that one of his reasons for writing music was "that the weary and worn or the man burdened with affairs might enjoy something of solace and refreshment." Coupled with this im-perturbable philosophic attitude towards God and his fellow man was a certain shrewdness and practicality of nature, and a well-developed sense of humor, which colored his music and contributed to its popular-ity. Perhaps the fact that he had married a Xantippe of a wife helped him to take life philosophically and in his daily stride; and there is a comforting touch of demos about his work which endears it to us today and assures its outlasting a great deal of the aristocratic art of its period.

This feeling of democratic familiarity, of Jack's-as-good-as-his-neigh-bor spirit that we have with Haydn's music, is nowhere better dem-onstrated than in the nicknames which have become associated with certain of his works, names that suggest something of their appeal and easy amiability. We somehow cannot imagine calling anything which Beethoven wrote, or Brahms or even Mozart, a *Dudelsack* or a *Lark* or a *Frog* quartet or a *Surprise* or a *Hen* or a *Clock* symphony! And yet these whimsical appellations seem somehow appropriate when they are applied to Haydn's compositions, even though we may not always know their meaning any more than we do that of some of the terms in Mother Goose. Something of the composer's spirit has survived in them.

The most rewarding beauties in Haydn's symphonies came in the last years of his life, after he had worked out the constructive principles of their form and had come into stimulating contact with Mozart. But there is much of interest along the way, in the works he wrote at the time he was connected with Prince Esterházy's little court orchestra, which he led dressed in a uniform of blue coat with silver buttons, a white collar, and a pigtail wig. He served this family for twenty-nine years, during which time over eighty symphonies came from his pen, including a set of six written for the *concerts spirituels* in Paris. The wealth of material contained in these works is only beginning to be realized, largely through the recent activities of musicologists, conductors, and recording companies. His very first symphony, written in 1759, shows the influence of the various instrumental styles then current: the Italian *sinfonia,* the Austrian contemporary composers, Leopold Mozart and Georg Mann, and the fashionable Mannheim group of symphonists. Like all the other first forty symphonies, this needs a harpsichord continuo to fill in the missing harmonies. He soon begins to show more personal individuality, and in number 13, which employs four horns and contains a minuet and a real Haydnesque finale, we come upon what may be called his first fully mature symphony. From then on, his development is notable, with all sorts of experimentation in form and scoring, and now and then a work of outstanding musical excellence. Between 1780 and 1790, he appears to have become the fully matured artist in his symphonies 44-48; but it is not until the so-called Salomon symphonies, written for an impresario in London (Nos. 93–104), that we recognize all the familiar hallmarks: such things as the long curtain-raising introductions (not inevitable, but usual), his phrase extensions, his sudden modulating jumps from key to key, and the amusing "pussyfoot" returns that he so often makes to the principal theme.

There are good reasons why Haydn's quartets, insofar as the modern listener is concerned, are his finest works. We need not make the historical adjustment when listening to them that is necessary in his symphonies, where his orchestration sometimes seems slight and limited. He seems to have put everything of himself into these chamber-music works: experience had proved that the four instruments making up the string quartet provided the perfect, concise, and self-contained combination in music, whereas further experimentation with timbres was always possible, and he liked to try this, sometimes with rather constricting results.

It was from his experiences in London, where he had been much impressed by the oratorios of Handel, that Haydn came to the resolve to write oratorios. Although his two works in this genre, *The Creation* and *The Seasons,* are not often played today, a study of them shows that they are not primarily vocal works with orchestral accompaniment, as the Handel oratorios are, but rather orchestral works completed and enhanced by chorus and soloists. *The Creation* begins with an imaginative "representation in chaos" which looks forward to Romantic chromatic practices; three archangels and the heavenly choir carry on the narrative through six days of creation; in the choruses Haydn outshines Handel's humanity and perhaps equals his sublimity. Based on a series of nature descriptions taken from James Thomson's poem of the same name, *The Seasons* is a tender and lyric work full of the Rococo conception of an ordered beauty, into which a definitely Romantic expressiveness is introduced. It is quite gentle and direct, with none of the Baroque intensity and tension that is to be felt in all of the Handel oratorios.

The Rococo influence is likewise strongly felt in the music which Haydn wrote for use in the church; a considerable amount of this has come down to us, although little of it is used in actual liturgical performances today. Beginning with such an early work as the *Missa Brevis in F,* through all the great set of Masses which Haydn wrote for the name day of his patroness, the Princess Esterházy,[11] we find the same kind of glorious color, laughing spirit, and gorgeous decoration that we see in the open, sunny, blue and gold Rococo churches of the period. And this in spite of the fact that a new spirit of sobriety, inspired by the determination of the French Revolutionists to wipe out all Rococo gaiety and lightheartedness from European life, had im-

[11] In his book *Haydn, His Art, Times and Glory* (New York: Rinehart), H. E. Jacobs thinks that Haydn's Mass settings were often written in friendly competition with his "little brother," Michael Haydn (1737–1806), who had settled down in Salzburg as an esteemed composer of church music and organist to the archbishop.

A SCENE FROM A HAYDN OPERA   (from a picture in possession of V. E. Pollack, Vienna) Thirteen violins and violas, one cello, two basses, two flutes, and a bassoon constitute the orchestra for this opera staged in the opera house at Esterház. Haydn himself is at the cembalo.

pelled the Catholic Church to seek a "purification from worldliness and sin" and to demand a "sincere, unconditional obedience and submission to dogma, even in the realm of the fine arts." Although Haydn was a good Catholic, he was also a true Austrian who delighted in the Baroque-Rococo determination to help church-goers forget the rather grim sobrieties of their daily lives; and so he paid little attention to this decree. The reformers criticized the superficiality of his religious works, as they did those of Mozart, and strongly resented the fact that, in the tonal and instrumental structure of their music, these composers recognized no fundamental difference between ecclesiastical and secular style. It is true that both sometimes complied with the extreme demands of the Church in the banning of the use of trumpets and drums and such "wicked and godless instruments" in ecclesiastical music, but, in general, it can be said that they went their own ways, expressing in characteristically Rococo fashion Haydn's fundamental belief that "since God has given me a cheerful heart, he will forgive me for serving Him cheerfully."

Few experiences are more rewarding than to review Haydn's development as a master of symphonic and chamber-music writing, music which is full of wisdom spiced with the best of good humor and cheer. Such a review cannot but make us realize anew that he was the composer of some of the most cordial, refreshing music ever written.

THREE MUSICAL TEXTS

The rather uncertain condition of instrumental music during the period of Haydn's development and experimentation is shown by the fact, as Sachs has pointed out, that three of the outstanding musicians of this period, "squeezed between a rapidly vanishing past and a timidly outlined future," took the trouble to write complete textbooks showing how the music of their time was to be performed and giving such careful details that these manuals provide us with a complete picture of the state of music between the times of Bach and Mozart.

In 1752, Johann Joachim Quantz, the chamber musician and court composer, wrote a hefty *Method for Playing the Transverse Flute (Versuch einer Anweisung die Flöte traversiere zu spielen)*. In 1756, the year of the birth of his son, Leopold Mozart issued a similar method for playing the violin, *Versuch einer gründlichen Violinschule*. And during the years 1753 to 1762 Carl Philipp Emanuel Bach published his *Versuch über die wahre Art das Clavier zu spielen,* an *Essay on the True Style of Playing the Clavier.* Quantz (1697–1773) was the most famous flautist and teacher of his time, having Frederick, "the most musical European prince of his time," as his best-known pupil. Quantz wrote three hundred concertos, which, together with the king's own one hundred twenty-one sonatas, provided most of the repertoire for the concerts at San Souci, the king's palace.

In addition to Quantz, this group included such well-known figures as the violinist Franz Benda and the harpsichordist Carl Philipp Emanuel Bach. Leopold Mozart, whose violin school gained a European reputation, proved himself to be as intelligent a teacher for his young son, Wolfgang Amadeus, as he was a wise father; in the early days of his son's success, Leopold traveled through Europe with him, displaying him as a *Wunderkind*. No less an authority than Haydn called C. P. E. Bach's clavier method the "school of schools." Sachs goes so far as to say that any conscientious musician who would understand the music of this period just before Beethoven must study these three instrumental methods, for "without them, he will necessarily distort the whole of music between Bach and Mozart."

FRONTISPIECE AND TITLE PAGE OF LEOPOLD MOZART'S BOOK ON VIOLIN
PLAYING

In Search of Mozart

All my musical self-respect is based upon my keen appreciation of Mozart's works. It is still as true as it was before the Eroica Symphony *was written, that there is nothing better in art than Mozart's best. We have had Beethoven, Schubert, Mendelssohn, Schumann, Götz, and Brahms since his time: we have even had Dr. Parry, Professor Stanford, Mr. Cowen, Dr. Mackenzie, and Sir Arthur Sullivan; but the more they have left the Mozart quartet or quintet behind, the further it comes out ahead in its perfection of temper and refinement of consciousness.*

Bernard Shaw: *Music in London*

The happiest artist is the one who furiously pursues his art without distraction from another world. It is when a man is torn between the passion of his intellect and the passion of his emotions that a crisis occurs.

Anonymous

MUSIC VERSUS LIFE

In discussing the types of music which Bach, Handel, and Haydn wrote, we have said that they were strongly conditioned by the events of their lives. The same cannot be said of Mozart. In his case, we are struck by the widely contrasting lines of his exterior and his creative life; they run, as has been often observed, in exactly contrary motion. His outward life started bravely and successfully in a number of grand tours all over Europe, displaying his powers as a *Wunderkind;* his middle years were given over to humiliating service for ungrateful patrons and underestimated labors for his family; at the end, after he had been crushed with debts and exhausted by overwork, came an early death and a pauper's grave. Creatively, his life progressed impressively in the other direction, from an early and almost unbelievable natural expressive ability to heights which represent the summits of musical composition.

It is easy to sentimentalize, as has been recently done by some of his biographers,[12] the great injustices and the crying wrongs of Mozart's life. We see reflected in his music something of the joys and the sor-

[12] Among the many Mozart biographies, that by Alfred Einstein (New York: Oxford Press, 1945) stands supreme.

THE MOZART FAMILY (painted by De la Croce in 1780-1781) Mozart and his sister ("Nannerl") are at the piano, Leopold is standing, and in the background is the picture of the mother, who had died in 1778. The intimate nature of the relationship between the family has been recently revealed through the publication of Emily Anderson's three-volume collection of the Mozart family letters.

rows, the humor and the gaiety, as well as the bitterness and the disillusionment, with which his life was filled. But, by and large, his life had only the most superficial connection with his music. His actual creative career was, as Margit Varro has so musically said, like a sustained melody which, through a long and consistently maintained crescendo, came finally to its triumphant climax. Underneath this, his physical life seems a modest and rather ineffectual counterpoint that, commencing on a promising note, ends in a complete silence.

THE TRAVELING PRODIGY

From his very earliest days (Mozart was born in Salzburg, January 27, 1756), this composer was plunged into a world of aristocratic patronage that was typical of the century. His father, Leopold, was fairly well known as a composer and was famous for his violin method, which was used all over Europe during the latter half of the eighteenth century. Wolfgang, as well as his sister Marianne, took to music as naturally as a duck to water: he was able to play the piano at three and to compose little pieces when he was five years of age. Later on, his father taught him the violin and the organ as well.

Convinced that he could exhibit his children as prodigies, Leopold took them on a tour of the fashionable world in 1762, presenting them in Munich and Vienna, and introducing them to the courts at both places with great success. This was the first of a number of similar tours that were undertaken during the next ten years, in the course of which the young Mozart was brought into contact not only with all the great court figures of the time in Vienna, Paris, London, The Hague, Florence, and Rome, but also with its outstanding musical personalities—such men as Johann Christian Bach (youngest son of J. S., at this time firmly established in London as a fashionable composer), Rameau, Baron Grimm, Sammartini (teacher of Gluck), Farinelli (the great *castrato*), Padre Martini (Italy's grand old man of the period), Piccinni, Jommelli, Gluck, and Haydn.

It is impossible for us to realize what a tremendous influence all these different scenes, these various styles of music, must have had on the young, precocious lad with the phenomenal memory and the unbelievable powers of musicianship.[13] It has been often said that his music is the perfect blending of the Italian and German and French styles: the explanation of this fact lies in these early tours which he took under the supervision and guidance of his astute father. Given his natural endowments, perhaps greater than those of any other musician, his thorough technical training at the hand of his father, and the unusual opportunity of knowing what all the great and near-great minds of the world had said in music, he had every right to look forward, at the end of his last tour, undertaken when he was twenty-one, to an appointment that would give him his just place in an appreciative world.

This he never found, although he spent the rest of his short life looking for it. Owing to a peculiar concurrence of circumstances—his own impractical nature, his inability or disinclination to fit, as Haydn had done, into a more or less menial position as musician to one of the courts of the time, and the very fact that the whole court system upon which such patronage depended was beginning to break down of its

---

[13] There are a number of stories regarding both of these. Perhaps the most impressive of them is the testimony of Schachtner, the court trumpeter at Salzburg, who said that Wolfgang's ear was so delicate that he could detect and remember to the next day a difference of half a quarter of a tone and so susceptible that he fainted the first time he heard a trumpet.

When he was in Rome in 1770, he went to the Sistine Chapel to hear Allegri's celebrated *Miserere;* when he came home after the performance, he was able to write out this entire contrapuntal composition, his copy needing only one or two corrections after he had heard the work a second time.

own weight—Mozart spent most of his mature life in Vienna, eking out a precarious existence by teaching, composing, and giving concerts, and by borrowing money wherever he could. In the last ten years of this miserable physical existence, while he was exhausting himself in an effort to keep one step ahead of his creditors and give his family a fairly comfortable and reasonable life, he wrote all his great music—masterpieces that could not pay even for the meager demands he made on society. But they have secured his enduring place among the world's immortals. He died in 1791, at the age of thirty-five, when most men are just beginning to learn how to live.

It is in his music that we must, after all, seek to know Mozart. Of all types,[14] and covering as wide a range as Haydn's, the six hundred authentic works which we have from his pen were written in the short space of twenty years—an average of over thirty compositions a year. It is quite possible to trace Mozart's course of development by means of representative compositions taken from different periods of his life; the interesting fact about such a procedure is that it shows how easily and freely Mozart wrote in the two general styles which we have men-

[14] The great Köchel catalogue, prepared by a Viennese botanist in an attempt to bring Mozart's hundreds of unnumbered works into some sort of decent order, lists the following classifications. This Köchel numeration is now universally used as a means of identifying the works of this prolific composer, the numbers referring to items in the catalogue.

Operas, 22
Church music, 60 various compositions—hymns, motets, Masses, etc.
Arias with orchestra, 54
Songs with voice and piano, 36
Choral works with orchestra, oratorios, cantatas, etc., 7
Music for several voices unaccompanied, 24 compositions, most of them canons
Miscellaneous choral works, 20
Symphonies, 52
Miscellaneous orchestral works, 96 *divertimenti,* serenades, dances, etc.
Concertos for piano and orchestra, 25
Concertos for violin and orchestra, 12
Other concertos, 14
Sonatas for organ and orchestra, 3
Sonatas for organ and strings, 14
String quintets, 5
String quartets, 24
String trios and duets, 5
Piano quartets, 2
Piano trios, 8
Miscellaneous chamber compositions, 15
Works for violin and piano, 38
Works for piano solo, 60 sonatas, variations, rondos, etc.
Works for piano four hands, 10
Works for two pianos, 2
Miscellaneous, 5 works for harmonica, mechanical organ, unspecified instruments

From a painting of 1770

THE FOURTEEN-YEAR-
OLD MOZART

tioned as developing at this time: the Rococo, *galant* style derived from
the court atmosphere and the more humanely appealing style of the
people, with its emphasis upon soul and sentiment, mounting at times
almost to Romantic frenzy.

The works of the year 1772 are the first, according to Wyzewa and
Saint-Foix (the French writers whose authentic work on Mozart has
done a great deal to stir up interest in his music), to show the hand of
a real genius. They possess something of the Romantic quality just
mentioned, showing that even this young lad of sixteen, trained according to the traditions of the eighteenth century and living amidst
all its glory, was beginning to respond to the new ideas astir in the
world—ideas which were later to shake it to its foundations and establish new political and humanistic ideals. But the little *Symphony in
C Major* (K. 200), written the next year, shows nothing of this ad-
olescent striving; it is music of pure delight, written by a youth to
whom the writing of music was as effortless as any of the procreative
processes of nature. Mozart never seemed to have any trouble with the

form in which his thoughts were to be clothed. In these works, as in all his music, it is crystal clear and perfectly suited to its purpose.

The year after the American colonists decided, in July, 1776, that they were and "of right ought to be, free and independent" citizens of their own land, Wolfgang sounded a Declaration of Independence of his own. Realizing that he could not go on forever as a sort of court servant to the tyrannical Archbishop of Salzburg, he began to cast about for new ways of advancing himself. Knowing that the career of a piano virtuoso offered possibilities, he commenced writing concertos and other piano music in which the virtuoso elements were, for the first time, emphasized. The lovely and dramatic *E Flat Concerto* (K. 271), composed for a French player, Mlle. Jeunhomme, shows this new instinct for keyboard display admirably. It was finished just before Mozart started on the last of his great tours, the journey to Paris, undertaken when he was twenty-one. He never achieved a more genuine, heartfelt emotion than that expressed in the *Andantino* of this work; and the cadenza just before the end of it is one which was written down by the composer himself (he usually left these to be improvised by the player) and shows us exactly how he wished these accessory virtuoso elements to sound. The coruscating rondo, brilliant and inspired, is full of youthful enthusiasm; it is a fine illustration of Italian lyricism adapted to the instrumental medium.

It was on this Parisian journey that the boy, now come of age, also achieved something of independence in the matter of his family relationships. Away from his father, who had thought it prudent to remain in Salzburg, and accompanied only by his mother, Wolfgang took advantage of his freedom by falling in love, not once, but over and over again. First it was a rather naughty cousin in Augsburg, then a Mlle. Rose, daughter of Cannabich, the conductor of the famous Mannheim orchestra, "a very beautiful and charming young girl," according to his own account; she was followed by Mlle. Gustl, daughter of the Mannheim flautist Wendling, and finally by Aloysia Weber, a gay young opera singer, daughter of the impecunious prompter and copyist of the Mannheim opera.

But nothing came of it all, even the expected opportunities in Paris. A capable young musician of twenty-two was an entirely different proposition for the Paris impresarios than the sensational young seven-year-old who had visited the city fifteen years before. In spite of a few performances of his works and a great deal of running to and fro, he finally had to write his father: "I have not yet got to know anyone.

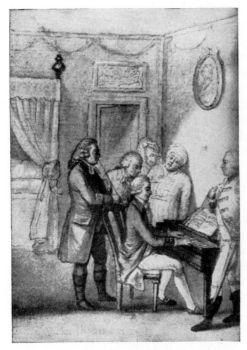

Courtesy of the Stadtmuseum, Salzburg

MOZART IN THE CIRCLE OF HIS SALZBURG FRIENDS   Colored drawing of about 1780 by Schütz

. . . They know what they have to do and that is enough." His mother, alone and homesick, became ill and finally died; and Wolfgang, disappointed and regretful, left Paris to return to his old life in Salzburg, where the prince bishop received him again and made him court organist at the munificent salary of 500 florins a year.

Here he lived for two years, unhappy and unknown. But out of this period there came some of his most delectable works, among them the spontaneous and perfectly constructed *Violin Sonata in B Flat* (K. 378), a *Sinfonia Concertante* for violin and viola (K. 364) which shows how wonderfully he understood the possibilities of both these instruments, and one of the finest symphonies, the *Symphony in C Major* (K. 338), a work which is deserving of more hearings than it gets. Ghéon characterizes this little masterpiece well when he says that Mozart never wrote anything which was firmer, more flowing, or more perfectly balanced, halfway between amusement and conviction, subtlety and ardor, grace and strength. He rather heretically adds that conductors might well substitute it for one of the three later Mozart symphonies they are always giving us—the *E Flat Symphony,* the *G Minor Symphony,* and the *Jupiter Symphony.*

In March, 1781, Mozart rather suddenly received a summons from the archbishop to join him in Vienna. The young musician immediately left his detested native city, never to return, except for a visit to his father. Vienna was his home for the rest of his life—not a very appreciative one, unfortunately, for the times and circumstances did not seem right there for the encouragement of a musician of Mozart's stamp. He established himself, however, and decided, much against his father's will, to marry. The bride of his choice was none other than Constanze Weber, the sister of the singer, Aloysia, who had jilted him in Mannheim. In the midst of all sorts of unpleasant domestic intrigue —for the girl's mother was as anxious for the marriage as Wolfgang's father was against it[15]—and the excitement incident to writing an opera, *The Abduction from the Seraglio,* on the very eve of his marriage, Mozart took time to write a serenade for his old friends, the Haffners, in Salzburg.

"My heart is restless, my head spinning," he wrote to his father. . . . "How can one think and compose something worth while in such a state. What will come of it?"

What came of it was some of the most graceful music he ever wrote, full of a gaiety and delicate perfection that suggests anything but the pain of the quarrels which he was suffering at the time of its composi-

---

[15] Even Ghéon suggests that Frau Weber may have taken advantage of the situation and "forced the young man to bring to light his still confused feelings in the form of a premature declaration." This is the way Mozart explains it to his father:

"Now to come to the written assurance of my honorable intentions towards the girl. You know that they have a trustee, the father being dead. Certain officious and impertinent persons must needs fill this man's ears (he knows nothing about me) with all sorts of stories about me—how there was need to beware of me—that I was perpetually with her—that I might jilt her, and that then the girl would be ruined, etc. The trustee swallowed all this—for the mother, who knows me and knows me to be honorable, let things take their course, and said nothing to him of the matter. For all our intercourse consisted in the fact that I lodged with them and afterwards visited the house daily. No man every saw me with her outside the house. This gentleman filled the mother's ears with his representations till she told me of it and begged me to speak to him myself as he was to come that very day. He came. We talked—the result was that he told the mother to forbid me all intercourse with her daughter until I had settled the matter with him in writing. . . . What other course was open to me? I had either to give my written promise, or agree not to see the girl. What man who loves with truth and constancy can absent himself from his beloved? Might not the mother, might not the beloved one herself, place the most dreadful interpretation upon it? I accordingly drew up a document, promising to wed Mademoiselle Constanze Weber within the space of three years. In the unlikely event of my changing my mind she should have a claim on me of 300 florins a year. But what did the divine girl do as soon as the trustee was gone? She asked her mother for the document, and said to me, 'Dear Mozart! I need no written assurance from you—I trust your word—thus!' And she tore up the paper!" (*Letters of Mozart,* translated by Bozman)

tion. (The "Haffner" *Symphony in D,* K. 385, was afterward arranged from this music.) Nothing he ever did better illustrates the complete disparity between Mozart the human individual and Mozart the artist. Overworked, distraught with alternate joy at his coming marriage and despair at his father's attitude, burdened with the thousand and one things incident to the production of an opera, he was nevertheless so little concerned with all these exterior details as to be able to write music of such quality as to prove a surprise even to himself, when he came to rearrange it later. Mozart once wrote to one of his benefactors that he would like to have everything good, pure, and beautiful; and seemingly he was able to will it so in his music, no matter what the exterior circumstances under which it was composed.

He was finally able to marry and settle down, his troubles, for the time being at least, over. Some of the fire in his blood was communicated to his music. Listen to the superb *Fantasia in C Minor* for the piano[16] (K. 396), composed at this time, and so powerful as to suggest Beethoven. He had more quiet in which to work and devoted a great deal of time to studying the works of Bach and Haydn. Out of this there came the great set of six quartets, modeled after Haydn's style and using all his technical means as well as some of Bach's contrapuntal skill. The first of these was written on the last night of the first year of his marriage. The second, in D minor (K. 421), was written down (it had probably been composed in his mind long before) during the night of his wife's first confinement; yet it shows no trace whatever of these circumstances. Of all his quartets, it is perhaps the most completely detached from the concerns of this world, its spirit entirely empyrean. The last of this set of quartets, the one in C major (K. 465), is celebrated because of its dissonant introduction. A great deal has been written about this, in an attempt to explain that it must be great because it is incomprehensible. The most obvious explanation would seem to be that, for once, Mozart simply did not achieve what he intended; the harmonies of these opening measures in this quartet remain as "confused, obscure, and artificial" as they were thought to be by the critics of the time. It is merely a piece of writing which does not come off when played.

[16] There are two C minor fantasias for the piano by Mozart; the one most frequently programmed is the later one, listed by Köchel as number 475. But this earlier work presents Mozart in a new light, especially as regards his piano music. While the classic style is carefully preserved throughout, there is a tremendous communication of emotional and physical power which can only be thought of as Romantic. If properly interpreted, this great fantasia is a gigantic introduction to the whole Romantic Movement in music.

In the early part of 1785, Leopold came to Vienna to visit his son. He wrote home to his daughter:

On Saturday evening we had Herr Josef Haydn and the two Barons Tindi with us, and the new quartets were played—the three new ones [K. 458, 464, 465] he has composed in addition to the ones we already know [387, 421, 428]. The new ones are a little easier than the first three, indeed, but excellently written. Herr Haydn said to me, "I tell you, calling God as witness and speaking as a man of honor, that your son is the greatest composer I know, either personally or by repute! He has taste, and, in addition, the most complete understanding of composition."

Letters of Mozart, translated by Bozman

At the end of March, Leopold returned to Salzburg. Father and son were never to meet again.

"These," Mozart once wrote during this period, "are the academies at which I have to play [he meant concerts which he must organize, for which he must sell the tickets, compose the music, and appear as soloist]:

Thursday, Feb. 26th, at the Galitzins
Monday, March 1st, at Joh. Esterházys
Thursday, March 4th, at the Galitzins
Friday, March 5th, at the Esterházys
Monday, March 8th, idem.
Thursday, March 11th, at the Galitzins
Wednesday, March 17th, my first private concert

Not a very light schedule for one who, in addition, must teach all morning long and try to find time to devote to composition as well. But the academies were occasions for which new music must be forthcoming. During his twenty-ninth and thirtieth years, Mozart was very much sought after for these fashionble affairs; and, if he had been at all provident in the usual sense, he could have been much better off financially as a result. But when he had money, he liked to spend it gaily, and it was his custom to give these rich patrons everything he had without receiving very much for it. We do not know whether his audiences realized what he was giving them; probably they did not. We of a later generation are the ones who have profited by all this activity, for out of this busy period there came the piano concertos and *Figaro*.

THE PIANO CONCERTOS

It was the custom in Mozart's time for piano virtuosos to improvise in public; and no one ever excelled Mozart at this, if we can trust the witness of contemporaries. Endowed with a facile musical imagination, a perfect memory, a brilliant technique, and an innate sense of what was beautiful, in his extemporary performances he seemed able to loose his daemonic powers to the full. In his twenty-five piano concertos, he came as near to putting this creative freshness and enthusiasm down on paper as in anything he ever wrote. In the best of these works, we feel that a perfect balance has been achieved between the piano and orchestra, the piano being at one and the same time an essential part of the ensemble, yet never overwhelming or competing with it, as so often happens in the later works of this sort.

THE LAST SYMPHONIES

Into many of these piano concertos there comes the feeling of sadness, reverie, melancholy—call it whatever we may—which we note in so many of his later compositions. This is likewise true of the last three symphonies, composed in the thirty-third summer of his life. Written in quick succession—the *Symphony in E flat* (K. 543) finished on June 26, the *Symphony in G Minor* (K. 550) on July 25, and the *Symphony in C Major (Jupiter)* on August 10—it seems as if he must have realized that the candle of his life was nearly burned out. His letters of the time are full of distress and misery: "if you could and would lend me 100 florins, I should be very greatly obliged to you . . . my circumstances are such that I must absolutely get money—in whom am I to put my trust? . . . if you should perhaps be unable to lend me so large a sum, I beg of you to lend me a few hundred gulden, at least until tomorrow."

Yet there is nothing of all this in these great works which mark the apogee of his creative ability: perfectly balanced, beautifully written, they seem as if they must have been the product of Augustan leisure and plenty. The *Symphony in G Minor* is the most popular of all Mozart's works—perhaps deservedly so. In the great *Jupiter Symphony*, there is more of the provenance of the Jovian attributes of lawgiving, of truth and justice royally dispersed, than of bolt-throwing or war. This work contains some of Mozart's most advanced and provocative writing, some of it definitely experimental and looking forward

MOZART in 1782 (from an incompleted portrait by Lange)

to the developments that were to come. It finishes with what is surely the most astonishing example of fugality since Bach.

During the remaining three years of his life, Mozart wrote very little music for the orchestra: he may have felt that he had already expressed everything he wished to say in these three great symphonies. The *Clarinet Quintet in A* (K. 581) was the only instrumental work of importance before the end; but what a work it is! As skillfully written and as full of deep feeling as anything he ever did, its melodies so fill our minds that nothing else seems to matter. All lovers of Mozart will be inclined to agree with Ghéon's statement that in this work, from the very first measure, there is nothing which seems to jar, "not a single gap, a superfluous ornament"; and yet in it there is a deep sorrow and a yearning sadness. The incomparably gay and Rococo *opera buffa, Cosi fan tutte,* and the strangely fantastic *Zauberflöte* also belong to these last years, as does the controversial *Requiem*. It is necessary to keep in mind the mixed origin of this work in listening to it—the fact that not all of it is by Mozart. Indeed, his friend Süssmayr claimed the authorship of the greater part of it, with justice, insofar as the truth may be known. But the glorious opening movement with its great double fugue shows Mozart at his best, even if comparatively little of the remainder (whether Süssmayr's or Mozart's) does.

The serious illness of his wife, who, after years of struggle with poverty and the strain incident to the bringing up of a family, finally broke down in 1789, hastened Mozart's end. The last months of his short life do not make pleasant reading: his attempt to finish the *Requiem;* his utter physical collapse and cruel passing; the hurried funeral, with no music and only a few friends; the committal of the body to a grave in the paupers' section of the cemetery, with no one but the undertakers present; and the unfortunate loss of record as to where even this poor tomb is located. But he was able to leave behind him abundant witness to the fact that he had reached the highest point of civilization to which the art of music has attained.

THE CLIMACTIC FIGURE OF THE CENTURY

In concluding any consideration of Mozart's place in musical history, we need especially to emphasize one point, namely, that he stands as the culmination of the eighteenth century, its last and most perfect product, and has little to do with the nineteenth century. His music is representative of the classic spirit of his time at its best; for it seems to dwell, to use the phrase of Sainte-Beuve, at the very source and center of all existence and to be able to move, as occasion arises, in any direction. In it there is none of the exaggeration and straining of emphasis which we sometimes find in the works of later composers; it seems to have assimilated completely the styles of all music up to its time and to have made them its own; there is in it that balance and proportion that was so dear to the minds of the period. Combined with all these qualities, there is a universality which makes this music unique and which needs no interpretation in terms of other composers.

All through the nineteenth century and the early years of the twentieth, Mozart, of course, had his ardent admirers; yet his real stature was oftentimes obscured during this period, which was more inclined to favor compositions of huge scope and strong expressiveness. Interpreters steeped in the traditions of the Romantic school have tried to make his music speak with the accents of the nineteenth century, feeling perhaps that Mozart's style was somehow small and limited.

Only now, with the recession of the Romantic tide, have we come to a full appreciation of his standing as one of the greatest geniuses of all time. As Rossini once said, Mozart is *the only one;* there has never been another like him. The scope of his accomplishment, as well as the depth of his universal greatness, will probably never be duplicated.

An Operatic Apex

MOZART AND HIS
OPERATIC BACKGROUND   Quite aside from their own individual qualities, the operas of Mozart deserve special consideration in any study of the history of music, for not only do they epitomize and aggrandize the tendencies which had manifested themselves in this style of writing up to their time, but they also laid the foundations for a great deal of the subsequent operatic works written in France, Italy, and Germany. Mozart's operas bring the eighteenth century to an end; they also start a new era, one which greatly influenced the Italian writers of the nineteenth century, as well as the Romantic reformers, Weber and Wagner.

We have seen how Mozart left untouched no species of music current in his day: church music, concertos, symphonies, chamber music, popular *divertimenti* and serenades, piano sonatas, operas—he tried them all. But there seems to be considerable difference of opinion among the critics as to the type in which he was supreme. A noted English writer on the opera[17] says, for example, that the works in which Mozart is most intensely himself are the operas; while an equally famous German critic[18] maintains that he was originally and

[17] Edward J. Dent.
[18] Alfred Einstein.

essentially an instrumental composer and that considerable "discrimination is indicated" in the matter of his operas. Where there is such a wide difference of opinion among the doctors, the ordinary listener may well be encouraged to form his own opinions; but, however we may rank the operas of Mozart, it is well to keep always in mind that their particular quality is due not only to the fact that their composer was a man of outstanding genius, but also that he wrote just when he did—at the end of the eighteenth century.

Review the scene briefly. Back of him stands the two-century-old tradition of Italian opera, a tradition based originally on the lofty ideals of truthfulness and freedom in vocal declamation, but which, in the course of its development, had become sadly debased and was chiefly concerned with the display of the melodic possibilities of the human voice. But always, even though the Italian *opera seria* was made up largely of a long series of floridly melodic arias, it maintained a certain aristocratic and graceful elegance which was peculiar to itself and which a genius such as Mozart could stir into new life. Paralleling this serious opera was the *opera buffa*—light opera—which, as we have seen, had arisen out of a derisive and lively parodying of the grand opera by those who felt its unnaturalness and wanted to do something to relieve it. By the time of Mozart, this light opera had achieved a definite superiority over its ostentatious predecessor because of its superior wit and sense of lively dramatic development. Here was a form ready for the vitalizing hand of a composer such as Mozart, its juxtaposition of elements from the classic comedy and its plots of inevitable disguise, mistaken identity, and the rest, with those of political and artistic parody and sentimental episodes, perfectly adapted to his naturally brilliant style.

But, most important of all was the rise of a newly developed and graciously skilled element of musical expression, the classic orchestra; capable not only of imitating the grace and elegance of contemporary singing, but also of infusing a new tenderness and emotion into music, this instrument became an outstanding feature of the period. Mozart's immediate predecessors had established the norm of its organization and had shown how to write music for it; and his own natural inclinations and early environment gave him a thorough grounding in its style. He it was who first successfully utilized this symphonic technique to give an adequate background to the vocal elements in his operas. There have been many others who have followed, but none who have surpassed him in this.

HIS OPERAS MIRRORS OF MAN

These are not only the materials which Mozart found ready to his hand; they do not in themselves explain the incomparable quality of such works as *Le Nozze di Figaro* or *Don Giovanni* or *Cosi fan tutte*. His great genius lay in his ability to take these elements that we have mentioned, these conventional styles and technical resources, and, through his powers of dramatic characterization, to weld them into a truthful mirror of human conduct. With all their eighteenth-century conventions, the operas just named are filled with real characters, each of them carefully delineated musically; they have dramatic continuity and climax; they are able to portray psychological motives of considerable complexity with deftness and surety. And they do all this without violating in any sense the principles of good musical form. Mozart did not hesitate to use all the means which he inherited from his predecessors—the aria, the overture, the recitative, and so forth: he added to these certain technical achievements perfected by his immediate precursors in the way of ensemble numbers by a group of singers; and the finale, a scene which in its very confusion of having all the characters singing at once and the audience not being able to follow anything clearly enough to know just what was happening, necessitated the fall of the curtain to bring the act to any sort of reasonable conclusion.

But, in using all these, he was wise enough never to allow the dramatic elements to overweigh his musical necessities, as his great follower, Wagner, often does; nor did he allow the possibility of a *coup de théâtre* to overbalance his inherent sense of dramatic propriety, as the Italians Donizetti, Bellini, and even Verdi are wont to do. Without being in any sense a reformer, Mozart was able to achieve, in the words of Alfred Einstein, a miraculous harmony of profound dramatic truth and characterization with perfect musical form. It is in this that his peculiar pre-eminence and distinction lie.

OPERA SERIA

His operatic works fall naturally into various groups: *opera seria, opera buffa,* and the German operas. Most of the *opere serie* were written during his youth and, with their rather slavish following of the convention of the Neapolitan school—sketchy recitative, bravura arias, and so on—are hardly representative of Mozart at his best. They comprise the following operas:

La finta Semplice, written in Vienna in 1768, but not produced until 1769 in Salzburg (The idea of the composer's writing this work came from the emperor, according to Mozart's father.)

Mitridate Re di Ponto, produced in Milan under the composer's direction in 1770

Lucio Scilla, ordered for performance in Milan, 1772

Idomeneo, the first mature work, written when he was twenty-five and, unfortunately, seldom performed today (Critics are united in proclaiming this to be his best serious opera because of its fine treatment of arias and concerted pieces.)

La Clemenza di Tito, written in haste on commission for the coronation of Leopold II, King of Bohemia, at Prague in 1791 (One of Mozart's few failures, it seems to have been impossible to give this work any semblance of dramatic life.)

OPERA BUFFA

In the field of the *opera buffa,* Mozart accomplished his greatest achievements, for it was this genre, so admirably cultivated by the eighteenth-century Italian dramatists, that he seemed to find most congenial. Rarely seeking heroic stature, the Italians nevertheless, better than anyone else, seem to have been able to hit off the lighter humors of the world; and they have created, time and time again, stage conventions which the world delightedly agrees to, however unlike life they may be. When the argument is not high, we can the more easily be pleased; we do not feel called upon for too critical an approach and are willing to accept the result as an amusing, satiric set of comedies, wonderfully suited to the exigencies of the stage. The leading eighteenth-century exponents of this Italian comedic spirit were Carlo Goldoni (1707–1793), who wrote many of his one hundred fifty comedies in France, where he settled as Italian master to the royal family, and Carlo Gozzi (1720–1806). Both men were natives of Venice and portrayed a comic, if somewhat conventionalized, picture of the events and life of their period; but they did more. It has been said that the one aim which steadily pervaded all Goldoni's writings, no matter what their comic or satiric qualities, was the advancement of honorable sentiments and the correction of the prevailing vices and follies of the day. In one of his plays, he says: "Nature has made us all equals, and nature has taught us that we are all made of the same clay." He contrived plots to show that the promptings of nature are virtuous and should be cultivated.

In this, Goldoni was ably seconded by the popular eighteenth-century French playwright, Beaumarchais, who, in his witty and shrewd comedies *The Barber of Seville* and *The Marriage of Figaro,* gave such a convincing picture of the decadence of the nobility and reflected so patently the feeling of the common folk of the time, that the latter play was personally banned by Louis XVI. It was only after the firm and independent author had fought this royal censorship for five years that *The Marriage of Figaro* was finally allowed production at the Théâtre Français in 1784. Its tremendous success is a matter of history; and it is still played the world over.

THE MARRIAGE OF FIGARO

Little wonder, then, that Mozart and his rather disreputable librettist, a Venetian by the name of Lorenzo da Ponte, former professor of rhetoric at Treviso and at the time the court poet of Vienna, selected Beaumarchais's popular comedy as the basis for an *opera buffa.* Da Ponte, whatever his other qualities, was a thorough man of the theater and was able to concoct a brilliant, scintillating libretto which exactly fitted Mozart's rapierlike wit and power of characterization. There is nothing of the original political allusion and universal import of the play left in the libretto: Da Ponte shifted the emphasis and tried merely to amuse in the Italian manner typical of the century; his plot of intrigue has no serious intentions whatever and centers upon the fickleness of a count who spends his life pursuing pretty girls, especially Susanna, the maid-in-waiting to his wife. The fact that Susanna is betrothed to Figaro, the count's valet and clever man of the world, makes for all sorts of amusing imbroglios. In the course of the opera's development, the plot becomes so involved, and there are so many subsidiary complots and cross intrigues, changes of disguise, and misinterpreted designs, that the confusion of the listener is complete, especially at the conclusion of the whole thing, where all the principal characters are wandering about in a dark garden scene, each of them misinterpreting the intentions of the others. But it does not really matter: Mozart keeps our interest throughout; everything is as light as a feather, perfect in its precision, gay as a marriage bell, completely formal and yet entrancingly human.

Without detracting in the least from the impetuous brilliance of the characteristic comedy of manners which Da Ponte had fashioned for him, Mozart brings the libretto to life through his score: the spirit, temper, and reality of the whole opera come from the music. Staged by means of a number of short scenes, it passes before we are hardly aware of its existence. The outstanding features, as we have hinted, are the solo arias and the concerted act finales; but even the recitatives, which up to this time had been largely formal and were used merely for getting over the action and most of the talk, are made an essential part of the make-up of the whole. *The Marriage of Figaro* is the first and almost the last opera of its kind,[19] inimitable in its perfection; it will always stand, in the minds of many of Mozart's admirers, as his most characteristic work—the consummate creation of a musician who was in the same degree a dramatist.

DON GIOVANNI

There has been a great deal of critical discussion as to whether or not Mozart's second great opera written in conjunction with Da Ponte, *Don Giovanni,* is a comic opera; and this in spite of the fact that the librettist definitely designated his work as a *dramma giacosa,* and that it was so considered by Mozart in composing the music. For this grand opera, in addition to its play of comedy, calls for certain depictions of tenderness, jealousy, and pride which are not to be found in *Figaro.* Mozart's genius again being equal to the task, the music of *Don Giovanni* has an intensity of expression and a dramatic amplitude that is hardly to be expected in the earlier work. Moreover, the nature of the subject demands a certain theatrical sense for the spectacular, which naturally takes it out of the more intimate and stylized atmosphere of the comedy of manners.

Time has probably been too benevolent to this libretto: because of Mozart's music, it has come to be considered a classic and so is usually treated by theater managers with undue solemnity and reverence; scholarly studies and monographs have been written about it as if it were one of the great works of the musico-dramatic stage. As a matter of fact, in spite of its threatening, melodramatic Statue, its frequent denunciations of the conduct of its libertine hero, its spectacular representation of his ultimate fate, it is a not overconvincing record of its

---

[19] As we shall see later, Rossini's *Barber of Seville,* based likewise on Beaumarchais, is worthy to be placed alongside of *Figaro;* but there are no others.

famous protagonist's progress through a series of merry pursuits of women to his inevitable doom in Hell, largely "lifted" from an earlier *capriccio drammatico* by the Italian librettist Bertati. Indeed, if it had been written in more modern times, it is almost certain that Mozart's adventurous librettist would have found himself involved in charges of plagiarism, so close is the resemblance between Da Ponte's libretto and its earlier model.

And the ironically delectable episode at the very end of the work, a closing sextet sung after Don Giovanni has traversed, in a cloud of theatrical smoke, the trap-door to Hades, gives the whole thing away and tells us what composer and librettist thought of their conglomeration of comedy and melodrama. So we need not take *Don Giovanni* too reverently; if it were not for the superb quality of Mozart's music, it would have, long before this, gone the way of its numerous prototypes.

Because of its many-sided characterizations, most connoisseurs consider *Don Giovanni* to be Mozart's outstanding work, some enthusiasts maintaining it to be the greatest and most perfectly co-ordinated opera ever written. Don Giovanni, the carefree, full-blooded, crafty libertine to whom life is merely a grand philandering adventure; his sly, lecherous confederate, Leporello; their feminine victims, Donna Anna, the daughter of Il Commendatore, virtuous and outraged; Donna Elvira, a grandam whose love Giovanni has scorned; Zerlina, charming, naïve, simple, the most desirable of them all; Il Commendatore, who loses his life at the very beginning of the opera as he attempts to defend his daughter's honor from Giovanni's wily attack; Don Ottavio, Anna's lover, whom she constantly (and, if the truth be told, rather tiresomely) beseeches to avenge the death of her father; Masetto, Zerlina's betrothed, a suspicious peasant resentful of the insults he must stand from his predatory superiors; and the awful, avenging Statue of the Commendatore, which finally achieves Giovanni's downfall: for all these Mozart has written characteristic music, his method of treatment being similar to that of *Figaro*. Arias, duets, and swiftly moving concerted numbers are connected by rapid-fire recitatives containing much of the life-giving dramatic elements. Mozart gives a great deal of his character delineation to his orchestral accompaniment, described by a contemporary as containing an "overpowering number of notes"; to which the composer retorted, "Just as many as are required." The vocal parts make consummate demands on the singers for fluent finesse of style, rapid singing, apt phrasing, ability to set forth long, lyric lines, fine focused tone, and consistent clarity of utterance—demands that

"The artifice and refinement of
the Rococo palace of Hellbrunn," near Salzburg

are unfortunately difficult of fulfillment today. So, because of these inherent difficulties of production, *Don Giovanni* remains for most of the present generation a classic sort of museum piece, instead of being the warm-blooded, melodramatic, and very human work its creators intended.

COSI FAN TUTTE

The third of Mozart's great comic operas, *Cosi fan tutte,* was written in 1789, only two years before his death. In some ways the most characteristic of all his works, representing the very quintessence of his bravura style at its lightest and wittiest, this opera was for many years thought to be inferior and second-rate. But recent restudy has given a better perspective, and we are coming to realize that, like the others, this little eighteenth-century comedy is a unique masterpiece, exquisite and dainty, fragile and witty, sophisticated and cynical. Its story, again by Da Ponte, is simple enough: two young officers, in a rash moment of boastfulness, decide that they will try the constancy of their loves, and, with the aid of a cynical philosopher and a willing servant, dupe the girls by pretending to go off to the wars. Returning in disguise, they pay court, each to the other's woman, with such ardor and charm that, although at first refused, they are finally accepted as lovers. Then comes the denouement—the return of the officers as their real selves, dismay, and final forgiveness; so it will always be: *cosi fan tutte*—"all women are like that."

Here is a perfect example of eighteenth-century *opera buffa,* with its sham and farce, its utter childishness and brilliant raillery. Ghéon well likens it to the artifice and refinement of the Rococo palace and gardens at Hellbrunn, near Mozart's birthplace, built by one of the prince bishops of Salzburg for the delectation of his inamorata. "The very refinement, harmony, and unexpectedness of all the sham fishes and singing birds, sham stalactites and automatons, the collection of grottoes and fountains, give one something of the same pleasure as certain works of Mozart—in particular *Cosi fan tutte.* Perhaps Mozart did not push artificiality quite so far, but he used nature rather as did the architect, building out of authentic pebbles and shells —authentic human emotion—a world at once real and sham, somewhat mechanical and yet alive, enchanted with its beauty and yet laughing at itself because it sees the ridiculousness of its narcissism. The scenes of *Cosi fan tutte* are like a succession of these fountains and grottoes. The duets and trios affect a symmetry that neither *Don Giovanni* nor *Figaro* possesses to the same degree. Less characterized, the voices are more content merely to satisfy the ear" (*In Search of Mozart*).

Looked at in this light, this last *opera buffa* must always be one of Mozart's most delectable works.

THE GERMAN OPERAS

The two German operas—*Die Entführung aus dem Serail* and *Die Zauberflöte*—are of importance historically as well as artistically. *The Seraglio,* as the first is usually called in English, written in 1782, was the first German opera to be composed by an outstanding man. In it, Mozart for the first time did full justice to the drama. Einstein feels that in *Die Entführung,* more than anywhere else, Mozart follows the suggestions of the text; his orchestra speaks a new descriptive language, and the whole work marks his complete emergence as a distinctive dramatic composer.

The Magic Flute, written to order to what seems to many present-day listeners a somewhat weird and confusing libretto by a practical show-man of the time—one Schikaneder—and produced only a month before Mozart's death in 1791, is a mixture of fairy tale, poetic fantasy, muddled symbolism, and powerful thought. What impresses everyone is the essential charm of the story and the magnificent quality of the music, music which in its overpowering strength, beautiful color, charming melody, and powerful rhythm sounds a truly German note in its symbolic solemnity and its romantic intensity. According to no less an authority than Wagner, this opera "laid the foundations and exhausted the possibilities of German opera," which is putting it rather strongly in view of the works he was later to compose! Another German critic has said that with this one work Mozart gained for German opera a position comparable to that held in the drama by Schiller and Goethe—an affirmation which a non-German would certainly question. But anyone can easily recognize in listening to this debatable masterpiece that, whatever its merits or demerits, it did open the mysterious door to a new age, as Dent has said. For with it, the first great work composed for the common man in the street instead of for the prince or the aristocrat in his palace, there begins a long, rich line of fantastic, legendary, romantic operas, a line which reaches from Weber to Wagner, and beyond to Debussy and Strauss and even Berg.

Which is, after all, perhaps distinction enough!

MUSIC BECOMES
MORE PERSONAL

The Romantic Ideal in Art

Hinaus ins Freie!
Goethe: *Faust*

CLASSIC VERSUS ROMANTIC:
HOW THE DEBATE BEGAN
If either Haydn or Mozart
had been asked, by an eighteenth-century counterpart of that ubiquitous
individual known in the twentieth as the "inquiring reporter," for an
opinion regarding the classic style in music, he probably would not
have known what the reporter was talking about. And yet, as we said
in the last chapter, the music of these composers has come to be considered representative of that style, so objective is its spirit, so universal
its appeal, and so almost ideally proportioned its structure.

It was not until well into the nineteenth century that people began to
talk about the difference between Romanticism and Classicism and to
discuss their qualities and characteristics, their advantages and shortcomings. In 1830, Goethe published this statement in his *Conversations
with Eckermann:*

> *The divisions of poetry into Classic and Romantic, which today is so general
> throughout the world and which has caused so much argument and discord,
> comes originally from Schiller and me. It was my principle always to work
> objectively in poetry: Schiller's to write subjectively. He thought that his way
> was right, and in order to defend himself wrote an* Essay on Simple and
> Sentimental Poetry. *Little by little, the idea spread throughout the whole
> world. Everybody is talking of Romanticism and Classicism. Fifty years ago
> nobody gave the matter a thought.*

There may be some disagreement among scholars as to the validity
of Goethe's claim of being the first to differentiate between Romanti-

Photograph courtesy of Bruckmann, Munich

LISZT AT THE PIANO, SURROUNDED BY HIS FELLOW ROMANTICISTS At his feet sits the Countess d'Agoult; in the chairs are Alexandre Dumas and George Sand; standing are Victor Hugo, Paganini, and Rossini. The painting is by Danhauser.

cism and Classicism in art; but there can be no question as to the truth of his statement that since his time there has been a great deal of talking and writing—perhaps too much—about these labels which have been more or less arbitrarily fastened not only on poetry, but on all the arts. Yet, with all this discussion, no one has ever fixed clearly the meaning of these "worn, smudged, and ambiguous words" or defined exactly the differences between them.

ETYMOLOGICAL ROOTS

Lucas, in his book *The Decline and Fall of the Romantic Ideal,* tells us that the first metaphorical use of the Latin word *classis* (meaning originally a "host," and applied to the class of Roman citizens who could afford the most heavily armed military hosts; all the others were *infra classem*) was that of Aulus Gellius, who distinguished a *classicus scriptor* from a *prolitarius*. And this connotation of *standard,* of belonging to the best class, especially if it was associated somehow with the civilizations of Greece and Rome, has remained with the word ever since. It was thus that the artists of the Renaissance thought of *classical;* and when the word was inserted into the English language, it was applied to anything which was thought to conform to the standards of classic antiquity.

The pedigree of *Romantic* is somewhat more complicated. The first Latin usage referred to a vernacular language, introduced by barbarian invaders, which by the eighth century had taken its place alongside the official Latin. It was called the *lingua Romanica.* Thus, the old French, and then the Provençal and the Spanish, and finally all the Latin vernaculars, came to be thought of as Romance languages, and the literature composed in them—made up of fictitious and fantastic stories in both verse and prose—was called *Romantic literature.* It was this meaning of the fictitious, unreal, fantastic, of the strange and fairy-tale-like that became gradually attached to a type of literature (and consequently other arts), as well as the temperaments associated with producing it and the forms which resulted therefrom. So that in a general sense the epithet *Romantic,* which began with meaning, in the seventeenth century, a lying sort of tale, assumed during the eighteenth the connotation of strange, unusual, fantastic, and was attached to such things, as Lucas observes, as "Gothic ruins, wild landscapes, and other delightful mixtures of terror and sublimity."

PRESENT-DAY APPLICATIONS

In all our present-day usages of these terms, there persist definite traces of these etymological meanings. We designate as classic such things as the Parthenon, the poetry of Sophocles or Horace, the prose of Demosthenes, not merely because they were produced by the Greek and Roman cultures, but also for the reason that they represent something standard, unique, ideal, which seems to stand somehow at the very source and center of all existence (to use Sainte-Beuve's phrase again), their natural freedom of form, their sense of balance and proportion, their sanity and reality, their peculiar blending of idealism and actuality representing a norm by which all other things of their class may well be judged. In the same sense we speak of the poetry of Milton, the plays of Racine, the sculpture of Michelangelo, the music of Mozart as classic, although these represent cultural civilizations that are far removed from those of Greco-Roman times.

Likewise, in the older usage, the term *Romantic* suggests anything which is out of the ordinary, highly imaginative, free and unrestrained, overpowering and remote—in a sense, attributes that are opposed to reason, balance, and calmness of spirit. Thus, *The Rime of the Ancient Mariner, The Arabian Nights, Macbeth,* and *The Afternoon of a Faun* can be thought of as Romantic, although they come from widely separated epochs in the world's creative history.

MISTAKEN USAGES

A number of unfortunate connotations have arisen from the wrong application of these etymological differences between Classic and Romantic. A common distinction often made is that in which Classicism, because of its particular associations, is considered as an appeal to reason, while Romanticism is described as being an appeal to the emotions. In a sense this is true, of course; but there is no such clear-cut difference between these terms. For it is easy enough to show that the supreme examples of both literature and music (the two arts which are most strongly affected by such differences) have at the same time form and balance, which appeal to the intellect, and those vast sweeps of emotion and devouring passion which traverse all human life. A great deal of the art which is strongly Romantic has also the control, balance, and reason which we think of as characteristically classic—the poetry of Schiller and the symphonies of Beethoven, for example. And anything more truly and destructively passionate than the hate of Electra and Clytemnestra or the overpowering terror of the final act of *Don Giovanni* can hardly be imagined!

Another distinction which is often made is that between the element of personal freedom and the rights of the individual—characteristics of Romanticism strongly emphasized, as we shall see, at the start of the nineteenth century—and the necessity which Classicism imposes of submerging such individualism in the interest of securing a perfect balance of the whole: in a word, of achieving general excellence rather than particular uniqueness. But the notes of individuality and freedom are strongly sounded in many a so-called classic: the despair of Molière's *Misanthrope* is individual; and the feeling that rises, sometimes poignantly, sometimes lyrically, out of so much of the music of Bach is very personal. On the other hand, some of the best Romantic art, such as the poetry of Coleridge (*The Rime of the Ancient Mariner* is one of the greatest of sermons on absorption in self) and Keats and the music of Brahms can hardly be said to be egocentrically personal.

There have been many other such distinctions. Goethe made the very sweeping statement that if a work is thoroughly good, it is bound to be classical; for "Romanticism," he assures us, " is disease; Classicism, health." Which leads us to speculate as to just how he managed to justify certain aspects of his *Faust*. A contemporary, Stendhal, confuses the issue still further by saying that Romanticism, at any time, is the art which is contemporary; Classicism is that which was produced yesterday. Thus, all good art would be first Romantic and then Classic. According to such a theory, Haydn's style was Romantic in his day, just as was Stravinsky's to those who first heard it in the early years of the twentieth century; whereas, both the *Surprise Symphony* and *Le Sacre du printemps* are now to be considered classics, belonging as they do to the past.

Plausible theories have also been worked out which show the whole history of Occidental art to have been a succession of three phases: a preclassic or symbolic stage, characterized by primitivism and the struggle to acquire technical facility; a classic stage, marked by an absolutely homogeneous unity of content and form; and a Romantic stage, an overdeveloped aspect of this perfect state, with emphasis laid on personal expression of feeling and new methods of saying old things, ending finally in incoherence and decadence.[1]

Probably the greatest of all these sources of confusion, however, is that which mixes the aesthetic-critical meaning with the historical application of these terms. The French, with characteristic logic, have avoided this difficulty by having two words to use for *Romantic:* they use *Romanesque* to designate the attitude towards life and art that we have just been discussing, while they confine their use of *Romantique* to the great historical movement which took place at the end of the eighteenth and the beginning of the nineteenth century and which has come to be known in English as the Romantic Movement.

THE SPRINGS OF THE ROMANTIC SPIRIT

In an earlier chapter, we had something to say regarding the causes which produced the gradual rise and spread of a new spirit in life and art during the eighteenth century—the feeling that the common man up until this time had had little opportunity for real freedom of thought in any political, religious, or social sense. In essence, this new spirit was,

---

[1] These theories are discussed thoroughly in Sorokin's *Fluctuation of Forms of Art.*

of course, a revolt which had become inevitable because of the extremes of the aristocratic governments then to be found in both Church and State; it was the result, as we have tried to show, of three parallel and sometimes conflicting tendencies of the era: the trend towards Enlightenment; the development of a rather overstressed Classicism; and the idea of Revolution which, when applied to social and political standards, caused the overthrow of the governing classes and the rise to power and position of the middle-class *bourgeoisie.*

The empirical and practical philosophy of Francis Bacon, as well as the necessity of having to prove everything clearly and mathematically before it could be accepted as true, arising from the philosophy of Descartes, made for a constant elevation of the reason at the cost of the imagination and led inevitably to an oversmugness and stuffiness of conception which could but stifle man's real originality and independence of thought.

The general conventions and artificialities that were to be found throughout the entire social structure created *l'honnête homme,* the individual whose personal existence was entirely subordinated to the general good of society. The conduct of such a correct, restrained, and elegant creature was ruled by a sense of decorum, of never offending what were accepted as the canons of good taste. It was society that set up the standards of thought and action during the seventeenth and eighteenth centuries, and any individual who did not conform to these standards was condemned.

The process of imitating and copying classic models had become common in all the arts. Its initiation during the Renaissance had at first been tremendously energizing because of the renewing of contact with the great minds of the past; but this had gradually deteriorated by the seventeenth century into a "grandeur of generality" that attached more importance to the manner in which an idea was expressed than to the idea itself. A pseudo-classicism was the result, which, instead of achieving the perfection, balance, and reasonable self-control that are the real attributes of the classic spirit, served rather to limit the creator's means to doing what had been sanctioned by tradition and approved by convention.

It was factors such as these which created the spirit of revolt epitomized in the cry of Goethe's Faust which heads this chapter: *Hinaus ins Freie!*—Away from all this and out into the open—a spirit of revolt which a continued acceptance of tradition and routine made unavoidable. This was the cry that was taken up by such leaders of the thought of the time as Rousseau and Schiller and Byron and that became so much a part of the people's philosophy as to change the whole political and cultural tone of Europe. It is this that the French have called *Romantique*.

Although we may never be able to define satisfactorily such a spirit, it is not difficult to see what it led to: a new understanding of and interest in the common people—the natural, unsophisticated type of humanity which dwelt in village cottages rather than in lordly halls. It pointed the way to the open country and the possibility of contemplating the beauties and terrors of nature as a means of relief from the burdensome routines of society; it suggested another convenient flight from the realities of the present by means of the consideration of times that were past and places that were distant; it insisted upon the importance, above all else, of exalting man's natural impulses and emotions—of a dedication of oneself " to unpath'd waters and undream'd shores"—with none of the confining restrictions of eighteenth-century rationalism; it tended to cultivate the picturesque and colorful, the strange and eccentric at the expense of the accepted and usual; it emphasized the principle of invention rather than that of imitation, of creating anew rather than merely following the models of the past; and, finally, it led man to look upon his artistic creations more in the light of a language of the emotions than as a means for the conveyance of ideas.

In general, the Romantic Movement was aesthetic rather than political, although some of the principles which underlay it were at the root of such political phenomena as the American Revolution and the French Revolution. It likewise caused something of a revolution in religious thought, in some places separating the Church and the State, abolishing the prerogatives which the former had held for so long; in others, it aroused the conviction that religion was not merely a matter of external creeds and formal organization, but one primarily concerned with the hearts and lives of men.

Eighteenth-century intellectuals and moralists had been sure that their age was the most advanced and "enlightened" the world had ever seen—with the possible exception of classic antiquity—and that the human reason, if given free scope, would be able to banish all ignorance and superstition and initiate a glorious era of reasoned progress. But it did not work out that way: the terrible horrors of the French Revolution and the Napoleonic Wars brought about severe disillusionment and led the clergymen and moralists of the latter part of the century to question the validity of the viewpoint of their predecessors. Was reason

THE OATH OF THE HORATIANS by Jacques Louis David (1784) The painting is characteristic of the neoclassic style of the late eighteenth century.

enough to guide man and show him the way to his highest destiny? Had not feeling and sentiment been neglected at the expense of logic? Was not the great medieval age of faith much better off than the much-vaunted and supersophisticated age of reason? Was not the vision of progress more concerned with the kingdom of man than with the realm of reason? The attempt to provide adequate answers to questions such as these led directly to the thinking which ushered in the Romantic Movement. It was this thinking that produced and reinforced reactionary movements in religion, politics, morals, and social life, without frustrating, however, the general trend of intellectual progress.

ROMANTICISM AS A FORCE IN ART

But it is Romanticism as a revolution in art that concerns us. Rousseau, its first great figure, a writer and a musician as well as a philosopher, stood firmly on the principle that man's emotions and instincts should be the guiding motives of his conduct. He thus opposed the principle of decorum and was insistent that, in order to get back to natural instincts, it was necessary to throw off the restraints and artificialities of society. Rousseau's somewhat paradoxical thinking was responsible for many of the rebellious ideas in life and art which were later adopted by society; because of this fact, it has been said that he influenced history more profoundly than any other single individual born within the Christian era.

In painting, Romanticism had been a potent force even as far back as the beginning of the seventeenth century, when Caravaggio, the brilliant Italian individualist, flung his challenge in the face of Renaissance Classicism. Later, men like Salvator Rosa, Richard Wilson, and Francesco Guardi kept alive the same spirit; and the "official" Classicism of the school of David and his followers in nineteenth-century France assured a Romantic outbreak there. These men, in an attempt to rebel against the Rococo graces and charms of painters like Fragonard, Watteau, and Boucher, reverted completely to Greco-Roman styles and topics. Géricault and Delacroix, the latter one of the most fervid of all the Romantics, embodied in their works the passion and turbulence of the new school, together with its disregard for convention and its emphasis on individual emotion. No better understanding of the fundamental differences between the Classicism of the eighteenth and the Romanticism of the nineteenth century could be gained than that to be obtained through a comparison of such pictures as David's *Oath of the Horatians* and Delacroix's *The Wreck of "Don Juan."*

The influence of Romanticism was by no means confined to France. It spread to other countries, where it had varying and lasting effects: in England its force was mostly felt in poetry. One of its earliest manifestations was the arousing of a love for folklore and poetry in all countries, a love which had sadly lapsed during the classic insistence on cultivation and refinement. Bishop Percy's famous collection of folk legends,[2]

---

[2] One of the most famous of these anonymous ballads is that of "Edward"; it has been the inspiration for several important pieces of Romantic music. Here are the opening stanzas:

"Why does your brand sae drop wi' blude,
    Edward, Edward?
Why does your brand sae drop wi' blude,
    And why sae sad gang ye, O?"

"Your hawk's blude was never sae red,
    Edward, Edward;
Your hawk's blude was never sae red,
    My dear son, I tell thee, O."

"O I hae kill'd my hawk sae gude,
    Mither, mither;
O I hae kill'd my hawk sae gude,
    And I had nae mair but he, O."

"O I hae kill'd my red-roan steed,
    Mither, mither;
O I hae kill'd my red-roan steed,
    That erst was sae fair and free, O."

Reliques of Ancient English Poetry, published in 1765, and the *Ossian* of James Macpherson, an epic made up of pretended translations of poems from a third-century Scottish bard and published in 1761–1765, were the first tangible results of this new ideal in poetry. These were copied and translated into other languages, especially the German, and had a strong influence on the development of the Romantic spirit in literature.

This spirit is to be felt in the works of all the poets who lived and wrote at the turn of the century—Wordsworth, with his portrayal of the way nature affects a "heart that watches and receives"; Coleridge, with his "strange power of speech"; Byron, with his spirit of hot revolt and insistence upon the rights of personal freedom; Shelley, and his hatred of tyranny and his vision of what man might become "between the cradle and the grave."

Eighteenth-century Germany had experienced a new propensity for indulging in emotional excesses for their own sake, a propensity that flourished naturally in the sentimental German soul and that had been strongly stimulated by the religious movement called Pietism, which had developed among the prosperous burghers of the late seventeenth and early eighteenth centuries. Although it did not have any official effect and gradually died out after 1740, Pietism encouraged many mental habits which had a profound effect upon later German life and German art. Particularly important was the idea that *feeling* was a human attribute which had to be encouraged at all costs;[3] it became very fashionable to be moved to tears in contemplating nature and art. For several generations after the middle of the eighteenth century, literature, correspondence, conversation, and art, especially the art of music, were full of this "flavor of sentimental debauchery," called *Gefühlsduselei* by the Germans. Much the same sort of sentimental nonsense was current in England at about the same time: late eighteenth-century English literature is full of images such as Many Meadows, the Harp of Aeolus, the Anaconda, the Glow-worm, and the

---

[3] Pietism was a natural reaction against the strong rationalism of the Lutheran clergy of this era, who seemed more concerned about purity of doctrine than they were about Christian faith and conduct. It took the form of a considerable movement, which, while proclaiming no new theology or doctrine, insisted upon a "faith of piety," each human being setting up a "priesthood of the Lamb in his own heart." Men were bid to present themselves as "naked spirits before God in simplicity and piety." Such a union was not to be *believed* or *proved,* but *felt.* "The heart should burn," insisted one Pietistic preacher, "just as a drunkard becomes filled with wine, so must man become imbued with the heartfelt spirit." What seems to us today as strange about so many of the texts of J. S. Bach's cantatas is due to this Pietistic influence.

ROMANTICISM IN PAINTING AND POETRY   Delacroix: *The Wreck of "Don Juan,"*
after Byron's *Don Juan*, Canto II

'Twas twilight, and the sunless day went down
  Over the waste of waters; like a veil,
Which, if withdrawn, would but disclose the frown
  Of one whose hate is masked but to assail.
Thus to their hopeless eyes the night was shown,
  And grimly darkled o'er the faces pale,
And the dim desolate deep: twelve days had Fear
Been their familiar, and now Death was here. . . .

At half-past eight o'clock, booms, hencoops, spars,
  And all things, for a chance, had been cast loose
That still could keep afloat the struggling tars,
  For yet they strove, although of no great use:
There was no light in heaven but a few stars,
  The boats put off o'ercrowded with their crews;
She gave a heel, and then a lurch to port,
And, going down head foremost—sunk, in short.

Then rose from sea to sky the wild farewell—
  Then shrieked the timid, and stood still the brave—
Then some leaped overboard with dreadful yell,
  As eager to anticipate their grave; . . .

Upas Tree, symbol of mysterious death, even though in that country, where energies were so largely devoted to the activities of handicraft and commerce, art was considered a thing of rather doubtful worth and extravagances of all sorts were likely to be frowned upon.

ROMANTICISM AND MUSIC

Musical instruments such as the pianoforte, capable of providing expression through the loudening and softening of their tones, became popular.[4] First constructed, as we have seen, by the Italians at the beginning of the eighteenth century in their desire to achieve expression in music and to make their musical instruments "sing," these keyboard instruments *col piano e forte* were being made and played in Germany as early as 1750. They were introduced into England some ten or fifteen years later, and by 1790 the grand pianofortes of the English manufacturers were noted throughout Europe for the sonority of their tone and the strength of their construction. In France, the wives and daughters of important *Directoire* figures, anxious to repudiate the Rococo pleasantries of the past, turned away from the harpsichord as a reminder of the old regime to the new instruments which were being made by Sebastian Erard, who had set up business as a piano manufacturer in 1796. Arthur Loesser points out in a remarkable treatise on the history of the piano[5] that this instrument was ideally suited to the life and times of the rising European *bourgeoisie:* "It is the easiest of all instruments to play a little, the perfect tool for persons of small talent or ambition," and since it quickly became a good-looking piece of room furniture and expensive enough to be proud of, it came to be considered the hallmark of a certain kind of social position, while the ability to play on it, even in the most rudimentary way, was thought to be a sure sign of advancing culture. All sorts of music particularly suited to its capabilities were written: strings of variations on popular opera

---

[4] Around 1750, the clavichord was still the favorite domestic instrument in Germany, largely because its delicate responsiveness to the touch made it a perfect instrument for expressing the finer shades of feeling, and because of the possibility of giving a prolonged *vibrato* effect to its tone by rocking up and down on its keys—*bebung,* the Germans called it. Even such a good composer as C. P. E. Bach wrote a *Farewell to My Silbermann Clavichord,* and songs about its possibilities of mitigating the "unspoken grief within the breast" became regular features of eighteenth-century German songbooks.

[5] *Men, Women and Pianos* by Arthur Loesser (New York: Simon & Schuster, 1954) is really a social study of the development of music!

melodies and well-known tunes; sets of dances, made up of country dances (*contredanses,* they were called) and waltzes, the latter a preeminent illustration of the "two most intoxicating virtue words of the age, the 'people' and 'liberty' "; cascades of program music imitating or suggesting sounds in nature, chiefly in the form of *storms* and *battles,* the most spectacularly popular of which, *The Battle of Prague,* remained for more than half a century, according to Loesser, the best-known long piece of piano music in existence, at least among the English and their cultural dependents;[6] and a peculiar outbreak of Turkish or Janizary pieces suggestive, it was thought, of the savage, barbaric people who had threatened European civilization so many times until they were defeated before Vienna in 1684.

Another musical fad suggestive of the new desire for Romantic expression in art was that for musical glasses—sets of drinking glasses which, when tuned by varying levels of water inside each glass and rubbed with a moist finger, gave forth a sweet, sustained tone. The practical-minded American, Benjamin Franklin, showed how this unusual instrument could be improved: he developed a mechanical "glass harmonica," whose celestial tone quality attracted the attention of Mozart and Beethoven. Still another characteristically Romantic instrument was the Aeolian Harp, whose "sequaceous notes," produced not by a human performer but by currents of air blown across its strings, wonderfully disposed the hearer for romantic sentiment.

All this emphasis upon *Empfindsamkeit* reached its climax during the decade between 1770 and 1780, during which time Goethe poured out his *Sorrows of Werther* (thereby causing a wave of sympathetic suicides throughout Europe) and Friedrich Maximilian von Klinger wrote a turbulent play called *Sturm und Drang,* thereby giving a name to this whole epoch.[7] Its two leading figures were Goethe and Schiller. The former was really a pioneering leader of his generation in science and philosophy, as well as one of the greatest creative artists of all time. Although he stood as a protagonist of classic form, his influence upon Schiller and the other artists of the time was that of a stimulating, bold individualist. It was the genius of these two artists which raised the Romantic Movement in Germany to respectability; and it is for-

[6] We have to remember that this kind of cheap program music attracted such first-rate composers as Weber, who wrote an *Invitation to the Dance,* and Beethoven, whose *Battle of Vittoria* gave him more immediate acclaim than anything else he ever wrote!

[7] In addition to *Werther,* Goethe's *Götz von Berlichingen,* Schiller's *Robbers,* Lessing's *Minna von Barnhelm* and *Laökoon* were characteristic *Sturm und Drang* works.

tunate for us that, in doing so, they produced some of the world's greatest literary masterpieces.

It is the very nature of such a spirit as Romanticism, however, to go to extremes, and it was these extremes that led a people as childlike and as imaginative as the Germans to an overexaggeration of literary fancy and symbolism which often bordered on the ridiculous. This can be seen clearly enough in the works of E. T. A. Hoffmann, who was an excellent musician as well as a facile writer,[8] and Jean Paul Richter, one of the idols of the composer Robert Schumann. One page of Hoffmann's fantastic *Kreisleriana* or Jean Paul's *Thorn, Fruit, and Flower Pieces* will show how strained was their struggle to bridge the gap which they felt to exist between the "real" and the "ideal." Music to them was the perfect art because it could best do this through the very nature of its abstractness, its immense infinitude, and its eternal quest of something that seems always to elude man. Jean Paul, addressing Music, said: "Thou speakest of things which all my endless life I have never found and never shall find."

LINKS BETWEEN LITERATURE AND MUSIC

And so these writers, together with their followers, tried to reduce all the other arts to the terms of music. For them, the colors of flowers sang, their forms resounded; music died away like a "stream of blue light." And Hoffmann confesses that after he had heard a great deal of music, "there takes place in me a confusion of colors, sounds, and perfumes; it is as though they all sprang up mysteriously together from some ray of light and then united to form a marvelous concert."

Hoffmann and Richter represent the connecting links between Romantic authorship and Romantic musical composition: it was through them that the literary ideals of the movement diffused into music. Schumann was a great disciple of theirs and did not hesitate to copy their style and imitate their imagery in both words and music.

[8] The following, written in 1810, shows Hoffmann's real understanding of both these fields, as well as something of his style:

"The instrumental compositions of Haydn, Mozart, and Beethoven breathe the same romantic spirit, a spirit which comes from a deep understanding of the essential property of music.

"Haydn conceives romantically that which is human in man; he is, therefore, more comprehensible to the majority. Mozart is able to grasp the superhuman, that which dwells in the imagination. Beethoven is able to stir within us fear, horror, terror, grief, and to awaken that endless longing which is the very essence of Romanticism."

TWO YOUTHS OBSERVING THE MOON by Caspar David Friedrich (1820) A German critic has defined Romanticism as that which appeals primarily and very strongly to the imagination and the emotions and which stresses the fantastic and emotional at the expense of the rational and normal. No better example of Romanticism in German painting and poetry could be given than this picture of Friedrich's or the little stanza by Ludwig Tieck:

"Mondbeglänzte Zaubernacht,	*Magic night of moonlight,*
Die den Sinn gefangen halt,	*Holding all our senses captive,*
Wundervolle Märchenwelt,	*World of wondrous fairy tales,*
Steig' auf in der alten Pracht."	*Come again with your old power.*

MUSIC'S NEW VITALITY

It may be said that the Romantic Movement in music was inspirited rather than inspired by that in literature; its greatest figure—Beethoven—arose quite independently of its direct line of influence, although he incorporated, as we shall see, the best of its ideals with those he received from the classic world of Haydn and Mozart. The real musical Romanticists are marked by the same characteristics as their brethren in the other arts; but music as a cultural factor in the history of the world received greater benefit from Romanticism than did any of the other arts.[9] The piano pieces of Schumann and Chopin, the symphonies of

[9] Some would add "with the possible exception of literature."

Brahms, the operas of Wagner, the tone poems of Strauss—all of them characteristically Romantic works—are greater than most of the things produced as a result of the Romantic spirit in literature, painting, or sculpture, because music is in essence a romantic art, allowing infinite reaches of the composer's imagination and stirring within the hearer responses which he is able to feel strongly but not to express definitely.

All the musical Romantics show a higher degree of nervous intensity than did their Classic predecessors; their melodies soar more fervidly, their stresses are more pointed, their dissonances sharper: they live, generally, at a higher degree of pressure. The great widening of operatic scope after Mozart gave these composers one main outlet for their Romantic tendencies; the influence of the development of instrumental music was another outlet. The new piano had expressive possibilities that were denied Bach and even Mozart; the orchestra was coming into its own as an expressive medium, though we have to remember with sympathy the weaknesses of the performers which Beethoven had to put up with. In general, it may be said that the freeing of imagination and personality at this time went along with the freeing of instrumental technique and potentialities.

HISTORICALLY SPEAKING

It is in its historic sense that Romanticism must be judged; as a principle it is firmly established in art. There is no question but that the thinking of its founder—Rousseau—is responsible for certain of the oversentimentalized social and political doctrines which have been carried over into the modern world. Like any violent reaction, necessary and wholesome in itself, Romanticism went completely out of bounds: the freeing of the individual's emotion and the intensifying of his imagination, which had been its original aims, degenerated into something which resembled mere frenzy, with a corresponding loss of a sense of balance and control.

This led the taste of the first third of the twentieth century to swing away from the whole idea; the intelligentsia of recent years have not hesitated to deprecate it roundly: the practice of "in dreams beholding the Hebrides" has not been overpopular. Irving Babbitt has written a set of books designed to emphasize the need for discipline in modern life as a means of protecting ourselves against the various forms of naturalistic excesses which were set in motion by the Rousseau philosophy. Yet if we seek the true values, the strengths as well as the weaknesses of Romanticism, we must conclude that the former outweigh the latter, certainly insofar as music is concerned.

The pages immediately following will show that, without Romanticism's impelling spirit of freedom, its insistence upon the right of the individual to express his emotions in his music—to make it an interpretation of life, responding to all the impulses of its period—we would of necessity have to relinquish some of the greatest joys of our art. The music of such men as Beethoven and Wagner, to mention but two composers of this period, shows the anguished conflict between man and the world in which he lives, the "feeling that life is no longer enough, that it is strangely, incredibly empty if one does not stray beyond its frontiers," which is the very essence of great art.

The great secret of Romantic power in music was that it could be experienced by so many different temperaments and through such various musical mediums: Beethoven with his orchestra and choir singing of the brotherhood of man and the fatherhood of God; Schumann flowing over with love songs in the year of his marriage; Weber delighting in the Germanic horrors of his Wolf's Glen; Berlioz dreaming of the thousands of performers necessary to carry out the grandiosity of his imagination; Wagner spinning his wondrous tales of gods and men and destiny; Brahms speaking alike with the Jovian accents of Olympus and with a tender sweetness that recognizes the futility of all man's existence here on earth; Strauss, with his vivid imagination and genial humor, depicting the foibles and weaknesses of humanity.

IMPULSE AND IDEA

It is curious that the juggling of these two terms, "Classic" and "Romantic," has never ceased since Goethe and Schiller started it a hundred years ago; and in this juggling most of the misconceptions of which we have spoken are constantly reappearing. As a matter of fact, in the widest sense all art must be both Classic and Romantic. There have been but two special powers, as Taine has well said, that have moved mankind—*impulse* and *idea,* which is but another way of saying the *emotions* and the *intellect, Romanticism* and *Classicism.* These have been present through the whole development of art—when the early Church was struggling to utilize artistic expression in painting, sculpture, and music as its medium for the impersonal communication of its beliefs; during the Middle Ages; during the time of the Renaissance; in the rationalistic centuries. Even today, when strong attempts are being made to eliminate emotional quality from music and painting and literature, they are active and always will be. It is this fusion which rises above the transient and the incidental in the perfection of the greatest art.

Beethoven the Liberator

In him, emotion is conciliated with reason.
Édouard Herriot

THE RIGHT MAN AT THE RIGHT TIME

The career of the first great Romantic composer, Ludwig van Beethoven (1770–1827), stands out as such a striking example of the best attributes of this movement in art that we are apt to forget that it developed in conjunction with those of a number of contemporary musicians now almost entirely forgotten, but in their day considered quite as significant and important as the self-willed and extravagant figure that stirred the musical life of Vienna to such depths in the early decades of the nineteenth century.

There was, for example, Luigi Cherubini (1760–1842), a Frenchman of Italian descent, one of the most famous composers of the time and Director of the Paris Conservatoire, with largely classical leanings, known today for half a dozen operatic overtures which, in the full light of the Romantic school that followed them, seem rather pale and thin.[10] Muzio Clementi (1752–1832) was another Italian who achieved distinction abroad, in England, where he had a most active and successful career as composer, teacher, music publisher, and piano manufacturer. Johann Nepomuk Hummel (1778–1837), pupil of Haydn and Mozart; Ignaz Moscheles (1794–1870); Carl Czerny (1791–1857)—all names very familiar to Viennese music lovers in Beethoven's day—were men who played an important part in the development of the technical resources needed to exploit to the full the possibilities of the new pianofortes. Johann Baptist Cramer (1771–1858) and John Field (1782–1837) were English exponents of the Clementi method, the latter having considerable influence upon the developing pianistic idiom of the young Chopin. Today, most of these men, if their names are known at all, are thought of as pedagogues—authors of studies that have bedeviled countless aspirants to pianistic achievement, their fame, as Churchill has remarked, "nothing but an empty name."

[10] It was the overture to his greatest opera, *Médée* (1797) which more or less set the pattern for the overtures in heroic style so wonderfully developed by Beethoven.

Courtesy of Reiffenstein Company, Vienna

ONE OF THE BEETHOVEN HOUSES IN HEILIGENSTADT It was here, in 1802, that Beethoven wrote the famous testament, one of his most important documents.

For my brothers Carl and — Beethoven

"*O ye men who think or say that I am malevolent, stubborn or misanthropic, how greatly do ye wrong me, you who do not know the secret causes of my seeming, from childhood my heart and mind were disposed to the gentle feelings of good will, I was ever eager to accomplish great deeds, but reflect now that for 6 years I have been in a hopeless case, aggravated by senseless physicians, cheated year after year in the hope of improvement, finally compelled to face the prospect of a* lasting *malady (whose cure will take years, or perhaps, be impossible), born with an ardent and lively temperament, even susceptible to the diversions of society, I was compelled early to isolate myself, to live in loneliness, when I at times tried to forget all this, O how harshly was I repulsed by the doubly sad experience of my bad hearing, and yet it was impossible for me to say to men speak louder, shout, for I am deaf. Ah how could I possibly admit an infirmity in the one sense which should have been more perfect in me than in others, a sense which I once possessed in highest perfection such as few surely in my profession enjoy or ever could have enjoyed—O I cannot do it, therefore forgive me when you see me draw back when I would gladly mingle with you. . . .*

"*Only art it was that withheld me, ah it seemed impossible to leave the world until I had produced all that I felt called upon to produce, and so I endured this wretched existence—truly wretched, an excitable body which a sudden change can throw into the worst state—Patience—it is said I must now choose for my guide, I have done so, I hope my determination will remain firm to endure until it pleases the inexorable parcae to break the thread, perhaps I shall get better, perhaps not, I am prepared. . . .*"

From the "Heiligenstadt Will"

There can be little question that Beethoven owes his dominating position in music history to the fact that he was a man of outstanding genius who happened to be born at exactly the right time. It was Goethe who remarked that the matter of genius was largely a matter of luck: "When I was eighteen," he said, "Germany was eighteen, too; a man could accomplish something then— I am glad I began when I did and not today, when the demands are so much greater." In the case of Beethoven, it was not only Germany but the whole of Europe which was eighteen when he was: the entire political and intellectual fabric of the last years of the eighteenth century afforded exactly the sort of background which was best suited to the development of his particular genius.

In all circles—political, intellectual, social, scientific, as well as artistic—there was a demand for greater freedom of thought and wider range of action, together with a strong swing away from the generally accepted modes of life and conduct. Rousseau became famous overnight by giving the answer he did to the question announced for competition by the Academy of Dijon, as to whether the progress of the sciences and arts had corrupted or purified society: "There is no doubt but that man was being ruined by the pressure of a corrupt society." Voltaire, through his nimble wit and unbounded energy, fought a one-man revolution against the superstition and corruption of the ruling and cultivated classes. Goethe and Schiller flaunted aloft their colorful banners proclaiming the right of man to complete intellectual and imaginative freedom. Everywhere there stirred a new conception of the status of the kingdom of man and fresh visions of the possibility of its progress.

Into the very midst of this teeming period was interjected a temperament ideally fitted by nature to take full advantage of its characteristics: Beethoven's life span comes at the very height of this revolution in thought and reaction against reason. And, although he died three years before Goethe published his famous statement claiming that it was an argument between the two poets which was responsible for defining the essential differences between Classicism and Romanticism, his work shows more clearly than does that of any other artist just what these differences were. By nature an individualist of the most pronounced type—"there is only one Beethoven," he was always to insist—he possessed other qualities which made him unique. Sincere almost to the point of crudity, he was absolutely disdainful of all shams and artificialities; his was a highly sensitive and passionate nature, but

CONTEMPORARY PENCIL
DRAWING OF BEETHOVEN
The sketch shows him as "he was
accustomed in his late years to
leap and run rather than walk."

it was coupled with an active and logical mind, one that was actuated by incessant intellectual curiosities;[11] the victim of some of the most cruel blows ever dealt to man by fate, he nevertheless believed in the necessity for human suffering and the value of spiritual courage.

Beethoven was linked by all his youthful training, as well as by his inherent intellectual sanity and balance, to the traditions of the past; yet his intense ardor and need for liberty of expression pushed him on into the freedom of that present in which he was fortunate enough to live. (It is hardly necessary to point out that such an intense individualism would have been impossible of expression, had Beethoven been born fifty years earlier.) He was forced by the circumstances of his career, by such facts as his never having married and his becoming

[11] Kuno Francke, in his book *The Social Forces in German Literature,* has this to say of Klopstock, Beethoven's favorite poet; in reading it, we realize well enough why the liberal-minded composer was so strongly attracted to, and influenced by, the Romantic poet:

"Klopstock was a true liberator. He was the first among modern German poets to draw his inspiration from the depth of a heart beating for all humanity. He was the first among them greater than his works. By putting the stamp of his own wonderful personality upon everything he did or wrote—by lifting himself, his friends, the objects of his love and veneration, into the sphere of extraordinary spiritual experiences—he raised the ideals of his age to a higher pitch; and although his memory has been dimmed through the greater men who came after him, the note struck by him still vibrates in the finest chords of the life of today."

completely deaf in the later years of his life, into an isolation from the world that made inevitable a constant and organic spiritual development such as has taken place in no other artist. And it was this spiritual development which was the motive for all his great music, an influence that finally led him to attempt expression of states of consciousness beyond the ordinary experiences of man.

Even in such matters as that of the freedom from patronage which the times made possible, Beethoven was fortunate. For he could never have lived under the rather humiliating circumstances which Haydn and Mozart took more or less for granted; his independent nature demanded economic and spiritual freedom, and these luckily were possible because of the spirit of the times. It seems as if never before or since have the characteristics of a composer fitted so well the background of the period in which he lived; nor has any period provided a composer with such stimulating surroundings in which to develop the peculiar characteristics of his genius. Whether we attempt to explain this in terms of daemonic control or resort to the more pedestrian but scientific recognition of the flowering of a temperament as due to accidents of circumstance and period, Beethoven's place in historical time must always seem a fortunate one. For he stood at the crossroads between the old and the new in music, on the great summit between the Classic and the Romantic, where he could look back reminiscently on the calm and pleasant spirit of the one, as well as forward into the exciting vistas of the other. Ideally fitted by nature for his place in the world, Beethoven took full advantage of all his endowments.

THREE-PERIOD BIOGRAPHIES

The three-period biographical treatment of great careers has long become commonplace—the division of lives into distinct periods of preparation, fulfillment, and retrospection. In the first of these, the biographer is wont to show the youthful enthusiasms of his subject and to describe him as one girding up his loins and preparing himself, by whatever means are suited to his purpose, for the race that is set before him. The second period occupies the mature years of discretion and is usually considered the most representative, the works produced in it bearing the truest characteristics of their creator's genius. The third is marked by the philosophic resignation so well phrased by St. Paul— "I have fought a good fight, I have finished my course, henceforth . . ."

Such a division is a natural enough one for Beethoven's life, but with this important distinction: with him there was no suggestion (as, for instance, with Haydn) of a retrospective awaiting of the end, his great work done. The compositions which came out of the last years of Beethoven's life—the five great string quartets and the *Ninth Symphony*—are the result of an inner development of such intensity as to make them the most spiritual creations of his whole life. In every sense of the word, we can say that Beethoven's was a career which was in process of flowering until its very end.

In following a three-period plan, these divisions are generally observed:

First Period, up to 1803

This comprises the first two symphonies, the first three piano concertos, well over half of his thirty-two piano sonatas including the *Pathétique* and *Moonlight* sonatas, the *Kreutzer* sonata for violin, and the six string quartets which comprise Op. 18. It was a period of gradual preparation, during which he completely assimilated the forms of Haydn and Mozart and learned not only how to follow in their footsteps but how to strike out on a bold path of his own. "I live in an atmosphere of music," he wrote at this time, "scarcely is one thing finished before I commence another. As I am writing now, I often do two or three things at a time."

Second Period, from 1803 to 1816

This includes symphonies 3–8, most of the remaining piano sonatas including the *Waldstein* and the *Hammerklavier*, the violin concerto, *Fidelio,* and the *Rasoumovsky Quartets* (Op. 59). It was a period of real maturity, marked by the appearance of an entirely new mood, first to be noticed in the so-called "Heiligenstadt Will," one in which the composer found out how to make his personal feelings serve as the spiritual stimulus for his music. During the first years of the new century, Beethoven was learning for himself what it meant to be a hero; instead of allowing his increasing infirmities to annihilate him, he realized he must face them: "I will take Fate by the throat—it shall not bend me completely to its will."

EROICA SYMPHONY

Certainly it is this idea of spiritual conflict which lies at the basis of the *Eroica Symphony* (Op. 55), the first outstanding work of his second period. Exteriorly, its generating force was the concept of Napoleon, whom Beethoven thought of as a savior of mankind and an exemplar of what the human will could accomplish; and he finished this great work and wrote his dedication of it with this concept in mind. It was only transitorily, however, that Napoleon satisfied his demands as a hero protagonist; Beethoven did not hesitate to erase his dedication upon hearing that Napoleon had proclaimed himself emperor: he exclaimed, "He is just like any other man, ready to tread the rights of man under his feet and serve nothing but his own ambition." *To the memory of a great man* was the dedication substituted for the one originally meant for the backsliding tyrant: the great man was Beethoven himself, although he may not consciously have meant it so. For the music is but a protraction, through a medium of which he was now complete master, of the spiritual experiences which he so pitifully tried to convey to his brothers in the "Heiligenstadt Will."

Sullivan, in his book *Beethoven, His Spiritual Development,* shows this more clearly than has anyone else: how Beethoven in the first movement of the *Eroica* expressed everything he knew of courage and defiance of fate; this is followed by the black despair of the second movement, cast in the form of a funeral march; in turn, there comes another indomitable rush of creative energy in the marvelous scherzo— "Oh! life is so beautiful—to live it a thousand times," he said at the moment; the last movement is based on a theme which we know, from appearances of it in other works, to have been associated in his mind with Prometheus, the Greek legendary hero who defied the gods and devoted his energies to benefiting humanity. The poetic idea, as well as the life cycle, was thus complete: first defiant courage, then utter and hopeless suffering and despair, this leading to a realization of the indestructibility of the creative force and the final liberation of Promethean strength which pushed him toward new heights of achievement. "Never before in music has so important, manifold, and completely coherent an experience been communicated."

In imbuing music with this personal, poetic meaning, Beethoven did not need to resort to any distorted structure; as a whole, this symphony keeps the traditional Haydn form, each movement being formulated in a manner that is well suited to its imaginative meaning. The first retains the conventional sonata structure, but the form is so shaped by the imagination as to make it almost a new entity, perhaps the greatest single movement in all symphonic literature. The idea of the funeral march was a novel one, but through it Beethoven was able to link his own personal suffering with the more objective human experience of death and the bitterness of the grave. The scherzo is an entirely new form, one based on the older minuet of Haydn but possessed of a spirit of such daemonic energy that we recognize it as the most characteristic of all the Beethoven innovations. By finally using a complex variation form,[12] Beethoven seems to suggest, according to Sullivan, the variety of achievement which was open to his tremendous energy, an explanation that for many satisfactorily disposes of the difficulties which critics have found in this movement.

In orchestrating this work, Beethoven did not hesitate to enlarge the bounds of his orchestral expression in order to develop fully the poetic significance of his ideas. There are many "irregularities" in his writing for the orchestra—he employs tone combinations with an ear to what they convey emotionally rather than to their sensuous appeal; he uses color as a means of expressing symbolically what he wants to say and employs a wide scale of dynamics in order to manifest his feelings. Here, as in everything else he did, he was absolutely individual, unlike anyone before or since.

CONCRETE THOUGHT EXPRESSED IN MUSIC

No one else has ever so definitely associated thought with music in the way that Beethoven did; for in his music he universalized conceptions awakened by the stirring events of the time—such concepts as liberty and heroism—as well as the more personal experiences of life.

---

[12] The variation form, which has been a favorite with composers and improvisators ever since the sixteenth century, when the writers of virginal music used it so freely, seems to have been especially attractive to Beethoven. His works, from the earliest period, are replete with variations of all sorts—melodic, rhythmic, and harmonic, especially the last. With him, it may be said that the variation became really a thematic development rather than the usual repetition in various guises of the same idea.

In addition to his separately published works in this form (some 29 all together, the most important of which are perhaps the 32 *Variations in C Minor* and the 33 *Variations on a Waltz Theme of Diabelli,* both for piano), a number of individual movements from various larger works are in variation form. Numbered among these are the slow movements of the Third, Fifth, Seventh, and Ninth symphonies; the last movements of the Third and Ninth contain also variations, as do the piano sonatas Op. 26, 14, No. 2, 109, and 111; the quartets in E and A major, Op. 124 and 132; and the *Kreutzer Sonata* for violin and piano, Op. 47.

MÖDLING

THE KALENBERG

THE LEOPOLDSBERG

Through terraces of vines, the way wound up the mountainside to the great green shady beechwood, which, in its cathedral-like stillness and silence, seemed endless. To Schubert's landscape belonged, too, the path on which Beethoven had composed his idyll, The Pastoral Symphony, and the vineyards, meadows, and valleys round the Kalenberg and the Schafberg, where the little dreamy wine villages in spring are pink with peach blossom.

Karl Kobald: Franz Schubert and His Times, *translated by Marshall*

Which is not to say that he wrote program music. It was a peculiar quality of his imagination which enabled it to fuse great thoughts with musical expression—to put into sonata, symphony, and string quartet such abstract ideas as those connected with liberty, equality, heroism, and struggle. And this expression is so definite that, if we possess any imagination at all, we can share Beethoven's mind. These concepts are so great as to revalue for us not only all music but all life, all emotion, and all thought, as Ernest Newman has said. "In every artist there is a touch of audacity without which genius is inconceivable," according to Goethe. Beethoven's audacity was in his attempt to combine concrete thought with abstract expression; he accomplished it so successfully as to enhance both, without transcending the natural limits of either. He stands as the supreme combination of the Classic and Romantic spirits, "dominating both periods, as a superior creator who increased the forces of the past by drawing on the still unreleased powers of the future," as Bekker has said in one of the best books yet written on Beethoven's life.

The works which he produced during these years of maturity are proof enough of the fact that this concept of heroism was constantly in his mind: the motto of the Third and Fifth symphonies, the Fourth and Fifth piano concertos, the *Rasoumovsky Quartets,* and the opera *Fidelio* might be set down as *per ardua ad victoriam.* There were relaxations, of course. Not even such a spirit as Beethoven's can live constantly on the heights, and we know from his letters that while he was busy with these great works, he refreshed himself by others of a different character. The Fourth and Sixth symphonies are lovely recuperative pauses after the heroic demands of the Third and the Fifth. He wrote some program music—such things as the *Battle Symphony* (Wellington's Victory), a work for which he had a strange liking, and which, when it was first produced, caused a greater sensation than all his other symphonies put together—and the *Leonore Overture No. 3.*[13] Besides, there was necessary a great deal of composition for the sake of keeping body and soul together, of "wandering about," as he himself put it, in the mountains, clefts, and valleys with a piece of music paper, writing down things for the sake of bread and money; "for to such a pitch have I brought it in this all-powerful land of the Phaecians that to gain time for a big work I must always first smear a lot for money." So we have an outpouring of lieder, variations, dances,

---

[13] Although written as an overture to the opera *Fidelio,* this is in reality a symphonic poem.

and so forth, works which can hardly be said to constitute any very important contribution either to musical literature or to their composer's reputation.

Third Period, from 1816 to 1827

From this period come the so-called "problematical works," the *Ninth Symphony,* the *Missa Solemnis,* and the last quartets, works which many of the admirers of the earlier Beethoven have not hesitated to describe as "difficult." The *Ninth Symphony,* which adds a chorus of voices to the usual symphonic instruments in order to express the grandeur of thought that was surging through its composer's mind, has nothing in it of human frailties or weaknesses. It is, in J. W. N. Sullivan's felicitous phrase, a revelation of existence as seen from the vantage point of a higher consciousness. In this music, Beethoven expressed the philosophy of his English contemporary, the poet-painter-mystic Blake: "He who sees the infinite in all things sees God. If the windows of perception were cleansed, everything would appear to man as it is, infinite. For man has closed himself up."

THE DIFFICULT QUARTETS

In writing of the *Ninth Symphony,* a contemporary asked: "On whom will the mission of surpassing these unattainable limits devolve?" The answer is, of course, on Beethoven himself. For in the five quartets written during the last years of his life, 1824–1826, he seems to be a man entirely loosed from the bondages of this world, one gazing into the mysterious reaches of eternity. Anyone listening to these quartets can but be bewildered; he is undergoing some sort of spiritual experience unlike any other he may have known, and yet the means for communicating this experience are so different that it is difficult to realize just what is going on. The physical aspect of such music as that of the *Quartet in C Sharp Minor,* Op. 131, for instance, is unlike anything else ever written. We may or we may not feel that this work contains the profoundest and most valuable experience ever conveyed by an artist; but the fact that Beethoven demands almost impossible interpretative clairvoyance from his players (and, one might add, from his listeners, too) does not make this music easy to apprehend. It may be music of another world, as some have claimed; but unfortunately, it has to be played in this. And the roughness of intonation which inevitably seems the result when this quartet is played can but offend the musical consciousness of many listeners, making this, and its brothers, "monsters of chamber music," as an unsympathetic critic has called them.

But we must listen beyond this. "I write for myself," said Beethoven at the time, and it is in a similar transfigured mood that we should try to listen. For here is

The prophetic soul of the wide world
Dreaming on things to come.

It was a dream which, from the first to the last part of his life, had been one of constant development; the very end seems to mark the highest stage of all—that of complete submission to his fate and of final resignation to whatever was to come.

THE EARLY

ROMANTIC COMPOSERS

AND THEIR PROBLEMS

Schubert, the Lyric Poet

A *lover of music and color, he beheld a vision of the very mind of music, and while within its trance, he composed a symphony upon the very soul of color. "Come to my earthly paradise," he seems to say, "to a land where the air is always balmy and the forest ever green, where life is but a pastime and music the only labor. Come to my golden land and feast upon beauty, where the richness of tones that thrilled you for a moment shall be your portion all the day long; and the dreams you once yearned to fold shall soothe you into forgetting that there is any such thing as passion or any such thing as pain."*

This is the land of Make-believe, eternally young and willfully fantastic with the spirit of romantic comedy. And in the last analysis, this land was the dream of this artist's short life—the goal of his aesthetic inspiration. He found for the strange, sweet spirit that had haunted his every conception a pictorial symbol as exquisite as the dream of life itself from which he never wished to wake. His single pervading spirit was made up of a mingling of a love of humanity, a poet's fondness of dreamy moods detached from an indifferent world, and an artist's passion for color, for light and shade. There are no jarring notes— the taste is always exquisite, the colors harmonious, the drawing arbitrary but emotionally expressive.

Other men before him had looked to the many-sided, many-colored life about them for their representations, but never with a thought of making light, color, and form symbolically expressive of personal emotions. When in looking at a beautiful thing our pleasure is for the first time stimulated less by our interest in the object itself than by our impression of its beauty, we have passed from the merely receptive to the appreciative stage of observation. Our eyes mean something to the world because the visible world means something to us. We have developed creative consciousness. We have begun to discriminate.

468

The significant thing about this man is that his influence seems to represent in the history of art just what the awakening to beauty means in the life of the individual. The romantic idyll which he introduced, and which served his lifelong purpose of self-expression, brought about a new epoch in music.

Duncan Phillips: *The Enchantment of Art*

Many a one who has gone through the exciting experience of learning that a thing which is beautiful can mean something to him because it has beauty, and not because it has some other connotations, will perhaps remember that it was the *Unfinished Symphony* or one of the *Impromptus* or a song of Schubert's which first awakened him to the fact that such beauty existed in music. In listening to one of these compositions, we are carried away not because of any such personal power as Beethoven was able to inject into his music, nor because of the clarity and ease of expression and the exquisite grace or tender sadness which is to be found in Mozart, nor because of such religious significance as we find in many of Bach's works. We love Schubert not only because, as was said above, the materials of art—melody (such as no one else has ever written), harmony, color, and form—are used as symbols expressive of personal emotion, but because they are used in such a way as to give concrete proof that pure beauty can exist in the tonal world and is worth cultivating for its own sake. It is a peculiar combination of deeply felt emotion and complete aesthetic satisfaction that makes Schubert's music unique.

A PARALLEL FROM ANOTHER ART

Lovers of this music may perhaps wonder why they have not come upon this apt description of its peculiar qualities and of the place of its composer in music history. The reason for this is that the author, Duncan Phillips, was writing, not about Schubert, but about an artist who lived some three hundred years before him and who worked in an entirely different medium—Giorgione of Castelfranco, one of the great painters of the Renaissance. We have quoted almost verbatim, the only words changed being those relating to the artist's name and the character of his art. The great similarity in the characteristics of these two men living so far apart in point of time has been commented upon before; but we have never seen such convincing proof of it as is given in Mr. Phillips's article as he goes on to say:

Before him . . . the oil medium had been introduced, and the scenes of scriptural story, the formulas of the faith, the saintliness of the saints, had

THE PASTORAL SYMPHONY   by Giorgione (about 1508-1510)

been depicted in colored pictures for the instruction of the people and the glory of the Popes. Before him in the works of such inspired dreamers and such masters of light and shade and line as Da Vinci and Botticelli, the principles of pictorial art had been molded. But Giorgione was the first not merely to revive the aesthetic spirit of the ancient Greeks, who had sought beauty for its own sake, but also to understand that the glorious possibility of art was to devote itself to an intensely personal expression. He aspired to no vast abstract beauty, but to detect, by means of the individual consciousness, the myriad concrete proofs that the world is beautiful; that there is beauty in the variable expression of the human face, in the trees and hills of home, in the lights of morning and the shadows of afternoon, in color and character, in music and old memories, in the evanescent moods of every passing hour.

All this, too, may be paraphrased so as to apply to Schubert. Before him, too, the principles and expressive mediums of his art had been perfected and great works of abstract beauty and tremendous scope had been wrought. But, in listening to most of his music, we are conscious not only that he was a composer aware of the possibilities of an art devoted to an intensely personal expression, but also that he was content that this expression should offer musical proofs of the beauty which is in the world. This beauty lies in the naïve simplicity of his utterance, the magic turning of his melodies, the glowing shifts of his tone colors, the graceful plasticity of his orchestration. He is as different from his great predecessors as Giorgione was from his: his music is that of a simple, kindly, loving man who knew little of this world other than that it was beautiful (and that because it was beautiful, there was much sadness in it), and who was able to sing this beauty.

Looking at such pictures as Giorgione's *The Tempest* or *The Pastoral Symphony* gives us the same sort of experience as we get in listening to the *Unfinished Symphony:* both artists were lyricists, the one painting his lyrics, the other drawing them from the depths of some instrument; both held the gift of easy persuasion, as a flower holds its perfume and with the same lack of concern as to impulse; both showed the most exquisite feeling in their expression, but neither had any need for story or program for his works; both knew how to organize materials without making us conscious of the process.

A MISAPPREHENDED COMPOSER

Because of the peculiar character of his music, Schubert has been the victim of misunderstanding. Through the misguided adulations of his sincere admirers, he has come down to us a pathetically oversentimentalized figure, completely baffled by the world and supremely unhappy in his life. The first of his biographers, Sir George Grove, pictured him as a man "born in the lowest ranks and moving in the society of his own class," with little cultural background, interested in nothing but his carefree, Bohemian existence. He described him as a provincial, untaught, intuitive genius who prodigally wasted his divine melodies on the desert air of *Biedermeier*[1] Vienna and died, poverty-stricken, exhausted by his life of neglect and want, just as he was about to receive for the first time proper academic instruction in music. And this general pattern has been followed by most writers since; the real facts place this greatest Romanticist in music in a different light.

A natural-born melodist, Schubert became the center of a group of young Viennese musical and literary enthusiasts, who, working hard at their art by day—the great mass of music which Schubert wrote during eleven years is hardly believable—met at different houses and on various country excursions for fun as well as for serious discussion. It was out of such an atmosphere that his music was born. Although he was by no means unknown or neglected in his native city, he never

[1] A term popularly used in Vienna to characterize the homely, bourgeois spirit.

received much publicity or actual money for his compositions; nevertheless, he kept right on composing, setting an extremely high standard for himself, always striving to equal, without in any sense copying, the work of his ideal, Beethoven. The works of his last year show a change of heart, however: the *C Major Quintet,* the *C Major Symphony,* the *Schwanengesang,* the last three piano sonatas—all have an added note of poignancy to them, although we can hardly think of their composer as being discontented, for any man possessed of such an inexhaustible flow of music which welled up out of his consciousness as freely as a spring of water out of the earth could not be really unhappy. There is no discrepancy between his life and his music; both possessed an indescribable sense of well-being, a simple sweetness, as well as a deep inwardness, which brings all these other qualities into relief.

SCHUBERT'S QUALITIES

It would be an injustice to think of this composer as being only a superb melodist. His genius as a harmonist (chiefly in the matter of modulations, where he achieved color and charm that have never been equaled) and as an orchestrater of unusual ability (especially when we consider the fact that he never had a chance to try out his effects on the orchestra) have been somewhat overshadowed by his superb lyricism. In the best of his work, his form is indissolubly linked with the material; yet in nearly everything he did there is a certain amount of diffuseness, due perhaps to his habit of rarely reshaping his ideas. But no matter how much he lapses, there is always present in his important music a certain sublimity, as Tovey has said, which marks it out from anything else ever written.

His masterpieces are, without question, his more than six hundred songs;[2] his two great symphonies (the *Symphony in B Minor* and the

---

[2] Schubert's pre-eminence in this form is so marked that we are inclined to forget his great contemporary Carl Loewe (1796-1869), who created a new genre in song, the so-called *ballad,* a vividly descriptive dramatic work usually set to a historical text. Outstanding examples of these are Loewe's *Edward, Archibald Douglas,* and *Prinz Eugen.* Although not so well known as Schubert's setting, Loewe's *Erlkönig* is magnificent.

Because Schubert is usually spoken of as the first great writer of art songs it must not be thought that he invented the form. Other German composers who wrote self-contained songs were Hassler, Bach, Gluck, Mozart, Beethoven, and Weber; but none of these gave more than momentary attention to the lied.

The boy Schubert was strongly influenced by some of his immediate predecessors and older contemporaries, notably by Carl Friedrich Zelter (1758–1832), a well-known Berlin musician of the time; by Johann Rudolf Zumsteeg (1760–1802), whose narrative and dramatic ballads were especially admired by the young composer; and by Johann Friedrich Reichardt (1752–1814), court conductor of Frederick the Great.

SCHUBERT IN THE COM-
PANY OF HIS FRIENDS IN
GRINZING In the background
of this sketch by Schubert's
friend, Schwind, can be seen the
Kalenberg and the Leopoldsberg.

Symphony in C Major); a few piano sonatas, notably the three written in 1828 (in C minor, A, and B flat); the *Death and the Maiden
Quartet;* the two trios for piano, cello, and violin, Op. 99 and 100; the
string quintets, Op. 114 (*Forellen*), with double bass and piano; and
Op. 163, with two cellos. On a somewhat lower plane, but lovely and
fresh and characteristic, are the *Moments Musicals,* the *Waltzes,* the
lyric piano pieces and the incidental music to *Rosamunde.* In addition,
there are such *pièces d'occasion* as the Masses, sacred and secular
choruses, male-voice music, four-hand piano pieces, etc.

And, having these, we should be content. On his death, Schubert
was mourned as having left behind him a "rich possession, but even
fairer hopes." One of his most ardent admirers calls his early death in
1828, at the very moment when his genius arrived at full maturity, the
"direst calamity which has yet befallen the world of music." Who
knows? Perhaps a wise Providence removed this gloriously inspired
naïve musician from the field of his labors while his native freshness
was still unimpaired. We can but look with trepidation on the fact
that, at the time of his death, this greatest of all lyricists, this Giorgione
of music, showed curious, unconscious strivings towards ends which

might well have proved to be beyond his reach. Or that, only a few months before he died, he had made arrangements to study with a professor of counterpoint—he, the composer of some of the most spontaneously conceived contrapuntal effects in all music!

At any rate, we are more fortunate in one way than he: we have the constant opportunity of hearing the glorious heritage which he left behind. It was not until long after his death that his compositions began to be widely played; as George Eliot put it,

Schubert, too, wrote for silence; half his work
Lay like a frozen Rhine till summer came
And warmed the grass above him.

But she hastened to add,

even so,
His music lives now with a mighty youth.

Mendelssohn and Schumann

When we want to be made unhappy we can turn
to others. It is well in these agitated modern days to be
able to point to one perfectly balanced nature . . . at
once manly and refined, clever and pure, brilliant and
solid. For the enjoyment of such shining heights of
goodness we may well forgo for once the depths of
misery and sorrow.

Sir George Grove on Mendelssohn

And so it is throughout human life—the goal we
have attained is no longer a goal, and we yearn and
strive and aim ever higher and higher, until the eyes
close in death and the storm-tossed body and soul lie
slumbering in the grave.

Schumann to his mother, 1828

A LUXURIANT DECADE

There was something essentially romantic about the way in which nature, at the beginning of the nineteenth century, provided composers to carry on after the deaths of Beethoven and Schubert; for no less than seven outstanding men were born between the years of 1803 and 1813. Of these, two became outstanding leaders in the development of certain phases of the Romantic Movement—Berlioz and Liszt; two—Schumann and Mendelssohn—were ardent heralds of its poetic-musical ideals; one—Chopin—developed into the greatest composer of piano music in the history of the art; the sixth—Wagner—whose development of opera into the music drama marked the culmination of the whole Romantic Movement, turned out to be one of the great figures of the world; and Verdi, the last, paralleled in Italian dramatic art the triumphant success of Wagner in Germany.

MENDELSSOHN AND SCHUMANN

Antipodal in most respects, Mendelssohn and Schumann may nevertheless be considered together. Both were North Germans, the one born in Hamburg in 1809, the son of a wealthy banker; the other born in 1810, into a cultivated, literary family of Saxony. Mendelssohn's first name was Felix, a good choice for one who seems to have known little but happiness in his life; rich, versatile in the best sense of the word (for he could paint, sketch, swim, write, and conduct almost as easily as he could compose), he matured early, passing easily from one triumph to another and becoming, in the latter years of his life, the outstanding musical figure of his day. Robert Schumann, on the other hand, decided on music as a career only after long struggle and grave doubts, and acquired his technical equipment (never really adequate) for composing only after years of difficult experiment. A man of real gifts and ardent temperament, he was a leader in various fields of activity, bringing his career to an untimely close by placing too great a strain on his emotional and creative powers. But his struggling gave him a great advantage over his more facile and objective contemporary. Mendelssohn had no need for curbing or restraining himself, and so his music is as lacking in conflict and deep feeling as was his life.

FELIX THE HAPPY

The favored son of a cultured family able to indulge his every wish, Mendelssohn was given the proper training and stimulation for the development of his precocious talent. He made his debut as a pianist when he was nine years old and produced during his eleventh year

MENDELSSOHN

over fifty compositions of various types. He achieved perfection in the orchestral overture which he wrote for a performance of Shakespeare's *A Midsummer Night's Dream* when he was seventeen, and this scurrying, elfin work remains, in many ways, the best thing he ever did. In his twentieth year, he conducted a performance of Bach's *St. Matthew Passion,* which was probably the most notable event in his career; for it gave an initial impulse to the study of the music of that forgotten master, the effects of which are still manifest. A number of journeys followed, to England (many of them), where he became a determining factor in the musical life of that country, to all parts of Germany, to Scotland, to Italy, to Austria. In 1835, he was called to direct the famous Leipzig Gewandhaus Orchestra and became the first of the great virtuoso orchestral conductors. This career was likewise of epoch-making importance, for, in infusing new life into a rather mediocre orchestra, he established the modern traditions of orchestral playing and interpretation.

During all these activities he devoted much time to writing music, his interest covering every field of composition. He finished four symphonies, of which the best is certainly *The Italian;* a number of concert overtures—if one would know this composer at his glowing, romantic height, let him listen to the *Fingal's Cave* overture; a violin concerto that has become the classic of its genre; a great deal of chamber music, of which the scherzos are inimitable and could have been written by no one else; an enormous amount of piano music, most of which has gone into discard, except the *Songs without Words,* short works having neat craftsmanship if little individuality; and a great deal of church and oratorio music, notably *St. Paul* and *Elijah,* most of it unheard today.

In all this music, there are qualities which correspond to those we commonly label Victorian. A prolongation of the rather inhibiting nineteenth-century elegance, it is refined, clear-cut, carefully formed, more or less superficial, always under gentlemanly control. But it lacks, unfortunately, any deep conviction or moving quality. Mendelssohn was a great lover of Handel and Bach, and his music has a certain natural classic restraint and careful balance; but he was at his best when embodying his romantic tendencies for gentle nature painting and tenderly expressed longing. It may be said that his outstanding characteristic was his marvelous technical proficiency. His idiom, while not great, was individual and beautifully clear, but it was submerged in the violent torrents which came later. It is not surprising, in view of the constant rotations of fashions in taste, that Mendelssohn's music, like other expressions of the Victorian spirit, is once again attracting interest.

SCHUMANN, THE STRIVING ROMANTIC

In a study of the Romantic Movement, the French aesthetician Basch has made the following striking statement:

> *Romanticism minted new values and raised a hero on its buckler. The Romantic hero, instead of treading life's path with the assured step of the classic hero, advances along it, groping his way, faltering, and staggering. Between himself and reality he sees an abyss which he is neither capable nor desirous of filling. With all his energies reinforced by the desperate consciousness of the uselessness of his effort, he strives toward those heights whose attainment has been forbidden, toward an infinity, a point beyond, which, owing to a contradiction he does not ignore, yet against which he cannot defend himself, he avidly seeks in the finite world here below. Hence, in his case, throughout his spiritual organism, there is a fundamental disharmony, a continuous dissonance which his morbid pride insists is superior to banal harmonies and flat consonances. Hence, in his whole physical constitution, there is a morbid fracture, yet one which he carries not as a blemish, but as a distinction and a pre-excellence.*

Quoted by Julien Tiersot in "Music and the Centenary of Romanticism"

M. Basch sees in Robert Schumann (1810–1856) the very incarnation of this spirit of Romanticism. He says that in order to understand him properly we must realize that it is his interior life which explains both the form and the content of his music. There is a feeling of "romantic disharmony," of "continuous dissonance" running all through Schumann's life like a leitmotiv, and all his music was born of it.

In almost every case, this disharmony of spirit proved fatal to continued success in these various branches of composition. His first attempts were the most spontaneous. Nothing he ever did surpassed his early piano things, the *Papillons* or the *Fantasiestücke,* the *Carnaval* or the *Kinderscenen;* the songs in the first two volumes, set to the romantic utterances of Heine and Eichendorff; the first and most spontaneous of his four symphonies, expressing the springtide happiness of his early marriage;[3] or his only successful great choral work, *Das Paradies und die Peri.* In all these we find exuberant and rapturous utterance, an alternation of minute images, quick changes of mood, a hovering between concentrated passion and lovely lyricism, overseriousness and pointed humor, mysterious poetic fantasy and graceful, obvious charm. The music is the counterpart, we are perfectly aware, of Jean Paul's fantastic poetry and Hoffmann's imaginative fancy; but, although it is clothed in a richly expressive and highly wrought style, there is in it a looseness of construction, a struggling toward an infinity beyond the composer's reach, that makes us painfully cognizant of its technical shortcomings.

Schumann as a creator of miniatures (the only successful wholes he ever composed are his songs and short piano numbers) did not possess the genius to pattern these units into consistently developed large works. His long compositions are mosaics made up of a number of closely set miniatures rather than organically wrought edifices; and so

[3] In writing to a composer who was about to perform this symphony, Schumann said: "Could you infuse into your orchestra in the performance a sort of longing for the spring, which I had chiefly in mind when I wrote in February, 1841? The first entrance of trumpets, this I would like to have sounded as though it were from high above, like unto a call to awakening; and then I should like reading between the lines, in the rest of the Introduction, how everywhere it begins to grow green, how a butterfly takes wing, and, in the Allegro, how little by little all things come about that in any way belong to spring. True, these are fantastic thoughts, which came to me after my work was finished; only, I tell you this about the Finale, that I thought of it as the good-by of spring."

Nothing has ever stated the Romanticist's approach to music more clearly or more revealingly than this letter.

CLARA AND ROBERT SCHUMANN

there is a great deal of repetition and monotony, of whimsical change and apparent lack of direction. His most regretful mannerism is a devotion to, and persistent use of, rhythmic patterns; he liked square-cut, even-measure phrases which often, after taking off hopefully, flop down to earth again with maddening regularity.[4] He was never able to master the mysteries of orchestration; tragedy was latent in this element of his technical equipment from the very start, Tovey assures us. And his symphonic works have to be most carefully treated to make them sound at all plausible. Somehow we cannot help wishing that the good qualities of these two men could have been blended—Mendelssohn's exquisite instinct for form and orchestration with Schumann's depth of feeling and poetic imagery. Then—but what is the use of imagining?

Yet, no one in his right mind, musically speaking, would be willing to dispense with Schumann's romantic, impetuous music; and, if his compositions were somehow to be removed from the repertoire of the pianists, their lot would indeed be desperate! He was able to introduce a breath of fresh air into an atmosphere which had threatened to become static. His harmonic originality, encouraged by his intimate sympathy with Chopin's pianistic innovations, and his melodic intensity both deserve special mention in any study of the music of this

[4] To be sure, Schumann often atones for these monotonous phrases by giving them an unusually effective harmonic development; but we can never get completely away from the wish that he had not become so tightly bound rhythmically.

period. In some respects, Schumann was a conservative pedant, as his writings[5] show only too well; in others, he was surprisingly liberal in his opinions. "Nothing is wrong which sounds right," he is supposed to have said; and, although he was not able to persuade himself that Wagner's music ever could sound right, he did not hesitate to introduce refreshing harmonies and even structural innovations into his writing.

Witness, for example, his fine *A Minor Piano Concerto,* which remains one of the great works in this particular form. It shows Schumann in his very best estate—warm, ardent, poetic, at times "dreaming with the pedal down," at times fiery with imaginative zeal; yet it is excellently constructed and stands as one of Romanticism's best monuments.

The same factor of essential disharmony continued to manifest itself during the later years of Schumann's life. After his outburst of concentrated composing, he tried conservatory teaching, concert tours with his wife (who was a famous pianist), giving private lessons, directing singing and orchestral societies; in none of these activities was he outstandingly successful. Yet he kept on with the struggle toward that infinity from which, as Basch says, he could not defend himself, writing a great deal of music and occasionally equaling his early power (for example, in the superb piano quintet and the piano concerto). The end was inevitable; the morbid fracture which Basch feels in the physical constitution of the typical Romanticist became in Schumann's case acute. In 1854, the mental disorder which had been developing for many years reached a climax, and he spent his last years in an insane asylum, completely mad.

It is but natural that, in as essentially a realistic age as ours, Schumann's subjective Romanticism should not be fully appreciated or his originality and significance realized. We can but feel in these days of reappraisal of the Romantic Movement that he is an overrated composer; but there is no need for indulging in that practice which the English picturesquely describe as "throwing out the baby with the bath water." Music, especially piano music, would be a great deal poorer without Schumann's picturesque and fervid utterances; and just because he was, perhaps, overzealous in his proclaiming of the poetic-musical ideals of his era is no reason why we should forswear the genuine enjoyment he can give us.

[5] Collected in two volumes, *Music and Musicians: Essays and Criticisms;* translated, edited, and annotated by Fanny R. Ritter. New York: Schuberth, 1877.

Berlioz the Unpredictable

*With all his efforts to go stark
mad, he never once succeeds.*

Mendelssohn

A SUPERSENSITIVE ROMANTIC

Théophile Gautier, the poet, novelist, raconteur, and journalist whose life span (1811-1875) coincided generally with that of the Romantic Movement in France, in his *Histoire du romantisme* passes in review all the contemporary poets, painters, pundits, historians, and so on, and comes to the conclusion that the spirit of the whole movement was incarnated in a trio consisting of a poet, a painter, and a musician—Victor Hugo, Eugène Delacroix, and Hector Berlioz.

Anyone reading the remarkable autobiography left behind by Berlioz[6] must come to the conclusion that, if an artist ever reflected perfectly the conditions of the epoch in which he lived, he was that artist. Born in 1803 in a little village near Grenoble, in the south of France, he was a typical child of his age, an age described by one of its own geniuses as an "ardent generation, pale, nervous, conceived by restless mothers in the intervals between battles—of exalted, suffering souls, enrapt in morbid dreams, whose heads were bowed in tears." His youth was passed in a world which was largely in French hands; for the forces of the French Revolution, embodied in the person of Napoleon, covered at that time all Europe from Russia to Spain. Berlioz grew up in an atmosphere of intoxicating struggle, continuous, straining warfare, cruel triumph, and utter, final disaster. No wonder the sensitive lad, wandering in the sunny fields of his native Dauphiné, his mind extremely receptive to early impressions, was given to indulging in solitary reveries or to seeking comfort in the study of Latin poets or the contemporary Romantics. A precocious, high-strung, overimaginative individual, he exhibited at an early age all the characteristics for which he later became famous: he fell so violently in love with a girl seven years

[6] The accuracy of this work is not to be trusted, for Berlioz had the artistic instinct for lying which makes a good storyteller. Tovey says that, as for accepting any of his own statements about his life or his works, one would be wiser to "hang a dog on the evidence of Benvenuto Cellini, supported by Captain Gulliver and Cyrano de Bergerac!"

his senior that the passion never left him all the rest of his life, although he did not see her again until the loneliness of old age forced him to seek her out and engage in correspondence so violent as to frighten her and force her to the conviction that he must be insane!

HIS EARLY CAREER IN PARIS

Berlioz showed his individuality in his early student days in Paris, where he had been sent by his father, a country doctor, to study medicine. After a short experience in the dissecting rooms of the medical school, the young student announced definitely that he was through with medicine for good and that music was to be his profession. The reasons for his choice seem to have been no more than a rather scanty knowledge of harmony and an ability to play the flageolet and the guitar! His parents threatened to cut off his income, but they could not shake his determination. Settling down in Paris, he took up his musical studies with frantic enthusiasm, quarreling constantly with his teachers, railing against all academic methods of instruction, violently inimical to the "soulless Italian music" with which he felt himself surrounded. He soaked himself in the works of Shakespeare, a passion which was inflamed by his falling in love with an actress who played the parts of Ophelia and Juliet; he read Goethe's *Faust* and took it for his inspiration; and, above all, he discovered the symphonies of Beethoven, the form of which showed him the path he must follow as he started on his own adventurous career.

A contemporary gives this picture of him at this period in his life: "a young man trembling with passion, and a head of hair—such a head of hair! It looked like an immense umbrella, projecting like a movable awning over the beak of a bird of prey. It was both comical and diabolical at the same time, something like the edge of a cliff, giving one vertigo."

THE FANTASTIC SYMPHONY

Maintaining himself by the sheer nimbleness of his wits and showing a courage that can only be called heroic, Berlioz struggled to secure the necessary technique for expressing the wild thoughts and emotions which were surging through him. His first essay at composition was a Mass with orchestral accompaniment, performed at the Church of St. Roch in 1825. This proved so unintelligible, both to executants and

HECTOR BERLIOZ

hearers, that he was laughed at for years in Paris. Nothing daunted, he kept on, writing, out of the intensity and misery of his unrequited passion for the Shakespearean actress (who later yielded and became his wife), a *Symphonie fantastique,* an audacious piece of program music in five movements, to which he appended the following statement as to its meaning:

A young musician of unhealthy nature and endowed with vivid imagination [he knew himself, certainly] has poisoned himself with opium in a paroxysm of lovesick despair. The narcotic dose he had taken was too weak to cause death, but it has thrown him into a long sleep accompanied by the most extraordinary visions. In this condition his sensations, his feelings, and his memory find utterance in his sick brain in the form of musical imagery. Even the Beloved One takes the form of a melody in his mind, like a fixed idea which is ever returning and which he hears everywhere.

THE HEIGHT OF HIS CAREER

In the year in which this was first performed, 1830, fortune smiled on Berlioz to the extent of his having a cantata accepted by the jury appointed to award the *Prix de Rome*. This gave him an opportunity to study and work in Italy for three years; eighteen months was all he could stand, however, and in 1832 he was again in Paris, adding to his labors as composer those of a music critic, the latter made necessary through his marriage in 1833. He did brilliant journalistic work for years on several of the Paris papers and wrote, in addition, such works as the symphonies *Harold en Italie*, *Roméo et Juliette*, and the *Carnaval romain* overture, all of which were well received by the public. This was the height of his career; after 1840 his health became impaired through overwork and emotional exhaustion, and he seemed no longer capable of the flights of genius contained in his earlier compositions. (That popular and fantastic work, *La damnation de Faust*, may be excepted.) His operas *Benvenuto Cellini*, *Beatrice et Bénédict*, and *Les Troyens* seemed to be only successes *d'estime*, although the latter brought him in enough cash to enable him, in 1864, to resign his position as newspaper critic, with the following characteristic outburst:

At last, after thirty years' bondage, I am free! No more feuilletons to write, no more commonplaces to excuse, no more mediocrities to praise, no more indignation to suppress; no more lies, no more comedies, no more mean compromises. I am free! I never need again set foot in a lyric theater, nor speak of nor listen to, nor even laugh at, the queer medley of music produced there. Gloria in excelsis Deo, et in terra pax hominibus bonae voluntatis!

Concert tours in England, Austria, Germany, and Russia brought him a certain amount of material and artistic success. For some reason or other, perhaps because of his fiery temperament, he seemed to be able to achieve greater recognition and better understanding abroad than he did at home. The French never gave him the honor he coveted, a professorship in the *Conservatoire*, although they elected him a member of the *Académie* and gave him the cross of the Legion of Honor. The evening of his life was darkened by the failure of *Les Troyens*,[7] and he spent his last few years wandering about Europe, a broken, disillusioned, disappointed man. He died on March 9, 1869. Few persons, Sitwell observes, can have been more pleased with oblivion.

At the very beginning of his career, Berlioz proudly announced that he had "taken up music at the point where Beethoven left it"; the interesting thing for the student of music history is that, in doing so, he evolved an entirely new type of expression—what later came to be

[7] Few have opportunity for hearing such a work these days; but Tovey, after hearing a concert performance of it, proclaims *Les Troyens* one of the "most gigantic and convincing masterpieces of music drama."

A CARICATURE
OF BERLIOZ IN
1846

known as the *symphonic poem,* created an entirely new set of orchestral sonorities, and established a new technique in writing for the orchestral instruments, which has remained the standard ever since. It is not always easy to realize these things as we listen to such a work as the *Symphonie fantastique,* for there is so much in it that seems tentative and awkward to ears which have grown accustomed to the later music it made possible—the works of Wagner, Strauss, Stravinsky, and so forth. But, if we keep in mind the fact that Berlioz wrote his masterpiece only seven years after Beethoven composed his last symphony, the position of this work in the history of music will be evident enough.

TALENT, TECHNIQUE, AND GENIUS

Berlioz was a relentless cultivator of program music, the first composer to devote his careful attention to this style of writing; and his intense

Romanticism often led him into impossible situations. He seems at his best in the expression of the macabre, the grotesque, or the tremendous —tempers not well adapted to the production of music. It is difficult to evaluate properly such a thing as his *Requiem,* a work which he felt was one of his best, a Romantic evocation of the terrors of the Judgment Day, requiring a tremendous chorus, five orchestras with groups of trumpets stationed to the north, east, south, and west in order to sound out the fearful melody that was to bring the dead from their tombs.

In order to tie together the various incidents of his program symphonies, Berlioz adopted what he called an *idée fixe,* or central theme which runs through all the sections, an idea which contained the germ of the leading-motive idea developed later by Wagner. Such a device, however, had been employed by earlier composers. Berlioz wrote his *Roméo et Juliette* symphony in order that he might depict feelings other than his own, suggesting, by means of characteristic themes, the actions of the characters and even their dialogue. Out of this there came Wagner's symphonic dramas, a fact which the latter himself acknowledged when he dedicated the score of *Tristan und Isolde* to the "great and dear composer of *Roméo et Juliette,* by the grateful composer of *Tristan und Isolde.*" In order to clarify and systematize the results which he obtained in his studies in orchestration, Berlioz wrote his famous *Traité d'instrumentation,* a book which has long held its place as the masterwork of its kind, a work from which his successors learned many of their secrets.

For these innovations and inventions, Berlioz will be remembered. But it is questionable that he will ever be a popular composer in the sense that Beethoven is. Although Berlioz's ideas are fertile enough, he never seems to coordinate them or bring them to their conclusion in a way that would make them fully communicable. For most listeners his melodies seem fragmentary and his harmonies often forced. The torrent of his imagination too often blocks the way to his technical achievement, with the result that his music frequently sounds bizarre and eccentric, in spite of its highly original moments. The very intensity of his attitude towards his art makes the average listener distrust him; and so, in spite of earnest and able propagandists who do not hesitate to claim Berlioz as one of the greatest composers, misunderstood and neglected, it is probable that he will never be widely popular; and that Grillparzer's contemporary description of him as "genius without talent" will seem apt for years to come.

Chopin and Piano Music

*For us Polish musicians Chopin is an everlasting
reality, an active power which exercises direct and spontaneous influence on the evolution of Polish music. It
is evident that in all our musical past it is the work of
Chopin which has the incontestable Polish style in the
deepest and noblest meaning of the word. Under this
aspect Chopin represents for us not only the symbol of
the genuine greatness of Polish music, but, even more
than that, he remains our master, who, by his wonderful art, solved the essential problem of every art—
how to attain in one's work the perfect expression of a
profoundly and universally human dignity, without
sacrificing one's innate traits and national originality.*

Szymanowski in the article on him in *The International
Cyclopedia of Music and Musicians*

THE SUPREME MASTER
OF THE SMALL FORM
Because of the
rather exterior events of his life, Frederic Chopin (1810–1849) has usually been put down as a typical *homme du monde* of the Romantic era:
born in Poland, the son of a native Polish woman and a Frenchman living
in Warsaw, he spent most of his short life in Paris. Here he came into
close contact with the brilliant social life of the French capital, as well
as with its great artists—Liszt, Meyerbeer, Bellini, Balzac, Heine,
Victor Hugo, and, especially, with Mme. Aurore Dudevant, who
under the pseudonym of George Sand was at that time creating a considerable stir with her Romantic novels. His association with these
artists, especially his characteristically Romantic affair with Sand, gave
him an intimate contact with the Romantic Movement in France, although he never came so definitely under its spell as did Liszt and
Berlioz, for his was essentially a lyric gift, and the pictorial, dramatic
approach to music, so common with other Romantic composers, was
entirely foreign and incomprehensible to him.

It is rather difficult to reconcile his rather prosaic life with the quality
of Chopin's output and its predominantly *spirituel*, rather melancholy
character. The only explanation, perhaps, is that the artist does not
need, in order to evoke moods, to experience them in the immediate

CHOPIN (painting by Delacroix)

present of real life. Much of his pleasure in his work comes from solving the problems of style, of mood evocation, of craftsmanship in structure. Chopin found his world of satisfaction in expressing himself mostly in small forms and on one instrument. He wrote chiefly one-movement, one-idea'd piano pieces, to which he gave the names waltzes, mazurkas, études, impromptus, and so forth, according to their style and mood. In them he created a new world of technique and expression. Rarely are there any clues as to their meaning; they are simply intense, concentrated, lyric outpourings in terms ideally suited to the instrument for which they were written. In very little was he indebted to others: slightly, to Italian lyricism in opera; and, as to the form of the *Nocturne,* to the brilliant Irish pupil of Clementi, whom we have already mentioned, John Field, who seems to have originated this type of essentially Romantic mood-piece. Chopin's music, as someone has said, breathes the piano spirit, incarnates the piano's soul, revels in the tone peculiar to the instrument, even turning its essential handicap—a lack of real sustaining power—to its own account, thereby establishing a style which has no tonal or technical resemblance to the orchestral piano effects of Beethoven or Liszt.

The fact that his natural tendencies led Chopin to choose the small, lyric forms for his expression does not mean that the results he achieved are to be thought of as inferior. Within the limits he chose, his music is highly organized, even though many of his pieces, in their broad outline, work out as simple three-part sectioned form (A-B-A). But there is more to them than this—a rhythmic organization of perfection, harmonic originality that has hardly been surpassed and yet is never eccentric, and the exploration in pure beauty of every pianistic resource, without a trace of the commonplaceness, vulgarity, or overemphasis which so often mars the works of his contemporaries. Liszt, a generous admirer of other men's art, said that Chopin was "imperious, fantastic, and impulsive," and that he was himself only when he had "cut adrift from all bondage and floated on his own wild will, swayed by the ever-undulating influences of his own mobile nature."

It is difficult for us today, more than a century after Chopin first used his "bewildering harmonies," to realize how novel they were at the time. Even his earliest works bear marks of great harmonic distinction and give us a sense of hearing something entirely new and fresh. For example, nothing like the opening measures of his Op. 6, No. 1 had been written before. He intermingled dissonances and consonances in a startling fashion and often evolved the most entrancing effects by decorating simple triads and seventh chords, the added tones throwing a veil of dissonance over the fundamental harmonies. In the hundred years since its invention, the piano of Chopin's time, as we have already seen, had been developed by the various European makers into a highly expressive medium of interpretation. By studying the effects made possible by the use of the new "damper pedal,"[8] Chopin became aware of the beauties afforded by introducing the upper overtones against a resonant fundamental chord. This led to even more complex and colorful harmonies, which, however, he managed in such a way as not to disrupt the melodic outline and essential euphony of the whole. Many modern listeners feel that Chopin's outstanding contribution to music was this unique and original harmonic construction; it is certain that it influenced such composers as Schumann, Liszt, Wagner, and Debussy.

A POET OF THE PIANO

Contemporary descriptions of Chopin's appearance give the exact picture which we might expect from much of his music: an aristocratic

---

[8] Liszt is authority for the statement that no master of the piano indicated the use of this device as frequently as did Chopin.

bearing and manner, clear-cut features, a high forehead, a thin, slight form—an individual bordering dangerously on the *genre précieux*. His playing was evidently flawlessly accurate and exceedingly brilliant, but very small-scaled tonally; he made a great deal of use of the "peculiar yieldingness in tempo" that is called *rubato*, a characteristic which fits his music well. Over everything there breathed a spirit of restless melancholy, derived from the prevalent *mal du siècle* and intensified by the background of depression that was prevalent in his native country, crushed under the overwhelming tyranny of Russia.

This explains the sudden outbursts of terrific power and fiery mettle which occur in some of Chopin's works—the polonaises, for instance; the deep color and invigorating character of the mazurkas; the thunder and surge of such a work as the *Ballade in G Minor;* and the deep-seated, brooding melancholy of the *Funeral March* and the enigmatic autumnal flight as of leaves in the night wind to be found in the last movement of the *Sonata in B Flat Minor*. But always in these, as in Chopin's other works, there is logic—the perfect shaping of formal means to expressive ends, whether he is enjoying the contrasting of moods as in the nocturnes, solving a problem of style as in the *Barcarolle,* or displaying a series of brief poetic panoramas of tone in the preludes.

It has become so customary to think of Chopin as a composer of small forms that we are apt to neglect his great mastery of the principles of formal organization. This is to be seen in countless of the smaller works, but it is particularly evident in the longer pieces—the études and parts of the sonatas. In the latter, he even maintains much of the classic formal outlines; but there is always present a spirit of organic development, even when he saw fit to adapt his means to the particular end he had in view. No matter how much he might cut himself adrift from bondage, to repeat Liszt's phrase, we can feel the essential element of organization in his music, that principle which some writers have called the "sonata principle." He was as ingenious a formalist as he was a harmonist.

CHOPIN AND THE ROMANTIC MOVEMENT

Although it was distinct from the more rugged and introspective Romanticism of the German composers, Beethoven, Brahms, and so on, Chopin's contribution to the whole Romantic Movement was a very important one. He was never a radical in the Berliozian sense or an intellectual *curieux* as was Liszt, whose interest in the music of other men interfered strongly with his own development; but Chopin's intensely personal lyrics are imperishable testimonials to the validity of the whole movement. Matthew Arnold's words on Heine could well be adapted to him:

> *The comfort of coming to a man of genius, who finds in verse his freest and most perfect expression, whose voyage over the deep of poetry destiny makes smooth! The magic of Heine's form is incomparable; he employs this form with the most exquisite lightness and ease, and yet it has at the same time the inborn fullness, pathos, and old-world charm of all true forms of popular poetry. Thus in Heine's poetry one perpetually blends the impression of French modernism and clearness with that of German sentiment and fullness.*

Liszt: A Soul Divided Against Itself

Der freundlichste der Freunde

From a contemporary description of Liszt

JEKYLL AND HYDE

To Liszt, Chopin's great contemporary, the piano was quite another instrument, one to be exploited for its own rather showy sake. The first of the great piano virtuosos, Liszt thought of the instrument in orchestral terms, both tonally and technically, and he tried to achieve on this essentially monochromatic instrument results that might suggest the rich sonority and color blend of the orchestra. Of course he did not succeed; but, in pursuing this particular ambition, he developed a method of writing which resulted in a great deal of flashy, overshowy music that is hardly representative of his real artistic stature. The essential Liszt is to be found elsewhere than in the purple passages and grandiloquent periods of so much of his piano music; but, in this, as in everything else in his life, Liszt was a heart divided, a soul knowing the tawdry from the true but always harkening after the cheap applause which the one so easily brings while yet aspiring to the truth that is its own reward. The appellation so often given him, the Dr. Jekyll and Mr. Hyde of music, is a good one.

LE GALOP CHROMA-
TIQUE executed by the
Devil of Harmony, 1843.
The original is a colored
cartoon of Liszt by an un-
known contemporary artist.

THE BASIS OF LISZT'S STYLE

To understand fully the reasons for Liszt's piano style, we must go
back to still another picturesque figure of the Romantic Movement, to
the dark, sardonic Paganini, the great Italian violin virtuoso who, during the early part of the nineteenth century, set Europe by the ears with
his transcendental playing.[9] This unbelievable figure, who was thought
by even sane-minded people to have been taught to play by the Devil,
caused everywhere what can only be described as consternation by the
performances he gave, not only of the pieces in the classic violin repertoire, but also of the new and curious type of pieces which he developed
for his instrument. This music, as described by Sitwell,[10] was a new
invention, comparable to the enlargement in the scope of poetry

[9] A contemporary critic thus describes Paganini's appearance on the stage:
"A sallow, haggard, ungraceful specter, with his instrument clutched rather than held
in his lean clawlike fingers: you would as soon expect melody from a sepulcher. A few
seconds elapse, the burst of applause subsides, and a change comes over the musician, so
sudden that you are already tempted to believe him a sorcerer. His figure grows erect, his
attitude commanding, his features stern and thoughtful.
"He commenced with a soft, streamy note of celestial quality, and with three or four
whips of his bow elicited points of sound that mounted to the third heaven and as bright
as the stars. A scream of astonishment and delight burst from the audience. . . . During
these effects a book caught on fire on one of the desks and burnt for some time, unob-
served by the musicians, who could neither see nor hear, though repeatedly called to by
the audience, anything but the feats of this wonderful performance."
[10] In his book on Liszt. In order to get the real character of this remarkable individual,
Sitwell's whole description should be read.

PAGANINI and the Royal Philharmonic Orchestra, by Daniel
Maclise

brought about by the Romantic writers: "all the romantic properties, mutterings of thunder, beating of rain, howling of wind, were there; and the human passions, anger, jealousy, daemonic laughter, could be imputed."

Liszt heard this extraordinary musician play when the latter came to Paris to give his first concert there in March, 1831. Paganini was then fifty years old, Liszt twenty; but the impact of the older man on the younger was of such terrific force that it changed the whole course of Liszt's life. For technical possibilities were revealed to the eager, impressionable youth such as he had never even dreamed of; and the potentialities of showmanship were disclosed to a nature only too prone to take advantage of them. Liszt has been called a combination of great actor and Hindu fakir; Paganini was his prototype in this.

PIANO MUSIC

For the next seventeen years, the world rang with the fame of the great virtuoso Liszt, the "Paganini of the piano." An apt phrase, but not one which conveys the whole truth: for to his fabulous technical achievements, which he modeled after those of Paganini, Liszt added a conception of the function and art of the interpreter that was unique at

THE YOUNG LISZT   He was the most romantic of all the musicians.

the time. While he did not deny himself the glory of dazzling the public as a virtuoso player, Liszt developed a high-minded conception of the interpreter as one who should strive to reveal the composer's inmost self—another manifestation of his dual nature. According to all the contemporary accounts, his playing "defied description in words." Would that the phonograph had been invented, so that we might compare his playing with that of our modern virtuosos!

From this concert period comes a great deal of piano music obviously designed for the programs which he played on his triumphal tours about Europe. Much of this music was actually written down and published after Liszt's retirement from the concert platform, but it was his long experience as a dazzler of the public which inspired its composition. In most of these piano pieces, nobility and showmanship go together: his showiness is at its best when sentiment is not involved, in such things as *La Campanella,* the amazing variations, or some of his fantasias on operatic airs or his transcriptions of instrumental pieces. (In passing, it may be said that Liszt was an insatiable "arranger" for the piano, the world's most astonishing practitioner of that subtly difficult art.) But, when he becomes concerned with such sentimental maunderings as those in the *Liebesträume,* he is wearisome. The best of his piano works are certain numbers in the *Années de pèlerinage* (*Years of Pilgrimage*), especially the *fantaisie-sonata* on Victor Hugo's poem, *D'Après une lecture de Dante;* and the dramatic, black-cloaked, romantic *B Minor Sonata.*

AT WEIMAR

In 1848, dissatisfied with his rather showy place in the musical firmament, Liszt accepted the position of court *Kapellmeister* at the little ducal court of Weimar in order to have more time for creative effort, undisturbed by the transient glories of the concert stage—so that he could, as he put it, "conquer the theater of my thought as I have done for my personality as an artist." Here he taught himself how to score for the orchestra, learned something of conducting, and from time to time moved out into the active concert world to sustain his reputation as a piano virtuoso.

Two great flaming Romantic personalities entered his life here: Princess Wittgenstein, with whom in 1847 he had begun what he thought was to be but another of the agreeable amorous adventures with which he beguiled himself; and Richard Wagner, then an exiled, thwarted composer, whose opera *Tannhäuser* Liszt had produced in 1849. It was the princess, who had left her Russian husband to live with Liszt at Weimar, who confirmed him in his determination to become known as a composer in the large orchestral forms. He worked out a new form, the *symphonic poem,* based on poetic ideas but ingeniously transforming their themes to suit the necessities of their programs. In developing this invention, based on Berlioz's model, Liszt wrote twelve symphonic poems, the best of which are no longer played; and two symphonies, the *Faust* and the *Dante,* which represent him at his best. His whole, huge execution of the Faustian concept in three character sketches devoted to Faust, Gretchen, and Mephistopheles is a thoroughly Romantic one, strongly poetic and effectively musical, and deserves more frequent playing than it gets.

The relationship of Wagner and Liszt was a close and complex one, each man reacting strongly on the other. Wagner, with the leechlike tenacity for which he was famous, fastened himself on the more noted and richer man, accepting all the financial and spiritual aid which Liszt was generous enough to give him, and all the time crying for more. On the other hand, it was Wagner's music, particularly his opera

LISZT'S MUSIC ROOMS IN WEIMAR It is so delicious in that room of his! It was all furnished and put in order for him by the Grand Duchess herself. The walls are pale gray, with a gilded border running round the room, or rather two rooms, which are divided, but not separated, by crimson curtains. The furniture is crimson and everything is so *comfortable*. . . . A splendid grand piano stands in one window (he received a new one every year). The other window is always wide open and looks out on the park. . . . His writing table is beautifully fitted up with things that all match. Everything is in bronze; inkstand, paperweight, matchbox, etc., and there is always a lighted candle standing on it by which he and the gentlemen can light their cigars.
Amy Fay: *Music Study in Germany*

Lohengrin, which opened Liszt's mind to the possibility of the music of the future, and his whole contact with Wagner was a refreshing and stimulating, if extremely trying, experience. He gradually began to glimpse what the younger composer was striving to do and tried in every way possible to help Wagner develop his ideas of the music drama. Unfortunately, neither Weimar nor Germany as a whole was ready for the things Wagner had in mind. In 1859, Liszt became so completely disgusted with the provincialism of Weimar as to leave it for Rome, where he spent many of the remaining years of his life, seeking consolation in religion, even receiving minor orders in the Roman Church.

THE LATER YEARS

In 1869, he emerged from this retirement and returned for part of each year to Weimar, where he lived simply in a little cottage and gave lessons to the pupils who flocked to him from all parts of the world. Thereafter he divided his life largely between Rome, Weimar, and Budapest, where he had been made president of the Hungarian Academy of Music; he traveled almost incessantly, giving his help wherever he thought it might be needed. A few piano compositions date from this last period, notably the *Mephisto Waltzes*. In 1886, he celebrated his seventy-fifth birthday by a triumphant grand tour, visiting London and Paris and playing for his admirers. Shortly after the finish of this trip, he went to Bayreuth, where his daughter, who had married Wagner, was striving to develop the great festivals devoted to her husband's music. He caught cold after one of the performances of *Tristan* and died on July 31 of that year.

Opinion will always vary as to the artistic value of Liszt's contribution to music; the character of a great deal of his work makes its excessive repetition almost insufferable. But his significance in history is clear. Locke, in the book *Music and the Romantic Movement in France,* shows just what this is. More than any other, Liszt established the poetic basis of program music and showed how thematic development in this style could be carried out. He turned away, as Beethoven and Berlioz had done before him, from the conception of art for art's sake to the theory of art as an interpretation of life. And this is what he tried to make his music. His powers were not sufficient for him to fully achieve his ideals, and he had many faults in common with the other Romantic artists. But his name will always be among the great names of music, the very first, as Sitwell has said, to come to mind when its nobler virtues are spoken of.

WAGNER—HIS PREDECESSORS

AND CONTEMPORARIES IN OPERA

Nineteenth-Century Italian Opera

Hush! the curtain rises.
Observe that very beautiful scene, how admirably those pillars are painted!
So well, that one almost fancies them real.
That is C., whom you will admire as much for her superior style of acting as the wonderful powers of her voice.
Those are indeed enchanting sounds; and how pleasing and modest in her manners!
Do you understand Italian?
Just enough to know what is going forward.
When the first act of the opera is over, you will be entertained with a short pantomime intermixed with dances.
This is the divertissement: the bill mentions a new dancer who is to dance a hornpipe in it.
The Prince of Wales is just come into his box: he speaks to the Duchess of L.
Between the acts amuse yourself by looking around this brilliant company.
How graceful these two dancers are!
You will see presently V. and A. who will much more surprise you.
Is it possible?
Judge for yourself; there they are.
I could not have imagined that art could have been carried so far.
We may, I think, fairly infer that it now has reached its utmost degree of perfection.
Indeed I think so. This evening's amusement has far surpassed every thing I expected.

Rev. Thomas Vivier: *French and English Dialogues upon Several Subjects; Exclusively Adapted for the Use of Young Ladies, 1814*

DIFFERENCES IN THE NATIONAL STYLES

No better starting point for a discussion of nineteenth-century opera could be found than one which shows the great differences that exist in national styles of humor as they are exemplified in the dramatic works of the various countries. For these differences had a great deal to do with the development of opera at the time. It was the distinctive quality of the old Italian high comedy, even when used by a German composer such as Mozart, which set the tone for early nineteenth-century opera. We have already had something to say about the origins and eighteenth-century traditions of this Italian comic genre. Before describing how it affected the operatic writing of the new century, we may well turn aside briefly and consider something of the comedic traditions of the other countries.

The French, who feel that they alone have been the true guardians of this spirit of comedy through the years, are much less personal and human than are the dramatic comedians of Italy and Germany. They have always had a leaning toward the satiric brand of comedy, one largely freed from sympathetic or human reactions. In the words of one historian of the theater, they like to place life on the rack and watch the result from a viewpoint that is impersonal and aloof, their sense of comedy arising out of the ability to ridicule the foibles and to describe the weaknesses of human nature. In this field of "detached comedy," their great seventeenth-century playwright, Molière, was a supreme master, and his feeling for satire and burlesque has strongly impregnated the French operatic stage down to the present day.

The eighteenth-century German *Singspiel* was a simple folk play consisting of spoken dialogue with musical numbers interspersed from time to time; it came out of the secularized medieval plays of a comic nature and possessed a rather broad and elementary sense of humor, bordering on buffoonery. These naïve folk works were not able to withstand the growing demand of the public for the more sophisticated Italian and French productions, and they became submerged in the advance of *opera buffa* and the operetta. The Anglo-Saxons have never had a national style of comic opera: not even their much-vaunted Gilbert and Sullivan is native, for most of its fun lies in the dialogue, and Sullivan's Englishness was only a minor element in his style, which drew largely on Mozart and on the French and Italian light operas for a great deal of its inspiration. *The Beggar's Opera,* a sort of English *Singspiel,* written some two hundred years ago, could have established a national style; but, like its German counterparts, it went down under the onslaught of the foreign invaders. The reasons for this precipitate retreat are obvious enough when we hear some of the works of Dibdin and Arne, which followed *The Beggar's Opera.* These works were simply collections of the ruddy, vigorous sort of tunes which England has turned out by the thousands during the course of the centuries; they have almost no dramatic value whatever.

THE ITALIAN SPIRIT

It was in the comic genre that the Italian spirit worked most effectively; it was scarcely at all successful in the tragic. The exceptions stand out so prominently as to establish the validity of such a statement. What, for example, did Donizetti make of Sir Walter Scott's tragedy of Lucy, the Bride of Lammermoor? Scarcely anything but a remarkable mad scene, lasting perhaps twenty minutes, in which the prima donna takes the stage and the drama flies out the window; while the same composer's masterpiece of comedy, *Don Pasquale,* has hardly any rival. It may have been this necessity for the predominance of leading vocal stars that dashed Italian hopes for tragic greatness in opera; but, whatever the reasons, the limitations of the stage or the vanity of singers, it must be admitted that the amusing Italian operas written during the late eighteenth and early nineteenth centuries constitute a type that has never been equaled.

THE RIDDLE OF ROSSINI

Who were the chief composers of this kind of opera? In addition to Mozart, there was Cimarosa, whose *Il matrimonio segreto* (1792) was in its day considered better than anything Mozart wrote; even today its frothy champagne can give great pleasure, although it is hardly to be mentioned in the same breath with the more heady draughts of Mozart. It was Cimarosa who served as a model for Rossini (1792-1868), a composer of much finer caliber and one whom Beethoven declared supreme in his particular field. Rossini's great masterpiece, *The Barber of Seville,* written in 1816, is in the true line of French-Italian comedy. Founded on the same plot as Mozart's *Marriage of Figaro,* it is worthy to stand beside that work in its clever characterizations, its patter songs, its verve and sparkling wit, its warm and sympathetic orchestration. The overture to this charming work sets the stage to perfection for the artificial comedy which follows in the best traditions of *opera buffa;* the famous patter song *Largo al factotum* has been the model for scores of others, including most of Sir Arthur Sullivan's; and the rest of the opera, because of its genial caprices and amusing situations, must always remain

ROSSINI

a favorite with the general public. Another of Rossini's comedies was *La Cenerentola (Cinderella)*, written immediately after *The Barber of Seville;* it has much of that opera's verve but nothing like so witty and sparkling a plot. This glittering, impudent work occupied Rossini for some three and a half weeks; the *Barber* took two!

Other operas by which this composer was well known in his day were *Tancredi, Semiramide* (Venice, 1823), *Moïse* (Paris, 1827), and, above all, the grand opera *William Tell* (1829), in which Rossini showed his ability to satisfy the requirements of the Parisians. A strong, powerful work, with plenty of musical scene painting and luscious melodies, *William Tell* demands singers of exceptional ability—for our generation, at least—and so is seldom heard. Its highly seasoned overture remains a favorite number in the repertoire of provincial bands.

Rossini was known far beyond the borders of Italy. In 1822, he visited Vienna, where his operas were produced with tremendous success. It is easy enough to trace the influence of his particular brand of melodic inspiration in the works of the German composers of the time —Weber, Schubert, and even Beethoven; and he, in turn, picked up from them many an idea as to orchestration and symphonic style. He developed so personal a mannerism of orchestral writing as to become known as *Signor Crescendo,* because of his method of working up

A PERFORMANCE AT THE OPÉRA COMIQUE IN PARIS, about 1780 (from a contemporary aquarelle now in the Opera Museum, Paris)

excitement. At the very height of his career, at a time when he was one of the most popular composers in Europe, he suddenly retired and wrote very little for the remaining forty years of his life, thus providing music researchers with one of the most curious problems in the history of the art.

Werfel attributes this retirement to a "veiled neurasthenia." It may be that, beneath the surface, he did not feel his success to be complete; that his rather cynical arrogance, which probably hid an excessive sensitiveness, turned to pique, and this combined with a strain of natural laziness to bring about his long silence. Chorley, the English critic, shrewdly believed that Rossini may have expected people to beleaguer him for more works; they did not, and his chagrin developed into obstinate refusal to write any music at all. In Italy he had been king; when he removed to Paris, he found himself in the cross currents of official cliquism. Wagner, when similarly beset, fought like a demon; Rossini, a lesser man, who was often in ill health, was no fighter. Whatever the reasons may have been, *William Tell* marks at once the height and the end of his career.

DONIZETTI AND BELLINI

At the beginning of the second quarter of the century, Paris took Vienna's place as the center of European musical activity. One of the chief reasons for this was that, no matter what the political or economic situation of France might be, whether she had an emperor, a king, or a republic, the government supported the opera as a matter of national pride. And, naturally, this well-supported institution became the goal of all composers, Italian as well as French. Paris was then, as she has remained since, the international center of the artistic and intellectual activities of the Continent. So, although we find that the outstanding writers of operatic music of the period were born and trained in Italy, they almost invariably deserted the Italian for the French scene.

Two of these early nineteenth-century Italians are still remembered, although most of their works are more honored by breach than by performance—Donizetti (1797-1848) and Bellini (1801-1835). It seems obvious enough today that both these men wrote too hastily and without careful-enough preparation to give their works any great staying power; but, in their time, they were the rulers of the smart Parisian *monde*. In addition to comedies, they composed a number of nationalistic-romantic works, after the manner of the Byron-Scott school, whose influence was making itself felt in Italy as elsewhere. These happened to chime in well at the time with national aspirations; and so many a patriotic libretto was used, no matter what its national setting might be, the better to minister at the altar of Italian freedom.

We find such characteristic Bellini titles as these, expressive of either the patriotic or the melodramatic-romantic sentiments of the literary spirit of the age: *The Pirate, The Capulets and the Montagues* (that is, Romeo and Juliet), *Norma* (The Druid Priestess), *The Puritans.* Bellini did not live long enough to produce an imposing list of works; but Donizetti, in his fifty-one years, turned out an astonishing number of operas—some sixty-seven in all! This fact alone suggests to us that we can hardly expect anything but the slightest of construction in these works, although it is well to remember that there are other kinds of operatic quality than that to be found in the long-gestated music dramas of Wagner. Some of Donizetti's titles are: *Alfred the Great, The Castle of Kenilworth, Elizabeth at Kenilworth, Lucy of Lammermoor* (*Lucia di Lammermoor*), based on Scott's romantic novels, *Anne Boleyn, Hugo, Count of Paris, Tasso, Mary Stuart,* and *Don Pasquale,* which Ernest Newman says has no rival in Italian comedy except perhaps Rossini's *Barber.* Here is a galaxy of romantic and historical people; not, it need hardly be said, a galaxy of portraits, but rather of dramatic figures given over to the stage conventions of opera. The great majority of these works do not now hold the stage, even in Italy; but in such works as do persist, we can trace the whole range of Italian powers in melodrama, and, above all, in comedic style.

Donizetti's melodramatic works were popular in a day when the drama was in rather dire straits; his librettos for the Paris opera, by the prolific Frenchman, Scribe,[1] are after a too-familiar pattern. But we have to consider these works, as indeed we must consider all of their time, in the light of the fact that the dramatic output of the first half of the century was exceedingly feeble (these were the days of Hugo and Dumas and Bulwer-Lytton) and with the understanding that to the Italians of the time opera meant almost nothing but singing. The audiences were remarkably exigent in that regard and remarkably careless about almost everything else. In particular, the orchestral parts are often extremely thin and the plots the merest novelettish cliché. Even when a good novel is adapted for the opera, the dramatic result is almost always deplorable, unity and proportion being sacrificed to musical high spots.

Take as an example such a plot of Donizetti's as *The Elixir of Love* (*L'Elisir d'amore*), an opera remembered now by but one air, *Una furtiva lagrima,* a favorite of Caruso's. In it a quack doctor sells a pretended love potion to a peasant, so that he may be able to win a wealthy bride from a soldier. When the peasant turns out to be wealthy, the

---

[1] No artist has been more felicitously named; for Scribe wrote over a hundred opera librettos in the course of his life for different composers, including Auber, Meyerbeer, Boïeldieu, and Halévy.

maid relents, finding that, after all, she does love him. The love complications in such comedic works as *Don Pasquale*, however, do not require any test of logic. We have only to regard them with the eye which the amused observer Goldoni (1707-1793) employed when, following Molière, he fashioned his comedies of character, observing and delineating social oddities with a deft touch. If Donizetti and his fellows could have kept always to the level of the best Goldoni comedy, they would have built more securely. But it is useless to judge these operas from too elevated a dramatic standpoint; most of our pleasure in them comes from noting the manipulation of familiar characters and properties and marking how much passion the composers could infuse into threadbare sentiments and commonplace situations.

Such single airs of Donizetti's as have survived represent some of his best skill; for example, the *Spirto gentil* from *La Favorita,* the sad farewell to worldly affairs of the hero who loved the king's mistress. In Caruso's singing of this, we find much of the attraction of that kind of opera in the easy overcoming of vocal difficulties. Now that we no longer have singers who can do these arias in the grand manner, they lose most of their appeal. Of another kind is the "Mad Scene" from *Lucia,* where all manner of florid decoration surrounds themes of this extended *scena,* which is one of the greatest vocal tests for any soprano. But the inherent touching quality of Scott's drama here has power to make us forget some of the staginess: the heroine, believing her lover false, marries another man, and the lover, coming back, thinks, in turn, that she has been false to him. Under this great grief, Lucy's mind deserts her; and the special pathos of the mad scene, which lifts it out of the ordinary, consists in her delusion that all her troubles are over and that she is to marry her beloved. The expression of her joy, though in decorative terms now outmoded, has a certain simple appeal for the sympathetic hearer; and there is no doubt that Donizetti found here a language which is both tuneful and emotionally apt. It is, however, in light comedy of the quick-riposte kind, such as we find in *Don Pasquale,* that his Italianate art shines most gaily.

Of Bellini's operas, almost the only one revived of late years is *Norma;* but *La Sonnambula* (The Sleepwalker) made in its day the reputations of both Jenny Lind and Patti. Here the sentiment is, for us, rather heavy, but it is worth while to observe the delicacy of its expression in such an air as *Sovra il sen;* and a good example of pathetic expression is the sleepwalking air, *Ah, non credea.* In *Norma,* there is the famous prayer *Casta diva* ("Chaste Queen of Heaven"), sung by the heroine, the Druid Priestess, one of the most taxing bits of vocal music ever written. There is some danger in judging any of these now rarely heard composers by single extracts: if, for instance, we were to judge Bellini by the duet in *The Puritans* in which the two gentlemen swear fidelity to their cause ("Sound the Trumpet"), we should probably find him heavy-handed, even clumsy. This is far from the truth; for most of Bellini's melodies have a grace, a tenderness, and a charm that make them distinctive. If his instrumentative and harmonic constructive gifts had been on a par with his melodic ability, he would have loomed as a much greater figure in the history of opera.

The influence of Italian opera upon the likings and the habits of both the English and the Americans is well worth marking, for it explains much that has been slow in the development of music in these two countries; a devotion to opera of the Italianate type on the part of society gave the plain man few opportunities to hear any other kind of music. It is, in fact, impossible to understand the development of music in Europe without realizing the force of middle-class convention, a force which was moulded, in turn, by upper-class social leaders, royal patronage, and idolatry of the foreigner. It was all these that made the Italian opera popular in European countries, especially in England. And anyone reading the history of music in the United States during the nineteenth century will realize that, to most of the people who had opportunities for hearing it, music meant the Italian opera.

Nineteenth-Century Opera Outside Italy

Music may be looked upon as a sort of thermometer that registers the degree of sensibility of the different peoples, according to the climate in which they live.

Grétry: *Mémoires,* 1789

We love so many things in France that we do not really love music.

Debussy

VARIOUS TYPES OF FRENCH OPERA

We have seen how avidly, at the time of Rameau, the French took to the popular tuneful comic operas which the Italians imported into Paris. Under the aegis of such composers as Duni (an Italian), Monsigny, and Dalayrac, they set about creating a school of comic opera of their own. In the *opéra comique,* the connecting dialogue was always spoken, whereas the Italian *opera buffa* kept to the traditional recitative. Later on, at the beginning of the nineteenth century, the spirit of seriousness and revolutionary earnestness gave a new turn to *opéra comique,* a concern with grave and solemn subjects. For operas of the comic genre, the term *opéra bouffe* was employed. And, in distinction to both, there evolved the *grand opéra,* embodying everything the term implies—florid vocalism, plenty of spectacle, and as much opportunity as possible for the ballet that was so beloved by the French. The grand opera was, in its way, as typical of the stateliness and grandeur of the autocratic state as were the other artistic manifestations of the spirit of the time—the Empire furniture and architecture.

We have mentioned the French operatic works of Grétry, Méhul, and Cherubini as standing between the worlds of the eighteenth and nineteenth centuries in Paris. Cherubini (1760-1842) was the great man of his time; today we are apt to think of his music, on the few occasions we have of hearing it, as following the traditions of Gluck but without his humor and finesse. Another Franco-Italian, Spontini (1774-1851), settled in Paris, in 1803, after a successful career as an opera composer and producer in his native land. His first great success was *La Vestale* in 1807; in 1820, he became general music director to the Prussian court in Berlin and was active there until his success was obscured by the rising demand for German as distinct from foreign opera set to German words, a demand that was stimulated by the success of Weber's *Freischütz.* Recent Italian revivals of such works as Cherubini's *Medea* and Spontini's *Agnese di Hohenstaufen* have given both these composers something of a vindication after long years of neglect, proving them to be composers of real, viable operas, and not merely historical figures of the vital transitional period between the eighteenth and nineteenth centuries. Something of the dynamic influence of Berlioz has also been suggested; his operas have had little success with the non-French public. The best known of them, *Benvenuto Cellini* and *Béatrice et Bénédict,* are occasionally revived by the French in a spirit of reverence. But they have, in spite of Berlioz's essential theatricalism in life, little dramatic value. The French have never seemed able to grasp the spirit of melodrama in opera, as did the Germans; and so there is no influence in France similar to that of Weber in Germany, with all due respect to Berlioz's classically inspired, daemonic art. Boïeldieu (1775-1834) is sufficiently remembered by an overture or two, that to *La Dame Blanche* being the most popular. His operas, however, are little but song *scenas,* put together, for the most part, against a mildly thrillerlike background. Auber (1782-1871), one of the longest-lived of composers, was able to make the best of two worlds, those of comic and grand opera. In his two score of operas, he frolicked with the greatest of French ease, address, and versatility, and yet with a certain timidity, which was partly temperamental and partly the result of not developing his structural sense. In his *La Muette de Portici* (also known as *Masaniello*), he was able to dig deeper. This work came out at a time (1828) when revolution was again in the air and deals with the Neapolitan patriot who led his people against Spanish tyranny. A performance of this work in Brussels in 1830 proved to be the torch which set fire to the revolution there against the Dutch. It may be noted that Verdi was, similarly, a rallying center in the fight for Italian freedom. These are strange surroundings for music, these stirrings amidst the destinies of nations!

So Auber, though he never thrilled before or again to the immediate excitement of social or political incentives, kept on in a sort of romantic playboy fashion, scarcely knowing whither the new Romantic spirit might lead, and too often allowing it to be overlaid with the cheapness of the penny thriller.

MEYERBEER THE MAGNILOQUENT

In this place, we must also remember Meyerbeer, who, though treated at more length elsewhere, comes into the French scene as yet another of those composers of mixed origin who played a striking part in the development of French art, having been lured to Paris by the brilliant success possible there. One writer on the history of opera thinks that the opera house in Paris (built in 1861-1875), so familiar to every visitor to that *ville lumière,* might well have been designed as Meyerbeer's monument, so masterfully heavy is its construction and so oppressive its wealth of ornament.

GERMAN OPERA OF THE NINETEENTH CENTURY

The roots of nineteenth-century German opera, out of which there came the rich fruit of the Romantic operas of Weber and the music dramas of Wagner, were planted, as has been shown, in the native *Singspiel* or its poor but attractive relative, the *Zauberpose* (fairy pantomine). But the efforts of the worthy composers of the early *Singspiele* proved to be largely without natural life, still-born imitations of Italian opera performed in the German language. They lacked the warming influence of the Romantic spirit that was soon to spread over the whole country and prove such a stimulus to German artists; and they unfortunately did not have the inspiring example of Mozart and his *Don Giovanni* and *Die Zauberflöte,* or of Beethoven and his mighty muse, to aid them in their enterprise. All these influences helped to mould the form and to shape the substance of the German national opera when it finally arrived. Even Beethoven's opera *Fidelio,* in spite of the composer's evident distaste for the form and his inexperience in handling voices, showed how powerfully affecting the Romantic spirit in opera might be, when directed by a great mind.

ITS BIRTH WITH WEBER

The actual birth of German opera may be said to date from the time of Weber (1786-1826) a musico-dramatist, whose style from the beginning of his work was an individual one and not a mere imitation of those who had preceded him. His opera *Der Freischütz* is a perfect expression in music of the spirit of the legends and fireside tales of daemonic power and romantic human prowess, of love stories and darkling fate, that had been so happily injected into German literature by the Romantic Movement. *Sturm und Drang* mingled with Classicism in Germany without mutually destructive effects: Schiller and Goethe, Herder and Richter wrought powerfully but not internecinely, as have so many literary figures in other lands. The German spirit of these early years of the nineteenth century could say, with Whitman of a later age, "I am large; I contain multitudes."

We have seen how Romanticism came to Germany about 1800. Politics, inevitably, became mingled with literature, but the various phases of the Romantic spirit had ample depth of earth in the national temperament, and some of them cast strong roots clear back to the Middle Ages. The Revolution of 1848, a revolution which flamed over the greater part of Europe, broke up many associations and uprooted many fine growths, as well as some which by then had become weak and cumbersome. And, in the latter part of the century, the national spirit became increasingly tinctured with the philosophies of other countries. We can say again (as of Beethoven) that one of the happiest facts about Weber's short career was that he was the right man at the right time, a time when the national consciousness was ready to flower in a natural way, without those wasteful defiances and war cries which so often accompany new ideas.

THE GERMANY OF NATURE AND LEGEND

It is the natural genius of the German forests, with their mysterious songs and tales, which we find predominant in Weber's music. He understood and could depict simple, homely things. His style struck fire immediately, for it was folky in its speech and friendly in its feeling. Even hostile critics have had to admit a certain "inevitable beer-gardeny obviousness." He had not the all-powerful grasp of Wagner, nor the rapid-fire skill of Mozart. The end of *Der Freischütz* is hurried and unspacious; so, for that matter, is the end of most of the Italian and French operas of the time. But no dramatic stroke, no passage of however few chords, misses its mark; Weber was as accurate a harmonic shooter as was the bedeviled hero of his opera.

His every overture forms an almost complete synopsis of the story which follows: vividly before us parade hero and villain, as well as the minor characters. The overture to *Der Freischütz*, for instance, contains four or five leading themes, besides sufficient serenity of melodic beauty and urgency of rhythm to please anyone who might prefer to know nothing of the drama, lest such knowledge take the edge off his musical appetite. Weber's apt harmonies light up a scene as with a flame—that is, if we are able to hear them with pre-Wagnerian ears! His uses of the brass are surprisingly advanced for his time, and his broad, flowing tunes could hardly be bettered, while in the overtures there is little waste of time or material in getting from theme to theme.

The heroine's air in *Der Freischütz* (*Leise, leise*), sung by Agatha as she is waiting in the moonlight for her lover, is typical of Weber's writing. The tenderness of the opening is exquisite, and there is something attractively simple-hearted about the curves of the melody: they are so full of feeling without being sentimental. It is in his hunting and drinking songs that Weber strikes one of the familiar and folky notes which give his operas such wide appeal, to both the simple and the skilled. There is an obvious parentage to many of the ideas in Wagner's early opera, *The Flying Dutchman*, a parentage to be sought in Weber's melodic flights and his orchestral intensity. Wagner first heard *Der Freischütz* when he was but eight; and five years after that Weber was dead. Notable among the heritages Weber left to his great successor was an effective and consistent use of recurring musical ideas

National Gallery, Berlin

CARL MARIA VON WEBER
(portrait by Caroline Bardua)

at dramatically significant points in the development of the drama, a device which Wagner was later to employ so startlingly.

This is especially to be noted in *Euryanthe,* the work which in Weber's own mind represented his best attempt to establish a German grand opera as the equivalent of the Italian *opera seria. Euryanthe,* in Weber's words, is to be considered as a "dramatic essay which counts upon the collaboration of all the sister arts for its effects and is ineffectual if deprived of their assistance." Unfortunately, it is burdened with such a foolish libretto as to make it almost impossible of enjoyment by a present-day listener, however sympathetic he may be to Weber's ideals in writing it. "To make excisions within so organic a whole as this grand opera is impossible, if the composer has thoroughly thought out his work," continues Weber. Here, in essence, is the theory which Wagner was to use later in developing his music dramas. As a noted German critic has put it, in *Euryanthe* the seed was planted from which the whole form of the music drama was to grow; and Wagner did more than perform an act of piety, when he began his career as a conductor in Dresden, with a performance of this opera.

Weber's attempt to capture national feelings and enthusiasms must not be forgotten in a summary of his qualities; for this was an aspect of his Romanticism which added spice to his style. He was able, largely through his handling of the orchestra, to give a characteristic color to each of his works: *Der Freischütz* is, of course, darkly mysterious with the atmosphere of the German forests; *Euryanthe* is gallantly chivalrous with the chivalry of medieval times; *Oberon* and *Turandot* (the latter being incidental music which he wrote for Schiller's play) paint in fantastic colors the daintiness of fairyland and the glory of the East.

FORETELLING WAGNER

In everything he did Weber was feeling his way toward the synthesis that was afterwards achieved by Wagner. The later composer had a greater sense of balance, as well as a much stronger grasp of his materials; but it was Weber, so little taught but so admirably inspired, who moved German opera into a position on which Wagner could later build. This was his greatest glory, although he would certainly deserve a place in music's hall of fame for his own inimitable qualities.[2]

MEYERBEER

Giacomo Meyerbeer, born Jakob Liebmann Beer (1791–1864), has been abused about as much as any composer in the world, partly with reason, and partly, unjustly. It has been said of him that he "wrote only for effect" and would hang about the stage, listening to remarks from all sorts of people, and altering his music accordingly. But such expedients had the good quality of working; they made Meyerbeer what he was, a master of effects for effect's sake. And there have been plenty of artists in other spheres who, in their time, were regarded as great, and whom time has found out. So why pick particularly on Meyerbeer? He was no fool and did not trust to merely a few overpowering moments for his effects; he took plenty of care about all his moments. If he did not have sufficient ideas to fill them all according to modern standards, he was at least able to make a definite impression on his contemporaries, who were struck with his bold shaping of drama and his ceaseless activity in diversifying his expression.

One of the best reasons for his success was the fact that he happened to fit the mind of his day extremely well, the day after the revolutionary turmoils in France, when the new urges and demands of the com-

---

[2] We might well add here that in addition to Weber's contributions to operatic development, he was important as the forerunner of the Romantic composers of small piano pieces of independent form—the *Klavierstücke,* as the Germans call them. His use of this style led directly to the piano pieces of Schubert, Schumann, Chopin, Liszt, and a host of minor figures. He is considered also one of the pioneers in the writing of music for *Männergesangvereine* (men's song societies).

mon man were being more and more considered. Meyerbeer was able to dramatize common problems, and so he seized the imagination of the public. After a precocious career in Italy and Germany, he came to Paris in 1826 and made a brilliant hit with his *Robert le diable,* a furious melodrama in which the lost souls of nuns were given over to evil. He followed this up with other spectacular and novel subjects: the great explorer, Vasco da Gama, in *L'Africaine;* history brought to life and made larger than life in *Les Huguenots,* which treats of the struggle of Catholics and Huguenots in France; the Anabaptist uprising of the sixteenth century, and its great figure John of Leyden, in *Le Prophète.* He made sure that his novelties would catch the ear of his time; and he also took care that the best casts of prima donnas should grace them: Jenny Lind, for example, making her first appearance in *Robert,* in 1847.

For all these works, Meyerbeer wrote music of power which sometimes rose to heights of real grandeur. Such a thing as the "Blessing of the Swords" from *The Huguenots,* for instance, is terrific; there is no other word for it. But he was not able to sustain such a mood; he was incessantly changing his style to catch the public ear, with the result that his operas lack consistency and spontaneity. They seem forced, overpompous, and grandiose to us today; yet they made Meyerbeer the man of the hour in Paris in the '30's, just as Weber had been the man for the decade before in Germany. Even a slight acquaintance with such a career as his should teach us not to trust present appearances. How easy it is to reckon a Meyerbeer the equal of a Weber, or even, if he chime with the mood of the time, as greater! The whole lifework of such a spectacular figure should prove clearly enough that things are not always what they seem and that a facile temporary success may prove to be the best and surest passport to oblivion.

CONTEMPORARIES

A whole host of German opera writers contemporary with Jakob Beer has been accurately, if not very elegantly, described as "small beers." There was Marschner (1795–1861), who was perhaps more of Weber's lineage, since he manifested an ardent interest in the doings of the devil. His *Hans Heiling* is full of the supernatural Romanticism of the period and so has great interest for Germans, but not much for anyone else. Marschner's greatest misfortune was to live too long. Before he had written his last opera, Wagner was on the scene with his *Rienzi*

THE TWENTY-EIGHT-YEAR-OLD WAGNER OF THE PARIS YEARS The earliest known picture of the composer, this is a pencil drawing by Kietz.

and *The Flying Dutchman,* and the lesser man was soon lost in the excitement engendered by these powerful works.

Then there was Flotow (1812–1883)—almost exactly contemporary with Wagner. Even the shortest extract from his one-time popular *Martha* shows the grace of this composer's talent. His invention, however, was by no means equal to his ability for writing tunes, and so he has not survived. Nicolai had such a very short life (1810–1849) that we can well deplore the loss of a man who could achieve the Shakespearean sparkle of *The Merry Wives of Windsor,* a work which he wrote but a few months before his end. Lortzing (1801–1851) had the good fortune to be brought up amid stage surroundings and to be an operatic singer himself. His fortunes were as changeable as his skill was limited. But he had a certain sense of good-humored fun, and his *Czar und Zimmermann* (Czar and Carpenter), telling of the adventures of Peter the Great of Russia, has survived (at least in Germany) because of these simple humors, while serious works by the score have died. Perhaps, as much as anything, the lighter works of these composers survived because (as Professor Dent has suggested) they speak an international language and contain so many bits of music by the admired classical writers.[3]

---

[3] Perhaps we like them for the same reason that the man enjoyed *Hamlet*—because it contained, he found, so many well-known quotations!

Richard Wagner and the Music Drama

Langsam und schmachtend

WAGNER'S PLACE IN HISTORY

It is not difficult to summarize briefly Wagner's position in history: to say that, inspired more or less by what he considered to be the ideals of the Greek dramatists, he envisioned a sort of superart, in which the separate arts of music, drama, the dance, and painting were to be combined. And that for the carrying-out of these ideals, he had to invent a new type of musical language, one which was made up of short themes (*Leitmotive* or leading themes, he called them), each of them representative of ideas and personages in the operatic story; and that, in doing so, he achieved the reform of opera which had been attempted at various times and by various composers ever since the Italians made it an instrument for vocal display rather than a means of conveying emotions.

But there is more to the subject than this. Otherwise it would never have been possible for Gilman to express the opinion that *The Ring of the Nibelung,* that enormous conglomeration of looose ends, contradictory motives, and unbelievable magic, was not only the hugest thing ever attempted by one creative mind, but that it is also, in the ultimate sense of the word, the greatest. The thing which explains Wagner, which gives him an unparalleled place in art history, is the fact that he was able to make all the multifarious activities of his tremendously alert mind—all his dramatic theories, his elaborate philosophic beliefs, his theatrical plots—the excuse for some of the most vital and deeply moving music ever written. He himself claimed—and very probably believed—that, in opera, poetry and drama and the arts of the stage should have an equal rank with music. But, fortunately for us, he had more than the courage of these convictions: using Beethoven's symphonies as models, logically developing in the music which he wrote for the stage the same principles which the earlier composer had employed in his works for the orchestra, Wagner achieved effects which transcended all his ideals.

With Wagner, in spite of his carefully elaborated theories, the stage drama was merely the outward form for shaping the musical ideas he had in mind, just as the sonata, the rondo, and the other traditional forms had conditioned the inspiration of Mozart and Beethoven. The drama, working itself out on the stage, was the means for instigating the music which accompanies it in the pit. And the modern researches of German critics, especially those of Alfred Lorenz, show conclusively[4] that the structural principles of architectural form underlie all Wagner's mature music and that it is as "formal" as are the symphonies of Beethoven.

It is the music, not the play, which is the important thing in Wagner. Contrary to general opinion, the drama with him was really nothing but a guide to the dramatic development which is constantly taking place in the music. Since he happened to be a less-talented dramatist and poet than he was a composer (unlike most opera composers, he himself constructed all the librettos for his operas), his works contain a good deal of second-rate and third-rate drama, as well as a considerable amount of poetry that, to put it mildly, is little better than literary doggerel. But this is of minor importance in comparison with the fact that he was a first-rate musician and one, moreover, who was deeply moved by the contemplation of the innate tragedy of man's existence, a tragedy which inspired most of his plots for the stage. The real difference between his music and the music of Bach and Beethoven lies not so much in its structure as in the fact that, unlike them, Wagner was essentially a man of the theater, and so depended on the dramatic stage for the instigation of his musical ideas.[5]

His love for and dependence on the theater go back to his earliest

---

[4] See Lorenz's monumental four-part work, *The Secrets of Form in Richard Wagner.*
[5] Both Bach and Beethoven, as we have seen, depended somewhat on exterior associations for their inspiration, Bach being strongly moved by a world of visual images and Beethoven by idealistic concepts.

days. He was reared in a stage atmosphere: his family, its members typical German *bourgeoisie* of that period, was keenly interested in the theatrical life of Leipzig, where Wagner was born in 1813. His stepfather (some of Wagner's biographers, including the careful Newman, lean to the belief that he may have been his real father),[6] Ludwig Geyer, was an actor and a playwright and a considerable figure on the German stage of the time. Others of his family, including a brother, a sister, and a niece, made distinguished careers for themselves in drama. Indeed, Johanna Wagner, the niece, became one of the best-known operatic singers of her generation and was of considerably more importance in the eyes of the world of that time than was Richard. In his autobiography, Wagner tells us:

> *What particularly attracted me to the theater—by which I mean the stage itself, the rooms behind the scenes, and the dressing rooms—was not so much the desire for entertainment and distraction, as it is with the theatrical public of the present day, but the provocative delight of being in an element that opposed to the impressions of everyday life an absolutely different world, one that was purely fantastic, and with a touch of horror in its spell. Thus to me a stage setting, even a wing representing merely a bush, or a costume, or even a characteristic part of one seemed to have come from another world, to have a sort of ghostly interest, and I felt that the contact with it must be a lever to lift me from the commonplace reality of the routine of daily life to that enchanting demon world.*

Could anything be more revealing as to the real source of his mature inspiration? His whole afterlife was occupied in some sort of connection with the footlights, from the early posts as opera conductor in such provincial towns as Würzburg and Königsberg, where he learned the practical details of his profession, to the climax of his career at Bayreuth, where he built his own theater and superintended the production of his own works.

WAGNER AS ROMANTICIST

Of all composers of this epoch, Wagner may be said to exemplify most completely the Romantic spirit. We have shown how the revolu-

[6] The appendix to the second volume of Newman's monumental *Life of Richard Wagner* gives a good summary of the arguments which lend credence to the idea that Geyer was Wagner's father. It also shows the probability of Wagner's mother being, not the daughter of a humble baker, as has been supposed, but the natural daughter of one of the ducal family of Weimar, Prince Constantine, a brother of Karl August, the Grand Duke who did so much to help Goethe. If this is true, it would go far towards explaining Wagner's genius.

tion in aesthetic ideals which marked the last part of the eighteenth century was coincident with, and partly the result of, the social and political ferments preceding the American and French revolutions; and how one of the artistic results of this rise of democratic idealism was the rediscovery of that huge reservoir of folk poetry which the classicists, in their scholastic refinement, had taken the trouble to forget. It was this Romanticism, revived in the literary productions of the men of the latter part of the eighteenth century—Percy in England, Macpherson in Scotland, Herder and Goethe in Germany[7]—which affected so strongly the aesthetic atmosphere of Wagner's day. When this was combined with the spirit of revolutionary ardor that was then so strongly alive, it produced an environment which proved impossible for one of Wagner's eager and impetuous temperament to resist.

This explains Wagner's absorption in the great legends from out of the Germanic past, the *Nibelungenlied,* the *Tannhäuserlied,* and the *Heldenbuch,* works which the new Romantic interest in folk poetry had brought forth from their long isolation in libraries. And so we find that all his mature works, with the exception of *Rienzi,* were drawn from folk sources, their dramatic outlines being evolved in his mind very early in his career. It explains, also, Wagner's dissatisfaction with being considered merely a Romantic artist and the necessity he felt for action when the opportunity arose. He became embroiled in an abortive attempt at revolt against the crown of Saxony, in 1848, to such an extent that for the most critical period of his life he was banished from his own land.

In fact, at this time it must have seemed that the years comprising the first half of Wagner's life had been given over to futile attempts at getting himself established; now, viewing them so long after the event, they seem necessary for what was to come later. Moving restlessly about in a precipitate flight from his creditors, he lived for a while in Paris, where he vainly attempted to capture the interest of that great center of operatic activity with his *Rienzi* (a work boldly written in the Meyerbeerian manner, beating even that lavish, pretentious

---

[7] As we have seen, Percy's *Reliques of Ancient English Poetry* (1765) rescued a large number of old English folk songs and ballads from oblivion; Macpherson's so-called Ossianic poems, probably largely translations into the vernacular of many of the bardic legends of the Celtic race, were published 1761–1765. Herder's *Voices of the Folk in Song* (1779), called the first international anthology of folk literature in the modern world, based most of its material on Percy. These, together with Goethe's great *Faust,* were striking manifestations of the rediscovery of the power of emotion to be found in the legends of the people.

composer at his own game); then he moved back to his native Saxony, where he supervised and produced operas at the Dresden theater, including his own *Flying Dutchman* and *Tannhäuser*. The Dresden authorities declined his new *Lohengrin;* this fact, together with Wagner's own natural leftist tendencies and his ardent enthusiasms for what he considered the rights of man, led to an actual participation in open rebellion against the Saxon authorities and his banishment to Switzerland. Here he settled for thirteen years and worked out in theory and practice the ideals of his *Wort-Ton-Drama* fusion of words, music, and action in opera which was to play such an important role in the development of his musical style.

During his first few years in Switzerland, he wrote no music at all. He had come to a distinct impasse. So far, the pursuit of his new ideals had brought him nothing but failure, artistic misunderstanding, and banishment from a country he was trying to save. Here, in his new environment, he had time to work out rationally in his own mind the ideas which up to this time had been pursued mainly by instinct. This he did by means of a long series of prose works—*Art and Revolution, Opera and Drama, The Art Work of the Future*—works which, although they contain the essence of his theories, make rather heavy reading today.

We know now that these prose works were in reality the result of Wagner's attempt at this time in his life to find himself, to justify intellectually what he felt to be true. They contain many statements which do not agree with the principles he put into actual practice; for it was only natural, as Newman has observed, that in Wagner's convulsive efforts to restore to the drama the rights which had been filched from it in ordinary opera, he was led to many eager overstatements. It is by observing what he did rather than what he said that we can come to a real conclusion as to his ideals.

PRACTICE

The importance of these theoretical works lies in the fact that they cleared Wagner's mind for the music which was to follow them. In his earlier Dresden days, he had written a libretto for an opera to be called *Siegfried's Death,* taking his material from the *Nibelungenlied*. When he came to work it over later, he found it to be unsatisfactory, in that it did not make intelligible the motives which lay back of the actions of the two main characters, Siegfried and Brünnhilde. Thus, he was

WAGNER WITH
HIS FAMILY
AND FRIENDS
The group is seen
at Bayreuth in the
later years of Wag-
ner's life.

forced to write another libretto dealing with the youth of Siegfried, the hero of the Nibelungen story, and then another to explain the history of Brünnhilde's former existence, and still a fourth to show how the curse arose which provided the motivation for the whole drama. Thus, there came into existence the text of the tetralogy, *Der Ring des Nibelungen,* comprising the four operas, *Das Rheingold, Die Walküre, Siegfried,* and *Götterdämmerung* (Twilight of the Gods). Wagner started to compose the music for this in 1853; four years later, after finishing the music for *Das Rheingold, Die Walküre,* and part of *Siegfried,* he began to feel the drag of the stupendous task and the necessity for some sort of relief from it.

This took the form of two new works along entirely different lines, works which we now consider the greatest he ever wrote—*Tristan und Isolde* and *Die Meistersinger,* the first an outburst of the most volcanic emotion that life can hold in store, the second one of the most universal of all art works in the sympathy of its understanding and the warmth of its action. Resuming work on the score of *Siegfried* in 1869, he completed the Ring with *Götterdämmerung* some twenty-five years after he had first sketched its libretto. In the meantime had come all his elaborate theories as to the necessity of creating an operatic medium compounded of word language and tone language and stage pictures.

Parsifal, finished in 1879 and first given at the theater which Wagner finally succeeded in building for the special performance of his works, has always meant different things to different people. To some, it stands as a sort of sacred symbol of a religious ideal; to others, it is simply an old legend not too skillfully retold; there are those who see in it only a deceptive and somewhat shoddy theatricalism. Nietzsche, Wagner's one-time friend, found it "much too religious"; the liberal-minded American critic, James Huneker, thought it hardly fit for stage reproduction; and yet Newman calls it the "purest spiritual aspiration the human soul has found voice for." There is something to be said for all these viewpoints.

Such a record of achievement—the composition of eleven operas, several of them containing as great music as has ever been written, in a period of forty years—is impressive enough under any circumstance. But, when considered in the light of Wagner's lifelong struggle against economic difficulties and his inability to secure anything like adequate recognition for his works until the later years of his life, it seems almost unbelievable. In all the annals of the artists' struggle against life, no career stands out more nobly than does Wagner's. He had, as someone has remarked, a disconcerting way of leaping from peak to peak of his development, like some inspired Apollonian goat, that did not make for the popularity of his music insofar as the majority of his contemporaries was concerned. As soon as one work was finished, sometimes even before, he was away on another tack, often one that was entirely different; and so it was difficult for the public, as well as for his interpreters, to follow him.

Wagner's career, as we look back on it, seems a rather ignominious series of retreats from creditors and government officials; yet, in the midst of all his temporal troubles, his faith in his mission in the world never faltered. Time and time again he was almost beaten by circumstances; but, fortunately for us, aid always arrived in time to revive his spirit and enable him to go ahead with his life. The amount of physical courage and indomitable energy necessary to carry on a creative career under such circumstances is impossible to realize. But, in trying to estimate it, we must never forget our great debt to those who came to Wagner's aid during these dark years: Liszt, who gave him large sums of money from time to time, as well as a great deal of artistic encouragement; Cosima, Liszt's daughter, who married Wagner in 1870 and provided the domestic tranquility that was needed so that he could finish his work; Ludwig II, young king of Bavaria, who at the time of Wagner's deepest despair, invited him to live in Munich and provided opportunities there for the first performances of both *Tristan* and *Die Meistersinger,* as well as later, through the granting of a credit of 100,000 thalers from the royal treasury, making possible the opening of Wagner's ideal *Festspielhaus* in Bayreuth. This theatre, with its carefully planned auditorium built after Wagner's plans, still remains one of the few places in the world to hear Wagner's dramas as they were meant to be heard. Under the guidance of three generations of the Wagner family, Bayreuth has kept abreast of the latest developments in theatrical techniques and production styles, and is a most potent force in European musical and theatrical life.

Since World War II Wagner's grandsons have tried to make his music more relevant for contemporary audiences through radical reforms in stage design and lighting, as well as through attempts to reveal the psychological bonds which link these music-dramas with the world of archetypal myth. These reforms have been a potent force in the gradual re-establishment throughout the world of Wagner's pre-eminence as a composer, following the anti-Teutonic complexes resulting from the war and its consequences. But it seems to have taken the results achieved through the modern processes of recording to re-convince today's listeners of the genius which produced such a stupendous creation as *Der Ring des Nibelungen* and the fact that it represents one of the great monuments to human daring.

Wagner's achievements as a musician overshadow the contributions he made to other fields of artistic activity. His was an avid mind which reached out into all phases of intellectual expression and his prose works contain a great deal of subtle thinking that has strongly affected the aesthetic ideals of later generations.

WAGNER, THE CULMINATION OF AN EPOCH

In these writings, Wagner had a great deal to say about his work being the "Music of the Future"; as a matter of fact, it was really the culmination of the past, especially the immediate past. In him there were brought to consummation, in one tremendous mechanism, the constructive principles which Beethoven developed in his symphonies; the nationalistic feelings and love for nature which had been introduced into music by Weber; the operatic effectiveness of Meyerbeer; the orchestral virtuosity of Berlioz; and all the literary and artistic Romanticism of his century. Out of these, there came that magnificent composite which, for lack of a better term, we call Wagner's *tone language,* a language which, in the richness of its orchestral palette, the elaborate working-out of its themes, the power of its dramatic speech, the perfection of its technical achievements, the amazing universality of its thought, the sumptuous beauty of its style, and the epic grandeur of its utterance, has not been equaled. So great was the spell which it cast on succeeding generations that no real successor to Wagner has ever appeared.

Which is not to say, of course, that Wagner had no real significance as a musical pioneer. Although from our modern point of view the Music of the Future appears to have been so firmly rooted in the past, its harmonic content (with the constant insistence upon dissonances which are for the most part unresolved) was such as to accustom the ears of later generations to the fact that such dissonance can be both beautiful and effective. Thus, the way was opened for the use of even greater quantities of dissonance, and the path prepared for the complete break with tonality, which came around the turn of the century. It is certainly not too much to claim that Wagner is the most important link in the long chain which stretches between the early attempts of the nineteenth century to revolt against the accepted ideals of tonality, and the twentieth-century composers Schönberg and Berg.

Largely stimulated by Wagner's own pioneering ideas, tastes have greatly changed since his death in 1883; after an unparalleled success in all the civilized countries of the Western world, his music stands in sharp contrast to our mid-twentieth-century ideals. And the fact that its nationalistic tendencies were seized upon by the Nazis as a backdrop for their political heroics has not increased its popularity today. Wagner's musical language, with its encompassing nobility, its heroic strength, its sensuous loveliness, and its epic grandeur, is not a language suited to the expression of the contemporary ideals of a non-Romantic, abstractionist-inclined, practical-minded generation. In days clouded by a global struggle for existence, it is difficult to take his "gods, demi-gods, and quarter-gods" as seriously as he meant us to take them. Nevertheless, it is reasonable to suppose that Wagner's music, no matter what the vagaries of contemporary taste, will endure because it meets so successfully the supreme test of all art: the ability to take some great and individual human theme—love, pity, desire, greed, grief—and treat it so that it has universal significance and expresses supreme truth. Wagner is one with Michelangelo and Shakespeare in this respect, which is, after all, a fair enough portent for the future!

Other Operatic Developments in Italy,
France, and Germany

VERDI

The earlier career of Giuseppe Verdi (1813–1901), the grand old man of Italy in whom musicians of all countries can delight, was almost exactly contemporary with that of Wagner and pursued its Italianate ways little influenced by the turbulent operatic style which was developing so mightily in the north. Verdi was in essence a simple peasant, but he developed types of skill that no other Italian musician ever possessed. He was happy in a long life, which gave him time to write twenty-seven operas, and most marvelous in the use he made of his later years, a time when most men would have been content to rest on their laurels.

Verdi was born in a small hamlet in the north of Italy, where his father was the local innkeeper; as a young boy, he showed signs of musical sensitiveness although he displayed no marvelous talent. He received his first musical instruction from the local organist, whose post he eventually inherited. Through the interest of a prosperous local merchant, Verdi was taken to Busseto, a small city in the vicinity of which he lived most of his life, and given lessons by the cathedral organist and director of the local orchestral society. This worthy musician, a good teacher and something of a composer, recognized the boy's aptitude and soon delegated some of his duties at the cathedral and at the Philharmonic Society to his fifteen-year-old protégé.

As soon as Verdi had achieved something of a local reputation, it was decided that he must go to Milan, where in 1822 he applied for entrance to the *Conservatorio*. Because he was eighteen years old (the age of admission to this famous music school was between nine and fourteen, and the pupils were supposed to leave when twenty), he was refused admittance; he settled down to study privately with Lavigna, the *maestro al cembalo* of the Milan opera. This study gave him a good grounding in the works of the Italian masters, especially Palestrina and Marcello; his public career as a composer may be said to have begun with the opera *Oberto, Conte di San Bonifacio,* undertaken at the suggestion of Masini, the director of one of the minor Milan theaters. Verdi took three years to finish this work, which was finally produced, not at the comparatively obscure theater for which it was intended, but at La Scala (1839), one of the greatest of Italian opera houses. The performance can hardly be called a success. "There is much in this opera," wrote a contemporary critic, "in common with the style of Bellini, above all an abundant, perhaps too abundant, wealth of melody. But where the words demand energy and passion, the vocal line is often languid and monotonous." This is in strong contrast to the later Verdi, who is often criticized for being too violent and intense.

In this work and in those which followed it—*Un giorno di regno* (1840, a complete failure), *Nabucodonosor* (1841, the work which laid the foundation for his later success and fortune, for it made its composer the fad of the times), *I Lombardi* (1843, an even greater success, due partly to the attempt which the Church made to suppress it), and *Ernani* (1844)—Verdi followed the operatic fashions of the time, adding to his natural gifts for melody and strong dramatic characterizations a special patriotic touch, which greatly strengthened works otherwise not particularly remarkable.

Between 1844 and 1851, the year which saw the production of the opera *Rigoletto,* Verdi's first enduring success, nine operas were written, an average of more than one a year. This composer never thought of himself other than as a man earning his living by providing good salable products, which in his case happened to be operas rather than oranges or orchids; but his inborn sense of truthfulness and his feelings as an artist were never overshadowed by his native shrewdness and business ability. Always he sought self-development and gradually achieved a composing technique which carried him to the greatest heights ever achieved in Italian opera.

From the viewpoint of today, it is hard to agree with the critic of 1851 who said that the orchestration of *Rigoletto* was "remarkable, marvelous, the orchestra speaking and weeping alternately and arousing every passion." The works of these middle days of the '50's—*Rig-oletto, Il Trovatore, La Traviata*—still hold the stage because of their simplicity and the energy of their melodies, their naïve dramatic truthfulness, and their innate psychological integrity. In spite of plots which today seem ridiculous—as one writer has remarked, it is doubtful whether anyone in the audience at a performance of *Il Trovatore* has a clear idea of what is happening in the last act—the concentrated and carefully developed emotional excitement of these works makes its effect and carries the audience along with torrential force.

Many of the twenty-seven operas which Verdi wrote were failures; but he never faltered, and in the end he learned to use the orchestra, particularly the wood winds, with a great deal of skill. One of Verdi's greatest assets, as well as a serious handicap, was the fact that throughout his whole life he was uninfluenced by his contemporaries. In a letter to a friend, written in 1875, he said:

> *I am unable to say what will emerge from the present musical ferment. Some want to specialize in melody like Bellini, others in harmony like Meyerbeer. I am not in favor of either. I should like a young man, when he begins to write, never to think about being a melodist or a futurist or any other of the devils created by this kind of pedantry. Melody and harmony should only be means to make music in the hands of the artist. If the day ever comes when we cease to talk of melody or harmony; of Italian or German schools; of past or future, etc., etc.—then perhaps the kingdom of art will be established.*
>
> *Another calamity of the present time is that all the works of these young men are the products of fear. Everybody is excessively self-conscious in his writing and, when these young men sit down to compose, their predominant idea is to avoid antagonizing the public and to enter into the good graces of the critics.*
>
> *You tell me that my success is due to a fusion of the two schools. I never give either of them a thought . . .*
>
> Quoted in Toye: *Giuseppe Verdi*

It is this strong self-reliance that gave the works of Verdi's middle years a certain lack of flexibility.

After the highly productive years, he could afford to take more time in writing; he composed but seven operas in thirty years. *La Forza del destino* (1862) marks a transition point in his career and points the way to the later and much more elaborate style of *Aïda,* written in 1871 for the khedive of Egypt. It was not until *Othello,* however, written when he was 74, that Verdi came into his own. Set to a book which his musico-poetic friend and adviser, Boito, took from Shake-

Casa di Riposo per Musicisti, Milan

VERDI (from a painting by Giovanni Boldini)

speare, this score may be said to represent the logical climax of the Italian operatic style, a style which always gives the stage precedence over the orchestral pit, which relies on the power of vocal melody rather than on orchestral resource to intensify mood and provide climax, and which looks upon the vocal ensemble not as a hindrance to dramatic development but as an opportunity to give expression at one and the same time to the various and often different sentiments of the singing actors on the stage. In its conception and execution, *Othello* is magnificent theater, and, as a modern critic has said in reviewing a revival of this work, there has seldom if ever occurred in the musical theater such a happy welding-together of movement, incident, and speech or such a sublimation of all three in inspired song.

When he was eighty, Verdi gave to the world his *Falstaff*, in which he seems to be once more striking out on a new line altogether, although the roots can be found in his earlier works. But what a difference between root and full-grown tree! *Falstaff* has a quicksilver speed and sheen: never has so rich a comedic spirit been embodied in music. Here sparkles the quintessence of Shakespearean sport and humor.

Hearing a first-class performance of this opera—such as those Toscanini used to direct—leaves one breathless. There is no room here for the prima donna's spreading periods or for the hero's holding-up of the dramatic action; everything is teamwork and rapierlike play, with a few moments of extended song. But how every flash of melody and turn of orchestration tells!

It used to be thought necessary to point out the strong Wagnerian influences in these later Verdi works. The example of Wagner may have stimulated Verdi's imagination, but there is not a trace of the Wagnerian conception of opera to be found in the Italian composer's style. Wagner thought of the opera fundamentally as a philosophic and symphonic conception, to be treated when necessary in a nontheatrical style. Dent has put it well in saying that often we see the Wagnerian characters only dimly through a rich orchestral haze. With Verdi, as with the long line of his Italian forebears, the opera was, above everything else, a vehicle for the vital projection of the drama: the characters stand in front of the orchestra, which provides them, at least in his late works, with a suitable and effective accompaniment. Accepting the conventional operatic procedures as those best adapted to his style, Verdi used them in such a way as to come close to providing the lyric theater with its most ideally balanced and integrated scores.

PUCCINI

Reviewing the activities of the post-Verdian Italian composers of opera provides little matter for great excitement. One name stands out above all the others—Puccini (1858–1924), who ranks in the great succession of openly sentimental, tune-making, voice-loving Italian melodramatists. His operas lack real integral development, but the way they pile up is often wonderfully rousing. Every move on the stage tells, for this composer had a perfect theatrical sense; and his stories and librettos were ideally designed for an end steadily held in view from the moment of the opera's first conception. His treatment of ideas has the not-too-common merit of adapting a style which is always recognizable as his to a plot which may be laid in any country or in any time. However critical we may be, we feel that it would be a disgruntled listener who, coming away from *La Bohème*, did not feel thoroughly satisfied with its Frenchness; from *Tosca*, with its Italianness; from *Madam Butterfly*, with its Japanese atmosphere; or from *Turandot* with its *chinoiserie*. Perhaps the fact that *The Girl of the*

GIACOMO PUCCINI

Golden West has not held the boards anything like so well as those other works is due to Puccini's failure to evoke anything resembling the Wild-West, Buffalo-Bill atmosphere which the libretto demands. But his sense of the stage as a generalized quality, and of particular atmosphere in varying works, together with his directness, his cutting superfluities, and his skill in placing his big scenes, his high lights, and the inevitable throb of his climaxes, must be recognized by the student of opera.

Mr. Newman finds, as the central element in Puccini, "a self-pity that tried to heal itself of its wounds by lavishing pity upon others." This element did not crystallize until late in his life; and it is not impossible to find in Puccini's work, together with this self-pity, a certain personal hardness and curious cruelty. It is not always easy to distinguish between what is core, edible pulp, and rind, nor to separate the moving elements in the composer as a man and as an artist. We may note, in passing, that Puccini immensely admired Wagner, whom he knew to be an infinitely greater artist than himself or the rest of the men of his time. If, as someone has neatly said, he is so often to be found writing in Italics, it was partly because he had found that this was the individual way which fitted his mind and heart and realized that Germanics would be a misfit, and partly because he shrewdly knew that for success on the post-Wagnerian stage, effects must be swift, brief, cumulative, and shorn of undergrowth—shorn, even, of the philosophy which his latest work makes us think he was growing into. He had the born dramatist's eye for situations, curtains, big scenes; and, taking the long perspective of nineteenth-century opera, where, outside Verdi, could any similar vividness in this special respect be found? Though most operagoers have always thought infinitely more about the singers and their tunes than about anything else, there is in Puccini's works, marked or unmarked, the additional excitement of this big-scene element; there is also his special skill in delineating heroines, and women characters in general (more distinctively than men), a quality appealing additionally to the women in his audiences in an era of novel reading and the rise of the cinema.

It may be found that musicians are not so susceptible to some of the qualities in Puccini's music which delight the layman. They complain that so many of his tunes bear a family likeness; but what other element so such pleases the lovers of popular tunes, who, if they were presented with a different idiom in each, would never get them by heart and would therefore never like any of them? It is no small measure of Puccini's skill that he was able to hold the interest of millions in his tunes; if his tunes had been too much alike, he could not have done so.[8]

Those whooping, soaring tunes, always carefully calculated for climax and vocal capacity, with the violins playing in octaves with them, prove irritating to some music lovers, yet are the very epitome of the sensuous machinery of Puccini's skill. The number of his different ways of attack is surprisingly limited, but his use of them is so skillful that the great majority of people like his music immensely and never complain of its being monotonous.

The curious and rather sad thing about him is that, just as he seemed about to take a new turning, he died. His new way would hardly have been as wonderful as that of Verdi in *Falstaff,* but his posthumous *Turandot* (and, to a similar extent, *Gianni Schicchi,* which more nearly adopts the standpoint of the *Falstaff* writing) seems to promise fresh pleasures for opera lovers, whether they happen to be devotees of

---

[8] Some day it might be profitable (musically, if not financially) to delve into the foundations of success in popular music. One of them is, undoubtedly, the art of reminding simple people of things they know and like, without being too reminiscent; but the degree to which reminiscence can be carried in such levels of musical art is very much greater than that which more experienced hearers will stand. On this score alone, we can expect some difference between musicians and laymen in the estimate of composers like Puccini.

Puccini's or not. And all such fresh pleasures in music need to be cultivated: there are not too many of them!

LESSER ITALIANS

Outside Verdi and Puccini, the tale of the late-nineteenth-century
Italian opera composers is thin enough. But it would be ungrateful to
pass by *Cav.* and *Pag.* (the familiar abbreviations of the two short
operas, *Cavalleria rusticana* and *Pagliacci,* which have formed such a
staple diet for opera lovers ever since they were written) without a
word of appreciation, if only for their exciting effect on any who were
fortunate enough to hear them in their heyday—the '90's.

It is interesting to compare a Puccini aria (such as *Vissi d'arte*) with
a favorite from Mascagni's *Cavalleria*—the *Voi lo sapete,* for example.
In the latter, we have again manifest the Italian poignance, in a scene
wherein the deserted maiden sings of her love for the man who has
betrayed her and whom another girl has attracted. There is little to
choose in the sentimental coloring, but a wider comparison of the two
composers would show the superior resource and musicianship of Puccini. It is not, perhaps, easy to convince *Cavalleria* lovers of the difference because so many of them were brought up on the music in youth;
such early loves are apt to be lasting, whatever the quality of their
object. A clever critic suggested that the reason Mascagni (1863–1945)
has been liked best when at his worst is that only then is he most truly
himself—sure of himself, unassailed by doubt, unmoved by any impulse (as Puccini was moved) to experiment and to probe wider worlds
of feeling. Mascagni has never lacked flashes of the true imaginative
spark; but the whole man was never able to catch fire from them. That
was his tragedy. At one time, he was called the true successor of Verdi;
but, since *Cavalleria,* written when Mascagni was twenty-six (it won
a prize in an operatic-writing contest), not one of a dozen or more
other operas of his has caught the easy ear of the public.

Leoncavallo (1858–1919) is another one-work man about whom
there is no more to say than about Mascagni; less, indeed, for his scope
was slighter. Both these composers were caught up in the *verismo*
craze of the time—a theory that operas and plays increase their artistic
value through the depiction of the ugly and vulgar as well as the good
and beautiful—stemming from the great success of Bizet's *Carmen* in
France. The famous Prologue from Leoncavallo's *Pagliacci* is a happy-
enough idea dramatically, though its sentiment is pure humbug—that
the sighs and tears from the other side of the footlights are real.

The Italian-German composer Ermanno Wolf-Ferrari (1876–1948) is known for two gay operas, *Il Segreto di Susanna* (Susanna's Secret) and *Gioielli della Madonna* (The Jewels of the Madonna). Italo Montemezzi (1875–1952) is scarcely known save by one opera, *The Love of Three Kings,* in which the absence of a distinctive style is largely compensated for by a keen stage sense of melodrama. It has an ingratiating effect of summarizing certain of the most attractive Wagnerian and Puccinian qualities, but it is not in any sense a great work. Umberto Giordano (1867–1948) was very successful with a series of stage works, those having the greatest appeal being *Andrea Chénier* and *Madame Sans Gêne.* Franco Alfano (1876–1954), Riccardo Pick-Mangiagalli (1882–1949), and Alfredo Casella (1883–1947) all achieved considerable attention in Italy, although their operas are little known on other European stages. One cannot but wonder whether the days of Italian operatic greatness are over—at least, for the present.

IN FRANCE

We need to beware, when considering nineteenth-century opera, of letting our minds be too fully occupied with the activities of the two really big figures, Verdi and Wagner, and failing to realize the essential qualities of such lesser men as Gounod, Massenet, Saint-Saëns, Bizet, and the rest. The characteristics of these French composers, be they personal or national, can be detected only by hearing a great deal of their music, and that is difficult, even in Paris. Halévy (1799–1862), for instance, is remembered solely by *La Juive,* an opera whose libretto was written for Rossini and rejected by him. In this work, the last opera in which Caruso appeared (in 1920), it is easy to see how the racial remembrance of persecution and sorrow has moved its Hebrew composer. But in the rest of his operas, Halévy shows very little sense of stage character and depth of dramatic feeling; besides, the deceptive attraction of that great luminary, Meyerbeer, seems to have been impossible to resist.

A SENTIMENTALIZED "FAUST"

What need be said of Gounod (1818–1893)? Since his great charm lay in a certain sensuousness, it is easy to abuse him, especially when we realize how he maltreated Goethe's *Faust* and Shakespeare's *Romeo and*

Juliet. And yet, for years after its first production (in 1859), *Faust* was a musical favorite in all countries,[9] with its stirring scenes, its melodiously gilded music, its Romantic plot, and its gay, lively ballet music. In general, it may be said of Gounod, as it was of Sullivan, the English operetta composer, that he was "too much at ease in Zion"—his effects were too easily and too cheaply achieved. The ballet music is often heard; but, in most of the modern productions of *Faust,* how trivial is the dancing! We, who have been brought up on the Russian ballet, not to speak of the modern abstractionists, are apt to forget the place which the ballet held in French opera; and we must hear and see with different apparatus, if we can, the nineteenth-century French opera ballets, which seem to tend to kill what little dramatic reality we can find in these works.

Gounod is a combination of delicate sensuousness, entirely charming melody, and mild melodrama. Infinitely the greatest of these is his melody. Remembering that he was the composer of one of the world's most famous operas, let us enjoy this melody without too much sniffing and pass on to other French talents.

A PARODIZING BOULEVARDIER

Offenbach (1819–1880) is not easy to classify; he loved to do everything in a big way. This, a characteristic of the Paris of his day, the Second Empire, was fully appreciated; yet, when a law was passed forbidding more than four characters on the scene at one time, as a form of protection for bigger enterprises, Offenbach could make the operetta form a huge success. He was a witty parodist: the Greek legends, so nobly treated by men like Gluck, were to him subjects for skits and jests; and he treated many of them in such clever works as *Orphée aux enfers* (1858) and *La Belle Hélène* (1864). Romanticism, that movement of liberalism, took on this humorous aspect in the French taste of the '50's and '60's, and Offenbach could throw together two or three of these extravagant and parodying works in a year.

Yet his *Tales of Hoffmann,* a posthumous work, reveals a deeper power. This was revised and partly orchestrated by Guiraud; but its composer knew that it was his masterpiece, and there remains the question whether, if he had begun earlier to dig deeper, he might not have

---

[9] A noted American critic, punning on the term given by Wagner to the special theater which he had built for the production of his operas, the *Festspielhaus,* dubbed the Metropolitan Opera in New York the *Faustspielhouse.*

OFFENBACH

produced more of such works. Speculation is idle: enough that his inventions have delighted millions and that his art has been well assimilated by many a composer since. We English-speaking peoples are most conscious of it in the works of Sullivan.

A GENIUS AND SOME TALENTS

Bizet (1838–1875) is remarkable in that, after writing a number of operas that were not notable successes but which stand musical scrutiny exceedingly well, he wrote one at the very end of his life, *Carmen,* that has remained one of the most popular of all operas, for it is as full of drama as his other works were short of it. It seems as if this composer's exquisite taste in the spinning of light harmonic webs was not sufficient to assure success until he came to the one subject which fired his imagination—that of the highly temperamental and irresistibly charming Spanish cigarette girl, Carmen. This is one of the happiest "accidents" in the whole history of opera; for this work, produced only three months before Bizet's untimely death, remains an unalloyed delight as well for the unsophisticated listener as for the jaded musician.

Hardly ever has a composer of real worth become so completely obscured by his work as Bizet. His correspondence, published a number of years ago, does not in any sense reveal the sort of man we should expect from hearing such a work as *Carmen*. Instead of a lively, independent musical liberal, we find an industrious, gifted, careful musician, who thought of his profession only as a means for acquiring honors and making money.

He early received recognition for his undoubted gifts, and in 1857, before he was 19, he was given the *Prix de Rome,* which was the highest official honor that France could bestow on a young composer. Several works came out of his study in Rome: *Don Procopio,* to an Italian libretto, and *La Guzla de l'emir,* the latter destroyed after it had been accepted at the Opéra Comique. But his later operas, *Les Pêcheurs de perles* (The Pearl Fishers), 1863, and *La Jolie fille de Perth* (The Fair Maid of Perth), 1867, each received eighteen performances during his lifetime, despite the fact that they show but little originality of melody, harmony, or orchestration. Bizet then undertook three more works for the French theater, leaving them all unfinished in order to work at his one-act opéra comique, *Djamileh,* which was berated by the critics because of its Wagnerian tendencies.

In spite of this long list of failures and half-completed attempts at writing operas, another theater manager asked Bizet for a score, this time for incidental music to a play by Daudet, *L'Arlésienne.* Although in its original form this music was a failure, the composer later presented it without the drama and achieved considerable success with it. In this music (usually heard in two orchestral suites), redolent of the south, Bizet for the first time let himself go and wrote as he actually felt, without consideration for effects. The result is music beloved by all who have heard it and thought by some to be better music than that in *Carmen*.

Notwithstanding the fact that Bizet's librettists destroyed much of the original strength of Mérimée's story on which *Carmen* is based, and that Bizet himself had no thought of achieving authentic Spanish atmosphere in it, he was able to provide such unusual harmonies, modulations, and orchestral color as to make his opera a great success. As someone has well said, it is the spirit of dramatic fervor and the musical quality of this work which triumphed over its obvious weaknesses. It was the first of a long succession of *verismo* operas, works which emphasize sordid and brutal subjects rather than the usual noble, inspiring, or humorous ones.

A statement that throws a great deal of light on French taste is the

GEORGES BIZET

one, taken from a French history of music, to the effect that the "musician who really ruled the theater between the years 1880 and 1910" was J. Massenet (1842–1912). Possessed of a certain delicacy of sentiment and lightness of craftsmanship, these works of Massenet's—*Hérodiade* (based on the story of St. John the Baptist and Salome), *Thaïs, Manon, Werther* (bowdlerized Goethe), and *Le Jongleur de Notre Dame*—give a strange suggestion of being hardly more than musical rose water and glycerin—glutinous masses of sentimentality faintly perfumed with the odor of romance. Yet Massenet was something of an innovator in his replacement of spoken dialogue by a form of recitation with orchestral accompaniment similar to the *melodrama,* thus allowing a quicker delivery of the words than would be possible in singing and avoiding the stiffness of recitative. In this, and the fact that he tried to reflect every nuance of the feeling of his characters, he paved the way for the greater work of Debussy in *Pelléas et Mélisande.*

Massenet's teacher, Ambroise Thomas (1811–1896), is of even lesser import, though he is remembered for his setting of Goethe's *Mignon.*

It can hardly be maintained, in reality, that either literary or musical taste was on a very high level in nineteenth-century France, in spite of the fact that it was the only country which officially patronized literature through supporting an academy of literary artists. It was Scribe, the facile librettist and playwright, who set the standards; he was able, between the years 1820 and 1850, to "create a play frame so perfectly articulated, so facilely constructed, that any sort of sentimental stuff could be tacked on it and made plausible. His was the supreme triumph of mechanics over dramatic content. Even while innocent of any of the larger virtues of the dramatist—he knew nothing of character drawing and little of dramatic grip in the profound sense—he made hundreds of plays that pleased untold audiences. He mastered theatrical device, filled his pieces with obvious type figures, pathetic incidents, skillful ravelings and unravelings, clever sayings, happy endings, etc., and developed a formula for theatrical effectiveness" (Cheney: *The Theatre*).[10] In brief, he gave the people what they wanted: a smooth article and a sweet concoction. And it was this taste which created the demand in French dramas and librettos throughout most of the century.

It was a long time before genius or poetry or incisive characterization came into the music drama, in Germany in Wagner and in France, in a subtler way, in Debussy. It was one of the strange moves of fate that enabled Debussy, whose music is hardly dramatic at all, to write the only French opera that can genuinely be called a masterpiece—*Pelléas et Mélisande*. But this did not come until 1902. Before then, it must be allowed that, with a mild outburst into "realism," as when Bruneau set Zola's *Attack on the Mill* or when Bizet wrote *Carmen* or when Charpentier (1860–1956) charmed us lyrically in *Louise* at the end of the century, there is little but melodramatic Romanticism of a weak sort in any French opera of the period, with the possible exception of two by Chabrier (1841–1894), whose *Gwendoline* and *Le Roi malgré lui* show definite Wagnerian tendencies.

Saint-Saëns (1835–1921), a curious mixture of classicism and sentimentality, wrote, daringly, upon the Biblical story of Samson and Delilah, a theme which so shocked the English that they refused to allow this work, which was highly popular elsewhere—first produced by Liszt at Weimar in 1877—on their operatic stages until 1909! Saint-Saëns carried French versatility to its extreme; he did not hesitate to

[10] "It is said that Heine on his deathbed, when his breath was failing, was asked if he could hiss; and his answer was: 'No, not even a play of Scribe's' " (Cheney).

attempt all manner of things; but only *Samson et Dalila* has kept the boards. Édouard Lalo (1823–1892), in his *Le Roi d'Ys,* treated an exotic subject with imaginative delicacy.

As early as 1830, Halévy made a ballet of *Manon Lescaut,* one of the sentimental tales by the Abbé Prévost that several composers (including Puccini, Auber, and Massenet) delighted to set. There have been a number of other French ballet composers: everyone knows Delibes's charming *Coppélia* music, brought out at the time of the Franco-Prussian War; and the ballet suites of Luigini (a Frenchman in spite of his name) have been done to death on every conceivable occasion.

Dukas, who has so long been thought of merely as the composer of the witty tone poem, *L'Apprenti sorcier,* wrote a delightful opera, *Ariane et Barbe Bleue,* a setting of a Maeterlinck fantasy with a decidedly Wagnerian tincture. The operas of Fauré (1845–1924) are almost unknown outside Paris as are his other distinguished works. *Penelope* (1913) is one of his few contributions to the lyric stage, but his music to the play *Shylock* is well worth hearing, and that for *Pelléas et Mélisande* forms an interesting study in comparison with Debussy's. Vincent d'Indy (1851–1931) is another neglected French composer. He was a follower of Franck, and his *La Légende de Saint-Christophe* (1920), a kind of combined oratorio and opera, contains some delectable music, while such extracts from *Fervaal* as can ordinarily be heard reveal a great talent. No résumé of French operatic activities, however brief, would be complete without mention of André Messager (1853–1929), writer of a great number of melodious operettas, which had a phenomenal success in France and England.

There seems to be only one conclusion possible after surveying France's contributions to the operatic form: although there was a great deal of activity, very little that is worth while came of it, and, although many of the decisive moves in the development of this form were made in Paris, the French have contributed few first-rate operas to the international repertoire. It seems that the capacity of this people lies more in writing music for plays than in producing indissoluble music and drama.

IN GERMANY

Peter Cornelius (1824–1874) is better known by his songs and choruses than by operas; but there is one, *The Barber of Bagdad,* which is still remembered kindly. The composer was a nephew of a well-known German painter and grew up in an artistic milieu. He was a great friend and disciple of Wagner's and did most of his work in the circle of the Wagnerians. Having a stronger sense of style than most of his contemporaries, he was not entirely swamped by the tremendous vigor of the great figure of his epoch. He was a quiet soul, fervent, generous, and simple. His music deserves more recognition than it has ever received; but his gift was more lyric than dramatic, and he was wise to confine it to those subjects which gave him the right feeling of freedom.

It is fitting that we add here, because of the contemporary popularity of one of his operas, the name of another operatic composer who is little known today—Karl Goldmark (1830–1915). *Die Königen von Saba,* first produced in Vienna in 1875, became known the world over; Goldmark spent ten years in writing it, lavishing on its glowing score his natural warmth of expression and love for Oriental color. He wrote, in addition, six other operas, chamber music, and songs, besides a great deal of orchestral music.

AN ISOLATED FIGURE: HUMPERDINCK

One other German opera composer, this time of the post-Wagnerian period, deserves special mention here: Engelbert Humperdinck (1854–1921). (Richard Strauss, the greatest of all German opera composers since Wagner, is dealt with in a separate chapter.) Humperdinck is known for two operas—his charming, heart-on-sleeve *Hänsel und Gretel,* still a good draw for lovers of sentiment, and *Die Königskinder.* It is perhaps unfair to complain that Humperdinck was so often nearly Wagnerian, and then not quite: he did well to keep so much of his own soul in that day. While he lacked the forging power of the greater man, he never wrote an ugly or a careless page. There is ample beauty in his music, much more than one might expect from his busy life as critic and professor. Criticism never seemed to sour him, and his music sounds anything but academic. The happy display of German toys in *Hänsel* is never vulgar, for Humperdinck had good taste as well as a lively imagination, gifts sometimes denied to Germans. In *Die Königs-kinder* he seems to be seeking deeper and trying to build more boldly; and sometimes in it he comes very near to a great nobility of feeling which is not readily found in the work of that day. But it is high

PLATE FROM THOMAS WILSON'S "DESCRIPTION OF GERMAN AND FRENCH WALTZING," 1816 The waltz began with the march, partners standing side by side with arms held in the position shown in Figure 1, or, alternatively, Figure 2. Soon the dancers began the slow waltz, Figures 3 and 4; the more lively *sauteuse* followed, with jumping steps, Figures 5, 6, and 7. Then came the *jetté,* in which the couples whirled about in quick tempo in the position shown in Figure 8; and Figure 9 shows the final pose.

promise, usually, rather than complete fulfillment of noble expression. One can but feel drawn to this rather lonely figure of the Wagnerian epoch.

It would be ungracious to forget here those great providers of the Viennese gaieties of the century: the Johann Strausses, father and son, as well as the lesser composers, Von Suppé and Millöcker. Johann Strauss the elder was made conductor of the court balls of Vienna in 1845. His son established his own reputation, first, through a series of summer concerts in St. Petersburg from 1855 to 1865. From 1870 on, he wrote mainly operettas; merely to catalogue his and his father's works would be an immense task. Everyone should hear young Johann's *Die Fledermaus* as it is sung by his compatriots, not as it is done by heavy-handed Anglo-Saxons; it belongs to the gay Viennese life of the period, which paralleled that of mid-century Paris, when so many minor composers flourished there, and represents the Offenbach operetta as seen and heard through another volatile nation's eyes and ears. But Strauss the younger was a much better musician than was

JOHANN STRAUSS
WITH HIS OR-
CHESTRA IN THE
VOLKSGARTEN,
VIENNA (drawing
by F. Kaliwoda in the
Historical Museum,
Vienna)

Offenbach, and his waltzes[11] and operettas have never been surpassed.

Which should not be interpreted to mean that some wonderfully sparkling additions have not been made to the Viennese operetta repertoire since the time of the Strausses. In 1905 the Hungarian composer Franz Lehár introduced *The Merry Widow* to a smiling society, and she has been a most welcome guest on every light-opera stage in the world ever since. In 1908 the native-born Oscar Straus converted Bernard Shaw's *Arms and the Man* into an operetta whose very name has become a household word everywhere— *The Chocolate Soldier.* Today, in spite of wars and effects of wars in Vienna, the tradition still holds.

[11] The waltz first appeared as a prominent dance somewhere about the end of the eighteenth century, its vogue being particularly pronounced during the 1820's and 1830's. It seems to have descended from the old German *Ländler* and to have had a special fascination for the Viennese, who, Beethoven complained toward the end of his life, were waltz-mad. Chopin, too, found that people would rather attend the astonishingly numerous balls than his recitals. A distinguishing feature of the dance was the various posturings of the arms, which liberty of gesture excited violent comment from many onlookers of the period, who complained of "the undue freedom with which the ladies were treated, and the obliging manner in which the freedom was returned by the females" (Burney).

THE LATER ROMANTICS

Johannes the Great

Strength, honesty, and sympathy—these have been the qualities which have carried the message of Brahms to the whole world.

W. J. Henderson: *New York Sun*

A COMPOSER LONG MISUNDERSTOOD

In the year 1900, the people of Boston, who liked to pride themselves on living in the Athens of America, built a proud new home for the great symphony orchestra which one of their wealthy citizens had developed for their musical enlightenment. In describing this new symphony hall, a paragraphist in one of the town's most important papers added to his description of the building a quip to the effect that the architects had forgotten to provide one thing—to add to each of the numerous and handsomely designed *Exit* signs over the various doors the line

In Case of Brahms!

Five or six years before this, Bernard Shaw, who started his writing career in the role of music critic and who put into his early critiques written for the London *World* some of the most searching and trenchant things that have ever been said about music, perpetrated this fatuity:

To me it seems quite obvious that the real Brahms is nothing more than a sentimental voluptuary with a wonderful ear. For respectability's sake he adopts the forms academically supposed to be proper to great composers . . . but you have only to compare his symphonies and quintets with those of Beethoven and Mozart to become conscious that he is the most wanton[1] of composers . . .

[1] The *Oxford Dictionary* gives the following definitions for this: "sportive, playful, capricious, irresponsible, luxuriant, wild, motiveless, random, serving no purpose"!

542

and that when his ambition leads him to turn his industry in any other direction, his charm does not turn with it and he becomes the most superficial and irrelevant of formalists.

A more sympathetic but anxious American critic of the same period, W. J. Henderson, felt called upon to warn his readers that a man is not "necessarily a mere formalist because he clings to the old-fashioned sonata form. Brahms's compositions show a completeness of architectonic detail, superimposed upon a symmetrical and organic development, such as are to be found in those of no other symphonist except Beethoven. Why deny the late Viennese master depth of feeling because he fashioned the expression of that feeling with all the force of a gigantic musical intellect? Brahms's music grows slowly in public favor because it is not easy for the careless hearer to grasp its inner spirit. But it is not true that to be real music demands a Swinburnian diction. Some day, I think, if not soon [this was written in 1898, a year after the composer's death], the world will see how profoundly representative of his nation and his time Brahms was, and he will be hailed, as Milton was, an organ voice of his country. The irresistible seriousness of Germany has never spoken with more convincing accent than in the music of Brahms. There is a feeling in this music which is far removed from any possibility of a purely sensuous embodiment. It may take time for the entire musical world to come under the spell of this austere utterance, but Brahms had the happiness of knowing ere he died that wherever music was cultivated, his individuality had at least made itself known."

These echoes from the last decade of the past century make rather strange reading today when Brahms is firmly ensconced in the circle of the gods along with Bach, Beethoven, and others. Why the doubt and hesitation and misunderstanding of the nineties—this feeling that Brahms (and to a large extent Bach as well, if we read the criticisms of the time aright) was an "inaccessible intellectual," a "recluse of the mind who dwelt in solitude, wrapped in speculations beyond the ken of common souls"?

THE REASONS

The answer is a simple one. Suddenly in the midst of the swirling vortex of Romanticism, in the period when music exuded personality, flamed with passion (Wagner's great works were just becoming known), and glowed with poetry, there appeared this serious, sober-

JOHANNES BRAHMS

hued artist who insisted on the necessity for restraint in expression and who, instead of composing in the admired free forms of the Romanticists, revived the vigorous sonata form of the classicists. And, because he insisted on form and careful intellectual manipulation in his writing, he was thought to have abjured imagination and forsaken feeling.

Today, it is possible to realize the error of such a theory. But to contemporaries Brahms was not a figure to fire the imagination: there is little question that his placid, rather sedentary, life favored the legend of his dullness, his heaviness in orchestration, his stodginess in thought. And his rugged simplicity of character, his essentially intellectual method of developing his genius, his hatred of all easy methods of attaining popularity made his own path difficult. It was only after coming to realize the great depth of feeling which is in his music and the lofty method of his communicating it that his fellows began to realize that "here was a truly great man, great in his elementary nature, great in his almost Biblical manner of expression." And this conviction, once attained, has grown so steadily that today we are in danger of taking his uniqueness and individuality too much for granted.

It is easy enough to be wise after the fact. But, if those who so completely misunderstood Brahms had only turned to such an early work as his now famous song, *Liebestreu (O versenk' dein Leid, mein Kind)* from his Op. 3, written when he was twenty, they would have found plenty of evidence which refutes their charges of coldness and intellectuality. In this short work, there is present the essential essence of Brahms's style, for it is compelling in its emotional force and indescribably poignant in its feeling; and it is constructed with the extraordinary mastery of form that was thought by his critics to be the evidence of his concentration on structure, to the neglect of emotional content. Henderson has pointed out the fact that this one work is an unanswerable demonstration of the error of such a theory: "Brahms felt to the bottom of his soul; he had the human sympathy and the divine imagination which enabled him to publish his conceptions in perfected form."

BRAHMS'S PLACE IN MUSIC

No better summary of this composer's place in music could be desired; it can be applied to all his great works:[2] the four symphonies—the majestic, exultant, but somber First, the lovely, lyric, and warmly idyllic Second, the alternatingly passionate and serenely contemplative Third, and the austere Fourth; the two great piano concertos, in reality symphonies with a richly interwoven piano part added to their gorgeous orchestral fabric; the mysterious and deeply felt *Requiem;* the beautifully written songs, which someone has called the most confidential communications of a solitary and almost abnormally sensitive soul ever written. In his piano works, while he provides a great deal of matter demanding the highest technical dexterity on the part of the executant, he avoids the "shimmering superficiality" so often written into music of this kind; his compositions for piano solo range from the graceful and lilting Hungarian dances and waltzes to the warmly expressed

[2] As was the case with every other composer, Brahms was not always on the heights; sometimes his imagination failed him and he had recourse to padding. His critics were not entirely wrong: there is considerable of what can only be called extraneous matter in some of his works, especially in the earlier chamber music. The following list of his compositions will show how wide a field he cultivated and how busy he was during his creative years:
Orchestral works: 9, including 4 symphonies, 2 overtures, 1 set of variations
Vocal music: 33 chorus and quartet compositions, including the *Deutsches Requiem*
Vocal music: 365 songs and duets
Chamber music: 24 quartets, quintets, trios, etc.
Concertos: 4
Piano works: 15 solo numbers and sets, excluding studies and exercises; 8 collections of duet music for piano
Organ works: 3, including 2 sets of chorale preludes.

Sonata in F Minor and *Sonata in F Sharp Minor,* both of them monuments of his genius.

A North German in every fiber of his being, Brahms was born in Hamburg in 1833. The son of a poor local musician, he was brought up under circumstances which must have proved revolting to him and which may have accounted for some of his later personal eccentricities. After years of careful preparation, some of them given over to concert tours with the Hungarian violinist Reményi, some spent in quiet retirement at the little court of Detmold, absorbing the works of the classic masters, Brahms settled in Vienna in 1872 and spent the rest of his life in the congenial atmosphere of that warm-blooded, lively city. Thus, his later music shows a peculiar combination of hereditary North German traits and environmental South German ones, of a natural, impulsive Romantic temperament moulded by industrious and eager study of his great predecessors.

In his life, as in his music, Brahms was interested in the universal side of human nature rather than in its personal, eccentric aspect; and, because he usually showed a gruff exterior, assumed partly to cover up his extremely sensitive nature and partly to ward off snobbish flattery, he was thought gauche and crude. His intimates were men and women of direct, unassuming nature; it made no difference whether they were of high or humble estate. He had no use for society and spent a great deal of time avoiding it after he had become one of the great men of Vienna. Brahms could be called "religious" in the ethical sense of the term—none other could have written the *Requiem* or the *Four Serious Songs,* the latter his last compositions and his final self-revelation. But he was, nevertheless, a fatalist, gazing with warm eyes at the beauties of this world while realizing their essential futility. Because he recognized in Bach a kindred spirit, he turned to him as to a great god: all his life he worshiped at this shrine, and his music, both in its solid structure and its expression of profound thought and deep emotion, gained thereby.

Although he spurned many of the outer graces of life, Brahms was a man of real culture; he read widely and thought deeply during the quiet days of his rather lonely life. A contemporary describes him as shunning all hackneyed and worn-out texts when seeking materials for songs, adding the statement that "very few persons are as little given to favoring the ordinary as he is." It is because of this fastidiousness of taste and the simple strength of his character that Brahms is a good mentor. Which is not to say that he was by any means at all times the

BRAHMS'S WORKROOM IN VI-
ENNA, 1872 (etching by Schmutzer)
Nothing illustrates better the essentially simple and human quality of
Brahms's life than this intimate glimpse
of the room in which he worked, taken
from a contemporary etching.

solemn classicist. There was in him a strain of wilder Romanticism that
is not always sufficiently appreciated. It comes out in the first piano
concerto and can be found as late as the clarinet quintet, Op. 115,
where the impassioned feeling in part of the slow movement is a
remarkable outburst, made more significant by the contrast with the
coda, in which we may perhaps hear resignation of spirit. Alfred
Einstein has spoken of "the paradise of melodic purity out of which
sprang his waltzes, his Hungarian dances and gypsy songs, and his
folk-song arrangements." In the quintet we may all join Brahms; and
it is a happy discovery for many that Brahms had his lighter side. The
works mentioned above have served, for many a music lover, as a door
of introduction to the master's storehouse; thus having entered, the
neophyte need never glance fearfully at that other door labeled "In
Case of Brahms."

In the universal delight in the dance, Brahms joins the early Strausses
(the Johanns) and the late expert (Richard), with a host of composers
of the eighteenth and nineteenth centuries, including even Mozart and
Beethoven and ranging clear through to Tchaikovsky and his successors. In the three sets of piano waltzes (the Op. 39 and the older and

the newer *Liebeslieder* series, the last two having vocal parts also),
Brahms affectionately framed in miniature the best of German sentiment in this long-cherished form.

These traits diversify and round out a nature gloriously lavish and
lyrical. As Basil de Sélincourt has said, even the epic with him was
lyrical. He represents, this thoughtful writer adds, one of the inevitable
stages of reflection on the artistically religious standpoint that art is
indistinguishable from the pure essence of the good. "Bach's is still
the attitude of cosmic union; his inspiration is direct; it is as if the voice
of the Creator were flowing through him. Beethoven is aware of cleav-
age; he is a Titan of revolt, a Prometheus affirming the divine and
drawing its fires from heaven. The spirit of Brahms is a spirit of atone-
ment and reconciliation; tragedy is recognized and accepted; and now
the purely human longings and raptures revive; a passion of luxuriant
beauty, mingling joy and pain, flows through his music" (London
Observer).

Sélincourt goes on to speak of Brahms's assurance of truth, of his
sublime regal aloofness, while living a hearty, commonplace life, enjoying his beer and sausages. In the realm of feeling, he is king: "for
common men, feeling is action and memory of action; for him, feeling
and memories of feeling clustered where he alone could enact them,
in his imperious forms of sound."

Hugo Wolf and Styles in Song

To think of his songs one by one is to see defiling
before the eyes a veritable pageant of humanity.

Ernest Newman

THE LIED, A CHARACTERISTIC GERMAN FORM

The German word
lied literally translated means simply "song"; to the music lover, however, it has come to have a special significance because of its association
with a particular kind of song developed by the Austro-German
masters. In Italy, one of man's most cherished possessions has always
been a beautiful singing voice, and Italian composers have written most
naturally and spontaneously when composing vocal music; so we

expect Italian songs to emphasize melodies constructed for the display of beautiful voices. In France, where art is more a matter of fastidious discrimination and good vocal material is not so abundant, songs are more adroit and cleverly sophisticated than spontaneous. In Germany, owing to a number of causes, among them the innate dramatic sense of the people and their capacity for deep feeling, songs have developed into a sort of miniature music drama in which text, tune, and accompaniment play co-equal roles. The expression of the proper dramatic mood or the general philosophical concept contained in the words is as important to the lieder composer (and the lieder singer, as well) as the attainment of a beautiful melodic line or the provision of a suitable accompanimental background, which has dropped any suggestion of the classic figured bass and which elaborates every possible harmonic detail.

It was Schubert who first evolved the lied as a definite musical form, although some casual experiments in this field had been made by composers before his time, notably by Mozart and Beethoven. When, at eighteen, Schubert wrote his famous *Gretchen am Spinnrade* and *Erlkönig*, the lied was born. Listen to these songs interpreted by a master singer, and the characteristics we have mentioned will immediately become evident: the breadth and expressive quality of the accompaniments, often suggesting elements of tone painting; the eloquence of the musical constituents, the melody and harmony; and the union of all these to form a mood picture which conveys the very heart of the text. So it is with such songs as Schumann's *Im wunderschönen Monat Mai*, Franz's *Im Rhein, im heiligen Strome*, or Brahms's *Feldeinsamkeit, Von ewiger Liebe*, or perhaps the most poignant of all, *O Tod, wie bitter bist du* from his *Vier ernste Gesänge*. A study of any of these will give an insight into the whole nature and purpose of the lied.

THE STYLES OF ITS COMPOSERS

Each of the outstanding lieder composers made his own distinctive contribution to the form. Schubert's was that of lovely melody, a melody which fits the mood of the text exactly. Schumann, being a pianist, emphasizes the accompaniment, without undue neglect of the vocal line; in general, his songs are more powerful and suggestive but not often so spontaneous as Schubert's. The desire of Robert Franz (1815–1892) in his songs was not realism, but "peace and reconciliation." Brahms favored the strophic form as the most suitable relation between melody and accompaniment, but his striking individuality and his insistence on formal finish are to be found in every song he wrote. It remained for Hugo Wolf (1860–1903), a composer who concentrated on the writing of songs as Chopin had on piano compositions, to bring to the lied some of the principles of the Wagnerian music drama. Which is to say that Wolf used a dramatic instrumental score for the basis of his songs, a score which vividly characterizes and powerfully portrays the thoughts and moods of the words, making use of definite motives as thematic material, and above this superimposes a vocal line which makes no pretense of melodic continuity but rather aims at a faithful rendition of the words.

WOLF'S MASTERY

Wagner was Wolf's god: both masters proceeded to their work from an identical standpoint, that of making music the perfect expression of poetic ideas. But Wolf also based his writing solidly on the work of his predecessors in Romantic song writing and, coming last, was able to avail himself of all their achievements. We find in the Wolf songs, quite a few of them written at white heat, sometimes as many as three in a day, the final consummation of the process of gradual evolution that was started by Schubert and reinforced and made more dramatic by Wagner.

One of the greatest of Wolf's songs, *Prometheus,* from the Goethe cycle, shows his genius at its best, as well as his close affinity with Wagner. It was written in one of those intense outbursts of inspiration and creative energy, outbursts which were followed by periods of complete sterility and utter despair. A favorite method of working was that of composing cycles of songs from the works of various poets—Mörike, Kleist, Eichendorff, Goethe; he also set translations of poems from Italian and Spanish sources, works which comprise the *Spanisches Liederbuch* and the *Italienisches Liederbuch.* A feature of all Wolf songs is their carefully composed piano accompaniment, sometimes so elaborate as to overshadow the vocal part. The composer also orchestrated some twenty of his total output of two hundred sixty songs.

Forced by practical necessity to undertake the uncongenial work of a Viennese newspaper critic, Wolf made many influential enemies during his lifetime through his powerfully expressed articles on some contemporary musicians, notably Brahms. These men were able to prevent the appreciation of his genius, and his works never attained during his lifetime the popularity which was their due, in spite of the valiant efforts of several societies formed for the express purpose of spreading a knowledge of his style. But, after his premature death in an insane asylum, his name became famous throughout the musical world as the great master of German lied, one whose range of expression was as remarkable as its intensity of utterance. Characteristic examples of his songs are *Anakreons Grab, Auf einer Wanderung,* the three *Harfenspieler* from Goethe, *Gesang Weylas,* and *Verborgenheit.*

Richard Strauss

There is no such thing as Abstract Music; there is good music and bad music. If it is good, it means something; and then it is Programme Music.

Richard Strauss

STRAUSS'S LONG CAREER

Born during the flaming days of Romantic expression and living halfway through the non-Romantic twentieth century, Richard Strauss (1864–1949) was the center of the German music world in one capacity or another for well over fifty years. He has been variously described: as the heir of Wagner;[3] the last of the great Romantics (those who look upon him in this light contrast him with Mahler as the first of the German moderns); the greatest of all composers of program music; a bold harmonic innovator and dissonantal experimenter; and as the only opera writer since Verdi and Wagner whose scores are likely to be compared by posterity with the works of those immortals. Not so many years ago, it was thought that his career had been more or less a topsy-turvy one: that he was greatest in such youthfully exuberant works as his symphonic poems *Don Juan* and *Tod und Verklärung,* written when he was an unknown twenty-three-year-old *Kapellmeister* of the Royal Opera in Munich, and merely

[3] He himself said: "I have a complicated mind; someone like me had to come after Wagner so as to make his position clear."

facile and rather sterile in such works as *Die ägyptische Helena, Ara-
bella,* and *Daphne,* composed when he was a sixty-five-year-old world-
renowned figure. From the better vantage point of today, we can see
that this "progress in reverse" estimate of this last great German figure
in music is not an accurate one; that, although the fires of his early
genius were naturally damped during the later years of his career (he
continued to compose prolifically until a year before he died), they
burned more or less fitfully to the very end.

There can be little doubt about the phenomenal genius of these early
works. Before he wrote them, Strauss had been largely occupied in
training himself for the brilliant career opening before him. Born into
a musical family of Munich, he started his composing career in the
classic vein, writing a symphony, a wind-instrument serenade, and a
violin concerto while he was still in his teens. Coming into contact with
an ardent disciple and propagandist of the Liszt brand of Romanticism
—one Alexander Ritter—Strauss abandoned these earlier tendencies and
entered wholeheartedly into the folds of the new program-music school.
Several important conducting posts gave him a thorough mastery of
the orchestra and of how to write for it, and this, combined with his
native genius, enabled him to produce effects which up to his time had
hardly been dreamed of. If this seems overstatement, listen to the
terrific gusts of hot-blooded passion which sweep through *Don Juan,*
or the mysterious, intense brooding, the understanding comprehension
of *Tod und Verklärung,* the sparkling wit and devilish roguery of *Till
Eulenspiegel:* these are new things in music, and important ones. Superb, consummate craftsmanship is in all these works, and a colossal
energy which comes only when young men of genius and vivid imagination are working at white heat.

In these program pieces, Strauss was able to realize the ideal form of
the symphonic poem envisaged by Liszt. He found in this an opportunity to display his brilliant qualities at their best: an inimitable sense
of orchestral color, coupled with an ability to use it; a searing intensity
of expression, a universal emotionality; extraordinary powers of characterization. At the time these works were first produced, the great
topic of discussion at all the musical *conversazioni* was Strauss's bold
harmonic innovations and terrific dissonantal experiments; today, no
one would think of even suggesting these as a conversational topic, for
they have long been accepted as a matter of musical course and have
become a part of every composer's expressive technique.

Beginning with *Also sprach Zarathustra,* a musical realization of the

RICHARD STRAUSS
(from a painting by Max
Liebermann)

Nietzschean superman—a tremendous, daring attempt that is only
partially successful—a new tendency is to be noted. Scored for an enormous orchestral force, the work contains some of Strauss's most wonderful inspirations, particularly the pages at the beginning (the so-called
"sunrise music"), which really do suggest the "portals of eternity
swinging slowly asunder." But—and this is the crux of the matter—
there are stretches of rather aimless, commonplace music which seem
to be only striving for bombastic, sensational effect. This tendency becomes still more apparent in the tone poems which followed, *Don
Quixote, Ein Heldenleben,* and the *Symphonia domestica.* The first of
these contains a marvelous portrait of Cervantes's immortal hero, together with one of his faithful henchman, Sancho Panza; but it also
contains some overrealistic imitations that tend to distract the listener
and draw his attention from the spiritual quality of the portrayal. *Ein
Heldenleben* describes the exploits of a hero, obviously Strauss himself,
with a great deal of meaningless verbosity and almost shameless triviali-

ties. The *Symphonia domestica,* dedicated to his rather difficult wife, depicts scenes in the Strauss menage which are sometimes amusing without being in any sense inspiring. A later symphonic poem, *Eine Alpensinfonie,* is a huge, sprawling, rather washed-out picture of life and nature as experienced in the Alps.

The best of these tone poems can stand superbly on their own feet as music pure and simple; nevertheless, Strauss has insisted on associating them all with programs. When he first gave them to the world, it was the composer's practice to announce officially that he wished them to be taken as absolute music rather than as the elaboration of the specific details of a schematic program; then would follow, by one means or another, the issuing of information as to the ideas which were in the deviser's mind when he wrote the music and with which the audience had to familiarize itself if it was to comprehend the full significance and completely grasp the inner meaning of the composer's score. Time and time again this happened, until the peppery admirer of Strauss, Ernest Newman, was moved to protest: "with each new work, there is the same tomfoolery—one can use no milder word to describe proceedings that no doubt have a rude kind of German humor but which strike other people as more than silly."

THE OPERAS

It is through his fifteen operas that Strauss will probably be best known to posterity. In the best sense, these may be said to derive from Wagner, to some extent from Mozart, and even more from Gluck. The general style of his writing—his harmonic richness, the clang of his orchestration, the boldness of his dissonances, as well as his extraordinary flair for drama and the theater—stems from Wagner. The intuitive ease of his invention and his unusual gift for characterization suggest Mozart, whom he admired above all other composers. And the Olympian majesty of his approach to classic themes and his ability to move about easily in all sorts of theatrical situations come from Gluck.

Strauss was fortunate in the inventive power of his librettists; the early *Salome,* a masterpiece based on an erotic, horrible, but fascinating subject, is an adaptation of Oscar Wilde's play treating of the scorned love of the pagan Judean princess for Jokanaan the Prophet. *Elektra* is a lurid re-interpretation and re-creation of Sophocles, with a libretto by Hugo von Hofmannsthal, an Austrian dramatist of uncommon ability, who furnished Strauss with some of his finest librettos, especially that of *Der Rosenkavalier.* This is a treatment in comic and romantic fashion of a glittering Rococo theme, set in the Vienna of Maria Theresa, with moods alternating from wistful tenderness to boisterous rowdyism, from captivating charm to ridiculous horseplay; but everywhere, throughout the whole score, there is melody, ingratiating, incessant, exuberant melody, and plenty of catchy Viennese waltz rhythms. Full of sparkling life, the music of *Der Rosenkavalier* bespeaks Strauss's supreme mastery of craftsmanship and represents, many feel, the summit of his powers.

But the later operas have their virtues, too, and display other and perhaps less evident facets of his genius. *Ariadne auf Naxos* is a combination of modern opera and the spirit of Italian *commedia del arte;* in *Die ägyptische Helena* and *Die Liebe der Danaë*, Strauss and Hofmannsthal treat well-known classic subjects from new angles and with new decorative twists. *Die Frau ohne Schatten* is a rather abstruse treatise on humanity, so abstruse, in fact, that it has rarely been done outside Germany. *Daphne* is a legend shrouded in symbolic mist and pastoral legend. *Capriccio,* Strauss's last work in operatic form, completed in 1941, is a stylish modern conversation piece on the artistic relationship between words and music.

"From now on," Strauss is supposed to have said at the completion of *Capriccio,* "it will be all for harps." But this was not to be; in the remaining eight "Indian summer years" of his life, he completed a number of important works which show his inventive powers as active and fresh as ever: a work for string orchestra, the *Metamorphosen;* the oboe and second horn concertos; a duet concertino; two wind symphonies; and, above all else, the *Vier letze Lieder* (Four Last Songs).

All these works, as well as his later-period operas from *Ariadne* to *Capriccio,* show plenty of evidence of Strauss's expert musicianship, his wide range of ideas, and his powers of invention. In them, he moved progressively away from the big impressiveness of the post-Wagnerian idiom, although he never abandoned it altogether. A great deal of this music lacks the glowing fervency of his early days, and, in it, there are obvious weaknesses of emotional content and lack of communicative emphasis. In Germany, this later music of Strauss has been loudly hailed as the last word in musical revelation; it has not been similarly acclaimed elsewhere, but there is a general agreement as to its sensuous fluency and its unmistakable personal style. To realize this, it is but necessary to compare the soprano monologues from two of his operas: that of the Princess in *Der Rosenkavalier,* written in 1910, and that of the Countess from his last work, *Capriccio,* composed some thirty years later. Both are unmistakably by the same hand, although the first is naturally more warmly materialized; both employ the same soaring *cantilena*, springing directly from the meaning of the text and backed by the same rich, surging, radiant orchestral texture. No other composer could possibly have written either; and, although they are separated by a wide stretch of years full of rich achievement, they both show the same aspect of the composer's genius, the same ability to project unmistakably a musically significant theme so that no one could possibly miss it.

Strauss has attracted considerable attention as a writer of songs; the few that are best known are straight-forward, honest expressions of emotion which seems to have been deeply felt. Some of the later songs, written during the *Zarathustra, Quixote, Heldenleben* years, are less evidently inspired, but they are exceedingly well put together. At the very end of his career, in 1947, he wrote what may turn out to be his best works in this form, the *Vier letzte Lieder;* these show that his musical and poetically expressive powers were still at their height, and they contain a sense of achievement and an intimacy of expression which are to be found in none of his earlier music. Scored for orchestra and soaring soprano voice, the four songs are supremely moving in their calm acceptance of the fulfillment of life and their unfearing presentment of death; they constitute a sublimely intense postlude to a long life, fully and richly lived, and sound a poignant note of farewell to the world and the music which Strauss loved so dearly. At the same time, they clearly place him as the last composer of gigantic stature.

THE PLACE OF STRAUSS

1964, the hundredth anniversary of the birth of Strauss, provided an opportunity for the re-evaluation of his place in contemporary music history. It has become evident that he was the last composer to cope successfully with all the problems inherent in musical composition as they presented themselves in his time. The last great representative German composer, he obviously drew his sustenance from the rich soil of his heritage, and stands as its final product. The peculiar combination of blazing inspiration and obvious platitudes in his music makes it difficult to accept it as the work of a first-class composer. But its tremendous sweep, its rich orchestral language, and its communicative power make it impossible to rate it as the work of a minor figure. Strauss had a very definite notion of what his ultimate place would be in musical history. He is said to have described himself as a "minor figure with a bit part in the last act"; but as Irving Kolodin has well said, to be worthy of the company of such major players as Bach, Haydn, Mozart, Beethoven, Schubert, and Wagner, even a bit player would have to be a star.

César Franck and Musical Mysticism

A man of shining genius, loyal of heart and strong of soul, who seemed to have known the angels.

One of his pupils

The affirmation of incompetence pushed to dogmatic lengths.

Gounod on Franck's symphony

A BELGO-FRENCH COMPOSER

César Franck (1822-1890), though born in Belgium, is usually accounted a French composer, one of the few refreshingly original talents which that country developed in the late nineteenth century. After Berlioz, France fell upon thin times, in which neither the mingled classicism and sentimentalism of Saint-Saëns nor the theatrical and melodramatic operas of Gounod gave her a place in the front rank of the world's musical work. Chopin may perhaps be accounted partly French, but only by adoption; Franck's whole working life was spent in Paris, after his entering the *Conservatoire* there in 1837. His was a quiet and uneventful career: to most of his associates he was nothing more than a worthy organist and professor. Much of his time was spent conscientiously in giving music lessons to those who were not too anxious to receive instruction. Sundays always found him in his beloved organ loft at St. Clothilde, where for nearly forty years he performed his duties as an ardent church musician and a devout Christian. These tasks comprised his whole existence, until, one day in 1890, while going about such business, he was injured in a street accident, and died—as he certainly would have wished to die—in harness.

By profession, he was a church organist, and his music has become greatly beloved by his confreres, for he gave them a few of the finest things in their rather limited repertoire. There was something about his mind and, above all, his heart, a combination of simplicity and mysticism, which appeals strongly to church musicians, less strongly, perhaps, to those outside that circle. In addition to his organ works, Franck left an indelible impression on two other fields, those of the orchestra and chamber music. He left behind no great amount of music; much of the best of it was written in his late years. As a rule, he composed but one work in each of the large forms: one symphony, one piano concerto, one string quartet, one quintet, one violin sonata, and a handful of tone poems and piano and organ pieces. These are all precious to the lover of choice, inward things, for they are informed by a wonderful harmonic sense that alone would mark out Franck as a pioneer, one of the distinctive men of a great century. The pioneer is not necessarily a great composer; often he simply suggests new ways of looking at things, while others, many of them smaller men, work them out. It was Franck's good fortune to be able, in his modest corner of life, to work out, himself, so many of his new ideas that he stands alone, as easily recognizable as Berlioz or Delius; and this in spite of there having arisen a small school of his pupils, men like D'Indy and Chausson, who employed much of his personal idiom.

HIS INDIVIDUAL STYLE

In addition to his peculiar harmonic style, the chromaticism of which, once recognized, can never be mistaken, Franck developed what has come to be known as the "cyclic" form. In essence, this consists in the use of one or more themes whose development (in varied shapes) in several movements of a large work is a unifying feature of the whole. Liszt's use of "motto" themes had exhibited this element of construction, usually in a rather obvious manner, his thematic metamorphosis rarely being subtle although often broadly effective. Franck's use of such themes is as pervasive mood-influences, rather than simply as labels. The quintet is an excellent example of the employment of this device, as is the composer's most popular work, the *Symphony in D Minor*.

THE SYMPHONY

The first thing which is noticed about this symphony is the fact that it has been so strongly influenced by the composer's organ style: the sustained quality of its orchestration does not always make for greatest effectiveness, while its often rather rambling improvisatory character is better adapted to the organ loft than the concert hall. But it has its great moments, not all of them as "mystical" as its disciples have tried to make them out. Included in its utterances are some sentimentalities, which dangerously suggest the *boulevardier* rather than the religious mystic, and these are unfortunate enough to cheapen the essential nobil-

CÉSAR FRANCK
(from the painting
by Rougier, 1888)
He is seated at his
organ in the Church
of St. Clothilde.

ity of the whole. In 1889, when this work was first heard, it would have been surprising if Franck's sense of chromaticism had not been influenced by Wagner; but he is never bogged, as another organist-symphonist, Bruckner, so often was, by failure to trim his own peculiarly, sometimes clumsily, cut sails to the Wagnerian winds that carried him so powerfully on. At its first performance, the symphony was received with ridicule by the authorities and with cold indifference by the public. When his friends asked for his opinion, Franck answered happily, "Oh, it sounded well, just as I thought it would."

HIS STRENGTH AND WEAKNESS

There are here, as in most of the Franck works, certain little melodic tricks which some regard as weaknesses: the way he has, for instance, of making a melody center upon the third of the key. And his combination of naïveté with a sort of innocent bombast offends the taste of others, who think that Franck has too palpable a design upon our emotions; such people are apt to associate signs of aspirations with low cunning, a judgment which does not hold in Franck's case. The majority of music lovers are content to bask in the sunshine of experience which this composer's music affords; in a certain sense, he is narrow and limited in his feeling, but narrow-channeled waters are often found to run deep, and there is in their flowing a concentration of power that bears us strongly along.

Franck's best works are probably the three great organ *Chorals* (the name implies only that their thematic bases are melodies of a religious cast), especially the one in A minor (No. 3). This, one of the last things he wrote, opens rhapsodically and has a glorious development, perfectly suited to its medium. By no means all those who have heard the symphony, and perhaps some of the piano works,[5] realize the riches contained in these organ and chamber-music compositions. Wherever we listen in Franck, we have the revelation of a nature at once open and noble, innocent and yet informed, together with a manifestation of subtle craftsmanship. He wrote a great deal of church music of a rather hackneyed character, most of which had better be ignored; but, in his large-scale works, originality of a rare order is backed by an elevated intimacy, a brooding sense of otherworldliness that does not often become weak or vague. These are qualities which tend to strengthen the listener's spirit while it exalts and renews it.

The Viennese Twins—Bruckner and Mahler

Not until we know them well are we in a position to reject their music.

Pitts Sanborn

A VIENNESE MASTER

Any visitor to the Vienna of 1880, when the Austrian capital was in the heyday of its glory

[5] Of the sixteen works which Franck wrote for the piano, only two, the *Prélude, Choral et Fugue* (1884) and the *Prélude, Aria et Finale*, are often played. In addition to the symphony, he wrote six other works for orchestra that are hardly ever heard, with the exception of the delightful *Variations symphoniques* for piano and orchestra.

and the center of European interest in music, might have noticed wandering about the streets a peculiarly square-cut figure in black clothes of an obvious country style, with a broad-brimmed soft hat covering a shaggy, rugged head. This was Anton Bruckner, the simple, sincere, modest professor of organ, harmony, and counterpoint at the conservatory and lecturer in music at the university. If the visitor had been curious enough to follow this rustic-looking man to his modest rooms on the top floor of a house in the Schottenring, one of the city's busiest thoroughfares, he would have found, according to contemporary accounts, a severe-looking apartment meagerly furnished with a worn piano, an armchair, and a chest of drawers on which would be found some open scores and a wooden crucifix.

But our suppositious visitor would hardly be aware of these external surroundings; for it is most likely that his interest would be centered in the striking personality of a young musician who was so often to be found in the apartments of Professor Bruckner—a pale, intense, and extremely dynamic young Hebrew student of the conservatory and the university, Bruckner's private pupil and friend, Gustav Mahler. The names of these two figures of the twilight of Austrian Romanticism have become inextricably linked together, and with good reason: for never were two composers more closely akin spiritually. Both were Austrians born in the provinces and thrown together in the cosmopolitan crucible of the late nineteenth-century Vienna; both were intense, almost fanatical worshipers at the shrine of Wagner; both were natural Romantics, with a desire to carry on the traditions and grandeurs of the master's orchestral style, and yet possessed of a peculiar naïveté of spirit which made such expression difficult, if not almost impossible, for them; both were essentially saints and mystics, as well as men of inordinate ambitions and unfortunately uneven capacities when it came to composing. All of which is to say that both wrote a number of huge, sprawling, eclectic works, which do not hesitate to storm the highest heavens or plumb the lowest depths; which are of excessive length and intense earnestness; and which contain passages of almost unbelievable banality alongside some of great beauty and tremendous power. It is impossible to come to any just estimate of these scores, unlike anything else in music and speaking so personal a language, unless the hearer can see life as did their composers. As the doubters have so often remarked, it is difficult, after hearing a Bruckner or a Mahler symphony, to decide whether one has been hearing good stuff in spite of some bad moments or some poor stuff that has its good moments!

Stadtische Sammlungen, Vienna

ANTON BRUCKNER   (painting by Bératon)

Bruckner came of an Upper-Austrian family of school teachers; he had planned to follow the family tradition, but his natural talent for music stood in the way and so he entered the monastery of St. Florian to study music. Largely self-taught, he became a master of counterpoint and an expert organist, at first in the monastery church and later in the Cathedral of Linz. After eleven years of service there he went to Vienna, where he was appointed Court Organist and Instructor of Organ at the Conservatory. After receiving the post of University Lecturer in music in 1875 he was able to extend his composing to the writing of symphonies, having produced three settings of the Mass, the first written in the 1860's. However, he made slow progress against the prejudices and partisanships of the strongly entrenched Brahms circle, one of the members of which described his attempts at development as "symphonic boa-constrictors." In spite of constant rebuffs, he kept on writing and succeeded in having his symphonies played. But the Viennese remained largely oblivious of his stature as a composer until his *Seventh Symphony* received tremendous acclaim in Germany in 1884. Eight years later a spectacular performance of his next symphony finally convinced Bruckner's countrymen that he was a composer capable of expressing their own characteristics in a unique manner which only they could understand. His reputation outside Austria spread slowly, however, and it was not until many years after his death that his greatness as a symphonist was finally recognized.

Bruckner's genial melodic vein is typically Austrian and often suggests that of his compatriot Schubert, although the monumental sound of his orchestra and the epic quality of his musical thought constantly remind the listener of Wagner. Perhaps nothing better suggests Bruckner's background as an organist than the kind of improvisatory meanderings in which he so often indulges. He has nothing of Beethoven's architectural genius. Although the general outlines of his huge forms can be heard easily enough, his structures are too artless and too discursive to be always effective. He is apt to wander leisurely all around an idea rather than to tackle it directly: "I find many alluring paths which, however they may retard, do not obstruct my objective," he said. The monotony of rhythmic and thematic repetition that results is often maddening. It was his misfortune not to be very prolific in ideas and so he had to spin those he did possess to so great a length that they often become tiring. Symphonies that last an hour and a half are doomed to be declared "too long" by the unconverted.

Yet the simple devotion and unquestioning faith that is in this music is evident to every unprejudiced listener. And the nobility of its utterance and the sumptuousness of its color (strongly reminiscent of the Austrian Baroque architecture Bruckner knew so well) make a profound impression, especially on those coming to these works for the first time. The best known and most often played of the symphonies are the *Third* (1873), dedicated to Wagner, the *Fourth* ("Romantic"), written in 1874, the *Seventh* (1881–83), and the *Eighth,* his self-confessed masterpiece (1884–90). Their composer never seems to have been entirely sure of just what he wanted to say in these symphonies, or of how he wanted to say it. So he would often agree to their revision by well-meaning friends and conductors who were anxious to help him "improve" them. Consequently, there has been considerable argument as to which of several versions should be used in playing them today. Conductors pretty well agree, however, that the original versions (*Originalfassungen*) not only sound better but also give the listener a more adequate idea of the intensely personal quality of these unique works.

A profoundly religious man as well as a thoroughly schooled musician, Bruckner made an ideal church music composer. Of his three settings of the Mass, that in E minor (1866) is the most characteristic, with its happy blend of neo-medieval and Romantic styles. Other sacred works are the *Te Deum* (1884) and *Psalm CL* for chorus and orchestra.

MAHLER, A MORE COMPLEX CHARACTER

Mahler was a much more complex character. A Jew, with tremendous intensity of emotion and psychic sensibility, he had a divided spirit, one which alternately believed and doubted, which possessed lofty and noble ideas, often attempting to comprehend the whole of the universe, and yet which did not hesitate to enjoy almost unbelievably childish devices in order to do so. At least, this composer was a simple and believing infant in many ways; yet in actual life he was what one writer has called an eternal Old Testament prophet, restlessly pursuing the problems of life and death in order outwardly to confirm his inner faith. Even his friends did not fully understand him. As a man, especially in his capacity as conductor and opera director he seems to have been hard, violent, hot-tempered; yet as an interpretative artist, he was often as tender and sweet and simple as a child.

During his stormily active career he held a number of posts as *kapellmeister,* in Kassel, Prague, Leipzig, Pest, Hamburg, and, finally, in 1897 at the court opera in Vienna. During his ten years at this last position, he had ample time to prove his extraordinary ability as organizer and conductor and the institution flourished as it never had before and never has since. His popularity in this musical city was unusual, in spite of the fanatic and ruthless vehemence with which he pursued his artistic ideals and the unfortunate brusqueness with which he expressed himself when dealing with his fellows. In 1907 he resigned in Vienna and came to New York, where he became the principal conductor of the Metropolitan Opera, and, later, of the Philharmonic Orchestra, which organizations he completely reformed at a fatal cost in nervous and physical energy. In 1911 he broke down physically and was compelled to return to Vienna, where he died in May.

Not content with the universal acclaim paid him everywhere as a great director and conductor, Mahler sought distinction also as a creative artist. He wrote nine symphonies (leaving, in addition, clear thematic sketches for a performing version of a tenth), as well as several important song cycles for voices and orchestra. These enormous works can be called symphonies only by courtesy, for they have little in them suggestive of the traditional symphonic form, not even in the number

MAHLER (after a
painting by Fritz Erler)

or arrangement of their movements. As in Bruckner's works, there is
in these Mahler symphonies music of exalted and unparalleled beauty;
but it is often contiguous to passages that are banal and inclined to be
over-sentimental. Perhaps it was because he so often strove in these
works to render certain physical conceptions that are impossible to express, even in music, that Mahler sometimes fell short. When he did
keep within the natural confines of his art, as he did in the magnificent
Das Lied von der Erde (probably his finest work), he wrote as heart-
searching music as has ever been put on paper.

There is little question that his ardent spirit and controversial temperament tried to do too much—to revolutionize the great opera thea-
tres and symphonic organizations of his time, as well as leave posterity
music which would honor his name. In everything he wrote there can
be felt a fever of nervous excitement and exhaustive tension; he worked
at white heat and his music consequently suffers. His was a peculiarly
personal way of expressing himself with the orchestra, a way that was
powerful, dynamic, and unconventional, and which was the result of

long years of practical experience with this instrument. Nevertheless, he seemed to be at his best when writing for the voice, a fact that may have been the result of his long career as an opera director. Each of his symphonies has its own distinctive character. The *First* (1889) is the most readily accessible since it contains folk-like thematic materials and, like all the others which were to follow, alternates moods of exaltation and tranquility. The *Second* (1895), the so-called "Resurrection Symphony," calls for two vocal soloists and a chorus in addition to an enormous orchestra. In the *Eighth,* Mahler tried to express the essential contradictions of his nature through the means of a double chorus of mixed voices, a boy's choir, and an enlarged orchestra. His song cycles, especially the *Kindertotenlieder* and *Das Lied von der Erde,* written in 1901 and 1907, are true symphonies; it is said that only superstition kept him from calling the latter his Ninth Symphony.

This wonderful work, composed after Mahler's strong spirit had been broken through his strenuous efforts to conquer the universe, has been well called a "voice from the grave." A profoundly moving testament, it is one of the most affecting utterances of all time. Mahler wrote this cycle for tenor and contralto with orchestra during the last years of his life, at a time when he knew his days were numbered. Set to words adapted from Chinese poets, *Das Lied von der Erde* is music that is solitary, haunting, unique—the work of a man on whom the darkness has already fallen. There is nothing in all music quite like the effect of the end of its closing movement, when the contralto tranquilly repeats the one word *ewig . . . ewig* (eternal . . . eternal). Properly interpreted, this seems not only the farewell of an estranged spirit to an alien world, but indeed the end of the ardent, impulsive, lovely but doomed, Romantic spirit.

THE PRESENT STATUS OF THESE COMPOSERS

The present increased interest in the music of both Bruckner and Mahler has been due on the one hand to the activities of such organizations as the International Bruckner and Gustav Mahler Societies and on the other to the devoted interpretations of such conductors as the late Bruno Walter, who was imbued with the same intuitive and psychic spirit that is present in the music. The works of both these men have become increasingly popular throughout the English-speaking countries, in spite of a world that has turned anti-Romantic. These composers seem to have a special appeal to present-day listeners for exactly opposite reasons:

A PAGE FROM THE SCORE OF MAHLER'S *EIGHTH SYMPHONY*—THE "SYM-
PHONY OF A THOUSAND"

Bruckner for his simple sincerity, his sublime faith, and his heroic utterance; Mahler because he reaches out to our period and warns us with terrifying prophetic utterance of the wrath to come, reflecting the weariness of his own age as well as predicting the despair of our own.

A Lone Northerner—Sibelius

It is impossible to define religion—least of all in words. Perhaps music is a mirror.

The thing that has pleased me most is that I have been able to reject. The greatest labor I have expended, perhaps, was on works that have never been completed.

On the whole, one is merely a tool. This wonderful logic—let us call it God—that governs a work of art is the forcing power.

Sibelius

Statements such as these readily explain the decline which the music of Jean Sibelius (1865–1957) has suffered during the present century. At the time of his seventieth birthday in 1935 Sibelius was looked upon, both in this country and in England, as the greatest of the post-Romantic composers, not only because of the bardic strength of his utterance, but also because of what he had done to revolutionize symphonic form. He was the only composer of that period who enjoyed both popular and intellectual esteem in these two countries. His seven symphonies and at least five of his tone poems were steadily programmed and highly regarded. Writing at the very height of the Sibelius movement, the English critic Constant Lambert prophesied that the Sibelius symphonies would have a more profound influence on future generations than the music of composers such as Stravinsky and Hindemith who had made a compromise with vogue.

It is now very evident that Lambert was not a very accurate prophet. The music of Sibelius seems to be largely ignored by the American and English composers of today (it was never very popular in France or Germany) and has had no influence whatever on contemporary musical thought. There are a number of reasons for this. The music of every composer who was popular in his own day seems to go out of fashion in the generation after his death. This was as true of the music of Sebastian Bach as it has been of the music of more recent composers such as Hindemith and Vaughan Williams. The chances are that, given time, such imbalances of judgment correct themselves, provided, of course, that the music is good. Sibelius spoke with a very individual voice and certainly deserves a more honored place among composers than that granted him by the musicians of today.

What is more important, Sibelius's present reputation is the result of the great change in aesthetic fashions since the days of his popularity. An ardent Romantic, as well as a great Nationalist, he suffers particularly in an age such as ours, suspicious of all romantic utterance and wary of all kinds of provincialism. Finally, it is only natural that in the prevalent appropriation of all advanced thought by the advocates of atonality and serialism, music such as that of Sibelius which makes no conspicuous use of disturbing experimental devices, should largely be forgotten. But there can be no question that if, and when, there is a resurgence of Romantic tendencies in the future, Sibelius will be one of the composers whose music will be revived.

HIS CAREER

Although there is in all of Sibelius's best music a suggestion of the instincts and traditions of his native Finland, he was well along in life before he had the opportunity of hearing the Finnish folk tunes on which he is supposed to have based his style. Sibelius himself confirms this; but nevertheless it is obvious that the great national epic the *Kalevala* absorbed his constant interest and that its tales of heroism, its wild, colorful idylls and scenes of fantastic tragedy inspired his best music, including the tone poems *En Saga, The Swan of Tuonela,* and *Pohjola's Daughter.* But to put everything he wrote into a neat pile and label it Finnish Nationalism is to miss completely the fresh and unique talent of this composer.

QUALITIES OF SIBELIUS'S STYLE

Sibelius's particular quality lay in his peculiar fusion of manner and matter, of nationalism and personality, as well as his persistent experimentation with and constant re-creation of symphonic form. Each of his seven symphonies achieves results that are quite different from those of the others. This constant departure from accepted norms is the reason for the epithet "synthetic symphonies" so often applied to Sibelius's works by their detractors. In reality, such variability of style is a marvelous demonstration of the freshness of invention which persisted throughout his whole career.

In the very first measures of his *First Symphony* (1898–99) we are aware of an entirely new voice speaking, one whose accents are worth listening to. And throughout all the others, the richly variegated and strongly contrasted *Second* (1902), the most popular of all his works, the joyous *Third* (1904-07), full of the vigor and health of the high hills, the introspective, imaginative, and unusually concentrated *Fourth* (1911), the rhapsodic and darkly mysterious *Sixth* (1923), the one-movement *Seventh* (1924), we are conscious of unique imaginative freshness and constantly varied formal structure. Indeed, it is difficult to realize that the *First, Fourth,* and *Seventh Symphonies* could have been written by the same man; and yet it is impossible to think otherwise. For they are all the result of a strikingly original mind which did everything in its own way; and still they all hang together by a logic of their own, without following in any sense but the most general, traditional methods of development.

The music contains certain characteristic methods of building, heard most easily, perhaps, in the *Second Symphony*. One of the most fundamental of these is Sibelius's habit of not exposing a theme in full until late in the movement, treating bits of it, hinting, suggesting, and, we may think, at times hiding it, until its presentation comes with a splendid panoply of irresistible vigor. Other characteristic traits are his liking for a busy, exciting opening section, his abrupt breaking off of a train of thought in order to start another—yet without the disjointed effects that might be feared—and his remarkably fresh and different-sounding orchestration, each combination carrying the conviction that the idea was born thus in its creator's brain, clothed in this specific orchestral dress, and only thus to be expressed.

THE COMPLETE INDIVIDUALIST

The one thing that placed Sibelius in an entirely different category from his contemporaries, however, was the fact that he concerned himself so largely with the content of what he was saying, rather than becoming principally interested in the manner of its delivery. Being a man of real individuality, with an extremely vivid imagination and a sensi-

Davart

SIBELIUS

tive reaction to his environment, he had something very definite to say. And he found that he could say it in more or less conventional terms capable of being understood by everybody, without it being necessary to adapt such completely untraditional devices as polytonality or twelve-tone rows in order to attract attention. He was not ashamed to put feeling into his music—deep, unaffected feeling—nor to give it direct connection with life. Repeated hearings of his music clear up any strangeness that may be felt when listening to it for the first time. And everything in these works falls logically into its proper place. So it would seem that there are good reasons for supposing that his best music will one day regain its former popularity.

Thus, like every other good composer, Sibelius had his characteristic traits, one of the most striking and exciting features of which is its un-expectedness—it is impossible to forecast the shape that his symphonies will take. Sometimes he followed the typical nineteenth-century models as in the *First Symphony* (1899), with its haunting melodies, melancholy changes of mood, and piled-up climaxes. There are some places (the most obvious are in the *Second Symphony* (1902)) that remind us of Liszt, Borodin, or Tchaikovsky, but which always seem to bring new luster to old practices. Sometimes he strove for extreme restraint and lack of sensuous appeal, as in the *Fourth Symphony* (1911), his least assimilable work. Sometimes he pursued extreme concentration and terseness, as in his last, somber *Seventh Symphony* (1924), which is quite free in form and very episodic in the use of its thematic materials.

There are lapses. Now and again a movement does not seem to fit its context, does not build fully into the works as a whole. Sibelius seems, at moments, to be rather too easily pleased with his themes, and so sometimes repeats them almost *ad absurdum*. There are family resemblances in his figures that seem more than a little casual. Like César Franck, Sibelius lacked a certain versatility of human contact: his music often seems over-introspective and sometimes seems to strain for individuality. One does not always come from hearing this music with a sense of ease. But one cannot fail to be braced and stimulated by curiosity, as well as by a feeling of keen interest, in this composer's strikingly personal way of carving out his ideas.

A DIVERSITY OF WORKS

Concurrently with his symphonies, Sibelius wrote a number of tone poems which, as we have said in another place, were largely inspired by nationalistic themes. They include the two very popular pieces *Finlandia* and *Valse Triste*. Because of its strongly patriotic character, the former was prohibited in the land of its birth during the years of unrest under the Russian regime. The latter was taken from incidental music written for a Finnish play. Neither of them is Sibelius at his best, but they are not as cheap as they are often made by popular interpreters. Sibelius wrote a surprising amount of piano music, none of it significant, and there is a great deal of what the Germans call *Kapellmeister Musik*, well-written and quite uninspired, for choruses, the theatre, and so on. Then there are the songs, a few of them based on ancient runes; but the majority are simply what used to be called drawing-room songs of a better character. Sibelius seems wisely to have kept his most independent thoughts for his large-scale works, such as the symphonies and the *Violin Concerto* which he composed in 1903 and revised in 1905. A dazzling virtuoso piece with a brilliant solo part, spacious themes, and stirring rhythms, this is not as personal or characteristic as the symphonies and so has become the most international of all his works. Its eloquent ardor and vigorous sweep have kept it popular through the years.

The critics and professionals of today are apt to distrust a composer who has turned out a large amount of music that is not of the highest quality; and they are inclined to consider those works that have secured a place in the repertoire to be freaks. This is certainly not true of Sibelius. Although a considerable amount of his output did consist of ephemeral potboilers, such compositions as the *First* and *Second Symphonies* (which a 1940 critic criticized as being vulgar and provincial), the *Fourth* and *Seventh Symphonies,* the *Violin Concerto,* the symphonic poems *Swan of Tuonela* and *Pohjola's Daughter* speak with a strong, individual voice that was new and provocative at the time they were written, and which refuses to be silenced by the sophisticated scorn of the modern puritans.

The Twilight of the Romantics

Man must abide
His going hence, even as his coming hither:
  Ripeness is all.
Shakespeare

A SUNSET GLOW

We should not let our judgment of an artist or a group of artists be too strongly influenced by the fact that they can be described as *fin de siècle:* it is a natural tendency to conclude that the artistic products of such men necessarily represent a definite tailing-off from the great line. As we must always remember, the assumption that there are certain logical aesthetic trends which tend to produce certain types of artists is only a convenient device for the clarifying of art history; the records show that, time and time again, such periods have waxed and waned, fashions in art have come and gone, while great works have continuously been produced, despite the conditionings of such periods and trends.

Nevertheless, the fact that such late Romantics as Elgar, Bax, MacDowell, D'Indy, and the rest spent their creative careers in a world which had largely outgrown its original enthusiasms for the Romanticism they professed had a decided effect on their work. For it is difficult for an artist to develop his personality fully in an environment which is not completely congenial, one from which he cannot readily extract the materials he needs for the weaving of his own personal artistic patterns. He is likely, under such circumstances, to grow somewhat self-conscious, to tend toward mannerisms which are suggestive of inhibitions and restraints on his natural spontaneity.

ELGAR: THE ENIGMATIC ENGLISHMAN

Elgar (1857–1934) is a good example of this. The most outstanding of a group of composers who, around the 1890's, were engaged in attempting to revive something of the past glories of English music, he seemed to have been conscious his whole life long that, as he expressed it, "nobody really wanted his music." Born in a musically meager period and country, he had to struggle through all the early part of his life against the lack of proper social background, an important factor in the musical life of the England of his day. He did not attend any of the official academies and so was not "in the swim"; the son of a provincial parish organist, he had to make his own way through merit alone. Naturally enough, he did not seem to make much headway, at least to outward view, for many years; engaged in a number of rather unimportant posts, he was really preparing himself so that when, after a few smaller works for chorus, he finally got a hearing (in 1899) for the set of orchestral variations to which he gave the name *Enigma,* his place as the outstanding composer of England was assured.

From then on, his success was complete; work after work followed, for both chorus and orchestra. Among the most important of these were the oratorio *The Dream of Gerontius* (considered by many of his admirers to be his best work) in 1900, the *First Symphony* (1908), the *Violin Concerto* (1910), the *Second Symphony* in 1911, and a great symphonic study, *Falstaff,* in 1913. He was showered with honors and degrees, made a member of many foreign academies, knighted (later made a baronet) and given the jealously guarded Order of Merit; he was invited to France and the United States to conduct his works. And yet, through all these years of outward success, in spite of all the honors which a repentant world seemed anxious to bestow, it is impossible not to feel in Elgar's works a certain sense of frustration, as if he was unconsciously being inhibited from expressing his full self as a composer. This resulted in definite mannerisms: a peculiar resort to an insistent series of harmonic and melodic sequences; tremendous bursts of nervous energy, which often culminated in a sort of self-conscious swagger that

FAURÉ

he ʼ
ing
whi
was
Ern
rath
are
mor
stret
is a

A
latei
duri
193ۮ
Ron
Frar

THE EBULLIENT CHABRIER

A different aspect of French character is seen in Chabrier, already mentioned in the section on French opera, whose zest and glowing ardor hold many attractions. He is widely known by a few compositions, in which gusto and good humor are hardly matched by formal balance. His *España,* a Spanish rhapsody on original themes, reflected a new tendency in music—an enthusiasm for things Spanish, which was to be cultivated frequently during the next generation. A lyric sense and a pointed humor and exuberance mark Chabrier as one of the Good Companions of music, whose acquaintance will brighten the life and cheer the heart of any listener.

FAURÉ: A FOUNTAINHEAD

Another French composer of the time who, like D'Indy, is very much overneglected, is Gabriel Fauré. If a few of his songs are familiar, his very considerable output of chamber music has but rarely been given the place it deserves in the art of this period. It has happened to more than one listener that first impressions of Fauré have to be revised, to the composer's advantage, on rehearings. There is in his music a curious deceptive simplicity and fluency, something which suggests a

The Russians

Lying midway between Europe and Asia, the West and the East, Russia is a fascinating study, both in its history and in its art. Its original inhabitants were Slavs, but there were so many repeated invasions by the Scandinavians from the west and the Mongols from the east and south, that little progress was made toward the establishment of a nation until the sixteenth century. It was Ivan the Great, chieftain of one of the largest principalities in the country, who drove out the Mongols, united the various tribal units, and established dominion over a territory which reached from the Arctic to the Urals. He was the first of a long line of absolutist monarchs who were to rule Russia; it was his grandson, Ivan the Terrible, who took unto himself the title of "Czar of all the Russias," a custom which was followed by all his successors. In passing, it may be noted that it was this Ivan who later was taken as the subject of one of Rimsky-Korsakoff's operas, and that it was Boris Godunov, subject of the novelist Pushkin's epic and Moussorgsky's opera, who was appointed to help Ivan's son, Feodor, to rule. The Russion nationalists had at hand plenty of colorful events in the long history of their country.

During the Middle Ages, Russia was strongly influenced by the civilization of the great Byzantine Empire to the southeast, an empire which was the medieval inheritor of the Greco-Roman traditions. The Ivans, when they founded their kingdom, considered themselves the direct successors of the Byzantine emperors and so took the title of "Head of the Orthodox Greek Church." This eastern, ecclesiastical influence was to continue as an important factor in the country's culture long after Russia had joined the family of European nations during the reign of Peter the Great in the eighteenth century.

The period between Ivan the Terrible and Peter the Great, nearly two centuries, was marked by a gradual expansion of the country into Asia, an expansion which was carried on largely by peasants and Cossacks, adventurous frontiersmen who led the vanguard of this territorial penetration and carried the influence of the established church and the czar clear to the plains of eastern Asia. The enlarged Russia was essentially Oriental in character, its customs and habits being Asian rather

the virtuoso pianist plenty of opportunities for displaying his ability. Busoni's most notable achievement in opera in a new style, *Doktor Faust,* was left unfinished; it was completed by Jarnach and first performed in 1925.

THE COSMOPOLITAN BLOCH

One other composer destined to leave a considerable mark on his age must be mentioned here, since his humane and richly expressive art put him directly in the Romantic succession, in spite of his using a sharper-edged, more dissonant tool than those before him had employed. This is Ernest Bloch (1880–1959). Born in Switzerland, he came to New York in 1917 and worked in this country for the rest of his life. Some of his most important works were written here, where he lived largely in retirement (except for the five years he was Director of the Cleveland Institute of Music), working slowly and continuing to develop his very individual style.

The sources of Bloch's inspiration varied. During his earlier European period he followed those trends of his time which best suited the essential characteristics of his nature, combining the Romantic rhetoric of Liszt with the colorful orchestration and sonorous utterance of Strauss. The important work of this period was an opera, *Macbeth,* first produced at the Opéra-Comique in Paris in 1910. In his second period he expressed his most intense feelings and developed his most eloquent powers as a Jewish nationalist: "It is the Jewish soul that interests me," he said, "the complex, glowing, agitated soul that I feel vibrates throughout the Bible." This inspired, among other things, the *Trois Poèmes juifs* (1913), the *Israel Symphony* (1912–16), and the intensely Romantic *Schelomo,* Hebrew rhapsody for cello and orchestra (1916). His last, rather neo-Classical period was characterized by a greater interest in structure; among its most important works were two *Concerti grossi* (1925 and 1955), the *Violin Concerto* (1958), the *Suite Symphonique* of 1945, and the *Second String Quartet* (1946).

For Bloch, music was not a doctrine concerning abstract form or experimental tonalities. Rather it was the expression of strong, personal emotion, as well as an opportunity for heroic utterance. While he never followed the fads and fancies of his day, he did not hesitate to use dissonance and radical harmonies when needed for a particular expressive purpose. A man of real worth, splendidly earnest, finely equipped technically, Bloch was one of the most impressive figures of his time. Unfortunately, there was a slackening of his powers during the last years of

art of the Italian and French operatic composers. This exotic development, centered in St. Petersburg and Moscow, had no influence whatever on the lives of the people.

In literature, the taste of the first part of the eighteenth century was French, followed later, as in the other countries, by a swing toward the Romantic style. It was not until the Russian writers of the early nineteenth century, stimulated by the rise of a distinctly nationalistic mode of expression in other lands, began to turn their attention to the history of their own people that anything distinctive or important was produced. As long as the Russian artist, far removed from the centers of European culture, tried to imitate the models of France, Germany, and Italy and abjured his native background, he remained sterile. But once Pushkin, who had started writing poetry in imitation of the European Romantics, began to immerse himself in the colorful past of Russia and to study native poetry, he was able to produce such works of brilliant imagery and impassioned expression as *Russlan and Ludmilla* and *Boris Godunov*. Other outstanding writers followed—Gogol (1809–1852), Turgenev (1818–1883), and Dostoevski (1821–1881) —who used folk themes and did not hesitate to discuss the abuses under which the common people suffered. It seemed as if it was not until these artists had established contact with their native soil and found beauty in the spirit of their own people that they were able to assimilate the great traditions of European culture and produce works which are comparable with those written in other lands. Nineteenth-century Russian literature is a unique admixture, produced by a combination of western-European influences, Byzantine thought, native strength, and a peculiar preoccupation with the sorrows and sadnesses of humanity's common lot.

THE RISE OF TWO SCHOOLS

This century saw also the rise of a definite Russian school of composers. These divided themselves into two groups: first, those who built their nationalistic ideals on the basis of European foundations and believed that it was only a thorough knowledge of what had been written by the composers of the past that could give the Russian nationalist the power to speak his own language eloquently; and second, those who broke completely with European traditions and attempted to go to the people for inspiration and guidance. The amateur Glinka was the initiator of this latter movement; he was followed by Dargomijsky and the talented circle of dilettanti—Balakirev, Borodin, Rimsky-Korsakoff,

than Eur
generatio
of Christ
It was
of his rei
Russian s
and those
dominatio
state of s
his politic
Russia the
ized his p
means to
tion of hi
extended t
world; her
lished: bet
Russian ci
was finally

CHANGES I

A nation
naturally su
tecture and
fifteenth ce
Byzantium
such as the
During the
eighteenth
copied and
Petersburg,
classic style
glories of N
classic mode
taste against
During th
other than t
European cul
eenth centur

the virtuoso pianist plenty of opportunities for displaying his ability. Busoni's most notable achievement in opera in a new style, *Doktor Faust,* was left unfinished; it was completed by Jarnach and first performed in 1925.

THE COSMOPOLITAN BLOCH

One other composer destined to leave a considerable mark on his age must be mentioned here, since his humane and richly expressive art put him directly in the Romantic succession, in spite of his using a sharper-edged, more dissonant tool than those before him had employed. This is Ernest Bloch (1880–1959). Born in Switzerland, he came to New York in 1917 and worked in this country for the rest of his life. Some of his most important works were written here, where he lived largely in retirement (except for the five years he was Director of the Cleveland Institute of Music), working slowly and continuing to develop his very individual style.

The sources of Bloch's inspiration varied. During his earlier European period he followed those trends of his time which best suited the essential characteristics of his nature, combining the Romantic rhetoric of Liszt with the colorful orchestration and sonorous utterance of Strauss. The important work of this period was an opera, *Macbeth,* first produced at the Opéra-Comique in Paris in 1910. In his second period he expressed his most intense feelings and developed his most eloquent powers as a Jewish nationalist: "It is the Jewish soul that interests me," he said, "the complex, glowing, agitated soul that I feel vibrates throughout the Bible." This inspired, among other things, the *Trois Poèmes juifs* (1913), the *Israel Symphony* (1912–16), and the intensely Romantic *Schelomo,* Hebrew rhapsody for cello and orchestra (1916). His last, rather neo-Classical period was characterized by a greater interest in structure; among its most important works were two *Concerti grossi* (1925 and 1955), the *Violin Concerto* (1958), the *Suite Symphonique* of 1945, and the *Second String Quartet* (1946).

For Bloch, music was not a doctrine concerning abstract form or experimental tonalities. Rather it was the expression of strong, personal emotion, as well as an opportunity for heroic utterance. While he never followed the fads and fancies of his day, he did not hesitate to use dissonance and radical harmonies when needed for a particular expressive purpose. A man of real worth, splendidly earnest, finely equipped technically, Bloch was one of the most impressive figures of his time. Unfortunately, there was a slackening of his powers during the last years of

art of the Italian and French operatic composers. This exotic development, centered in St. Petersburg and Moscow, had no influence whatever on the lives of the people.

In literature, the taste of the first part of the eighteenth century was French, followed later, as in the other countries, by a swing toward the Romantic style. It was not until the Russian writers of the early nineteenth century, stimulated by the rise of a distinctly nationalistic mode of expression in other lands, began to turn their attention to the history of their own people that anything distinctive or important was produced. As long as the Russian artist, far removed from the centers of European culture, tried to imitate the models of France, Germany, and Italy and abjured his native background, he remained sterile. But once Pushkin, who had started writing poetry in imitation of the European Romantics, began to immerse himself in the colorful past of Russia and to study native poetry, he was able to produce such works of brilliant imagery and impassioned expression as *Russlan and Ludmilla* and *Boris Godunov.* Other outstanding writers followed—Gogol (1809–1852), Turgenev (1818–1883), and Dostoevski (1821–1881) —who used folk themes and did not hesitate to discuss the abuses under which the common people suffered. It seemed as if it was not until these artists had established contact with their native soil and found beauty in the spirit of their own people that they were able to assimilate the great traditions of European culture and produce works which are comparable with those written in other lands. Nineteenth-century Russian literature is a unique admixture, produced by a combination of western-European influences, Byzantine thought, native strength, and a peculiar preoccupation with the sorrows and sadnesses of humanity's common lot.

THE RISE OF TWO SCHOOLS

This century saw also the rise of a definite Russian school of composers. These divided themselves into two groups: first, those who built their nationalistic ideals on the basis of European foundations and believed that it was only a thorough knowledge of what had been written by the composers of the past that could give the Russian nationalist the power to speak his own language eloquently; and second, those who broke completely with European traditions and attempted to go to the people for inspiration and guidance. The amateur Glinka was the initiator of this latter movement; he was followed by Dargomijsky and the talented circle of dilettanti—Balakirev, Borodin, Rimsky-Korsakoff,

Moussorgsky, and Cui. These two circles never met; both made important contributions to Russian music, giving it, together with the parallel developments in literature, a place among the most important manifestations of the nationalistic spirit of the nineteenth century.

THE COSMOPOLITES

I often begin to write with the intention of using one or another popular Russian song. Sometimes, as in the finale to the Fourth Symphony, *this comes of itself, quite unexpectedly. As to the Russian element in general in my music—the relation to the popular songs in melody and harmony—I grew up in a peaceful spot, saturated from earliest childhood with the miraculous beauty of Russian popular song, so that I love to the point of passion every expression of the Russian spirit. In short, I am Russian through and through.*

Bowen and Von Meck: *Beloved Friend*

This was the attitude of Tchaikovsky (1840–1893), the greatest of all the Russians, toward his own nationalism. Posterity, however, hardly bears him out; for we are able to realize today that this most popular of all the Muscovites was a cosmopolitan rather than a national composer: his music, although strongly colored with Russian temperament, shows definite German influences and is never far out of touch with French *esprit*. With the exception of Rimsky-Korsakoff, he was, moreover, the only real craftsman in the whole lot, having been thoroughly trained under the aegis of Anton Rubinstein, the founder of the St. Petersburg Conservatory and the outstanding pianist of Europe at the time. Since Tchaikovsky placed high value on the necessity for training and hard work as factors in musical composition, he was disclaimed by the amateur talents of the *Kutchka* (that band of five friends of Russian nationalism—Balakirev, Cui, Borodin, Moussorgsky, and Rimsky-Korsakoff) and looked upon as a traitor to real Russian music.

TCHAIKOVSKY

Of all the composers in the world, it is difficult to think of one with a more direct appeal to a large number of people than Tchaikovsky: his music needs no explaining. He described composition as being a lyric process of soul confession, pouring itself out through the medium of sound just as the lyric poet pours himself out in verse; and these confessions have been such as to make a wide appeal to all sorts and conditions of men. At first, Tchaikovsky was looked upon as a Russian barbarian by those outside the country, but the latter years of the nine-teenth century saw the whole world at his feet. It is only in recent years that his popular domination of the symphonic literature has been challenged by others. Today, he, like so many of the Romantics, has lost caste: his emotional outbursts have taken on a threadbare, heart-on-sleeve aspect. He has become "popular" in the most derogatory sense, musicians admitting his ability as a craftsman while deploring his overemotionalism, sometimes rising to hysteria, and his lush Romanticism.

As a matter of fact, only when we place Tchaikovsky against his proper background are we able to come to anything like a fair estimate of his music. He was a peculiar amalgam of individual characteristics: he was a Russian, first of all, an arch Romanticist living at the very zenith of that epoch; he possessed an unusually sensitive temperament, one which was tragically unsuited to normal living and which cast a dark shadow over his life, often making it almost intolerable; finally, he was driven by a strong creative urge which gave him no rest and which ensured a constant growth in artistic stature to the very end of his life.

A TYPICAL RUSSIAN

In their art, the Russians have never been content with mere state-ment; they must always exaggerate. And it was his Russian spirit that gave Tchaikovsky his emotionally blanketed locution and his peculiar alternation of melancholy and almost hysterical gaiety, grief and joy, shade and light. In this sense he was, as Stravinsky has remarked, "the most Russian of us all." The whole idea of suffering and expiation, of tremendous emotional struggle and tragic consequence which so strongly flavors many of his works was, moreover, part and parcel of the thinking of his time: he may be well thought of as the apotheosis of the Romantic Movement; this coincidence of Tchaikovsky's being a Russian and a Romanticist accounts for his strong popular appeal. The dark tragedy of his personality is explained by the letters he wrote to his rich patron, Mme. Nadejda von Meck, whom he was careful never to meet, although she gave him liberal financial and spiritual support through the most difficult part of his life. His letters explain also why some of his music—perhaps the most potent of it— was a necessary "casting out of a demon, an exorcism by the major art of expression." The fact that he was a thorough craftsman, driven by a healthy love for creation, gave us so much of that which is cheerful and effective in his music, perhaps three quarters of the whole. We are too often merely conscious of the overemotional Tchaikovsky and are liable to forget the composer of the *Casse-noisette Suite,* the *G Major Suite,* the *Romeo and Juliet* fantasia, the early symphonies.

HIS WIDE RANGE

His was an astonishingly wide range of expression—from near-genius, through cheerful mediocrity, to utter banality—with a compellingly attractive sincerity and directness from which we cannot escape. He wrote six symphonies, of which only three—the Fourth, the Fifth, and the Sixth—are played in present-day concerts. They contain some of his finest moments, which, while hardly comparable with the best of Beethoven and Brahms, are nevertheless inspired and tremendously moving; and there are others which are dreadfully weak and trite. There are few listeners, even today when it has become hackneyed through overplaying, who are not greatly moved by a performance of the *Sixth Symphony,* if it is interpreted with dignity and sincerity. But there are parts of the Fourth and the Fifth which certainly contain some of the noisiest and most banal music ever written by a great composer. The overture fantasia *Romeo and Juliet,* composed in Tchaikovsky's twenty-ninth year (1869) and dedicated to Balakirev, is moving in a real Shakespearean sense. Another composition of the same sort, *Francesca da Rimini,* is effective after the Lisztian manner, with perhaps too much of a striving after effect for effect's sake. The *Casse-noisette (Nutcracker) Suite,* the orchestral *Suite in G,* the *Capriccio Italien,* and the *Serenade for Strings* are brilliant examples of their type. The *Piano Concerto in B Flat Minor* is full-blooded, lusty, strenuous in a rather vulgar way, but still appealing. Such notoriously purple patches as the *Marche slave* and the *Ouverture solennelle 1812* were never taken seriously by their composer, who admitted to the latter's being "very showy and without artistic merit because I wrote without warmth and love."

Tchaikovsky's eight operas have not held their places in the repertoire; the best of them is *Eugen Onegin,* in which his talent for lyric expression of the Italianate order is given full scope. His was not a dramatic temperament in the theatrical sense: and, although he knew well enough, as his letters show, what an opera demands, he did not have theatrical qualities sufficient to sustain interest for very long. Most of the songs show very little individuality: in them, he merely says things that Schumann and the other German Romantics have said much more effectively.

Tchaikovsky merits neither the undue adulation with which he was received at the turn of the century nor the rather sniffing condescension with which he is greeted today. He outlived completely the extreme spirit of Russian nationalism, if, indeed, he ever believed in it strongly. And, although his music may not express the soul of Russia, it was inspired by the Russian spirit and shaped by Russian consciousness; the result, since Tchaikovsky was more of a genius than most of his nationalistic confreres, may well be of greater permanence than the utterances of the nationalists.

OTHER RUSSIAN COSMOPOLITES

We need but mention one other important cosmopolite of Tchaikovsky's time, Anton Rubinstein (1829–1894), who, although he had great aspirations as a composer, is largely forgotten today. The later Alexander Glazunov (1865–1936) and Serge Rachmaninoff (1873–1943) stand out as cosmopolitan Russians. The former had something of Tchaikovsky's blend of instrumental color without any of his genius. The latter had a distinguished international career as composer as well as virtuoso pianist and orchestral conductor. His style, derived from Liszt and Chopin and strongly influenced by Tchaikovsky, was nevertheless his own, with its broad rhapsodic sweep and sonorous harmonies. Although such works as his *Second Piano Concerto* (1901) and his *Second Symphony* (1908) belong to the pre-World War I era, they have a strong appeal and nostalgic attraction, even for a non-Romantic era.

THE RUSSIAN *Kutchka*

The group known as the Big Five or *Kutchka* looked upon Michael Glinka (1803–1857) as their prophet patriarch. A rich nobleman, he possessed, according to Tchaikovsky, a colossal talent, which suffered, however, through his unwillingness to subject himself to regular and thorough training. He worked as a dilettante, whenever the mood came, and in this, as in the general characteristics of his music, he set the style for the group of nationalists who followed. Not only did Glinka and his fellow nationalists incorporate the spirit (and often actual melodies) of Russian folk tunes into their music, but they relied on dramatic intensity and natural feeling to take the place of constructive principles.[1] How effective such a procedure could be may be judged from Glinka's *Kamarinskaya,* an orchestral fantasy on Russian folk songs, perhaps the most strikingly original thing he ever wrote. "All of us," admits Tchaikovsky, "the moment we need Russian dance tunes, borrow *Kamarinskaya's* contrapuntal and harmonic designs quite openly. In this one short work, Glinka succeeded in concentrating that which the smaller men have accomplished only through heroic effort."

GLINKA'S PATRIOTIC OPERAS

But when it came to longer works, a procedure such as this did not suffice. Glinka's two operas, in spite of some original beauties, are strikingly uneven and tiresomely repetitious mixtures of Italianate tradition and folkish development. The first, *A Life for the Czar* (1836), was based on a strong nationalistic libretto dealing with the historic enmity of the Russians and the Poles; the second, *Russlan and Ludmilla* (1842), while it has less of the folk element, emphasizes the Eastern, Oriental element which permeates so much of Russian art. While there is a great deal of picturesque color in these works, there is also an unfortunate amount of conventionality; the years have more than justified Tchaikovsky's judgment: "We are proud of Glinka, but we must admit that he did not fulfill the task his genius put upon him."

DARGOMIJSKY

Dargomijsky (1813–1869), the other composer who was the inspiration of the *Kutchka,* tried to rationalize the operatic setting of words; he wrote one opera, *Roussalka (The Water Witch),* in which he tried

---

[1] Perhaps more than is the case with any other people, the Russians have preserved individuality of expression in their folk songs and dances: folk art of all kinds in Russia is very much alive today, encouraged by the post-Revolution government in power there. A number of features characterize Russian folk and dance tunes and make them sound unusual to Occidental ears: the use of short, two-measure phrases and sharply defined, animated rhythms; a tonality suggestive of the music of the Greek Church; an affinity of style and coloring with the tunes of other Slav countries, together with their love for extravagance, their bravado of expression, and their gift for improvisation. As might be expected in so huge a land, the dances are of widely varying types, many of them making use of wild steps and vigorous motions. The best-known peasant dance is the *gopak,* which, starting in a tranquil, melancholy fashion, ends in a tremendous outburst of primitive vitality.

to incorporate his principles of careful regard for the integrity of the text. But it is of little importance, aside from the fact that it gave more than one hint to Moussorgsky, and so, in turn, to Debussy, when it came time for him to write his *Pelléas et Mélisande.* A later work, *The Stone Guest,* left in an incomplete form by the composer and finished by his friends, Cui and Rimsky-Korsakoff, became known as the bible of the Russian school. In addition to his operas, Dargomijsky wrote a great number of songs.

BALAKIREV

It was Mily Balakirev (1836–1910) who founded the famous Russian Five and who was for years the most active spirit in the establishment of a significant Russian school. He and his associates, basing their ideals on the parallel movement in literature, wished to free Russian music from all "foreign influence and to make it an art for Russians alone, employing the Russian language only where words were necessary." They turned to the native folk song for their sources and were sincere in their desire to throw off all the traditions of Italian, French, and, especially, German music, which they felt had enslaved Russian art so long. Meeting at one another's houses in St. Petersburg, they would often spend the whole night talking, as only Russians can talk, about inspiration, talent, the abominations of rules, the advantages of antiprofessionalism, what constituted Russian art—time which Tchaikovsky thought[2] might better have been spent in learning something of the fundamentals of composition. There is no doubt that the group possessed talent, although Balakirev, its leading personality, never made much of his gifts: he is known today almost entirely by his Oriental fantasy for the piano, *Islamey,* and his orchestral tone poems, *Russia* and *Thamar,* the latter used for a Diaghilev ballet.

BORODIN

Borodin (1834–1887), a professor of chemistry in the Academy of Medicine, was one of the few Russian nationalists who attempted the writing of symphonies. The sense of design, not necessarily of classic German design, but form in any keen sense, was woefully lacking in all these Russians; even Tchaikovsky realized his weakness in this respect. And the three Borodin symphonies, written at intervals when, because

[2] In spite of his lush Romanticism, Tchaikovsky had a good deal of the professor in him.

of sickness, the composer could steal some time from his busy professional life, suffer in this respect. For a listener familiar with the great German works in this field, these symphonies are apt to pall because so little happens, and the orchestration is bound to seem awkward. But they, as do Borodin's quartets, possess many colorful moments and plaintive melodic touches, exciting enough in themselves. The tone poem *In the Steppes of Central Asia* depicts the passing of a caravan in the sandy wastes; it is a small thing, but colored to perfection. His opera *Prince Igor*, left in an unfinished state at his death and completed and edited by Rimsky-Korsakoff and Glazunov, is effective largely because of the generous measure of ballet which it contains.

Like so many of its kin among the Russian operas (most of the nationalists wrote them), *Prince Igor* carries conviction because of its composer's enthusiasm and interest in incident, rather than because of any inherent balance and proportion. It was fortunate that Borodin was happiest on the stage; his thoughts flowed freely there, and he never seems at a loss as to what he wanted to do. Since its barbaric thrills come off well, this opera holds the boards.

MOUSSORGSKY

Moussorgsky (1839–1881) was by far the most original of the Five: in his short life, which drink and drugs cut off when he was little more than forty, he produced not only the greatest of Russian music dramas but likewise a few individual works which may well stand as representative of the very best music his nation has produced. *Boris Godunov*, written in 1874, completes the cycle started by Glinka's *A Life for the Czar* forty years before. Its portrayal of rough humors, dissolute monks, the terrors of conscience and remorse, the remarkable part it gives to the chorus of people, its sense of strange, wild history (which, in spite of many diversions, nevertheless seems inevitable and irrevocable)—all make it a work apart, something unlike any other opera ever written, and one possessed of a compelling and fascinating attraction. Based on Pushkin's great story, its libretto deals with the early days of Russian history and the ruthless Boris, who, arriving at supreme power, killed all those who stood in his path—an uneasy career, which led to final remorse and tragic death; this text gave Moussorgsky full opportunity to show his great dramatic sense, and the results are overpowering.

Moussorgsky worked at *Boris* most of his life, making two versions of it, one in 1868 and another in 1872; these were afterward altered, revised, and reorchestrated by his friend Rimsky-Korsakoff, in an attempt to "correct" some of the composer's crudenesses and heighten some of his dramatic effects. This Rimsky-Korsakoff edition is the one generally used in theaters; but, since the original Moussorgsky edition was published in 1928, one of the burning aesthetic questions has been, "Which of the two is the more effective?" It is a question of little moment: Rimsky-Korsakoff was a thoroughly effective man of the theater and one of the most brilliant orchestraters in the whole history of music; he unquestionably deleted some of Moussorgsky's Russianism, but he left the work as a whole more practical and more effective.

Khovantchina, a later opera, has not been successful. Its history of religious dissension drags heavily; the play does not hold together even so well as does *Boris,* out of which whole sections have been carved at various times without affecting its dramatic continuity, so loosely is it woven together. The music of *Khovantchina* is happiest when it is most frankly pictorial; otherwise it has little interest.

Other well-known Moussorgsky works are the popular piano pieces *Pictures at an Exhibition,* which a number of men have orchestrated, Ravel's arrangement being by far the best; and the two interesting song cycles, *Songs and Dances of Death* and *Sunless.* These latter vary in quality: some of them are superb, with a singular blend of powerful imagination and experience, digging deep into human hopes and fears ("Field Marshal Death" is a good example); others are quite characterless.

Being a member of a small landholding family, Moussorgsky grew up amid folk legends; above everything else, he liked to emphasize his simple birth and lack of musical training, boasting that his genius was the richer because it had never been tamed. Later in life, he deepened; but he was always quite satisfied with his intuitive way of expression. It seemed as though he was born to be at once a fire-eating realistic pioneer and a rather simple-minded employer of the national idiom; he had a direct lyrical sense, which it is worth while trying to separate from his realism when estimating his place in music history. He was frequently inspired, but he was not a great builder,[3] and his originality often led him into blind alleys; we ought to be able to enjoy his music without deifying it or him.

---

[3] Cecil Gray has quoted Tchaikovsky as saying that this is an essential Russian characteristic: "there is a profound lacuna in our intellectual organization—the capacity for logical thinking, the spirit of method, and the feeling for continuity are entirely lacking in us."

CUI

César Cui (1835–1918) was of French descent, an expert on fortification by profession. When he had time to write music, he composed rather coquettish and meticulous pieces, most of them of small scale, entirely forgotten today. His influence was of more importance as a critic than as a composer.

RIMSKY-KORSAKOFF

Rimsky-Korsakoff (1844–1908) was the only composer of the *Kutchka* to secure a thorough musical education, thereby proving himself a renegade to the ideals of its founding. By profession he was a naval engineer, and he acquired, in his trips through the East, a love for Oriental color and rhythm which stood him in good stead later on. When he was thirty and had already attracted considerable attention as a composer, he decided that he could go no further without more knowledge of musical theory; so he went to Tchaikovsky, then a professor in the Moscow Conservatory, for guidance. Thorough study and enormous industry made him an orchestral craftsman and a composer of several works of some importance, outstanding among them being that "gorgeous and unfailing Russian picture book in tone," *Scheherazade.* His operas are seldom heard outside Russia, although *Le Coq d'or,* a symbolic fairy tale, has been played both in England and in America. Everyone can yield with real delight to the spell of its queen's song, or to "The Song of India" from the opera *Sadko;* but, in general, these works depend too much on color and do not give enough of the real Russian spirit to satisfy the foreigner for long.

In addition to being a composer, Rimsky-Korsakoff was an excellent teacher: Stravinsky and Respighi were among his pupils, and his treatise on orchestration has become a standard text the world over. A cultivated man, he possessed real literary gifts, and his charming autobiography, *My Musical Life,* is a good picture, impressive because of its honesty, of the whole Russian movement.

They were a fascinating company, these members of the *Kutchka,* stimulating to one another, with enormous pluck and self-confidence but little first-rate criticism (not even from themselves), and curiously childlike in many ways. They were typical products of their age, the like of which we shall hardly see again, representing one of the many aspects which the Romantic Movement assumed as it matured and developed during the course of the century.

LATER RUSSIANS

Not so many years ago Alexander Scriabin (1872–1915), with his new and individual harmonic structures, seemed the forerunner of a new era;[4] today he is an almost forgotten figure, except for his piano pieces based on Chopin's techniques and his own method of inventing new harmonies, though his big, overblown works, *Poem of Ecstasy* (1908) and *Poem of Fire* (1910), occasionally appear on orchestral programs as the sumptuous descendants of the Lisztian-Strauss tone poems. Scriabin is considered today a pioneer in harmonic construction who, by anticipating a freer use of the twelve chromatic tones, opened up new prospectives, rather than a composer who attempted, as he put it, to obtain a "glimpse of higher spiritual planes."

Among the composers of Tchaikovskian tendencies may be mentioned Nikolai Medtner (1880–1951), who worked both in the large classical forms and in sets of fairy tales in sonata form, both styles firmly rooted in classical and romantic traditions. Anatol Liadov (1855–1914) also wrote orchestral pieces, based on Russian legends, that remain in the Russian repertoire, though they are not played anywhere else. Sergei Taneiev (1856–1915) chose for the most part the less picturesque paths of chamber music; he was also a theorist of note. Anton Arensky (1861–1906) followed closely in Tchaikovsky's footsteps, notably with a popular set of variations on a tune by the older composer. Alexander Gretchaninov (1864–1956), though he wrote in larger forms, including the opera, is best known for his wonderful settings of the liturgy of the Russian Church. Mikhail Ippolitov-Ivanov (1859–1935) worked for some time in Tiflis, where he studied the native music and put into his popular *Caucasian Sketches* (1895) his impressions of this particular brand of Russian semi-Orientalism. There are two Tcherepnins, Nicolas (1873–1945) and Alexander, the son (*b.* 1899). The father was a pupil of Rimsky-Korsakoff who, after some years of conducting Russian opera and ballet music in Paris, settled there permanently. The son, even more of an internationalist, was somewhat influenced by Prokofiev and concertized and lived in the Far East as well as in Paris and this country, where he came in 1949 as a teacher.

---

[4] An important critic of the early years of the twentieth century said that Scriabin's works represented the chief advance in musical consciousness since Beethoven's time.

The Czechs

One of the first coun-
tries to achieve national independence in music was Bohemia, a
division of the Austrian Empire that has since been known as Czechoslovakia. Peopled mainly by a race of Slavs—the Czechs—which had
a distinctive language and literature, and, for many centuries, its own
kings, Bohemia was traditionally a part of the Holy Roman Empire.
Thus, although the national feeling of her people was strong, the
country early became inextricably concerned with German affairs and
permeated with strong Germanic influences; and when, in 1526, panic-
stricken because the Turks were at her gates, she elected a Hapsburg
as king, she automatically became part of the Austrian domains and
remained a dependent state for almost three centuries. The nationalism
that centers in legends and folk tales of the country's heroes had ample
opportunity to develop; for the Czechs, a "small island in a large
German sea," as someone called them, continued to struggle bitterly
against the Hapsburg influence all through their years of humiliation
and fostered a store of patriotic fables and folk heroes to help bolster
their desire for independence—independence won in 1919, lost in 1939.

SMETANA

When, in the general literary and Romantic stir of the early nineteenth century, these old folk tales and ancient elegiacs were unearthed and the middle classes began to realize their significance, the
stage was set for the appearance of a national genius. Smetana (1824–
1884) was the first to celebrate in music the peculiar virtues and
prowess of Bohemian (as distinct from German or Austrian) natures
and aspirations. His operas and his set of six symphonic poems, linked
under the name of *My Fatherland,* create the very spirit and atmosphere of Bohemia. One of these latter, *Vltava* (*The Moldau*), is a
most successful example of objective pictorialism in music, tracing as
it does, with eloquent orchestral description, the course of the country's
largest river.

The one operatic work of Smetana's that is known the world over is his colorful comedy *The Bartered Bride;* charming and attractive as it is, this opera is by no means his finest. Travelers who have been fortunate enough to hear it in Prague or in one of the other Bohemian theaters at Bratislava or Brno, give the palm to *Libussa,* an opera which a widely traveled critic has called "one of the most majestic creations ever conceived for the lyric theater." *Dalibor,* the third of Smetana's operas, is characteristically national in that it is based on the life of a fifteenth-century Bohemian warrior who kept the realms of King Wladislaw in constant turmoil; like all Smetana's works, it contains music which is wonderfully rich and vital, with a real flavor of the soil. When first produced, in 1868, it seemed to the contemporary critics to be over-Wagnerian and insufficiently nationalistic; today, it seems more strongly Czech than even *The Bartered Bride.*

DVOŘÁK

Anton Dvořák (1841–1904) was perhaps a greater man, whose principal field of activity was orchestral and chamber music. An intuitive composer of the Schubert type, he suffered somewhat from the over-adulation of foreigners, who were too easily satisfied with the local colors which he provided in such profusion. There is an engaging simplicity in Dvořák, which led him (with, perhaps, something of peasant shrewdness) to push the folk motive sometimes beyond judiciousness. Too often he was satisfied with ideas that are inferior; even in his mature chamber music (his quartet, Op. 105, is a good example), which, aside from the *New World Symphony,* represents him at his best, there are exasperating cheapnesses, especially in the matter of melodies.

Nevertheless, no composer is a more genial companion. Brahms influenced Dvořák and secured recognition for his spirited *Slavonic Dances,* originally written as piano duets and lavishly employing Bohemian mannerisms both in melody and in rhythm.[4] Together with a certain amiable diffuseness, Dvořák's work is distinguished by real creative genius and marked by a wonderfully intimate and endearing

---

[4] The first of these dances to become familiar to outsiders was the polka, remarkably popular in the '40's of the last century (when it was comparatively new even to its native land). The works of Smetana and Dvořák have familiarized us with the furiant, with its frequently changing rhythm, whose name suggests its character; the redowa, of mazurka type; and the dumka, a title remembered in a chamber work by Dvořák (*Dumky Trio*). The dumka, alternating between hectic gaiety and sadness, is actually an imported dance, native to South Russia.

ANTON DVOŘÁK (lithograph
by Max Švabinský)

sentiment, as well as by a strong intensity of feeling. He wrote a
number of symphonies, although the *New World,* composed while he
was in temporary residence in the United States, in an attempt to
show American composers how they might cultivate their art through
folk channels, is almost the only one often heard. His nine operas are
not performed outside Bohemia, since they are local and slight in subject and comparatively weak in development.

Like the instinctive instrument that he was, Dvořák responded to
almost any influence which was going; but it was the response of a
highly individual nature, tasting here and there, and never for a moment copying or needing to copy. His own nature was too full and too
fresh to need anything more than a few contacts with good models; for
the rest, shrewdness, immensely hard work, simple dignity, and nationalist enthusiasm were sufficient, because he had the touch of near-
genius that transmutes all into art. Without it, no amount of pains-
taking nationalism signifies anything; it becomes simply peddling
parochialism, wearisome because so near to childishness.

Since his day very few Czechs have made a great stir outside their
own country. Perhaps the best known so far is Janáček (1854—1928),
who delved deeper than Dvořák into folk music but never met with

as wide recognition because he swung to the side of a fairly mild extremism in harmony, writing in a style that made no concession to a possible market and its demand for "tunefulness." Leoš Janáček was active in the musical life of Brno, the capital of his native Moravia, throughout most of his life; but it was not until the production of his opera *Jenufa* in 1904 that his importance as a national composer was established. Altogether he wrote ten operas, the most important of which, in addition to *Jenufa*, were *Kata Kabanová* (1921) and *The Cunning Little Vixen* (1924). Most of them are based on Pan-Slavic subjects and written in a concentrated musical idiom that emphasizes the stark drama and sustained intensity of their plots; they employ a peculiar type of structure based on the continued variation of a few themes.

Because of the effectiveness of this elliptical style, the delicacy of their expression, and the luminous quality of their orchestral scoring, Janáček's operas have increasingly attracted music lovers of many countries and have been produced with great success in England and the United States, as well as throughout central Europe. In addition to these dramatic works, Janáček wrote in other forms: the *Glagolithic* or *Festival Mass* is exciting in its power and originality; and the earlier symphonic tone poems *Taras Bulba* and *Ballad of Blaník* show his magic way with an orchestra. As with many other composers, Janáček's originality began to be recognized only after his death.

OTHER CZECHS

Other Czech composers include Vasa Suk (1874–1935), highly respected in Russia, where he achieved a reputation as an opera conductor; Karel Kovařovic (1862–1920), whose series of nationalistic operas have become very popular in Prague; and Alois Hába (b. 1893), who became famous for his experiments with intervals of less than a semitone, basing his works on a division of the octave into 48 or even 72 tones.

As if to show what a native conductor and composer could do with good tunes and a full-blooded, lusty style, Jaromir Weinberger (b. 1896) has contributed one of the best comic grand operas in the repertoire: *Schwanda, The Bagpipe Player,* a work which has had performances all over Europe in a number of languages. It was first given in German at the Metropolitan in 1931.

The Poles

The name Poland runs like a colorful thread through all European history: peopled by a fiery and turbulently independent race of Slavs who were akin to the Russians and the Czechs, this country freed herself from the Holy Roman Empire during the fourteenth century. Situated between Germany and Russia, with the Slovaks and the Magyars on the south, Poland has always been one of the danger spots of Europe; at the crossroads of Europe, she has been frequently overrun by her covetous neighbors.

In 1386, a union of Poland and Lithuania made a strong military country, which, however, was not able to maintain its individuality against the designs of the envious monarchs to the west and south. Frederick the Great of Prussia and Maria Theresa of Austria between them made the first partition of the country in 1772; others followed in 1793 and 1795. But a number of patriots, by means of uprisings and revolutions, kept alive the spirit of nationalism, until, in 1863, they were finally overwhelmed by Russia, and the country was made a province of that huge empire. The inevitable miseries and gallantries entailed in such a series of wars, especially when the people involved are as excitable and as impressionable as the Poles, are the very stuff on which the spirit of Romanticism thrives.

NATIONAL MUSIC

As in other lands, the popular dances have reflected national character and aspirations. The polonaise has for hundreds of years been the greatest expression of courtly ceremonial and patriotic fervor. From the sixteenth century, when Henry of Anjou was made king of Poland, the polonaise was used to introduce court balls and other occasions of ceremony, and, by the eighteenth century, it had become a part of every national festivity. Even the popular poetry was modeled on the rhythm of the dance.

Liszt, in his life of Chopin, describes the method of dancing the polonaise. The host opens the ball by choosing a partner and heading with her an elaborate parade around all the rooms of the house and all the garden paths. On returning to the ballroom, the host's partner is claimed by another man, and a corresponding shuffle of partners takes place all around. This goes on all through the evening, each leader trying to outdo his predecessors in the invention of steps and gestures indicative of the great pride, courage, and gallantry of the Polish nation.

The dance found its way tentatively into the classical suite, but it has been far more brilliantly celebrated in the music of Chopin, as has its companion, the mazurka, which has been described as the feminine counterpart of the masculine polonaise. Both are in three-time: the mazurka's gait is the gentler, its first pulse being divided into two, often unequally (three quarters and one quarter); the polonaise has a stronger, springing effect in its subdivision of all three pulses, the first into a half and two quarters, the others into halves.

ITS FLOWERING IN CHOPIN

It was Liszt who first pointed out that Poland's national characteristics were epitomized in Chopin's polonaises: "Although Chopin was born too late and left his native land too early to be initiated into the original character of the polonaise as a national dance, he was able to supplement what others imparted to him in regard to it by his own imagination and nationality." The best of these works—such things as the C sharp minor and the E flat minor, Op. 26; the A major and the C minor of Op. 40; and the *Fantaisie polonaise,* Op. 61—must always stand as Poland's greatest music. Their dark tempestuous despair, alternating with pages of rarest poetic beauty, make them like cannon buried amongst flowers, as Schumann put it; those who would realize the power of Poland's spell should listen to these works played by a Polish artist such as Paderewski or Artur Rubinstein.

The nationalism of the great pianist Ignace Paderewski (1860–1941) was of a rather mild type, which seems strange in view of the fact that he was such a strong patriot and was elected the Prime Minister of the Polish Republic established after the First World War. His opera, *Manru,* a *Polish Symphony,* and a *Polish Fantasy* for piano and orchestra, do little more than exploit, in acceptable terms of general romance, a few native airs.

SZYMANOWSKI

The only other composer who raised high hopes for this country's music was Karol Szymanowski (1882–1937). He can scarcely be claimed as a real nationalist because of the combination of so many different trends in his style. Starting under the domination of Strauss, he changed from German to Russian influences and then veered toward Impressionism, finally finding his inspiration in folklore in such works as his ballet *Harnasie* (1926). His treatment of the national Polish dance, the mazurka, has special significance. Internationally he is best known for his *Symphonie concertante* for piano and orchestra (1934); his real contribution to Polish music, however, was the cultivation of a new attitude toward the problems of sound, form, and technique—an attitude which strongly stimulated the ideals of the younger Polish composers who followed him.

Around 1926 an infiltration of neo-Classicism came into Polish music and a whole generation of composers developed this style after World War II. The best known of these men are Antoni Szalowski (*b.* 1907), with his brilliant *Overture* for orchestra (1936), and Mihal Spisak (*b.* 1914) and his *Symphonie concertante* of 1948. After this came an attempt to seek a more fruitful synthesis between contemporary musical language and the elements of native tradition, always powerful in such a land as Poland. The first composer to exemplify this tendency was Witold Lutoslawski (*b.* 1913).

The Scandinavians

SCANDINAVIAN
NATIONALISM
During the Middle Ages, the people who constitute those nations we call Scandinavian—Denmark, Norway, and Sweden—were among the most powerful and adventurous in all Europe. Through their vigorous business and colonizing enterprise, they penetrated the lands lying south along the Baltic and even settled as far away from home as England, France, and southern Italy; they occupied Iceland and Greenland, seized Finland, and entered Russia. Fundamentally a Germanic people, the Scandinavians had many common racial characteristics, although their languages have always been

divided by certain dialectical differences. All through their history, they have kept more or less together: theirs have not been the intense struggles and rivalries that have marked the growth of the other European countries, although they have engaged in plenty of good, hard fighting at one time or another. Lutheran in religion since the sixteenth century, fundamentally agricultural or commercially minded, these people do not seem at first blush to constitute a type from which we could expect a national art of importance. Yet they have a splendid artistic tradition going away back to the time of the Norsemen and have produced some of the most characteristic and interesting artists in the whole field of nationalism: Hans Christian Andersen, on whose fairy tales the whole world has been reared; Björnson and Ibsen, humble-born writers of a peasant nation—Norway; Grieg, whose engaging, simple-hearted piano pieces and songs have made his name known the world over; Anders Zorn, the painter and etcher of Swedish scenes; and, in our own generation, Selma Lagerlöf, the Swedish novelist.

GRIEG THE BELOVED

When Scandinavian music is mentioned, one name comes to everyone's mind, that of Edvard Grieg, born in Bergen in 1843. He came to maturity at the same time as the great figures in Norwegian literature, Björnson and Ibsen, and contributed quite as much to the international repute of his country as did they. Educated in Germany, he determined early in his career that his music would strive to embody the spirit as well as the rhythms and melodies of his beloved land; he succeeded so well in his aim that he became known, in addition, as one of the most original composers of his time. Aside from his *Piano Concerto,* a great favorite, and his violin and piano sonatas, his work was composed mostly of miniatures—chiefly short piano things. In these, he was particularly happy, for his was an inventive rather than a constructive genius; such things as his *Wedding Day at Troldhaugen* and the *Norwegian Dances* pose no problems, but they are lyrically fresh and unconventionally attractive. To realize how fully his music fits the spirit of his people, one must see a performance by a Norwegian cast of the Ibsen drama *Peer Gynt,* for which he furnished the incidental music: the arts of Grieg and Ibsen in many of the scenes of this great masterwork come recognizably from the same folk fount.

EDVARD GRIEG (from a painting
by Elif Peterssen, Oslo Museum)

OTHER NORWEGIANS

In addition to Grieg, Norway has given us a great deal of most acceptable music of folk-song cast, both in songs and in symphonies; operas appear to be few. Svendsen (1840–1911) was partly national, partly cosmopolitan; both his *Carnival in Paris* and his *Norwegian Artists' Carnival* are well known. Sinding (1856–1941) stands high in the Grieg succession, with a very prolific output, including that hardy perennial, *The Rustle of Spring*. His contemporary, Börgstrom (1864-1925), wrote some symphonic poems, notably one on the subject treated by Ibsen in his play *John Gabriel Borkman*. Others are D. M. Johansen (*b.* 1888), who is said to use impressionistic technique in a newer national, "primitive" way; Arvid Kleven (*b.* 1901); and L. I. Jensen (*b.* 1904)—the latter two of modern tendencies. In general, however, the proximity of German culture has tended to preserve very strongly the Romantic trend in Norwegian music.

SWEDEN

There is less of interest to report here, since Sweden has not produced a composer so readily enjoyed by the plain man as Grieg the

Norwegian; the novelist's art has not lacked at least two world figures, Strindberg and Lagerlöf. It may be, for reasons that are not often clear, that one country produces its greatest artists in some particular direction; there may also be cycles in these things—great poets at one period; later, great scientists. Sweden possessed a considerable number of the latter in the nineteenth century, but her music, in which the German influence largely predominates, has not been exciting.

It was Gustavus III, called the King of Song, who gave the first impetus to Swedish national music. In the century after him, the nineteenth, the study of folk song was pursued by Häffner; Geijer was a poet as well as a historian; and Berwald (1796–1868) is probably the only Swedish composer of the older school whose work was much performed in his own country. Berwald's was a personality by no means entirely swamped by German Romanticism, but there was little chance in his day for any art but that of the Germans to make headway, and so he was not widely known, even in his native land. In passing, it may well be noted that Sweden's fame at this time was carried abroad rather by singers than by composers: there are few people who have not heard of music lovers of past generations rhapsodizing about the lovely singing of Jenny Lind, the Swedish nightingale, and Christine Nilsson.

Other composers of the mid-nineteenth century are Lindblad, a song writer, and Wennerberg and Landblad, writers of church and choral music. Hallström attempted opera, while the name Söderman is well known to almost every choralist. Kurt Atterberg (*b.* 1887), engineer and critic, as well as composer, has become known chiefly because he was the winner in a contest that was foolishly instituted some years ago to finish Schubert's *Unfinished Symphony;* his contribution honored neither Schubert nor himself. In addition, he has written several symphonies and operas, showing varied if not entirely co-ordinated talents. G. Nyström is said to glance back to Grieg's straightforward simplicity and melodic charm, and possess, in addition, something of French impressionistic style, with a dash of the piquant sauce that so often is used today—Stravinsky's best. But Swedish composers, in general, seem to have been content to let the majority of modernisms in music go by, though they have shown themselves anxious to use them in the other arts.

DENMARK

We have a less clear idea of the essence of the Danish national spirit than we do of the Norwegian. Most music lovers could probably name but one Danish composer, Gade (1817–1890), who, founding his work on folk songs, achieved a sort of Scandinavianism that seemed effeminate to Grieg, so tinctured was it with the elements of Germanism. Other important names among the Danish composers are Laub (*b.* 1852), who carefully studied folk and dance songs; Eduard Lassen (1830–1904); Carl Nielsen (1865-1931), who wrote in all the larger forms, and who is best known by his symphonies, in which neoromanticism is treated in pungent, modern fashion, with traces of Germanic mysticism; and Paul Klenau (1883–1946), a composer of sensitive, lyrical music. Most Danish musicians, like their fellow artists in other fields, have taken their color and inspiration from the lands which so closely hem in their little country. The representative national opera is *Elverhöi,* written in 1828 by Friedrich Kuhlau (1786–1832), a native German. The great cultural center of Denmark is Copenhagen, whose operatic and concert life has greatly stimulated national development.

FINLAND

Ethnologically, the Finns are a people entirely distinct from the Scandinavians; but their history has been so closely bound up with that of Sweden that they are often considered as Scandinavian. Finland was part of the independent national state of Sweden, instituted in the sixteenth century under the renowned Gustavus Vasa; in the nineteenth century, the country was allocated to Russia as a result of the Napoleonic Wars, an arrangement which became extremely unpopular with the people and which helped make for a strong feeling of nationalism throughout the land. It was not until the end of World War I that the Finns were able to see the consummation of their dream of centuries—the establishment of an independent country, which took place in 1919.

As might be expected from their close connection with the two peoples, the folk songs of Finland show both Russian and Swedish characteristics. There is a prevailing melancholy to most of them, with frequent outbursts of fantastic and demonic power, a characteristic which is prevalent in Russian music. In addition to this folk-music background and the strong spirit of nationalism engendered by a political past that was full of oppression, the composers of Finland have been greatly influenced by their national folk epic, the *Kalevala.* This set of poems, which until the last century existed only in the memory of the peasants, was collected and set down by ardent nationalists and has strongly affected the spirit of both literature and music. No less a figure than Sibelius has called this great Finnish saga of early gods and wild nature an "heirloom from the distant land of runes and magicians coming from the solitudes of the boundless forests, full of yearning and mystery." On the facing page is a typical passage from this work, describing the bringing of fire into the world of man.

Sibelius, the leading Finnish musician, went directly to the *Kalevala* for the inspiration of a number of his orchestral works—*The Swan of Tuonela, Tapiola, Pohjola's Daughter.* And his popular folk rune, *Finlandia,* wonderfully expresses all that we have tried to suggest as characteristic of the soul of this people—the melancholy yet spirited melodies and rhythms of their folk music, their love for scene and legend, the humiliation of their long captivity.

In addition to Sibelius, who is discussed elsewhere, a number of Finnish composers have become known: Armas Järnefelt (1869–1958), who, like many another became familiar through one or two of his small pieces, Erkki Melartin (1875–1937), Selim Palmgren (1878–1951), Toivo Kuula (1883–1918), Yrjö Kilpinen (1892–1959), Aarre Merikanto (1893–1958), and Uno Klami (1900–1961). Palmgren is the best known of these men; his five piano concertos are good examples of his talent, which did not run to both strength and length but seems happiest in brief impressions of nature and in general Romanticism which has been compared with that of Mendelssohn. He was not as strong a nationalist, however, as Kuula, who loved to explore the imaginative riches of the Kalevala legends.

On the whole, the Scandinavian countries have hardly fulfilled the promise and the early hopes that were aroused by the advent of such individual composers as Grieg and Sibelius. Those we have mentioned, though we have few opportunities of hearing their music, are known sufficiently for us to realize that if any outstanding genius dwelt among them, we should have been aware of it long before this.

Therefore was the night unending,
And for long was utter darkness,
Night in Kalevala for ever,
And in Väinölä's fair dwellings,
Likewise in the heavens was
    darkness,
Darkness round the seat of Ukko.

Life without the fire was weary,
And without the light a burden,
Unto all mankind 'twas dismal,
And to Ukko's self 'twas dismal.

Ukko, then of Gods the highest,
In the air the great Creator,
Now began to feel most strangely,
And he pondered and reflected,
What strange thing the moon had
    darkened,
How the sun had been obstructed,
That the moon would shine no
    longer,
And the sun had ceased his
    shining.

Then he stepped to cloudland's
    borders,
On the borders of the heavens,
Wearing now his pale blue
    stockings,
With the heels of varied colour,
And he went the moon to seek for,
And he went to find the sunlight,
Yet he could not find the
    moonlight,
Nor the sun could he discover.

In the air a light struck Ukko,
And a flame did Ukko kindle,
From his flaming sword he struck
    it,
Sparks he struck from off the
    sword-blade,
From his nails he struck the fire,
From his limbs he made it crackle,
High above aloft in Heaven,
On the starry plains of heaven.
When the fire had thus been
    kindled,
Then he took the spark of fire,
In his golden purse he thrust it,

Placed it in his silver casket,
And he bade the maiden rock it,
Told the maid of air to rock it,
That a new moon might be
    fashioned,
And a new sun be constructed.

On the long cloud's edge she sat
    her,
On the air-marge sat the maiden,
There it was she rocked the fire,
There she rocked the glowing
    brightness,
In a golden cradle rocked it,
With a silver cord she rocked it.

Then the silver props were shaken,
Rocked about the golden cradle,
Moved the clouds and creaked the
    heavens,
And the props of heaven were
    swaying,
With the rocking of the fire,
And the rocking of the brightness.

Thus the maid the fire was rocking,
And she rocked the fire to
    brightness,
With her fingers moved the fire,
With her hands the fire she tended,
And the stupid maiden dropped it,
Dropped the flame the stupid
    maiden,
From her hands the fire dropped
    downward,
From the fingers of its guardian.

Then the sky was cleft asunder,
All the air was filled with windows,
Burst asunder by the fire-sparks,
As the red drop quick descended
And a gap gleamed forth in
    heaven,
As it through the clouds dropped
    downward,
Through nine heavens the drop
    descended,
Through six spangled vaults of
    heaven.

Translated by W. F. Kirby

The Spaniards

When J. B. Trend, who has written a great deal about Spanish music and art, says in an article in *Grove's Dictionary of Music and Musicians* that "to the majority of people in Spain the only serious music is folk song," he is speaking not of peasants, but of educated people. It is this fact which explains the small number of composers that modern Spain has produced, for the public attitude is bound to influence the interest in serious art, although it may not entirely direct it. The chief weakness of nationalism in Spain is that those composers who have arisen have not availed themselves of their great historic past, of such music as that of Victoria, for instance, whom we have already discussed. In Russia, as we have seen, the mistake was in refusing to learn from the past of other nations. Always, nationalism in music, as in its political and social aspects, seems to tend toward some form of narrowness. Yet, in itself, it is a fruitful thing.

We have seen, in examples from various lands, the reaction of church music on profane music, of aristocratic troubadour art on the music of the people, of nationalism on the spirit of internationalism, and so on. But, in all discussions of Spanish music, there is a factor of special importance, one on which there has been a great deal of discussion among the experts—the authenticity of its sources. Those who pretend to know say, for example, that the music of Falla is purer in its evocation of the true Andalusian spirit than is that of Albeniz. These discussions may well be left to the experts, for music lovers in general can enjoy the sense of the dance and the sound of guitars, drums, castanets, and tambourines heard in so much of this music, together with the rich ornamentation which so attracts northern ears and the springing rhythms which set the feet astir.

There is an old Spanish tale of a court of morals that may well indicate what our attitude towards this music should be. Apparently the seemliness of one of the Spanish dances was being tried; a demonstration was decided upon, in order that justice might be done. Some gypsy dancers were called in: they had not been at work many moments before the learned judges began to twitch in sympathy, and finally they threw off wigs and gowns and joined in the dance!

SPANISH DANCES

R. Johnstone, in his history of dancing, has said that Andalusia, the province in the southernmost part of Spain where a large proportion of the inhabitants are descendants of the Moors, is the classic home of the dance. Whether this be true or not, there can be little question that much of the beauty and languorous expressiveness for which Spanish folk music has become famous can be traced to the Orient, together with many of the cadences and ornaments employed so profusely in this music and the instruments—mandolin, guitar, tambourine, and castanets—used to accompany it.

The classic sixteenth-century and seventeenth-century Spanish dance was the *chaconne,* a slow dance with three beats in a measure, framed on a ground bass; it was taken over later by the classic composers of the eighteenth century, who used its characteristic features with striking success. Popular eighteenth-century dances were the *fandango,* the *bolero,* and the *seguidilla,* the latter the most general of all Spanish dances, each province having its own particular version. The fandango starts in slow time and is danced by a single couple, the speed increasing as the dance proceeds. Every so often, stops are introduced, the dancers remaining motionless and sometimes singing short *coplas* appropriate to the moment—a feature to be found in the other Spanish dances. The successful performance of a good stop and an expressive pose is greeted by the onlookers with the cry *Bien parada!*

The bolero, with its insistent rhythm of ♩ ♫♫ ♫ ♫ seems to have been strongly influenced by other dances—the *saraband,* the *chaconne,* and the *polonaise;* it has been brought vividly to the attention of modern listeners by Ravel's stirring orchestral version.

"The ardent melody, at once voluptuous and melancholy, the rapid clank of castanets, the melting enthusiasm of the dancers, the suppliant looks and gestures of the partners, the languorous grace and elegance of the impassioned movements—all give to the picture of the seguidilla an irresistible attraction," according to Baron Duvillier. In this dance, the *bien parada* is very important; the dancers "stand motionless and, as it were, petrified, in the position in which they are surprised by the certain final notes of the air. Those who manage to do this gracefully are applauded with repeated cries of *Bien parada! Bien parada!*" The *coplas* interpolated in the seguidillas are usually improvised by local poets to suit the particular situation.

Another well-known Spanish dance is the *jota* (ho'tä), the national dance of the province of Aragon in the north. Often included in religious ceremonials, the interpolated *coplas* are then of religious character, usually celebrating the birth of our Lord; when the jota is used in secular fashion, the *coplas* deal with that universal subject, love, often in a cynical fashion. Evelyn Porter, in her interesting description of Spanish dances, quotes a typical *copla:*

> *On Monday I fall in love; on Tuesday I acknowledge it; on Wednesday I propose; Thursday I am accepted; on Friday jealousy is aroused; on Saturday and Sunday I start looking for a new love.*

Other Spanish dances, developed later, are the *habanera,* which takes its name from its native city of Havana and is used so effectively by Bizet in his *Carmen;* the *tango,* adapted by the Spaniards from their colonial compatriots in South America; and the *farruca,* of Andalusian gypsy origin, declared by Morales, one of the outstanding authorities on Spanish styles, to be the most musical of all the national dances.

The most widely known songs come from the mountainous districts of Andalusia: the traditional Andalusian *cante hondo* is serious, somber, even tragic. The word *flamenco* is the modern and best-known term for this type of song, with its strange intervals of less than a semitone, its repeated notes, short compass, and ornaments for special significance at high moments.

INTERNATIONALLY KNOWN COMPOSERS

As in Russia, the works that have turned twentieth-century attention to Spain have been written almost entirely by composers of the last century. It was a Spanish Jesuit professor and writer, Antonio Eximeno (1729–1808), and his insistence that national song should serve as the basis for the art music of each country that started the nationalist movement in modern Spanish music. This dictum was taken up by Felipe Pedrell (1841–1922), another literary man as well as composer, expounded in his pamphlet *Por nuestra música,* and illustrated by his dramatic triology *Los Pirineos* composed in 1889–91 and produced in Barcelona in 1902. In addition Pedrell composed a great deal of other music, including symphonic poems and other operas, brought to light many of the great treasures of Spain's musical past (including a complete edition of the works of Victoria), directed the reform of religious music in Spain, and had as pupils three of the most distinguished Span-

Courtesy of The Hispanic Society of America

A MODERN SPANISH DANCE—THE ARAGONNESE JOTA (painting by Joaquïn Sorolla y Bastida)

ish composers of the turn of the century: Isaac Albeniz (1860–1909), Enrique Granados (1867–1916), and Manuel de Falla (1876–1946). Little wonder that he is still looked upon as the leading figure in modern Spanish music, though little of his music has gained general recognition outside of his native land.

Albeniz lived mostly outside of Spain; he started his foot-loose career by running away from home at the age of thirteen, traveling as far

THE MARQUESA DE PONTEJOS
(a painting by Goya) The Rococo
charm and elegance of the Spanish
court figures of his time are beautifully portrayed here.

afield as Cuba and the United States and supporting himself by playing in concerts. After later studies at the Brussels and Leipzig Conservatories, as well as in Budapest, he settled in Paris where, inspired by
Pedrell's championship of nationalist music, he composed a rhapsody
for piano and orchestra, *Catalonia* (1899), and the remarkable set of
twelve piano pieces *Iberia* (1906–09). Full of nationalistic suggestions,
these virtuoso pieces were strongly influenced by Impressionistic techniques; many of them have been orchestrated by other composers and
have become standard orchestral fare the world over.

Granados began his career as an opera composer, at first with little
success. It was not until he started on a series of piano pieces inspired
by the paintings and etchings of Francisco de Goya y Lucientes (1746–
1828), one of Spain's greatest artists, that Granados attracted world
attention. Later he took a number of these picturesque and imaginative
pieces and introduced them into an opera, *Goyescas,* its libretto based
on scenes from some of the Goya paintings. This was given its first

performance at the Metropolitan in New York in 1916, with enormous success. It was on his return from this premiere performance that Granados lost his life in the torpedoing of the ship on which he was traveling. In addition to this *Goyescas* music, Granados is well known for his brilliant and very characteristic *Spanish Dances,* four volumes of piano music full of the fire and color and spirit of the popular songs of his homeland.

The best known of these Spanish composers is de Falla, who worked at home in the early years of his career, organizing folk festivals and seeking out authentic sources, gradually gaining esteem as the leader of modern Spanish music, as well as the preserver of the most faithful forms of its folk art. In 1907 he went to Paris, where he became friendly with Debussy and Ravel, whose influence definitely determined his style. In 1914 he returned to Spain and devoted his whole attention to composition, often traveling abroad to conduct performances of his works. He wrote a number of stage works, including an opera, *La Vida breve* (1913), which became popular in many countries, the ballets *El Amor brujo* (1915), in which mystic lore and gypsy wizardry play a part, and *The Three Cornered Hat* (1919), full of humorous gallantry and fascinating piquancy, and a marionette show, *El Retablo de Maese Pedro* (1923). His great masterpiece is the work for piano and orchestra *Nights in the Gardens of Spain* (1909–13), a wondrous recreation of the scenery as well as the soul of his land.

In 1926 at the suggestion of the famous harpsichordist Wanda Landowska, Falla composed a *Concerto for Harpsichord* (or piano) *and Five Solo Instruments* in the style of a classic chamber concerto. While less Spanish in nature than most of his works, freer in tonality and harmony and more classic in structure, this is nevertheless very characteristic of de Falla and blends Spanish modernism with traditional aristocratic purity and grace. Like all these Spanish composers, Falla wrote a number of piano pieces, ranging from his over-popular *Ritual Fire Dance,* through the Andalusian *Four Spanish Pieces,* to the *Fantasia Bética,* the last a sort of epitome of all his creative styles.

After living in Granada for many years de Falla went to Argentina at the end of the Spanish Civil War; here he lived in seclusion and died in obscurity.

His style, the result of a peculiar mixture of Impressionistic techniques, Andalusian idioms, and Spanish Classicism, is absolutely unique and unlike anything else in all music. Musicians are attracted to its purity and color, and are appreciative of its structural strength; concert-goers like it because of its marvelous color and rhythm. More than any other Spanish composer of his time Falla made his aim that of fine art rather than the mere exploitation of nationalism. He did more than any other individual to make a place for Spanish music—an exciting as well as constructive place—without having to beg for its acceptance on purely nationalistic grounds.

This is not true of the music of Joaquin Turina (1882–1949), however. Although his style contains elements of Impressionism as well as French Romanticism assimilated from his stay in Paris from 1905 to 1913, it seems to make a special point of being Spanish. Assembled from small ideas stated and restated rather than developed, Turina's music is popular because of its pictorial qualities. Lighter in nature and weaker in structure than the music of de Falla, it nevertheless speaks with a personal accent that is immediately appealing.

The difference between the music of these two composers is obvious if we compare their two big pieces for solo piano and orchestra. Turina's *Rapsodia sinfónica* is a long one-movement work made up of a series of Spanish tunes expanded into contrasting sections, with no overall design or particular exploitation of the solo instrument. Falla's *Nights in the Gardens of Spain,* in spite of its programmaticism, was conceived as a carefully constructed three-movement work, taut in structure, yet sensually suggestive and romantically expressive in nationalistic terms.

Turina wrote for all media, though he may be said to have specialized in chamber music, piano pieces, guitar music, and songs. His principal orchestral work (originally written as a chamber music work and rescored for string orchestra) is *La Oración del torero,* not so much a Bull Fighter's Prayer as a medium for displaying the various colors and effects possible from the stringed instrument family. Much of his piano music is frankly nationalistic, with such programmatic titles as *Impressions of Spain, Gypsy Dances,* and the like. His songs are some of the loveliest now available for recital programs.

A composer who should be mentioned here as important in another field is Tómas Bréton (1850–1923), conductor of the Madrid Opera, who devoted himself largely to the development of the *zarzuela,* the Spanish adaptation of opera comique, containing spoken dialogue intermingled with music. Bréton's *La Verbena de la Paloma* (1894) is the standard example of comic zarzuela, as is his *La Dolores* (1895) of the serious type.

There has been a great deal of effective cross-pollination between the arts of Spain and France. Goya's vivid canvasses showed Delacroix his way and anticipated the discoveries of the Impressionists. And both Debussy and Ravel wrote music that is redolent of the beauties of the country to the south which both of them loved but never visited—such things as *Soirée dans Grenade* and the orchestral suites *Ibéria* and *Rapsodie espagnole*. Yet another, earlier, affinity should also be noted, that between the music of the Spaniards and that of the Russians. Glinka, the first of the Russian nationalists, made a lengthy stay in France and Spain after he had lived several years in Italy in order to absorb something of the Italian operatic style. And we have, as the result, such pleasant souvenirs as his *Jota Aragonesa* and *Night in Madrid*, both of them rather typical applications of the nationalist ideas to the life of a foreign country.

LATER TENDENCIES

The importance of Spanish musical activity at this time is highlighted by the fact that two Spanish instrumentalists of this period achieved world fame, both as players and composers: the violinist Pablo Sarasate (1844–1908), whose works still figure prominently on concert programmes of violin music; and Pau Casals (*b.* 1876), the violoncellist, who has been called the greatest of all instrumentalists. Casals was very active in Spain as a player and composer up to the time of the Civil War; since then he has lived outside the country, in France, Puerto Rico, and the United States, busy as conductor, soloist, and teacher.

The mere mention of some of the other prominent Spanish musical names shows the scope of the country's musical life at the time of the lamentable civil war that was fought there in the interim of the two World Wars, a catastrophe for all Spanish art. Angel Barrios, born in Granada in 1862, composed operas and instrumental works, as well as furnishing his fellow townsman, Andreas Segovia, with some of the best music used in bringing the guitar to the appreciation of the contemporary musical world. Amadeo Vives (1871–1932) devoted his energies to composing zarzuelas, while Jesus Guridi and Oscar Esplá, both born in 1886, collected and edited folk music, Esplá developing a modal scale of his own in order to fashion this native music into his orchestral compositions. Joaquin Nin (1879–1949), born in Havana, became internationally known as a pianist and composer of strongly nationalistic piano works.

The Hungarians and the Rumanians

Had a sweetheart, mourned her loss long years
  and years,
Thought her dead, and every day gave her my
  tears.
Now I find her 'neath another's roof and
  shield,
But, no matter, more was lost at Mohács field.

Hungarian Folk Song

THE BACKGROUND OF HISTORY

This reference in one of the oldest and most popular of Hungarian songs, is to the battle of Mohács in 1526, through which Hungary lost its independence and its opportunity of maintaining itself as a major European power. During the Middle Ages, the Hungarian kings, beginning with Stephen the Great in the eleventh century, by their brilliant ability and strong military prowess, had been able to form a monarchy of such an extent that it compared favorably with the vast kingdoms of England and France. Their subjects, the Magyars, were a homogeneous people orginally descended from Asian nomads and possessed of a fierce spirit of national pride; especially was this true of the ruling nobles, as strong and self-sufficient a group as was to be found in all Europe. When, on the battle-field of Mohács, the Turkish sultan Suleiman ii, who had advanced into Europe in the hopes of seizing the Holy Roman Empire, met the Hungarian army and killed the Magyar king, as well as the flower of Hungarian chivalry, the blow to the national pride was overwhelming. At the very time the nationalism of the other European countries was being fostered, that of the Magyars was lost completely. Divided into three subject states in 1547, Hungary for over a century and a half possessed not even a semblance of national unity.

But the spirit of nationalism, as we have seen, thrives on adversity; during this long period of national captivity, the Magyars became more desirous than ever of attaining their independence. In 1699, after sixteen long years of struggle, the Turks were finally driven out; but the country, instead of achieving its freedom, became united with the dominions of the Austrian Hapsburgs. Time and time again during the next century, the spirit of nationalistic revolt flared up, only to be ruthlessly crushed by such reactionary conservatives in Vienna as Metternich and Schwarzenberg. Finally, in 1867, taking advantage of a temporary accentuation of the spirit of liberalism within the Austrian empire, the Magyar patriots were able to elevate their country into a constituent part of the Hapsburg monarchy; the dual monarchy of Austria-Hungary was formed, in which the kingdom of Hungary was a separate entity, with its own constitution and parliament, and the flaming spirit of the Magyars was finally appeased.

Whoever visited the gay city of Budapest, the capital of Hungary, before the Second World War came away with the feeling that he had become intimately acquainted with the folk music of that country. For on every side he heard the gay melodies and infectious rhythms that Liszt used in his *Hungarian Rhapsodies* and Brahms in his *Hungarian Dances*. A native Hungarian, Liszt spent a considerable part of his varied career in Budapest and became tremendously interested in the folk music of the country, making a special study of and writing a book on the gypsies and their music. Brahms came to know these fascinating tunes through his long association as a young man with the Hungarian violinist Reményi; and he, like Liszt, made rich capital of their natural appeal.

Modern research, however, has shown that these two misguided Romantics were mistaken in their choice of material representative of the Hungarian spirit. The Liszt-Brahms themes are now considered by investigators as being nothing but cheap examples of a type of popular amusement music that is really not Magyar in spirit. Bela Bartók (1881–1945), Zoltán Kodály (*b.* 1882), and other scientific researchers went about Hungary and the adjacent countries, collecting thousands of folk tunes which they regarded as distinctively Hungarian. And these two composers have used these tunes as the basis for a national idiom which they felt stems from the very roots of their national culture.

BARTÓK AND KODÁLY

Bartók wrote a great deal of music of all kinds, passing through a number of different stylistic phases. He started his career with music suggestive of the older European styles; his opera *Bluebeard's Castle*, his earlier orchestral suites, though flavored with nationalistic traits, are quite different from the peculiar blend of poetic fervor, radical tonal experiments, and "audacious *gaminerie*" that characterizes his middle period. In his later years, very largely spent in the United States, he found a new tonal language, which, while still harsh and abrupt, did not disdain to woo the hearer and try to communicate to him something of the composer's enthusiasm. Since these important works really belong to the contemporary period, they are discussed in a later chapter.

Kodály is, in general, a somewhat more ingratiating composer, who treated his melodic and harmonic materials in a characteristically nineteenth-century manner, with touches here and there of Impressionism. In celebration of a 1923 national anniversary he wrote his first outstanding work, the noble *Psalmus Hungaricus,* a striking choral composition in which the nationalist influence is conveyed by direct, even fiery, response to the words, rather than by the mere use of folk tunes. He continued this type of choral writing, for which he has shown a real affinity, with his *Budavári Te Deum* in 1936, written for the two-hundred-fiftieth anniversary of the delivery of Budapest from the Turks. His best known composition and greatest success was the national opera he wrote in comic style in 1926, *Háry János,* about a preposterous national hero, genial liar, and general humbug. The orchestral suite drawn from this opera has become a well-known repertoire piece everywhere, along with his two suites of folk dances arranged in a modern manner, *Marosszék Dances* (1930) and *Galanta Dances* (1934).

Kodály has combined his work as a composer with the careers of teacher and musicologist. He has long been associated with the Academy of Music in Budapest and his students there include some of the most important names in Hungarian musical life; most of them have considered their most important task to be the continuation of Kodály's struggle to preserve the essential Hungarian character of their national folk music. He has become famous the world over as a researcher in the field of folk music and has played an important role in international folk music circles. As the great modern figure of Hungarian music, Kodály has remained an active leader in the musical life of his country, occasionally traveling outside to teach and lecture. As late as 1965 he visited the United States.

The serious musician naturally has a high regard for scientific research in his field of art. It is entirely to the good that Bartók and Kodály and the rest have searched out the real from the false in the tunes of Hungary. We cannot but raise the question, however, as to whether the treatment which these men have given this material is consistent with its essential nature. There are plenty of critics who assert that modernism is merely a reversion to the primitive; and some aspects of it certainly seem so—the extremely percussive use of the piano by Bartók, for instance. The play of modern primitivism on material which is really primitive is likely to produce something unusual and strong; much can be argued as to values here: whether the old gets fair enough play when the new is mixed with it, and whether the old really retains much meaning when treated with modern dissonances.

DOHNÁNYI

One other important Hungarian composer must be mentioned here, Ernst von Dohnányi (1877–1960), who has been well described as the last flowering of the Hungarian Romantic era. His folk-influenced music is not so extensive as that of the other two, more famous, Hungarian composers; nor did he apply himself to this subject with their intensity, one might perhaps say "fanaticism." His *Ruralia Hungarica Suite* (1924) represents the type of folkiness which most people find palatable; his powers as a composer were admirable and so the result is refreshing. To a certain Brahmsian background he added a delightful skill in key manipulation, a sense of humor, and a particular adroitness in the use of the variations he introduced into so many of his works.

There are few composers whose works may be more readily recommended to music lovers who appreciate craftsmanship, and yet who do not greatly care for idioms that go beyond the nineteenth century. Dohnányi's *Second Quartet,* Op. 15, and the *F sharp minor Suite for Orchestra,* Op. 19, as well as the humorous *Variations on a Nursery Song for Piano and Orchestra,* Op. 25, give a good idea of this composer's sterling musicianship and good companionship.

Born in Bratislava, Dohnányi was influenced largely by Hungarian and German sources. He became famous as a concert pianist and also attracted attention as an outstanding conductor. Late in life he assumed the role of educator, spending considerable time in this country.

THE RUMANIAN ENESCO

Probably no other country owes so much of its musical development to one man as does Rumania to Georges Enesco (1881–1955). Born in Liveni, Rumania, he was trained in Vienna and Paris, where he studied with Massenet and Fauré. Skilled as a concert violinist, he also played the cello, organ, and piano, and became famous as a conductor in both England and America, as well as central Europe. Later in life, he turned to teaching, his most famous violin pupil being Yehudi Menuhin. An international figure of renown, his unusual musical versatility was shown on the occasion of the sixtieth anniversary of his first public appearance at the age of eight, when he played a farewell concert in New York in 1950 at which he appeared in the capacity of violinist, pianist, conductor, and composer.

As a composer, Enesco is best known for his *Rumanian Rhapsodies,* two neo-Romantic orchestral compositions written in 1901 and 1902 that are distinctly colored with a nationalistic spirit and an idiom that is much more accessible than that of Bartók. The same complaint has been made about the gypsies' deforming of the real folk music in contributing, not original ideas, but their own decorative flamboyance to material of which they do not understand the real nature. Enesco was fortunate in being able to combine a feeling for nationalism with fresh ideas of craftsmanship, thus making the result acceptable to the average listener. In addition to these very successful pieces, Enesco wrote an opera, *Oedipus,* which was produced in Paris in 1936, as well as three symphonies, a violin concerto, and a *Symphonie concertante* for cello and orchestra.

But his greatest contribution to Rumanian music was the establishment of national prizes for new works by young composers, to be distributed at an international contest held every other year in Bucharest. This has resulted in what Nicolas Slonimsky has described[1] as a proliferation of Rumanian composition in the last twenty years that is staggering—symphonies and operas, concertos and chamber music, piano pieces and songs being produced in quantities and almost instantaneously published. As specific examples of this Slonimsky cites Dimitri Cuclin (*b.* 1885), who has already written eighteen symphonies which are dutifully performed and published in Bucharest. So the spirit of Enesco still dominates the activities of contemporary Rumanian music.

The English Tradition

AN OVERDUE RENAISSANCE

For a number of reasons British music rocked in a long period of the doldrums between the time of Purcell in the seventeenth century and that of Elgar, whom we have

---

[1] In an article in *The Musical Quarterly* of January, 1965 on modern composition in Rumania.

spoken of elsewhere as the acknowledged head of English composition during the nineteenth century. There were a number of composers of Elgar's generation who, in any extended account of English music, would deserve fuller treatment than we can give them here. We mention them briefly in appreciation of the heavy task they faced and the spirit with which they produced music which, though based on a good classic training, did attempt to bring out something of the essential English spirit. Sir Alexander Mackenzie (1847–1935), Sir Charles Stanford (1852–1900), and Sir Hubert Parry (1848–1918) stood for the classic values in Victorian England, each of them contributing something fresh, according to his nature, to the general development of his country's music. Sir Arthur Sullivan (1842–1900), generally associated with the thirteen light operas which, written in collaboration with the satirical light dramatist Gilbert, have brought him everlasting fame,[2] had a lively, fluent instrumental style as well, quite suggestive of Mozart and Mendelssohn in its melodic inspiration and technical resourcefulness. Others of this time were J. B. McEwen (1868–1948), a lowland Scot who trod his native heath with swinging step and whose music combined a philosophic introspection with French Impressionism; and Frederick Delius, whose music we have treated at length elsewhere as representing the best possible expression of the nostalgic, the sweet, yet not sentimental, evocative power of the English countryside.

Sir Granville Bantock (1868–1946) was an eclectic who ranged the world for his impressions and, since he was attracted to subjects with mystical overtones, wrote a great deal of program music bearing titles connected with literature or legend. Dame Ethel Smyth (1858–1944) was a composer whose music roamed widely and whose style (in her opera *The Wreckers,* for instance) is apt to be patchy. Yet she had plenty of vitality, humor, and intensity, qualities which distinguish her inimitable books of reminiscences of the period in which she lived and worked. A man whose nature remains a mystery to many was Gustav Holst (1874–1934), who, while maintaining a close affinity with his better known contemporary, Vaughan Williams, struck out a very distinctive path for himself. His *Planets Suite* shows as well as anything he wrote the range and personality of his style. In his later works there is to be felt an increasing raggedness, even a forbidding tinge—a withdrawal that is not easy to penetrate and which has not increased the

---

[2] Beginning with *Trial by Jury* in 1875, the best known of these are *Pinafore* (1878), *The Pirates of Penzance* (1880), *Iolanthe* (1882), *The Mikado* (1885) and *The Yeomen of the Guard* (1888).

general recognition of the worth of such works as *The Hymn of Jesus* (1917) and *Egdon Heath* (1928). Rutland Boughton (1878–1960) wrote operas and choral works based on Celtic and Arthurian legends; his *Immortal Hour* (1914) had remarkable success.

The British love for choral singing, but not for opera, gave to these composers of the English Renaissance some of their best opportunities, and a great deal of the reputation of most of them was, in fact, made in the field of oratorio. But this meant a limitation of their chance of becoming known abroad, partly because of the obvious difficulty of language and partly because few Continental nations have taken to choralism as strongly as have the British. The composers who found congenial the Elgarian tincture of mysticism, or the broad national tunefulness which irradiates the music of Purcell, made reputations that are higher in England than in the rest of the musical world.

The most notable gap in late nineteenth-century British music seems to arise from the paucity of composers born between about 1870 and 1890. The losses of World War I account for some of this shortage, though one or two of the men who were killed had already shown that they had something to say which England would have been glad to hear—men like George Butterworth (1885–1916) and Ernest Farrar (1885–1918) and Ivor Gurney, born in 1890 but who, mentally injured, lingered until 1937. These were composers of the quiet sort, musing on friendly English scenes, mostly stirred to some extent at least by Vaughan Williams and his passion for the countryside. In general, however, it would appear that the fading of the Romantic impulse washed some of the life and faith out of this generation of English composers.

Later, E. J. Moeran (1894–1950), though of Irish descent, found some inspiration in the English scene. His music glowed with gentle warmth, his *Songs of Springtime* being as good an example as any of English music that is native without being naïve—the besetting sin of the folksong school. Another composer of this period whose choral writing has had considerable success is Herbert Howells (*b*. 1892), who followed in the British-classical lines of Parry and Vaughan Williams.

Philip Heseltine (1894–1930) was a strange dual personality. Under his own name he edited a considerable amount of old music, wrote some delicate, sensitive songs, and took up the cause of another English composer closely related to him in spirit, Frederick Delius. Under the pen name "Peter Warlock" he assumed a more robust and even swashbuckling character—a sort of Elizabethan born out of his time, someone called him.

Constant Lambert (1905–1951) was one of those creative artists whose gifts were so various that they hindered his full development of any one of them. He was active as a ballet conductor and journalist as well as a composer. His best work was the ballet *Rio Grande,* set to a scenario by Sacheverell Sitwell, which tries to evoke the exotic atmosphere of Brazil with the use of jazz elements. We have already mentioned his *Music Ho!,* published in 1934, as a collection of trenchant criticism.

Is There a German Nationalism?

As a people made up of the most extraordinary mixing and mingling of races, perhaps even with a preponderance of the pre-Aryan element, as the "people of the center" in every sense of the term, the Germans are more intangible, more ample, more contradictory, more unknown, more incalculable, more surprising, and even more terrifying than other people are to themselves:— they escape definition and are therefore alone the despair of the French. It is characteristic of the Germans that the question, "What is German?" never dies out among them.

Nietzsche: *Beyond Good and Evil*

An anecdote about the Englishman, the German, the Frenchman, and the Russian, who agreed to write in one brief extemporaneous sentence the definition of their respective nations, presents the German character. According to the story, the Englishman wrote, "I am"; the Frenchman, "I love"; the Russian, "I sin." When the German's turn came to read out his definition of himself, he asked to be excused so that he might take a walk and "think it over."

Demiashkevich: *The National Mind*

A SPIRIT DIVIDED AGAINST ITSELF

The title of this section brings us face-to-face with a basic question which no book that attempts to interpret the human spirit in music can possibly neglect, however difficult it may be to provide anything like a real analysis of the creative spirit of the nation which, above all others, has produced an abundance of the purest musical genius. The difficulties of this question are perhaps best epitomized by a comparison of the great Germany of the past with that of the spirit-frightening Germany of later times, a comparison which always make us wonder whether they can possibly be reconciled.

The quotations cited from Nietzsche and Demiashkevich suggest a duality or, perhaps better, a plurality in the German spirit, which accounts for the violent contradictions in German life and method: Demiashkevich defines this conflict as being between the two souls which Goethe discerned as lodging side by side in the German breast —that of "totalitarianism" and that of "infinitism." On the one hand, there is the passion for wholeness and unity which causes this people to sink all considerations in the pursuit of a worldly, practical end; on the other, there is the mystical, self-communing aspiration for the infinite, for divine truth and absorption in a higher sphere of being. In trying to explain the course of German history through the years, Demiashkevich propounds the theory that there has always been an alternation, with corresponding spiritual failing or progress, of these two opposed elements.

Further, he points out what we all readily realize, that the German temperament is basically of the Dionysian order as opposed to the Apollonian—that it is essentially of the mystical, metaphysical, prophet-seeking type and has few of the precise, rationalistic, analytic tendencies represented in the French character. In art, the Apollonian spirit may be said to be represented by sculpture, architecture, painting; the Dionysian, by music. It is no accident that the French have produced some of the greatest painting and architecture of the world; the Germans, the greatest music.

PHASES OF GERMAN HISTORY

When the Germans first appear on the stage of history, they do so under the urge of a totalitarian impetus, as savage warriors, who, in the fourth and fifth centuries, overran the Roman Empire; this caused them to drive forward in an irresistible conquest of all Europe, a drive which was succeeded by a quiescent epoch—from the sixth to the ninth century—of infinitism. During this time, their native qualities made them easy proselytes to the gospel of Christianity, and the whole period is marked by outstanding developments in art and good living.

Then followed a revival of the totalitarian spirit at the expense of infinitism: during the period of the tenth to the thirteenth century, there were further drives for the conquest of the southern and eastern parts of Europe, drives which culminated in the Holy Roman Empire of the German Nation of Otto I (what modern Germans call *das erste Reich*). Then, Demiashkevich points out, came another great epoch of infinitism, from the fourteenth to the seventeenth century, which reached its zenith in the terrible religious wars of the sixteenth and seventeenth centuries. The latter, although they took the physical form of armed conflicts between German Protestants and Catholics, were in reality expressions of the national longing for the infinite, of a desire to attain a suitable triumph for eternal religious truth. During this time, Germany was weak politically and militarily; but she contributed mightily to the artistic, philosophical, and scientific progress of the world. Madame de Staël, a sympathetic French observer of the German scene, puts it in this fashion:

> *This division of Germany, fatal to her political force, was nevertheless very favorable to all the efforts of genius and imagination. In matters of literary and metaphysical opinion, there was a sort of gentle anarchy, which allowed to every man the complete development of his own individual manner of perception.*

Then, slowly at first, commencing with the efforts of Frederick the Great, there started a new totalitarian drive for world supremacy, a drive which reached its zenith only recently. But before it received its greatest impetus from Bismarck, the founder of *das zweite Reich,* there ensued the greatest *Blütezeit* (literally, "flowering time") the nation has ever seen. The best qualities of German infinitism seemed to come to fruition during this period, when the nation was in process of development: this was the time of the most significant literary Romanticists, Goethe and Schiller, of the hosts of Romantic musicians, Beethoven, Schubert, Schumann, Wagner, Strauss, and the rest; when the German artists soared in search of a "supernational, infinite truth and beauty," which they found revealed to them in the beauties of nature, the principles of religion, and, above all else, the struggles and aspirations of mankind.

GERMAN MUSIC UNIVERSAL RATHER THAN NATIONAL

It has been these elements of infinitism, so strongly present in the German's character, that have made his art universal rather than merely national. Nothing could be more purely German than the music of Bach or Beethoven or Wagner or Brahms; and yet the essential char-

acteristics of these great spirits—all of them Men spelled with a capital
M, to borrow Napoleon's phrase describing Goethe—appeal to the
world at large. The longing of the German spirit for a communion with
nature, and its adoration for, and realization of, the beauty which is in
the world, to be found so strongly in the music of Beethoven and
Brahms, are understood everywhere. The universal yearning for the
infinite, the ardent desire for the realization of spiritual truth that we
sense in the music of Bach, makes this provincial Thuringian organist
the most international of all composers. Romanticism, with its native
mysticism, its personal probings and aspirations, was essentially a German movement—a "Dionysian revolt against the domination of the
French rationalistic enlightenment and triumph associated with the
names of Voltaire and Diderot." The music of two early German Romantics, E. T. A. Hoffmann (1776–1822) and Louis Spohr (1784–
1859), containing chromatic progressions and characteristic modulations, is no longer played. It was not until Weber's *Freischütz*, with its
magic horn calls, its huntsmen's choruses, and its eerie haunted glen,
that the German spirit really came into music. The typically Romantic
figures of Schumann, Wagner, and Strauss could have come out of only
a nation such as the German; and yet this music is as popular in Paris,
New York, and London as it is in Berlin, Munich, and Vienna!

It must be recognized, of course, that any such attempt as we have
made to define the German nature and to apply such definition to the
course of the country's musical history cannot be considered a complete,
exclusive explanation; for too many factors of a socio-political nature
are involved to allow one easy account to explain any nation's art. It is
a commonplace of history that the existence of so many small, independent states in the Germany of the eighteenth and early nineteenth
centuries greatly fostered the development of the nation's music, opening up posts for executive musicians and composers which otherwise
would not have existed. But it is exceedingly dangerous to make the
statement, as one English writer has recently suggested, that Germany's
preeminence in music over the other nations "probably lies largely in
the greater opportunity she offered." Such leadership and superiority
are better explained by the duality of German nature than by the mere
accident of political growth; but it is weak oversimplification which
accounts for the greatness of a nation's art through any specific cause.
All that we can be sure of is the fact that there seems to be something
in the make-up or working of the German mind which accounts for the

creative, universally appealing musical triumphs of the past and the comparative sterility of the present.

Which is not to say, of course, that there have been no manifestations of what we can call a nationalistic spirit in later German music. Humperdinck's operas were strongly tinged with real German flavor. Hans Pfitzner (1869–1949) suggests Romantic, Germanic ideals: *Die Rose vom Liebesgarten, Das Herz, Das dunkle Reich, Von deutscher Seele*—the very names of these operas and cantatas could belong to none but German works. His greatest success was with the opera *Palestrina* (1917), an effective dramatization of incidents in the life of the great Italian composer, rather turgidly set to music which is Germanic rather than Italianate.

It seems wise, however, not to press too closely the explanation of totalitarianism and its consequent disasters at the end of World War II as accounting for the weakness of the German music which followed it. This weakness seems to have arisen from a lack of faith that cannot be accounted for by socio-political upthrusts alone, since it was shared by other countries who maintained a democratic system entirely opposed to the sort of totalitarianism which was rampant in Germany and later in Russia. The recognition of the duality of the German mind is useful in trying to estimate what nationalism has meant to that people's art, and in showing that this is something quite different from the more self-conscious nationalism of the various other European countries whose music, in the freeing years of the nineteenth century, attracted the world. That there is an essential conflict between totalitarianism and infinitism in German music is evident enough, and there has been a real struggle on the part of the younger Germans after the disasters of the two world wars to secure for their country a place in the creative life of the world commensurate with its achievements in the past.

THE MODERN REVOLT

The Rise of Realism

Artists who do not use nature weary the public.

Alfred Stevens

THE TEEMING NINETEENTH CENTURY

T he development of the Industrial Revolution, the rise of the power of the Machine, the encouragement of the spirit of Scientific Progress, the formulation of the doctrines of Socialism—all these characteristic nineteenth-century manifestations, together with their attendant philosophies, affected art in many different ways, the most direct being through spelling the doom of handicrafts the world over. Another has been the fostering of a cult of *realism*—the reverence for things which can be realistically depicted—a type of art which has little to do with man's aspirations or idealizations but which rather emphasizes the pragmatism rampant in the contemporary world. The realists, whether writers, painters, or musicians, did not hesitate to use the ugly for the stuff of their art; they often felt that it suited their purposes better than that which was beautiful. This spirit flourished more strongly in literature than in the other arts; but its influence was felt in painting and sculpture and, a bit later —around the turn of the century—in music and architecture.

IN LITERATURE

The list of realist authors is legion. In France, Flaubert (whose *Madame Bovary,* published in 1857, is looked upon as the first great realistic novel), Daudet, De Maupassant, Zola (a radical politician as well as artist), Bourget, and above all the others, Anatole France, poured out a series of works dealing with humanity in its veristic aspects, some of them somber and sodden in character, others witty and

634

sardonic. In England, George Meredith and Thomas Hardy concerned themselves with the pitiful and realistic struggle of people for existence; Henry James studied the leisured classes of two continents—people on a different, but no less realistic, plane; Bernard Shaw, in a brilliant series of plays, essays, and novels, set forth a personal version of the current philosophy; H. G. Wells combined the marvels of science with a study of social problems; Samuel Butler's skeptical *Way of All Flesh* carried the realistic concept to its ultimate conclusion, for it made no attempt to take seriously either life or death.

In Norway, the dramas of Björnson and Ibsen; in Germany, the stories and plays of Sudermann and the plays of Hauptmann; in Italy, the novels and plays of Pirandello taught a progressive and intense— often grim—objectivity. The works of Russia's realistic writers were especially effective, owing to the political struggle inherent in their background for so many years: Tolstoy, Chekhov, Gorky took delight in showing what a miserably weak cog in the machinery of Russian life the common man was, and portrayed with pessimistic realism what they saw as the inevitable futility of his existence.

IN PAINTING

Even in the earlier part of the century among the painters who adhered to the doctrinaire dogmas of the David-Ingres school, there existed a strong tendency towards realism, especially in portraiture. And the Romantic painters Delacroix and Géricault, in spite of their overtheatricalism and exaggerated emotional expression, did not hesitate to represent nature and natural objects in a thoroughly realistic manner. As a matter of fact, realism in painting may be said to go back to Caravaggio (1573–1610); but, due largely to the opinions of the theorists, especially those of Charles Adolphe Dupresnoy (1611–1668), it had come to be considered an inferior type of painting.

So when the independently minded, defiant young Gustave Courbet (1819–1877) started to paint his lusty scenes from everyday life, the critics thought to confound him by calling him a realist. He gladly accepted the challenge, gathered an active group of disciples around him, and, posting on his studio door the sign *G. Courbet, Realist*, brought a cameralike eye to bear on all sorts of subjects, often mixing with it a vivid creative imagination. Corot, with his lovely, vaporous landscapes; Goya the Spaniard, who painted and etched the most telling exposé of war's horrors the world has ever seen, as well as

SUMMER   by Claude Monet

portraits which were candid enough to show the sitter as he actually was; Daumier, with his swift, telling technique, withering irony, and amazingly forceful method of expression; Toulouse-Lautrec, who injected the bitterness of his private life into the pictures of Parisian scenes which he painted; Degas and Manet, who brought an element of design into their essentially factual way of looking at things—these are the great names in realistic painting. Lesser men followed the same tendencies and became even more popular: Morland, Wilkie, and Landseer in England and Millet in France.

IMPRESSIONISM, REALISM'S LAST FLING

Finally there arose the school of *impressionists*—men like Monet, Sisley, Pissarro, Seurat, and Renoir—whose pictures were the result of a sincere attempt on their part to make an even more exact, natural recording of nature than their predecessors had done. Impressionism is, as has often been said, the last phase of realism, the final fling of the artists who tried to reproduce on their canvases what they felt nature revealed to their eye. Its exponents called to their help some of the new discoveries which science had made, discoveries which showed the phenomenon we know as color resulting from the breaking-up of light waves; in order to gain the greatest possible realism in this respect, these impressionists, instead of mixing their colors on a palette, broke them up into tiny smears placed on the canvas in close juxtaposition, leaving the mixing and the blending of them to the eye of the beholder. This made the color seem much more alive and gave a fresh, open-air quality to their work, which was in pleasing contrast to the older studio technique. Thus, the whole problem of painting came to be bound up largely with but the one idea, the realistic rendering of light and color; forms were dissolved into color patches, patterns became unconventional and largely accidental, subject did not matter. The most familiar, commonplace objects became material for pictures —washwomen, bridges, factories, open-air scenes from everyday life, the sea—all painted as visual *impressions* caught under certain light conditions. One writer has rather wittily described this type of painting as reality dissolved in a luminous fog.

But if we can accept this impressionism for what it is—"an exalted poetry of nature expressed through light and color"—a new world of beauty is revealed to our eyes. All the men concerned with this movement possessed definite personalities and produced individual results: Monet is supreme in his rendering of the play of light and color over nature; Seurat, with his technique of pointillism, the use of minute, evenly spread dots of color, exalted the episodes of everyday life; Renoir, the greatest of them all, painted joyous, buoyant pictures which made use of impressionistic color in an architectural sense. Musicians are specially interested in these artists because of their direct effect on the works of Debussy and his followers.

SYMBOLISM

A parallel movement in literature was called *symbolism*, which was first established as a theory and illustrated in poetry by Stéphane Mallarmé. His ideal was the result of the success achieved by the painters: "to name an object is to sacrifice three quarters of the enjoyment which comes from the pleasure of guessing bit by bit. To suggest, that is our dream." He strove for an "ideal poetry," freed from all subservience to subject matter, which, as he put it, depicted not the object itself but the effect produced by the object. Together with Verlaine and Rimbaud, who were the immediate predecessors of symbolism, and Maeterlinck, Valéry, Gide, Stefan Georg, Hopkins, Joyce, and Eliot, who were strongly influenced by it, Mallarmé wrote a tenuous sort of verse that is frankly sensuous in sound and suggestive rather than exact in its meaning, poetry which he beautifully described as a voyage in quest of the unknown. Words were used much as the colors of the impressionistic painters, as symbols evocative because of their sound and certain subconscious sensations, rather than as means for conveying ideas: the central thought contained in a passage was of less importance than what one was led to read between the lines. The *opus magnum* of symbolism was Mallarmé's famous *L'Après-midi d'un faune*. It was this masterpiece of vague loveliness and poetic imagination that inspired Debussy, as we shall see, to attempt to transfer to tone the symbolism which he felt the poet had tried to convey through words.

REALISM IN THE OTHER ARTS

Sculpture and architecture reflected some of the same tendencies of realistic expression, although not so strongly. The natural realism of Dalou's *Triumph of the Republic* was widely copied by sculptors everywhere. Rodin (1840–1917), the great man of the time in sculpture, essayed all sorts of symbolic subjects by means of an individual way of expression that was a peculiar combination of imaginative mysticism and brute strength. Imagination of a high order was also infused by the American, Saint-Gaudens, into his realistic conceptions; and the Belgian, Meunier, saw in the ordinary workman, engaged in his everyday task of earning a living, an aesthetic subject of highest value. Architecture became eclectic in character, in an attempt to combine practicality with tradition; but there was a decided swing toward functionalism— that is, the adapting of form to the necessities of function and environment—an idea which the present day has made so largely its own.

Music did not show the effects of the current trend in the same way as its sister arts. Through all the rush of this realistic era, most musicians continued to see visions and dream dreams. Composers as imaginative as Elgar, Delius, and Sibelius made great contributions to their art during this period; but they did so largely by isolating themselves completely from the world, Elgar by retiring behind the gruff exterior of a conventional Englishman, Delius by losing himself in the quiet isolation of a provincial French village, and Sibelius by remaining in the lonely wastes of Finland. There were, of course, definite realistic trends, illustrated best by the works with which Richard Strauss startled

THE BREAKFAST OF THE BOATING PARTY   by Renoir

a bewildered world: the sensational operas *Salome* and *Elektra* and
such tone poems as *Also sprach Zarathustra, Tod und Verklärung, Ein
Heldenleben,* and the *Symphonia domestica.*

The bestial, sordid, veristic one-act operas *Cavalleria Rusticana* and
Pagliacci, with their stories taken directly from what well might have
been real events in the life of contemporary Italy, were followed by a
whole flock of operatic shockers in other countries. These included
such things as Massenet's *Navarraise* (1894), Puccini's *La Bohème*
(1897) and *La Tosca* (1900), Charpentier's *Louise* (1900), and, as we
have said, above all others Strauss's *Salome* (1905) and *Elektra* (1909).
Realism has continued to hold the interest of operatic composers right
down to the present day. In 1935 the popular composer George Gershwin, after saturating himself with the idioms and styles of American
Negro music, wrote his folk opera *Porgy and Bess,* which has become
a classic of its kind throughout the musical world. And the Italo-
American Menotti has adopted this veristic style for his successful
shockers, *The Medium* and *The Consul,* while *The Saint of Bleecker
Street* (1954) concerns itself, in a way that is perhaps more effective
than moving, with the rather squalid life of Italo-Americans in New

York's Little Italy. Menotti sums up the ideals of this school well by saying, "I offer no solutions. I am satisfied if I shock, that is, if I create strong emotion."

In strange contrast to these realistic works, and yet in a way their direct result, are Debussy's orchestral poems *L'Après-midi d'un faune* and *La Mer* and his rather rarely heard masterpiece, the opera *Pelléas et Mélisande*. That these are perhaps the most artistically successful incarnations of the spirit of this whole period is due to the indefinite nature of the art they represent rather than to any difference in the ideals of the artists who created them. In the literal sense, they are the first great modern works in music.

Debussy and Impressionism

Nature disengaged by the Impressionists from all contingency, interpreted into logical harmonies of tones and of lines, gives, besides plastic joy, intimate experience of an intellectual order.

Georges Lecomte

DEBUSSY'S LIBERATING INFLUENCES

The summation in music of those tendencies of the nineteenth century which made modern art inevitable came in the person of Claude Debussy (1862–1918), who devoted his life to answering the question he boldly put to his generation: "Is it not our duty to find the symphonic formula which fits our time, one which progress, daring, and modern victory demand?"

There are two aspects from which to view Debussy's position as one of the great men of art; it is difficult to decide which is the more important. First, he was the creator of some of the most sensitively conceived, poetically original music ever written—music which showed that the principles and ideals of the impressionists and the symbolists could be carried out even more successfully in a transient and impalpable art than in one in which the creator's vision must of necessity be fixed on canvas or paper. And second, he was one of music's great liberators from the shackles of traditions that had become outworn, the initiator of new and hitherto undreamed-of possibilities. If genius has ever given wings to music and sent it soaring up to heights to which it could not have risen otherwise, Carl Engel says, it did so through the liberating influences which Debussy introduced. His aim, like the aim of all the great liberators in art, differed materially from that of his predecessors; to reach it, he had to find new ways. Quite aside from the fact that they are outstanding and, if contemporary opinion provides any criterion, lasting works of art, *L'Après-midi d'un faune* and *Pelléas et Mélisande* opened up such new visions and suggested such new horizons that it is impossible to see just what the end will be. Debussy was the first of the new moderns in music, and, so far at least, he is the greatest.

UNITIES IN THE ARTS

Any thought of this composer brings up the subject of the impressionist school in music, of which he was the most distinguished member. We have already shown that, in painting, this school, which has provided us with so many tenuous, atmospherically vague expressions, was in theory the result of an attempt on the part of the artists to be even more exact and scientific in their renderings of nature. When they came to put their theories into practice, however, the impressionists gave us pictures which, in their color lyricism, their evanescent beauties, their soft-focus loveliness, approach the suggestiveness of music and poetry. In producing such pictures as Pissarro's *Early Morning,* Monet's *Summer,* or Renoir's *The Breakfast of the Boating Party,* the artists may or may not have been consciously aware of trying to make their subject matter brilliant and alive through their use of "broken color." But the person who looks at these pictures gets far more than an effect of lovely color and light: he receives somehow a suggestion, an impression, of the feeling which the artist experienced as he painted them. There is, in these pictures, a peculiar sense of unreality, a tendency to present illusion rather than fact, to draw as near as possible to pure sensation and emotion, without any of the usual trappings and mechanics of art.

It is little wonder that these Parisian painters of the 1880's stimulated their contemporaries in poetry and music to follow their ideals; for this style of impressionistic[1] expression suits the arts of poetry and music even better than it does that of painting. Out of the heated aesthetic

---

[1] The term *impressionist* was first applied in derision to one of Monet's canvases.

discussions of the Paris of those days, there came two movements which closely paralleled that of the painters—symbolist poetry, with its attempt, in the words of its leading exponent, to "evoke in a deliberate shadow the unmentioned object by illusive words"; and impressionistic music, with its attempt to provide "colored hearing" and "orchestral verse." Thrown together in the maelstrom of artistic controversy which rocked Paris at the time, artists like Verlaine, Mallarmé, Debussy, Manet, and Pissarro strongly affected one another's opinions and shaped one another's conduct. Debussy intended at one time to take up painting as his profession and so was naturally disposed to see in the new technique of the impressionists ideas which could be transferred to music; he placed his chords, for instance, in close and unusual successions, much as his fellow artists laid their colors on canvas; and he did not hesitate to proclaim that his music could depict "various experiences and special effects of light."

THE SCHOOL OF MUSICAL IMPRESSIONISM

There is as definite a school of musical impressionism as there is of painting. Its leading figures did not always follow Debussy's lead in technical procedure, but they incorporated in their music the same general tendencies. Debussy, Delius, Ravel, Falla, and the rest were primarily absorbed in the possibilities of color as an expressive medium; they looked on the communication of feeling as one of the most important elements in their music; and they were content to let the form of their work grow naturally out of its materials. So we are justified in calling them *impressionists* and in thinking of their compositions as characteristic manifestations of the general artistic tendencies of their time.

Strictly speaking, the term *color* belongs purely to the visual arts, where its use is in connection with the sensations produced on the eye by rays of decomposed light. But we have borrowed the term freely for the other arts: we speak of color in music, for example, in attempting to describe aural sensations produced by such specific factors as the *timbre* or tone quality which results from certain instruments; or the result of the management of key relationships within the course of a composition; or the particular manner in which a composer chooses and arranges his harmonies. In poetry *color* is used to refer to the choice of exact words and fit phrases, which the poet makes in order to create a certain illusion. Can anyone deny the color that is inherent in Edward Rowland Sill's description of a tropical morning at sea?

Off to the East the steady sun track
  Golden meshes fill—
Webs of fire, that lace and tangle,
  Never a moment still.

Liquid palms but clap together,
  Fountains, flowerlike, grow—
Limpid bells on stems of silver—
  Out of a slope of snow.

Sea depths, blue as the blue of violets—
  Blue as a summer sky,
When you blink at its arch sprung over
  Where in the grass you lie.

Dimly an orange bit of rainbow
  Burns where the low west clears,
Broken in air, like a passionate promise
  Born of a moment's tears. . . .

It is hardly necessary to suggest that the use of color in painting has been one of the art's chief glories from its earliest beginnings. It is not until we come to the impressionist composers, however, that we fully realize how important an agent this can be in music: the cool, lovely, and yet brightly tinted hues of Debussy, the blaze of glorious ambient color with which Ravel invests his orchestra in such a work as his second *Daphnis et Chloé* suite, the melting and shifting of Delius's peculiarly shaped color masses—all these were new elements in music, elements which have established themselves so firmly in our affections that we would never willingly forgo them.

THE COMMUNICATION OF FEELING

"How can music ever be a mere intellectual speculation or a series of curious combinations of sound that can be classified like the articles in a grocer's shop? Music is an outburst of the soul; it is addressed and should appeal instantly to the soul of the listener. It is not experimental analysis like chemistry." This characteristic remark of Delius's may be said to be representative of the attitude of the whole impressionistic school as to the importance of communicating feeling in art. Monet's lovely picture *Summer* holds us spellbound not merely because of its light nuances or its color harmonies: we immediately react to it because it communicates to us the indescribable feeling of radiant fulfillment and peaceful contentedness associated with midsummer, a happiness which is mixed with a sense of nostalgia and regret, for

    June is short
And we must joy in it and dance and sing
And from her bounty draw her rosy worth.

It is the communication of just such feeling that we get in Delius's wonderful tone poem *In a Summer Garden;* Debussy makes us feel the fleeting emotions of the drowsy faun in his *L'Après-midi d'un faune,* and the intoxicating fragrance of the summer night in his *Ibéria;* in his *Nuages,* he shares with us his melancholy in watching the undying aspect of the sky and the "slow passage of clouds dissolving in a gray agony tinted with white." There is nothing descriptive about this music; it simply strives to evoke in the listener's mind something of the feeling which its creator experienced in writing it. And when the composer possesses as sensitive an imagination and as sure a technique as Debussy or Delius, the result is unforgettable.

The symbolists tried to do the same thing with words, putting them together in such harmonious combinations as would suggest to the reader, as one of their principal apologists has put it, a mood or condition which is not actually mentioned in the text but was nevertheless paramount in the poet's mind at the moment of conception. The reader of Mallarmé or Verlaine in the original French will be able to testify to their success. Even to those unacquainted with the language, such lines as the following from the opening of *L'Après-midi d'un faune* are evocative of emotion:

Ces nymphes, je les veux perpétuer.
                              Si clair,
Leur incarnat léger, qu'il voltige dans l'air
Assoupi de sommeils touffus.
                         Aimai-je un rêve?
Mon doute, amas de nuit ancienne, s'achève
En maint rameau subtil, qui, demeuré les vrais
Bois memes, prouve, hélas! que bien seul je m'offrais
    Pour triomphe la faute idéale des roses.

FORM EVOLVED FROM FEELING

Because of their absorption in other things, the impressionists have often been accused, sometimes quite unjustly, of a neglect of form. They had little to do with structure in the ordinary formal sense—with repetition and arrangement of details, subjects and developments, fillings and passage work, and the rest of the paraphernalia. The shape of their works was bred, rather, out of the nature and sequence of the ideas they were attempting to express—their form arose naturally out of their materials. We cannot say that Henley's poem *Margaritae sorori* lacks form simply because it does not follow classic practice; it is the nature and force of the thinking which evolves its perfectly congruent shape and which gives it form in the true sense of the word:

A late lark twitters from the quiet skies;
And from the west,
Where the sun, his day's work ended,
Lingers as in content,
There falls on the old, gray city
An influence luminous and serene,
A shining peace.
The smoke ascends
In a rosy-and-golden haze. The spires
Shine, and are changed. In the valley
Shadows rise. The lark sings on. The sun,
Closing his benediction,
Sinks, and the darkening air
Thrills with a sense of the triumphing night—
Night with her train of stars
And her great gift of sleep.

So be my passing!
My task accomplished and the long day done,
My wages taken, and in my heart
Some late lark singing,
Let me be gathered to the quiet west,
The sundown splendid and serene,
Death.

Sometimes—very often—this method of expression yields little more than a sort of sensuous loveliness; but the real masters—Renoir, Delius, Debussy, Mallarmé—provide their works with actual structural skeletons, even though they may not be orthodox ones. To say that *L'Après-midi* or *Sea Drift* or *Le Déjeuner des canotiers* lacks form is to display complete ignorance of the meaning of the term. For these works, rhapsodic though they are, are knit together with surety and freedom of technique, their shape and articulation, like that of the poem of Henley's, evolving from the inside instead of being the result of standardized schemes applied exteriorly.

INFLUENCES

Biographers have given a great deal of attention to the influences which helped shape Debussy's revolutionary ideals. Two visits to Bayreuth fastened on him the spell of the old magician, Klingsor, as he called Wagner, and there are many purple Wagnerian patches in these early works, try as Debussy might to rid himself of them. Somewhere around 1894, he discovered Moussorgsky and recognized in him a real kindred spirit. Massenet, whose music he found to be "vibrant with thrills, transports, and would-be eternal embraces," and Grieg, the northerner with the individual harmonic gift, helped him find himself; as did the eccentric Eric Satie, the composer of the *Pieces in the Shape of a Pear* and *Airs to Make You Run*. Possessed of so unusually sensitive an ear that he was said to have been able to recognize instantly the overtones of bells, trumpets, and other instruments, Debussy obtained new vistas of possibilities through hearing the exotic music and native instruments which were brought from the Far East to the Paris World's Fair of 1889–1890. His close association with the symbolist poets and the impressionist painters and his absorption of many of their spiritual and technical ideas have already been described. The character of the artistic milieu in which he lived during these years gave direction to his whole career.

IDEALS

But all these would have been of little avail if Debussy had not been an artist as well as an innovator. The sources of his peculiar style of writing may be traced, but his manner of using them was his own. Feeling that Wagner's tremendous, exhausting grip on music had led it into "sterile and pernicious ways" which exaggerated almost to a point of caricature the ideals of development and repetition left by Beethoven, Debussy announced boldly that he would strive to achieve a kind of music "free from motives and themes, founded in reality on a single continuous theme which nothing would interrupt and which would never return upon itself. There will be development that is logical, compact, and deductive, rather than mere restatements of the same characteristic themes with hasty and superfluous 'filling in.' Such development will not be merely professional, the sort of rhetoric which is the result of academic training, but will have universal and essential psychic connotation"[2] (Oscar Thompson: *Debussy, Man and Artist*).

FULFILLMENT

These ideals came to fulfillment in the tone poem *L'Après-midi d'un faune* (1894), planned at first as the prelude to a triptych based on

[2] Taken from a verbal description of Debussy's arguments during a symposium of the symbolists at Pierre Louys's home, described in Fontainas's *Mes Souvenirs du symbolisme.*

DEBUSSY
(a contemporary etching)

Mallarmé's poem of the same name; the other two numbers, an *Interlude* and a *Paraphrase,* were never written. There can be little question that this work is Debussy's masterpiece; for it is music which is so individual and so free from the ordinary and accepted conventions of composition, and yet so poetically suggestive and intensely evocative, that the very fact of its composition still seems today one of the great miracles of music. Even more suggestive in mood, passionate in utterance, and colorful in expression than the poem which suggested its composition, it nevertheless reveals the composer's consummate craftsmanship and the masterful logic of his theoretical reasoning. At the time it was written, nothing exactly like it had existed before; and nothing finer has been written since.

HIS SOLITARY OPERA

Closely associated with this work and marking the summit of Debussy's career stands the opera *Pelléas et Mélisande,* based, with the author's permission, on Maeterlinck's shadowy and symbolic play. Written more or less in protest against the grandiose tyranny of Wagner's music dramas, in which, according to Debussy, the music so arrogantly predominates, this opera is an almost perfect materialization of its composer's theories concerning musical works for the stage: that the music should live the lives and work out the destinies of the protagonists in the drama, beginning where speech fails, "expressing the inexpressible, appearing as if from shadowy regions to which she returns from time to time."[3]

Coming upon Maeterlinck's play in the summer of 1892, Debussy seems to have been inspired by a single reading of it, but it took ten years to get his inspiration on paper. First produced at the Opéra Comique, in 1902, *Pelléas et Mélisande* established its composer's place as the leading man of the time; yet it was five years before this work was heard outside France. Because of its ineffectiveness as pure stage material, this opera will probably always be limited in its appeal; but it must remain as one of the great landmarks in dramatic music. For no other opera has ever been written in which the text is so naturally declaimed or in which the spiritual background of the drama is so beautifully developed by the orchestra. In every sense, it is the antithesis of Wagner; its constant restraint and lack of emotional climaxes give it a peculiar sense of mysticism, however, that, profound and sincere as it is, is poorly suited to the requirements of the stage. This, coupled with the fact that there is little of sustained melodic interest in either the vocal or the orchestral score, and the rather fugitive character of the music make it a work for the chosen few. But what a world of loveliness there is in it for them!

THE NOCTURNES

During the time of its maturation, Debussy produced his set of three *Nocturnes—Nuages, Fêtes, and Sirènes*—for orchestra, in which his impressionistic, painterlike tendencies were perfectly illustrated. The title has a decorative rather than a musical implication, Debussy insisted: he was not concerned with the structural form of the nocturne, but rather with what the word suggests in the way of "diversified impressions and special lights." If a choice had to be made as to which single work of Debussy's contains his most individual, personal expression, it might well fall on *Nuages*. Both the peculiar quality of its harmonies and the characteristics of its orchestration suggest the effects sought by the impressionist painters through their use of vibrations of color and light; only, in Debussy's case, the imaginative concept is so

---

[3] Quoted from Debussy's own words.

sensitive and the possibilities of the medium so limitless that this work must be put down (with the possible exception of *L'Après-midi d'un faune*) as the crowning glory of the Impressionist Movement.

THE LAST YEARS

Most critics will agree that after *Pelléas* there is little advance in Debussy's style; rather, perhaps, a decline, for the composer seems in his later writing to try to carry his medium beyond its natural limits, making it more definite in line and color, more robust, and, therefore, less individual. Belonging to this period is the set of three symphonic sketches, *La Mer,* the composer's most extended orchestral work, full of gorgeous tonal images suggestive of the varied aspects of the ocean. But the tautening of structure, the increase in complexity of texture, the leaning toward more orthodox expression evidenced throughout the three integrated sections of this work do not always fit the composer's individuality as well as do some of his earlier things.

OTHER WORKS

Debussy's output includes music in other fields. His best works for the piano, especially the two sets of *Préludes,* all of them written after he was forty, constitute some of the most idiomatic music ever penned for this instrument, which, because of its essential characteristics, is so well adapted to the impressionistic medium. The fifty songs that Debussy wrote cover all periods of his life from his fourteenth year on; unfortunately they can never be very popular outside the French-speaking countries because of the unusually close association between their texts and their musical settings. He made one notable essay in the field of chamber music—the early *String Quartet,* written in 1893. In his later years, when the fire of his genius had somewhat died down, he turned again to chamber music; unfortunately, his three *sonatas pour divers instruments* (1915–17) suggest that the one-time rebel had become a conventionalist, their striving for effect being a poor substitute for their composer's former limpidity of expression.

HIS NEW TECHNIQUE

Debussy might have taken for his device that of one of his famous compatriots: *Après moi le déluge.* It was his ideas of revolt against the harmonic conventions accepted by all composers from Bach to Wagner that opened the door to the reforms which have come into music since his time. More than any other composer, he thought of music as a series of harmonic progressions, everything beginning and ending with the chord; and the fundamental principle of his revolt was that of escape from the chordal combinations which were usual within a given key. He did not try to destroy tonality as his successors have done, for his compositions have a general key center which determines their course; but he did not hesitate to introduce chords that are unrelated according to the older harmonic system and entirely foreign to the key. It was in this way that he achieved so much of his vagueness and impressionism.

Before his time, the foundation of all music was consonance, with dissonances freely and often purposely introduced; his harmonic ideals led to dissonance's being regarded as an end in itself and not merely as a means for setting off and emphasizing consonances. He used all sorts of dissonant chords freely—sevenths, ninths, elevenths, and so on— without any idea of resolving them according to the demands of the academicians. Chords to him were complete units, capable of employment in any combination or succession—consecutive fifths, fourths, seconds, sevenths, or whatever "forbidden" series the composer's fancy might dictate. He loved to run constituent members of chords in parallel lines, much like the practice of the old medieval masters of organum. And he delighted in enhancing the color richness of his fabric by establishing a definite chordal bass and then festooning it with all sorts of unusual and entirely unorthodox chords. By technical means such as these, Debussy strove, as he put it, to "rid music of that legacy of clumsy, falsely interposed traditions under whose weight the art seemed likely to succumb."

Another important item in his repertoire of effects was the use of unusual scales: the pentatonic or five-tone scale, in which the shortest step is the whole tone, found in so much primitive music; the seven-note church modes—Phrygian, Dorian, and so on; and the so-called whole-tone scale, consisting of six whole tones. The unusual sound of so much of Debussy's music has led to the belief that he used these exotic scales more frequently than was actually the case; like all great artists, he knew the value of and necessity for restraint, and when he did introduce an exceptional scale or chords based on it, it was always with a certain definite effect in mind.

In order to achieve the vague, half-uttered impressions that so attracted him, Debussy avoided the cadences which are usual in music as the devil avoids holy water; likewise, any long-drawn, definite melodic utterances were carefully eschewed. And, to secure rhythmic freedom, there are elaborate and carefully considered alternations of bar values in many of his compositions—in *L'Après-midi d'un faune,* they fluctuate between 9/8, 6/8, 12/8, 3/4, and 4/4—as well as between various conflicting and cross rhythms. We have mentioned his detestation of the usual devices of composition—sonata form, development, variations, and so forth; to him, "discipline was to be sought in freedom and not in the outworn philosophies fit only for the feeble-minded." [4] His natural painter's instinct taught him to outline his form in much the same way as a painter frames his picture. Think of the number of his music forms that are the result of visual images: *L'Après-midi,* the *Nocturnes, La Mer, Images, Ibéria, L'Ile joyeuse, Jardins sous la pluie,* and many more; in all of them, Debussy builds up his form just as a painter does within the natural boundaries and limitations of his picture.

THE GREAT ARTIST-REFORMER

The advent of this painter-poet-musician-reformer provided an ideal answer to the cry heard in all the aesthetic discussions on music during the closing years of the nineteenth century: "After Wagner, what?" For we may say of Debussy, the musical revolutionist, as it has been said of certain other figures in history, that if he had not existed, it would have been necessary to invent him. After the tremendous struggles of the Romanticists and the overpowering Teutonic exuberances of Wagner, music needed some strong antidote if it was to continue any kind of healthy existence. And this is what Debussy's inquiring mind, intrepid insurgent tendencies, sensitive musical ear, cool, unclouded imagination, aristocratic Gallicism, and forward-looking vision provided.

If he had possessed no qualities other than these, Debussy would still have been one of the great milestones which mark the process of musical development. But he had, in addition, those indefinable qualities which go to make up the supreme artist—surety of vision, clarity of expression, universality of feeling; and so we look upon him as one of the significant figures in music, the composer of works which, while they mark the beginnings of modern ideals, also happen to be among the greatest masterpieces of the art. Already Debussy the Revolutionary

[4] His own words.

has become Debussy the Classic, and the works he bequeathed to posterity have joined that assemblage which for so long has withstood the onset of modernism throughout the ages. For the average listener, *L'Après-midi d'un faune* is as classic a work as Beethoven's *Eroica Symphony* or Brahms's *First Symphony*.

Ravel

In art, nothing is left to chance.
Ravel

RAVEL THE CLASSICIST

Historians of the art of painting are fond of quoting Cézanne, the leading figure of that art during the post-impressionist period, to the effect that he wished to make of impressionism an art which was "solid and durable, like that of the museum masters." The same ideal may be said to have inspired the composer Maurice Ravel (1875–1937), Debussy's contemporary and logical successor, although he may not have been consciously aware of striving to live up to it.

Twenty-five years ago the names of the radicals Debussy and Ravel were linked on musicians' tongues in much the same way as those of Bach and Handel or Haydn and Mozart; but it has become increasingly clear that, although the younger man seemed to employ the general compositional technique of his older colleague, fundamentally he was quite a different type of individual—a conservative and a classicist, with little of Debussy's desire for reform and hardly any of his warm, sensuous, human qualities. A hearing of almost any typical Ravel work—the second *Daphnis et Chloé* suite (1910), the *String Quartet* (1903), or the *Piano Concerto* (1932)—will reveal the truth of this to even the casual listener.

Ravel was a classicist not only in his use of rigid formal devices, such as that of sonata form, but in such general tendencies as his aristocracy of taste, his clarity of expression, and his frugality of means. Like Debussy, he had a fondness for archaic things, especially the music of his compatriots, the early clavecinists; but, in echoing the spirit of things

L'ESTAQUE by Cézanne   This is one of the many studies Cézanne made of this subject. He tried, as he said, to combine the principles of impressionism with the "solid and durable ideals of the museum painters."

past, he did so by having recourse to a world of imagination that is generally outside our visible one, in which human emotions are not present but attributed to mystic or legendary figures. In this sense, too, he was a Classic, one who saw the world from an impersonal, mystic viewpoint, entirely different from Debussy's eminently sensuous outlook. It was natural for Ravel, therefore, to limn his melodies and rhythms clearly and to make them an integral and component part of his structure, in contradistinction to the practice of his predecessor.

A CONSCIOUS DEVELOPMENT OF SELF

Ravel possessed neither the richness of nature nor the depth of feeling of Debussy, and his natural creative gift was less spontaneous. It was only by dint of tremendous energy and constant industry that he made himself a distinguished artist; his was a fastidious method of creation, that of a careful and conscious search for just the right and the most significant expression: his whole art, as one of his friends said, consisted

RAVEL   at the height of his career

in the rejection of the useless. "Bare essentials must ever have been for him his constant main article of faith; but these were no poor and beggarly phantoms, for he was keenly alive to the phenomenon of the world; his imagination discerned its mysteries—a world re-echoing with harmonies, colored with soft and fanciful tints." [5] It is because of this discarding of all superfluities that some critics think his work may stand the shocks of time better than the work of some of his contemporaries.

He did not hesitate to select what he found most suitable for the development of his style from the works of his French predecessors—Fauré, Chabrier, Satie, and, above all, Debussy;[6] when it came to orchestration, an art in which he was consummate master,[7] he chose Rimsky-Korsakoff as his mentor. By the time he was twenty-eight, he had, through hard work and careful selection, achieved his own natural manner of speech: witness the *Jeux d'eau*, that most glamorous of impressionistic piano pieces; the set of three poems for voice and orchestra

---

[5] Jean-Aubry in *The Chesterian*, January, 1938.
[6] It is said that in Ravel's last illness he asked that *L'Après-midi d'un faune* be played for him.
[7] A contemporary critic quite justly describes the second *Daphnis et Chloé* suite as the most brilliant and exciting score for sheer orchestral effect in the literature of present-day music.

—*Scheherazade;* and the *String Quartet.* Afterwards, there was nothing for him to do but improve this style through more industry and fastidious selection.

HIS WORKS

In 1907, there appeared the *Spanish Rhapsody,* the first of Ravel's works to draw attention to his mastery of orchestration; then came the *Mother Goose* set of five children's pieces, written as a suite for piano duet in 1908 and afterwards orchestrated by the composer (1912); the *Daphnis et Chloé* music was written originally for performance as a ballet, in 1910, and then arranged for concert performance in two orchestral suites, the second of which will probably prove to be Ravel's masterpiece, so warm and human is its glow, so unearthly its shimmer of orchestral color, so fresh and vivid its sense of life; *L'Heure espagnole,* a witty and sardonic musical comedy, was produced in 1911; the suite originally composed as a set of piano pieces (in 1914–1917) and later orchestrated, *Le Tombeau de Couperin,* pays devoted respect to the spirit of the precise and ordered classicism of the eighteenth century; *La Valse* is a brilliant postwar caricature on themes of Straussian flavor; a piano trio appeared in 1916; the concerto for piano and orchestra (not to be confused with another concerto for the left hand, which Ravel composed for the one-armed pianist, Wittgenstein), not finished until 1931, was a composition which particularly pleased its composer, for he felt that he had been able to pour his thought "into the exact world he dreamed of"; finally, in 1928, came the incredible *Bolero,* written on commission as a ballet, a *tour de force* of rhythmic monotony and orchestral brilliance which, as one Frenchman has wittily pointed out, invalidates the gastronomic aphorism so often heard in his country to the effect that the sauce will excuse the fish by rending the fish to nothing and making the sauce everything. His sardonic opera-ballet *L'Enfant et les sortilèges* and his brilliant set of three piano pieces, *Gaspard de la nuit,* could have been written by no other composer.

To those attracted to art that is precise, sophisticated, symmetrical, Ravel's music will always appeal; for these attributes gradually took precedence over the impressionistic style which is so evident in his earlier works. Almost more than any other composer, he is able, through one means or another, to delight—by his wit rather than his humor, his dextrous manipulation of colors and sonorities, his varied use of dance forms.[8] A contemporary characterization of him as being "amusing yet artistically upright" is just; in this he upholds the best traditions of his country.

Delius, the End of a Chapter

Music is an outburst of the soul; it is addressed and should appeal instantly to the soul of the listener.

Delius

TWO GENERAL CATEGORIES

It seems natural to divide the art which has come into being during the course of the centuries into great, opposing categories. There is, for example, that type which is associated with other values—religion, morals, idealism, philosophy, and so on—art which may be called, in general terms, spiritual, since its main objective is to uphold a world of eternal and supersensual values. In contrast, there is the art which has been created for art's sake, sensate art, with its main purpose that of providing sensuous pleasure. Then there is the distinction which can be made between art that is, on the one hand, planned, clear-cut, rationally calculated, conceived primarily in an intellectual, unemotional sense, and to which some sort of intellectual approach seems essential; and that which is, on the other hand, essentially spontaneous, intuitive, emotional, symbolic, warmly human, and naturally appealing. Various terms have been given to these opposing categories in an attempt to describe their differences: the first has been called Greek, Apollonian, Classic; the second, Gothic, Dionysian, Romantic. But, whatever the name given, the investigators of the phenomena of art dynamics, as well as the historians of the various arts, have not failed to note the existence of such strongly marked divisions, together with the fact that there has been some sort of rhythm in their appearances during the course of art history.

---

[8] One critic has taken the trouble to count the number of dance forms with which Ravel occupied himself: there are thirteen of them—minuet, pavan, furlana, tambourin, gigue, rigadoon, rondo, habanera, malagueña, waltz, tango, fox trot, and bolero!

In between, of course, there are all sorts of admixtures and gradations, some of them combining a greater proportion of the characteristics of the one category, others employing more of the other. There can be no question that the greatest artists, men such as Michelangelo, Shakespeare, Mozart, and Beethoven, to mention but a few, have intuitively kept a careful balance between these two qualities. Such a work as the Sistine Chapel mural of Michelangelo's, bringing as it does all the world's glory, as well as the joy and tribulations of man, into one carefully achieved expression, is an almost unbelievable combination of these opposing tendencies. The lesser men, however, have instinctively leaned toward one or the other pole of these trends, according to their natural endowments.

For instance, there are the meticulously created phrases of such English poets as Denham and Waller of the seventeenth century, or their greater successors in the next, Dryden and Pope, for whom, as one of them has expressed it:

True ease comes from art, not chance,
As those move easiest who have learned to dance.

Or there is the sensuous beauty of Verlaine's natural poetry, which comes perhaps as near being pure feeling as the art of literature has provided; or the intuitive mysticism of such men as William Blake and Francis Thompson, with their sense of rapturous revelation that has little concern with reason. The seventeenth-century Poussin, whose hard, carefully composed painting became the foundation upon which the whole structure of French classic tradition was reared, stands in strong contrast to the tempestuous force and the intuitive, fanatic power of the later Van Gogh, who seemed to have the ability to transmute emotion directly into paint. That these tendencies are sometimes concomitant can be shown easily enough by a comparison of the cool, sophisticated, mannered, consciously manipulated art of Ravel with that of his fellow impressionist and contemporary, Frederick Delius, for whom life and art were almost entirely matters of feeling.

DELIUS, THE INTUITIVE ARTIST

Perhaps no artist, whatever his medium, has ever succeeded quite so perfectly as has Delius in achieving the ideals of those to whom art is essentially an intuitive, emotional, dynamic expression. No one else,

THE OLD BRIDGE AT GREZ-SUR-LOING   Delius lived in the small village on the southern border of the Fontainebleau forest for many years and wrote most of his music there. Grez was a resort for artists, and this bridge, which adjoined Delius's garden, was the subject of many a well-known painting by men such as Corot, Edward Munch, and Carl Larson.

not even Debussy, has made his art so completely suggestive of sensations and emotions without the necessity of the intervention of thought or judgment, has allowed the ear so completely to "devour the brain." Delius named one of his earlier pieces *Over the Hills and Far Away:* no more suggestive title could possibly be found for music such as his, for, with its first measures, we are immediately transported out of our usual selves into a land of faery fancy which has no counterpart on this earth, which has in fact never existed except in man's imagination. What matters with Delius is not technically calculated effect; rather does he strive for illusions, and so almost more than any other of his generation he should be called an impressionist.

There are technical reasons for his being classified under this insignia of his period: in listening to such typical works as his *On Hearing the First Cuckoo in Spring, The Walk to the Paradise Garden,* or *In a Summer Garden,* we may be reminded of Debussy—and also Grieg, and even Wagner, perhaps. But Delius's is impressionism with a difference, for somehow he was able to make the musical idiom used by his contemporaries (he was born in 1863, only a year after Debussy) his own personal expression to a remarkable degree. Except in superficial details, such as the use of some Griegian harmonies, his style is as individual as that of any composer who ever wrote. Someone has well said that Delius fused melody and harmony together in a way which makes it impossible to consider them separately—"he invented melodic harmony."

But the thing which makes this peculiarly emotional medium of Delius's so effective is the spiritual nature which was back of it, a nature like that of no other in music. Delius was an ardent lover of beauty, as many a composer had been before him; but to him beauty was something which was not only connected with the world about him: it was rather to be found in contemplation after an event, in regarding that which is left to man after the show of life has passed on. One of his biographers speaks of the "wind as from a far country" which blows through all his most characteristic scores. It is this nostalgic longing for something that is unattainable, that has never existed, combined with a poignant tenderness that is sometimes almost unbearable, which makes the music of this composer unique. If one would experience this to the utmost, let him listen to the setting with which Delius has invested the words of Whitman in his cantata *Sea Drift,* words which are almost autobiographical insofar as Delius is concerned:

Oh troubled reflection in the sea!
Oh throat, oh throbbing heart!
And I singing uselessly, uselessly all the night.
Oh past! Oh happy life! Oh songs of joy!
In the air, in the woods, over fields.

We may intuitively claim this music as an expression of our own souls, or we may never be able to realize its peculiar beauty; but we shall have to admit that it is unlike anything else in the history of the art—a still, small voice, perhaps, but an absolutely unique one.

THE END OF ROMANTICISM

There seem to be no half measures about this music: if one leans naturally toward the romantic type of art, he likes it the moment it is first heard; if one's tastes are instinctively classic, the sound of it will be immediately and forever distasteful. As so many critics have remarked, Delius can never be an acquired taste; the listener cannot grow into him, as he does into Mozart or Brahms. Because of its peculiar sense of detachment and its fine-grained expressiveness, Delius's music is extremely difficult to interpret successfully. Not only must its interpreter be enamored of its spirit and feel its peculiar spell; he must, likewise, have consummate technical skill—that art which conceals art—sufficient to hold together its delicate, tenuous fabric and imbue it with life. The interpreter's task is not simplified by the fact that, until Delius found out how to dispense with the classical forms and shape his thoughts perfectly according to their emotional demands, he was liable to show only too clearly his lack of formal training. As so often heard, this music may sound meandering and dull; but when played under the direction of a conductor such as Sir Thomas Beecham, it will always be for those who can respond to its magic some of the most beautiful ever written. For these listeners, even though they may belong to the materialistic postwar generation, which knows little of the world of which Delius sang, the passing of this unique figure marks the end of a chapter in music. These works, charged as they are with the sadness of a transitory and evanescent world, give the listener a peculiar sense of finality; for it seems as if with them the spirit of Romance has passed from the world.

The Aftermath

THE DIFFERENCE BETWEEN
GERMAN AND FRENCH ART

One noted German critic has said of Debussy's music that in it there is no passion, no deep feeling, and no real emotional expression; rather, it is hardly more than "suggestive sound" observed with an almost unrivaled refinement. "His is an altogether sensuous art, without any marked moral quality, without religious feeling or metaphysical overtones."

Nothing shows better the line of complete and seemingly unbridgeable demarcation that exists between the thought of the German and of the French people. In the art of the one, style or manner of expression has come about as the result of an overwhelming emotional impulse and all its attendant moral, religious, and metaphysical implications. Beethoven's symphonies and Wagner's music dramas are really the revelation of the German soul and mind: the fact that they are colossal works of art simply means that the native genius of these composers was able to forge, out of the molten surge of their emotions, the structure best fitted to contain them. In all French art at its best, on the other hand, emotional implication comes as the result of a superb building of style. Berlioz and Debussy are two good cases in point. The Romanticism of the first was bounded by the composer's conceptions of what could be done with the orchestra; of Debussy, by the suggestive new manipulation of sound colors. But to deny the reality or validity of such emotion is to show oneself insensitive to most essential qualities of these composers.

DEBUSSY'S INFLUENCE

It need hardly be said that such a pronouncedly German view of Debussy is by no means universal; no other single composer in the history of music, with the possible exception of Wagner, ever gave such a completely fresh and stimulating turn to the music of his time. Just as the influence of his confreres, the French impressionistic painters, made an indelible impression on all art produced since their day, so Debussy's technique and style reached out into all countries and influenced, in one way or another, almost every composer of prominence. Moreover, by disregarding aesthetic conventions and compromises, Debussy acted as a liberator of the music of his country from the spell of German domination and restored its direct line of connection with the masters of the eighteenth century. In France his style became quickly modified by other elements, notably those to which a growing intellectualism gave substance and encouragement.

SOME OTHER FRENCH IMPRESSIONISTS

French art has always been, of all national styles, the most nearly eclectic; for Paris, since the days of the early universities, has been the great cosmopolitan city of the world, absorbing into her life, as into her art, ideas and ideals from all the world. But because Paris is the brain of France, these elements have been subjected to the test of French logic and their validity judged by a very exacting critical standard. So we do not expect to find either staleness or overemphasis on any one aspect prevalent for any long period in Parisian art. Both Florent Schmitt (1870–1958) and Albert Roussel (1869–1937) were in the best sense of the word French *eclectics,* strongly influenced by Chabrier, Fauré, and above all others, Debussy. Schmitt's music has, likewise, a note of German magniloquence that is not very common in the French art of his period. This, as well as his strong dependence on Debussyan techniques, is shown in his vivid orchestral *Tragédie de Salomé* (1911), written for performance with mimed dancing. Its unusual harmonic intensity and dramatic use of the orchestra make this one of the most important post-Debussyan scores, second only to Ravel's *Daphnis et Chloé* as a vital product of the French imaginative style.

Although Roussel received his training under D'Indy's influence in the *Schola Cantorum,* he early developed a taste for the mysterious and exotic; out of this came the ballet *Festin de l'araignée* (1913), "The Spider's Feast." Following the trends of the 1920's, Roussel took up neo-Classicism and wrote three symphonies in that style.

Jacques Ibert (1890–1962) was another of the French composers who early in the century came under Debussy's influence; he was inspired as well by Ravel's precision of thought (a characteristic which may be said to underlie all the best French art) and wrote some effective works combining the best characteristics of Impressionism and neo-Classicism. His series of attractive travelogues, *Escales* (1924), is best known.

IMPRESSIONISTS IN OTHER COUNTRIES

There were some Italian writers of orchestral music who followed in the footsteps of their French Impressionistic colleagues. The best known was Ottorino Respighi (1879–1936), a pupil of Rimsky-Korsakoff. Respighi combined his master's colorful orchestration with Impressionistic techniques to produce some brilliant symphonic poems evocative of various aspects of the Italian landscape. *The Fountains of Rome* (1917) and *The Pines of Rome* (1924) have become repertoire favorites the world over because of their happy blend of Italian melody and Impressionistic coloring.

A few individual composers in other countries stand out because of their devotion to Impressionistic ideals: the Alsatian-American Charles M. Loeffler (1861–1935), the Englishman Cyril Scott (*b.* 1879), who wrote a number of slight piano pieces à la Debussy, and Charles Griffes (1884–1920) in America. But in general the younger men turned more and more from Debussyan Impressionism toward the veristic triumphs being achieved by Stravinsky in Paris during the first decade of the new century.

THE TWENTIETH CENTURY

Con-tempo: with the times. Contemporary music is the most interesting music that has even been written, and the present moment is the most exciting in music history. It has always been so.

Igor Stravinsky

THE PROBLEMATIC PRESENT

*All forms of imitation should be held in contempt; and all forms
of originality glorified. We should rebel against the tyranny of
the words* harmony *and* good taste. *A clean sweep should be
made of all stale and threadbare subject matter in order to express the vortex of modern life—a life of steel, pride, fever and
speed.*

From the 1910 Manifesto of the Futurist Painters

STANDS MUSIC WHERE IT DID?

evel-
opments in the twentieth century have produced an art quite different
than we have been concerned with to this point. The term *music* can be
used in its common meaning for the art which passed under that name
up to the beginning of this century; aesthetic changes since then make
a common meaning less certain. Something revolutionary happened
during the early years of the century, something that precipitated a
series of reactions exceeding in violence and rapid sequence anything in
the long art history of mankind. To understand how these changes
affected all the arts, and especially music, it is necessary to review briefly
the social and political backgrounds of Europe at the turn of the century.

We have noted the nineteenth century's firm belief in progress, and
how this belief produced self-confidence which colored the thought of
the whole era. A well-known anthropologist described it: "Democracy
in government, brotherhood in society, equality in rights and privileges
and universal education—all foreshadow the next higher plane of society to which experience, intelligence and knowledge are steadily leading." (Lewis Henry Morgan, 1818–1881) After Napoleon's downfall
in 1815 the trend in most phases of European intellectual, social, and
artistic life was upward, and at the end of the century there seemed no
limit to achievement.

The three great European capitals of the time—Paris, Vienna, and
London—teemed with artistic talent. Painters flocked to Paris, musicians to Vienna, and London glowed in the warmth and splendor of its

Edwardian age. It seemed, as one historian said, as though something had to happen to put an end to a period of such brilliant achievement. What did happen was, of course, World War I. In one sense the war was an expression of a spiritual malaise which, paradoxically, had been engendered by a number of desirable conditions, among them a long period of peace and a marvelous growth of material prosperity in all the principal countries. In his great history of this era, Winston Churchill describes how the nations, unsatisfied by their material achievements, turned toward strife, both internal and external. "One might almost think," he adds, "that the world wished to suffer." As always, it was the artists who felt most keenly the sense of dissatisfaction with the past, despair for the present, and foreboding for the future.

The best of these artists, however, did more than merely give vent to such sentiments as those contained in the quotation at the beginning of this chapter. It was their attempt to revolt against the smugness of their times, combined with their natural experimental curiosity, that led to the development of new media and techniques in all the arts. Out of these early experiments there evolved the kind of music, painting, writing, architecture, and sculpture we think of as "modern." An entirely new type of artistic expression, one which reflected profound esthetic, political, social, and economic changes, evolved from such pioneer pre-

Collection, The Museum of Modern Art, New York
Gift of Mr. and Mrs. Zadok

LONDON BRIDGE by André Derain

WATERLOO BRIDGE by Claude Monet

World-War I experiments as Picasso's *Les demoiselles d'Avignon* (1907), Schoenberg's *Pierrot lunaire* (1912), and Stravinsky's *Le Sacre du printemps* (1913). To understand these changes as they are found in music, it will be helpful to learn something of developments in the other arts, especially painting, during this time.

SOME BEGINNINGS IN PAINTING

In 1905, the year usually given for the founding of psychoanalysis by Freud, a group of young avant-garde painters prepared an exhibit of pictures which attempted to evolve an intense form of personal expression through the use of all sorts of exotic shapes and violent colors. Called *Fauves* (Wild Beasts) by an exasperated critic, they used startling discords of intense vermillion and green and violent explosions of sky-blue and vivid orange, held together by broad brush strokes and weird patterns. Some idea of how sharply the *Fauves* broke with the art of the late nineteenth may be gained by comparing André Derain's picture of a London river scene, painted in 1906, with one of Claude Monet's Impressionistic treatments of the same subject, painted a few years earlier. Even black and white reproductions, in which the subtleties of color and atmosphere are almost completely lost, show the extent of Derain's revolt against the past. The imaginative and atmospheric concepts of the Impressionists are rejected in favor of distorted perspective and heavy black lines and deep shadows. Smudges of paint and wide brush strokes give a rich surface texture that is itself an expression of strong emotion and complex psychic states.

The same desperate intensity of feeling, and a similar revolutionary method of expressing it, may be felt in Schoenberg's *Erwartung,* written in 1906, only three years after Derain's picture was exhibited in Paris. Growing up in the intense Romantic atmosphere of musical Vienna, Schoenberg had shown up to this time how completely he could exploit the idiom of Wagner, Richard Strauss, and Gustav Mahler. In *Erwartung,* however, he turns from this post-Romantic style and uses unorthodox devices to convey his heightened emotional message. He utilizes extremely dissonant harmonies that have no tendency to resolve or relate themselves to any tonal center. His fragmented melodic lines cause the voice as well as the instrumental parts to leap wildly about, without following a succession of tones which sound "musical." His rhythms are irregular, his orchestration bizarre and grotesque, and the text strongly suggests Freudian concepts. All this was before he settled into his advanced style of "composing with twelve tones related only with one another," as he described it; or before Stravinsky, his revolutionary counterpart in Paris, had begun the series of experiments which were to help change the whole course of music history.

In painting, the developments initiated by the *Fauves* led directly to varying paths of free invention. A group of Expressionist painters, with whom Schoenberg had been very closely associated, carried their experiments with color, line, and form to the point where subject matter and even representational elements were eliminated in an attempt to emphasize subjective experiences. Any one of Wassily Kandinsky's (1866–1944) series of *Improvisations,* painted around 1912, will illustrate this Expressionistic school of painting. In the same way Schoenberg tried to divorce his music from traditional practices through the destruction of tonality and to produce his effects through dissonant harmonies that have little or no tendency to resolve, fragmented melodic lines, irregular rhythms, grotesque and bizarre orchestration. And, just as Kandinsky strove to convey his subconscious feelings by allowing the colors to flow onto the canvas almost spontaneously, with little attempt to control them, so Schoenberg expressed his personal conflicts and anxieties through distorted harmonies and melodies.

Pablo Picasso and Georges Braque were the major figures in another group of avant-garde painters, the Cubists, who dissolved natural forms into their essential volumes and planes, thereby utilizing a sort of fourth dimension in which objects are shown not as they are seen at any particular moment, but rather in different aspects at different moments. One of the earliest forms of modern art, Cubism was also one of the most fruitful, even though there were few painters who remained entirely faithful to its tenets. It was particularly influential in the period immediately following World War I.

Twenty-one years after the last shot was fired in this war, a second one broke out. The period between these struggles was marked by growing political tension in Europe, by unparalleled prosperity, and then a devastating economic depression. The intense intellectual and aesthetic experimentation of the earlier decades continued unabated. Reacting to the disillusionment that followed World War I, as well as to the abstract tendencies implicit in the work of the Cubists, artists now strove for expression that would be characteristic of what they hoped would become a more stable social order. Painters, architects, sculptors, and designers based their new styles on the fewest possible elements of design and leaned more and more towards abstraction. Picasso and Braque continued their Cubist experiments, striving for a fusion of Fauvist color and Cubist principles of form. Picasso, always the Romanticist, went his own restless way, with sudden changes of style and abrupt reversions and re-directions, his pictures becoming increasingly powerful, combining savagery and sophistication in a manner that marvelously mirrored the times. "Strangeness was what we wanted to make people think about," Picasso explained, "because we were quite aware that our world was becoming very strange and not exactly reassuring." Braque, more the classicist, strove for more balanced expression and subdued color; in many ways he is the most typical artist of the period, his 1937 *Woman with a Mandolin* being an excellent summary of its ideals.

At the end of World War I came an outbreak of nihilistic art called *Dada*. Centering in Paris, it rejected the moral, social, and aesthetic ideals of the past. The Dadaists held that, since European life had lost all meaning, its art must be chaotic and orderless—a viewpoint that has maintained surprising vitality down to the present. Another direct outgrowth of the war was a phase of German Expressionism called the *New Objectivity*, which reflected the artist's feeling of helplessness at the state of corruption and natural degradation he felt all about him. More positive were the ideas of the Constructivists ("new and constructive art for a new social order") and those of the Dutch *Stijl* group,

RECUMBENT FIGURE by Henry Moore in the Tate Gallery, London

WOMAN WITH A
MANDOLIN by
Georges Braque

*Collection, The Museum of
Modern Art, New York
Mrs. Simon Guggenheim
Fund*

LES DEMOISELLES
D'AVIGNON by
Pablo Picasso

*Collection, The Museum of
Modern Art, New York
Acquired through the Lillie
P. Bliss Bequest*

SCHERZO WITH THIRTEEN by Paul Klee

Collection, The Museum of Modern Art, New York

which advocated a purification of art through the elimination of subject matter and the substitution of constructive elements made up of lines and planes.

These ideas affected all the western world and were ably disseminated through an international group of artists gathered at the *Bauhaus*, a school of design founded in Germany in 1919. Many of these concepts were incorporated into an international style of architecture developed by a group of architects that included such prominent men as Walter Gropius (designer of the Bauhaus building), Mies van der Rohe, and Le Corbusier. These men subscribed to the principle of functionalism—the theory that the aesthetic content of a building is not as important as the degree to which it fulfills its efficient purpose. This international style has spread over the whole world and influenced a good proportion of the architectural design of the mid-century years.

Surrealism had as its aim the exploration and exploitation of the world of inner consciousness revealed by the research of Freud and his followers. Originally a literary movement with the Czech writer Franz Kafka as its inspiration, Surrealism had its painterly beginnings in a manifesto of 1924, which sought to bring together in one artistic expression the outer world of reality and the inner world of expressionistic experience. The aim of the Surrealistic painters seems to have been to shock the beholder's consciousness so violently that he would try to find some explanation of a picture in the hidden mysteries of his subsconscious existence. The technique was effective not only in painting but also in literature and music, and was widely used by some experimental writers and composers.

COMMON CHARACTERISTICS

As the result of all this activity there developed certain characteristics that may be said to be common not just to painting but to all the art produced during his time; a brief consideration of these characteristics should be very helpful in trying to understand and appraise that art in which we are particularly interested—contemporary music.

1. The rejection of emotion as the basis of art—the idea that feeling and sentiment can serve as inspiration to a creator. The fact that the modern age has been ashamed and afraid of emotion has thus been explained by the English philosopher Alfred North Whitehead: Art is the result of aesthetic experience that has been powerfully felt; in contemporary creation, somewhere between the impulse of the original feeling and its manifestation in art, a kind of Freudian censor seems to

intervene: the emotion is not permitted to be communicated in modern art except in disguise, symbols, wit, and satire being the masks most favored by contemporary creators. Cocteau, as spokesman for the avant-garde artists of the earlier years of the century, railed against what he called "music of the bowels," and demanded that music supply the hearer with plastic apparitions, to be heard objectively at a magic distance—whatever that means. And Stravinsky put himself on record many times as saying that music cannot in any way express ideas or emotions, its sole purpose being to "establish order in things."

2. The abhorrence of what may be called overstatement. Such a conception precludes everything in artistic expression except the barest essentials and is responsible for, among other things, emphasis on the functional in architecture, and the machine-like streamlining of everything we use. The creative exaltation which we have seen so strongly present in Baroque and Romantic art is anathema to the modern artist. For it he attempts to substitute direct, terse, sometimes even brutal expression.

3. The gradual evolution of the idea of non-representation in art, the abjuring of any notion that painting should be representational of objects present in the visible world, that literature necessarily has to mean something, or that music should try to suggest or convey emotional concepts or describe events by having a program attached to it.

4. Consequent to this, the concept that art possesses complete autonomy, the insistence that it exists as an absolute in itself rather than as a means of transmitting experience, communicating feeling, suggesting ideas, or picturing objects. This concept was brushed aside for the modern idea that art does not necessarily have to "mean" anything, but simply "be." As early as 1890, Busoni (see page 580) demanded that we "free ourselves from architectural, acoustical and esthetic dogmas: let art be pure invention in forms and colors."

5. The development of all kinds of abstraction in pattern, design, color, sound, and so on. There should be no question of art's reconstituting life by representing it. The painter Matisse summed this up by saying that the modern artist's aim should be to render art through the sensation of life itself and not through imitation of nature.

6. The desire of the artist to surprise and shock audiences in the hope of integrating them with the performer. Through this means the artist hopes to break through the general apathy concerning art which artists feel exists on the part of the public and to penetrate the ordinary reactions of individuals largely occupied with everyday problems of living.

7. The negation of the idea that art is necessarily connected with beauty, an idea widely held since the time of the ancient Greeks. Art does not always interest us because it is ennobling or exalting. The experience of the artist, his knowledge of the world about him, his innermost thoughts—these may be unpleasant, tragic, fatal.

Many, but obviously not all, of these traits of contemporary art can be recognized as reactions against the ideals of Romanticism and the metaphysical outlook it fastened on the artistic world of the nineteenth century.

TECHNICAL CHANGES IN MODERN MUSIC

To realize how these new theories have affected the development of modern music, it is necessary to understand something of the technical changes during the twentieth century. First of all, the traditional ideas of harmony, tonality, consonance, and dissonance have changed. The composers of the early part of this century initiated a revolution that altered the whole course of music history by abandoning the idea of tonality: that music has somehow to be related to a central tone, or *tonic*. Wagner and Debussy had already stretched the traditional harmonic structure so that its elements could not easily be recognized as centering around a particular tonal point. Later composers used new sounds and individual harmonies—especially dissonances—in an attempt to alter the concept of tonality without destroying it altogether. Ultimately, however, the twelve-tone school rejected the principle of tonality completely.

A number of technical devices were used by twentieth-century composers in their efforts to expand the language of music. Among these was a new way of building chords by basing them on intervals of fourths rather than thirds. This new *quartal* harmony gave a freshness, a sort of out-of-focus effect, to the music of certain composers, some of whom added still other intervals to their chords, thus forming still more dissonant combinations.[1] Continued acquaintance with the new chordal formations which had thus come into the language of music made it possible for tonal combinations that at first sounded strongly dissonant to seem less wild, and finally to be accepted as consonant. This gave

---

[1] Finally composers came to use what they called *pandiatonic* chords, made up of any or all the tones of the diatonic or natural scale as it is produced on the white keys of a keyboard instrument. This permitted combinations of seconds, fourths, and fifths, as well as thirds.

dissonance a new significance: it became, in contemporary jargon, emancipated—that is, freed from the need to be resolved according to older concepts. Thus was abandoned the long-maintained distinction between consonance and dissonance, a distinction which had given nineteenth-century music much of its essential power and quality. To the composer of this century, as Schoenberg said, dissonances are only remote consonances and chords are used entirely as individual entities, each existing entirely for its own sake, without any relationship to what precedes or follows it.

Another device was using several planes of tonality at the same time. This principle of *polytonality,* vividly illustrated in certain parts of his ballet score *Petrouchka,* was employed by Stravinsky in his earlier scores, as well as by a number of his followers. Still another device was *atonality,* a practice which gives the hearer no feeling of key relationship whatsoever. It was initiated by Schoenberg and exploited by his pupils Berg and Webern.

In addition to these new concepts of harmony, new ideas were advanced concerning the make-up of melody—the kind of tonal succession that is able to be perceived as a recognizable entity. There were innovations also in rhythmic patterns and, of course, in new formal structures made necessary by the new compositional techniques. On the whole, the attempts at rhythmic unorthodoxy have proved somewhat disappointing, in that the extreme complication brought about by different rhythmic patterns in many parts results in a dwindling of the piquancy which the more spacious and leisurely rhythmic combinations enabled one to apprehend easily and enjoy thoroughly. And the complications of the totally organized works produced by the theorists, while sometimes formidable intellectual feats, can be followed only with the greatest difficulty by the unassisted ear.

THE DIFFICULTIES OF HEARING MODERN MUSIC

Perhaps the chief technical factor which stands in the way of immediate understanding of modern music is the use of so much dissonance. We have already indicated that the term *dissonance* is a relative one, the significance of which has changed from time to time. Any listener who has had sufficient experience can easily prove that chords which seemed incomprehensible in one period of his own musical development have become quite intelligible in a later one. But the use of polytonality and atonality is something else. The chief difficulty, for both composers and listeners, when the bounds are broken in all directions at once—for key, harmony, melody, form—is that, however logical the process of unified advance may seem, its composers are unable to use all the new elements at once, and the listeners appear unable to take in more than one or two of them at a time. Thus, the old communication between artist and public, which never before broadly failed, has been broken to such an extent that for a great proportion of the faithful public who call themselves music lovers the new developments mean nothing, and the music reaches neither the intellect nor the heart.

We have to beware, however, of a too dogmatic insistence on the necessity of full public participation. To understand the position of contemporary art, we have to remember the immensely flamboyant, full-flavored, certainly overgrown nineteenth century. Every form of Romanticism grew large and lush, so that even the least aesthetically cultured listener could wallow to his heart's content—an idea which has been much emphasized by the modernists. This is not to argue that the lushness of Romanticism was all a mistake; it is merely to understand the thinking of the modernist as he contemplated the Gargantuan century of emotional release and to agree with him that this can never be duplicated. What, then, is to take its place? The answer to this question must be given by the bulk of modernist composers to the bulk of the twentieth-century public. In spite of the start which has been made in introducing this music to general audiences, the contemporary concert programs of such musical centers as New York and London contain a relatively small proportion of it. As late as 1964 a reporter reviewing the general musical situation of the Western world noted that "few European audiences respond to modern music. As in America, there are various cliques and schools, the products of which are heatedly discussed in very small circles throughout Europe. But the general public could not care less." (Harold C. Schonberg in *The New York Times*.) Of course, we should also remember that the relative size of what is spoken of as the "general public" has grown with the growth of democracy. Today we are concerned about the artistic taste of practically all parts of the population—this was not true of the more aristocratic societies of earlier centuries, even the nineteenth.

A SIMULTANEOUS ADVANCE ON ALL FRONTS

What the listener must realize is the immense difficulty of the composer's advancing triumphantly on so many new fronts at once; so we seek for signs of fruitful evolution rather than merely those of fretful revolution. There are two considerations which seem as likely as any to be useful guides in such a search: first, that great composers of the past never sought to make radical changes in all departments of their art; and second, that the most revolutionary composers have never been recognized in after-ages as the greatest. The law of artistic life seems to decree that a composer cannot have it both ways: he must either risk his life in strong revolution or work it out in more peaceful and much gentler evolution. In an age impatient of law, whether of nature, art, or man, it is salutary to seek those laws which time appears to have demonstrated as valid. This is certainly one of them.

There are far too many possibilities in the suggested revolutions of modernism to be worked out in one generation—or perhaps in several. Composers who seek to wield all the new weapons at once are likely to become entangled and fail in communication, the operative end of their striving. If there were any sound assurance as to which of the elements —the new harmony, melody, rhythm, or form—was the best on which to concentrate, the artistic situation might become clarified and the probability of establishing sure communication between artist and public would be brighter. In all these developments the great problem is that of selection—a conscious responsibility for the composer which, apparently, was never a shackle to the men of old times, but which has proven so today. While the modern composer is faced by an enormously greater complexity of possible materials, he does not seem to have the dominating, driving force that would keep him, single-minded, on an irresistible course. The cynic may observe that what this really boils down to is that there is a shortage of the kind of genius that seemed in plentiful supply during the preceding centuries. But what is wanted is not genius alone, but a greater sense of direction in the minds of artists in general, as well as a greater awareness of their responsibilities—the fact that they should be the leaders as well as the mirrors of their generation.

The Impact of Stravinsky

Technique is the whole man.
Stravinsky: *Conversations*

A NEW INDIVIDUALITY DEVELOPS

There is an immense gap in communication that is felt by all listeners when they compare their understanding of composers from the last century—of, say, Brahms and Wagner—with that of the modernists. We have shown some of the reasons for this gap. There is one composer, Igor Stravinsky (*b.* 1882), who serves as an admirable bridge between these two territories; he began, with exciting freshness, in the tradition of Russian pictorial nationalism and in his later years arrived, full-armed, in the camp of the moderns. In between there were all sorts of varied and interesting combinations of his two styles.

Stravinsky was born in Oranienbaum, near St. Petersburg, the son of a famous bass singer at the Imperial Opera. He received most of his early training under Rimsky-Korsakoff and so it was natural that his first works should fall into his master's modes of thought. When he was twenty-three he wrote a symphony which makes use of folk-song material in the Rimsky-Borodin-Glazunov tradition; a work written a few years later, *Fireworks* (1908), adds suggestions of yet another influence, that of Dukas and his *L'Apprenti sorcier*. It was not until the ballet *The Firebird,* written in 1910, that Stravinsky's individuality began to crystallize. There are still two ghosts which hover over the pages of this score—and pretty solid ghosts they are—those of Rimsky-Korsakoff and Debussy. The music set to the various scenes of this Russian fairy tale changes abruptly from old to new and back again; but certain characteristics of the idiom that we have come to recognize as Stravinsky's are here apparent, especially the arrangement of the rhythms into ingenious patterns and the use of constantly clashing chord members and chord combinations.

TWO LONELY MASTERPIECES

His next two works, also written for the Russian Ballet, *Petrouchka* in 1912 and *Le Sacre du printemps (The Rite of Spring)* in 1913, carry

Photograph by "Anthony"

SCENE FROM STRAVINSKY'S BALLET *PETROUCHKA*

these tendencies to a logical and effective climax. In addition, they make striking use of the device which earlier composers had hinted at but which became almost a mannerism with Stravinsky—the simultaneous use of several tonalities, at the same time keeping the essential harmonic language diatonic. There are also clever manipulations (after Debussy's style) of constituent chords running in parallel lines, an elaboration of the ancient organum.

But these two works are much more than mere adaptations and developments of the work of other composers; they have a physiognomy of their own and stand out as unified works of art written in an entirely new style. In fact, they remain strangely isolated and lonely masterpieces, both of them dealing in a characteristic Russian manner with fantastic subjects beyond ordinary experience—one reason for their phenomenal success. The puppet Petrouchka looks at life with the detached observation of the cynic and shows the comedic existence which man-the-machine leads in a largely disinterested world. *The Rite of Spring* suggests the primitive worship of our ancient ancestors and, with startling new means, attempts to project the mind of twentieth-century man back into the dark, unexplored realms of prehistory. Above anything else he ever wrote, this powerful score sets forth the features of Stravinsky's new tonal language: the clashing power of dissonances, the excitement possible from polyrhythms, the peculiar acerbic quality of his polytonalities, and his very individual manner of orchestration that gives a sense of transparency to all his scores. It raises to perhaps a

STRAVINSKY   (from a drawing by Picasso)

higher power than any music ever written the nervous excitement and emotional tension through rhythm which so many followers of Stravinsky tried to imitate. Although this remarkable tour de force and veristic triumph has become an accepted classic, it is not difficult to imagine the tremendous antagonism (as well as enthusiasm) it aroused at the time of its first production in Paris just before World War I.[2]

CONTINUED EXPERIMENTS

The Rite of Spring represents Stravinsky at one peak of his creative career; in it he seems to have expressed his most individualistic and imaginative ideas. Living in the stimulating milieu of Paris in the 1920's, he was caught up in the sweep of the new movements then surging so strongly there and changed his style to suit the new aesthetic theories of the day as they came along, just as did his contemporary, Picasso. In fact, his contemporaries seemed to consider one of the most attractive attributes of Stravinsky's style the way he constantly changed it. His ideas about the kind of music he wanted to write, the way his music should be interpreted and, indeed, the very nature of music itself, never became fixed or final. His whole creative career has been marked

[2] Today its effect is largely one of delayed shock as we come to see what influence Stravinsky's explosion had on later music.

not only by changes in style but by direct contradictions of earlier ideas.

For example, after the tremendously complex orchestral forces demanded by his earlier works, he wrote a number of compositions that were much more economical in expression and needed much smaller interpretative forces. These include chamber music scores, piano pieces, songs, and such reduced ballets as *Les Noces* (1917–23), scored for four pianos, percussion, and chorus, *L'Histoire du soldat* (1918), needing only seven players, *Pulcinella* (1920), and the one-act operas *Mavra* and *Renard* (1922).

In another change of style, Stravinsky abandoned his luxurious color and propulsive dissonance in favor of neo-Classicism, now fashionable after having been earlier promulgated by Busoni and incorporated in the early works of Prokofiev while Stravinsky was busy with his lush *Petrouchka* and *Le Sacre* scores. Strictly speaking, "neo-Classicism" is a misnomer, since the neo-Classicists were more influenced by the contrapuntal writing of the Baroque period than they were by the later style of the Classic era. But "neo-Classicism" is accurate insofar as it indicates a relatively intellectual approach to art. One of the early influences in the New Music of the century, neo-Classicism was characteristic of its period in its emphasis on structural form rather than communicative and emotional content. This "back-to Bach" movement, with its use of dissonant harmonies, emphasis on contrapuntal structure, revival of eighteenth-century forms, de-emphasis of orchestral resources and color, and general tendency toward impersonal and objective expression, began to attract Stravinsky's attention about 1920, as is shown by his declaration at that time that classic ballet is the triumph of studied conception over vagueness, of the definite over the arbitrary, of order over chaos. "I am thus brought face to face with the eternal conflict between the Apollonian and the Dionysian principles. The latter assumes ecstasy to be the final goal, that is to say, the losing of one's self, whereas art demands all the final consciousness of the artist. There can be, therefore, no doubt as to my choice between the two."

With Stravinsky's *Octet for Wind Instruments* in 1923, neo-Classicism came into its own. The same idiom prevails in his *Piano Concerto* of 1924 and *Serenade for Piano* of 1925. Later chamber music scores of this period include *Duo concertant* for violin and piano (1932), *Concerto for Two Pianos* (1935), and *Dumbarton Oaks Concerto* (1938). More extended forces were used in the *Capriccio* for piano and orchestra (1929), the *Violin Concerto* (1931), the *Symphony in C* (1940), and *Symphony in Three Movements* (1945). The spirit of Greek classicism hovers over the opera-oratorio *Oedipus Rex* and the ballet *Apollon Musagète* (both 1927), and there is an added attitude of religiosity in the choral-orchestral *Symphony of Psalms,* written in 1930 "for the glory of God and in honor of the Boston Symphony Orchestra." This neo-Classical period of Stravinsky's career may be said to have ended in about 1935, though a number of later works show the influence of the same aesthetic.

There has been a wide divergence of opinion regarding these neo-Classical works. For the devotees they show Stravinsky's unique power to hammer synthetic material into shapes that are at once consequential and personal. For the detractors and apostates (their number has increased through the years) they represent, with exceptions like *Oedipus Rex* and *The Symphony of Psalms,* the rewriting of a single piece over a period of forty-five years. The unbiased observer can only note that not a single work of Stravinsky's after the *Symphony of Psalms* has had lasting success. Even the much-praised opera *The Rake's Progress,* a sort of morality play inspired by Hogarth's celebrated paintings on eighteenth-century life, has never had any real success, though it has been produced in the world's greatest opera houses. This debatable work, its style hesitating between the abstraction of fable and the realism of stage drama, was first produced in Venice in 1951, with the composer conducting.

Another caprice of Stravinsky's was the conversion of the ideas, manners, and even themes of earlier composers into his own terms. He copied Pergolesi in *Pulcinella,* Tchaikovsky in *Le Baiser de la fée* (1928), the Netherland contrapuntalists in his *Mass* (1948), the Elizabethans in his *Shakespeare Songs* (1954), and the ideas and techniques of a number of opera composers, especially Mozart, in *The Rake's Progress.*

Stravinsky's last and most surprising switch in style, which chagrined some of his most ardent disciples while reinstating his position as a leader with some of the younger men, was a change to the serial, twelve-tone procedures of his long-time rival Schoenberg. In the works written after his seventieth birthday, Stravinsky showed himself more and more responsive to ideas which in his earlier years he had strongly opposed; the result was, as Aaron Copland said, that "all sorts of composers [including Copland himself, we might add] started experimenting with tone-rows to which they had hitherto been irreconcilably opposed." Stravinsky's works of this last period include the 1942 *Cantata,* a *Septet* (1952), *In Memoriam Dylan Thomas* (1954), *Canticum Sacrum* (1956), *Agon* (1957), *Threni* (1958), *Noah and the Flood* (1965), *Abraham and Isaac* (1964), and *Variations in Memory of*

Aldous Huxley (1965). Of all these serial works concerned with pattern rather than content, this last seems, at least on first acquaintance, the least fragmented and the most approachable.

Throughout his long career Stravinsky never hesitated to think of himself as an artisan as well as an artist—ready and willing to provide music for all sorts of occasions and with whatever resources were available. He expected, of course, as a successful twentieth-century figure, to be well paid for his services. From his first ballet commission in 1909 through the various jobs ordered by patrons eager to be associated with his fame, the fashionable International Festivals in Venice, down to the unfortunate television dance-drama of 1963, *Noah and the Flood*, Stravinsky succeeded admirably in advancing his financial as well as his artistic interests. All his compositions, even the inconsequential ones, have been recorded for posterity, and his ideas about music as an art will be available for future generations. Although his earlier efforts as an author can hardly be called brilliant,[3] he continued his earlier pontifical pronouncements about music and its composition in a series of volumes written in collaboration with Robert Craft. These slim volumes also contain a number of unflattering portraits of his fellow composers and contemporary artists, many of them etched in acid, as well as some bad-tempered, even vicious, articles on those who had the temerity to disagree with him or criticize his music. In fact, Stravinsky the octogenarian is not a particularly appealing figure. Idealized throughout the first half of the century, especially in this country,[4] as its outstanding musical personality and leading composer, in 1963 he was dubbed "The Angry Old Man of Music" by one of his principal depreciators. A more lenient posterity will certainly forget the asperities of his later years and will remember him as one of the seminal figures in the shaping of modern music.

[3] His autobiography, *Chronicle of My Life*, appeared in 1935 and was published in an English edition in 1936. The Charles Eliot Norton lectures, which he delivered in French at Harvard, were published in 1948 in English as *Poetics of Music*.

[4] He became an American citizen in 1945 and has lived here, largely in Hollywood, since 1939.

The Twelve-Toners

*When one observes well, things gradually be-
come obscure. One begins to realize that one
is not destined only not to guess the future
(only to delineate it) but also, to forget the
past, already set forth.*

Schoenberg, translated by J. D. Bohm

ANOTHER GREAT MAN OF MODERN MUSIC

A second composer of tremendous significance in the history of modern music was Arnold Schoenberg who, born in Vienna in 1874 and strongly influenced throughout his earlier years by its musical backgrounds, became an international figure, living and teaching in this country for the last eighteen years of his life, from 1933 to 1951. The new techniques which he finally evolved, those of the twelve-tone school, were extremely difficult for the layman to appreciate or even understand; so Schoenberg more than any other composer, even Stravinsky, felt it necessary to explain the new elements of his style and his reasons for striking out in what he considered to be new directions. This, together with the character of the Expressionistic movement,[5] of which he was an effective representative, has not made him a popular composer. It is possible that posterity will consider him more important as an innovator than as a creator; it was his theories and his explanation of them that focused the attention of the music world of the 1920's and 30's on the compositional procedures which were to affect the whole course of twentieth-century music.

Like all the great revolutionaries in art, Schoenberg based his changes on the foundation of a thorough knowledge of the music of the past. He early gained practical knowledge of music through having to play in

---

[5] As we have said, this term has generally been used to signify a kind of art arising from inner experience rather than from outer reality. It used agonized, often violent, and even exacerbated expression, distorted accentuation, heightened and constantly maintained tension, in order to communicate its concern with the inner life of man. A sort of tortured Romanticism in an age become anti-romantic, it has become familiar through the painting of the three K's—Kandinsky, Kokoschka, and Klee—and through the works of such writers as Joyce, Kafka, Faulkner, and Tennessee Williams, the dancing of Martha Graham, and the films of Bergman and Fellini.

orchestral groups and arrange popular music. His first performed work was a *String Quartet* (1897), followed two years later by the string sextette *Verklärte Nacht,* a work stemming directly from the chromaticism of Wagner and filled with the spirit of Romanticism. *Gurrelieder,* started in 1901 and finished ten years later, was a huge score which for sheer size and ardent Romanticism rivaled the major works of Strauss and Mahler. Another nineteenth-century-inspired piece was the symphonic poem *Pelléas et Mélisande* (1905), entirely different from the later *Kammersymphonie* (1907), in which Schoenberg employed technical departures from tradition: chords based on fourths instead of thirds and dissonances without resolution. It was during this period that Schoenberg became interested in painting and was strongly influenced by the theories of the Expressionistic painters, especially Kandinsky. He gradually attracted attention as a coming modernist, drawing into his personal circle such progressive-minded students as Berg, Von Webern, and Wellesz, all of whose music was influenced by their master's developing theories. The *Second String Quartet* of 1908 was the last work Schoenberg wrote with a key signature. In this he added a voice part in the manner of Mahler and in the last movement arrived at almost complete atonal expression, abjuring everything resembling what he had hitherto considered melody.

SCHOENBERG'S MIDDLE PERIOD

The works written from 1909 to 1913 show Schoenberg coming to final grips with the intricate problems of his slowly developing advanced style, marked by the complete rejection of tonality and the evolution of a new kind of writing. The most important of them are *Three Piano Pieces,* Op. 11; *Six Little Piano Pieces,* Op. 19; *Five Orchestral Pieces,* Op. 16; *Erwartung,* Op. 17 (see page 668); and *Die glückliche Hand,* a drama with music, Op. 18. The composition which marks the end of this experimental middle period (and one of the epoch-making works of the whole century) was the 1912 *Pierrot lunaire,* a set of twenty-one songs each with a different orchestration and different structural form. Its scoring calls for a reciting voice (a blend of speaking and singing), piano, flute, clarinet, bass clarinet, violin, viola, and cello. In this work for the first time Schoenberg's experimental music seems to come to life and not to be the mere embodiment of his theories. And in it there is a hint, in the incessant repetition of certain main themes, of the means he finally adopted of giving some sort of unity and coherence to this new type of writing.

A NEW PRINCIPLE

The device Schoenberg used was that of basing each piece, not on a repeated theme, but on what he called a *tonerow,* an arrangement in some fixed, arbitrary order of the twelve tones of the chromatic scale. These tonerow patterns became the basis of both the melodies and chords of his compositions; they were always used complete but could be transposed to any one of the other eleven steps of the chromatic scale. And since each of these series could be inverted (turned upside down), reversed (played backward), or reversed and inverted, they provided forty-eight possible modifications, the rule being that the tones must always occur in the same order in the series and must be presented in full before the series was used again.

Here is the basic series or tonerow of the first large-scale work in which Schoenberg used this method of construction, his 1925 *Suite for Piano:*

This should be thought of as the structural element from which all the details of this work are derived. Everything is drawn directly from this basic series, its modifications or transpositions:

Inversion of the Basic Series or Tonerow

Reversion of the Basic Series or Tonerow

Inversion of the Reversion

The tones in the row may also be presented vertically in the form of chords, thus providing the harmonic as well as the melodic materials of the composition. At the very beginning of the Prelude to this Suite, Schoenberg uses this basic series as follows:

Basic Series

Basic Series Transposed

(Permission granted by Gertrud Schoenberg)

This kind of composition goes on through the five numbers of the Suite, dictating its materials as well as the order of their presentation.

The mechanistic method of producing music without any sense of tonality and without the traditional methods of constructing chords is an extremely complicated one for the composer and an almost incomprehensible one for the listener. In providing what he considered a complete release from the limitations of the tonal system, Schoenberg intellectually created tonal relationships of such complexity that even experienced listeners find them difficult. Evolved during a period of some twelve years in which he wrote no music at all, Schoenberg's method of composing with "twelve tones related only with one another," as he described it, was an attempt to will into being an entirely new way of writing music. Perhaps because it tried to give a sense of equilibrium and organization to counter the destruction and absurdity of its time, this serial principle appealed to other composers of that era as well.

Schoenberg used the serial technique for many of the works of his last period, including those he wrote after coming to the United States. Notable examples are the 1936 *Violin Concerto,* the *Piano Concerto* (1942), and the unfinished opera *Moses and Aaron,* a work of unusual power and expressiveness, even in its truncated form and, in the opinion of many, Schoenberg's masterpiece. It is interesting to note that in some of his best American works he relaxed somewhat from the strict application of his system: in them, tonal elements exist alongside serialism, making these works somewhat more accessible than his earlier compositions. Included among these are *Suite for String Orchestra* (1934), *Ode to Napoleon* (1942), and a cantata, *A Survivor from Warsaw* (1947).

SCHOENBERG'S PRESENT POSITION

It has often been said that one of the hallmarks of genius is its power to set in motion the imagination of others. In this sense, Schoenberg was certainly a genius, for his break with the past and his discovery of free tonality through the use of the twelve-tone system opened up a new and logical road that has proved to be the main musical highway of the mid-twentieth century. It was his logical linking of the late Romanticism of Mahler with the theories of free tonality that attracted the attention and aroused the enthusiasm of his outstanding pupils Alban Berg and Anton von Webern. These three formed what has come to be known as the twentieth-century Viennese School, based firmly on musical tradition and yet pointing directly to a new musical future.

And yet, if we are to believe his letters, he wanted to be known as a composer and not as a pioneer. "I do not compose Principles," he declared, "but music." "My method of composing with twelve tones was not introduced as a style to be used exclusively, but rather as an attempt to replace functional qualities of tonal harmony." He railed at some length against the over-analysis of his works, since this could result only in seeing what had been done, not in what the music was. He rather wistfully said that the one thing he longed for more than anything else was to be taken for a better sort of Tchaikovsky—"a bit better, but that's all; or if anything more, that people should know my tunes and whistle them."[6]

Unfortunately, the music in which Schoenberg uses this principle of free tonality[7] does not mean much more to the man who whistles Tchaikovsky's tunes today than it did to the average music lover at the time he wrote it. For the man in the street, the shoots of tone and bits of color in the later Schoenbergian works, their use of counterpoint without any underlying harmonic association to make it intelligible, their manufactured forms—all tend to make this music so complicated and over-elaborate that he cannot grasp its content. No matter how absorbing all these devices may have been to Schoenberg and those who followed him, they give little hope that such music will be known and appreciated in the Tchaikovskian sense now or in the foreseeable future.

[6] *Arnold Schoenberg Letters*, selected and edited by Erwin Stein: translated from the German by Eithne Wilkins and Ernst Kaiser. New York: St. Martin's Press, 1965.

[7] His method of absolute chromaticism—the use of twelve tones related only to one another—is often called *dodecaphony*, a rather pretentious term for the twelve-note system. This theory was, in fact, anticipated by others, especially Josef Matthias Hauer, another Viennese. But these earlier men did not derive compositional techniques from such an idea, as did Schoenberg.

TWO SCHOENBERG DISCIPLES

Hodeir makes the perspicacious observation[8] that Schoenberg remained an exceptional creator only so long as he was busy destroying; he ceased to be truly creative when he tried to construct. In a general way this is true: like the Moses of his opera, Schoenberg may be said to have shown the way to a Promised Land, but was never able to enter it. None of his twelve-tone compositions has proved to be as significant for the future as the works of two of his pupils and followers, Alban Berg (1885–1935) and Anton von Webern (1883–1945).

The only composer who has been able to make the Schoenberg system intelligible to the general listener was Berg. His talents enabled him to adopt the difficult technical processes of this new idiom to the necessities of musical construction in such a way as to produce compositions that communicate as well as challenging the listener's power of apperception. Not only did Berg learn Schoenberg's technical facility, but he was able to extend and humanize his master's ideas in a manner that makes them more accessible and comprehensible.

Like Schoenberg, Berg was born in Vienna and grew up there in the midst of a warm Romantic tradition dominated by the music of Schumann, Brahms, Wagner, Richard Strauss, and especially Mahler, who was at that time the director of the Vienna Opera. This atmosphere fostered the young musician's natural tendency for dramatic, romantic expression. And it was no accident that the work which first brought him fame and has turned out to be his masterwork was the opera *Wozzeck,* produced in 1925 after occupying him for nearly ten years. Berg's earliest works were all written under the watchful ear of Schoenberg; these comprise a *Piano Sonata,* Op. 1, and a set of songs with a strong Wagnerian flavor. His first steps toward transcending the bonds of tonality were taken in Op. 3, a *String Quartet,* written in 1910. Two years later he composed a song cycle with orchestral accompaniment, the so-called *Altenberg Lieder,* which foreshadowed his later opera in many details, especially the incorporation of large formal schemes into their dramatic structure. This peculiar dual emphasis on structural form and dramatic content was characteristic of all Berg's mature work: in *Wozzeck,* for example, each scene of the opera (there are sixteen altogether) is fitted onto the framework of a large symphonic form, al-

---

[8] André Hodeir, *Since Debussy: A View of Contemporary Music.* New York: Grove Press, 1961.

though, as Berg himself stated, no one in the theatre is aware of the fugues, inventions, sonata fragments, variations, and passacaglias which shape the music and form an integral part of its structural fabric.

Wozzeck is not only one of Berg's greatest works; it stands as the only major opera to be completed since Debussy's *Pelléas et Mélisande* was produced at the beginning of the century. The extraordinary fusion of music and drama shows its composer as the great dramatic genius of the period, able to extract maximum intensity from a rather sordid plot dealing with the woes of the insulted and injured of the earth. Berg saw the Büchner play from which he drew the libretto of his opera in 1914. He instantly recognized this story of a poor soldier driven to crime and madness by the wretchedness of his lot and the brutality of the world about him as being ideal for his purpose. Setting to work at once, he finished the libretto in 1917 and the score in 1921, employing some of Schoenberg's technical processes and using an adaptation of the tone-row, as well as a type of rhythmic declamation based on the *sprech-gesang* of *Pierrot lunaire*. He combined with these certain features of the German musical theatre in use since the time of Wagner—pure vocal declamation, the leitmotiv, and the expressive use of orchestral color. Some of his harmonies are diatonic, some not; some passages make use of scales, others of serial rows. According to the purists, Berg used the tonerow without grasping its full significance. This may or may not be true; what is important is that in this work Berg outstripped his teacher in the manipulation of his composing techniques and in so doing provided us with one of the century's indubitable masterpieces— one whose characters no longer belong to any one time or place but are rather universal symbols of human heartbreak and futility.

In the few years that were left him after the writing of *Wozzeck*, Berg produced a *Chamber Concerto* for piano, violin, and thirteen wind instruments (1925). This is the most abstruse of his compositions. Although later serialists pronounced it a hopelessly Romantic piece, it furnished further proof that the twelve-tone system can be employed to communicate emotional meaning. His next work was the *Lyric Suite* of 1926, generally considered his best purely instrumental work. It too displays his essentially dramatic nature, as is evidenced by the names given its various movements: *Allegro giovale, Andante amoroso, Allegro misterioso, Adagio appassionato,* and *Largo desolato.* The piece was originally written for string quartet, but Berg later arranged the three middle movements for string orchestra (1929). His second opera, *Lulu,* on which he spent the last seven years of his life and which he left unfinished, was first produced in Zurich in 1937 in a two-act version, although there seems to be evidence that Berg had essentially completed the sketches for the last act before his death in 1935. Based on two plays by the German Expressionistic playwright Frank Wedekind, *Lulu* is a bitter social commentary on the time when it was written, full of sex and violence, tragic irony, and intense expressiveness. Its crucial final scene has to be performed in a truncated version, because of the refusal of Berg's widow to allow its reconstruction from sketches left by the composer. In spite of its complex musical structure, its sordid dramatic material, its unrealized tension, and its uneven artistic style, *Lulu* is an over-powering work, splashed all over with genius.

Berg broke off the orchestration of this work in 1935 to write his *Violin Concerto*, which many consider his musical last will and testament. Inspired by grief over the tragic death of a young friend, this piece contains music of transcendent beauty and is strongly emotional in its depiction of the tragedy of life, yet tranquil in its reconciliation of life and death. Based on a formative tonerow, as well as on two traditional melodies, it employs a sort of loose tonality in its attempts to reconcile the procedures of serial and more traditional harmonic methods. Its Romantic qualities are enhanced by an alternation of consonance and dissonance, and a gradual build-up to an emotional climax, giving a sense of ebb and flow to the music entirely lacking in strict twelve-note composition.

ANTON VON WEBERN

It is usual to include Webern (he dropped the prefix late in life) as the third member of the famous Viennese contemporary composer triangle. As a matter of fact, although Webern was born in Vienna and that city became the center of his whole existence, and although he studied with Schoenberg and became the close friend and associate of Berg, his talents and temperament were entirely opposed to theirs, and the music he wrote possesses quite different characteristics. If Schoenberg and Berg belonged to the twilight years of German Romanticism and accepted the possibility—even the desirability—of the co-existence of tonal and atonal elements in their music, Webern made a clean break with the tonal concepts of the past and tried to renovate the language of music in entirely new terms.

Following the path pioneered by Debussy nearly a quarter of a century earlier, Webern became occupied with the possibilities of using music as sound—that is to say, with sound for sound's sake rather than as a means of communication between composer and listener. After some early works produced during his formative years with Schoenberg, Webern became principally concerned with the mechanical problems arising out of his attempt to achieve the utmost purity and economy in musical expression: how to avoid the repetition of materials;[9] how to secure the most delicate possible sonorities, with the tone color of each instrument exploited with the greatest possible skill; how to produce completely contrasting effects in instrumentation, giving precise directions as to how each individual tone should be produced; how to gain the subtlest dynamic levels, making expressive use of silence as well as sound; how to negate any sense of flowing continuity in music by avoiding accentuated rhythms or apparent metrical patterns; how to controvert any feeling of melodic line by using wide leaps and awkward intervals as structural elements and paying no attention to the natural capacity of the human voice or orchestral instruments; how to provide some sort of structural unity in this discontinuous style by extending the Schoenberg serial system for determining the order of the notes in a tonerow to include all the components which go into a musical work: tone colors (*klangfarben*), registers of instruments, intensities with which the notes are played or sung, dynamic levels—even silences. Put briefly, how to develop a completely new musical language that would provide a kind of recondite sensual pleasure.

For a man of Webern's uncompromising nature, this difficult task took a great deal of time—hence the small number of his works (thirty-one) and their brevity. He was content to tackle the various technical problems one at a time; when the solution was found, the piece was finished. Webern became, in the minds of his followers, a sort of musical Columbus, a daring explorer into a hitherto uncharted tonal world. He is often called the first really modern composer and he became the idol of younger men anxious to express themselves in a language that had no relationship with the past.

One of the reasons so little of Webern's music is played is its difficulty for listeners steeped in the older traditions; another is its unsuitability for concert programs. His *Five Pieces for Orchestra* (1913), for example, take only four-and-a-half minutes to play, with the fourth piece lasting only nineteen seconds; and the *Symphony for Small Orchestra* (1928) lasts only ten minutes, devoted largely to the manipulation and coloring of single, individual tones—a procedure not very well suited to holding the interest of an audience. This symphony, together with the works which followed it (the 1954 *Concerto for Nine*

[9] "Once started, the theme expresses all it has to say and must therefore be followed by something new" was his description of the process of composition.

Instruments is the best known) should be thought of as the ancestors of all the so-called post-Webern pieces written around the middle of the century.

The general effect of these compositions was disconcertingly negative insofar as the general public and the critics of the time were concerned. But this made little difference to the gentle, quiet, yet determined man, who was thoroughly convinced of the rightness of his position and ultimate acceptance. Even his accidental death at the hands of an American soldier caused little stir, and it was not until a number of years later that his influence began to be felt. Realizing how closely the particular aesthetic conceptions of the mid-century period corresponded to the ideals for which Webern strove all his life, it is not difficult to see why he became the rallying figure of the avant-garde composers of that time. As revealed in his lectures and letters, Webern seems to have been quite a different personality from that which is usually inferred from his ivory-towered music. Obviously a warm, sympathetic, and very human individual, he might be astonished at what these admirers have done in his name.

A Contemporary Iconoclast

We could learn, from the folksongs studied, how best to employ terseness of expression, to cultivate the utmost excision of all that is non-essential. And it was this very thing, after the excessive grandiloquence of the Romantic period, that we thirsted to learn.

Béla Bartók

Contemporary with Stravinsky and Schoenberg and sharing with them a position of significance in twentieth-century music, was another iconoclast, Béla Bartók (1881–1945), whom we have already noted as a pre-eminent Hungarian nationalist who based his work on extensive researches in folklore. Bartók had an unusual combination of abilities, enabling him to do important work in scientific research and musicological investigation as well as to appear on the concert stage as a virtuoso and composer. Born in what is now Rumania, he received his musical education at the Royal Academy in Budapest where, after four years of study, he was appointed professor of piano in 1907. Shortly after World War I he joined his brilliant colleagues Kodály and Dohnányi as a member of the Music Directorate of this famous school.

BARTÓK'S EARLIER WORKS

The compositions of the earliest period of Bartók's creative career (1904–1911) were largely in the vein of the older emotional world of European music. All of them seemed to have been failures: "I have tried eight years to get somewhere; I am sick of it and have made no further efforts," he wrote after the rejection by the Budapest Opera of his *Duke Bluebeard's Castle*. The next year (1912) he went into self-imposed exile from professional music-making for three years, devoting his attention entirely to musicological studies. In addition to his professional disappointments, he had experienced a series of emotional crises which made his opera an autobiographical, symbolical piece with an ending of tragic despair—not exactly the sort of fare relished by operagoers.

In an attempt to pull himself out of his dejected state of mind, he started composing again, finishing a ballet, *The Wooden Prince,* in time for its premiere in 1917. The success of this happier work established Bartók's reputation. Encouraged, he went to work on a realistic pantomime, *The Miraculous Mandarin,* the story and music of which reflected in a tough, outspoken manner the ugly repellent world of the time. Though he finished writing it in 1919, the world premiere of this much-disputed work did not take place until seven years later and then it was withdrawn after one performance. Bartók's uncompromising music, with its powerful motorial drive, its strong, erotic realism, and the harshness of its story have not made this a popular work in either Europe or this country, though it is often programmed. But it did crystallize one of the essential characteristics of Bartók's creative philosophy: the hopelessness of man's struggle against the hostile world about him, and the fact that everyone must wage this struggle alone and in his own way.

THE MIDDLE PERIOD

This dark, brooding philosophy colored all the work of Bartók's middle period. In works such as the *Third* (1927), *Fourth* (1928), and

Fifth (1934) *Quartets* he seems determined to cut the bonds which linked him with the past, to write music of a problematical, intellectual nature, and to create sounds quite different from anything heard before in quartet music. During this period he traveled widely in Europe and came to the United States for his first visit in 1927. He returned the next year to Budapest to teach and compose, becoming one of the leading figures of his generation. One of his most influential works of this period was a set of 153 progressive piano pieces, *Mikrokosmos* (1926–1937), an attempt to provide, within a small scope and simple idiom, a summary of modern composition. The two *Sonatas for Violin and Piano* (1921–1922) and the *First Piano Concerto* (1927) are other works of this period.

THE LAST DECADE

In the *Sixth Quartet* (1939) and other major scores of the last decade of his life (the last half of which was spent in this country), Bartók again became interested in communicating sentiment and emotion, as well as in more intellectual experiments with form and sonority. In *Music for String Instruments, Percussion and Celesta* (1936), an example of his use of varied rhythms and flair for orchestral color, his *Violin Concerto* (1937), now a standard work in the modern repertoire, the very popular *Concerto for Orchestra*, commissioned by Koussevitzky in 1945, and the *Third Piano Concerto* (1945), his final musical testament, Bartók reached the height of his creative career.

A number of influences shaped Bartók's rather austere idiom, including the nineteenth-century masters Liszt, Wagner, Brahms, and Strauss; the French Impressionists and Stravinsky and Schoenberg; southeastern European folk music, with its modal melodies and scales, and rich, varied rhythms; and modern techniques of dissonance.

Bartók showed himself able to achieve out of the exciting experiments of his time music that reconciles the demands of the intellect and the desires of the heart.

The French Retreat
from Impressionism

The genius of Debussy is the starting point of the revolution in the musical language of our time.

Antoine Goléa

EXPERIMENTALISM

By 1920 the mainstream of musical modernism was flowing from the two principal sources, Stravinsky and Schoenberg, but all sorts of personal idiosyncrasies were developed by various composers. In this they seemed to be following the course of the visual artists of the time: anything different was the directive from Paris, especially if it ran counter to the traditional. The musical experimentalists put together all sorts of incongruous ingredients—complex and startling rhythms, jazz-band instrumentations, café and music-hall sentimentalities—in an attempt to shock or intrigue the listener, and thus secure his attention. In doing this they had a good model to follow: the earlier French composer Eric Satie (1886–1925), who wrote music which poked fun at the pomposity and stuffiness of the European society of his day, as well as at the kind of preciosity that had come into French art with the Impressionists. Although Satie did not start the study of music professionally until he was nearly forty, his simple, unconventional style made him a great favorite with the younger men, who looked to him as a leader in the artistic rebellion against the conventions of all the arts. Such earlier works as the program pieces *Trois Gymnopédies* (1887), the later ballet *Parade* (1917), and the symphonic drama *Socrate* (1918) had healthy, antiseptic values for their time, though they do not seem very important today. Satie's significance lay in his recognition that Impressionism had come to a dead end with Debussy and that future developments would have to follow other lines.

In 1920 Georges Auric, Louis Durey, Francis Poulenc, Darius Milhaud, Arthur Honegger, and Germaine Tailleferre were banded together as *Les Six* through articles written about them by a contemporary critic. This group had as its doctrine the spirit of contradiction against whatever existed and as its common aim "the going from drum to flute, from flute to drum, so as to reshape certain French qualities whose rings, as it were, were worn and leaking too much oil."[10] Although a great deal of fuss was made about this group at the time, only three of its composers can be said to have survived as distinct personalities—the rest have almost completely disappeared. One of the survivors, Francis Poulenc (1899–1963), was a paradox. He wrote a number of deft, flippant works strongly influenced by Ravel and Satie; perhaps the most characteristic of these was the opera-burlesque *Les Mamelles de Tirésias* (1944). He also wrote a weighty, tragic piece in the very best grand-opera tradition, *Les Dialogues des Carmélites* (1957), concerning a group of Carmelite nuns who refused to disband during the French Revolution and suffered martyrdom. He turned out a great deal of satirical, funny, jazzy music, as well as such exalted sacred works as the *Gloria* and *Sept Répons,* both written during the later years of his life. A great deal of his music seems vapid, threadbare stuff, and yet he composed some of the century's finest songs. He wrote many salon pieces for the piano, a number of chamber music works, some film scores and incidental music for plays, and several large-scale instrumental compositions, notably the *Concerto for Two Pianos* (1932) and the *Concerto for Organ, Strings and Percussion* (1956). In spite of his contradictions, or perhaps because of them, Poulenc has proved to be perhaps the most important member of *Les Six.*

Darius Milhaud, born in 1892, is one of the most prolific composers of the century, which is saying a great deal, for most twentieth-century composers have written a great deal. He has composed in all forms and experimented with a number of advanced techniques, yet has been able to establish a style recognizably his own. Suave and urbane, complex yet always clear, harmonically bold within a framework of polytonality (in the evolution of which he played a significant part), with melodies that are vital and fresh and rhythms that reflect the time, Milhaud's music has become popular in a way that the works of most of his contemporaries have not. Many of his pieces sound like nineteenth-century music of rather obvious statement twisted out of tonal focus, and these have already passed into oblivion. But his attempt, which time has proved to be not very successful, to use jazz in concert music, *La Création du monde* (1923) and his opera *Christophe Colomb* (1928)

---

[10] From a speech by the literary spokesman of the movement, Jean Cocteau, given at a gala anniversary concert devoted to the music of *Les Six* in Paris in 1953.

are typical of the period which produced them. Since 1940 Milhaud
has spent part of his time in this country, teaching in a number
of important posts and powerfully influencing the ideals of a number of
young Americans, among them some of the leading jazz composers
of the day.

Arthur Honegger (1892–1955), Swiss by parentage but French by
inclination, seems to have got free more surely than the rest of the
group from its defiant desire to shock and surprise—this in spite of the
tremendous success of his sensational realistic portrait of a locomotive
in full flight, *Pacific 231,* the piece which first brought him fame, in
1924. But Honegger turned away from the rather easy success of this
symbol of the machine toward a more classical, architectural style, and
in so doing manifested the double-nationalistic character of the influences which shaped his music—a coupling of the essential Germanic
traditions with Gallic grace, wit, and clarity. In addition to his desire
for solid formal structures, there were other German traditions which
motivated his style: a tendency toward polyphony, and the belief that
music is a means of communicating spiritual values rather than merely
attracting attention. "I do not follow the cult of the fair or music-hall,
but rather that of chamber music and symphony in their most serious
and austere aspect," he is supposed to have declared. He also felt the
need for a composer to write music that is accessible to large numbers
of listeners and yet free from the banality which would repel a sincere
musician.

These ideas seem to us strangely out of fashion for the Paris of the
1920's and 30's. Yet they are the secret of Honegger's most enduring
successes—*Le Roi David* (1921) and *Jeanne d'Arc au bûcher* (1935),
both of which colorfully decorate the somewhat dilapidated mansion of
oratorio, the orchestral *Pastorale d'Ete* (1920) and five symphonies
(1930–57), the last and best of which was commissioned by Koussevitzky, the conductor most responsible for making Honegger's works
known. More specifically French are the mimed symphony *Horace
Victorieux* (1921), the opera *Antigone* (1927), and the melodrama
Amphion (1931). Like all the other members of *Les Six,* Honegger
wrote in all styles, producing a tremendous quantity of chamber music,
piano music, and songs in addition to the types already mentioned.

The Neo-Classicists

*I consider that music is by its very nature
essentially powerless to express anything at all,
whether a feeling, a state of mind, a psychological state, a phenomenon of nature and the like.*

Igor Stravinsky

W e have described
some of the characteristics of neo-Classicism and shown how it influenced Stravinsky and those who followed in his footsteps. This chapter
includes brief descriptions of the most important exponents of this new
force.

Chief among them was Paul Hindemith, whom we discuss elsewhere (pp. 702–704). The others mentioned in this chapter effected a
union of classical and contemporary in various ways, according to their
temperaments and national backgrounds. Albert Roussel (1869–1937),
for example, formed his mature style out of the charm of French folk
melodies, the elegance of French classicism, the vitality of Baroque
rhythms, and the spice of French wit. This is well shown in all three
of his symphonies, the last commissioned in 1930 by the Boston Symphony Orchestra.

A pupil of Roussel, the Czech composer Bohuslav Martinu (1890–
1959) followed the neo-Classical mode in general, but used a number
of different techniques and combined the intellectual elements of his
period with a high degree of imaginative communication. He wrote:
"There are . . . new riches, a true development of our musical sensitivity in domains still to be explored. But one must be aware that this
enrichment can become an impoverishment if the spirit of the composer thereby loses all the riches accumulated in centuries of searchings
and finding." Of his last six symphonies, all of them written in this
country, the most successful has been the last, *Fantaisies Symphoniques*
(1955).

The younger Jean Françaix (*b.* 1912) has based his work firmly on the best classic traditions of his country and has written a great deal of chamber music in advanced but not serial style.

In Italy the tremendous strength of the operatic tradition resulted in neglect of any other kind of composition until late in the nineteenth century. It was not until the work of Alfredo Casella (1883–1947) that any sort of experimentation was tried in Italian instrumental music. Casella lived in both Paris, where he came under the influence of Stravinsky, and the United States. This background led to a style in which modern techniques were applied to old forms. But in spite of his cosmopolitanism, Casella never gave a convincing personality to his music. His best-known work is the choreography comedy after Pirandello, *La Giara* (1924).

Another composer interested in reviving Italian traditions is Gian Francesco Malipiero (*b.* 1882). He became absorbed in preparing editions of the complete works of Monteverdi and Vivaldi, a labor of love that helped determine the style of his own music, which can be described as national in essence and cosmopolitan in technique. His works include some twenty-five operas, four ballets, nineteen orchestral works, nine symphonies, fifteen choral works with orchestra, five piano concertos, seven string quartets, a mass of chamber music works, piano music, and songs. Hardly any of this enormous output is heard anywhere today.

The music of Vittorio Rieti (*b.* 1898), a pupil of Respighi and a resident of France as well as Italy who later became a naturalized American, is appropriately cosmopolitan in character, although influenced by Casella and activated by Stravinsky. Rieti has written in all forms, the most effective being the ballet and opera.

Willem Pijper (1894–1947) can be said to have determined the nature of Dutch music between the two wars and succeeded in giving it a place in the musical life of Europe. His style was influenced by late Romanticism (Mahler) and Impressionism and showed strong classic tendencies, although it employed contemporary techniques. Pijper became dominated by what he called the "germ-cell theory"—the development of a whole composition in an organized manner from a short motive or chord as a starting point. Perhaps his most characteristic work based on this principle was his *Third Symphony* (1926), dedicated to Monteux, who did much to make it known through Holland and abroad.

The first of the postwar German composers to attract wide attention was Boris Blacher (*b.* 1903). His strong, terse, direct music is uncompromisingly original and employs an unusual mathematical concept of rhythm (variable meters employed to suit mathematical progressions and permutations), as well as free atonal counterpoint. Blacher's classical leanings are manifested in his use of eighteenth-century forms for his instrumental music, although his operas and ballets show dramatic flair. His most famous work, little known outside central Europe, is the 1953 *succès de scandale,* the *Abstract Opera No. 1.*

The twentieth-century British composers have shown less reliance than their foreign contemporaries on the fashions initiated by Stravinsky and Schoenberg, though they have followed the non-Romantic trends and use some of the century's new techniques. William Wordsworth (*b.* 1903), a distant relative of the poet, has written symphonies and quartets classical in their austerity and compact use of form. Alan Bush (*b.* 1900), as a result of his interest in Marxism and consequent search for more immediate means of communication with his listeners, gradually moved away from his earlier serial procedures toward a tonal language more easily understood. His historical opera *Wat Tyler* (1950) has had considerable success. The *Clarinet Concerto* (1936) of Alan Rawsthorne (*b.* 1905) is one of the few extended essays for this instrument. Rawsthorne's style, not without asperity, shows a consistency lacking in many modern works. It is based essentially on the contrapuntal practices of the past and has vigorous rhythm, fluent melodic patterns (often departing from a tonal center), and real eloquence, all qualities appealing to the composer's countrymen.

Although Michael Tippett's (*b.* 1905) style is basically Romantic, its polyphonic complexity and attention to intellectual stimulation give it also a strong Classical cast. His best-known work is an oratorio, *A Child of Our Time* (1944), with a touching treatment of humanity under the stress of war which uses Negro spirituals in place of the customary chorales. The composer's subject here stimulated him to produce a score of great power. This was not the case, unfortunately, with his two operas, *The Midsummer Marriage* (1955) and the 1962 *King Priam.* In these the ineptness of the literary treatment seems to have dulled the composer's vision. The *Concerto for Orchestra* (1963) has some of the richness and color of Tippett's earlier style and shows, as one of his admirers has said, that "this most poetical, most serious and very passionate composer is among the very few who have been able to create worlds of their own."

Nikolai Lopatnikov (*b.* 1903), born in Russia but since 1959 a resident of the United States, has written instrumental music almost entirely. His works have been widely performed by orchestral and chamber music organizations in Europe and this country. His *First*

Symphony (1930) was vividly nationalistic, but his later works have been strongly influenced by the neo-Classical trends associated with Stravinsky and Hindemith.

Johann Nepomuk David (*b.* 1895), probably the most eminent living Austrian composer, has spent much of his life in Germany. The music of Bach has been his model and its study has made him a polyphonic classicist, known largely for his choral and organ works, to a lesser degree for his symphonic compositions.

The Austrian composer best-known on the international scene is Gottfried von Einem (*b.* 1918), whose music has been wittily described as being *nicht von Einem sondern von Allen*—not from one, but from all! Von Einem's eclecticism includes the advanced techniques of his contemporaries, elements of jazz, traditional harmonic usages, and general neo-Classical tendencies. His interest has been largely dramatic and he has written a number of works with striking dynamic and rhythmic effects, jagged vocal lines bordering on atonality, but with real communicative power. His best-known works are his operas, *Dantons Tod* (1947) and *Der Process* (1953), both first performed at the Salzburg Festival, where von Einem has been an outstanding figure. After these dramatic works, von Einem assumed a more classical style, pronouncing himself the successor to Viennese Classicism.

Hindemith—
the Compleat Musician

*Genius seems to be the ability to retain the
keenness of the first vision until its embodiment in the finished piece is achieved.*

Paul Hindemith

After Stravinsky the best known twentieth-century composer to espouse neo-Classical ideals was Paul Hindemith (1895–1965). Though he was an undisputed leader during the twenties and thirties, at the time of his death Hindemith's reputation and influence had considerably diminished, his music being thought of as academic by the new revolutionaries. But there has never been any disagreement about his significance as one of the great figures in the century's musical life. He was a practicing musician of high caliber: a professional violinist and violist, he also had a good working knowledge of all the instruments in the orchestra. He was an adequate conductor, a good pianist, one of the century's leading theorists, and a most respected musical educator, with fields of activity as widely separated as Turkey, Germany, and the United States, where he taught for a number of years at Yale University and the Berkshire Music Center in Tanglewood.

He received a sound musical training at Frankfort Conservatory and became concert master and ultimately conductor of the famous opera of that city. A representative man of his time, he turned away from Romanticism and back to the Baroque. His modernistic idiom made use of strong acerbic harmony, tremendous rhythmic drive, dry, rather artificially conceived melodies, skillfully controlled dissonantal counterpoint, and traditional elements of formal structure. He adhered to the principle of tonality but worked out his own ways of keeping within its limitations.[11] Like his great prototype J. S. Bach, Hindemith could and did write at the slightest provocation and, as was the case with his great exemplar, he sometimes overstepped the line between creativeness and verbosity. There was for him no such thing as an ivory tower: he seems always to have been busy in the orchestra pit, the concert platform, or the professorial chair. He had a sensible belief that music should be made to serve its own day and generation and not bother too much about the next. He wrote nine operas, five ballets and pantomimes, cantatas, a vast amount of orchestral music, including symphonies and concertos for various instruments, quartets, trios, and considerable vocal music. Among his specialties was a tremendous amount of *Gebrauchmusik* (practical music for everyday use) and *Hausmusik,* to be played and sung by amateurs at home. He made a very comprehensive attempt to establish a modern theory of harmony and wrote three books on it. In *A Composer's World* he had many pertinent things to say about the music of his time and about the art of music in general.

Like Schoenberg, Hindemith went through a process of strenuous

[11] In conformance with the spirit of 1922, Hindemith's *Third String Quartet* went by the name *Atonal;* in reality, it is based on a free use of the twelve chromatic tones about a center. Written before he became preoccupied with notions of order and proportion, this is one of the most effective works of the whole century.

development; from writing music with a strong Wagnerian background, he passed through a cerebral period, of which his two operas *Cardillac* (1926) and *Neues vom Tage* (1929), his work for viola and orchestra, *Der Schwanendreher* (1935), and his oratorio *Das Unaufhörliche* are representative. The four concertos that make up his *Kammermusik* (one each for violin, viola, cello, and piano, with chamber ensembles of various constitutions) are among the most exhilarating works of this period. Later he came to use a more communicative style, paying more attention to the need for establishing contact with his listeners. This warmer writing is first noted in his masterwork, the opera *Mathis der Maler* (1938), from which a popular orchestral triptych has been extracted. The ballet based on the life of St. Francis, *Noblissima visione* (1938), and the *Symphonic Metamorphoses on a Theme by Carl Maria von Weber* (1944) continued this trend and have joined the short list of Hindemith's works that can be called repertory pieces.

There is no doubt that Hindemith wrote too easily, too frequently, and too much. A great deal of his music is mechanization incarnate, immensely glib and fluent, often amusing and interesting in its salesmanlike dexterity of displaying many lines of goods to suit all possible fancies. But the best of his works will certainly survive any temporary eclipse they may have suffered, although coming generations may well wonder how a composer so responsive to form and so insistent on the need for honest craftsmanship and continuance of tradition could have lived and worked in the midst of the present century.

Twentieth-Century Nationalism

The slogan of nationalism will die as soon as it is realized that each nation is aiming at the same ideal of mechanical civilization.

Constant Lambert

We have noted that nineteenth-century Nationalism, while by no means the only important phase of the Romantic movement, provided the stimulus for some of its most spontaneous and appealing music. The same can be said of this powerful incentive during the twentieth century. There were, of course, significant differences between these two eras of nationalistic expression —differences which arose from the more scientific, less idealized temper of the later period. Twentieth-century researchers, through the use of recording equipment, were able to determine more exactly the specific characteristics of the folk music which could be used as a basis for this type of writing. And composers became more concerned with using this material objectively, accurately, and suitably than with exploiting it merely for picturesque effects.

The new interest in folk music paralleled an upsurge of interest in old music in general, with its freer rhythms, modal scales, unhackneyed melody, departures from regular structural patterns—all characteristics of special interest to composers attempting to free themselves from nineteenth-century dimensions.

THE NEW NATIONALISM

The nationalistic aspect of Bartók's and Kodály's music has been treated in other places. Here we need only remind the reader of the great difference in the results achieved by their method of treating folk tunes and those produced by earlier nationalistic composers such as Rimsky-Korsakoff and Dvořák. As Bartók explained it, several thousand melodies were noted down in a few years. In the most valuable part of this collection, the oldest Hungarian melodies, the material was discovered that could serve as the foundation of a renaissance in Hungarian art music. The appropriate use of this folk material was not the sporadic introduction or imitation of these old melodies, however, or their use in works of foreign or international tendencies. It was necessary for the composer to command this musical language so completely that it became the natural expression of his own musical ideas.

RUSSIAN NATIONALISM OF THE TWENTIETH CENTURY

For reasons not entirely musical, the Russians produced the most notable nationalistic music of the twentieth century, just as they had in the nineteenth. The differences in style between the idioms of these Russian nationalistic schools a century apart were due not only to changes in taste and techniques but also to the rise of a political system which demanded that the activities of the Russian artist, like all other activities of the Russian people, be devoted to the welfare of the nation as a whole rather than being merely the expression of the artistic and intellectual ideals of the individual artist.

In spite of the heavily oppressive political atmosphere of the Czarist Russia, the nineteenth-century Russian nationalists had been able to assimilate many of the general characteristics of European music and join them with the traits of their own nationalist tradition to produce some of the world's most attractive and communicative music. The political and cultural aims of the Soviet Union after the revolution of 1917, as evolved under Lenin, Stalin, and Khrushchev, were to identify the totalitarian rule of the party with the forces of legitimacy and stability, in the process glorifying the State as the only source of activity possible in Soviet society. Hence there could be no absolute freedom for the individual, be he a political commissar, a business executive, or an artistic creator.

THE DILEMMA OF THE RUSSIAN COMPOSER

This Soviet doctrine puts the Soviet creative artist on the horns of a real dilemma. On the one hand, he is ordered to follow the ideals of Socialist Realism as proclaimed and approved by the government as the safe path to pursue. This theory stresses the importance of art as an expression of great ideas and passions, affirms the beauty and dignity of man (as a component member of Soviet society, of course) and points out the necessity of creating art that has a meaning for a large number of people—and, incidentally, that can be used for political propagandistic purposes. It rejects what the Soviet authorities have called "bourgeois formalism," a term which implies the sacrifice of musical thought for the sake of form, and the use of the composer's technical skill to disguise the fact that he does not have anything significant to express. Such criticism was aimed directly at the practices of non-Soviet composers, especially the neo-Classicism of Stravinsky and the twelve-tone technique of Schoenberg. It has officially been proclaimed on such occasions as the famous "purge" of 1948, when the government's official theoretician publicly castigated three of the Soviet's leading composers for "disregarding the great social side of music." If the Soviet composer adheres to these ideals and dutifully follows the paths of Socialist Realism, he can be assured of government support adequately—and sometimes handsomely—given. What is more, he becomes aware that his music is wanted, that it will be published and played, and will probably become the subject of active discussion. In brief, he can become a significant figure in the cultural life of the country, respected and re-warded.

On the other hand, if he follows the ideals of Socialist Realism, the contemporary Soviet composer has to forsake one of the most cherished prerogatives of the creative mind—exploring the new resources and techniques that are possible in his art. He has to shut his mind and ear to the new experiments in modernism that are being made by his con-temporaries in other countries and confine his work to the possibilities inherent in the Soviet situation. There has been a constant struggle be-tween the opposing forces: the government demanding restriction and the artists asking liberalization. There have been periods of freeze-up, followed by periods of thaw. But it does not seem likely that the battle for complete freedom of artistic and intellectual expression will ever be fully won during the Soviet regime.

In spite of all the restrictions, Russia has produced some of the cen-tury's best compositions. What it might have done without these re-strictions is a fascinating subject for speculation.

TWO BRIDGE MEN

Reinhold Glière (1875–1956) and Nikolai Miaskovsky (1881–1950), the two men regarded as the last survivors of the nineteenth-century school of Russian Nationalists, in reality served to bridge the gap between Czarist and Soviet Russia. Trained in the traditions of the older generation, they were active as teachers of the new. Both were prolific composers who wrote in all forms without transgressing the borderlines of either the older harmonic style or the newer aesthetic re-quirements. Glière's principal work was the enormous *Third Symphony* (1909–11), on the subject of the Russian folk hero Ilya Murometz. His compositions approved by the new regime include the very popular ballet *The Red Poppy* (1927) and the two overtures *Twenty-Five Years of the Red Army* (1943) and *Victory* (1945).

Nikolai Miaskovsky deserves mention if for no other reason than the quantity of his output: he wrote twenty-seven symphonies, three of them after World War II. Although they contain attractive, colorful music, they are seldom played, even in Moscow; as late as 1961 his former student Khatchaturian complained that Miaskovsky's sym-phonies had disappeared from concert programs. It is difficult for West-ern listeners to know why.

SERGEI PROKOFIEV

The most spontaneous and highly gifted of the newer Russians was Sergei Prokofiev (1891–1953), a real composer and not, like many of his contemporaries, an inventor or theorist. The brilliance of his style, the versatility of his accomplishments, the natural appeal of his melodies, the lean, athletic quality of his rhythms, the cynicism and wry humor of much of his work, and, above all, his power of direct communication, made him one of the foremost men of his period. Even though Prokofiev's international popularity diminished somewhat following his death, a survey of American concert programs in 1962 showed him still leading all foreign modern composers in the number of performances of his works. More of his works have become classics than any other twentieth-century composer's. His *First (Classical) Symphony* of 1917, as well as the later *Fifth* (1944) have become regular concert repertory items, with the more lyric *Sixth* (1949) and *Seventh* (1953) played more and more frequently; his two violin concertos rank high in the repertory, while such piano works as the *Sonatas* (especially numbers 6, 7, and 8) and the *Second, Third,* and *Fifth Piano Concertos* seem to have been written with the present-day piano virtuosos in mind. *Lieutenant Kije* (1934) and *Peter and the Wolf* (1936) need no introduction to anyone who has heard any concert music at all; the score of *Alexander Nevsky* (1938) is certainly the best cinema music ever written; and *Romeo and Juliet* (1935–36) is coming to be recognized as probably the finest music ever written as a ballet score. Prokofiev's operas have not been as successful: *The Love for Three Oranges,* commissioned for Chicago in 1921, is best known; *The Flaming Angel,* completed in 1927, was never staged during the composer's lifetime and is only now appearing occasionally, even though its rich and intense music shows how much Prokofiev later sacrificed in attempting to conform to Soviet ideals; and his great epic after Tolstoi's novel, *War and Peace,* remains largely unknown outside the U.S.S.R.

PROKOFIEV'S CAREER

From his earliest days Prokofiev, in addition to being a brilliantly gifted performing musician, was a natural rebel, impatient with the past and quite certain of his own ability to better it. In his conservatory days at St. Petersburg he earned the reputation of an *enfant terri-*

ble, slashing away in such things as *The Scythian Suite* (1914) at the conventionalities. He left his native land shortly after the Revolution and in 1918 came to this country, where his sharp percussive pianism and "age-of-steel" compositions aroused a great deal of criticism. After the failure of his opera in Chicago he determined to live in the more congenial atmosphere of Europe, settling in Paris, whence he made frequent trips to all the great musical centers to play and conduct his music. In 1934 he returned to Russia, impelled not only by the desire to live again in his beloved homeland, but also by an awareness that it was there he could do his best work. He was immediately recognized as the leading composer of the Soviets and was given wide recognition and adequate financial support. Nevertheless, along with others, he was sharply attacked in the Central Committee's Decree of 1948 for being a "bourgeois formalist," and called merely an emigré who had had the good sense to return to Russia. All his works were temporarily barred from concert programs, though such restrictions could not be effectively maintained. In spite of the fact that he wrote a very dignified and reasonable reply to the canards of the committee, Prokofiev was terribly shaken by this attack, for he had sincerely tried to meet the aesthetic requirements of the Soviet government in the music he had written since his return to Russia. His last symphony *The Seventh* (1952), completely re-established his reputation with his countrymen and showed the world that he was still an important composer and not merely an exponent of Socialist Realism.

Prokofiev's music sounds much less revolutionary today than it did when it was written, for now we can easily realize that, in spite of its piled-up dissonances and twisted harmonies, it always keeps within the traditional framework of tonality. It is true that this music is seldom profound or universal, that its emotional range is somewhat limited, and that it too often depends on shock effects, especially in the earlier works. Nevertheless, its steel-age dynamism, tempered by innate Russian nationalism, gives it a special quality which, at its best, is unique. Prokofiev brightly and wittily expressed the rebellious spirit of his age; and so in the years to come his scores will probably sound as fresh as they do today.

DMITRI SHOSTAKOVICH

Dmitri Shostakovich (*b.* 1905) is the only composer of world renown to spend his entire working life under Communism, and so the Russians like to think of him as representative of their new order. The outside world is more apt to regard his career as a mirror of the stormy history of the arts in the first Marxist state. In his early years Shostakovich's energies were devoted largely to expressing contempt for the past. Although it is a work of exciting originality, written when Shostakovich was only nineteen and still a student at the Leningrad Conservatory, his *First Symphony* (1925) definitely bears the irreverent, sardonic stamp of anti-Romantic modernism. And such things as his satirical opera *The Nose* (1930), the incidental music to Mayakovsky's comedy *The Bedbug* (1929), and the fateful opera which changed the direction of his whole career, *Lady Macbeth of Mtsensk,* all held bourgeois society and its customs up to ridicule.

In 1930 Stalin decided to abandon, for the time being at least, his hopes for a Leninist revolution and concentrate on strengthening his party's power in Russia itself. Realizing that the arts could be of great help in such a re-orientation, he decided that their function would have to be changed: from being the destroyers of bourgeois ideals in the countries that were ripe for revolution, they would have to become supporters of the status quo in the Soviet Union. A suitable occasion for announcing such a fundamental change in political aesthetics came in 1934, after Stalin had attended a performance of Shastakovich's new and popular opera. Sitting directly over the orchestra's hard-pressed brass (so the story goes, at least) Stalin became incensed by the noisy musical style and the political implications of *Lady Macbeth of Mtsensk.* At any rate, a blistering blast in *Pravda* resulted in the withdrawal of the opera, as well as the composer's *Fourth Symphony,* then in rehearsal. In 1937 Shostakovich's *Fifth Symphony,* accommodatingly labeled a "creative reply of a Soviet artist to just criticism," was given its first performance. Since it turned out to be the composer's best and most popular work and did not transcend official restrictions, it restored Shostakovich to official favor.

Shortly after this came the war, and Shostakovich was used time and again as a shining example of what Soviet culture could produce. He wrote more symphonies, including the patriotically inspired *Seventh* (Leningrad), which has been played all over the world as a tribute to the composer's native city; the far greater *Eighth,* containing some of Shostakovich's most profoundly moving music[12]; and the light-hearted *Ninth* (1945), in which he seemed to return to the spirit of his youth.

Suddenly, in 1948, came a drastic denunciation of all Russian music,

[12] Written at high speed, it is as powerful a statement on war as has been made by any twentieth-century artist. It reveals more of Shostakovich's inner self than any other of his works.

especially that of Prokofiev and Shostakovich, by the formidable Zhdanov, Stalin's cultural executioner. Obliged to admit the error of his ways in two subservient speeches, Shostakovich wrote nothing of importance until the death of Stalin in 1953, when he produced the *Tenth Symphony* and the *Violin Concerto,* both among his better scores. In view of the gradual lessening of political pressures as part of the de-Stalinization process initiated by Khruschchev, the later works of Shostakovich are disappointing, only one really good score appearing during the next decade—the *Cello Concerto,* Op. 107. *Symphonies Eleven* (1957) and *Twelve* (1961) are hardly above the level of mediocrity, with little of their composer's earlier vigor; they reflect in a rather tired way the mannerisms of his earlier works. The *Thirteenth Symphony* (1962) had to be withdrawn after an unforgettable first performance because it included in its setting a poem on anti-Semitism. The fact that Yevtushenko the poet and Shostakovich the composer readily complied in making the dictated changes in the score indicates that the Soviet authorities were still by no means willing to recognize the artist as a free agent.

This decade saw the rehabilitation of the two Shostakovich works rejected during the Stalin era: the *Fourth Symphony,* first played in 1961, and the opera *Lady Macbeth of Mtsensk* under a new name, *Katarina Ismailova,* in 1962. The former is a kind of missing link between the youthful *First* and the mature *Fifth Symphonies.* Strongly influenced by Mahler, one of Shostakovich's great gods, and full of ideas not always satisfactorily developed, it explores a new world of independence and leads directly to the *Fifth.* Those who attended the performances of *Lady Macbeth* given in this country in 1935 remember that, while it was hardly the negation of opera or the leftist monstrosity that Pravda tried to make it out, it was not a very good work, with coarse, vulgar naturalism and loud, overblown orchestration. Evidently Shostakovich tried to remedy these defects by making some changes in the orchestration, altering some of the awkward vocal lines and composing some new, less realistic orchestral interludes.

The success of Shostakovich as one of the leading composers of this century rests on solid musical grounds. His harmonies, in spite of some occasional cacophonous outbursts, are solidly diatonic, with Mahlerian chromatic leanings. He has a gift for melody and an instinctive sense of orchestral color, handling the different instruments with consummate skill. His structural ability, especially in the larger forms, enables him to build logically, always keeping a grand linear continuity in spite of his predilection for unexpected details. There are many major shifts of mood to provide contrast and sustain interest—from impudent (sometimes boisterous) humor, through romantic lyricism, to moments of epic, Beethoven-like grandeur.

For all his imaginative power and structural ability, Shostakovich often gives the impression of not being entirely sure of himself. His music, like that of Mahler, is frequently vague and full of unresolved tensions and unachieved effects. In such cases, especially in the later works, we have nothing but fussy details, big noise, and rhetorical gestures. The causes of these inequalities are hard to determine. It is too simple to interpret them as merely the result of political pressures. The sources of an artist's inspiration are complex and lie deep within his personality, as well as in the circumstances of his existence.

OTHER TWENTIETH-CENTURY RUSSIANS

The music of Aram Khatchaturian (*b.* 1903) is more fully in the nationalistic tradition than that of either Prokofiev or Shostakovich. An Armenian by birth, Khatchaturian exploits the rich vein of his native folk music, writing in the style of Russian orientalism without actually quoting folk songs. A most competent craftsman, he has composed in all the various forms, especially the concerto. In such works as the *Piano Concerto* (1936), *Violin Concerto* (1940), and *Concerto for Cello and Orchestra* (1950), he utilizes the exciting possibilities of his native dance styles in a florid and rhapsodic manner. The "Sabre Dance" from his 1942 ballet *Gayane* has become part of the world's popular repertory, and some of his incidental theatre and film music is fairly well known outside Russia. Though he was included in the 1948 criticism of the Central Committee for his modernistic tendencies, he has gone on in his own way, insisting that Soviet composers should be allowed varied means of achieving the results demanded by Social Realism. Because of his position as professor at the Moscow Conservatory and his activities as a conductor, he has had great influence on contemporary taste in Russia.

Dimitri Kabalevsky (*b.* 1904) is a simpler native talent, one content to supply in symphonies, concertos, and chamber music the demands for optimistic, tuneful, uncomplicated music. He is best known in the West for his piano music and a 1940 orchestral suite, *The Comedians*. In 1962 Kabalevsky wrote what he called a *Requiem* to a text by the contemporary Russian poet Rozhdestvensky. Like the *War Requiem* of Benjamin Britten, this work has none of the characteristics of the liturgical requiem, but celebrates those patriots who died to save their country in two brutal wars. It had its first performance in the English-speaking world at Rochester, New York, in 1965.

Another leading Nationalist is Tikhon Khrennikov (*b.* 1913), whose strong rhythmic style is based largely on folk material. Khrennikov is known chiefly for his patriotically inspired works; his music is little played outside Russia. Some of his operas still repertory pieces in Russia include the early *Into the Storm* (1939), the satirical *Frol Skobeyev* (1950), and the effective *The Mother* (1957), based on Gorky's novel of the 1905 Revolution.

Another opera composer is Ivan Dzerzhinsky (*b.* 1909), whose success with *Quiet Flows the Don* in 1935 has not been repeated. His 1960 *The Fate of a Man* particularly disappointed the critics, who tried to explain its failure as due to Dzerzhinsky's "creative irresponsibility." The most successful of the younger opera composers seems to be Rodion Shchedrin (*b.* 1932), whose opera dealing with life on a collective farm, *Not Love Alone,* was successfully produced at the Bolshoi Theatre in 1961.

Works of the oratorio-cantata genre have become popular with Soviet authorities because of their adaptability to official policy. Many of these odes to peace, victory, collective farming, forestation, and the like may serve well as propaganda pieces, but those that have been exported seem very dull, Shostakovich's *Song of the Forest* (1949) being no exception. But observers of the Russian musical scene have been impressed with the work of Georgii Sviridov (*b.* 1915). In his *Pathetic Oratorio* of 1959, Sviridov set the words of Vladimir Mayakovsky, the chief poetic spokesman of the Revolution, to a musical idiom which, though necessarily conventional, is highly communicative and deeply moving.

Many younger Soviet composers have recently emerged as the result of the government's lavish support of a system of musical education that is probably the most elaborate in the world.[13] Included in this group are Vadim Salmanov (*b.* 1912), Moissei Vainberg (*b.* 1919), Galina Ustvolakaya (*b.* 1919), Andrei Volkonsky (*b.* 1933), and Boris Tishchenko (*b.* 1940), none of them known outside Russia. Although a few of these younger men seem to have succeeded in introducing

---

[13] A recent survey by Boris Schwarz in *Contemporary Music in Europe* (New York: G. Schirmer, 1965) gives the astonishing total of 1,966 children's music schools, 187 specialized secondary schools, and 23 conservatories for college-age students in the Soviet Union today. Especially gifted children are educated in 22 Central Music Schools, many of them attached to conservatories, which offer a combined curriculum of general education through high school with music.

some adventurous innovations, including a few brief dodecaphonic essays, into their music, their future within the circumscribed circle of Soviet art remains uncertain.

The accomplishments of twentieth-century Russian nationalism have been considerable: it has brought great enjoyment to millions who had never had an opportunity to hear music; it has preserved and extended the achievements of the musical past and educated composers to the necessity of maintaining constant contact with the general masses. But unless it can find some way of giving composers freer opportunities to work out their own salvation, its music seems doomed to obsolescence.

Two English Nationalists

Have we not all about us forms of musical expression, which we can take and purify and raise to the level of great art? The composer must live with his fellows and make his art an expression of the whole life of the community.

Vaughan Williams

The strength of British music, even before Elgar in the late nineteenth century, has been in poetic conception rather than introspective content. This is a perfectly natural phenomenon, since the poetic is the dominant art tradition of England, just as painting is of France, and music is of Germany. When this strong poetic conception is united with marked technical skill, as with such composers as Ralph Vaughan Williams (1872–1958) and Benjamin Britten (*b.* 1913), the result is significant music—music which expresses the spirit of the composers' native country in the same indefinable yet indubitable way that the music of Prokofiev and Shostakovich communicates the spirit of Russia.

VAUGHAN WILLIAMS

One of the chief resources of English poets and composers has been their rich heritage of folk material; and a rather remarkable school of English folk composers arose during the latter part of the nineteenth century, stimulated by Cecil Sharp and his English Folk Dance Society, and by a revival of interest in the older English musical styles, especially Tudor church music and Elizabethan madrigals. The leader and most important figure in this new school was Vaughan Williams, a composer to whom the folk idiom—above all, its modality—seemed a most natural musical speech. Trained in the Romantic tradition, he became involved in the folk-song movement early in his career, even going out into the country villages to gather melodies, some of which he used for his earliest works, the *Three Norfolk Rhapsodies,* written in 1906. His popular string *Fantasia on a Theme of Tallis* (1910) was based on an anthem by one of England's best known early church composers, and a folk opera, *Hugh the Drover* (1911–14), glorified in both story and music the life and virtues of simple people.

Vaughan Williams's symphonic nationalism is best shown in such works as the *London Symphony* (1914), a sort of Edwardian view of the city, and the *Pastoral Symphony* (1922), which reflects the peculiar charm and quiet beauty of the English countryside. As his scope widened, he almost imperceptibly integrated some of the technical procedures of the time into his folkish way of expressing himself to form a distinctly personal and less parochially English style. In his *Fourth Symphony* (1935) he broke completely with his earlier works and launched into what seems even today a bitter, harsh, dissonant tirade against the injustices and cruelties of the period just before World War II. This rather un-English change of style was followed by the grave and melodious *Fifth Symphony* in 1943, probably the best of his nine symphonies, with a twelve-minute epilogue for muted orchestra, suggestive of the "final echo of a vanished world" that is one of the finest imaginative concepts of the whole century. The *Sixth Symphony* (1948) has the strong dramatic quality of the *Fourth,* as well as some of its irascible temper. The *Seventh* (Sinfonia antartica), 1952, is hardly a symphony at all but a picturesque travelogue *à la* Richard Strauss's *Alpine Symphony,* made up of materials previously used for the sound track of a film on the Antarctic. The *Eighth* (1956) and *Ninth* (1958) return to the more mellifluous if less striking style of his earlier works.

Vaughan Williams displays his nationalistic tendencies also in a wonderful lot of vocal works set to powerful English texts, beginning with the King James version of the Bible and continuing through Chaucer, Shakespeare, Milton, and Bunyan to Coleridge, Shelley, Tennyson, Hardy, Housman, Meredith and Walt Whitman. The most typical are *The Lark Ascending,* a romance for violin and orchestra (1914), and *On Wenlock Edge,* for tenor, string quartet, and piano, set to the lines of A. E. Housman, as pure an evocation of national spirit as has ever been put on paper. Vaughan Williams did not hesitate to enter the highly competitive fields of film and church music, and contributed significant compositions to each—works which might serve as models for lesser composers who turn out these types of music by the yard.

The love of good tunes is evident in everything this composer wrote. His most natural way of expressing himself was in non-chromatic, largely modal harmonies and smoothly flowing counterpoint. He had little sympathy with many of the advanced technical developments of his time. There are certainly some novel, and often terribly dissonant, tonal combinations in his later works, but they are always achieved by the natural movement of the individual parts and not inserted merely for effect. He would often indulge in musical sonorities, especially in his later works; yet the exercise of any technical process for its own sake, in the manner of the twelve-tone writers, was anathema to him. This, together with the usual posthumous neglect of all creative artists by the generation immediately following and the present-day tendency to remove all humanistic associations from art, has led to an unfavorable reaction against Vaughan Williams on the part of up-to-date listeners. Their judgment is that he, like Sibelius, is old-fashioned. Yet it is impossible to think that music so much of a piece of life as that in the best of Vaughan Williams's symphonies will not prove a permanent passport to fame.

BENJAMIN BRITTEN

The nationalism of Benjamin Britten (*b.* 1913) is of a much subtler character than the brusque heartiness and modal charm of Vaughan Williams. Britten's nationalism is the result of atmosphere rather than feeling; it takes shape from the rhythms and inflections of sophisticated English prosody rather than from the folk rhythms and dances or antiquated styles of the past; it has a fashionable facade of nervous brilliance rather than the straight-forward thrust of emotional expression. If its dramatic effectiveness often strikes the listener as contrived and clever, it is nevertheless skillfully achieved through means that are most impressive. In short, this Englishman is apt to suggest the recherché and ingenious rather than the poetically rooted consciousness that is common to most English artists. Still, Britten is the only contemporary composer whom his countrymen, even those who think modern music difficult, do not hesitate to call the oustanding composer of the mid-twentieth century, and they are proud to claim his 1962 *War Requiem* the Western world's twentieth-century masterpiece.

Britten was a precocious Suffolk boy who graduated from the Royal College of Music when he was twenty-one and came to the United States in 1939, feeling that he might find conditions more conducive to the development of his talent. While here he wrote a number of works, including the tart *Violin Concerto* (1940) and orchestral *Sinfonia da Requiem* (1941). In 1942 he returned to England and wrote an opera commissioned by Koussevitzky for performance at the Berkshire Festival. This work, entitled *Peter Grimes*, was produced in 1945 and brought Britten world fame. The chamber operas which followed, *The Rape of Lucretia* (1946), a classically derived work, and *Albert Herring* (1947), an English genre piece, did not fulfill the promise of deepening characterization inherent in *Grimes*. *Billy Budd* (1951), based on the Melville story, was more successful, but *Gloriana,* composed for the coronation of Queen Elizabeth II, did not turn out very well. *The Turn of the Screw* (1954), its libretto drawn from a Henry James story, suffered from a non-operatic text, and Britten did not seem able to maintain the suspense essential to its dramatic development. *The Little Sweep* or *Let's Make an Opera* (1948) and *Noye's Fludde* (1958) were written in the Hindemithian sense of *gebrauchmusik.* The big-scaled *Midsummer Night's Dream* (1960) seems contrived and affected in comparison with its gossamer-like Shakesperian prototype.

Some of Britten's best works outside the opera include the early *Ceremony of Carols* (1942) for treble voices and harp; the *Serenade* for tenor solo, horn, and string orchestra, set to varied English poems and a fine example of this composer's ability to shape his music to the especial nature of English lyrics; the ubiquitous *Young Person's Guide to the Orchestra,* a series of variations on a theme of Purcell; the *Cello Symphony* of 1961, a monumentally constructed work which shows Britten's mastery of abstract formal construction, as well as the dark and dour side of his imagination; and the *War Requiem,* written for the re-consecration of Coventry Cathedral in 1962.

This last work constitutes a sort of summary of Britten's achievements and unites a series of bitter, agonized, anti-war poems by Wilfred Owen, a young British poet killed in World War I, with the liturgical serenity of the Latin Mass for the Dead. The interplay and conflict between these two texts provides the motive power of the music, which calls for a full orchestra, a chamber orchestra, a mixed choir, a boy's choir, and three vocal soloists. In spite of Britten's virtuosic treatment of the vocal and instrumental parts, the essential message of this enormous work—the pity and futility of war—seems to be more impressively conveyed by its literary than by its musical components. Britten's eclectic style, while clear and distinct, simply does not match the power and intensity of the words.

In 1963 Britten was invited to compose a work commemorating the hundredth anniversary of the founding of the International Red Cross; the result was the *Cantata Misericordium,* a setting of the parable of the Good Samaritan, with Latin text for tenor and baritone, chorus, and small orchestra. This cantata, like the *War Requiem,* exemplifies the theme of compassion for persons overcome by forces beyond their power which runs through many of Britten's works.[14] Unfortunately, like the *War Requiem,* it points up the strange lack of communicative power that can be felt in much of his music. Essentially a classical-minded composer devoted to the development of control, Britten is a superb workman, a resourceful orchestrator, and a natural lyricist. But in the process of sublimating the raw materials of his imagination into the polished products of art, something seems to lessen the impact of the music. Perhaps it is a limitation of emotional powers—he can express compassion, but seems unable to communicate overwhelming passion; perhaps it is over-preciosity. Whatever it is, it precludes the universal appeal which works of this kind must have if they are to join the ranks of great masterpieces.

The New Romantics

Our goal is an iridescent music which will delight the aural senses with delicate, voluptuous pleasure and at the same time express noble sentiments.

Messiaen

We have seen that revolt against nineteenth-century Romanticism was one of the most important sources of the striking change which characterized the music

---

[14] Other examples are *Peter Grimes, Billy Budd,* and *The Turn of the Screw.*

of the twentieth century. The passing of time naturally brought a lessening of the necessity for music which had to show, above all else, determination to break with the past. A series of world-shaking political and economic upheavals which cried out for intense emotional expression brought an inevitable reaction against the unnecessary absolutism of neo-Classical doctrine, together with the re-realization that the Romantic attitude toward art is essential to its very existence.

So there began another shift in the Apollonian-Dionysian (Classical-Romantic) pattern characteristic of the development of artistic styles throughout all history. Although it revived interest in program music with poetic or dramatic content, re-emphasized the need for listenable melody, and re-affirmed the pre-eminence of emotional expression as a necessary requisite of music, it also added a new poignancy to the Romantic type of expression by absorbing some of the technical innovations developed during the preceding quarter of a century. The classical trends of the twenties had deflated some of the overpowering *panache* of the earlier style, as well as improving on the technical facilities of the nineteenth-century composers. The emotional content of the New Romanticism was thus more tersely conveyed; and new technical devices were used, though they were never allowed to overshadow the excitation of feeling. In short, the New Romanticism, while using the past, adapted itself to the present. Some of the composers who had made their reputation as intransigents reflected the trend toward a new romanticism in some of their later works, notably Bartók in his *Concerto for Orchestra* (1944), Hindemith in his *Symphonic Metamorphosis on Themes by Weber* (1944) and Prokofiev in his last two symphonies, written in 1949 and 1955. But there was also a whole group of new Romantics, with a wide variety of temperaments.

BRITISH EXAMPLES

A number of British contemporaries belong in this group. Among the more conventional was Arthur Benjamin (1895–1960), a pupil of Stanford and the writer of several significant stage works, notably the operas *A Tale of Two Cities* (1950), a warmly successful treatment of Dickens's novel, and *Tartuffe,* a mildly dissonant embodiment of Molière's scintillating play. The latter was left unfinished and was completed from his sketches for its premiere performance in 1964.

Edmund Rubbra (*b.* 1901) let his interest in Oriental philosophy color his Romanticism, and his style often borders on polytonality.

The most important figure among the English New Romantics is

William Walton (*b.* 1902). Although he started his career as a smart anti-Romantic, Walton developed into an unashamed and outspoken exponent of this style. Basing his composition firmly on old foundations and using modern devices with direction and restraint, he has written works of real quality, as well as more facile music for films. His satirical *Façade,* based on the surrealistic poems of Edith Sitwell, created something of a furor in London when first produced in 1923. But it is much more than a youthful *jeu d'esprit;* in it Walton showed himself a composer of perception and sensitivity, able to convey the delicate shades of meaning in the poet's symbolism. A *Viola Concerto* (1929), two *Symphonies* (1935 and 1960), a *Violin Concerto* (1939), and a brilliant and effective oratorio, *Belshazzar's Feast* (1931), based on words from the Bible arranged by Osbert Sitwell, are works of stature. The opera *Troilus and Cressida* (1954) is a very successful stage piece in spite of its rather awesome background—much more successful than most Anglo-Saxon attempts at musico-dramatic composition. The 1962 *Variations on a Theme of Hindemith* was written as a mark of respect and assumes at times a stylistic character very suggestive of Walton's great contemporary.

British to the core, Walton's way of writing is nevertheless thoroughly Romantic, with warm expressive lyricism, deep, uninhibited sentiment, and rich orchestral texture. His music has a strong sense of tonality in spite of its modern harmonic structure. Its rhythmic patterns, derived from his early fascination with Stravinsky and with jazz, are strikingly powerful, and lend motility. He was knighted in 1951 in recognition of the immense popularity of his music with his countrymen.

A GERMAN ROMANTICIST

The outstanding German representative of the New Romanticism is Carl Orff (*b.* 1895); the most manifest twentieth-century attribute of his music is its use of rhythm as a vitalizing force. Instead of continuing the elaborate tonal experiments of his contemporaries, Orff has sought to revive the old single-voice-with-accompaniment style, adapting it to modern tastes by adding dissonant counterpoint, lively rhythmic patterns, and a carefully adjusted union of melody and speech. Early in his career he became interested in progressive educational methods and helped found a music school in Munich, where he has spent most of his life, to promote rhythmic education. To promulgate this new educational method, he published a set of exercises, *Schulwerk* (1930–33), which has influenced music education. Concern with simple melodies and rhythmic patterns has led Orff to avoid intellectual pretensions and to write in a straight-forward, completely tonal style, vitalized by fascinating rhythms and spiced with clashing polyphony. His music is easily accessible and very interesting to the average listener.

Believing in the theatre as a means of education, Orff has written a number of lyric dramas which make use of medieval materials—fairy tales and legends—for their librettos. His musical settings give these texts strong support and powerful impact, even though they do not have a striking physiognomy of their own or expand according to the usual musical formulas. His two best-known theatre pieces, *Der Mond* (1938) and *Die Kluge* (1942), are based on Grimm fairy tales. Another, *Die Bernauerin* (1945), is an opera in the style of a dramatic ballad; *Antigone,* set to a German adaptation of the Sophoclean tragedy, is written in a kind of dramatic recitative, with accompiment for four pianos, fifty-nine percussive instruments, double bass, and heavy brass.

The work which made Orff world famous is one of his three song cycles, *Carmina Burana* (1937), a "scenic oratorio" of intriguing charm, set to the old Latin and German words of some thirteenth-century student poems discovered over a century ago in the Bavarian monastery of Benediktbeuren. This has been given with such enormous success that the specific qualities of Orff's two other scenic oratorios, *Catulli Carmina* (1943) and *Trionfo di Afrodite* (1953), have unfortunately been obscured.

OLIVIER MESSIAEN

The leading French exponents of twentieth-century Romanticism show quite different qualities. Olivier Messiaen (*b.* 1908) was a member of the so-called *Jeune France* group[15] which followed *Les Six* in Paris. In 1946 these young Frenchmen issued a manifesto in *Le Revue Musicale,* France's most respected musical magazine, which stated plainly that their movement aimed at re-integrating music as "humanism reborn" and added that "to exclude emotion is to drain the very essence of music." Messiaen was the leading figure in documenting the truth of this statement and so became the leader of the New Romanticism in Paris, the very citadel of neo-Classicism.

Like all good French musicians, Messiaen studied at the Paris Con-

[15] The other members were André Jolivet (*b.* 1905), Yves Baydrier (*b.* 1908), and Daniel Lesur (*b.* 1908).

servatoire and, like many of them, on graduation became an organist in one of the fashionable churches of Paris. After a rather harrowing war experience, which included internment in a Silesian prison camp in 1942, he was appointed professor of harmony at the Conservatoire, where he had as pupils some of the best men of the next generation, including Jean Barraqué, Karlheinz Stockhausen, and Pierre Boulez. Messiaen's first major work was a set of four organ meditations, *l'Ascension* (1933), reflecting his deep desire to express Christian mysticism through music. His next work, *La Nativité du Seigneur* (1935), continued his predilection for program music of a religious-descriptive nature, a predilection which resulted in a number of other extended organ compositions. His principal orchestral work is the grandiose *Turangalila Symphony* (1948) in ten movements and strongly influenced by Messiaen's Oriental leanings. It shows his mystical sense, his love of nature (which includes a study of the songs of birds), his attempts to imitate the rhythms of Hindu music, and especially his vivid, exotic sense of orchestral color, which leads him to employ all sorts of unusual orchestral combinations and new orchestral instruments.

For those accustomed to the older types of Romanticism, Messiaen's music is a monstrous mélange. While it most certainly stands at the opposite pole from neo-Classicism, its wide range of resources, tonal ambiguity and polytonality, constantly shifting rhythmic subtleties, and exotic new sonorities make it difficult for many listeners, especially those who are not in full sympathy with the composer's expressed desire to "open a few new doors and pluck off a few, still distant, stars." It may well be that Messiaen's importance as a twentieth-century figure will lie in his activities as a teacher rather than as a composer, for it was his revelation of the possibility of employing rhythmic structures that are independent of sonorous structure that is considered, by French critics at least, to be the source of the totally serialized music that was developed by the next generation.

OTHER EUROPEAN ROMANTICS OF THE TWENTIETH CENTURY

In Paris the neo-Romantic movement of the second quarter of the century was carried on by a number of other composers, none of them strong enough to turn back the onslaught of the twelve-tone style engineered there around the middle of the century by René Leibowitz. All the French composers of the postwar period wrote pleasantly and fluently, but with little to say that was important or original. Jolivet was a typical *amuseur,* interested in new ideas in painting, playwriting, and literature before he turned his attention professionally to music. While he did not hesitate to use all the advanced techniques of the time, he insisted on the need for expressive lyricism in music. As musical director of the Comédie Française, he wrote much for the theatre, including a comic opera, *Dolores* (1942), and several ballets and "radiophonic legends." Baudrier and Lesur advanced the neo-Romantic cause in an influential article which they wrote in 1946, "Towards a New Romanticism." They composed orchestral works of a programmatic nature, as well as organ and chamber works.

Henry Barraud (*b.* 1900), a composer of somewhat more conservative tendencies, has been an important figure because of his position as director of the official French radio network Radiodiffusions Française. Henri Sauguet (*b.* 1901) has written a number of theatre and film scores which, like the music of his friend and associate, employ a seemingly simple style for the expression of sophisticated ideas. The romantic element is strong in his works for the theatre, of which the opera *La Chartreuse de Parme* (1939) is best known. Maurice Duruflé (*b.* 1902), a pupil of several well-known French organists, has written much church music, including a much-used *Requiem* illustrative of his aversion to tonality set up on any absolute system. Henri Dutilleux (*b.* 1916) has incorporated some Impressionistic techniques into his very personal style, as is clearly evident in his *First Symphony* (1951). In his *Second Symphony* (1959), he assimilated into his natural atonal idiom a flavor of jazz. Jean Michel Damara (*b.* 1928) has written several ballets and some orchestral and chamber music which avoids serialism in its attempt to be new and different.

Scattered through the other European countries are a number of characteristic Romantic composers whose creative careers embraced the second quarter of the century. In Italy the leading men are Ildebrando Pizzetti (*b.* 1880) and his pupil Mario Castelnuovo-Tedesco (*b.* 1895). A native of Parma, Pizzetti became well known for his operas, many of them counterparts (astringent, chromatic harmonies, and all) of the mediaeval mystery plays. In this country his best known work is an opera based on T. S. Éliot's *Murder in the Cathedral,* which received its first performance at La Scala in 1958. Pizzetti also wrote a quantity of choral, orchestral, and chamber music. He was appointed professor of composition at the Santa Cecilia Academy in Rome, and served as its director from 1948 to 1951.

Because of his religious background, Castelnuovo-Tedesco was obliged to flee from Mussolini's Italy in 1939 and came to the United

States, where he became active as a film composer. He also wrote fluent and agreeable chamber and choral music, including a number of songs for the lyrics from Shakespeare's plays.

An Austrian neo-Romantic composer of international repute during the second and third decades of the century was Franz Schreker (1878–1934). From the time of the production of his first full-length opera, *Der ferne Klang,* in 1912 until his death a year after the Nazis forced him to resign his teaching post in Berlin, six of his eight operas were performed all over central Europe, and Schreker was considered the great hope of German-language opera. But because of the change of direction away from his typical Romantic-Impressionistic style, his operas have suffered almost complete eclipse.

Other Austrian Romantics of this period include Ernest Toch (1887–1964) and Paul Pisk (*b.* 1893), both of whom emigrated to the United States in 1935–36 after considerable creative activity in Austria and Germany. Toch was a full-blooded Romantic who worked in a basically tonal idiom cleverly adapted to modern tastes. He had considerable influence on the writing of a better type of film music than that which had been turned out by Hollywood, though he by no means confined his efforts to this métier. After coming to this country he composed four symphonies, as well as some chamber music and piano pieces. Typical are his *Pinocchio, A Merry Overture* (1936), and *Third Symphony* (1955).

Pisk, a pupil of Schoenberg and Adler in Vienna, is known here as a musicologist and teacher rather than as a composer, although his music was frequently heard in Europe between the wars. His divided loyalties have enabled him to combine a characteristic Viennese Romanticism with a tendency toward classic formalism.

Aside from Carl Orff, the most active German neo-Romantic is his pupil Warner Egk (*b.* 1901). A genial Bavarian like his teacher, Egk has written in a non-complicated, colorful, strongly melodic, and largely tonal style. Such works as his setting of Ibsen's *Peer Gynt* (1938) and Gogol's witty comedy *The Inspector General* have become very popular in central Europe.

Other Twelve-Tone Composers

Structure—one of the key words of our era.

Boulez

SOME HISTORY

In 1939 it seemed that the Schoenberg movement had ceased to exist. Berg was dead, years before his time. Webern's small voice, never very strong, had fallen silent. And Schoenberg himself was teaching in California and writing no music. "I have not composed for the past ten years," he wrote in a letter to a friend, giving as the reason "unbearable depression." It was, strangely enough, in Paris that the twelve-tone current was re-introduced into the bloodstream of European musical life to become again the fashionable composing technique of the younger generation.

By the end of World War II the musical situation in Paris had lost all the brilliance gained at the time of *Les Six*. The music of Schoenberg and his followers had been banned in Nazi-occupied Paris. Once the city was cleared of the Germans and order restored, however, an effort was made, as we have seen, by the *Jeune France* group to establish a new type of Romanticism. At that time, though Milhaud and Poulenc had gone to Vienna to learn about the twelve-tone style of Schoenberg and Berg, the music of these composers was hardly known in Paris. The music now popular with Parisian audiences was that of Prokofiev, Hindemith, and Stravinsky. Suddenly, in the very year the occupation forces left the city, there came another "Austro-Boche" (the term is Debussy's) invasion, this time a cultural one, in the form of dodecaphonic music introduced by young composers having their first fling in the musical world.

The invasion centered around René Leibowitz (*b.* 1913), a nationalized Pole whose family had settled in Paris and who had spent three years in Berlin and Vienna studying the techniques of Schoenberg and Berg. Leibowitz published two rather explosive books, *Schoenberg et son ecole* in 1947, and *Introduction à la musique de douze sons* in 1949. These had a powerful influence on the young composers of the day who had become impatient with the music of the *Jeune France* group. A number of these young men who had been students of Messiaen at the Conservatoire became involved with the processes of twelve-tone composition after study or contact with Leibowitz. Combining the style and aesthetics of dodecaphonism with ideas regarding *inquiétude rythmique* received from Messiaen, these younger composers initiated an entirely new type of serial composition.

PIERRE BOULEZ

The leader was a brash, aggressive young intellectual, Pierre Boulez, born in the Loire district of France in 1925. Like several other composers of his generation, he had studied mathematics and science before deciding to take up music professionally. He entered Messiaen's Conservatoire class in 1944, at the same time studying counterpoint with the wife of Honegger and, later, twelve-tone composition with Leibowitz. On taking up the serial technique, Boulez turned against Messiaen, publicly accusing him of writing "bordello music." Nevertheless, it on his master's concept of music as a form of intellectual exercise that Boulez based his aesthetics. In 1946 he became music director of the newly formed theatrical group of Barrault-Renaud, a post which gave him opportunity to develop his practical techniques and to devote more time to composition.

Although all his early works were twelve-tone scores, Boulez soon realized, as he said, that there were other things in serial music than the mechanical manipulations taught him by Leibowitz. In his *Second Piano Sonata* (1947–48) he developed a series of experiments with the object not only of expanding the ideas of Webern but, indeed, of founding a new musical language by extending the serial organization of the tonerow to all the other components of music, thus serializing rhythm, tone color, and dynamics, as well as pitch. His aim may be described as an attempt to produce a serial kind of music so basically different from tonal music as defined by the works of the past that it could not be considered the same art. Although it can hardly be called a repertoire piece, this sonata started the trend among younger composers toward total serialism.

Boulez became a fashionable avant-garde composer during the 1960's, more talked about than played because of the massive complexity of his music for performers as well as listeners. His admirers claim that he stands as the culminating figure in a line that starts with Bach and descends through Beethoven and Debussy. In all his works that have become accessible to concert audiences—this *Second Piano*

Sonata, Le Marteau sans maître (1955), and the long-incompleted *Doubles,* started in 1958—the same general characteristics are recognizable: driving motility; short, ejaculatory utterances whose speed and rhythmic diversity make them difficult to grasp; sudden outbursts of violence followed by periods of silence; flashing sparks of sound patterns alternating with harsh, almost unbearable percussive effects.

This attempted synthesis of all the creative currents since the end of the nineteenth century, as Boulez describes his style, is more easily appreciated in the kaleidoscopically colored *Le Marteau* than in the severely monochromatic *Second Sonata.* Indeed, in spite of its formidable, densely organized structure, *Le Marteau,* a suite of nine movements based on three short, rambling poems set for contralto, interspersed with sounds produced on six instruments (including a gamelan-like percussion group), is rather beguiling in its succession of unusual sounds. But the sonata, with special ways of hitting the piano specified by the composer—the new fore-arm position, the rigid attack—is extremely difficult for most listeners. Its chief interest lies in the exciting-looking score and the virtuosity necessary for its performance. To the unassisted ear, the music never emerges in any purposeful shape, and the final impression is curiously negative and confused.

Originally conceived as a four-minute piece, then expanded to a work twice as long, and finally made the center of a larger three-part form, *Doubles* is a good example of Boulez's "work-in-progress" method of conceiving the shape and form of a work as he writes it. Perhaps because he is a practical musician and extremely effective conductor as well as composer, Boulez is aware of the tremendous problems which have to be solved by all advanced composers.

Obviously it is impossible to evaluate music such as this until the idiom becomes less obscure; and any evaluation is going to be difficult for those superfluous listeners (the term is Boulez's own) who cannot feel the necessity of a new twelve-tone serialized language or for its use in everything a composer writes. For this is exactly the implication of Boulez's style. His apologists think of his music not, as most listeners do, as a sort of sonorous mathematics, but as the most powerful kind of expression possible—"a cry from the depths, the unanimous protest of an age against the overwhelming cruelty of our condition."[16] They feel that, in writing it, Boulez is transposing into music the terrible disorder of the world today. On the other hand, there are those, like Jacques Chailley, professor of Music History at the Sorbonne, who feel that Boulez is completely out of touch not only with the public, but with

---

[16] Quoted from Antoine Goleá, author of *Vingt ans de musique contemporaine.*

his art. M. Chailley amusingly shows[17] how a Boulez work actually in existence might have been composed simply by juggling numbers without any reference to the ear.

LUIGI DALLAPICCOLA

Some twentieth-century composers have been strongly influenced by the Schoenberg-Webern doctrines without trying to alter them as drastically as did Boulez. One of these is the Italian Luigi Dallapiccola (*b.* 1904) who, born in a small northern town, came early into touch with the Austro-German musical traditions and literature, a fact important for his later development. After studies at the Florence Conservatory (where he was later to serve as professor), he studied the music of Berg and Webern, and used their methods in his compositions. But Dallapiccola's career covers over three decades and evidences a wide range of styles; there are many influences detectable in his works, among them the clarity and economy of Italian Renaissance polyphony and the long, lyric lines of Italian opera.

Dallapiccola's output has been conditioned largely by vocal concepts, even when he is writing for instruments. This is clearly shown in such a pre-twelve-tone piece as his 1939 *Canti di prigionia,* a set of songs based on texts by famous prisoners and expressive of the composer's turbulent feelings about events just preceding World War II. It also comes out in the series of instrumental moods and images making up the fourteen-minute *Varazioni per Orchestra,* written in 1954. Dallapiccola showed that the twelve-tone technique can be used with dramatic effect in opera in his 1948 *Il prigionere,* as well as in his *Job,* produced in Rome in 1950. His 1964 *Parole di San Paolo,* set to St. Paul's famous eulogy of charity, shows his unusual ability to couple words and notes, as well as his characteristic alteration of the tonerow to achieve washes of tone color. Although Dallapiccola has written some of the most accessible twelve-tone music, it is little known to the average listener, perhaps because the composer has not been able fully to express his belief that "man, with his joys and sorrows, still stands for something."

SWISS DODECAPHONISTS

The leading Swiss composer, Frank Martin, born in Geneva in 1890, has said that although Schoenberg (together with German and French Traditionalists and Impressionalists) has influenced his style, he is

[17] In his book *40,000 Years of Music,* New York: Farrar, Straus and Giroux, 1965.

opposed to the revolutionary doctrine of atonality, since it represents complete tonal anarchy. "Abstract art is an art without a future—and for me, without a present,"[18] he has said; yet all his works between 1932 and 1937 were in strict twelve-tone style. This paradox was later resolved through his development of a musical language using tonerows in conjunction with major and minor triads and restoring some of the traditional harmonic functions to the older styles. This attempt to reconcile dodecaphonic and traditional practices was Martin's real contribution to contemporary style; it influenced a number of other composers and helped strengthen the impact of twelve-tone music.

Yet it resulted in a rather Esperanto-like musical language that does not have any striking characteristics. Martin's best works are a dramatic oratorio in post-Romantic style, *Le Vin herbé* (1942); *Six Monologues* from the Hofmannsthal morality play *Jedermann* (1943); a *Petite Symphonie Concertante* (1945); and an opera, *Der Sturm,* after Shakespeare's *The Tempest* (1955), filled with Romantic and Impressionistic references.

Another Swiss composer of considerable international repute is Wladimir Vogel (born in Russia in 1896), whose adaptation of the Schoenbergian technique is similar to that of Martin. Vogel has become known for experimentation with speech-melodies based on Schoenberg's handling of the *sprechtstimme;* his most ambitious work, *Worte,* employs two declamatory solo voices against a string orchestra and uses twelve-tone techniques.

Two other Swiss composers have attracted attention through their works for the musical stage: Heinrich Sutermeister (*b.* 1910) and Rolf Liebermann (*b.* 1910). Both feel that the opera should fill a fundamental social need, using means radically different from those employed earlier, and stunning and shocking if necessary. Liebermann is best known in this country, however, for his *Concerto for Jazz Band and Symphony Orchestra,* first played at that mecca for devotees of the more advanced modernism in music, the Donaueschingen Festival, in 1954. It is based on a twelve-tone row and attempts, not very successfully, to bridge the gap between contemporary techniques in "straight" music and the improvisatory style of jazz.

DIVERSE FIGURES

Another distinguished Italian composer, Goffredo Petrassi (*b.* 1904), has been aptly described as an off-and-on dodecaphonist. His early in-

---

[18] This and similar quotations from various contemporary composers are from a French radio *enquete,* an enquiry on modern music conducted by Radiodiffusion Française in 1955.

fluences, Casella and Hindemith, gave his music a solid neo-Classical foundation. Petrassi has written a number of religiously inspired choral works, the best known of which, the *Coro di Morti* (1941), employs various contemporary styles—tonal, polytonal, and atonal. In his orchestral works, particularly the five piano concertos, he has employed twelve-tone procedures, following Dallapiccola's manner of utilizing them for his own Italianate ends and discarding them when not needed.

Like the other members of the Viennese circle of dodecaphonists, the Austrian-born Ernst Krenek (*b.* 1900) came to the style in his thirties, after having meandered through all the styles, as he described it. Starting with post-Romanticism, he turned to neo-Classicism for some of his earlier chamber music works, including four *String Quartets* (1921–24) and a *Symphony for Wind Instruments and Percussion* (1925). A later phase embraced what he called the "aggressive idiom of atonality and its organizing agency of rhythmic force." Combining this with jazz elements, he composed his most popular work, the opera *Jonny spielt auf,* a sensation when it was first produced in Leipzig in 1927, as well as at the Metropolitan in New York in 1929. Then came a neo-Romantic phase and finally, in 1933, the adoption and consistent use of the twelve-tone system.

His first important work in this style was the opera *Karl V,* commissioned by the Vienna Opera; its premiere performance was prevented by the Nazis and first performed in Prague in 1938, the year Krenek emigrated to the United States. He has taught and lectured in a number of universities in this country and has composed a great deal of music, all of it employing the century's advanced techniques and far away from the brassy insouciance of *Jonny.* Krenek's career is something of an epitome of the creative phases of twentieth-century music. Perhaps, in the autobiography which he is said to have deposited with the Library of Congress not to be opened until fifteen years after his death, he tells what he really thinks of the various phases of twentieth-century music as they were mirrored in his career.

An almost exact contemporary of Krenek is Stefan Volpe, born in Berlin in 1902 and also a resident of the United States during his later creative years. Although many of his compositional attitudes were developed early, in association with the Expressionist painter Klee and Kandinsky, he did study composition with Schrecker and Webern in Vienna. Most of his major works were composed in Jerusalem, where he lived four years, teaching in the conservatory there before coming to this country in 1938.

The work for which he became known here was his *First Symphony,* written in 1955–56 and given its first performance (at least as much of it as could be prepared for the occasion) in New York in 1964. Tremendously complicated and densely organized, the entire work was derived from the twelve notes of an initial tonerow, the structural field of whose pitches was analogous, according to the composer, to those of physical bodies in a force field. Whatever effect it had seemed the result of an enormous apparatus designed to create a kind of intellectual tour de force and to make it bigger than any other serial work yet written. For most listeners it did not differ greatly in character from other post-Webern works except, perhaps, to be more incomprehensible.

Another German composer who has mixed the serial style with more traditional ways of writing is Wolfgang Fortner, born at Leipzig in 1907 and professor at Heidelberg, Dortmund, and Freiburg-am-Breisgau. Fortner has kept the tonal fabric of his music clearly apparent, though his Reger-like contrapuntal textures often seem ill at ease in the twelve-tone fabric.

A Spanish-born dodecaphonist who has tempered his loyalties to that system with the use of partial tonerows, polytonal passages, and even frankly tonal chords is Roberto Gerhard (*b.* 1896). After studying with the great Spanish pedagogue of the time, Pedrell, as well as with Schoenberg in Vienna, Gerhard settled in England, where he has been busy with works which combine the style of his Spanish antecedents with serial techniques. His 1950 *Violin Concerto* is his most attractive work.

Another foreign-born composer of this era who did most of his work in England was Mátyás Seiber (1905–1960), born in Budapest and a pupil there of Kodály until he left for London in 1935. He composed works of every kind, the earlier strongly permeated with Hungarian flavor: an opera, several operettas, chamber music, jazz treated in a folk-song style, and even a book on jazz percussion playing. His best-known work is the cantata after Joyce, *Ulysses,* premiered in London in 1949.

Andreas Mihály (*b.* 1917) is another pupil of Kodály who has gradually veered toward the post-Webern school, as have György Kurtág (*b.* 1926) and András Szöllösy (*b.* 1921). In fact, as contact with the outside world became more possible after 1956, the younger Hungarians have become more and more taken with the new music and proficient in its techniques.

POLISH DEVELOPMENTS

But the iron-curtain country that has shown the warmest hospitality to contemporary music is Poland. As in other countries under Soviet domination, the trends toward modernism in Poland began with music of a strongly nationalistic character, written in accordance with the official commandment: music must always be somehow connected with folklore. Then followed a gradual infiltration of neo-Classical ideals, beginning about 1926 and culminating in the works produced at festivals of modern music held in 1956 and 1958. About this time contact with the chief centers of advanced music in the West was resumed. With the election of Gomulka as leader of the Communist party there came much greater freedom in cultural developments. Musical scores and recordings came into the country and the younger composers were stimulated to follow the new Western experiments in sound structure and organization of musical material.

The music of the most eminent of the postwar Polish composers, Witold Lutoslawski (*b.* 1913), illustrates how the new technical devices were gradually absorbed into a personal style. Lutoslawski's *Concerto for Orchestra* (1954) was based on folk motives as raw material; his 1958 *Funeral Music,* dedicated to the memory of Bartók, while intensely emotional, was based on a tonerow which gives the suggestion of a basic series altered each time it appears; while his later works, *Jeux vénitiens* (1961) and *Trois Poèmes d'Henri Michaux* (1963), boldly explore all the possibilities of the new techniques. Other Polish composers who have adapted the tonerow procedures for their own purposes are Kazimierz Serocki (*b.* 1922), Tadeusz Baird (*b.* 1928), and Wlodzimierz Kotonski (*b.* 1925).

ENGLISH SERIALISTS

The two best-known native-born English serialists are Elizabeth Lutyens (*b.* 1906) and Humphrey Searle (*b.* 1915). The former adopted a personalized dodecaphonic technique in 1935 and is said to have destroyed all her earlier works written in Romantic and atonal idioms. A number of her compositions were performed at the International Society for Contemporary Music, which was founded in 1922 to further works such as those of Luytens. Searle, a private pupil of Webern in Vienna, is an Expressionist in the same sense as Schoenberg, Berg, and Webern; but he has attempted to modify his twelve-tone procedures with purely English patterns and styles. In addition to a *Symphony* (1952) and several settings of Edith Sitwell's poems for speakers, men's chorus, and orchestra, Searle has attempted to make an opera out of one of the theatre-of-the-absurd plays of Ionesco, *Tueur sans gages,* under the English title *The Colonel's Photo.* It was given its first performance at Frankfurt in 1964.

Brought to the fore by the vogue for new music which existed in London around 1960 (a vogue which did not last), a group of younger English serialists emerged as significant figures in the musical life of their country. This group includes, according to Andrew Porter,[19] Alexander Goehr (*b.* 1932), Peter Maxwell Davies (*b.* 1934), and Harrison Birtwistle (*b.* 1934), constituting the "Manchester Group"; Rodney Bennett (*b.* 1936) and Nicholas Maw (*b.* 1936), members of a Royal Academy group; Thea Musgrave (*b.* 1928), a Scottish composer; and Australian-born Malcolm Williamson (*b.* 1931). All these composers seem to have kept in touch with contemporary European developments, assimilating those they have found useful (including serialism) and discarding those whom they do not like (including total serialization, aleatory techniques, and electronic developments).

HANS WERNER HENZE

Hans Werner Henze, born in Gütersloh, Germany, in 1926, has rapidly become the most performed and highly regarded German composer since World War II. Thoroughly trained theoretically (in the *Staatsmusikschule* in Braunschweig and the *Kirkenmusikalisches Institut* in Heidelberg, and as a pupil of Fortner and Leibowitz) and practically (as theatre and ballet director in Konstanz and Weisbaden), since 1953 he has devoted most of his time to composing, living in Italy. He has pursued a quite different path from that taken by his contemporaries who have had as their goal the breakdown of older concepts and a new ordering of tonal materials. Henze has been old-fashioned enough to maintain interest in personal expression. And for this purpose he has developed an individual style which, though based on post-Webern techniques and embracing something of everything that has been going on in Europe, has richness, a sense of scale and proportion, and imaginative intensity.

His rapid rise is attested by the fact that, while the first performance of his opera *König Hirsch* was greeted in 1956 with abuse by the music lovers of the very musical city of Berlin, eight years later his music was being performed with great acclaim in all parts of Germany. In 1961 a very conservative English critic hailed a performance of Henze's cantata *Novae de Infinite Laudes* as an immortal masterpiece and called its

---

[19] Editor of *The Musical Times,* a magazine which, under his leadership, has stoutly championed the cause of contemporary music.

composer the most prodigiously gifted man of his generation. And in 1962 Henze's *Fifth Symphony* was commissioned and performed on the occasion of the opening of Lincoln Center in New York, while his *Third Symphony* was introduced to the American public by the Chicago Orchestra at a special UNESCO concert in 1963.

Although he started his career as a symphonist, completing his *First Symphony* in 1947 for Darmstadt, Henze's fame rests chiefly on his works for the theatre. His first work in this field was a one-act melodrama, *Das Wundertheatre,* after Cervantes, produced in 1949. Then followed *Boulevard Solitude* (1957), which adapted the Manon Lescaut story to modern Paris. His most substantial operatic success so far has been *The Stag King (Il re cervo),* which started as *König Hirsch* in 1956 and was metamorphosed in 1964 into an adult fairy-tale phantasmagoria. Its complex libretto contains elements of almost everything that has developed in the Western theatre for centuries, including Italian *commedia dell'arte* and German nature-worship. Henze has set all this to atmospheric music that ranges in style from soaring, extended arias with eccentric vocal lines through atmospheric atonal tone-painting of great beauty to highly dissonant, "pulverized," powerful expressionism. The result is a mixture of romantic enchantment and sophisticated modernity—a sort of contemporary *Magic Flute.* In 1959 came another opera, *Prinz von Homburg,* and the ballet *Undine,* both popular repertoire pieces in Germany. The 1961 *Elegy for Young Lovers,* composed to an English libretto by W. H. Auden and C. Kallman, the librettists of Stravinsky's *Rake's Progress,* has not achieved the success of Henze's earlier works, partly because of its involved and unsatisfactory libretto. *The Young Lord,* premiered in Berlin in 1963, reverts to tonality, since its composer felt that atonality was unsuitable for such a comic opera—it does not "radiate cheerfulness but rather evokes a sort of undefined anxiety."

Henze's concert scores have attracted considerable attention, especially the *Novae de Infinite Laudes,* a tremendously difficult oratorio based on the cosmological reflections of Giordano Bruno, a sixteenth-century philosopher, and several cantatas written for radio. Henze has also composed concerted works for piano, violin, and cello with orchestra, and chamber-music compositions.

In all this variety of forms, Henze has employed an amazing variety of compositional techniques, using tonality, polytonality, atonality, and serialism with equal ease. Not hesitating to integrate traditional and new materials, Henze makes no concessions. Interspersed between outbursts of sustained harmonies, vivid splotches of orchestral color, and the varied surfaces of his tonal textures are obdurate passages that demand concentrated listening. And the stylistic references in his music are varied: at one moment he suggests the rhythmic devices of Stravinsky, at another the tone colors of Berg or the pointillism of Webern. Yet he always sounds like himself, and his music has such an affirmative quality, such poetic sense of mood, so much dramatic tension and rhythmic excitement that it "works" in the same sense that the music of Richard Strauss does.

Because Henze has been able to appeal widely to the generally intelligent public, we have to look back to the triumphs of Strauss at the turn of the century to find parallel success for a young, advanced composer. So Henze is criticized by the extremists as anachronistic and old-fashioned, but it does not seem to bother him. As late as 1963 he said he was aware of the danger of saying that music can carry a message of human condition—of love, for example, or forgiveness. "But nevertheless I believe it wholeheartedly."

The Avant-Gardists

Avant-garde (F. Vanguard) 1: those who create, produce, or apply new, original, or experimental ideas, designs and techniques in any field, especially in the arts; 2: a group (as of writers or artists) that is unorthodox and untraditional in its approach; 3: sometimes, a group that is extremist, bizarre, or arty and affected.[20]

DEFINITION OF THE TERM   In our account of the development of music in history we have attempted to show (1) that this development through the centuries has involved constantly changing techniques, (2) that such changes have been marked by increasingly complex systems of organization and expression, and (3) that each of the new directions music has taken was headed by certain ad-

---

[20] A definition given—concocted, we suspect—by the music editors of *The New York Herald Tribune* for the heading of their special issue of May 17, 1964: "The Avant-Garde --What It's Doing, Where It's Going."

venturous spirits who, in the words of the quotation above, have produced or applied original or experimental ideas, designs, and techniques in the practice of their particular art.

In this sense J. S. Bach, Haydn, Berlioz, Wagner, and Debussy may all be described as the avant-garde creators of their time. Bach's *The Well-Tempered Clavier* was the first complete realization of a newly worked out system of temperament. Haydn was the first to make the sonata form really work. Berlioz was the first to realize fully the possibilities of using instruments for their particular tone color. A century ago Wagner's music was considered the music of the future. And anyone who has listened to the shimmering sonorities of *L'Après-midi d'un faune* immediately realizes what a new world of color and imagination Debussy opened to his hearers. Obviously, the advance of music (this is also true of the other arts) has been dependent on this kind of avant-gardist, the creative artist who seeks new and untraditional ways of expressing himself.

Avant-garde also has the meaning listed under (3) in the definition —extreme, affected, "arty." Every period of music history has had this kind of avant-garde activity. We do not have to go very far back to find it in Scriabin, with his special color-keyboard, designed to project the changing colors he felt necessary as a background for his symphonic scores, and his "universal art," which was to unite the impressions of the senses with religious experiences. Or in Luigi Russolo (1885–1946), the Italian futurist who divided his orchestra into six groups, which produced noises ranging from explosions to shrieks and groans. Or Alois Hába (see page 604) and his use some forty years ago of intervals smaller than the semi-tone. All of them are gone, and largely forgotten.

But it is doubtful that any period of art history has been so marked by avant-garde *bizarrerie* as were the years of the 1950's and 60's. It is natural, perhaps, in an era of mass culture that all kinds of artistic activity, especially those which produce new and unusual results, should become a sort of status symbol. And painters, musicians, poets, and sculptors who supply these demands find it necessary to change their artistic wares constantly in order to keep themselves in the public eye. So the latest thing one year is likely to be "old hat" the next.

As a result there developed a particular kind of avant-garde artist, who tried to secure admirers, followers, and purchasers through expressing what he called the "living spirit of the time." The writers produced literature that was often incomprehensible. The painters, abetted by their dealers, kept things stirred up with a number of publicity-gaining movements, among them Abstract Expressionism—improvised abstractions of form and color—Pop Art, the assembly and transformation of real-life objects into art—and Op Art, concerned with portraying movement, real or illusory. Those who wrote and directed motion pictures concerned themselves largely with attention-attracting devices such as risqué themes, abstract, unintelligible sequences, subliminal plots, and psychological probings. The composers, who no longer had the destruction of tonality as a novelty (by this time tonality was as extinct as the dodo) sought other avenues of aggressive inventiveness.

This they did in various ways. Like all other contemporary artists, they realized that the world's run of attention was almost entirely on science. So it was natural to turn to modern physical theory for ideas and inspiration. The avant-garde composers began to talk about parameters, formants, acoustical continuity, variants, the continuum, sound atoms, time fields—all terms related to quantum physics.[21] Aware of the advances in electronics and acoustics, many also turned to these special fields for some of their effects. Instruments capable of electronically generating, manipulating, and transforming sound made possible certain compositional and projective procedures never before dreamed of.

This period, which also saw the invention of the computer, provided a suitable environment for the development of a type of abstract, artistic expression that has very little relationship to the kind of art, described by St. John Chrysostom in the fourth century, that can "withdraw our minds from earthly cogitations and lift our spirits up to heaven." Quite the contrary! The particular concern of this type of avant-garde composer has been the development of new ways to produce and manipulate sound—which he considers the principal element of music. And in order to attract attention to their novel ideas, composers such as Stockhausen and Cage have not hesitated to indulge in all sorts of neo-Dadaist pranks, with results that have not enhanced their reputation with most observers of the contemporary scene.

CHARACTERISTICS

Among their new ideas of producing and manipulating sound, the avant-gardists seem to have found the following significant:

(1) *The production and development of electronic music.* Briefly,

[21] The principal means of propagandizing the scientific approach to composing has been a magazine, *Die Reihe*, published in Vienna, in which such composers as the German Stockhausen, the Frenchman Boulez, the Belgian Pousseur, and the Hungarian Ligeti explain their theories, state their formulas, and display their charts. This type of theoretical explanation was described by John Backus, an American professor of physics, as "pure bluff designed to impress the reader," in an article in *Perspectives of New Music*, Fall 1962.

this kind of music may be defined as organized sound evolved for and performed on some sort of electronic device and designed to be sent through speaker systems. It has been made possible by a number of recent inventions by means of which existing sounds or noises can be recorded as well as artificially created by sound-wave generators.[22] Since these sounds can be manipulated, mixed, or arranged in any combination, they provide composers with a completely new set of sonorous materials. These include all sorts of dynamic and rhythmic transpositions, in addition to transformation of pitch and structural patterns, new sound colors, and the opportunity to work directly with their material as a painter can, without a performer. In short, this constitutes a revolution of unparalleled proportions; its value depends in part, as is the case with all revolutions, on the quality of the creative intelligence shaping the materials.

(2) *The use of aleatoric or chance methods in composing.* The concept of chance or aleatoric music came both from an increased awareness on the part of the composer of the role of chance in modern life and from his desire to give the performer a more creative part in the music played. The work generally credited with heralding this idea is Stockhausen's *Piano Piece XI,* written in 1956. The shape and contents of this piece depend on the order in which the pianist chooses to play its nineteen fragments, using any of six different tempos, scales of dynamics, and kinds of touch. The composer's only stipulation is that when one of the fragments has been played three times, the piece is finished. The element of chance offered in this piece was a comparatively modest one, consisting simply of the order in which the player's eyes happened to fall on the different sections of the music. But it obviously implies that any score might be realized in a number of different ways, each of them quite different from the others. As aleatory composing became more fashionable, all sorts of extraneous means were used to determine the order in which the choices were to be made.[23]

(3) *The increased use of percussive effects.* One almost universal practice among avant-garde composers is the use of every possible means of producing percussive effects. The traditional percussive instruments (drums, cymbals, tam-tam, and the like) are not sufficient for their

---

[22] Distinction is made between music which applies these electronic devices to sounds of non-musical origin (*musique concrète,* developed by the French) and that which uses as its raw materials sounds from conventional instruments and the human voice, developed largely in this country. The Germans have used sounds produced by wave-generators rather than non-electronic sources.

[23] The Italian avant-gardist Donatoni calls for the reading of newspaper headlines to determine the "articulation" of his *Quartetto IV* (1965).

purposes, even when used in solo or ensemble groups. Composers like Stockhausen call for added percussive timbres produced electronically, as well as grunts, whistles, claps, bangs, clicks, and the like by the performers to punctuate their particular fusion of instrumental and vocal sounds.

(4) *The enrichment of tone color.* Schoenberg's theories of tone color and its expressive possibilities have been further developed by avant-garde composers, who have taken advantage of all the scientific and electronic advances made in the production of tone color since his time. In addition to the textures produced by electronic means, some interesting color changes, gleaming sonorities, and sparkling textures have been produced by new instruments such as those developed by the Baschet brothers in Paris from 1957 to 1965. Materials for the vibrating, energizing, and amplifying components of these instruments include metal and glass rods, aluminum cones and cylinders, and plastic balloons.

(5) *The insistence that all audible phenomena be used in music— that is, that noise and its antipode, silence, is as essential to music as tone.* According to John Cage, the high-priest of the avant-garde group emphasizing this belief, "composers should no longer be concerned with tonality or atonality, Schoenberg or Stravinsky, or even with consonance and dissonance, but rather with Varèse, who fathered noise into the century's music." Following this dictum, the music of Cage and his followers is made up of a collage of sounds produced by "prepared pianos," scrapings on sheets of glass, recordings of street sounds, and the like. At the opposite extreme, the importance of silence in music is suggested by such means as a cellist sitting slumped over his instrument and, during fifteen minutes of the piece, doing nothing but make an occasional silent pass of his bow above its strings.

(6) *The realization that acoustical space is an essential factor in music making.* Boulez, for example, in *Doubles*, seats the members of the orchestra in an entirely new manner: "when tone-colors follow each other rapidly they should not be delayed because of the obstacle of distance; the ear of our time demands stereophonic listening in its desire for clarity and movement." Electronic music, of course, offers limitless possibilities of producing this desired quality of sound (a desire that has been greatly fostered by techniques used in recording and radio transmission) through the build-up and collision of sound images within certain prescribed acoustical conditions by means of various arrangements of speaker systems.

(7) *The concept of music as theatre.* The use of sound as a sort of

musical theatre has been a particularly congenial concept to mid-century avant-gardists. This theatre finds its dramatic material in its own performances, in the blending and mixing of tones, noises, sights, actions, designs, colors, words, objects, and people. These are all put together in a series of unplaned acts so as to give a feeling of artistic unity. In a way this seems to be a twentieth-century version of Wagner's *Gesamtkunstwerk*, or total art, and is the exact counterpart of the "happening," a type of visual-art assembly popular with avant-garde painters.[24]

A number of avant-garde concepts are sometimes incorporated into a single composition, but usually the composer is satisfied with using only one or two at a time. Much of the experimentation has taken place in Europe, where festivals such as those held at Donaueschingen, Palermo, and Venice have provided opportunities for the performance of the most advanced music. But this country too has produced a number of active avant-garde composers, following its natural inclination to break easily with tradition.

ACTIVE AVANT-GARDISTS

Any summary of the activities of this period would probably list Karlheinz Stockhausen as its most lively and active composer. Born in Attenberg near Cologne, Germany, in 1928, Stockhausen has used a wide variety of styles and has worked in a number of different countries. He started his career as a scientist interested in physics and acoustics, and so it was natural that he should be attracted by the new electronic experiments and the means for projecting sound into specially designed acoustical surroundings. A pupil of Martin in Cologne and Messiaen in Paris, he began his composing career with works for conventional instruments: *Kreuspiel* (1952), *Kontra Punkte* (1953)—strongly influenced by Webern—and *Zeitmasse* (1956), in which he introduced cadenza-like passages giving the performer unusual freedom. This first

---

[24]Perhaps the music-as-theatre concept can be understood through a description of *Originals*, a work of Stockhausen produced in New York in 1964. Instead of surrounding his auditors with sounds, Stockhausen seems to have attempted to secure their participation in what he had to offer through the framework of an improvised drama so absurd that it aroused either enthusiastic approbation because of its novelty or violent disapproval because of its incoherence. The cast of this music theatre included, in addition to musicians, jugglers, acrobats, goldfish, noisy birds, a chimpanzee, hens, assorted dogs, poets, and actors reading lines from Shakespeare and Greek dramatists, boys building things out of wooden blocks and sound engineers fighting each other with antennas from walkie-talkies. The music was provided by a female cellist perched on a balcony rail and playing Bach, groups of saxophone players and percussion thumpers, a pianist playing an instrument stuffed with flowers, and a tape recorder.

notion of controlled chance was further developed, as we have seen, in *Piano Piece XI,* of the same year.[25] In *Gruppen* (1955–57) this energetic innovator showed his interest in the spatial dimensions of music; it was written for three orchestras, each of them controlled by an independent conductor, placed so as to surround the audience. The orchestras play in different tempos, occasionally meeting in common rhythm, sometimes echoing and answering each other, and so forth.

Like other disciples of Webern, Stockhausen has expanded the master's serial procedures to all the elements of composition—rhythm, timbre, dynamics, and densities, as well as pitch. He has composed a number of works employing voices with electronic and instrumental music, notably *Gesang der Jünglinge* in 1956 and *Momente* in 1962. In the latter, as we have said, he tried to improve the fusion of instrumental sounds and enlarge his percussion group by including clinks, claps, and the like, furnished by the chorus. Moreover, this is a composition written so as to be able to integrate any new version of order or relations of existing materials desired by the conductor.

Like many of his confreres in all the arts, Stockhausen has written and lectured vigorously and extensively in support of his attempts to solve the musical problems of his time. Endowed with a keen mind, a vivid imagination, and a desire to "embrace, re-order and transform the entire realm of all experience," he is certainly one of the most exciting and provocative figures among the postwar composers.

Another active German composer of this school is Giselher Klebe (*b.* 1925), who, like Stockhausen, has employed a wide variety of modernistic techniques but has tried to fuse them into a style of his own. His long list of compositions, few of them known outside his native land, includes works that are classically conceived, dodecaphonic pieces strongly influenced by Schoenberg and Webern, and highly experimental essays in color and rhythm. He has written a number of operas, the best known being *The Robbers, Alkmene, Figaro Gets Divorced,* and *Jacobowski and the Colonel.*

Italy has been particularly prolific in producing avant-gardists, divided largely into three groups working in Rome, Florence, and Milan, each possessing, in characteristic Italian fashion, its own ideological viewpoint. In Rome there developed a sense of freedom among the younger men, each of whom tried to follow his own inclination rather than trail along after a fashionable theory. Their works are serial, pointillistic, jazz-inspired—whatever style has appealed to the various mem-

---

[25] At this piece's first performance in New York in 1957, David Tudor played two entirely different versions on the same program.

bers: Fermio Sifonia, Boris Porena, Domenico Guaccero, and Aldo Clementi. In Florence the influence of the veteran twelve-tone composer Dallapiccola has been very strong: the first internationally performed composer since Respighi, Dallapiccola made Viennese serialism the orthodox Florentine style.

It was Milan, however, with its electronic studio, that became the real center of Italian avant-garde activities. Among the composers associated with that city are Luciano Berio, Bruno Maderna, Luigi Nono, Niccolo Castiglioni, and Vittorio Fellegara. The works of Maderna (*b.* 1920) and Berio (*b.* 1925) are representative of how these composers have been able to combine serialism with the new electronic developments. Moderna's 1954 *Serenade,* probably his most readily accessible work, is written for eleven instruments, including the rather unconventional mandolin; Berio's *Différences* (1958–60) combines five conventional instruments with magnetic tape music recorded before the concert begins. His *Circles* is written for a singer-speaker projecting an e. e. cummings poem over an unusual instrumental combination, with much of the music supplied by improvisation. Nono (*b.* 1924) has used a totally serialized technique to produce a number of powerful and rather violently expressive works. A real Italian in that he expresses himself most effectively in works for voices and instruments in combination, Nono has produced a number of radical compositions for chorus and orchestra which reflect his commitment to Communist philosophy. These include *Il canto sospeso,* which uses the letters of resistance workers as texts; the *Cori di Didone,* with words fragmented into all sorts of unintelligible sounds; and *La Victoria de Guernica,* inspired by Picasso's famous picture of Spanish civil-war atrocities. His opera *Intolaranze* (1960), an extremely difficult two-act work, is a political blast at intolerance which combines twelve-tone music with electronic tape music and uses film and television projections.

Contemporary with these localized groups, a bevy of composers (including the *giovani,* or youngsters) were attracted by the theories and practices of John Cage and followed the lead of the American in his desire to abolish all conventional attitudes toward music. Their principal leader is Franco Evangelisti (*b.* 1926).

A number of contemporary French avant-gardists have followed the lead of Boulez. Those most often mentioned are Michel Philippet, Michel Ciry, Michel Farro, Maurice Le Roux, Gilbert Avery, and especially Jean Barraqué (*b.* 1928). The last was a pupil of Langlais and Messiaen in Paris, a member of the research group that developed *musique concrète* and, according to his admirers, a composer who has made some of the most important contributions to his art since Debussy. This is difficult to confirm, for Barraqué has not written much, and his recorded scores are not easily available. His most important works seem to be *Sequence* (1950–55), a setting of three poems by Nietzsche, *Le Temps Restitué* (1956–57), *Au-delà du Hasard* (1959), and *La Mort de Virgile,* unfinished, and intended to be the composer's great life work; it employs soloists, vocal ensembles, choirs, chamber groups, several full orchestras, and in addition projects tape music stereophonically.[26] Like Boulez, Le Roux was a pupil of Messiaen and Leibowitz; he was the first film composer to write serial music (the music for *Bitter Victory* is an example), and he has written a ballet inspired by Saint-Exupéry's *Le petit prince.* Again like Boulez, he has become an orchestra conductor, devoting himself to the propagandizing of contemporary music.

As indicative of the widespread avant-garde revolution that has swept all Europe, even the countries behind the Iron Curtain, mention should be made of such Dutchmen as Kees van Baaren (*b.* 1906), who followed Pijper as the leading teacher and inspiration of the younger men, his pupil Peter Schat (*b.* 1935), Jan van Vlijmen (*b.* 1935), and Louis Andriessen (*b.* 1938). One name stands out above all others in the Scandinavian countries, that of Bo Nilsson (*b.* 1937), the wonder boy of Swedish post-Webern constructivism. In Greece the modern Orpheus tunes his lyre atonally, as Nicolas Slonimsky puts it in a recent article on the music of that classic land. Jani Christou (*b.* 1926) and Yorgo Sicilanos (*b.* 1922) wrote in an atonal program style; their contemporary Yannis Xenakis (*b.* 1922) composed what he called *stochasti* music, put together according to the mathematical theories of probability, sets, and symbolic logic. But it was not until the 1930's that a lively generation of dodecaphonic composers was born; the principal men in this group, many of whom studied and worked in Germany and Austria, are Yannis Ioannidis (*b.* 1930), Stephanos Gazouleas (*b.* 1931), and Theodor Antonian (*b.* 1935).

Even in the Communist world, according to the latest reports, the newest, most contemporary avant-garde ideas are being accepted. After having been shut off for many years from contact with the West, there seems to have come a time of intellectual and ideological change in these countries, of which the revolution in the arts is only one manifestation. Travelers report that in all the Eastern European countries the intelligentsia and the artists seem determined to make a break with the

[26] Hodeir treats the music of Barraqué in some detail in *Since Debussy.* New York: Grove Press, 1961.

past and to establish an intellectual and artistic independence based on the latest developments of the West. Beginning with the anti-Stalinist revolt in 1956, the Poles have gradually acquired an almost complete artistic-intellectual freedom, the most striking example of which is the big annual Warsaw Autumn Musical Festival, catering to a wide public eager to welcome the newest and most advanced ideas. And there is an Experimental Studio of Polish Radio and Television, established in 1958, which has been especially encouraging to composers.

Among the older generation of Polish modernist composers we have noted Lutoslawski (p. 607) and Tadeusz Baird (p. 732). The younger generation, which has imbibed all the present-day Western tendencies and uses avant-garde techniques with the greatest ease, includes Wojciech Kilar (*b.* 1932), Krzysztof Penderecki (*b.* 1933), and Henryk Górecki (*b.* 1933). According to recent reports, there is very little tonal music being produced in Poland today; the old-timers are the twelve-tone composers and the serialists; the younger generation is occupied with all kinds of experiments, including happenings.

The same condition applies to a somewhat lesser extent in the other Eastern European countries. Although there has been considerable freedom achieved by other artists, the Czech composers seem to have had a harder time of it in establishing new stylistic trends, though there are private concerts which program the newest things from East and West. Revolutionary trends are apparent in Rumania, Bulgaria, and Hungary, though as yet nothing comparable to what has happened in Czechoslovakia and Poland. How far things will go in Russia with the appointment of a new secretary of the Soviet Composer's Union remains to be seen. There is evidently some serial and twelve-tone music allowed in private concerts, and the younger musicians seem to be well informed on all the avant-garde developments taking place outside Russia.

Whither Music?

There are a number of ways of evaluating the developments and changes we have seen taking place in the music of the present century. To the forward-looking, adventurous listener they constitute progress. To those of more conservative tastes, especially those whose musical experiences have been almost exclusively with the music of the past, they often seem retrogressive. To those who view art and music in historical perspective, they appear to be contemporary examples of the changes in technical procedure and aesthetic attitudes that have marked the course of art and music through their entire history. But to the musical philosopher, these changes have implications that may well portend not merely change but the end of music as we have known it.

Even such a brief survey as we have made shows that there are grounds for such a prediction. Not only have composers such as Boulez and his followers announced as their aim the total dismantling of music and its total reconstruction under new laws, but the composers of this era seem generally to have become unconcerned with the fact that the general public never even tries to understand them or what they are doing. Not having any need, as they see it, for the kind of individualized expression which up to this time has been the very lifeblood of art, they are satisfied to devote their time and energy to devising mathematical formulas and experimenting with them for their own delight, quite oblivious of the enormous gap which exists between them and the public.

Although many contemporary composers realize that without the understanding of a wider public their activities can have no support in the future, they do not see that such understanding depends on communication. And communication depends, as recent experiments in interpersonal relationships have proved, on the fact that the response of one member of a relationship conditions the statement of the other. This does not mean, any more than it does in normal conversation, that the poet or musician should not say what he intends to say. It does mean that, since communication cannot be one-sided, the creator must say what he has to say in forms capable of being apprehended by his audience. The great artists of the past have always been fully aware of this; and the creative artist who complains that he is not understood and blames it on his audience while making no attempt to remove the barriers between him and his public, is refusing to accept the most elemental principle of communication.

We have seen what these barriers are. But there are additional reasons for the contemporary listener's inability to like much of the music that has been produced during his time. Never before have so many changes taken place in music in so short a time as those we have been describing. Not only has there been lost the one common denominator of tonal unity which has made all the music written up to the beginning of this century accessible to everyone within the circle of European culture, but the total dissonance, the manufactured melodies, and the pulverized rhythms of the new musical language have proved to be largely incomprehensible. As a result, this new kind of musical expression has seemed to be nothing but another one of the contemporary activities dominated by science, its conception governed by calculation rather than imagination and its users having the mark of men engaged in programming a computer rather than of creative artists engaged in enlarging the vision and strengthening the spirit of men.

Disturbing also for the contemporary listener are the new means of creating and reproducing music available to composers. The results can appear on magnetic tape, without any necessity of performance through playing; this tape can be projected through loud speakers, recorded for later production or preservation, or transferred to listeners thousands of miles away. All these new resources for producing and reproducing sound remove any need whatsoever for the creative incitement of the performer, up to this time an essential and determining factor in the production of music, because of the specific quality of this particular art. Since this new music can be conceived, created, and reproduced through means entirely mechanical, it tends to become more and more impersonal and to lose most of its distinctive glories as art.

As the century draws nearer its close, there is a divergence among musicians as to the possible future. There are some who wishfully feel that the systematic denigration of the Romantics instituted by Stravinsky and reinforced by the severely mechanistic outgrowths of the serialists is but a temporary phenomenon—one of the swings of the pendulum of fashion caused by the changes in creative temperament inevitable in every period of history. Such persons are inclined to think that the kinds of music that have developed since the early part of the century are transitional, like the various forms of painting which have evolved during the century and which, after exerting influence, have been displaced by others. Writing in late 1964, the music critic of *The London Times* noted that there were perceptible signs of change in the general musical climate, and that we are about to re-enter a period in which works evocative of vision and imagery and full of the intangible, sensuous beauty of this world, would again come into their own.

Only a few months later, however, Hermann Scherchen, the German conductor who has proved himself qualified to speak because of his long and distinguished career as an interpreter of both traditional and modern music, expressed a quite different opinion. Realizing, as everyone these days has to, that science is inevitably reshaping our environment as well as influencing our thought, Scherchen declared that science will be the determining factor of the art of the future and that the music of the next era will be inspired by entirely different psychological stimulations from those which have been the source of traditional art—fancy and imagination. Indeed, he brings up the pertinent question as to whether there will be any necessity at all for the type of art that has existed up to this time.

Only time can tell which of these prophecies will prove correct—or whether, perhaps, there will evolve a style somewhere between these two extremes. The whole century has been engaged in the production of a new kind of music: we were promised it in the twenties and were still looking hopefully for it in the thirties. But it seems hardly to have emerged beyond the experimental stage. Perhaps, when and if it does come, it will indeed fill needs never felt in less complex times.

AMERICAN MUSIC

I hear America singing.
Walt Whitman

IN THE NATIVE GRAIN

Various Phases of Activity

$\mathcal{A}$ccounts of American music and the place it occupies in the world today are apt to be either chauvinistic or meager, according to whether the observer has conservative or progressive leanings. Moreover, these accounts are not apt to consider adequately the two fields which have characterized musical activities in the United States—folk music and popular music. To a certain extent, this is true of most descriptions of nationalistic art: historians are likely to consider straight or academic art of more aesthetic importance than folk or popular art. Such an account is particularly unjust in the case of American music, however; for, whether we are reluctant to admit it or not, the outstanding contribution which the United States so far has made to twentieth-century music has been in the popular field—specifically in (1) jazz, (2) what has come to be known as "pop" music, and (3) works written for the musical theatre.

The various forms of our popular music, whatever their other qualities, often have vitality because they express the essential spirit of their time and place of origin. This type of music has been our most viable export, as eagerly sought in Europe (even in Soviet Russia at the time it was officially banned) as in Australia or the Far East.

In fact, the tremendous vitality of this phase of American musical activity has often been advanced as one of the causes of the relative weakness of serious music in this country. There can be little doubt in the mind of the impartial observer that the composers of serious music in the United States have not played a role commensurate with that of the creative workers in the other arts. In spite of the handicaps of over-industrialization and philistinism inevitable in all newly settled and rapidly growing countries, our creative artists have long since gained an important place in world literature, painting, and architecture—so much so, indeed, that it can be reasonably claimed that today we set the pace in these fields, as we long have done in technology. So also in musical *performance* we at least equal the Europeans and, in certain

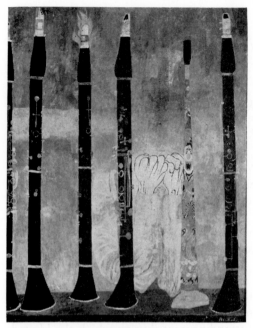

Courtesy of The Detroit Institute of Arts

CLARINETS AND TIN HORN
by Ben Shahn Born in Lithuania,
Shahn has lived for most of his life
in the United States and has become famous as a social observer.
This is his symbolic comment on
American music.

ways, better them. But America has produced few, if any, serious composers of first-rate importance and international significance.

The reason could well be, as we have said, that so much of the country's creative energy has gone into the production of popular music.
The law of supply and demand has necessarily had something to do
with this: the music called for by the alienated masses that have come
to occupy a significant role in the life of our country is not easily reconciled with what more traditional societies call "art." There are, of course,
other reasons. But certainly, at least up to the beginning of the seventh
decade, the twentieth century's authoritative voice in American music
has not been that of the serious composer.

THE AMERICAN FOLK TRADITION

As its name implies, folk music is music that is in the possession of
the masses of the people within a country—what may be called their
musical vernacular. It has existed among all nations, as we have seen,
from the earliest days of music, and a great body of it has survived in
the various countries and according to the different traditions. This
music belongs to the people not only because it comes into their consciousness naturally, without formal instruction, but because they them-

selves can play or sing it. Obviously, folk songs must be of a nature common to the great majority—they must treat of the people as they are, tell of their history, sing of their joys and sorrows, and voice their hopes and aspirations.

American folk music was drawn from far and near: early settlers and later immigrants brought with them the songs and dances of their own lands and many of these have survived practically unchanged, as in the case of folk tunes in the isolated sections of the eastern Appalachians. Folk-song collectors have found the people there singing the old Scottish and English ballads of the time when their forebears came over from Europe. Such music as this has been of little importance, of course, in the development of a real American folk-song type, since it impinged so slightly on the general life of the nation.

But a great many European folk ballads and dances have taken root in the changed life of America and been affected by its freedom, stimulated by its struggles, and salted by its humor. The mainstream of this music has been the traditional songs brought by the English-speaking peoples who settled a large part of colonial America. Grafted on to produce an entirely new fruit have been the customs and habits, the sentimentality and wit, the slogans, the "layout and lingo" of life in a pioneer country. Adding its own flavor has been the rhythmic genius and harmonic subtlety peculiar to the Negroes, brought into the music of the country in the early days of its history. The result is what Carl Sandburg, the American poet, picturesquely called a "rag bag of strips, stripes, and streaks of color" from all parts of the earth—something as indigenous to this country as its skyscrapers: as old as the medieval ballads brought into the Appalachians and yet as new as the latest oil gusher.

There are thousands of these ballads and ditties; one of the best collections is Sandburg's *The American Songbag,* a book which contains nearly three hundred of the most characteristic tunes and verses, gathered by the compiler and his friends from coast to coast and from the Gulf of Mexico to Canada. If one would secure the real flavor of this national folk idiom, he should go through this and similar collections carefully; such songs as "My Name It Is Sam Hall," or "I Ride an Old Paint," or "I'm Sad and I'm Lonely," although they could have come only from the United States, are as representative of the common feelings of humanity as anything ever written or sung.

In general, Americans have always considered as folk songs certain songs of traceable ancestry, such as "Dixie" and "Old Folks at Home." This tendency, abetted by the particular social and technical conditions

THE QUILTING PARTY, Anonymous, 1840–1850   The American folk spirit in art is seen in this oil painting, found in Massachusetts. It is in the collection of Mrs. John D. Rockefeller, Jr., New York.

of mid-nineteenth-century American life, encouraged Tin Pan Alley and Hollywood to produce topical songs suitable for such purveyors of entertainment as night club and radio shows. So there ensued a veritable flood of such "folk songs" during the 1940's and '50's, some of them manufactured by urban synthetes, others imported from backwoods balladeers and country singers, all of them popularized by traveling soloists and singing groups, by radio and television singers. A do-it-yourself movement swept the country during this era, and amateur folk singing, accompanying oneself on the guitar, became the fashion, especially among young people. This rather barren ferment paved the way for a more constructive type of activity and extended the frontiers of American folk music to include a diversity of interests: city as well as country performers; the songs of talented individual composers, such as Woody Guthrie and Josh White; the activities of outstanding interpreters such as Burl Ives, Pete Seeger, Richard Dyer-Bennet, Joan Baez, and Ella Fitzgerald; the introduction of jazz and blues elements; and the use of contemporary folk songs in such political activities as those connected with the labor and civil rights movements. Since they reveal various attitudes on subjects such as religion, sex, and social position, these movements are of historical importance, and they have produced songs of considerable musical interest.

AMERICAN POPULAR MUSIC

Early popular music on this continent was little but a weak simulation of European types; life in the early days was given over largely to serious, pioneering effort, with no time or opportunity for amusements of any sort except in the biggest cities. One of the first performances of entertainment music of which we have a record was of *The Beggar's Opera* in 1750, before there was even a United States. This combination of social satire, a plot that gave opportunities for dancing as well as singing, and a popular ballad kind of music had been patched together by John Gay and Christopher Pepusch as an antidote to the fashionable vogue for Italian opera in England. (See page 345.) It drew upon people from the streets of London for its characters and was so successful that it became the prototype of many of the musical shows which followed it, including the famous Gilbert and Sullivan operettas of the nineteenth century. This first performance in New York inspired a number of similar efforts by American composers, the best known being *The Archers,* written by the English-born Benjamin Carr in 1796, based on the story of William Tell and thus antedating Rossini's famous opera by thirty-three years.

The first popular musical entertainment indigenous to the American scene was the Negro minstrel show, a combination of folk vaudeville and topical songs of a Negroid character. Popular for some sixty years, these shows had their origin, it is believed, in the singing of a song about a Negro called Jim Crow by Thomas Rice in Pittsburgh in 1830. The performers in minstrel shows were white men with blacked faces who sang what were thought typical Negro songs; characteristic Negro dancing, banjo playing, and similar features were added. The popularity of the Negro minstrels extended as far as England, where they were a feature of every British resort at the end of the nineteenth century. The most famous minstrel company was the Christy Minstrel Troupe, which introduced the songs of Stephen Foster, many of them written especially for it. Foster was a talented melodist and poet of folk-like lyrics which, based on Negro subjects, depicted the joys and sorrows of life among the colored people. Such songs as "Old Folks at Home" and "Old Black Joe," though completely antipodal to the ideas of the

PHASES OF MUSIC IN AMERICA   No better summary of the development of music
country home of Mr. and Mrs. Lawrence Tibbett. At the extreme left is a suggestion of
has been so closely bound up with the life of the country. The left center suggests the
background the artist has painted a characteristic American farm and village church, thus
center two cowboys "render" some of the music of the Western plains. The

present-day Negro, became popular throughout the English-speaking
world because of their sentimentalism and plaintive melodies.

THE AMERICAN MUSICAL THEATRE

The earliest American musical show to combine all the various elements characteristic of this type of theatrical entertainment—songs and
star singers, dancing and ballet girls, and special kinds of theatrical
effects—was *The Black Crook,* produced in New York in 1866. It may
be regarded as the progenitor of the sophisticated variety shows that became popular in this country during the early days of the twentieth
century. The mainstream of the American musical, however, had as its
source the English Gilbert and Sullivan series of operettas and the
Johann Strauss models imported from Vienna. The musicals began to
assume importance around the turn of the century, with works such as

Photograph by Juley; courtesy of Lawrence Tibbett

in America could possibly be found than this mural, painted by William Yarrow for the
the music of the Negroes, which, although not American in any true sense of the word,
romantic era of Stephen Foster and his songs that have gone around the world; in the
intimating the great role they have played in the spread of native music. In the right
modern college youth and his amusement music occupies the rest of the picture.

DeKoven's *Robin Hood* (1890) and the attractive *Babes in Toyland*
(1903), *Mlle. Modiste* (1905), and *Naughty Marietta* (1910) of Victor Herbert, an Irish-born musician whose style was nevertheless characteristically American. Another outstanding figure in the American
popular music of this period was John Philip Sousa (1854–1932),
whose nationalistic marches, written for his own concert band, are still
played by military bands the world over. Nothing ever produced in this
country better demonstrates the "youthful spirit, optimism and patriotic
fervor" that was noted by a foreigner during its pioneer days.

It was the headway gained at this time that gave impetus to that
particularly American institution, ragtime—syncopation applied whole-
sale to music. This kind of popular music originated with the Negroes
and became popular with the whites because of its happy, infectious
nature. Its idioms were widely imitated and intensively developed by
many professional composers of popular music during the first decades

of the century. Irving Berlin's characteristic *Alexander's Rag Time Band* (1911) is usually considered the first piece of published ragtime, though plenty of this kind of music had been composed and sung long before. Its progeny among the pop songs were numerous and, through the infusion of other folk elements, were gradually metamorphosed into jazz.

The first flood tide of the American musical theatre swept Jerome Kern's *Showboat* into New York in 1927. Written by an American composer on an American theme taken from a popular American novel, this was not merely a theatre piece containing a few appealing tunes (its "Old Man River" has never been excelled as a pop tune) held together by a loose plot, but rather a closely knit entity with dramatic development in both text and music. Its tremendous success stimulated the production of a number of other works of similar nature, including George Gershwin's *Of Thee I Sing* (1931), a satire on the political life of its day and the first musical ever to receive the distinction of a Pulitzer Prize; the notable and very distinctive Rodgers and Hammerstein series beginning with *Oklahoma!* in 1943 and continuing with such shows as *South Pacific* (1948) and *The King and I* (1951); Cole Porter's lively adaptation of Shakespeare, *Kiss Me Kate* (1948); Irving Berlin's brash *Annie, Get Your Gun* (1946) and *Call Me Madam* (1950); Frank Loesser's hardboiled picture of American gangsterism, *Guys and Dolls* (1950); Lerner and Loewe's charming transformation of Shaw, *My Fair Lady* (1956); and Leonard Bernstein's *West Side Story* (1957), full of the raw power of racial strife. Although nothing that has been produced since has been able to equal the striking individuality and indigenous virility of these shows, there have been some interesting experiments suggestive of even greater possibilities for the future.

THE DEVELOPMENT OF JAZZ

Authorities on jazz, another distinctive contribution which this country has made to the art of music, are apt to disagree violently on many details of its history, including the origin of its name. There is general agreement, however, that this music is the result of a number of widely differing sources, including European harmony, Euro-African melody, and African rhythm, and that the effect is a kind of music entirely different from anything earlier.

Characterized by rhapsodic, improvisational expression based on a fluid, rhythmic foundation, jazz emerged from the activities of a number of talented Negro musicians—singers, trumpet players, trombonists, pianists, and drummers—earning a living as members of entertainment and dance bands in the teeming life of New Orleans' "back-town" around the turn of the century. By 1900 there had come into existence in the lively melting pot of this picturesque Latin-American city, with its blend of West African, European, and Central-American Caribbean influences, a kind of music which struck the public as something entirely new.[1] This style of playing, which became known as Dixieland when it began to be used by white musicians, spread over the whole country (the experts seem to differ on the historical details) until it became the rage of the self-titled "Jazz Age" of the 1920's.

THE SPREAD OF JAZZ

Aside from New Orleans, the centers important in the development of jazz were in Chicago, New York, St. Louis, and Kansas City, each developing its own style of composing and playing, and priding itself on its own jazz interpreters. Over the years a number of developments have occurred in this indigenous American product, each of them typical of its time and characterized by a definite type of expression. In the earlier years the Dixieland and Chicago styles, derived directly from the original New Orleans jazzmen, used small bands, which gave flexibility and encouraged improvisations. Another early development was "symphonic jazz," the use of concert devices by such big bands as that of Paul Whiteman, whose Æolian Hall concert in New York in 1924 brought George Gershwin to the attention of the public. Many of the best-known jazz players of that time were members of Whiteman's band, and his position and influence brought jazz to the closer attention of serious musicians. The later Swing period (from 1935 to 1945) saw a mass conversion to the cause of jazz on the part of the American people. During this time large ensembles of twenty or so became popular, all the players striving for mass rhythmic effects rather than individual flexibility or spontaneity, except from on-the-spot soloists, often the band leader or the drummer. Catering to thousands of their listeners

[1] Marshall Stevens, in *The Story of Jazz* (New York: Oxford Press, 1956), claims that we can pinpoint the different tribes responsible for the African influences in jazz. He says that the strongest European influence was that of the French quadrille and march music then current in New Orleans. And he indicates that Negro work songs, spirituals, blues, and ragtime were the chief American influences.

JAM SESSION by George von Physter   The lithograph is from *Down Beat*, the trade paper of the swing movement, and appears also in *Destiny*, a sketchbook of the lives of popular musicians.

who loved to dance, such big bands, especially those of Benny Goodman, Tommy Dorsey, and Artie Shaw, achieved enormous popular and financial success.

Even before this hectic era ended there was a revolt against these strenuously blasting groups, and small-band jazz re-appeared, playing a revival of the New Orleans style and what later came to be known as "rebop," "bebop," or just plain "bop." The revival of the earlier and more relaxed New Orleans style made enthusiastic converts for jazz, especially among middle-class whites of the entire world. This was the time when mass audiences everywhere began to know and enjoy and imitate this music which the American Negro had developed some thirty years before. And this was the era when jazz began to be studied as an aesthetic force. Books about it were written in France,[2] England, and Belgium, as well as in this country. Jazz began to be thought of as art rather than merely amusement. Bop, which constituted a more powerful revolt against the commercial swing era, featured certain erup-

[2] Some of the best critiques of jazz have been written by André Hodeir for the French magazine *Jazz-Hot*. A number were translated and published as *Jazz, Its Evolution and Essence*. New York: Grove Press, 1956.

Courtesy of Hansen-Williams, Inc.

THE MOOD OF SWING   One of the most famous of swing bands, Duke Ellington's, is shown in action.

tive elements, such as unusual modulations and additional flatted chords, as well as more advanced harmonies and more complex melodies. There resulted a complicated, deliberately confusing music which gave new importance to improvisation; its chief exponents were the saxophonist Charlie Parker and the trumpeter Dizzy Gillespie.

LATER DEVELOPMENTS

Again there was a revolt, this time featuring progressive or "cool" jazz, which was relaxed and calm, in direct contrast with bop. Centering on the West Coast, this style explored the more intellectual possibilities of the jazz idiom and placed a premium on subtlety of expression and variety of musical effects. Although large bands were still in fashion, they featured small combinations within themselves, often led by classically trained musicians, who did not hesitate to employ chromaticism, polytonality, highly involved rhythms, and dissonant intervals. Miles Davis and Lennie Tristano were the principal figures in this intellectualizing of jazz, a movement which reached its peak as early as 1955.

Since then there have been attempts on the part of some jazz composers to write what they call "classical jazz"; the difficulty here is that of assimilating into the elements they have borrowed from classical composers the characteristics indigenous to jazz: the subtle rubato that makes it swing, and the opportunity to improvise. Gunther Schuller, the so-called "third-stream" man, maintains that such a blend is possible and is only a matter of time. And such organizations as the Dave Brubeck Quartet and the Modern Jazz Quartet have been successful in embroidering jazz materials with advanced techniques and polyrhythms.

It is well to remind ourselves that the fanatic devotion which jazz seems to kindle in listeners from Sidney, Australia, to Reykjavik, Iceland, is due to its being a separate and indigenous art composed, as we have said, of European harmony, Euro-African melody, and African rhythm; and that it therefore does not need the addition of other, more sophisticated features. Nevertheless, there have been a number of attempts to combine jazz with concert music: by such composers as Milhaud in *Le Bœuf sur le toit* (1920) and *Le Création du monde* (1923), Honegger in the 1925 *Concertino,* and Copland in *Concerto for Piano and Orchestra* (1927). Although none of these was very successful, in recent years there have been somewhat more sophisticated attempts to develop a modern jazz style that would accommodate the more serious and intricate techniques of concert music. Dave Brubeck (*b.* 1916), a composition student of Milhaud, has attempted to create a jazz-symphonic style in what he calls *Dialogues,* in which, as one listener has observed, he puts a jazz combo and a symphony orchestra together on stage, steps aside, and hopes they won't fight. This, of course, is only a negative way of achieving a reconciliation between the two worlds, and so defeats its own end.

The problem of incorporating the important thought processes and techniques of jazz in a new style based on the older traditions does not seem to have been so difficult in the field of opera. A number of works combining traditional operatic forms with various manifestations of jazz were written during the 20's and 30's—notably, in Europe, Krenek's *Jonny spielt auf* (1927) and Kurt Weill's *Rise and Fall of the City of Mahagonny.* In America the outstanding work of this type has been George Gershwin's *Porgy and Bess* (1935).

Classical Music
in the United States

EARLY BEGINNINGS
$\qquad$In connection with music, the term
"classical" is unfortunately used in several confusing ways. Here it simply means music that is antithetical to "popular." Until the turn of the century any description of the course which this kind of music followed in this country is largely a record of serious, ambitious effort, without results sufficient to lift localism into world importance. Various reasons could be given. One is the comparative youth of the country: when the Mayflower sailed for America, Schütz was laying the foundations of the great structure of German music; and the early years of the colony of New York correspond to the period when Bach was busy with his organ and church compositions! Another is the difficulty which all art, and especially music, encounters in a pioneer society, where life is given over largely to earning sustenance and developing natural resources. Finally, it was necessary to integrate the many conflicting traditions and complex idioms of expression inherent in the different racial strains which comprise the nation.

In general, the story is one of the gradual adaptation to local conditions and native soil of the ideals and principles of the great body of musicians whose activities during the eighteenth and nineteenth centuries we have chronicled in this book. This process produced what one of our best-known composers has called "museum art"; it did not create what he considers American music until a school of twentieth-century composers developed, able to speak directly to the people in a language it was able to recognize as its own.[3] The story ranges from the early efforts of Francis Hopkinson (1737–1791), whom *Grove's Dictionary* calls the only native musician of distinction in early America, to the surprising cultural phenomenon of today, the mass distribution of music (both good and bad) throughout the wide spaces of our continent by means of radio, records, and stereo tape.

[3] Aaron Copland, the composer quoted, gives this definition of an American composer: "one who can speak in a language which expressses fully the deepest reaction of the American consciousness to the American scene."

LOWER MANHATTAN by John Marin   More than any other American painter, John Marin (1870–1953) was able to convey his excitement about nature and urban life in his watercolors. This one, composed from the top of the Woolworth Tower, is one of his best.

EARLY SOURCES

The principal sources of classical music in the United States were English and German. The English were the first settlers along the Atlantic seaboard, and their influence was long predominant; and many of the early musicians who came to this country were German. But it would be merely tiresome to try to list all the influences on the evolving musical taste of the young country. Certainly one of the strongest was the development of a fine musical tradition both in composition and in performance at the Moravian settlements of Bethlehem, Pennsylvania, and Winston-Salem, North Carolina. Another was the immigration of German artists which took place in the early part of the nineteenth century.

After the American Revolution, the musical life of the country passed from such untrained native hands as those of William Billings

(1746–1800)[4] into the more skilled hands of foreigners. Prominent among these early foreign musicians were the Philadelphians Alexander Reinagle (1756–1809), an English teacher, concert manager, and composer; and Benjamin Carr (1769–1831), one of the first conductors to perform a Beethoven symphony in America and composer of the pre-Rossini ballad opera on William Tell which we have mentioned. In New York, James Hewitt is said to have brought the music of Stamitz and Haydn to America. In Boston, Gottlieb Graupner, a player in the orchestra which Salomon assembled for Haydn in London, helped found two of the country's earliest musical organizations, the Philharmonic Society in 1810 and the Handel and Haydn Society in 1815.

The most picturesque of these early foreigners who cast their musical lot with America was Anthony Philip Heinrich, who wrote a number of compositions requiring an orchestra of Berliozian dimensions. Father Heinrich, as he was called by his admirers (they also dubbed him the "Beethoven of America") was easily the most commanding figure of the composers in America before 1860 and was the first to display such nationalistic tendencies as those evidenced in some of his compositions: *Pocahontas, the Royal Indian Maid and the Heroine of Virginia and Bride of the Wilderness;* and *The Wild-wood Spirit's Chant or Scintillations of "Yankee Doodle", forming a Grand National Heroic Fantasia scored for a Powerful Orchestra in 44 parts.* Another important figure of this period was Louis Gottschalk (1829–1869), who made successful tours of Europe as well as the United States, playing his own piano works and conducting his orchestral compositions. The Latin character of his music made it very popular, and such things as his *Gran Tarantella for Piano and Orchestra* and *Nuit des Tropiques* are still listenable.

Around mid-century, opera began to attract attention, with performances of French and Italian works. The first of these were sung in French in New York, where for years a most distinguished operatic tradition was cultivated. Adapted and arranged versions of grand operas were produced up and down the Atlantic seaboard, together with the very popular ballad operas. Hopeful American composers were producing operas by the hundreds, and a number of remarkably elegant provincial opera houses were being built. Researchers have arrived at the rather rough figure of two thousand as the number of American operas written since 1850; although a few have had sporadic performances,

---

[4] Billings was a tanner turned composer; his hymn tunes (six collections of them appeared from 1770 to 1794) won great favor with their simple melodies, effective choral effects, and novel attempts at fugal counterpoint.

none has joined any permanent operatic repertoire. *Leonora* (1845), by William Fry, stands as the first American opera to be written in the grand style, and George F. Briston's *Rip Van Winkle* (1855) is the first grand opera on an American theme. To complete the record, Frederick S. Converse's *Pipe of Desire* was the first American opera to be given at the Metropolitan Opera, in 1909.

Beside the musical societies already mentioned, others were founded in American cities: the St. Cecilia Society of Charleston in 1762, probably the earliest of them all; the Musical Fund Society in Philadelphia in 1820; and the New York Philharmonic Orchestra in 1842. The great pioneer in orchestral music among Americans, Theodore Thomas, made the first concert tour with his orchestra in 1869. In 1881 the Boston Symphony, the first of the American orchestras to achieve an outstanding world position, was founded. And in 1884 German opera, under the aegis of Leopold Damrosch, began its long run in the United States.

The Founders

The entry of American music into the world arena was made by a group of New England composers headed by John K. Paine (1839–1906), who studied in Germany and was appointed to the first professorship of music in this country, established at Harvard in 1875. The traditions he established there were carried on by a group which included Arthur Foote (1853–1937), George W. Chadwick (1854–1931), Edgar Stillman Kelley (1857–1944), Horatio Parker (1865–1919), Mrs. H. H. A. Beech (1867–1944), and Henry F. Gilbert (1868–1928). With the exception of Kelley these were all New Englanders; most of them had studied in Europe and all of them espoused the spirit of late Romanticism absorbed there. The first generation of Americans to be thoroughly trained composers, they did much to raise the technical standards of our native music; but though several of them made attempts at writing "non-European" music, they had nothing very individual to say, and very few of their works are heard today.

The first American composer who did succeed in expressing something of the spirit and ideals of his native country and in achieving a reputation abroad was a man of this generation—Edward MacDowell (1861–1908). A native New Yorker who had studied in Germany with Joseph Raff, a disciple of Mendelssohn and Liszt, MacDowell is best remembered for the series of small piano pieces, *Woodland Sketches, Fireside Tales,* and *New England Idyls,* which painted a romantic picture of American scenes, rather than for the two piano concertos, five symphonic poems, and two orchestral suites which he considered his important works. Even for a twentieth-century American there is something endearing in these cameos of old days, Puritan times, Indian ways, and the like. And though his attempts to translate something of the spirit of the New World into sound seem rather mild today, MacDowell did in a small way what Walt Whitman accomplished in a greater way for growing-up America.

THE NEXT GENERATION

Again in the next generation a number of New Englanders carried on the decorous traditions of the earlier group, though such a composer as Frederick S. Converse (1871–1940) did not hesitate to use the more advanced harmonies of his European confreres. Henry Hadley (1871–1937) combined a successful conducting career with composing; he too used fairly advanced and even exotic harmonies on occasion. In his numerous orchestral works Daniel Gregory Mason (1873–1953), a member of a distinguished family closely associated with American music for three generations[5] kept strictly to the ideals of the Romantic school, especially Brahms.

A foreign-born composer active at this time was Charles Martin Loeffler (1861–1935). Brought up under several different racial influences—Alsatian, French, Russian, and Ukranian—he developed a sophisticated personal style which, together with Impressionism, had a powerful effect on American composers: it turned their attention from German to French influences and established an entirely new orientation in American music. Loeffler's *Pagan Poem* (1906), written for chamber orchestra and later orchestrated for full orchestra, is a real tour de force.

Among the composers to follow the new French lead was John Alden

[5] His grandfather was Lowell Mason, hymn writer and pioneer of American school music activities. His father was a co-founder of one of the best American piano manufacturing firms. And his uncle was William Mason, a pupil of Liszt and one of the great concert pianists of his day.

Carpenter (1876–1951), a Chicago businessman who late in life devoted himself entirely to composing. He used a mellifluous, mildly contemporary style, spiced with some Impressionistic devices, to depict American urban life in such works as *Adventures in a Perambulator* (1915) and *Skyscrapers* (1926). Edward Burlingame Hill (1872–1960) wrote several books about contemporary French music and composed a considerable number of orchestral works in the Impressionistic manner. Arthur Shepherd (1880–1958) introduced a strong tendency toward Impressionism in his essentially Romantic style. Deems Taylor's (*b.* 1885) charming *Through the Looking Glass Suite* (1921) is an Impressionistic tonal picture of Lewis Carroll's famous story. Taylor's two operas, *The King's Henchman* (1926) and *Peter Ibbetson* (1931), are in a pure Romantic vein; although they set records for performances of American operas at the Metropolitan, they have disappeared from the repertoire.

The most gifted of the Impressionists was Charles T. Griffes (1884–1920), who in an unfortunately short life produced some sensitive piano pieces and several orchestral works of interest: *The Pleasure Dome of Kubla Khan* (1912), *The White Peacock* (1917), and *Poem for Flute and Orchestra* (1918). His early death robbed American music of one of its most promising composers.

AN AMERICAN ORIGINAL

The reputation of Charles Ives (1874–1954) has changed considerably in recent years. From being thought of as a maverick of interest largely because of his use of tonalities, rhythms, and other modernistic inventions in ways that anticipated Schoenberg and Stravinsky, he is now looked on as the "grandfather of American music," and probably its outstanding composer. Time will probably show that the truth lies midway between these two extremes.

An original experimenter, son of a small-town Yankee band master, Ives studied music at Yale and decided that the professional career of musician could not support the kind of life he wanted. So he entered business and devoted himself to music without having to earn a living from it. He wrote a great quantity of music that exploited all sorts of dissonant harmonies, conflicting rhythms and keys, fractional intervals, polytonal counterpoint, and polyrhythmic structures. He developed a montage way of composing that made use of a number of patriotic tunes ("Columbia, the Gem of the Ocean" seemed a special favorite), folk melodies, and hymns to create a sense of mood or induce nostalgic memories. This sometimes resulted in music of a highly original and imaginative nature; the second movement from *Three Places in New England* (1903–14), descriptive of the sights and sounds evoked by a visit to an old Revolutionary War camp, shows this montage-quotation style at its best. Another result was music of extraordinary difficulty for both performers and listeners, filled with pyrotechnic and dissonant complexities and turgid expression, as in the monumental *Second Piano Sonata* (subtitled Concord, Mass. 1840–1860), inspired by and suggestive of the philosophical, social, and economic life of New England of that period.

In addition to music evoked by ideas, experiences, and emotions such as the *Three Places in New England, The Unanswered Question* (1908), and "In the Night" from his *Theatre Orchestral Suite* (1904–11), Ives wrote five symphonies, four quite unorthodox string quartets, a considerable amount of chamber music, piano music (including a set of quarter-tone pieces), choral works, and over a hundred songs. Most of this remained unknown until after World War II, when a performance of the *Third Symphony* by one of his friends brought Ives the 1947 Pulitzer Prize and some recognition from the general public. The New York Philharmonic programmed the *Second Symphony* in 1951, exactly fifty years after it was written, thus completing public acceptance of the Connecticut Yankee as a significant composer. In 1965, nearly fifty years after it was written, Ives's *Fourth Symphony* received its first performance; largely a rendering in orchestral terms of material originally conceived for other purposes, this had to be pieced together from the composer's scrawled and poorly organized manuscript. An enormous score that may turn out to be his most representative work, it employs Ives's usual technical procedures and shows, even more than most of his works, his lack of skill in articulating what he wanted to say.

There is danger, in such belated recognition of the freshness and communicative power of the music of Ives, that its real significance be over-rated. The fact that he was a fascinating figure, ahead of his time, a man with ability to evoke the particular atmosphere and flavor of his native land, does not necessarily make him a great composer. Probably because he never had the opportunity to hear most of what he composed, his music is uneven, often unnecessarily rough and crude, and it lacks homogeneity of style. It may well be that *Three Places in New England* contains some of the best music yet written by an American.

But the *Second Symphony,* as well as many other things in Ives's folk-loric repertoire, can hardly be considered masterworks, either of conception or of imagination.

OTHER COMPOSERS OF THIS GENERATION

A New England contemporary of Ives and, like him, a powerful figure in the American scene, is Carl Ruggles (*b.* 1876). His harmonic style as it finally developed was completely atonal, but he used it to communicate emotion, which he felt to be the real purpose of music. This is apparent in even the names of his big orchestral works: *Men and Angels* (1920), *Men and Mountains* (1924), and *Portals* (1926). The music is of such intensity that they have been described by critics of the period as "volcanic eruptions of gorgeous sonorities." But they have been but little played; Ruggles's position in contemporary music is best described by the title of yet another of his pieces: *Vox Clamans in Deserto*—a voice crying in the wilderness.

Lazare Saminsky (1882–1959) was a Russian-born composer who was very active for many years in this country as a teacher, writer, conductor, and leader of Jewish musical activities.

Another Russian-born American of this generation was Louis Gruenberg (1884–1964), a pupil of Busoni. His two most important works were inspired, strangely enough, by Negro themes: a composition for tenor and chamber orchestra, *Daniel Jazz* (1919), and an opera based on the well-known O'Neill play *The Emperor Jones,* performed at the Metropolitan in 1933.

The work of Wallingford Riegger (1885–1961), who for many years before his death was hailed as the dean of American composers, is a sort of composite of all the composing styles employed by his compatriots. His first efforts were in the Romantic chromatic style of his teachers, Max Bruch in Berlin and Edgar S. Kelley in this country, an influence clearly evident in the *Piano Trio in b minor* (1919–20). Then came an Impressionistic phase, shown best in some of his piano pieces, notably the 1927 *Blue Voyage.* Finally, starting with *Study in Sonority* (1927), there emerged a style based on arbitrarily selected tonal centers in the Schoenbergian manner. He used this style for all his later works, but always in a personal way, combining with it, whenever he felt them necessary, the traditional elements of tonal writing. He claimed that this process gave him "new possibilities of texture, of melody (albeit in a new guise) and of form, all of them expressive of the age in which we live, without losing anything of the universally human."

There is little question that of all Americans using the twelve-tone technique, Riegger has used it most expressively. There is nothing doctrinaire in his music; the turgid prolixity that marks many serial compositions is absent in such a work as the *Third Symphony,* commissioned and first played in 1947. Following the classic conception of form used in a four-movement symphony, this is an outstanding example of Riegger's individual approach to the problems of form, melody, rhythm, and texture. His contemporaries rank this symphony high in the list of the American achievements of this century; whether it will find similar favor with audiences is an open question.

In addition, Riegger wrote three other symphonies, over twenty orchestral pieces, works for band, brass, and string ensemble, a great many chamber music works, pieces for both piano and organ, ballet scores, vocal works, and songs.

AN EARLY AVANT-GARDIST

In the span of less than a single lifetime virtually every aspect of our society, including our reactions to art, has been affected by the tremendous impact of science and technology. This impact was clearly predicted years ago by Edgar Varèse (1885–1965), the Franco-American composer: "The future composer of symphonies will consult the scientist in his laboratory instead of the violin-maker in his garret." When he made this prophecy Varèse, who came to this country in 1915 after an active career in Paris and Berlin, was busy writing music for sounds that he realized could better be produced if the scientist in his laboratory and the engineer in his workshop would only get together with the composer. Since that time increasing experimentation with electronically synthesized music has made possible the realization of Varèse's prophecy. And two generations of composers have followed him in writing this new kind of music.

In every sense of the term a professional avant-gardist, Varèse seems always to have been ahead of the game. The first work which showed his determination to cut himself loose from earlier musical tradition was *Hyperprism* (1923), for wind instruments and percussion. The only things that seem to have interested him were sonorities and the exploration of new sounds; it was with this work that Varèse fathered the idea that music must be, first and foremost, *sound,* and that since noise is sound, it is as useful to music as the so-called musical tones. His next work, *Intégrals* (1925), was still more daring in its expression of those twentieth-century characteristics which, according to Varèse, "crush the

American individual: over-organization, institutionalism, herd-repressing unkultur." Other works of the same nature followed: *Amériques* in 1926; *Ionisation,* for forty-one percussion instruments and two sirens (1931); *Equatorial,* for bass, trumpets, trombone, organ, percussion, and theremin (1934); and *Density 21.5,* for unaccompanied flute (1935).

In *Deserts,* first heard in Paris in 1954, Varèse began to use electronically produced sound. For the Brussels World's Fair in 1958 he wrote a work, *Poème Électronique,* which contained both human and electronic sounds; it was projected into a large pavilion by hundreds of loud speakers so arranged as to give a sense of universal spatial dimension. As evidenced by their fanciful names, Varèse thought of his pieces as program music, symphonic poems that employ sound rather than tone as material. For him, scientists are the poets of today, and art means keeping pace with the speed of light; there was no room in his music for private feeling or emotional reverie. In its attempt to return to music's primitive sources of rhythm and noise, its abjuration of melody and harmony, its insistence on individual dissonance, his music embodies the spirit of our age and evokes the imagery of our machine civilization. Because it needs a special kind of score, a great many unusual instruments, players of the utmost skill, and a forceful, precise conductor accustomed to its special demands, this music is not often played. Its scientific nature makes it especially suited to recording, however, and much of it has been made available through this medium. Varèse's eventual place in history will probably be that of a revolutionary innovator.

The Composers of the Twenties and Thirties, Continuing into the Forties

Although it is not possible to draw a clear line between the styles of the Americans of this generation, they may be divided into several general groups according to the dominant characteristics of their music: those with strong Romantic leanings, inclined toward the more traditional means of expression; those who advanced the then-fashionable ideals of neo-Classicism; those who tried to form an eclectic style combining the best of the Romantic heritage with more modern concepts and contemporary techniques; and the eager experimenters, who were concerned with the development of new techniques and the widening of the listener's experiences. These composers were aided in their struggle for recognition by the gradual emergence of a fondness for contemporary music, by a fashionable swing toward a native American school, and by a general prosperity which encouraged the support of art in general. Most of the composers of the time, whatever their consciously induced American-ism, were strongly influenced by the dissonances and polytonality of Stravinsky's earlier style, the later Stravinskian neo-Classical ideals as interpreted to them by Nadia Boulanger, the French school of the 1920's, and the Schoenbergian revolt. These strong European influences led to a disconcerting similarity of style and uniformity of content, and spread a rather thin, neutral surface over the musical utterances. In general, American composers used tonal or pandiatonic harmonies, and they followed the same general contemporary trends toward economy of means, contrapuntal texture, and free rhythms.

THE OUT-AND-OUT ROMANTICS

Howard Hanson (*b.* 1896) is a pure Romantic who, remaining true to his Scandinavian heritage, has written a number of things strongly reminiscent of Sibelius. Of his five symphonies, the best known are the *First* (Nordic) and the *Second* (Romantic), composed in 1922 and 1930. He has written tone poems in an expanded Lisztian idiom and contributed to American choral literature in such works as the *Lament for Beowulf* (1925) and the 1935 *Songs from Drum Taps* by Whitman. His opera *Merry Mount,* based on a New England theme, was produced at the Metropolitan in 1934.

In spite of his prolific career as a composer, Hanson will perhaps be best remembered for his championship of two causes, neither very popular at the time: that of Romantic expression in an age opposed to any kind of effusive sentiment; and that of the native American composer. As head of the Eastman School in Rochester for forty years, Hanson taught several generations of young composers and gave them the chance to hear good, live, carefully prepared performances of their works.

Frederick Jacobi (1891–1952), born in San Francisco, lived and worked principally in New York. He spent considerable time with the Pueblo Indians in New Mexico, and his early works were influenced by his study of their music. His later works, such as the *Concerto for Cello and Orchestra* (1932) and *Hagiographa, Three Bible Pictures* (1938), are examples of his Hebraically oriented, conservatively Romantic style.

Another strong American Romantic is Douglas Moore (*b.* 1893), who used his particular kind of Romanticism for expressing characteristically American traits. Moore's songs, set to texts by outstanding American poets, convey the rhythms and natural inflections of American speech. His operas, especially *The Devil and Daniel Webster* (1938) and the *Ballad of Baby Doe* (1956), enhance the spirit of the native legends on which they are based without distortion or pretension. His orchestral pieces, such as *The Pageant of P. T. Barnum* (1924), *Village Music* (1942), and *Farm Journal Suite* (1947), picture an era when people were not afraid to be warmhearted and even sentimental.

An interesting Romantic figure of this period is William L. Dawson (*b.* 1898), a Negro graduate of Tuskegee Institute, where he has been active as composer and choral conductor. His big, sprawling *Negro Folk Symphony* (1932, rev. 1952), in three movements, is suggestive of the American Negro's historic past, his troubled present, and his hopeful future.

THE GREAT GERSHWIN

Many good reasons could be given for the fact that George Gershwin (1898–1937) is the best known nationally and internationally of all American composers. Above all is Gershwin's gift for establishing an immediate and powerful connection with his listeners, a gift which we recognize in composers as different in character as Beethoven, Schubert, Wagner, and Tchaikovsky. Whether or not one is particularly fond of the type of music in which Gershwin excelled, it is impossible to miss the appropriateness of almost everything he wrote.

When he was growing up, Gershwin had a chance to assimilate some of the most vital elements in American folk music—the jazz, ragtime, and blues he heard on the New York city streets. In addition, he was the lucky possessor of one of the most astounding lyric gifts in all music, as well as an attractive, quirky, ebullient personality. It was out of these elements that he wove his magic spell, after starting in one of the most stereotyped and stultifying jobs in American music—writing and plugging Tin Pan Alley tunes. Even here, from the very beginning of his career, his distinctive gifts were evident and he soon wrote some of the most refreshing and unconventional Broadway show tunes of his time.

He soon became interested in what he thought of as serious music and adapted its particular and distinctive style to his own ends. The eventful appearance of the piece he wrote to show what he could do along this line, the *Rhapsody in Blue,* with orchestration by Ferde Grofé, started Gershwin on his road to fame. First played at a concert hall in New York on Lincoln's Birthday, 1924, this attempt to "make a lady out of jazz," as it was then described, was tremendously successful and encouraged Gershwin to go on to a *Piano Concerto* in the same vein, and with his own orchestration. The first performance of this work was given the next year with the composer as soloist; and this, in turn, was followed by the rhapsodic *An American in Paris* in 1928.

Gershwin's crowning achievement is usually considered to be the work—he called it a folk opera—which he made out of *Porgy and Bess,* the novel and play by Dorothy and DuBose Heyward depicting Negro life on the Charleston waterfront a number of years ago. Although it has a weak libretto and its operatic development shows Gershwin's inexperience in this kind of writing, its insouciant lyrics (by Gershwin's brother Ira) and striking tunes have made this hodge-podge stage piece an international hit ever since it was first produced in Boston in 1935. It has gradually won world recognition as a kind of period-piece Americana; its dramatic situations belong to a past era of this country's life, however, and whether it will survive under the changed social conditions is something of a question.

It is easy enough to point out Gershwin's weaknesses as a composer: he never learned how to develop the tunes he so easily invented in a way that would hold a listener's attention through an extended movement; he lacked the kind of musico-dramatic technique that is necessary to shape a number of separate tunes into a coherent operatic whole; and many of his tunes are slick and his harmonies mawkish. That he was aware of his compositional faults is evident, for he worked with a number of different teachers at various stages of his career in an attempt to improve his style. Fortunately, there was not enough of such study to lessen the sparkle of his originality or dull the flow of his melody. What really counts in his music is the intensity of its feeling, the lyric appeal of his tunes, the rhythmic verve and exuberance of his whole musical personality. His death at the early age of 38 removed a genuine creative talent from the American scene.

Randall Thompson (*b.* 1899) is a composer of a quite different type. Not strongly attached to any particular trend in composition, he has busied himself with many different forms of music. Writing in a strongly conservative Romantic style, he has become best known for his choral works, especially the *a cappella* motet *Alleluia* and cantata *The Testament of Freedom,* set in 1943 to words by Thomas Jefferson. One does not have to look further than their complete command of choral techniques to account for the popularity of these works.

TWO CLOSELY ASSOCIATED AMERICAN ROMANTICS

Although Samuel Barber (*b.* 1910) can hardly be thought of primarily as an opera composer, his two works in that genre have received unusual support from that greatest of all American operatic enterprises, the Metropolitan Opera in New York. His first opera, *Vanessa,* set to a Henry James-like libretto by his friend Menotti, had its premiere at the Metropolitan in 1958, remained in its repertoire for two years, and was revived five years later. His second, after Shakespeare's *Antony and Cleopatra,* was commissioned by the Ford Foundation and scheduled for the opening performance at the Metropolitan's new house in Lincoln Center in 1966. Although Barber came to opera writing comparatively late in his career, his interest in this form of music was a natural one, since his aunt was Louise Homer, one of the great American opera singers, and he himself was trained as a singer as well as composer.

The first works to establish his reputation, however, were orchestral, the *Adagio for Strings* (1936) and the first *Essay for Orchestra* (1938). Essentially Romantic in nature and using conservative tonal harmonies, they are products of a genuinely creative talent inspired by a highly poetic imagination. First introduced by Toscanini, these two short pieces have become known throughout the entire musical world. Other works belonging to this first period include the *Overture to the School for Scandal* (1932), the *First Symphony* (1936), and *Dover Beach,* a piece for solo voice and string quartet (1931).

In his compositions of the next decade, Barber showed a greater awareness of the contemporary practices of his fellow composers. His harmony became more dissonant, though still largely tonal; he adopted some of the Stravinskian rhythmic procedures; and his melodies were more strongly chromatic. Representative works which show these significant changes are *Concerto for Violin and Orchestra* (1941), *Cello Concerto* (1945), the brilliant *Piano Concerto* (1962), the choral works *Knoxville-Summer of 1915, Prayers of Kierkegaard* (1954), and the ballet *Medea* (1935). Even in his most advanced pieces, with their intense chromaticism and contrapuntal complexities, Barber seems able to maintain the traditions of the past, while altering them to suit his purposes. The important thing about his music is its sense of movement;

no matter how complex it may be, it seems always able to draw its listeners into its incessant flow. And since it is the product of feeling rather than of contrivance, since it seems to be fully realized rather than merely experimental, it is able to hold the listener's attention and give him a sense of satisfaction and achievement. This has not endeared Barber to his more radical confreres or to the *cognoscenti,* who consider him out of date and not of his time.

"I feel that I am the only revolutionary in contemporary music, because I will not be conditioned by the modern idiom." This is the personal assessment of his own position in contemporary music by Gian Carlo Menotti (*b.* 1911), a close associate of Barber and, like him, a composer in revolt against the composition procedures of the twentieth century. An Italian-born writer of operas, Menotti received almost all his musical training in this country and has lived and worked here since 1928. He is unique in that he is the only American composer of operas with enough audience appeal to remain in the permanent operatic repertoire; this is because of his gift for devising dramatic situations (he writes all his own librettos), his ability to provide expressive singing lines, and his skill in adapting these specific qualities to the particular requirements of the American public.[6]

His feeling for theatrical effect is evident in his very first operatic effort, a short opera-buffa, *Amelia Goes to the Ball,* staged in Philadelphia in 1937, to be followed by another of the same type, *The Old Maid and the Thief,* in 1941. The more serious *Island God* was not very successfully produced at the Metropolitan in 1942, and Menotti's real stature was not revealed until *The Medium* was staged in New York in 1946. This had a long run and was subsequently given all over this country and Europe with such success that its performances mounted into the thousands, proof that its composer knew exactly how to provide the dramatic elements necessary to hold the attention of a general audience. In 1950 *The Consul* continued and expanded Menotti's development. Its story deals with a particular type of suffering engendered by the tragedies of our time, and this added to its strong appeal. A third opera to continue this particular facet of Menotti's creative power was *The Saint of Bleecker Street* (1954) which, although it won a Drama Critic's Award and a Pulitzer Prize, has never proved popular. Two short works, *The Telephone* (1947) and *Amahl and the Night Visitors,* on the other hand, have been most successful in attracting listeners; the latter, a Christmas television show, has been a feature

---

[6] It is characteristic of the American attitude toward opera that many of Menotti's works have had to be produced as Broadway shows rather than as operas in opera houses.

of American Christmas programs every year since its first showing in 1951. In 1963 Paris saw the first performance of an opera commissioned by the Opéra there, *Le Dernier Sauvage;* revised and partly re-written, this comic opera was given its Metropolitan premiere as *The Last Savage* in 1964. A "church opera," *Martin's Lie,* and a cantata, *The Death of the Bishop of Brindisi* (1964), have attracted some attention since then; and there have been other experiments, a ballet, *Sebastian,* in 1944, a madrigal ballet, *The Unicorn, the Gorgon and the Manticore,* commissioned by the Coolidge Foundation in 1956, and an opera, *Maria Golovin,* written expressly for the International Exposition in 1958. Another television opera, surrealist this time, *Labyrinth,* proved a complete failure, while Menotti's excursions into absolute music, a *Piano Concerto* in 1945 and a *Violin Concerto* in 1952, have not been repeated. He was also the librettist and stage director for Barber's *Vanessa* and, it may be assumed, had an important influence on its composition. His great financial success has enabled him to organize and support an ambitious "Festival of Two Worlds" in his native land, with the idea of bringing together the creative resources of Europe and the United States.

Like Wagner, Menotti possessed an intuitive sense of the theatre that has enabled him as dramatist to provide opportunities which as composer he can turn into music. And he has been able to do this in a carefully calculated manner so as to interest average audiences. It has often been said that, unlike most of his contemporaries, Menotti does not hesitate to pull the heartstrings of the many rather than the legs of a few. This means that he intentionally deals with such sentimental simplicities as truth, love, duty, and death, and uses dramatic situations that are not complicated. He possesses the fortunate gift of being able to fuse music and words into an inseparable whole that sweeps his listeners along emotionally. But he does not seem to be able to do more than this. When called on to write music that develops dramatically, he has shown little of the power of Puccini, his obvious nineteenth-century precursor. While Menotti's dramatic music is hardly "nothing but watered-down Puccini," as some of his detractors maintain, it lacks the impact, the ability to delineate character, intensify mood, and build to overwhelming climax that makes the music of the older master powerful. It is certain that Menotti's slenderer gifts will never be able to hold the interest shown by opera lovers the world over in the music of Puccini for over half a century.

THE NEO-CLASSICISTS

Characteristic of the neo-Classical ideals followed by a number of the important composers of this generation is Walter Piston (*b.* 1894), whose composing career has been closely associated with his academic career at Harvard, where he taught from 1926 until 1960. A classicist by nature and training, Piston is an outstanding American representative of the Boulanger-Stravinsky tradition; his style has attracted attention as much for the distinction of its materials as for the skill with which these materials are manipulated. Purely musical ideas and their development in a strong formal design are always predominant considerations. Piston feels that his *Fourth Symphony* (1950) comes nearest to solving the problems he envisages between communicative expression and formal design. His earlier works, such as the 1937 *Concertino for piano and chamber orchestra,* show his penchant for using special technical devices, especially the kind of linear counterpoint favored by Stravinsky. His later symphonies (his *Eighth* was premiered in 1965) are more melodious and direct, and therefore seem more grateful. But with the exception of his 1938 ballet suite, *The Incredible Flutist,* Piston's music can hardly be thought of as appealing to the average listener.

Another composer long associated with academic teaching is Roger Sessions (*b.* 1896). Highly regarded by his contemporaries as a man of profound culture and strong intellectual power, Sessions has exerted a powerful influence on American students through his teaching at Smith College, The Cleveland Institute (where he himself studied with Ernest Bloch), the New School in New York, the University of California at Berkeley, and Princeton University. He spent eight years studying in Europe—six in Italy and two in Germany—and since returning to this country in 1933 has been a leader in promoting contemporary music and composers.

That there is a strain of Romanticism in Sessions is clear from his early *Black Maskers Suite,* written in 1923 while he was under the influence of Bloch. But in most of his music he attempts to fuse the various elements—structural outlines, thematic materials, orchestral colors —into a harmonic density that makes his work difficult to listen to. His style, which obviously derives from Stravinsky, though influenced also by Schoenbergian ideals, is severe and strong, hovering between atonal chromaticism and dodecaphony. In addition to five symphonies, he has written some austere chamber music, two piano sonatas, a few keyboard pieces, a *Mass* (1958), and two operas, *The Trial of Lucullus* (1947) and *Montezuma* (1947), which had its premiere in Berlin in 1964.

Born the same year as Gershwin, and as thoroughly American in an entirely different way, was Roy Harris. With his origins in an Oklahoma log cabin he may be said to represent the pioneer spirit of this country's wide open spaces, in strong contrast to the urban nationalism of such composers as Gershwin and Copland. Harris was largely self-taught until he won a fellowship to go abroad in 1927 to study with Boulanger in Paris. He gradually evolved a sturdy neo-Classical essentially diatonic style that employs polytonal counterpoint and does not hesitate to strive for special effects in order to convey moods Harris considers typically American: "noisy ribaldry, a sadness, a grasping earnestness which amounts to suppliance towards those deepest spiritual yearnings within ourselves, and finally, a struggle for power."

All these moods are suggested in Harris's *Third Symphony*, written in 1938. This is his best work, and one he does not seem to have been able to duplicate. Its consistent architectural achievements, strong and rather homespun character, and striking themes made Harris one of the chief protagonists of American music. Although he has written a great deal since and has held numerous teaching positions in various American colleges, he seems gradually to have disappeared from the American scene.

Quincy Porter (*b.* 1897), a more traditional composer, was until 1965 a professor of music at Yale. A violinist and violist himself, he has concentrated on chamber music, writing in a typical neo-Classical style, with fine craftsmanship.

LEADER OF HIS GENERATION

Another important composer of this generation is Aaron Copland, born in Brooklyn at the turn of the century. The general consensus of critical opinion at the half-century mark would probably have named him the most significant American composer of the time. Active as a teacher, lecturer, pianist, conductor, general propagandist, and composer, he became the center of a powerful group that aroused high hopes for the creation of an indigenous American music. Yet because of the strange turn which music took as the century progressed and the startling changes in its language after the middle of the century, any hopes that Copland and those assembled about him might have had for the development of such an American school were swept away, and they were left stranded amidst a powerful backwash of post-Webern serialism—in reality, American composers without a country.

Like that of any significant composer, Copland's style is an amalgam of environmental and hereditary influences. It reflects his urban Jewish origins, American penchant for rhythm, neo-Classical training (he was another of Boulanger's American pupils), considerable intellectual powers, and a generally serious attitude toward life. In spite of the severe, highly cerebral, Stravinskian-influenced compositions of his earlier years (the 1930 *Piano Variations* and the 1935 *Statements for Orchestra* are examples), Copland has been genuinely concerned with becoming an American composer with a style that would assure communication with the music-loving masses rather than with a cultivated minority.

To this end he has consciously used materials and media in a number of his works that appeal to a large public, writing music that is simple and direct, easy to listen to (sometimes too easy, as in the *Lincoln Portrait* of 1942, written to stir up patriotism after the Pearl Harbor disaster), and immediate in appeal. Notable successes in this vein have been the popular Latin-American travelogue *El Salón México* (1937), a light-hearted treatment of rural Americana in the ballets *Billy the Kid* (1938) and *Rodeo* (1942), an orchestral suite made out of a ballet score on a primitive American theme, *Appalachian Spring* (1945), and the genial *Concerto for Clarinet and String Orchestra,* commissioned by Benny Goodman in 1948. All these are American-sounding pieces, as is his most important symphony, the *Third,* written in 1944–46 and described by a sympathetic foreign listener as portraying the "cocky, back-slapping optimism and the gleaming precision action of a prosperous, industrial age."

In his later compositions Copland returned to his earlier, more severe style. The 1950 *Piano Quartet* was written in his former, tough, concentrated manner, and he made a severe orchestral version of the already formidable *Piano Variations.* In 1962 he attempted (not very successfully) to join the ranks of the dodecaphonists in *Connotations for Orchestra,* written for the opening concert of the new Philharmonic Hall in New York. Copland's one attempt to write for the lyric theatre, his 1954 *Tender Land,* plainly shows that he is not a dramatic composer, in spite of its deeply felt lyricism. His *Music for a Great City,* patched together in 1964 from an earlier film score, is a big, four-movement work in his earlier style, with plenty of noise but little substance.

Anyone listening attentively to the younger composers or the film scores produced in Hollywood before mid-century will recognize Copland's influence on the American music of that time. He himself wrote a number of effective film scores, including *Quiet City* (1939), *Of Mice and Men* (1939), *Our Town* (1940), and *The Red Pony* (1948), and many composers in this field copied his general style and mannerisms, just as did those in the more serious field of symphonic writing. In all these Copland-influenced pieces written in this country before the onset of serialism, we hear the same kind of technical competence, the same rather somber scoring, the same lack of intense personal involvement, the same little plaintive motives—all in the proper places.

LATER NEO-CLASSICISTS

Paul Creston (born Joseph Guttoveggio in 1906) is another composer of Italian parentage who has made significant contributions to American musical life. A native of New York, he was trained there and has been active in its church music and orchestral circles. His is a rather somber style; he makes use of traditional materials in quite traditional ways, although he shows a strong leaning toward modal harmonies. A number of his compositions have been recorded, including several of his symphonies; especially noteworthy is the *Third,* subtitled *Three Mystery Symphony* of 1950, dealing with the nativity, crucifixion, and resurrection.

Belonging to the group of composers especially admired by their confreres and the contemporary critics,[7] Eliot Carter (*b.* 1908) received his training and inspiration from a number of sources: Ives, Holst, Harvard, and Boulanger. He has combined his musical interests with an intensive intellectual curiosity and so has acquired a viewpoint that regards music not only as aesthetic experience but as scientific discipline. Carter's reputation as one of the most significant composers this country has produced has been established largely by his chamber music works, especially his two *String Quartets,* the first completed in 1951 and the second in 1959. Both these works are somewhat reminiscent of the Bartók quartets and, like them, bristle with cerebration and surge with energy, particularly rhythmic energy, which Carter employs as an essential dimension of his structure alongside of and parallel to its other elements. But the Carter quartets have little of the breadth of vision or warmth of communication that make the Hungarian master's works in this genre remarkable.

Carter has summarized his whole approach to music-making by say-

[7] Characteristic descriptions: "Carter's *First String Quartet* is one of the handful of truly significant works that open the second half of the century." "With his second quartet Carter reveals his right to be regarded as one of the most distinguished of living composers."—New York *Times.*

ing that he tries to give musical expression to experiences anyone living today must have when confronted with the remarkable changes and relationships that have been uncovered in the human sphere by psychologists and novelists, in the life cycle of insects and marine animals by biologists, and in every domain of science and art. Nevertheless, his works are more admired by professionals because of the competence with which their materials are manipulated than by the public for their expressive content.

William Schuman, a man whose extra-curricular activities as business executive and educational director have almost obliterated his reputation as a composer, was born in New York in 1910. From the very beginning of his musical career, which did not start until he was twenty, he has been connected in one way or another with some musical activity of his native city: as a publisher's editor, as a college teacher and choral director, as president of the Juilliard School, and finally as General Director of the Lincoln Center of the Performing Arts. As a composer influenced by Roy Harris, with whom he studied, he is best known for his strongly rhythmic, big-scale, rather emotionally reserved works, especially his *Third* (1941) and *Eighth* (1962) *Symphonies*. His most popular and very characteristic works are the *American Festival Overture* of 1939 and the 1956 *New England Triptych,* which pays homage to the early New England composer William Billings by using three of his tunes as themes. Schuman's natural gift for choral writing is shown in such things as his settings of Whitman's poetry in *Pioneers* (1937) and *A Free Song* (1942). He has also provided the score for several ballets, including the powerful *Undertow* (1945), *Night Journey* (1947), and *Judith* (1948).

In his composition as in all his other activities, Schuman has shown himself a typically successful American figure: well trained for what he wants to do, aggressive, effective, respectful of but not particularly concerned with tradition, and apt to measure success by activity.

ECLECTIC COMPOSERS OF THESE GENERATIONS

One of the earliest of these was Leo Sowerby (*b.* 1895) who, although he busied himself with all kinds of music, was especially interested in organ and church music, his rather unorthodox harmonies and stringent dissonances stirring up considerable excitement in these rather placid fields of activity. Sowerby's best-known orchestral work, *Prairie* (1929), was inspired by the poem of another midwestern artist, Carl Sandburg.

The Three Penny Opera, carried on the traditions of European socially significant plays in this country. A pupil of Boulanger and Schoenberg, he used a harshly dissonant style well suited to the treatment of such a work as *The Cradle Will Rock,* inspired by the social conditions during the Great Depression. This hybrid combines the characteristics of social drama, revue, and opera, held together largely by political implications. It made an impression when it first appeared in 1937, but attempts to revive it have shown that its principal interest is that of a period-piece pointing the way to later, more significant theatre works. In 1949 Blitzstein composed an opera *Regina,* using as his libretto a powerful American play with strong social implications; although this work shows its composer's dramatic power, its strength is the development of the play used rather than the music—a fatal fault for an opera. At his death Blitzstein was busy with an opera based on one of America's most famous trials, that of Sacco-Vanzetti; his sketches for this have been found and the work may yet materialize from other hands.

THE EAGER EXPERIMENTERS

Henry Cowell (1897–1965), although he wrote a vast amount of music of all kinds (over a thousand works according to his own account), held teaching positions in a number of schools and universities, and championed the cause of serious new music in this country, is best known as an experimenter, especially in ways of liberating harmony from its traditional connections and opening the ears of the world to new sounds. In these attempts to extend the horizons of music through research and experiment, Cowell helped prepare the way for the noise specialists and tape maneuverers. One of his chief contributions to these experiments has been the use of clenched fists, elbows, and even the entire length of the player's arm to produce what he calls "tone-clusters." He introduced these into many of his compositions, sometimes imitating the resultant effect in the orchestra, in order to surround his melodies and themes with clouds of tones and overtones. A number of these piano effects were recorded in pieces bearing unusual titles—*Amiable Conversation, Dynamic Motion, Advertisement,* and the like. The chief items on his long list of compositions are his symphonies, many of them quite romantic in nature, with folk elements and exotic touches.

Another member of the so-called "whiz-bang" group, George Antheil (1900–1959), is remembered today chiefly as the "bad boy of music." His *Ballet mécanique,* scored for anvils, airplane propellers, electric bells, auto-horns, and player pianos, made a tremendous stir in its day, thousands being turned away from its performance in Paris in 1927. Although Antheil's friend Ezra Pound described this music as a world of steel, its vision does not seem to have been very successfully realized if we can judge by its recording, and one wonders how much excitement its performance would stir up today in competition with recent works in this manner. Antheil wrote six symphonies in a more or less conventional style, as well as an exotic opera, *Transatlantic* (1929).

Another experimental composer is the Californian Harry Partch (*b.* 1901) who, to get away from what he considers our falsely tempered scale and its exhausted harmonic possibilities, evolved a scale of his own. Taking as his point of departure the melodies of spoken or intoned words, Partch divided the octave into 45 microtones, the use of which gives an effect of glittering instrumental rhythms and weird, wailing sounds. He invented and built a small orchestra of new instruments, mainly percussion and plucked strings, to play music based on this new scale, and composed for it such pieces as *Windsong,* for the 1958 film of that name, and *The Bewitched.* Although they have historical interest, these experiments largely lost their point after electronic instruments proved capable of producing intervals of any desired size and timbres of any quality.

The Composers of the Forties and Fifties

Merely to mention the names of the composers who came to maturity around the turn of the half-century is to show the ever-widening scope and broadening interests of American music. These men, who had available to them all the compositional techniques that had been developed during the first half of the century, chose their particular manner of handling musical resources from a kind of grab-bag containing a wide variety of styles and different kinds of techniques. Some of them kept rather strictly to neo-Classicism, which by this time had lost much of its *panache*. Others became interested in folklore and its possibilities. Still others reverted to a kind of neo-Romanticism. But most of them

music are an outstanding example of what may be accomplished in this important field. But only the future can determine which of the potentialities of this extraordinary musical personality will be further developed.

NEO-CLASSICISTS

Prominent among those mid-century Americans who have adhered to neo-Classical ideals is Arthur Berger (*b.* 1912), who has combined professional newspaper criticism and university teaching with his career as a composer. Berger has used stylistic elements drawn from both Stravinskian neo-Classicism and Webern dodecaphony to exemplify his belief that music is an autonomous art, a thing in itself rather than a response to life.

Norman Dello Joio (*b.* 1913), a member of a New York Italo-American musical family that gave him a background of church music, Italian opera, and jazz, all of which helped him determine his style, studied with Hindemith and became interested in Schoenbergian techniques. Consequently he developed a fluent, neo-Classical style in which he writes easily and freely, and which befits his lyrical heritage. He has turned out an enormous amount of music: orchestral pieces, such as the *Meditations on Ecclesiastes* (1956) and *Variations, Chaconne and Finale* (1947), concertos, songs, and choral works, and several operas, including *The Trial at Rouen* (1955), *The Ruby* (1955), and *Blood Moon* (1961).

Roger Goeb (*b.* 1914) and Ben Weber (*b.* 1916) are two Midwesterners fortunate enough to have had a symphony recorded by no less a figure than Leopold Stokowski. Goeb's *Third Symphony* (1951) is a characteristically dissonant neo-Classical work; Weber's *Symphony on Poems by William Blake* (1950) achieves a more Romantic atmosphere suitable to its title through a flexible adaptation of dodecaphonic techniques. Both these men, like most of their confreres, have written a considerable amount of chamber music.

Alexei Haieff (*b.* 1914), a characteristic product of Stravinskian neo-Classical internationalism, is a Russian-born composer who came to this country in 1931. His music has all the usual traits of this style: strongly dissonant counterpoint, rhythmic vitality, and a general lack of any personal involvement.

David Diamond (*b.* 1915) has tried to blend the neo-Classicism which he developed during his studies with Rogers, Sessions, and Boulanger with a neo-Romantic trend toward clearer melodic lines and more basic tonal harmonies. The result has been some fresh, though uncompromising, works of considerable difficulty for most listeners.

Robert Palmer (*b.* 1915) is still another neo-Classicist, concerned with the development of purely musical ideas and totally organic structures.

Vincent Persichetti (*b.* 1915) has devoted his considerable ability to attempting to fuse the many and varied influences of his period into a personal style. The rather bland results lack authority, however, for Persichetti's synthesis is artificial. It is largely tonal, though he manipulates his counterpoint so as to produce polytonal relationships; it emphasizes rhythmic vigor and diatonic rather than chromatic lines. He has been particularly active in the choral fields.

Characteristic of the present-day Negro's attitude toward his racial backgrounds, Ulysses Kay's (*b.* 1917) music has no nationalistic flavor and no programmatic connotations whatsoever. He manipulates the usual neo-Classical counterpoint with skill; his harmonies are strongly dissonant; his rhythmic impulse drives his music steadily onward; and his orchestration is competent. In a word, he is a good neo-Classicist whose music sounds very similar to that of all his like-minded contemporaries. Kay's *Serenade for Orchestra* (1954) is one of his best-known works; a Guggenheim Fellowship has helped him write a seven-cast, full-evening opera, *The Game*.

THE ECLECTICS

Although originally inspired by the ideals of Stravinskian neo-Classicism, Irving Fine (1914–1962) achieved a more generic cosmopolitan style in his later works, such as the string orchestra lament, *Serious Song,* composed in 1959. Befitting his New England background, his music makes its points through understatement.

Hugo Weisgall (*b.* 1912) has shown strong affinity for writing expressionistic operas. A native Czech, he has lived in this country since 1928 and has been active here as conductor and teacher as well as composer. Highly dramatic in the mid-European manner and employing all the mid-European techniques, Weisgall's style is well adapted to the tensions of such dramatists as Wedekind and Strindberg. This is well shown in his settings of their plays, *The Tavern* (1950) and *The Stranger* (1952).

Norman Cazden (*b.* 1914) has combined the careers of composer and musicologist. His eclectic, rather academic style has distinctive folk-loric touches, making use of the materials he has gathered in various parts of New York State. *Three Ballads from the Catskills* (1949) and a musical play *Dingle Hill* (1958) are typical.

At the beginning of his career, George Perle (*b.* 1915) was attracted to the twelve-tone system, and the greater part of the considerable amount of music he has written since 1939 is in this style. Like others of his contemporaries, however, Perle has found it expedient to modify the rigidity of the tonerow technique by occasionally allowing purely musical ideas to function on their own level, as in his 1953 *Rhapsody for Orchestra.*

George Rochberg (*b.* 1918) has devoted his efforts to adapting the twelve-tone system to fit his need for expression. His 1958 *Second Symphony* shows what he has been able to do in combining a dodecaphonic vocabulary, serialist techniques, and large-scale forms.

Leon Kirchner (*b.* 1919) is a product of the exciting West Coast musical atmosphere of the 1930's and 40's. He is one of the few men of his generation to emphasize the need for expressiveness in music. "Many contemporary composers, dominated by the fear of self-expression, have sought the superficial security of current style and fad worship, and have made a fetish of complexity," he has said. "Idea, the precious ore of art, is lost in a jungle of graphs, prepared tapes, feedbacks, and void minutiae." How far Kirchner, with his advanced idiom and complex constructional principles, has succeeded in recovering the humanistic ideals of an earlier age can best be judged by listening to the work for which he is best known, the *Piano Concerto* of 1952–53, an enormously scaled, three-movement work that makes virtuosic demands on both soloist and orchestra.

A GROUP OF EXPERIMENTAL COMPOSERS

The leading figure among the experimental composers of this era is John Cage (*b.* 1912). Those familiar with his attempts to remove all personal intention from music and make all audible phenomena its proper tools will recognize him as one of the most important figures in modern art, strongly influencing a whole generation not only of musicians, but painters, poets, and dancers as well—and this in spite of, or perhaps because of, his irritating mannerisms and propensity for presenting himself unfavorably to the public eye.

Growing up in an intellectual climate that fostered all sorts of radical experiments, Cage studied with Schoenberg, Cowell, and Varèse. In order to develop further Cowell's ideas on piano technique, Cage initiated what he called a "prepared" piano: a piano so fitted with gadgets—screws, thumbtacks, rubber bands, coins, and the like—that its tone is transformed into an ensemble of softly percussive sounds. It was his performance on this instrument, together with the music that he wrote for it, that first attracted public attention. He has furthered other experimental ideas that have become part and parcel of avant-garde techniques: random or aleatory compositions, which, in their attempt to escape the straight-jacket of structuralism, depend on such chance devices as a cast of dice or toss of a coin to determine what materials are to be used and how they are to be manipulated; the exploration of the negative as well as the positive principle of composition through the production of such works as *4 Minutes and 33 Seconds* (1954), consisting of a silent period of this duration during which a player sits at a piano without playing a note; happenings, a form that has become popular in all the arts; and the use of electronic equipment to produce all sorts of new and entirely different sounds.

Since a considerable amount of Cage's music has been recorded, every listener can form his own estimate of its value as art. But there is no question as to its influence on mid-century aesthetics.

The work of Harry Brant (*b.* 1913) vividly illustrates the effect of science on the arts of this period. His efforts as a composer have been directed to producing *directional* rather than *ensemble* sounds, thus emphasizing the effects which are produced in stereo recording. His scores call for various groups of performers to be placed in different locations, each of them playing in different keys, rhythms, and tempos. Among his compositions are the appropriately titled pieces *Signs and Alarms* (1953) and *Grand Universal Circus* (1956).

Lou Harrison (*b.* 1917) is of the Varèse-Cowell-Cage lineage. He has been influenced by all the fads and fashions of the period—dodecaphony, neo-Classicism, and exoticism, the last derived largely from his extra-musical activities. He has shown considerable interest in developing ways for the improvement of constructing instruments and has written a number of "sinfonias" for percussion orchestras, in addition to some relatively conservative orchestral pieces.

Milton Babbitt (*b.* 1916), one-time instructor in mathematics and later professor of music at Princeton, has become one of the leading figures of the 1960 avant-garde through his experimental work with electronic music. Earlier he was known for his espousal of a rigidly constructed type of writing based on the logic of the twelve-tone method, his aim being, he said, "a really autonomous music that does not depend upon analogies with tonal music." To this end he applied the serial techniques formerly used in tonerow manipulation to every aspect of his music: its rhythmic and dynamic elements, its various timbres, even its instrumental registers—all are serialized.[9] He has written a number of these cerebral manipulations, among them *Three Compositions for Piano* (1947), *Composition for Twelve Instruments* (1948), *Composition for Tenor and Six Instruments*.

The fact that for most listeners these compositions sound exactly like what they are—tonal mathematics—does not concern Babbitt in the least. He believes that the serious composer today must accept isolation from the general public as the price he must pay for being the harbinger of developments that are necessary if music is to evolve in the future as it has in the past. Babbitt's intellectually structured music is not as important, however, as the experiments and developments he has made with electronic media. As early as 1947 he became interested in trying to adapt the principles of the twelve-tone system to the non-pitch elements which can be produced by the manipulations of tapes and similar electronic processes. He has been a leading spirit in the center which Princeton and Columbia Universities have set up for research in this kind of music. Babbitt's principal work in this field is *Composition for Synthesizer* (1964).

The two other composers largely responsible for the development of electronic music in this country are Otto Luenig *(b.* 1900) and Vladimir Ussachevsky *(b.* 1911), both of whom have worked at Columbia. Their *Rhapsodic Variations for Tape Recorder and Orchestra* (1954) and *Poem of Cycles and Bells* show what they have been able to do in this new medium.

Still Another Generation

As the number of younger American composers increases, it is obviously impossible to mention them all. In general it may be said that the composers of the generation born between 1920 and 1930 have become more and more intrigued by the inherent possibilities of even greater complexity, although a few

[9] Some claim that he antedated Boulez in this serialization of all the elements of music.

have seemed aware of the increasing danger of their music becoming obscure in its striving to be intricate. The influence of jazz becomes more evident, especially its emphasis on the importance of improvisation and the significance of the performer in the final result.

THE INFLUENCE OF JAZZ

Hall Overton (*b.* 1920), a pupil of Riegger and Milhaud, is representative of these trends. A long association with jazz affected his more serious writing, though he has made no attempt to combine the two styles. His best-known works are his *Second String Quartet* (1954) and his *Second Symphony* of 1962.

Mel Powell (*b.* 1923) has had a checkered career as jazz pianist in Benny Goodman's band, member of the Army Air Force Band, popular Hollywood musician, student of Schillinger,[10] Toch, and Hindemith, and finally university professor. Out of this varied experience has come a carefully woven, meticulous style especially well suited to chamber music. Powell's later works were strongly influenced by the pointillism of Webern, as is evident in the intense expressivity of his *Filigree Setting for String Quartet* (1959).

Gunther Schuller (*b.* 1925), the acknowledged leader of the so-called Third Stream—those composers who have tried to combine jazz and advanced compositional techniques—has been active as a lecturer, horn virtuoso, teacher, conductor, and composer. A practising musician who served as a player in several important American orchestras, a writer who believes that the creative artist should try to communicate with his public and not limit himself to specialized audiences, and a skilled composer who has been influenced by the rhythmic freedom and improvisatory freedom of modern jazz, Schuller has seemed to be the one personality able to bridge the gap between contemporary techniques and popular appreciation, as well as to arouse enthusiasm for modern music among general, as opposed to elite, listeners.

His orchestral suite *Seven Studies on Themes by Paul Klee* (1959) is an attempt to do just this. Based on pictures by the famous surrealist painter (who was himself a musician), the technical methods used in these pieces vary according to the composer's reaction to each of the paintings chosen: serialism and non-serialism, tonality and atonality, abstract and programmatic expression exist side by side, and the whole

---

[10] This Russian-born teacher and theorist had an important influence on a considerable number of American composers through his system of composition based on rigid mathematical principles. A number of composers of popular music, including George Gershwin, found his instruction very helpful.

THREE PHASES OF CONTEMPORARY AMERICAN ART

Collection, The Museum of Modern Art, New York

NUMBER 1 by Jackson Pollock (1948)

result is intelligible and amusing to an average audience, as has been often proved in performance. Schuller's specifically jazz works include a 1959 *Concertino for Jazz Quartet and Orchestra* and *Conversations* (1959). His abstract concert pieces include *Music for Brass Quartet* (1961) and *Fantasy Quartet for Celli* (1958).

OPERA WRITERS OF THIS GENERATION

Jack Beeson (*b.* 1921) spent the early years of his life in Muncie, Indiana, the town which a famous sociological study showed to be the typical American town of 1929. This may have prompted him to concentrate on characteristic American themes, making an opera out of William Saroyan's play *Hello, Out There* and basing *The Sweet Bye and Bye* on the adventures of a famous American woman evangelist. In 1965 his verismo portrait of *Lizzie Borden*, painted in dramatically vivid colors, received its premiere at the New York Civic Opera. This story of one of the most famous of American murders was most enthusiastically received.

The career of Robert Kurka (1921–1957), an American of Czech descent and one of the most talented composers of his generation, was

SWEET WILLIAM by
John Chamberlain
(1962)

CURRENT by Bridget
Riley (1964)

Collection, The Museum of Modern Art, New York
Philip C. Johnson Fund

tragically short. Although he wrote a number of instrumental works, including two symphonies and five string quartets, he will be remembered by his opera *The Good Soldier Schweik,* after a novel by the Czech writer Jaroslav Hasek. Like Berg's *Wozzeck,* it narrates the trials of the "long-abused, victimized and patient comman man." Finished after the composer's death from his sketches, it shows Kurka to have been a composer on the way to real distinction.

Lee Hoiby (*b.* 1926) and Carlisle Floyd (*b.* 1926) have made their names as opera writers. The former, a pupil of Menotti, has written in the Romantic vein; *The Scarf* was introduced to the Spoleto Festival of 1958 and *A Day in the Country* was produced by the New York City Opera. Floyd won recognition with *Susanah* (1955), an American folk adaptation of the familiar Biblical tale of Susanna and the elders, which showed a remarkable ability on the part of the composer for realizing dramatic potentialities, an ability that was unfortunately not fully sustained in his later *Wuthering Heights* (1958), set to his own libretto fashioned from Brontë's novel.

Ned Rorem (*b.* 1923) has achieved a considerable reputation as a writer of songs that are lineally descended from the great Romantic composers of this genre. Great hopes were held for his opera based on Strindberg's play *Miss Julie,* produced in New York in 1965, hopes that were unfortunately unjustified; for, like so many American operas, this work lacks dramatic development, though it contains a number of interesting lyric bits.

AN INCREASED AWARENESS OF ROMANTICISM

John LaMontaine (*b.* 1920) reflects his generation's increased awareness of the significance of Romanticism as a musical quality. His 1958 *Piano Concerto* brought him a Pulitzer Prize and his orchestral work *From Sea to Sunlit Sea* was chosen for President Kennedy's inaugural concert.

The post-Romantic William Bergsma (*b.* 1920) is well known for his choral and instrumental works, many of which have been recorded. Characteristic are *The Fortunate Islands* (1947) for string orchestra and the opera *The Wife of Martin Guerre* (1955).

William Flannigan (*b.* 1926) is another American composer with a special flair for vocal writing. A perceptive reviewer and critic, as well as composer, he has displayed two distinctive personalities: as critic he has been able to comment objectively on all the musical trends of his time; as composer, he has refused to conform to the fashions of the day and has written simply and clearly, in a straightforward, tonal style. Characteristic is his cantata written with Edward Albee, *The Lady of Tearful Regret* (1958).

AN OUTSTANDING NEO-CLASSICIST

Andrew Imbrie (*b.* 1921), on the other hand, is a neo-Classicist, his style largely dependent on contrapuntal texture. Born in New York, he studied composition on both the east and west coasts, principally with Sessions, and since 1949 has been on the faculty of the University of California at Berkeley. His *Violin Concerto* (1950–54) has gradually established its place as one of the few orchestral masterpieces of this century because of its power of communication. And this in spite of the density of its texture, the complexity of its structure, the difficulty of its chromatic language, and its carefully polished craftsmanship. What really counts here, as with all good music, is the fact that the composer had something to say and knew how to say it with directness and immediacy, even though he employed the technically difficult language of his time. In this respect Imbrie's *Concerto* strongly resembles the violin concertos of Berg and Bartók.

COMPOSITE STYLES

Daniel Pinkham (*b.* 1923) is a characteristic New England product, in both his training and his career. His music has not been strongly caught up in the turmoil of current fashions and so has a distinctiveness and clarity not always to be found in the works of his contemporaries. He has written in all forms, paying special attention to chorus and choral music, including a chamber opera, *The Garden of Artemus* (1948).

Peter Mennini (shortened to Menin) was born in Erie, Pennsylvania, in 1923, the younger of two talented members of the family to become professional musicians. He has been prominent as director of two famous American music schools, the Peabody Conservatory in Baltimore and the Juilliard School in New York. His eclectic, strongly rhythmic compositions include seven symphonies (number seven, the *Variation Symphony*, was given its premiere in 1964); they are generally neo-Classical in style, without extreme dissonance, and tend toward diatonic harmony and counterpoint.

Lucas Foss, born Fuchs in Berlin in 1922 and resident of the United States since 1937, is a musical internationalist and universalist, so much so that his greatest problem as a composer has been to forge all the influences to which he has been subjected—German Romanticism, neo-Classicism, Copland Americanism, French experimentalism, Stravinskian rhythmic propulsion—into an integrated style of his own. He has engaged in a wide variety of activities: pianist, conductor, teacher, avant-garde propagandist. He was closely associated with Koussevitzky at Tanglewood as one of the first students there; he succeeded Schoenberg as professor at the University of California; and he assumed the duties of the conductorship of the Buffalo Orchestra. With all this, he has gradually developed as one of the chief exponents and champions of new music, and has taken part in some of its most unusual experiments.

Foss's first American work, a cantata based on Carl Sandburg's poem *The Prairie,* received its premiere performance in 1944. In it he tried, not very successfully, to grasp some of the *ethos* of his new homeland. His short opera *The Jumping Frog of Calaveras County* (1950) after the story by Mark Twain, was another such attempt. Several Biblical cantatas, *The Song of Anguish* (1945), *Song of Songs* (1946), the 1953 *Parable of Death,* and a setting of *Psalms* (1956) show his continuing interest in vocal writing. In *Time Cycle* (1960) he advanced into more clearly defined modernism, using serialism, atonalism, and other contemporary devices to depict the transience of time. In his attempt to transfer some of the improvisatory freedom and spontaneous excitement into concert hall music, Foss joined the ranks of the Free-Art Improvisors by forming a small ensemble group which he himself led, to create its own harmony, counterpoint, and form in on-the-spot improvisations, without the limitations of written music. *Echoi* (1963) for four soloists, is an example of what he achieved in this manner.

William Sydeman (*b.* 1928) has proved to be one of the most prolific composers of his generation. His works are typical of the period—abstract, without tonal orientation, and developed largely through the juxtaposition of contrasting sound patterns rather than the manipulation of tonal materials. Characteristic are the *Orchestral Abstractions* (1963) and *Study No. 3 for Orchestra* (1965); like most of the music of this era, these can be best described as "works not to like or dislike, but nevertheless, hard to ignore."

ELECTRONIC MUSIC

Two prominent experimenters are Milton Feldman (*b.* 1926) and Earle Brown (*b.* 1926). Both are disciples of Cage and have attempted to follow his ideas regarding chance or aleatory music, the use of all possible phenomena as tools for music, and the development of electronic music. Feldman, through his studies with Riegger and Volpe, seems to have absorbed at least some of the serial procedures. Brown, because of his studies in engineering and experience as a recording engineer, acquired an understanding of electronic equipment that has stood him in good stead. Characteristic works are *Durations* (1960–61) by Feldman and *Light Music* and *25 Pages* by Brown. Scored for lights, electronic equipment, and full orchestra, *Light Music* has to be performed in cooperation with an electronic studio; *25 Pages,* according to the composer, is capable of being played in any sequence; each page may be performed either side up; events within each system may be read either as treble or bass; the total time duration is between eight minutes, twenty seconds, and twenty-five minutes; and the piece may be played by any number of persons up to twenty-five.

Charles Wuorinen (*b.* 1938) has been a very active worker and experimenter in the field of electronic music, as well as a composer of more traditional works. In such a work as *Orchestral and Electronic Exchanges,* begun in 1964, he combines orchestral performance with tape recording, the basic material being presented in the tape part and commented on in the orchestral part. The 1965 *Chamber Concerto for Oboe and Ten Players* is in a typical disjointed post-Webern style, with insistence on extreme instrumental effects, especially those produced by the percussionists.

In Summary

The position of the artist, especially of the musician, in the United States has changed appreciably during the course of the twentieth century. The life of the creative artist in any epoch of history has never been easy. But, as the American novelist Thomas Wolfe said in his *Story of a Novel,* it may well have been during the early part of this century one of the hardest lives that man has ever known. This was so not only because the country's "run of attention" worked against the artist's life and tended to stifle his growth but because it was necessary for the American artist to find the power and energy for his existence, for the articulation of his speech, for the very substance of his art, in the dense complexities and peripheral activities of the nation's life.

In spite of these difficulties, the twentieth-century creative artists of this country did make tremendous forward strides. Although the country as a whole can hardly be said to have been art-conscious during the century's early decades, by mid-century American painters had not only been able to absorb all the important European techniques of Expressionism, Cubism, Surrealism, and the rest but had evolved a flourishing contemporary school of their own—Abstract Expressionism—which influenced the painting techniques of the rest of the Western world. The changes which the American architects of the first half of the century forced on the International style during the period between World Wars I and II were significant enough to influence the architectural thinking of all the Europeans. And it was during this time that the United States produced a school of writers which, starting in the 1920's and continuing through the next two decades, attracted sufficient international attention to gain six American Nobel Prizes in literature.

In music, however, at least in concert music, our composers have never been able to attain a position of leadership. Just as the American composer of the century's early decades was dominated by European influences, so the men who came later simply joined—some years afterward—the musical trends which had sprung up in Europe after World War I. At one time there seemed a good possibility that a distinctive American school of composition might develop out of the activities of the group which centered around Copland and included such men as Harris, Piston, Thomson, Barber and, later, Schuman and Della Joio. But we have shown how these once significant figures in American music were either completely carried away or were left stranded in the backwash of the tremendously powerful stream that swept out of Europe after World War II with the discovery of Webern and the re-discovery of Schoenberg. The younger men of the next generation, feeling that the music of the composers of the '20's and '30's had little or nothing to communicate to them, trouped to the standards of the post-Webern dodecaphonists. It was no longer the works of these masters of the past— Copland, Harris, Piston, Barber, and Schuman—that interested them, but those of Riegger, Carter, Babbitt, Stockhausen, and Boulez, together with the experimentalists with tapes and other devices. These postwar Americans were, of course, simply following the trends which developed in all the other arts at this time.

But unfortunately for them, the composers were not able to duplicate the success which their avant-garde confreres in painting, sculpture, and architecture have had in reaching the American public with their innovations. Today's public, with plenty of prodding on the part of museum directors, dealers, and collectors, has become acquainted with, and interested in, the works of the non-objective painters, the Abstract Expressionists, the "junk" and "op" artists, the abstract sculpture of Moore, Hartung, and Lipton, the mobiles of Calder, the architectural designs of the followers of Gropius, Mies van der Rohe, Pier Nervi. Back in the thirties and forties, this was also true of music: such avant-gardists of that time as Bartók, Hindemith, Poulenc, Barber, Copland, and Harris were talked about and their music was listened to by relatively large numbers of people. Even if the concert-goers did not like what these composers wrote, their music stirred up a great deal of interest and they were the recognized leaders of the musical world.

Now the very names of the new generation composers (with the possible exception of Cage, whose ability to get himself before the public we have already noted) are unknown to the public. Their music is listened to only by other composers or by select audiences. Whatever the reason, it is only too obvious that the same American public which has become enthusiastic about contemporary painting, sculpture, and architecture has shown very little enthusiasm for contemporary concert music.[11] As we have remarked, the composers have done very little to improve the situation.

This is not to say, of course, that music has been neglected by the American public during the gradual cultural renaissance which has been taking place during this century, a renaissance that has produced a rise in interest in the arts by a mass public unparalleled in history. Insofar as music is concerned, this interest has been manifested largely in improving the technical quality of our performances, the enlargement of physical facilities through such devices as the arts council and the cultural center, and the securing of adequate government support for both the creators and the performers of music. The technological and economic changes of the past decades have helped foster this interest and have created a market for the arts which is one of the fastest-growing markets in the world. The demand for concert tickets, for new and improved recording and reproducing machines, for more and better musical instruction, has increased enormously—indeed, consumer spending in the arts has risen, according to the economists, better than

[11] Evidence of the wide gap between the American contemporary composer and his public is the fact that there were no Pulitzer Prizes given in the field of music for the years 1964 and 1965. These prizes, awarded each year for outstanding achievements in journalism, letters, and music, are given on the recommendation of an advisory board representing what may be described as intelligent journalistic opinion.

six times the outlays for spectator sports. There is more civic pride in symphony concerts and opera companies than ever before, just as there is more private and foundation support for artists. In short, the arts, and especially music, seem to have provided the people with a new kind of status symbol.

If this is to be more than a cultural boom, however, the future must become more concerned with spiritual changes and not be content with purely physical ones. Attempts must be made to create Great Audiences as well as Great Auditoriums in which to house them; the American public must come to realize that there is more to what it has come to think of as "culture" than the building of centers for performing arts. Solicitude for training taste must match attention to the development of performing skills. Listeners must become aware of the need for supplementing their repertoire with new types and modes of musical expression, rather than letting themselves remain satisfied with the heritage, however rich, from the past.

How this can best be accomplished or, indeed, whether it can be accomplished at all, is a matter for the future to disclose.

Music in the Other Americas

We are apt to forget that a full hundred years before the Pilgrims set foot on Plymouth Rock in 1620, an intrepid Spanish explorer, Hernándo Cortéz, battled inland from Vera Cruz to what is now Mexico City, conquered this powerful capital of Montezuma and substituted for its flourishing Aztec civilization the ideals of the European Spanish empire. Included in Cortéz's forces were musicians who helped found the first music schools on the American continent. From Mexico this European musical tradition quickly spread to the other parts of colonial Spanish America. Long before the English and French traditions were established in North America, a vigorous musical life had arisen in the lands south of the Rio Grande. Combined with this Spanish background was a peculiar mixture of native elements which helped give the music of Latin America, both popular and serious, a character and flavor quite different from that of any other nation in the world.

So we have, in Latin America, a music made up of components of the European style (Spanish in most countries, Portuguese in Brazil), music surviving from the early original inhabitants, and music brought in from Africa by the Negroes. This Latin-American music is particularly rich in emotion, quite direct and simple in content, rhythmically complex and fascinating, melodically haunting and, above all, alive.

These hybrid elements are more readily observed in the dance music, which in more recent years has become extremely popular in ballrooms the world over. Such dances as the tango, conga, samba, maxixe, béguine, and habanera are known far beyond the borders of Latin America and serve as excellent representatives of its folk spirit.

There have been a number of important composers in these countries. The Brazilian composer Antonio Carlos Gomes (1839–1896) started a tradition of opera-writing unequalled by any of the other Americas. To date, over fifteen hundred ballets and operas by Latin American composers have been written, a number of which have been presented on European stages. The Overture to Gomes's opera *Il Guarany* (1870) has become one of the best known of all South American orchestral pieces. Alberto Nepomuceno (1864–1920) used thematic material from Brazilian folk music in his orchestral works and may be said to have been the precursor of the important Brazilian nationalistic school. Following him were the nationalists Oscar L. Fernândez (1897–1948) and Francisco Mignone (*b.* 1897).

The most outstanding of Latin American composers, and one of the important world figures in the music of his time was Heitor Villa-Lobos (1887–1959). Although he may be called a nationalist, since so much of his music was derived from the natural exuberance of Brazilian folk melodies and rhythms, he developed an eclectic style which combined folk resources with European values and produced results that far transcended a simple nationalistic spirit. Largely self-taught, widely traveled, and tremendously energetic, Villa-Lobos wrote an enormous amount of music that has been played everywhere. His series of works with the title *Choros,* for example, ranges from small chamber music works to vast symphonic scores that require huge orchestral resources. His monumental series *Discovery of Brazil* is made up of four suites of ten pieces, all of them containing gorgeous splotches of exotic color and every sort of sophisticated polytonal technique. He composed a number of operas based on folk tunes; and his series *Bachianas Brasileiras* is an attempt to amalgamate the universal spirit of Bach's music, which Villa-Lobos considered to be deeply rooted in the folk music of every country in the world, with the harmonic, contrapuntal and melodic atmosphere of the folklore of the northeastern regions of Brazil—truly a strange combination, but one that resulted in some first-class music, such as that in the fifth number of this set, one of the most haunting pieces written during the whole century.

The best known of the younger Brazilian composers is Claudio Santoro (*b.* 1919), who started as a twelve-tone composer but later, after study with Boulanger and a trip to Russia, adopted a simpler, more diatonic style so that he could become a "composer of the people." His music, exemplified by the *Seventh Symphony* (1964), resembles that of Shostakovitch in its exultant quality and impressive handling of colorful tonal masses.

Argentina is another South American country with a large and productive music history, which began with the early activities of the missionaries who attempted to teach European arts and crafts to the native Indians. The first important contemporary Argentine composer was Alberto Williams (1862–1952), who founded the Conservatory of Buenos Aires and, strongly influenced by the music of César Franck, composed a great deal in the traditional style. Because of the prominence of the Teatro Colón in the life of the country, there has been considerable activity on the part of Argentinian opera composers. Felipe Boero (*b.* 1884) has been especially prominent, his 1929 *El Matrero,* with its story of life on the Argentine pampas, proving a great success. The two Castro brothers, José Matia (*b.* 1892) and Juan José (*b.* 1895) have been active both as composers and conductors, as well as in the *Grupo Renovación,* devoted to radical musical experiments. The most prominent member of this dissenting group is Juan Carlos Paz (*b.* 1897), who has written works in neo-Classical, atonal, polytonal, and twelve-tone styles. The outstanding figure of the younger Argentinians is Alberto Ginastera (*b.* 1916), whose works, though naturalistic, use advanced procedures. His ballets *Panambi* (1940) and *Estancia* (1941) and his *Piano Concerto* (1961) have become known in this country through recordings; and his opera *Don Rodrigo,* produced in Buenos Aires in 1964 and New York in 1966, created something of a furore with its twelve-tone score.

In Mexico, Carlos Chávez (*b.* 1899) and Silvestre Revultas (1899–1940) set out to write music that was expressive of their people. Chávez started his composing career along pseudo-European lines; like the other men concerned with the recent artistic renaissance which has taken place in Mexico, he discovered the folk art of his country, and since that discovery has drawn his inspiration largely from it. Such orchestral works as *Sinfonía India* (1936) and *Xochipili Macuilxochitl* (1940) are derived directly from this source. Yet in them and in a number of his other works, Chávez has succeeded in amalgamating the folk tradition with real musical form in such a way as to give them extreme clarity of expression and definiteness of outline. His nationalistic qualities have been likened to those of the somber, severe paintings of his noted countryman José Clemente Orozco (1883–1949).

Revultas, on the other hand, used Mexican folk dances in a much more direct, spontaneous way; his compositions are picturesque and gay, but have little of the organizational quality of Chávez's works. *Homage to Federico García Lorca* (1936) based on Indian and Hispanic rhythms and *Sensemayá* (1938) are characteristic.

Blas Galindo (*b.* 1910), a composer of Indian descent, seems to be the most likely successor to Chávez in his application of the neo-Classical style to native materials. Other men of this generation in Mexico include Daniel Ayala (*b.* 1908), Salvador Contreras (*b.* 1912), and Pablo Moncayo (1912–1958).

Humberto Allende (*b.* 1885) and Domingo Santa Cruz (*b.* 1899) have been prominent in Chilean music, the latter having served in a number of important educational positions, including the presidency of the organization which controls all of Chile's concert activities.

Cuban music is of special interest because of its cross-breeding of Spanish and Negroid influences with fascinating results, especially in dance music. Even such European-trained composers as Joaquin Nin (1879–1949) and his son Joaquin Nin-Culwell (*b.* 1908) were affected by this influence, as were the later Alejandre Caturia (1906–1940) and Amadeo Roldán (1900–1939).

These Latin Americans, aided to a great extent by the various Central and South American governments, have succeeded in producing native schools of music having a strongly nationalistic point of view and yet incorporating the best of contemporary techniques and modes of thought.

A SELECTED BIBLIOGRAPHY

The following makes no claim of being a complete bibliography. It is simply a list of books on music that have proved valuable to the authors of *Music and History* and which they pass on to their readers to widen their interests and supplement their knowledge.[1]

GENERAL REFERENCE

Grove's Dictionary of Music and Musicians (New York: St. Martin's Press) first appeared in 1879–89 in four volumes. The first standard reference work in English, it has since appeared in further editions, the last under the editorship of Eric Blom in 1954 in ten volumes. This is generally considered the most comprehensive reference work in the English language, although the articles are not always authoritative.

The New Oxford History of Music (London: Oxford) is a standard work by English writers that was meant to replace *The Oxford History of Music* issued at the beginning of the century. It was planned to cover the whole history of music in ten volumes, each paralleled by a series of illustrative recordings. Although all the records have been issued, so far only three volumes have appeared: *Ancient and Oriental Music; Early Medieval Music to 1300;* and *Ars Nova and the Renaissance.* These have been criticized as not always in line with the results of the most recent investigations in their particular fields.

International Cyclopedia of Music and Musicians (New York: Dodd Mead), originally edited by Oscar Thompson, was issued in its ninth edition in 1964.

The Oxford Companion to Music (New York: Oxford), edited by Percy Scholes, is the most readable of all the general encyclopedias and has been kept up to date by new editions, the latest of which was the ninth, issued in 1955.

The Harvard Dictionary of Music (Cambridge: Harvard) by Willi Apel is an outstanding reference work, but contains no biographies. The 13th edition was published in 1961. A smaller companion, *A Brief Harvard Dictionary* (1960), contains material of interest to general readers.

Die Musik in Geschichte und Gegenwart (Kassel; Barenreiter), probably the best of all the general reference works, is available only in German. The first volume was issued in 1929 and the twelfth in 1965.

Baker's Biographical Dictionary of Musicians (New York: Schirmer) 1965 edition was completely revised by Nicolas Slonimsky. It contains an abundance of factual data on the lives of musicians, together with the dates and titles of their major works and the dates of their first performances. Invaluable, since its information has been most carefully researched and is as reliable as is humanly possible.

[1] "§" indicates paper edition.

The Columbia Encyclopedia (New York: Columbia), third edition 1963, gives the general reader the essential facts concerning music and music history, together with information as to where further data can be found.

Schering's *Geschichte der Musik in Beispielen* (New York: Broude) is the authoritative work for those who demand printed scores of the music they hear.

A Historical Anthology of Music by Davidson and Apel (Cambridge: Harvard, 1949–1950) is a two-volume work that concerns itself with printed examples of early music.

Masterpieces of Music before 1750 by Parrish and Ohl (New York: Norton, 1951) is an anthology of musical examples from Gregorian Chant to J. S. Bach; it has a parallel series of recordings.

An Illustrated History of Music (New York: Reynal, 1959) has fine illustrations and comments by the noted French musicologist Marc Pincherle.

Dictionary of Musicians from Earliest Times to the Present, Saintsbury (New York: Da Capo, 1965).

A General History of Music (New York: Dover, 1957) by Charles Burney was written by a friend of Samuel Johnson and of the other leaders in politics, music, art, and literature of the time. It was the result of observations made during a long trip through Europe and was first published in 1776–89. Naturally, Burney's ideas on the history of music have been enlarged by modern research; nevertheless, this very readable book remains one of the best sources of information about the society, customs, and civilized life of Europe at that time.

The following are works of general musical criticism:

The Pleasures of Music (New York: Viking, 1951), edited by Jacques Barzun, is a reader's choice of great writing about music from Cellini to Shaw.

Music Ho! (London: Faber & Faber, 1934) by Constant Lambert contains some brilliant observations about modern music in general.

Men, Women, and Pianos (New York: Simon and Schuster, 1954), by Arthur Loesser, contains an amusing commentary on music in general, as well as some sage observations on its title-pieces.

Music and Society (London: Dobson, 1950) Wilfred Mellers speaks his mind regarding the place of music in the societies of the past and present.

Lexicon of Musical Invective (New York: Coleman-Ross, 1953) by Nicolas Slonimsky. An informing and amusing collection of musical criticism gathered by a Russian-born musicologist well acquainted with all aspects of musical activity here and abroad.

The Language of Music (London: Oxford, 1960§) by Deryck Cooke. Poses the question: What kind of an art is music? Answers it by stating that it is an art meant to express and evoke emotion and shows how a large-scale musical work functions expressively.

Journey Toward Music (New York: Dutton, 1965). Victor Gollancz, one of England's important publishers, and an enthusiastic music lover, criticizes music and musicians perceptively.

The following are in special fields:

Choral Music of the Church (New York: Free Press, 1965) by Elwyn Weinaudt

The Great Pianists (New York: Simon and Schuster, 1963) by Harold Schonberg

History of Orchestration (New York: Dover, 1935, paper) by Adam Carse
Cyclopedic Survey of Chamber Music (London: Oxford) Walter W. Corbett's great two-volume work was republished in 1963, together with a third volume bringing it up to date.

Annals of Opera 1597–1940 (Geneva: Societas Bibleographia, 1955) by Alfred Loewenberg. An outstanding achievement, listing in chronolgical order the exact dates of the first performances of some 4,000 operas, thus providing a catalogue of all operas performed up to 1940.

Crowell's Handbook of World Opera (New York: Crowell, 1961). Compiled by Moore, this gives information on everything connected with the long and checkered history of opera.

Opera Guide (New York: Dutton, 1965) by Gerhart von Westerman, edited by Harold Rosenthal. Provides historical data, musical analyses, and detailed synopses, and covers some works not hitherto available.

Complete Book of Light Opera (New York: Putnam, 1962) Lubbock. Treats all the important light operas, including the modern ones.

The History of Musical Instruments (New York: Norton, 1940) by Curt Sachs.

Donington's *The Interpretation of Early Music* (New York: St. Martin's Press, 1963) gives a detailed explanation of the ornamentation used in early music, together with numerous examples. Meant for specialists rather than general readers.

The Italian Madrigal (Princeton: Princeton U. Press, 1949), Alfred Einstein's monumental three-volume work gives a detailed description of the evolution of this form, together with the words and music of choice examples.

Anglo-American Folksong Scholarship since 1898 (New Brunswick: Rutgers U. Press). Scholarly but readable history of the backgrounds of the collecting of present-day folksongs by D. K. Wilgus.

High Fidelity Record Annual (Great Barrington: Wyeth Press, first volume 1955, tenth 1965). An annual publication containing critical reviews of new records. Written by the reviewers of *High Fidelity* magazine and organized by composer for easy reference, this gives advice both as to quality of performance and recording.

THE ARTS IN HISTORY

The Social History of Art (New York: Knopf, 1951) by Arnold Hauser. An extremely valuable and very individual study of the social and historical backgrounds that are manifested in the various changes of artistic style through the centuries. Although not entirely accepted by the professional art historians, this makes highly interesting and provocative reading for the general art student.

The Art of Music (New York: Crowell, 1960) by Cannon, Jolinson, and Waite. This study by three university professors covers the same general ground as *Music in History,* examining the manifestations of musical style in the light of the ideas of different historical periods, but in a more technically detailed manner.

Music in Western Civilization (New York: Norton) First published in 1941, this work by Paul Henry Lang refers the history of music to the general background of various historical periods.

In Curt Sachs's *The Commonwealth of Art* (New York: Norton, 1946), the most knowledgeable of all the German musicologists attempts to prove that all the arts have united in constant evolution to mirror man's aspirations, his spiritual backgrounds, and the social backgrounds of the different times in which he has lived.

The Arts and Their Interrelations (New York: Liberal Arts Press, 1949) by Thomas Munro. A general summary of the arts and ideas about them, including a comparison of their similarities and differences.

THE ORIGINS OF ART

Believing that art is a work of knowledge and that the world of art is a system of knowledge valuable to man, Herbert Reed, the English art critic has shown in his *Art and Society* (New York: Macmillan, 1937) how he thinks the plastic arts began. In a similar way Curt Sachs in *The Rise of Music in the Ancient World* speculates on the origins of music (see below).

MUSIC IN THE LIFE OF THE NEAR EAST

Sachs's *The Rise of Music in the Ancient World* (New York: Norton, 1943) covers all the different closely related musical styles of the ancient Eastern world, including the Egyptian, Hebraic, Chinese, Japanese, and Indian. It also treats the music of ancient Greece and shows how it was organically connected with the Orient. Gustav Reese's *Music in the Middle Ages* (New York: Norton, 1940) covers a wide field, beginning with the music of ancient times. It is largely concerned with style analyses of the music of the various early periods and is only recommended for special reference.

THE MUSIC OF THE HELLENIC AGE

Although it does not treat Greek music, Edith Hamilton's *Greek Way to Western Civilization* (New York: Mentor, 1948§) shows what the modern world has to learn from the Greek. It is written in a style that suggests Greek clarity and simplicity. Reese's *Music in the Middle Ages* (*op. cit.*) devotes considerable attention to the various systems of Greek music, while Edward Lippman's *Musical Thought in Ancient Greece* (New York: Columbia U. Press, 1964) shows the place held by Greek music in Greek life and quotes the speculations of the Greek philosophers on music. Difficult reading

ROMAN AND EARLY CHRISTIAN MUSIC

Reese's *Music in the Middle Ages* (*op. cit.*) treats Roman music briefly, but gives several long chapters to the beginnings of Christian chant and the growth of some of its chief branches. The second chapter of Oliver Strunk's *Source Readings in Music History* (New York: Norton, 1950) states the early Christian view of music as seen in the writings of the Church Fathers from Clement of Alexandria to St. Augustine. Professor Willi Apel's *Gregorian Chant* (Bloomington: Indiana U. Press, 1958) is a comprehensive historical and stylistic study.

MONODIC MUSIC OF A THOUSAND YEARS

Reese's *Music in the Middle Ages* (*op. cit.*) traces the development of the Gregorian Chant and its notation, as well as that of the secular monody of the period.

THE MUSIC OF THE MIDDLE AGES

Reese's *Music in the Middle Ages* (*op. cit.*) describes the development of polyphony in the various countries up to the middle of the fifteenth century. Manfred Bukofzer's *Studies in Medieval and Renaissance Music* (New York: Norton, 1940) is concerned with the English music of this period, as well as with the origins of the Mass and an analysis of some of the masses of that period. G. S. Bedrock's *Keyboard Music from the Middle Ages to the Beginnings of the Baroque* (London: Macmillan, 1949) concentrates on this special field. Although Nan Carpenter, the author of *Music in the Medieval and Renaissance Universities* (Norman: U. of Oklahoma Press, 1958) is mostly concerned with tracing the teaching of music in the universities of Medieval and Renaissance Europe, she also shows how this teaching influenced the music of the countries in which these universities were located—Italy, France, Germany, and England.

THE MUSIC OF THE RENAISSANCE

A comprehenive picture of every facet of Renaissance life—its people, politics, arts, commerce, literature, philosophy and manners—is given in the sumptuous *Horizon Book of the Renaissance* (New York: Doubleday, 1961). Gustav Reese's *Music in the Renaissance* gives a comprehensive, scholarly account of the musical activities of this period, beginning with the second half of the fifteenth century and continuing through the sixteenth. Wylie Sypher in his *Four Stages of Renaissance Style* (New York: Anchor, 1955, paper) pictures the cultural and social backgrounds of the various Renaissance periods, and describes the transformations in the forms of art and literature which took place during these different stages of the development of the Renaissance style.

MANNERISM—A TRANSITIONAL PERIOD

The general artistic backgrounds of this period (roughly 1520–1600) are wonderfully treated in Arnold Hauser's *Mannerism* (New York: Knopf, 1965), as well as by Sypher in his *Four Stages of Renaissance Style* (*op. cit.*). The life of its greatest composer, Gesualdo, is discussed in Cecil Gray's *Contingencies* (London: Oxford, 1946), and the particular qualities of his music are well described by Robert Craft in the article which accompanies the Columbia recording KL5718, *Don Carlo Gesualdo, Prince of Madrigalists*.

THE OVERTURE TO THE BAROQUE

The general social and artistic backgrounds that produced two of the most important generations of European culture (1610–1660) are given by Carl Friedrich in his *The Age of Baroque* (New York: Harper & Row, 1952§). The special musical features of this era are described in W. F. Bukofzer's *Music in the Baroque Era* (New York: Norton, 1947). D. J. Grout's *Short History of Opera,* second edition, 2 vols. (New York: Columbia U. Press, 1965) devotes considerable attention to the birth and development of the two great Baroque forms, the opera and oratorio. And Leo Schrade shows in his *Monteverdi, the Creator of Modern Music* (New York, Norton, 1950) the significance of this composer. A fine, overall picture is given in *The Baroque Era: An Age and Its Music* by Frederick Grunfeld (New York: Time, 1966).

THE MIDDLE AND HIGH BAROQUE

Romain Rolland's characteristic *Essays on Music* (New York: Crown, 1948) is a refreshing foil to the overspecialized treatment of the Baroque period by Bukofzer. Chapter Five of Curt Sach's *The Commonwealth of Art (op. cit.)* is especially good in its description of the Baroque style and how it developed out of the Renaissance and evolved into the Rococo. The eminent musicologist also shows the attitude toward the musical instruments used during the Renaissance and Baroque periods in his *History of Musical Instruments (op. cit.)*. A colorful picture of the court music of this time is given in Ernest Helm's *Music at the Court of Frederick the Great* (Norman: University of Oklahoma Press, 1960).

AND THERE WERE GIANTS
IN THOSE DAYS

Hans David and Arthur Mendel in their *Bach Reader* (New York: Norton, 1945) and Otto Deutsch in his *Handel: A Documentary Biography* (New York: Norton, 1955) have collected a great number of interesting and important references to these composers. The standard Bach biographies are Spitta's (New York: Dover, 1899), Terry's (New York: Oxford, 1928), and Schweitzer's (New York: Breitkopf and Härtel, 1923), translated by Ernest Newman. Although Schweitzer's theories are discounted by today's experts, his work remains one of the most important books on the subject, and his very original ideas deserve careful attention. *The Music of the Bach Family* has been treated by Karl Geiringer (Cambridge: Harvard, 1951) and is especially valuable because it is paralleled by a series of recordings. The standard Handel biography is that of Newman Flower, *Handel: His Personality and His Times* (London: Cassel, 1952).

THE MUSICAL DEVELOPMENTS OF THE
EIGHTEENTH CENTURY

The general characteristics of the Rococo style are described by Wylie Sypher in his *Rococo to Cubism in Art and Literature* (New York: Vintage, 1960§).

Adam Carse shows the development of the orchestra in the eighteenth century in his book of that name (New York: Broude, rept). Karl Geiringer's *Haydn: A Creative Life in Music* (New York: Norton, 1946) is a standard work, as is Alfred Einstein's *Mozart* (New York: Oxford, 1945). A very useful and practical biography and appraisal of Mozart will be found in John N. Burk's *Mozart and His Music* (New York, Random House, 1959). Otto Deutsch's latest documentary biography on Mozart was published in an English version in 1965 (Stanford, Stanford U. Press). Like his other works of this kind, this exemplifies the valuable as well as irritating aspects of *musikwissenshaftlich* activities. It contains a methodical and systematic assembly of every extant document relevant to Mozart except the letters, which are available in a three-volume edition translated by Emily Anderson (New York: Macmillan, 1938). But this process has produced a multitude of trivia that can be of no possible help in throwing light on the composer's life, his art, or the sources of his inspiration. Very valuable here as a general background book is Gilbert Highet's *The Classic Tradition* (New York: Oxford, 1950), since it gives the general characteristic of the classical tradition in the different arts during the various periods.

MUSIC BECOMES MORE PERSONAL

Although it may seem difficult to define Romanticism as a style, much has been written in attempts to describe this intensification of experience in art. Jacques Barzun has discussed its manifestations in literature, its governing purposes, and its historical causes in *Classic, Romantic and Modern* (New York: Anchor, 1961, paper).

It would seem that a more sympathetic historian of its musical manifestations could have been found than Alfred Einstein shows himself to be in *Music in the Romantic Era* (New York: Norton, 1947). More characteristically Romantic is Romain Rolland's *Essays on Music* (New York: Crown, 1948); his novel *Jean Christophe* remains one of the great works of the period because of his understanding of the essential Romantic traits. The standard Beethoven biography by Alexander Thayer has been revised by Eliot Forbes and handsomely reprinted (Princeton: Princeton U. Press, 1964). J. W. N. Sullivan's *Beethoven and his Spiritual Development* still maintains its position as one of the best books ever written on this composer. Daniel Gregory Mason's *The Quartets of Beethoven* (New York: Oxford, 1947) is a good guide to these rather puzzling works.

THE EARLY ROMANTIC COMPOSERS

Gerald Abraham's *A Hundred Years of Music,* first published in 1938 (London: Duckworth), in its discussion of the triumph, decline, and fall of Romanticism, treats the music of the composers from Berlioz to Stravinsky, as does Jacques Barzun in his *Berlioz and the Romantic Century* (New York: Columbia U. Press, 1950). Adam Carse describes his specialty in *The Orchestra from Beethoven to Berlioz* (New York: Broude, rept.). Otto Deutsch's *Schubert Reader* (New York: Norton, 1947) and Gerald Abraham's *Schumann: A Symposium* (London: Cassel, 1952) give details of the lives and music of these composers. André Gide's *Notes on Chopin* and Sacheverell Sitwell's *Liszt* (both

New York: Philosophical Library, 1956) are two beautifully written accounts of the music of these composers by two extremely capable nonprofessional musicians.

WAGNER: HIS OPERATIC PREDECESSORS AND CONTEMPORARIES

Ernest Newman's *Life of Richard Wagner* in four volumes (New York: Knopf, 1933–46) must always remain the standard work on this composer in English, simply because it was written by the man best qualified for the task. Newman also wrote a fine estimate of the importance of this most-discussed nineteenth-century composer in his *Wagner as Man and Artist* (New York: Vintage) and Jacques Barzun has compared him with two of the other great figures of his period in *Darwin, Marx and Wagner* (New York: Doubleday, 1941). A good history of the staging of the Wagner operas, as well as a description of the various new experiments along this line undertaken by his grandsons, is given in *Wagner at Bayreuth, Experiment and Tradition* by Geoffrey Skelton (London: Barrie and Rockliff, 1965). Francis Toye, the English critic, has written two good studies of the other two important nineteenth-century opera composers: *Rossini, A Study in Tragi-Comedy* (New York: Knopf, 1947) and *Giuseppe Verdi: His Life and Work* (New York: Knopf, 1946). Another valuable book is Frank Walker's *The Man Verdi* (New York: Knopf, 1962).

THE LATER ROMANTIC COMPOSERS

The standard work on Brahms is by Walter Niemann, translated by Phillips (*Brahms,* New York: Knopf, 1929). A good account is *César Franck,* written by his pupil Vincent D'Indy (New York: Dover, rept. §). No adequate account of Richard Strauss's music is available in English, but the composer's own *Recollections and Reflections* (London: Boosey and Hawkes, 1953) and the *Correspondence between Richard Strauss and Hoffmannsthal* (New York: Knopf, 1927) have been translated and give us an idea of his personal beliefs. The operas are well treated in William Mann's *Critical Survey of the Operas of Richard Strauss* (London: Cassel, 1964). *Tchaikovsky: A Symposium,* edited by Gerald Abraham (London: Drummond, 1946), contains an excellent account of the various aspects of this composer's work by eight English and one Soviet critic. Three of the most important late Romantics are compared in Dike Newlin's *Bruckner, Mahler, Schoenberg* (New York: King's Crown, 1947).

NATIONALISM IN MUSIC

National Music, Ralph Vaughan Williams (New York: Oxford, 1934)
Studies in Russian Music, Gerald Abraham (New York: Oxford, 1939)
Eight Soviet Composers, Gerald Abraham (New York: Oxford, 1943)
The Moussorgsky Reader, edited by Leyda and Bertennson (New York: Norton, 1947)
My Musical Life, Nikolai Rimsky-Korsakoff (New York: Knopf, 1923§)
Grieg: A Symposium, edited by Gerald Abraham (Norman: Oklahoma U. Press, 1950)

French Music from the Death of Berlioz to Fauré, Martin Cooper (London: 1957)

The Music of Spain by Gilbert Chase (New York: Norton, 1941)

Edward Elgar: His Life and Music, Diana McVeagh (London: Collins, 1955)

The Works of Ralph Vaughan-Williams, Michael Kennedy (London: Oxford, 1964)

The Music of William Walton, Frank Hawes (New York: Oxford, 1965)

Sibelius, Robert Layton (London: Dent, 1965)

THE MUSICAL IMPRESSIONISTS

The artistic, social, and political climate in which the Impressionists lived and worked is re-created in Francis Mathey's *The Impressionists* (New York: Prager, 1961 §), together with excellent reproductions in color and black-and-white that constitute a critical survey of the whole movement in painting. Oscar Thompson in his *Debussy, Man and Artist* (New York: Dodd, Mead, 1937) shows how the French Impressionist schools of painting and literature were reflected in music. The most complete Debussy biography is that by Edward Lockspeiser in two volumes (New York: Macmillan, 1962 and 1965). Rollo Meyers's *Ravel* was published in London by Duckworth in 1960; and Sir Thomas Beecham's intimate account of *Frederick Delius* was issued there by Hutchinson in 1959. Jaime Palissa has written *Manuel de Falla: His Life and Works* (London: 1954).

THE TWENTIETH CENTURY

The following cover the general field of twentieth-century music as well as the works of all its most important composers:

Music in Our Time, Adolfo Salazar (New York: Norton, 1946)

A History of Modern Music, Paul Collaer (Cleveland: World, 1961)

Musical Trends in the Twentieth Century, Norman Demuth (London: Rockliffe, 1952)

Music since 1900, Nicolas Slonimsky (New York: Coleman-Ross, 1949)

European Music in the XX Century, edited by Howard Hartog (London: Routledge-Kegan Paul, 1957)

Contemporary Music in Europe, symposium edited by Land and Browder (New York: Schirmer, 1965)

Since Debussy, André Hodeir (New York: Grove, 1961 §)

XX Century Music in Western Europe, Arthur Cohn (Philadelphia: Lippincott, 1965). Valuable for its list of recordings

Schoenberg and His School, René Leibowitz (New York: Philosophical Library, 1949)

Tonality in Modern Music, Rudolph Reti (New York: Collier, 1962)

The Agony of Modern Music, Henry Pleasants (New York: Simon and Schuster, 1955)

In addition, the following are worthy of special attention since they give the composer's ideas as well as many personal judgments on the music of others:

The Poetics of Music, Igor Stravinsky (Cambridge: Harvard, 1947)

Archive Productions of the Deutsche Grammophone Gesellschaft, MGM
This series, prepared by the History of Music Division of the DGG, presents works in their complete authentic form, based on original versions, and performed faithfully in the original style, often using historical instruments. But what makes these records especially valuable to present-day listeners is the fact that they are living, artistic manifestations and not merely academic interpretations. The technical qualities of these recordings are of the highest standard and many of them are available in stereo. A complete catalog is available, giving the details of each recording and its catalog number.

Storia della Musica Italiana, RCA Victor Italiana
Contains Italian items not to be found in other collections. Volume I covers examples from Gregorian Chant to Carissimi-ML 40000.

Music in Old Towns, Odeon
An unusual series of recordings by medieval and Renaissance composers centered in the towns of central Europe during these two periods. Among the 16 towns represented are Augsburg, Dresden, Hamburg, Lübeck, Munich, Nürnberg, Salzberg, and Vienna.

INDEX

(Figures in italics refer to illustrations.)